Wireless Technologies in Vehicular Ad Hoc Networks:

Present and Future Challenges

Raul Aquino Santos
University of Colima, Mexico

Arthur Edwards
University of Colima, Mexico

Victor Rangel Licea
National Autonomous University of Mexico, Mexico

Managing Director:	Lindsay Johnston
Senior Editorial Director:	Heather Probst
Book Production Manager:	Sean Woznicki
Development Manager:	Joel Gamon
Development Editor:	Myla Harty
Acquisitions Editor:	Erika Gallagher
Typesetters:	Jennifer Romanchak
Cover Design:	Nick Newcomer, Greg Snader

Published in the United States of America by
Information Science Reference (an imprint of IGI Global)
701 E. Chocolate Avenue
Hershey PA 17033
Tel: 717-533-8845
Fax: 717-533-8661
E-mail: cust@igi-global.com
Web site: http://www.igi-global.com

Library of Congress Cataloging-in-Publication Data

Wireless technologies in vehicular ad hoc networks: present and future challenges / Raul Aquino Santos ... [et al.], editors.
    p. cm.
  Includes bibliographical references and index.
  Summary: "This book explores different models for inter-vehicular communication, in which vehicles are equipped with on-board computers that function as nodes in a wireless network"--Provided by publisher.
  ISBN 978-1-4666-0209-0 (hardcover) -- ISBN 978-1-4666-0210-6 (ebook) -- ISBN 978-1-4666-0211-3 (print & perpetual access) 1. Automotive telematics. 2. Mobile communication systems. I. Aquino Santos, Raul, 1965-
  TL272.58.W57 2012
  388.3'124--dc23
                              2011045043

British Cataloguing in Publication Data
A Cataloguing in Publication record for this book is available from the British Library.

All work contributed to this book is new, previously-unpublished material. The views expressed in this book are those of the authors, but not necessarily of the publisher.

Table of Contents

Section 1
Theory and Application of the Physical and Medium Access Layers

Section 2
Theory and Application of the Network Layer

Section 3
Theory and Application of Higher Layers

Detailed Table of Contents

Section 1
Theory and Application of the Physical and Medium Access Layers

Chapter 1
Sergio Hernández Gaona, DGETA, Mexico

Empirical propagation models are extensively used in the area of communications to predict the behavior of radio signals because there are many variables which can affect their propagation. This chapter presents a state-of-the-art review of several of the most important empirical propagation models used to predict the propagation of radio signals in various outdoor environments. The objective of the chapter is to better understand the mechanisms that affect the dissemination of radio waves and present many of the most popular propagation models used to calculate a link budget. The three kinds of fading are presented in this chapter: path loss, shadowing, and fast-fading. The advantages and disadvantages of the different propagation models are then discussed in terms of fading, shadowing attenuation, margin delay, and Doppler spread.

Chapter 2
David W. Matolak, Ohio University, USA

This chapter provides a detailed description of physical layer characteristics for the mobile wireless channel for vehicle-to-vehicle (V2V) communication and networking applications. Maintaining signal integrity can be one of the most challenging problems yet to be solved due to low antenna heights and the constant movement between vehicles in a V2V environment.

Chapter 3
Corneliu Eugen D. Sterian, Polytechnic University of Bucharest, Romania

Direct inter-vehicular communications are presumably more difficult to perform than communications within a cellular network or between a moving vehicle and the roadside, where there is a large fixed infrastructure. This chapter maintains that the mobile channel between the two vehicles is so rapidly variable that it is not possible to measure it in real-time. Consequently, the author selects and considers only modulation and coding techniques for which the knowledge of the channel state is not necessary at both the transmitter and the receiver. The author uses space-time coding communication systems with two transmit antennas to provide a more real scenario. The author purposely avoids introducing very much theory because he maintains that all of the techniques mentioned in this chapter should not be a too difficult to implement. Finally, the author concludes his contribution by providing areas of opportunity for future research.

Chapter 4

Claudia Campolo, Università Mediterranea di Reggio Calabria, Italy
Hector Agustin Cozzetti, Istituto Superiore Mario Boella, Italy
Antonella Molinaro, Università Mediterranea di Reggio Calabria, Italy
Riccardo Maria Scopigno, Istituto Superiore Mario Boella, Italy

The main aim of this chapter is to serve as an introduction for readers interested in vehicular network design, with a special focus on the MAC layer. It includes a detailed description of the major features and operating principles provided by PHY and MAC layers of the IEEE 802.11p and IEEE 1609 standard suites to support Wireless Access in Vehicular Environments (WAVE). The last part of the chapter contains a brief survey of some relevant MAC proposals in the scientific literature that try to cope with the above-mentioned challenges related to vehicular network scenarios. Most of the proposals follow the concept of contention-based channel access. The authors then go on to propose extensions to the 802.11p MAC layer in order to achieve higher throughput and increase fairness.

Chapter 5

Riccardo Maria Scopigno, Istituto Superiore Mario Boella, Italy
Hector Agustin Cozzetti, Istituto Superiore Mario Boella, Italy

This chapter proposes some alternative MAC solutions for VANETs, based on a synchronous, slotted philosophy. After highlighting the limitations of the incumbent CSMA/CA solution, the chapter explains the rationale for a slotted standard and briefly introduces three solutions found in literature (namely MS-Aloha, D-TDMA, and STDMA). According to the authors, MS-Aloha, appears to be particularly versatile insofar as its functionality. Furthermore, it solves several open issues in terms of scalability. The characteristics of MS-Aloha are then presented and extensively discussed as the authors present simulations and quantitative metric results. The authors then go on the performance of CSMA/CA and MS-Aloha to gain a deeper insight and draw conclusions about these two common medium access mechanisms.

Chapter 6

D. Muñoz, ITESM Campus Monterrey, Mexico
R. Rodríguez, UANL Campus Monterrey, Mexico
S. Villarreal Reyes, ITESM Campus Monterrey, Mexico

This chapter describes different propagation scenarios in V2V communications based on practical Intelligent Transportation System applications. The intention is to study propagation impairments for modeling purposes. The authors maintain that it is important to consider the environmental characteristics of the scenario in order to choose the proper model to evaluate performance. The intention of this chapter is to explore how well current models fit the scenarios and to identify areas of opportunity for new model design. Many devices, including sensors, transponders, and communication radios of different kinds, co-exist in a typical urban scene. The signals sent by these competing devices can sometimes interfere with each other, causing possible electromagnetic coupling with external waves. Therefore, the integration of the various technologies is imperative, and more optimal conditions for physical interaction of the radio waves need to be provided. This is critical for automatic systems that control safety sensible information to function as required. Very strict standard electromagnetic compatibility restrictions and regulations are applied to vehicles. These emissions and immunity tests need to be re-engineered in the near future in order to consider new radio devices for communication among vehicles through sensors and transponders.

Section 2
Theory and Application of the Network Layer

Chapter 7

The author maintains that the idea of using geographical information in highly mobile nodes is to improve packet forwarding decisions. Before forwarding a packet, a node using location information only needs information about the immediate neighbourhood and the position of the destination. However, as an essential prerequisite for location-based routing, a location service is needed from which a node can learn the current position of its desired communication partner. The author goes on to discuss position based algorithms and compares several of the most common. Raul Aquino then proposes that in order to preserve location information about other nodes in the network, each mobile node must maintain a location table. He discusses the mechanism used to maintain updated tables and how to communicate this information throughout the network. Finally, the author simulates and presents results of a Reactive Location-Based Routing Algorithm with Cluster-Based Flooding.

Chapter 8

The author introduces his chapter by maintaining that Vehicular Ad-Hoc Networks (VANETs), characterized by their high mobility, cause wireless links between vehicles to unpredictably change and that this mobility makes it very challenging to establish and maintain communications in vehicular networks. As a result, the author adds, networking in these kinds of networks has become a very intense area of study. Consequently, research of ad hoc routing and medium access control strategies has become an intensive part of current study. The author presents a state-of-the-art discussion about different strategies to improve network stability in highly dense and dynamically-changing ad hoc network environments. This chapter presents a simulated evaluation of the LORA-CBF geographic routing algorithm that permits seamless communication in an ad-hoc WiMAX network and concludes by suggesting future areas of related research.

Section 3
Theory and Application of Higher Layers

Chapter 9

JA Guerrero-Ibáñez, University of Colima, México
C Flores-Cortés, University of Colima, México
P Damián-Reyes, University of Colima, México

Today, modern society faces serious problems regarding its transportation systems. There are more traffic jams, accidents, and fatalities, and CO2 emissions are increasing fast. The authors maintain that improving the safety and efficiency of transportation systems is imperative. Developing a sustainable transportation system requires better using existing infrastructure, adopting emerging technologies (e.g. embedded devices, sensors and short range radio transmitters), and developing applications capable of operating in wireless and spontaneous networks. This chapter is written to provide readers a more global vision of the issues related to developing applications for vehicular ad-hoc networks (VANETs). It also presents a classification and an overview of the top-level application domain. In addition, the chapter discusses the importance of information in vehicular networks and analyses the requirements for different types of vehicular applications. Finally, the communication schemes that underpin the operation of VANET applications, as well as the security threats they are exposed to, are studied.

Chapter 10

Marina Aguado, University of the Basque Country, Spain
Nerea Toledo, University of the Basque Country, Spain
Marion Berbineau, IFSTTAR, Institut Français des Sciences et Technologies des Transports, de l'Aménagement et des Réseaux, France
Eduardo Jacob, University of the Basque Country, Spain

Current challenges in mobility and sustainable development are closely related to increasing travel safety, optimizing the use of transport infrastructure, reducing operating and maintenance costs, and making public transport more attractive. The authors of this chapter propose that solutions to these major challenges depend to a great degree on political decisions, the development of good practices, and on the innovation and technology introduced through on-going Intelligent Transport Systems (ITS) programs and initiatives. "Intelligent Transport Systems" refers to those efforts to seamlessly blend information and communication technologies (ICT) to improve safety, efficiency, and competitiveness in cars, buses, railways, and mass transportation systems (goods & persons). These Intelligent Transport Systems rely on communication architectures, computation, databases, and geo-location information. This chapter covers taxonomy of these Intelligent Transport Systems and their underlying communication architectures.

Chapter 11

Jetzabel Serna, Universitat Politécnica de Catalunya (UPC), Spain
Jesus Luna, Technische Universitaet Darmstadt, Germany
Roberto Morales, Universitat Politécnica de Catalunya (UPC), Spain
Manel Medina, Universitat Politécnica de Catalunya (UPC), Spain

Vehicular Ad Hoc Networks (VANETs) currently represent a prominent field of research, which aims at improving everyday road safety and comfort. To achieve this, the authors propose deploying several potential applications that promise to provide extraordinary benefits, but will also represent important security challenges due to the unique characteristics of VANETs. This chapter addresses VANET security issues and discusses some commonly used security approaches. As a proof of concept, a Public Key Infrastrure-based protocol, able to cope with the interoperability issues among untrusted central authority domains, is presented, and the trade-offs between security and performance are empirically analyzed and stressed.

Chapter 12

Mahmoud Efatmaneshnik, University of New South Wales, Australia
Nima Alam, University of New South Wales, Australia
Asghar T. Balaei, University of New South Wales, Australia
Allison Kealy, University of Melbourne, Australia
Andrew G. Dempster, University of New South Wales, Australia

This chapter introduces the concept of Cooperative Positioning (CP) for vehicular networks, or more precisely, VANET, (Vehicular Adhoc NETwork) as an application of DSRC (Dedicated Short Range Communication). It includes a comprehensive review of available and hypothetical vehicular positioning technologies. Amongst these, the authors emphasize the importance of CP for Location Based Services, using DSRC. Furthermore, the authors address issues that need to be resolved in order to implement CP successfully with a standard DSRC infrastructure. The performance bounds of CP are derived. Ranging between vehicles is identified as the main hurdle to be overcome. Time-based techniques of ranging are introduced, and the bandwidth requirements are investigated. The robustness of CP to inter-node connection failure as well as GPS (Global Positioning System) dropout is demonstrated via simulation. Kalman Filter performance for CP is evaluated, and proven to be efficient under conditions such as the consistency of GPS signal availability, that of ranging between vehicles. CP has, however, shown to increase the positioning accuracy to 1-meter level, even in the deep urban valleys where vehicles frequently become invisible to navigation. Overall, CP is proven to be a viable concept and worthy of development as a DSRC application.

Chapter 13

Nitin Maslekar, IRSEEM-ESIGELEC, France
Mounir Boussedjra, IRSEEM-ESIGELEC, France
Houda Labiod, Telecom ParisTech, France
Joseph Mouzna, IRSEEM-ESIGELEC, France

Vehicular ad hoc networks (VANETs) represent an important component necessary to develop Intelligent Transportation Systems. Recent advances in communications systems have created significant opportunities for a wide variety of applications and services to be implemented in vehicles. According to the authors, most of these applications require a certain dissemination performance to work satisfactorily. Although a variety of optimizations are possible, the basic idea for any dissemination scheme is to facilitate the acquisition of the knowledge about the surrounding vehicles. However, the dynamic nature of vehicular networks makes it difficult to achieve an effective dissemination among vehicles. This chapter provides an overview on those challenges and presents various approaches to disseminate data in vehicular networks.

This chapter describes the authors' experiences and findings deploying a vehicular network architecture
supporting different communications technologies. Their approach has been developed taking into account key issues regarding mobility and security. These two aspects have been provided by means of the
NEMO and IKEv2 protocols, respectively. In addition, thanks to the EAP protocol, transported by IKEv2,
an extensible authentication method can be used to implement an access control mechanism. This work
also focuses on how the terminal is aware of the surrounding environment in order to boost the handoff
processes among heterogeneous networks using the IEEE 802.21 protocol. Apart from the description of
the on-board system architecture, a WiMAX/WiFi deployment has been set up at the infrastructure side
to validate the development of the mobility and security environment designed for vehicular networks.

Intelligent Transportation Systems (ITS) are the future of transportation. As a result of emerging standards, vehicles will soon be able to "talk" to one another as well as their environment. A number of
applications will be made available for vehicular networks that improve the overall safety of the transportation infrastructure. This chapter develops a method to impart chaotic motions to an Automated
Guided Vehicle (AGV). The authors state that a chaotic AGV implies a mobile robot with a controller
that ensures chaotic motions. This kind of motion is characterized by the topological transitivity and the
sensitive dependence on initial conditions. Due the topological transitivity, the mobile robot can scan
the whole connected workspace. For its scanning motion, the chaotic robot neither requires a map of the
workspace nor plans its global motions. It only requires the measurement of the workspace boundary
which the robot respects when it comes close to it.

Foreword

Raúl Aquino Santos, Arthur Edwards, and Victor Rangel have edited this new book to reflect the present and future challenges in wireless technologies for vehicular ad hoc networks. New technologies are being developed for vehicular ad hoc networks, and these networks provide an efficient method for today's complex vehicle communications. Emerging vehicular ad hoc networks in the forms of Vehicle-to-Vehicle (V2V) and Vehicle-to-Infrastructure (V2I) communications are a cornerstone of the envisioned Intelligent Transportation Systems (ITS).

By enabling vehicles to communicate with other vehicles via V2V communication as well as with roadside infrastructure via V2I communication, vehicular ad hoc networks will enable a variety of applications for safety, traffic efficiency, driver assistance, and infotainment. For the safety requirements, vehicular network technologies will be applied to reduce accidents so as to save lives and reduce injuries. Examples of such applications include vehicle breakdown and obstacle detection, lane departure warnings, accident warnings, collision warnings, over-height/over-width warnings, turnover warnings, work zone warnings, black box recorder to register accident forensics, and so on. For traffic efficiency, vehicular network technologies will be applied to improve the flow of traffic and reduce congestion, for example, cooperative adaptive cruise control, highway/rail intersection traffic management, congestion information for traffic control, electronic toll collection, et cetera. For driver assistance, vehicular networks can also provide accurate information and data, as well as good communications for drivers to improve safety and security, e.g., advanced navigation systems, parking information, real-time traffic information, various kinds of warning information, driver's daily blog, automatic emergency calls, and so on.

This book has provided wireless technologies from the physical layer to the application layer and new research challenges for vehicular ad hoc networks to realize the above exciting applications. First, this book describes the physical layer characteristics for the wireless channel, and identifies the distinguishing features of V2V channels. Due to the low antenna elevations, and mobility of both transmitters and receivers in the V2V environment, the V2V wireless channel can be one of the most challenging elements to ensuring reliable V2V communication. Hence, channel modeling and modulation and coding techniques for V2V communications are presented in this book. It then introduces a detailed description of the major features and operating principles provided by Physical (PHY) and Medium Access Control (MAC) layers of the IEEE 802.11p and IEEE 1609 standard suites to support Wireless Access in Vehicular Environments (WAVE). It further presents the alternative MAC solutions based on a synchronous, slotted philosophy. It also describes the channel impairments for V2V communications in ITS scenarios so as to identify areas for the new performance evaluation model design.

Second, this book presents technologies related to ad hoc routing and medium access control strategies for vehicular ad hoc networks. Due to high mobility, it is very challenging to establish and maintain a communication link in vehicular networks. Therefore, this book introduces WiMAX as medium access technology and geographic strategies for routing algorithms. Furthermore, it presents an evaluation of the LORA-CBF geographic routing algorithm that permits seamless communication in an ad-hoc WiMAX network.

Third, this book presents development challenges and opportunities of applications in Intelligent Transport System. It gives readers a global vision of the issues related to the development of applications for vehicular ad-hoc networks, and presents a classification and an overview of top-level application domains. It then presents the communication architectures on which Intelligent Transport Systems rely. It also addresses the challenges and issues with cooperative positioning, data dissemination, and heterogeneous communications for vehicular ad hoc networks.

Last but not least, security issues in deploying vehicular ad hoc networks are addressed, and the most outstanding security approaches are discussed. As a proof of concept, it presents a PKI -based protocol, able to cope with the interoperability issues among un-trusted CA (certificate authority) domains, and the trade-offs between security and performance are empirically analyzed.

I have known Dr. Santos since 2007 when I edited a book on Automotive Informatics and Communicative Systems: Principles in Vehicular Networks and Data Exchange. At that time, he contributed an interesting chapter of Inter-vehicular Communications using Wireless Ad Hoc Networks. From 2007 until now, he has shown the great passion and devoted his time and effort to this area. Thus, I highly recommend Dr. Santos's timely book. I believe it will benefit many readers and inspire them to conquer the challenges mentioned in this book for vehicular ad hoc networks.

Huaqun Guo
Institute for Infocomm Research, A*STAR, Singapore

Huaqun Guo *obtained B.Eng and M.Eng from Tianjin University in 1989 and 1991, respectively, and obtained M.Eng and PhD from the National University of Singapore (NUS) in 2001 and 2007, respectively. She was a Senior Engineer, Kent Ridge Digital Labs (KRDL), Singapore from 2000 to May 2001. She was a senior research staff, NUS from June 2001 to March 2003. She is IEEE Member from 2007, and IEEE Senior Member from 2009. Currently she is Scientist at the Institute for Infocomm Research (I²R), Agency for Science Technology and Research (A*STAR) in Singapore. She has published more than 40 papers in the international journals, conferences, and books. She is an editor of a book, Automotive Informatics and Communicative Systems: Principals in Vehicular Networks and Data Exchange. She is member of an Editorial Board, and TPC member and session chair for 16 internatinal journals and conferences. Her research areas include multicast, vehicular network, security, P2P computing, networked middleware, and multimedia communication system.*

Preface

Interest in inter-vehicular and vehicle-to-roadside communication has significantly increased over the last decade, in part because of the proliferation of wireless networks. Most research in this area has concentrated on vehicle-to-roadside communication, also called beacon-vehicle communication, in which vehicles share the medium by accessing different time slots.

Some applications for vehicle-to-roadside communication, including automatic payment, route guidance, cooperative driving, and parking management, have been developed to function within limited communication zones of less than 60 meters. However, the IEEE 802.11 Standard has led to increased research in the areas of wireless ad hoc networks and location-based routing algorithms, (Morris et. al., 2000), (Da Chen, Kung, & Vlah, 2001), (Füßler, et. al., 2003), (Lochert, et. al., 2003), (Kosh, Schwingenschlögl, & Ai, 2002). Applications for inter-vehicular communications include intelligent cruise control, intelligent maneuvering control, lane access, and emergency warning, among others. In (Morris et. al., 2000), the authors propose using Grid (Li, et. al., 2000), a geographic forwarding and scalable distributed location service, to route packets from car to car without flooding the network. The authors in (Da Chen, Kung, & Vlah, 2001) propose relaying messages in low traffic densities, based on a microscopic traffic simulator that produces accurate movement traces of vehicles traveling on a highway, and a network simulator to model the exchange of messages among the vehicles. Da Chen et al. employ a straight bidirectional highway segment of one or more lanes. The messages are propagated greedily each time step by hopping to the neighbor closest to the destination. The authors in (Füßler, et al., 2003), compare a topology-based approach and a location-based routing scheme. The authors chose GPSR (Karp & Kung, 2000) as the location-based routing scheme and DSR (Johnson, Maltz, & Hu, 2007) as the topology-based approach. The simulator used in (Füßler, et. al., 2003) is called FARSI, which is a macroscopic traffic model. In (Lochert, et al., 2003), the authors compare two topology-based routing approaches, DSR and AODV (Perkins, Belding-Royer & Das, 2003), versus one position-based routing scheme, GPSR, in an urban environment. Finally, in (Kosh, Schwingenschlögl, & Ai, 2002), the authors employ a geocast routing protocol that is based on AODV.

In inter-vehicular communication, vehicles are equipped with on-board computers that function as nodes in a wireless network, allowing them to contact other similarity equipped vehicles in their vicinity. By exchanging information, vehicles can obtain information about local traffic conditions, which improves traffic control, lowers contamination caused by traffic jams, and provides greater driver safety and comfort.

Vehicle collisions represent the great majority of automobile deaths and injuries. Although great advances have been made regarding passive safety systems (seat belts, air bags), and these systems have significantly reduced the number of deaths and injuries on streets and roadways, active collision avoidance systems are still in the development stage, and there is still much research and development to be done before these systems can actually be deployed.

In the United States, the Transportation Statistics Annual report (Transportation Statistics Annual Report, 2006) states that "highway travel times increased between 1993 and 2003 in all but 3 of the 85 urban areas (98 percent)", and "it took 37 percent longer, on average, in 2003 to make a peak period trip (from 6 to 9 a.m. and 4 to 7 p.m.)." The additional time spent commuting can cause greater fatigue or distraction as the attention span of drivers becomes taxed. Although the number of fatalities slightly decreased, "in 2005, 43,443 motorists and non-motorists were killed in crashes involving motor vehicles, up 1% compared with 2004, and about 2.7 million people were injured." Finally, the report mentions that "there were 1.47 fatalities per 100 million vehicles-miles of highway travel in 2005." One of the major causes of car accidents and fatalities is driver distraction. Distracted driving is defined by the United States Department of Transportation (USDT) (http://www.distraction.gov/) as: "any non-driving activity a person engages in while operating a motor vehicle. Such activities have the potential to distract the person from the primary task of driving and increase the risk of crashing."

Future developments in automobile manufacturing will also include new communication technologies. The major goals are to provide increased automotive safety, to achieve smooth traffic flow on the roads, and to improve passenger convenience by providing them with information and entertainment. In order to avoid communication costs and guarantee the low delays required for the exchange of safety related data between cars, inter-vehicle communication (IVC) systems based on wireless ad-hoc networks represent a promising solution for future road communication scenarios. IVC allows vehicles to organize themselves locally in ad-hoc networks without any pre-installed infrastructure. Communication in future IVC systems will not be restricted to neighbored vehicles travelling within the radio transmission range, as in typical wireless scenarios, the IVC system will also provide multi-hop communication capabilities by using "relay" vehicles that are travelling between the sender and receiver.

Another important aspect of IVC or RVC communication is the environment in which the vehicles are moving. It is known that different physical environments lead to different performances. For example, in an urban scenario, vehicles will suffer more multi-path interference than in a freeway scenario. This is primarily because the presence of buildings and other obstacles (trees, communication towers, billboards, etc.) in urban environments cause diffraction and scattering. Moreover, researchers must also consider the different velocities implicit in different scenarios. Generally speaking, drivers require more time and a greater distance to come to a complete and safe stop. Vehicles will travel at a higher velocity and be more widely spaced in a freeway scenario because drivers require greater reaction times than in urban settings. Distance and relative velocity, therefore, are very important because they significantly influence communications. For example, in urban scenarios, inter-vehicular distances are very small for prolonged periods of time due to reduced spacing from merging and frequent stops. Consequently, closely spaced vehicles can exchange more data than in freeway scenarios, where the distances and velocities between vehicles are substantially greater. It is important to recall that in peer-to-peer communication, the distance between peers must be small enough for the entire duration of the communication. Therefore, vehicles predictably maintain lower speeds and smaller spacing, frequently stop, and transmit greater uninterrupted information streams. The speed and spacing factors lead to considering the dynamics of vehicular movements, particularly inter-vehicular distance and their relative velocity and position as they move along to streets or roadways. Consequently, different models must be developed to predict vehicular movement in highly dynamic and varied real-world scenarios. Another issue that can affect IVC or RVC communication is the technology employed; each technology prioritizes different features, such as frequency, bandwidth, and transmission power.

One of the most obvious issues relating to inter-vehicle ad-hoc routing protocols is the velocity of the mobile devices. One of the effects of velocity is to make the signal strength highly variable. Chu and Stark demonstrate in (Chu and Stark, 2000) that the fading signals are in function of velocity. Based on simulations, they observed that the best performance is at lower velocities because the signals vary more slowly, thus creating little channel attenuation between bits of information transmitted.

There are many problems that affect communications in mobile communication environments, but the two main ones are multi-path delay and Doppler Shift (Rappaport, 2002). Multi-path delay produces frequency selective fading, so that signals suffer interference, and Doppler can affect shifts suffered by the carrier frequencies. Fading is caused by interference between two or more versions of the transmitted signal that arrive at the receiver at slightly different times. The versions, also called multi-path waves, combine at the receiver antenna to give a resultant signal, which can vary widely in amplitude and phase, depending on the distribution of the intensity and relative propagation time of the waves and the bandwidth of the transmitted signal. The phenomenon is known as constructive or destructive interference.

In the estimation of the radio coverage area of a transmitter and receiver, two simple large-scale and small-scale propagation models can be used. Large-scale models characterize signal strength over large T-R separation distances (several hundreds or thousands of meters). Propagation models that characterize the rapid fluctuation of the received signal strength over very short travel distances (a few wavelengths) or short time duration (on the order of seconds) are called small scale, or fading models.

This book is organized as follows:

Section 1 describes current theories and applications of the physical and medium access layers.
Section 2 analyses theories and their applications in the network layer.
Section 3 discusses how to integrate theory into different applications in the application layer.

In greater detail:

Section 1 includes the chapters titled: *Fundamentals of Empirical Propagation Modeling for Outdoor Scenarios; Channel Modeling for Vehicle-to-Vehicle Communications and Networking; Modulation and Coding Techniques for Inter-Vehicular Communications; PHY/MAC Layer Design in Vehicular Ad Hoc Networks: Challenges, Standard Approaches, and Alternative Solutions; The Challenge of a Future Slotted Standard for Vehicular Ad-Hoc Networks*; and *Channel Impairments for V2V Communications in ITS Scenarios*.

Section 2 presents: *Reactive Location-Based Routing Algorithm with Cluster-Based Flooding* and *Evaluation of the LORA-CBF Routing Algorithm with Selective Gateway in an Ad Hoc WiMAX network*.

Section 3 includes: *Development of Applications for Vehicular Communication Network Environments: Challenges and Opportunities; Communication Architectures and Services for Intelligent Transport Systems; Analyzing the Trade-Offs between Security and Performance in VANETs; Cooperative Positioning in Vehicular Networks; Data Dissemination in Vehicular Networks: challenges and Issues; Experience Developing a Vehicular Network Based on Heterogeneous Communication Technologies*; and *Unpredicted Trajectories of an Automated Guided Vehicle with Chaos*.

Raúl Aquino Santos
University of Colima, Mexico

Arthur Edwards Block
University of Colima, Mexico

Víctor Rangel Licea
National Autonomous University of Mexico, Mexico

REFERENCES

BTS. (2006). *Transportation statistics: Annual report*. Retrieved from http://www.bts.gov/publications/transportation_statistics_annual_report/2006/.

Chu, M., & Stark, W. (2000). Effect of mobile velocity on communications in fading channels. *IEEE Transactions on Vehicular Technology, 49*(1), 202–210. doi:10.1109/25.820712

Da Chen, Z., Kung, H.-T., & Vlah, D. (2001). Ad hoc relay wireless networks over moving vehicles on highways. *Proceedings in International Conference on Mobile Computing and Networking,* (pp. 247-250).

Distraction.gov. (n.d.). *Home page*. Retrieved from http://www.distraction.gov/.

Füßler, H., Mauve, M., Hartenstein, H., Käsemann, M., & Vollmer, D. (2003). MobiCom poster: Location-based routing for vehicular ad-hoc networks. *Proceedings in ACM SIGMOBILE Mobile Computing and Communication Review, 7*(1), 47–49.

Johnson, D., Maltz, D., & Hu, Y.-C. (2007). *The dynamic source routing protocol (DSR) for mobile ad hoc networks for IPv4.* http://www.ietf.org/rfc/rfc4728.txt. Request for Comments (Work in Progress).

Karp, B., & Kung, H.-T. (2000). Greedy perimeter stateless routing for wireless networks. *Proceedings of the 6th ACM International Conference on Mobile Computing and Networking,* (pp. 243-254).

Kosh, T., Schwingenschlögl, C., & Ai, L. (2002). Information dissemination in multihop inter-vehicle networks – Adapting the ad-hoc on-demand distance vector routing protocol (AODV). *Proceedings in the 5th IEEE International Conference on Intelligent Transportation Systems,* (pp. 685-690).

Li, J., Jannotti, J., De Couto, D., Karger, D., & Morris, R. (2000). A scalable location service for geographic ad hoc routing. *Proceedings of the 6th ACM International Conference on Mobile Computing and Networking,* (pp. 120-130).

Lochert, C., Füßler, H., Hartenstein, H., Hermann, D., Tian, J., & Mauve, M. (2003). A routing strategy for vehicular ad hoc networks in city environments. *Proceedings of the IEEE Intelligent Vehicles Symposium,* (pp. 156-161).

Morris, R., Jannotti, J., Kaashock, F., Li, J., & Decouto, D. (2000). A scalable ad hoc wireless network system. *Proceedings of the 9th wOrkshop on ACM SIGOPS European Workshop: Beyond the PC: New Challenges for the Operating System,* (pp. 61-65).

Perkins, C., Belding-Royer, E., & Das, S. (2003). *Ad hoc on-demand distance vector (AODV) routing.* http://www.ietf.org/rfc/rfc3561.txt. Request for Comments (Work in Progress).

Rappaport, T. (2002). *Wireless communications: Principles and practice*. Prentice Hall Communications Engineering and Emerging Technologies Series.

Acknowledgment

I would like to thank my wife, Tania, for her deep love and for giving me a wonderful family. To my lovely daughters: Tania Iritzi and Dafne for providing me many years of happiness. Also, I would like to thank my parents Teodoro and Herlinda for offering me the opportunity to study and to believe in God. Finally, I want to thank to my brother Carlos and my sisters Teresa and Leticia for their support.

I would like to endlessly thank my wife, Marilú, for selflessly dedicating her life to making my life worth living. Thank you for giving me my most precious children, Elisa and David, and for always firmly standing beside me. Thank you for walking life's path with me.

My special gratitude is for my wife Adriana, for her immense love, patience, and support for more than 20 years. My lovely kids: Mary Fer, Karen, and Miguel for making me such a proud dad. I would like to thanks my parents Paulino and Ma. Salud for being an immense source of inspirations throughout my life. Finally, I want to thanks Raul Aquino, for giving me the opportunity to contribute to this book.

Raúl Aquino Santos
University of Colima, Mexico

Arthur Edwards Block
University of Colima, Mexico

Víctor Rangel Licea
National Autonomous University of Mexico, Mexico

Section 1
Theory and Application of the Physical and Medium Access Layers

Chapter 1
Fundamentals of Empirical Propagation Modeling for Outdoor Scenarios

Sergio Hernández Gaona
DGETA, Mexico

ABSTRACT

The empirical propagation models are widely used to predict the behavior of radio signals. In this chapter some empirical propagation models for outdoors are reviewed. The objective of the chapter is to understand the mechanisms that impinge radio waves, and the most popular propagation models for outdoors that can be used to calculate a link budget. The three kinds of fading: path loss, shadowing, and fast-fading are described through the chapter. Some statistical concepts required for the shadowing calculation, like Probability Density Function (PDF) and Cumulative Distribution Function (CDF), are also explained.

MAIN FOCUS OF THE CHAPTER

Noise is an essential factor in wireless communications due to changing environmental conditions. The surroundings of a wireless network can very different at distinct places greatly affecting communication between nodes.

Noise can be divided into two kinds to analyze the effect of noise in wireless communications:

additive noise and multiplicative noise. Additive noise is inherent to the receptor and is usually stable. Multiplicative noise arises from many factors and objects that affect the wireless channel. As a result multiplicative noise can vary greatly from location to location. Multiplicative noise is the main factor of interest when analyzing a wireless channel and propagation models.

The multiplicative noise having no relation with either the transmitter or the receiver can be divided into three main fading processes (see

DOI: 10.4018/978-1-4666-0209-0.ch001

Figure 1. Fading processes. Adapted from (Saunders & Aragón-Zavala, 2007)

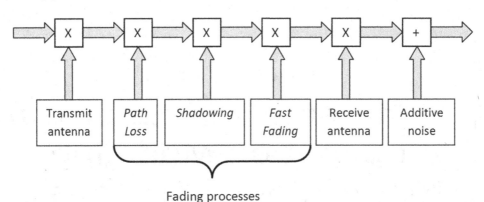

Figure 1): Path Loss, Shadowing (or slow fading) and Fast-Fading (or Multipath fading).

Some of the most important phenomena that generate multiplicative noise are the following:

- **Absorption:** This phenomenon occurs when objects absorb electromagnetic radiation and convert it into another type of energy such as heat or electricity. All the objects present in the environment generate different levels of absorption, for example, walls, trees, signs -- even the atmosphere.

- **Reflection:** Reflection occurs when electromagnetic waves hit an object which is much greater than the transmitted wavelength. When this happens, the signal is reflected by the hit surface (see Figure 2). Reflection takes place when the waves hit the ground, walls and furniture. When a wave is reflected, it can be partially refracted (Sarkar, 2003). The degree of reflection depends on the material's properties, like reflection, absorption and transmission. For example, a metal sheet has a nearly perfect reflection, whereas glass and paper have a nearly perfect transmission. Materials like brick have a certain degree of reflection, absorption and transmission (Webb, 1999).

- **Diffraction:** It occurs when there is an obstacle with sharp borders in the path between the transmitter and the receiver. When the waves reach the obstacle, they bend over the sharp borders (see Figure 3). Diffraction has an advantage: the waves can reach places where there is no line of sight; however, the attenuation is greater (Rappaport, 2002). The most important factor is the diffraction angle. With large angles of diffraction, the signal can surround an obstacle. On the other hand, a narrow angle can form a shadow behind the obstacle, where there will be no signal reception (Webb, 1999).

- **Refraction:** The refraction phenomenon occurs when electromagnetic waves pass from one material to another with different densities, causing a change of direction (see Figure 3).

- **Scattering:** Objects with rough surfaces reflect waves in several directions, which diminish the signal intensity. Scattering occurs when the medium through which the signal is propagating contains objects with dimensions smaller than the wavelength signal and the number of obstacles is high (Sarkar, 2003). The scattering level depends on the incidence angle of the signal, and the roughness of the surface. Some

Figure 2. Reflection effect

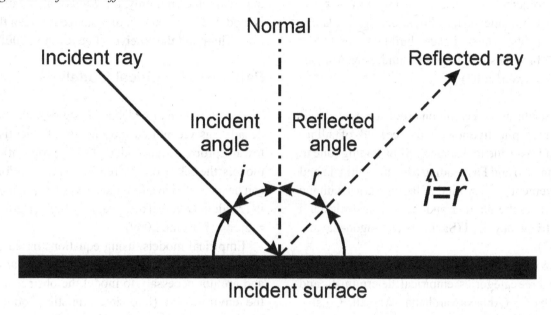

Figure 3. Refraction effect

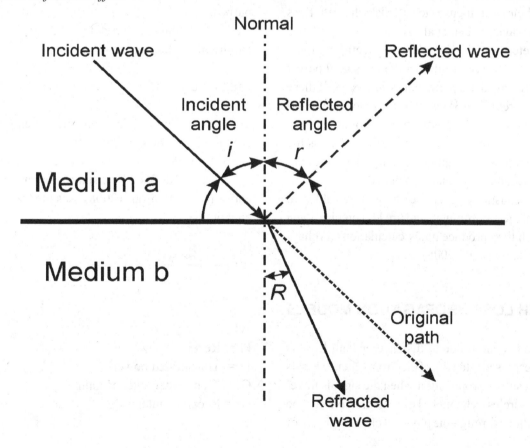

objects that cause scattering are water surfaces, uneven terrains, street signals, lampposts; stairs inside buildings and tree branches and leaves (Saunders & Aragón-Zavala, 2007).

Scattering is a common procedure that classifies multiplicative noise into three kinds of fading: Path Loss (due to distance), Slow Fading (due to obstacles) and Fast Fading (due to multipath and movement). Every kind of fading varies with the distance, the number and type of obstacles and the frequency used (Saunders & Aragón-Zavala, 2007).

Wireless propagation models can be classified into three categories: empirical, deterministic and stochastic (Abhayawardhana, Wassell, Crosby, Sellars, & Brown, 2005).

Empirical models are widely used because are very simple, easy and fast to calculate. These models are based on observations and measures, and their main focus is to calculate the Path Loss (Abhayawardhana, et al., 2005).

Deterministic models use electromagnetic propagation laws to determine the signal power to be received at a particular point. Many of these models require a 3D map of the place, including as many objects as possible to improve the precision. A drawback of deterministic models is the computer power required to calculate the attenuation (Abhayawardhana, et al., 2005).

Stochastic models use random variables to model the environment and are less precise, even though they produce quick calculations (Abhayawardhana, et al., 2005).

PATH LOSS PROPAGATION MODELS

The attenuation due to distance or Path Loss is the decreased intensity of electromagnetic signals that result of propagation when the signals travel in a wireless channel. This attenuation can be calculated through the physical characteristics of the channel. Commonly, this kind of attenuation is modeled as a function of distance between the transmitter and the receiver (Lee & Choi, 2008).

Path Loss Empirical Models

The proliferation of wideband systems in the last decade has recaptured the interest of scientists toward propagation models. Using propagation models, the behavior of wireless communications can be predicted in a fast and easy way, considering random factors if necessary (LaSorte, Barnes, Zigreng, & Refai, 2009).

Empirical models, using equations based on measurements, can be used in similar scenarios and are not necessary to model the obstacles in the environment (like deterministic models). These models have restrictions about frequencies, distances and antenna heights.

Some of these models can be employed beyond the established ranges, but only for comparative purposes.

The following section includes several outdoor empirical models for analysis.

Friis Equation

The Friis Equation is the foundation of empirical propagation models. This equation determines the proportion of received power against transmitted power, as defined by distance, antenna gains and wavelength. Itoua (2008) uses the following equation:

$$\mathrm{Pr} = \frac{P_t G_t G_r \lambda^2}{\left(4\pi\right)^2 d^2 L} \qquad (1)$$

Where:
Pr = Received power
Pt = Transmitted power
Gt = Transmitter antenna gain
Gr = Receiver antenna gain

λ = Wavelength (in meters)

d = Distance between transmitter and receiver (in meters)

L = Additional losses (not related to the system, $L \geq 1$)

Sometimes, antenna gains and additional losses are not used (Seybold, 2005) and the equation is simplified like this:

$$\Pr = \frac{P_t \lambda^2}{\left(4\pi\right)^2 d^2} \tag{2}$$

Commonly, the Friis Equation calculates the relation between received power and transmitted power. The following equation is used to calculate Path Gain:

$$\frac{P_r}{P_t} = G_r G_t \left(\frac{\lambda}{4\pi d}\right)^2 \tag{3}$$

Or without antenna gains:

$$\frac{P_r}{P_t} = \left(\frac{\lambda}{4\pi d}\right)^2 \tag{4}$$

It is important to take into account that the Friis Equation considers a location without obstacles, where the electromagnetic waves are traveling and there is no additional attenuation. In the real world these conditions are nearly impossible. Therefore, additional parameters must be considered to calculate the attenuation for each specific location (Saunders & Aragón-Zavala, 2007).

Free Space Path Loss

Path loss is the energy attenuation in electromagnetic waves when they propagate through space (Green & Obaidat, 2002).

Free Space Path Loss is derived from the Friis Equation. In other words, it is the relationship between the transmitted power and the received power:

$$L_{fs} = \frac{P_t}{P_r} = \left(\frac{4\pi d}{\lambda}\right)^2 \tag{5}$$

The lambda value can be substituted by $\lambda = c / f$, where c is the light speed in m/s and f is the carrier frequency in Hertz:

$$L_{fs} = \frac{P_t}{P_r} = \left(\frac{4\pi d f}{c}\right)^2 \tag{6}$$

However, it is common to express the Free Space Path Loss in decibels, using the following equation:

$$L_{fs}\left(dB\right) = 32.44 + 20\log d + 20\log f \tag{7}$$

Where:

d = distance in kilometers

f = carrier frequency in Megahertz

In the Free Space Path Loss equation, the power signal decreases inversely to the square of the distance (Lee & Choi, 2008).

Two-Ray Model

Free Space Propagation is very rare and occurs only in situations like transmission between satellites, where there are no obstacles. In terrestrial environments, there are different conditions that negatively affect electromagnetic waves. When the antennas are near ground level, there is reflection caused by the ground. If there are no obstacles, the receiver antenna receives at least two signals: the first signal is the direct ray that travels from the transmitter to the receiver and the second

Figure 4. Two-ray model. Adapted from (Garg, 2007).

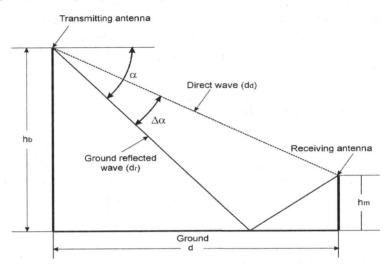

signal is the signal reflected by ground (Garg, 2007). The two signals are added at the receiver with a difference in phase because of the different distance each signal has to travel (Saunders & Aragón-Zavala, 2007).

When the ground reflected signal has been taken into account, the model is called the Two-ray Model, which is shown in Figure 4.

The Two-ray Model is used when the antenna heights are much less than the distance between them, and the reflecting surface is level (Garg, 2007). One condition to consider about the ground plane is that the distance between transmitter and receiver must be at most a few dozen kilometers. The equation for the Two-ray Model is:

$$\frac{P_r}{P_t} = G_t G_r \left(\frac{h_t h_r}{d^2} \right)^2 \qquad (8)$$

In decibels, the equation for the Two-ray Model is:

$$L_p \left(dB \right) = 40 \log d - 20 \log h_t \\ - 20 \log h_r - 10 \log G_t - 10 \log G_r \qquad (9)$$

Where:

d = distance in meters
ht = transmitter antenna height in meters
hr = receiver antenna height in meters
Gt = Transmitter antenna gain
Gr = Receiver antenna gain

Log-Distance Model

This model is based on the principle that the average received signal diminishes in a logarithmic way according to distance in both outdoor and indoor environments. The main characteristic of Log-distance Model is the attenuation exponent n (Rappaport, 2002). The equation is:

$$PL \left(dB \right) = PL \left(d_0 \right) + 10n \log \left(\frac{d}{d_0} \right) \qquad (10)$$

Where:

n = attenuation exponent
d = distance between transmitter and receiver
d0 = reference distance.

The attenuation exponent indicates the relationship between attenuation and distance and the reference distance is a short distance that depends on the signal coverage (in macrocells, this can be 1 km; in microcells, this can be 100 m or 1 m).

The reference distance always must be in the far field of the transmitter antenna. The value of d0 can be calculated using the Free Space Path Loss equation or can be obtained from measurements. n varies with the propagation environment. For example, in free space n = 2, when there are obstructions, n takes the higher value.

Dual-Slope Model

The Dual-slope Model is similar to Log-distance Model, but the dual-slope model uses two parameters instead of one (Saunders & Aragón-Zavala, 2007).

The equation for Dual-slope Model is:

$$L = 10n_1 \log\left(\frac{r}{rb}\right) + Lb \quad \text{for r} \leq \text{rb} \tag{11}$$

$$L = 10n_2 \log\left(\frac{r}{rb}\right) + Lb \quad \text{for r} > \text{rb} \tag{12}$$

Where:
Lb = reference attenuation when r = rb
rb = breakpoint distance
n1 = attenuation exponent when r ≤ rb
n2 = attenuation exponent when r > rb

There is a modified equation to avoid the abrupt transition between the two attenuations (Saunders & Aragón-Zavala, 2007):

$$L = Lb + 10n_1 \log\left(\frac{r}{rb}\right) + 10\left(n_2 - n_1\right)\log\left(1 + \frac{r}{rb}\right) \tag{13}$$

Ad hoc Model by Green and Obaidat

Green y Obaidat (2002) proposed a propagation model for links with LoS (Line of Sight) and antenna heights between 1 y 2.5 meters (typical for ad hoc networks).

In ad hoc networks, the antennas are at a low height. Therefore, the first Fresnel Zone is invaded by the surface where the antennas are located. Any object inside the first Fresnel Zone causes diffraction and attenuates the electromagnetic waves.

The equation for the ad hoc model is:

$$P_{LOSS} = 40 \log d + 20 \log f - 20 \log h_t h_r \tag{14}$$

Where:
f = carrier frequency in Gigahertz
ht = transmitter antenna height in meters
hr = receiver antenna height in meters
d = distance between transmitter and receiver in meters

Okumura Model

The Okumura propagation model is based on measurements realized in Tokyo in 1960. Today, it is sometimes used as a reference in many macrocell scenarios (Seybold, 2005).

The main problem of the Okumura model is that is entirely based on measurements and does not provide an analytical explanation. Furthermore, some of the parameters are obtained from the curves drawn by Okumura, which makes the calculation prone to errors (Rappaport, 2002).

The Okumura model uses an urban area as the main scenario for its calculations. It then corrects for factors that are applied to calculate different scenarios (suburban and rural). A weakness of the Okumura model is that it employs almost level ground in its calculations, making additional corrections necessary for other kinds of terrain (Seybold, 2005).

The frequencies recommended for the Okumura model are between 150 MHz and 1920 MHz (it can be extrapolated to 3000 MHz). The recommended distances are between 1 km and 100 km, with the antenna height at between 30 m and 1000 m (Rappaport, 2002).

The model is represented as:

$$L_{50}(dB) = L_{FSL} + A_{mu} - G(h_{te}) - G(h_{re}) - G_{AREA} \tag{15}$$

Where:

L50(dB) = Median attenuation measured in decibels

LFSL = Free Space Attenuation

Amu = median attenuation relative to Free space and nearly plain terrain, obtained from the Okumura curves.

G(hte) = Base antenna height gain

G(hre) = Mobile antenna height gain

GAREA = Environment gain, obtained from the Okumura curves.

The receiving antenna gain varies depending of antenna height:

$$G\left(h_{te}\right) = 20\log\left(\frac{h_{te}}{200}\right) \quad 1000 \text{ m} > \text{hte} > 30 \text{ m} \tag{16}$$

$$G\left(h_{re}\right) = 10\log\left(\frac{h_{re}}{3}\right) \quad \text{hre} \leq 3 \text{ m} \tag{17}$$

$$G\left(h_{re}\right) = 20\log\left(\frac{h_{re}}{3}\right) \quad 10 \text{ m} > \text{hre} > 3 \text{ m} \tag{18}$$

Hata Model

The Hata Model, also known as Okumura-Hata model is an empirical formula created to make it easier to obtain the values represented graphically by Okumura (Anderson, 2003). Garg (2007) mentions that this model is useful for frequencies between 150 and 2200 Mhz; however, many other articles point out that the model is adequate for frequencies between 150 y 1500 MHz.

This model is widely used in macrocells, using three kinds of scenarios: rural, suburban and urban. A rural scenario is an open space without

trees and buildings such as farms and rice fields. A suburban scenario contains some trees and houses. An urban scenario is a city or big town with tall buildings and many houses with two or more stories (Saunders & Aragón-Zavala, 2007). The three variants of this model are:

Urban scenarios:

$$L_{dB} = A + B\log R - E \tag{19}$$

Suburban scenarios:

$$L_{dB} = A + B\log R - C \tag{20}$$

Rural scenarios:

$$L_{dB} = A + B\log R - D \tag{21}$$

Where:

$$A = 69.55 + 26.16\log f_c - 13.82\log h_b \tag{22}$$

$$B = 44.9 - 6.55\log h_b \tag{23}$$

$$C = 2\left[\log\left(\frac{f_c}{28}\right)\right]^2 + 5.4 \tag{24}$$

$$D = 4.78\left(\log f_c\right)^2 - 18.33\log f_c + 40.94 \tag{25}$$

For big cities and fc ≥ 300 MHz:

$$E = 3.2\left(\log\left(11.75h_m\right)\right)^2 - 4.97 \tag{26}$$

For big cities and fc < 300 MHz:

$$E = 8.29\left(\log\left(1.54h_m\right)\right)^2 - 1.1 \tag{27}$$

For small and medium cities:

$$E = \left(1.1 \log f_c - 0.7\right) h_m - \left(1.56 \log f_c - 0.8\right) \tag{28}$$

In the last equations, hb refers to the base station antenna height, and hm is the mobile antenna height. This model is valid for base station antenna heights of between 30 and 200m and mobile antenna height of between 1 and 10m. The distance between antennas (R) must be in kilometers and the valid interval is 1 to 20. The frequency is in MHz (Pahlavan & Krishnamurthy, 2009).

COST-231 Hata Model

The COST-231 Hata Model, sometimes called the Hata model PCS extension, is an extended version of the Hata model, which permits the use of frequencies of between 1.5 and 2 GHz.

The following equation shows the COST-231 Hata Model:

$$L_{dB} = F + B \log R - E + G \tag{29}$$

Where:

$$F = 46.3 + 33.9 \log f_c - 13.82 \log h_b \tag{30}$$

The value for B is defined in Equation (23), E take the values defined in Equations (26), (27) and (28) according to the scenario. G = 0 dB for medium cities and suburban areas, or G = 3 dB for metropolitan areas (Saunders & Aragón-Zavala, 2007).

The frequency (fc) is represented in MHz, the distance between the base station and the remote terminal (d) is in kilometers and the antenna heights for the base station (hb) and mobile station (hm) are in meters.

Zhang & Chen (2008) present the COST-231 Hata Model in a different way:

$$\begin{aligned}PL =\ &45.5 + 0.7h_m - 13.82 \log(h_b) \\ &+ \left(44.9 - 6.55 \log(h_b)\right) \log\left(d / 1000\right) \\ &+ \left(35.46 - 1.1h_m\right) \log f + G\end{aligned} \tag{31}$$

The COST-231 Hata Model is restricted to locations where the base station antenna is above the roof of all nearby buildings (Parsons, 2000).

ECC-33 Model

The ECC-33 model is a modification of the Hata-Okumura Model, extrapolating the measurements obtained by Okumura and modifying the parameters for broadband systems (LaSorte, et al., 2009).

This model was developed by Electronic Communication Committee (ECC) and is adjusted for fixed systems (Ayyappan & Dananjayan, 2008). The ECC-33 model is represented in the following way:

$$PL = A_{fs} + A_{bm} - G_b - G_m \tag{32}$$

Where:
Afs = Free Space Path Loss
Gb = Base Antenna Height Gain
Gm = Mobile Antenna Height Gain.

$$A_{fs} = 92.4 + 20 \log d + 20 \log f \tag{33}$$

$$A_{bm} = 20.41 + 9.83 \log d + 7.894 \log f + 9.56(\log f)^2 \tag{34}$$

$$G_b = \log\left(h_b / 200\right)\left[13.958 + 5.8\left(\log d\right)^2\right] \tag{35}$$

$$G_m = \left[42.57 + 13.7 \log f\right]\left[\log h_m - 0.585\right] \tag{36}$$

Where:
f = Frequency in GHz.

d = Distance between base antenna and mobile antenna in kilometers.

hb= Base antenna height in meters.

hm = Mobile antenna height in meters.

IMT-2000 Vehicular Model

The IMT-2000 (International Mobile Telecommunications 2000) model, also known as 3G or 3rd generation, is a set of standards for cell phones and mobile telecommunications. This vehicular model is defined for macro cells with high transmission power (Garg, 2007) and areas outside of city centers, where there are high buildings. This model can be used in urban, suburban and rural areas (Zhang & Chen, 2008).

Garg (2007) defines the IMT-2000 model like this:

$$L_{50} = 40\left(1 - 4 \times 10^{-2}\Delta h_b\right)\log d - 18\log\left(\Delta h_b\right) + 21\log f_c + 80 \ dB \tag{37}$$

Where:

d = Distance between base antenna and mobile antenna in kilometers.

fc= Frequency in MHz.

Δhb = base antenna height measured from building average height in meters.

Zhang & Chen (2008), define the IMT-2000 model in a different way:

$$PL\left(d\right) = 40\left(1 - 4.10^{-3}H_{BS}\right)\log d - 18\log\left(H_{BS}\right) + 21\log f + 80 \ dB \tag{38}$$

Where:

d = Distance between base antenna and mobile antenna in kilometers.

f = Frequency in MHz.

HBS = base antenna height measured from building average height in meters.

This model has been used in measurements for frequencies around 2.5 GHz (Zhang & Chen, 2008).

SHADOWING MODELS

Shadowing is the attenuation effect caused by obstacles like walls and trees that are in the way of electromagnetic transmissions. The obstacles through mechanisms like absorption, diffraction and reflection act on electromagnetic waves and attenuate them. The obstacle position and properties (shape, size, thickness and material) are not predictable. That is the reason why the shadowing effects in considered a random effect, where the received power can vary even at the same distance (Lee & Choi, 2008).

Path Loss models allow us to calculate the median attenuation based on distance. Nevertheless, in practice, there are some variations between the upper and lower median values. These variations are caused by shadowing. To include these fluctuations, it is necessary to add an attenuation margin to the value obtained from a path loss model. The result will provide a more accurate calculation (Pahlavan & Krishnamurthy, 2009).

Shadowing is usually modeled, statistically, through a log-normal distribution. In the communications world, a log-normal distribution describes a variation of the mean signal measured in decibels similar to a Gaussian distribution (Anderson, 2003).

Variations in received power, as a consequence of shadowing, depends on the environment, but can reach up to 20 dB (Saunders & Aragón-Zavala, 2007).

Calculation of Attenuation Margin

To determine the attenuation margin to counteract shadowing in a link budget calculation is one way of improve the reliability of a propagation model. Importantly, however, the link distance is reduced

Figure 5. Probability associated with a Gaussian distribution. Adapted from (Montgomery & Runger, 2003).

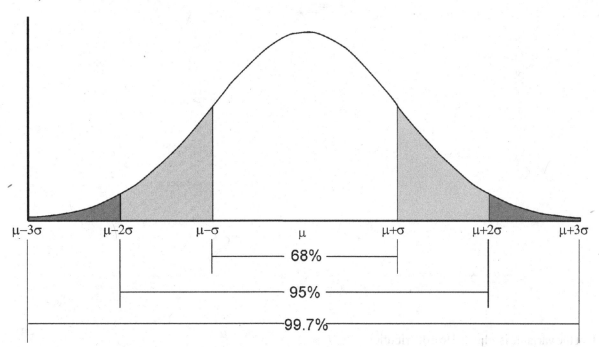

as a result of the attenuation margin (Pahlavan & Krishnamurthy, 2009).

Because of the random behavior of shadowing, the attenuation margin must be determined statistically and by probability. The following paragraphs define some of these concepts.

Shadowing has a log-normal probability distribution, which means that the power intensity of the signal at the receiver antenna, or the attenuation values calculated in decibels, follows a Gaussian distribution (see Figure 5).

In determining probability, a Probability Density Function (PDF) f(x) can be used to describe the probability distribution of a continuous random variable X. The probability that X is between a and b is determined for the integral of f(x) between a and b (Montgomery & Runger, 2003).

When there is a Gaussian distribution, the PDF (Spiegel, Hernández Heredero, & Abellanas, 1998) is defined in the following way:

$$f(x) = \frac{1}{\sigma\sqrt{2\pi}} e^{\left(\frac{-(x-\mu)^2}{2\sigma^2}\right)} \tag{39}$$

μ represents the mean, $\sigma2$ the variance and σ the standard deviation. When a variable has a PDF of the Equation (39), it is said that it has a distribution of $N(\mu,\sigma2)$, "normal distribution with mean μ and variance $\sigma2$" (Ogunnaike, 2010).

Shadowing is a random variable with a zero mean and normal distribution (as shown in figure 6) where the area under the curve always has a value of 1 (Montgomery & Runger, 2003). When the mean is zero, the Equation (39) can be simplified in the following way:

$$f(x) = \frac{1}{\sigma\sqrt{2\pi}} e^{\left(-\frac{x^2}{2\sigma^2}\right)} \tag{40}$$

There is a common process used to manipulate random variables under a Gaussian distribution. This process, called "standardize", that means

Figure 6. PDF for some dispersion values: σ=1, σ=2, σ=3 and μ=0, under a Gaussian (normal) distribution

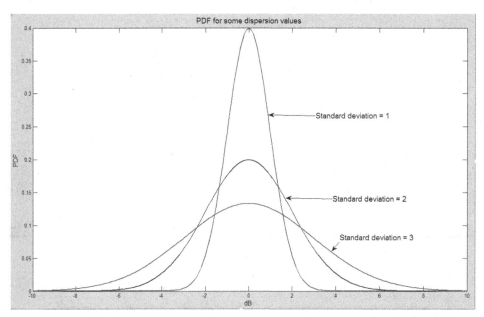

that the variable is adjusted to a distribution $N(0,1)$. This standardization (Ross, 2004) is made through the next calculation:

$$Z = \frac{x - \mu}{\sigma} \tag{41}$$

Working with a standardized PDF has some advantages: 1) it is possible generalize the probability calculation for every random variable through standardized probability tables, 2) some functions are included in mathematical software like MATLAB (error function, Q function) and, 3) The PDF is simplified (Tse & Viswanath, 2005):

$$f(z) = \frac{1}{\sqrt{2\pi}} e^{\left(-\frac{z^2}{2}\right)} \tag{42}$$

When standardized values are used to calculate the PDF, it is possible to calculate the probability of any random variable $N(\mu,\sigma2)$. Consequently, upon reaching the final calculation, one only needs to apply the inverse process calculated in Equation (41):

$$x = z\sigma + \mu \tag{43}$$

However, the PDF it is not very useful to calculate the attenuation margin corresponding to shadowing, so the Cumulative Distribution Function (CDF) is used. Figure 7 shows a graphic of the CDF. The PDF and the CDF have an intimate relationship: the PDF is the derivative of the CDF and the CDF is the integral of the PDF (Baron, 2006).

The CDF allows one to determine the probability that the random variable is between -∞ and a specific value. For example, for a standardized random variable with a Gaussian distribution, the CDF of 1.26 allows one to obtain the probability of the variable with values between -∞ and 1.26 or ≤1.26, as shown in figure 8 in the shadowed area.

Returning to Equation (39), the corresponding CDF is:

$$F(x) = \frac{1}{\sigma\sqrt{2\pi}} \int_{-\infty}^{x} \exp\left[-\frac{1}{2}\left(\frac{t-\mu}{\sigma}\right)^2\right] dt = \frac{1}{2}\left[1 + erf\left(\frac{x-\mu}{\sigma\sqrt{2}}\right)\right] \tag{44}$$

Figure 7. CDF for some dispersion values: σ=1, σ=2, σ=3 and μ=0, under a Gaussian (normal) distribution

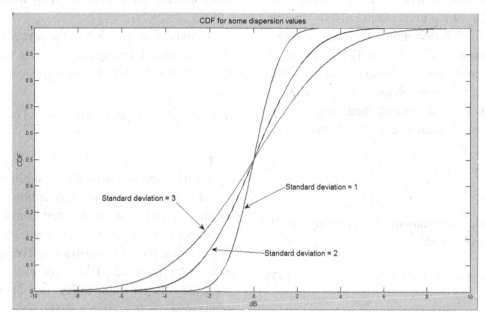

Figure 8. The probability that Z take values ≤1.26, equivalent to CDF(1.26) with a standardized random variable with a Gaussian distribution (Montgomery & Runger, 2003)

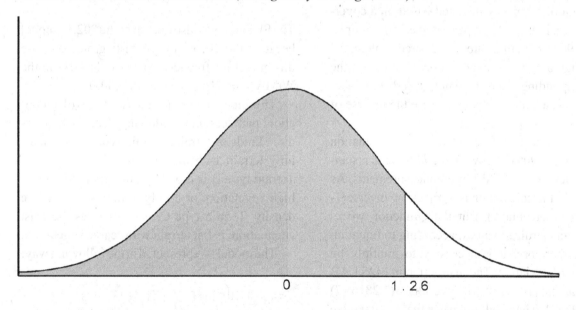

Where, erf is the *error function* available in many types of mathematical software like MATLAB. When the PDF is standardized, the corresponding CDF is simplified:

$$F(x) = \frac{1}{2}\left[1 + erf\left(\frac{z}{\sqrt{2}}\right)\right] \qquad (45)$$

There is a function that allows simplifying the attenuation margin calculation which is called the *Q function*, defined in the following way: 1 - the CDF of the normalized random variable with a normal distribution (Mathworks, 2008). Saunders and Aragón-Zavala (2007) define it as "the complement of the cumulative normal distribution". In Figure 8, the *Q function* of 1.26: Q(1.26) is the area without shadowing. The Q function can be calculated in the following way:

$$Q(z) = \frac{1}{2}\left[1 - erf\left(\frac{z}{\sqrt{2}}\right)\right] \tag{46}$$

From the last equations, the following equalities can be obtained:

$$CDF(z) = 1 - Q(z) = Q(-z) \tag{47}$$

$$Q(z) = 1 - CDF(z) = CDF(-z) \tag{48}$$

However, generally speaking, the attenuation margin of a link is calculated based on a coverage area, indicated by a percentage. For example, if a 90% coverage area is desired, calculated through a path loss model, one must obtain the corresponding value of z, when Q(z)=0.1. In cases like this, a better method is to use the inverse of the Q function.

If it is necessary to calculate the attenuation margin for 90% of coverage and there is a standard deviation of 7 dB in the measurements. As a result, the calculation is: Qfunction_inverse(1-desired_percentage). But the Qfunction works with standardized values; according to Equation (43), therefore, it is necessary to multiply by standard deviation. The instruction in MATLAB is: *qfuncinv(1-0.9)*7*, which results in (1.2816)(7) = 8.97 dB. The result indicates that to guarantee 90% coverage within the limit area, an attenuation margin of 9 dB must be added.

Log-Distance + Shadowing Model

This model is a variation of the preceding Log-Distance model, taking into count an additional attenuation value for shadowing:

$$PL(dB) = PL(d_0) + 10n \log\left(\frac{d}{d_0}\right) + Xs \tag{49}$$

Xs, which representing shadowing, is a random variable with a Gaussian distribution and zero mean. Commonly, Xs is obtained from measurements varying the distance between transmitter and receiver. It is common to use an average value of 8 dB for the standard deviation of shadowing, which results in a value of Xs=10.5 dB for 90% of the area coverage (Garg, 2007).

Stanford University Interim (SUI) Model

The SUI model is also known as the 802.16 model because the IEEE 802.16 task group propose this model for frequencies below 11 GHz in the WiMAX standard (Anderson, 2003).

This model takes in count two types of attenuation: path loss and shadowing. It also considers three kinds of terrain. Terrain type A represents hilly terrain with moderate to high vegetation. Terrain type B is mostly plain with moderate to high vegetation, or a hilly terrain with low tree density. Terrain type C, which causes the least attenuation, is flat terrain with scarce vegetation.

The model is represented in the following way:

$$L = A + 10\gamma \log\left(\frac{d}{d_0}\right) + X_f + X_h + s$$
$$\text{for d>d0} \tag{50}$$

Where:

d = Distance between base antenna and mobile antenna in meters.

d0= Reference distance (100 m).

s = deviation factor, a log-normal distributed value representing shadowing, with a value between 8.2 and 10.6 (Anderson, 2003).

$$A = 20 \log \left(\frac{4\pi d_0}{\lambda} \right) \qquad (51)$$

$$\gamma = a - b\, h_b + \frac{c}{h_b} \qquad (52)$$

Where:
hb= Base antenna height over the ground (10-80 m).
Xf= Correction factor for frequencies over 2 GHz.
Xh = Correction factor for mobile antenna height.

According to Zhang (2009) these factors must be calculated in the following way:

$$X_f = 6.0 \log \left(\frac{f}{2000} \right) \text{ f in MHz} \qquad (53)$$

$$X_h = -10.8 \log \left(\frac{h_m}{2} \right) \text{ For A and B terrains} \qquad (54)$$

$$X_h = -20 \log \left(\frac{h_m}{2} \right) \text{ For C terrain} \qquad (55)$$

The value of a, b and c is obtained from Table 1.

FAST-FADING

When it is necessary to calculate the link for a mobile system and the path loss and shadowing values have been considered, there are still are some variations in the received signal intensity when the mobile receiver is moved small distances (a few wavelengths). This is called the fast-fading effect (Saunders & Aragón-Zavala, 2007).

The fast-fading effect, also called multipath fading is a power variation of the electromagnetic signal caused by constructive and destructive interference in the signal components that arrive to the receptor through different paths. These

Table 1. Field parameters for the SUI model (Zhang, 2009).

Value	A Terrain	B Terrain	C Terrain
a	4.6	4.0	3.6
b	0.0075	0.0065	0.005
c	12.6	17.1	20

multiple paths are caused by objects near the path between the transmitter and receiver, provoking signal reflection and signal dispersion. The fast-fading effect is also modeled statistically (Lee & Choi, 2008).

When the transmitted signal is reflected for multiple objects in the path between transmitter and receiver, every signal arrives at the receptor with a random shift phase caused by the length of every path. Because of this, the signal intensity varies for short periods of time (Garg, 2007) and the time the signal arrives also varies (Parsons, 2000).

The signal intensity variations due to the multipath fading effect can be very high, in the order of 35-40 dB (Saunders & Aragón-Zavala, 2007).

To separate the fast-fading effect from the shadowing effect, the signal intensity of the receiver must be averaged at a distance of less than 10 m. specifically; the distance to be used must be between 5 and 40 wavelengths (Garg, 2007). For example, in a 2.437 GHz frequency, to separate the fast-fading effect from the shadowing effect, the measurements must be averaged at a distance between 61.5 cm and 5 m.

Depending on number and characteristics of obstacles that cause multipath fading, there are two possibilities: 1) There is LoS and 2) There is non LoS. In the first case, when there is a direct signal between transmitter and receiver and many secondary signals occurring simultaneously with less intensity, a Rice distribution can approximate the PDF. In the second case, when there are several signals with similar intensity, a Rayleigh distribu-

Figure 9. Delay spread caused by multiple signals traveling different length paths. Adapted from (Garg, 2007).

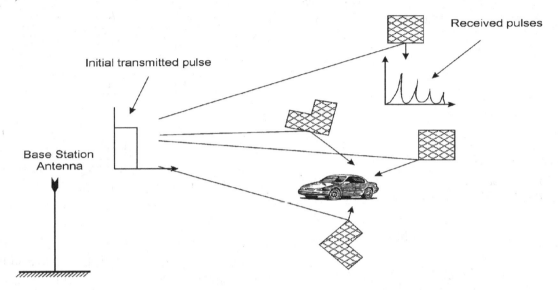

tion can be used to obtain the approximate PDF (Garg, 2007).

The multipath fading effect can provoke time variations or frequency variations. When the time is affected, is called delay spread; when the frequency is affected, it is called Doppler spread (Seybold, 2005).

Delay Spread

The effect of delay spread, also called time dispersion, is the signal delay suffered at longer distances. In other words, between the arrival of the signals with the shorter distances (LoS signal) and the signals with longer distances, there is a period of time or "delay". This is what causes the signal to spread (Garg, 2007) like as shown in Figure 9.

The delay spread effect can cause Inter-Symbol Interference (ISI). The ISI occurs when the energy of one symbol invades the area of another symbol, causing an increase in the Bit Error Rate (BER). The ISI problem is aggravated when the delay spread effects approaches or exceeds the symbol duration used by the system (Garg, 2007).

Doppler Spread

The Doppler shift is the apparent change in the signal frequency caused by transmitter or receiver movement, or both. When the receiver approaches the transmitter, the frequency seems to increase. When the receiver moves away from transmitter, the frequency seems to lessen. Doppler shift depends on the angle of signal arrival with respect to the movement of the mobile device (See Figure 10). The highest value for Doppler shift occurs at an angle of 0°, when the receiver approaches to transmitter in a straight line (Saunders & Aragón-Zavala, 2007).

The variation of Doppler shift, fd (Saunders & Aragón-Zavala, 2007) depends on:

$$f_d = f_c \frac{v}{c} \cos \alpha = \frac{v}{\lambda} \cos \alpha \qquad (56)$$

Where:

$c = $ Light speed.
$v = $ Vehicle speed.
$fc = $ Transmission frequency.
$\lambda = $ Wavelength.

Figure 10. Doppler effect. Adapted from (Saunders & Aragón-Zavala, 2007).

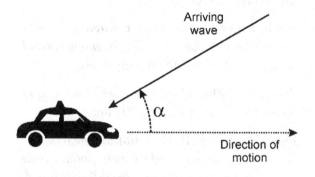

$\alpha =$ angle of arrival of the electromagnetic signal respect to the movement.

The maximum variation of Doppler shift fm, occurs when α=0, because cos(0) = 1, and the Equation (56) becomes:

$$f_m = f_c \frac{v}{c} = \frac{v}{\lambda} \qquad (57)$$

Nevertheless, the Doppler shift impact varies when the receiver approaches the transmitter (fc + fm) and when the receiver moves away from the transmitter (fc – fm), when the variation is within (fc – fm) ≤ f ≤ (fc + fm). In a multipath fading environment, every signal arrives at a different angle. That is when the Doppler shift varies with every signal, causing signal spread (Saunders & Aragón-Zavala, 2007), which is shown in Figure

Figure 11. Doppler spread. Adapted from (Saunders & Aragón-Zavala, 2007)

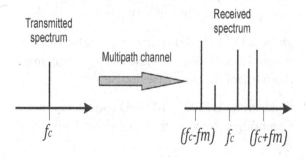

11. In conclusion, the Doppler spread is twice the maximum variation of Doppler shift (fm).

REFERENCES

Abhayawardhana, V. S., Wassell, I. J., Crosby, D., Sellars, M. P., & Brown, M. G. (2005). *Comparison of empirical propagation path loss models for fixed wireless access systems.* Paper presented at the Vehicular Technology Conference, 2005. VTC 2005-Spring. 2005 IEEE 61st.

Anderson, H. R. (2003). *Fixed broadband wireless system design.* West Sussex, England: Wiley. doi:10.1002/0470861290

Ayyappan, K., & Dananjayan, P. (2008). Propagation model for highway communication system. *Ubiquitous Computing and Communication Journal, 3*(4), 6.

Baron, M. (2006). *Probability and statistics for computer scientists.* Boca Raton, FL: Chapman & Hall/CRC.

Garg, V. K. (2007). *Wireless communications and networking.* Amsterdam, The Netherlands: Elsevier Morgan Kaufmann.

Green, D. B., & Obaidat, A. S. (2002). *An accurate line of sight propagation performance model for ad hoc 802.11 wireless LAN (WLAN) devices.* Paper presented at the IEEE International Conference on Communications, New York.

Itoua, S. M. (2008). *Effect of propagation models on ad hoc networks routing protocols.* Paper presented at the 2008 Second International Conference on Sensor Technologies and Applications.

LaSorte, N., Barnes, W. J., Zigreng, B., & Refai, H. (2009). *Performance evaluation of a deployed WiMAX system operating in the 4.9GHz public safety band.* Paper presented at the 6th IEEE Conference on Consumer Communications and Networking Conference.

Lee, B. G., & Choi, S. (2008). *Broadband wireless access and local networks: Mobile WiMax and WiFi*. Boston, MA: Artech House.

Mathworks, I. (2008). *MATLAB help (Version 2008b)*. Mathworks, Inc.

Montgomery, D. C., & Runger, G. C. (2003). *Applied statistics and probability for engineers* (3rd ed.). New York, NY: Wiley.

Ogunnaike, B. A. (2010). *Random phenomena: Fundamentals of probability and statistics for engineers*. Boca Raton, FL: CRC Press.

Pahlavan, K., & Krishnamurthy, P. (2009). *Networking fundamentals: Wide, local, and personal area communications*. Chichester, UK: Wiley.

Parsons, J. D. (2000). *The mobile radio propagation channel* (2nd ed.). Chichester, UK: J. Wiley. doi:10.1002/0470841524

Rappaport, T. S. (2002). *Wireless communications: Principles and practice* (2nd ed.). Upper Saddle River, NJ: Prentice Hall PTR.

Ross, S. M. (2004). *Introduction to probability and statistics for engineers and scientists* (3rd ed.). Amsterdam, The Netherlands: Elsevier Academic Press.

Sarkar, T. (2003). *Smart antennas*. New York, NY: IEEE Press. doi:10.1002/0471722839

Saunders, S. R., & Aragón-Zavala, A. (2007). *Antennas and propagation for wireless communication systems* (2nd ed.). Chichester, UK: J. Wiley & Sons.

Seybold, J. S. (2005). *Introduction to RF propagation*. Hoboken, NJ: Wiley. doi:10.1002/0471743690

Spiegel, M. R., Hernández Heredero, R., & Abellanas, L. (1998). *Estadística* (2nd ed.). Madrid, Spain: McGraw-Hill.

Tse, D., & Viswanath, P. (2005). *Fundamentals of wireless communication*. Cambridge, UK: Cambridge University Press.

Webb, W. (1999). *The complete wireless communications professional: A guide for engineers and managers*. Boston, MA: Artech House.

Zhang, Y. (2009). *WiMAX network planning and optimization*. Boca Raton: CRC Press.

Zhang, Y., & Chen, H.-H. (2008). *Mobile WiMAX: Toward broadband wireless metropolitan area networks*. New York, NY: Auerbach Publications.

ADDITIONAL READING

Almagro-Carrion, S., Cerdán, F., Cabrera-Lozoya, A., & Lujan-Fernandez, S. (2009). *A Mobile Approach for a Physical Simulation Model in Wimax*. Paper presented at the Fifth International Conference on Networking and Services, Valencia, Spain.

Amarasinghe, K. C., Peiris, K. G. A. B., Thelisinghe, L. A. M. D., Warnakulasuriya, G. M., & Samarasinghe, A. T. L. K. (2009). *Comparison of propagation models for fixed WiMAX system based on IEEE 802.16-2004*. Paper presented at the Fourth International Conference on Industrial and Information Systems, Peradeniya, Sri Lanka.

Barsocchi, P. (2006). Channel models for terrestrial wireless communications: a survey. Pisa: CNR-ISTI Technical Report.

Bensky, A. (2004). *Short-range wireless communication: fundamentals of RF system design and application* (2nd ed.). Burlington: Elsevier.

Dobkin, D. M. (2005). *RF engineering for wireless networks: hardware, antennas, and propagation*. Amsterdam, Boston: Elsevier/Newnes.

Goldsmith, A. (2005). *Wireless communications*. Cambridge, New York: Cambridge University Press.

Manning, T. (2009). *Microwave radio transmission design guide* (2nd ed.). Boston: Artech House.

Milanovic, J., Rimac-Drlje, S., & Bejuk, K. (2007). *Comparison of propagation models accuracy for WiMAX on 3.5 GHz.* Paper presented at the 14th International Conference on Electronics, Circuits and Systems, Marrakech, Morocco.

Pérez-Fontán, F., & Mariño-Espiñeira, P. (2008). *Modeling the wireless propagation channel: a simulation approach with Matlab.* Chichester, West Sussex, England; Hoboken, NJ, USA: Wiley.

Sharma, P. K., & Singh, R. K. (2010). Comparative analysis of propagation path loss models with field measured data. *International Journal of Engineering Science and Technology, 2*(6), 2008–2013.

Soma, P., Baum, D. S., Erceg, V., Krishnamoorthy, R., & Paulraj, A. J. (2002). *Analysis and Modeling of Multiple-Input Multiple-Output (MIMO) radio channel based on outdoor measurements conducted at 2.5 GHz for fixed BWA applications.* Paper presented at the Internationa Conference on Communications, New York.

KEY TERMS AND DEFINITIONS

Empirical Models: Propagation models based on measurements. The equations included in this kind of models are fast and easy to calculate.

Fading: Attenuation in the strength of radio waves due to distance, obstacles and other physical effects.

Fast-Fading: Fluctuation in the strength of radio waves, varying in very small distances. Fast-fading is a result of movement in the transmitter, receiver or both of them.

Noise: A disturbance that affects the strength of a radio signal.

Path Loss: Attenuation in the strength of a radio signal as a result of the distance traveled.

Propagation Model: A mathematical model that can predict with certain accuracy the distance that a radio signal can travel.

Shadowing: Also known as slow fading. Attenuation caused by obstacles between transmitter and receiver.

Chapter 2
Channel Modeling for Vehicle-to-Vehicle Communications and Networking

David W. Matolak
Ohio University, USA

ABSTRACT

This chapter provides a description of physical layer characteristics for the mobile wireless channel for vehicle-to-vehicle (V2V) communication and networking applications. Due to the low antenna elevations, and mobility of both transmitters and receivers in the V2V environment, the V2V wireless channel can be one of the most challenging elements to ensuring reliable V2V communication.

ORGANIZATION

We first define the environment and conditions for V2V communications, along with mention of anticipated applications and a current V2V communication system standard. A concise motivation for accurate channel characterization is provided, and a short description of the channel's effects upon communication system performance is also given. The distinguishing features of V2V channels are identified, particularly in comparison to more tra-

ditional channels such as those for cellular radio, public safety, etc. We focus on statistical models for small scale fading, but also include a short discussion of large and medium scale fading; a review of statistical channel characterization basics (in the delay, frequency, Doppler, and time domains) is provided as background. We then focus on how researchers are modeling the V2V channel. After noting some of the primary theoretical findings for V2V channels, we describe three classes of V2V channel models that appear to be the leading candidates for widespread use: these are deterministic (and quasi-deterministic) models, and two types

DOI: 10.4018/978-1-4666-0209-0.ch002

of empirical statistical models, the tapped delay line, and geometry-based. Example tapped delay line models are provided, and a geometry-based model is also described. The final section looks at some of the unique features of V2V channels, including statistical non-stationarity. This section also addresses multiple-input/multiple-output (MIMO), and multi-band models, and discusses V2V networking and channel estimation. We conclude with a summary and recommendations for future work in V2V channel modeling.

INTRODUCTION

Vehicle-to-vehicle (V2V) communications are envisioned to grow dramatically in the upcoming decade. Numerous projects, some of which come under the heading of Intelligent Transportation Systems (ITS) (US DoT, 2010), are being conducted by governments and industry consortia. As automobiles become more complex, and more and more vehicles travel, new features for safety and efficiency are needed. Thus, vehicular ad hoc networks (VANETS) are being researched (Bai, 2010). New short range communications for vehicle-to-infrastructure (V2I) communications (sometimes vehicle-to-roadside, V2R) are also being researched for multiple applications (Belanovic, 2010). Most important of all applications is safety (Gallagher, 2006), but numerous other applications are being studied to improve efficiency, reduce roadway congestion, and offer drivers and passengers new options for making travel more productive and pleasant (Papadimitratos, 2009).

Regardless of the application, the V2V communication signals will almost certainly travel by electromagnetic wave propagation. Past research has considered millimeter wave bands (Tank, 1997), (Wada, 1998) and even the ultrahigh frequency (UHF) band (Sai, 2009), but since both the US and European spectrum regulatory agencies have reserved spectrum in the 5 GHz band, this band is most likely for near-term V2V use.

Similarly, although several transmission schemes have been studied for use in the V2V setting, the modified IEEE 802.11a standard, denoted 802.11p (Zhu, 2003), (Jiang, 2008), or WAVE (for Wireless Access in Vehicular Environments) (Uzcategui, 2009) is most likely to see application, at least initially. This standard was originally (and sometimes still is) termed the Dedicated Short Range Communication standard (Jiang, 2006).

Regardless of frequency band, propagation channel characteristics are important (Parsons, 2000). The physical layer (PHY) must transfer information across the wireless channel efficiently and accurately so that higher layers of the communications protocol stack can operate properly (Stuber, 2001). Thus, good models for the PHY wireless V2V channel are essential for system analysis and design. This chapter discusses such models. Worth noting is that these models are usually designed for use in computer simulations of communication systems, which is done in concert with design, before any system deployment.

The next section provides some general and specific definitions for the V2V channel. It also provides more detail on frequency band of operation, and the WAVE standard. This section discusses distinct features of the V2V channel in comparison to more traditional channels, and also provides motivation for accurate channel modeling.

In the third section, we review the statistical characterization of wireless channels, beginning with a brief discussion of preliminaries. The focus then turns to the channel impulse response (CIR) and channel transfer function (CTF). Correlation functions for these channel characteristics are described, as are common simplifications of wide sense stationarity (WSS) and uncorrelated scattering (US). This section also provides comments on the need for statistically *non*-stationary (NS) characterization.

The fourth section describes types of V2V channel models, including theoretical models and the most popular empirical models, the tapped delay line channel model (TDLCM) and the geometry-based stochastic CM (GBSCM). Comments are also provided on deterministic models. The TDLCM and GBSCM are described in some detail.

Model refinements are discussed in the fifth section. This includes the NS considerations of multipath component (MPC) persistence and propagation region transitions. Example TDL and GBS models are provided. This section also addresses extension to multiple-input/multiple-output (MIMO) models and multi-band V2V Models. Brief discussions on V2V networking and channel estimation are also provided. The final section provides a chapter summary, the key conclusions, and remarks on areas for future work.

DEFINITION OF THE V2V CHANNEL

V2V Channel Features

For the purposes of this chapter, we define the V2V channel as the transmission medium between two vehicles traveling on established ("improved") roadways[1]. From the perspective of the transmitter (Tx) and receiver (Rx), a sufficient definition for the channel is the set of linear system parameters that describes all the electromagnetic wave components that travel from transmitter to receiver. We specify these parameters in the sequel.

On established roadways, the V2V channel will exist between vehicles of multiple types: automobiles, trucks, buses, etc. Antenna heights will be limited to a few meters, and for passenger cars, heights will typically be no higher than 2 m. Obstacles to propagation include buildings, other vehicles, walls, bridges, and other roadway construction objects, groves of trees or other vegetation, hills, road signs, etc.

Most currently-planned V2V systems are envisioned to operate over relatively short ranges, up to approximately 1 km (US DoT, 2010). Thus in most cases, transmit power levels need not be large. These short distances could yield reduced frequency of obstruction of the line of sight (LOS) path between Tx and Rx (compared with cellular), particularly on highways when traffic density is low, but in urban areas or in hilly terrain, or when vehicle density is high, a LOS path will often not be present.

V2V communication systems will operate in urban, suburban, rural and highway environments. In the latter two settings, link distances may change fairly rapidly.

Frequency Bands for V2V Communication, and the WAVE Standard

In principle, nearly any frequency band could be employed for V2V communications. Yet since V2V systems must coexist with other systems, orthogonality of spectral allocations is preferred. In general, too low a frequency implies narrow channel bandwidths, whereas too high a frequency means very large propagation path losses. The 5 GHz band, from 5.85-5.925 GHz, has been authorized by the Federal Communications Commission (FCC) in the USA. A similar band has also been allocated in Europe. This band has moderate path losses, suitable for the relatively short ranges envisioned for V2V communication. The 75 MHz of available bandwidth in the USA—part of the "unlicensed national information infrastructure" (UNII) in the USA—is a shared band, but the FCC has declared that transportation use is primary. This spectrum has initially been divided into seven 10-MHz channels, but aggregation to 20 MHz channels is possible in the future. One 10-MHz channel is reserved for priority messaging. Thus, most channel measurement and modeling efforts in this band focus on 10-20 MHz channel bandwidths.

This frequency band has been envisioned for vehicular use by the US Department of Transportation since the mid 1990's (US DoT, 2010). Initial work on communication systems used the term

Dedicated Short Range Communication (DSRC) standard (ASTM, 2008), but this standard was taken over by the IEEE 802.11p group (IEEE, 2008), and commonly goes by the name Wireless Access for Vehicular Environments (WAVE).

WAVE is a modified version of the IEEE 802.11a standard for wireless local area networks (WLANs), which specifies transmission scheme characteristics at the PHY and medium access control (MAC) layers. The transmission scheme is parallel orthogonal frequency division multiplexing (OFDM) with various modulation alphabet sizes; multiple user access is time-division based (Aggelou, 2005). Additional detail can be found in (ASTM, 2008) and (IEEE, 2010). Additional transmission schemes such as the IEEE 802.16e standards (Andrews, 2007) or LTE (Sesia, 2009) may be used in V2V systems of the future.

Challenges of V2V Channels vs. Traditional Mobile Channels

As noted, due to the low antenna heights, obstruction of LOS will be common in V2V communications, and far more frequent than in conventional systems such as cellular. Although some references (Reichardt, 2010), (Kaul, 2007) have begun to address the effects of antenna placement on vehicles upon the V2V channel characteristics, this topic has not been completely covered. Nearly all measurement campaigns have employed roof-mounted antennas; one exception is (Sen, 2008), in which antennas were placed inside vehicles (on dashboards). In V2V channels, significant scatterers may surround *both* Tx and Rx, not only one or the other, as in the traditional cellular setting.

Also different from conventional communication systems is the mobility of *both* Tx and Rx in V2V settings. This has the effect of inducing more rapid changes in the channel, up to twice as fast as cellular, if Tx and Rx are moving in opposite directions (Renaudin, 2011). Because of mobility, scattering objects such as other vehicles may cause significant local changes in the channel that

may persist or be transient. The more rapid time variation will mean that the traditional statistical channel models that assume wide-sense stationarity (WSS)—roughly, the invariance of channel statistics over a short time period—are applicable for shorter durations.

Figure 1 shows a conceptual V2V channel, in which the primary propagation obstacles are vehicles themselves, but in urban areas, signals can also be obstructed by buildings, civil structures, terrain, etc. Link distances in such urban areas may be very short, up to only a few tens of meters. For more open environments such as suburban and highway cases, stationary obstacles become less dense and achievable link distances can also increase. Yet even in these cases, as Figure 1 indicates, obstructions can be common.

For the purpose of specifying V2V channels, the use of multiple channel classes is convenient. This is also typically done in other systems, e.g.,

Figure 1. Diagrammatic depiction of V2V channel, illustrating multipath components

for the cellular case, the urban, rural, and suburban classes are used (Correia, 2001). Each class aims to represent a particular type of physical situation. For the V2V case, researchers have used urban, highway, and small city classes, among others. Some classifications (in addition to, or within such classes) also explicitly incorporate the presence of an LOS component or vehicular traffic density. Vehicular traffic density can make substantial differences in channel characteristics (Sen, 2008).

Significance of Accurate Channel Modeling

Regardless of the type of wireless communication system, accurate knowledge of the wireless channel characteristics is crucial. Channel knowledge is used in the design and performance prediction for any communication system (Parsons, 2000). From an engineering perspective, channel characterization should be in *mathematical* terms, since mathematical representations are useful for analysis, computer simulations and design. Channel models can be used to compare candidate transmission/reception schemes, and they can also be used to ascertain performance limits for each channel class. Modulation parameters such as transmission bandwidths and MAC parameters such as packet durations are only two examples of communication system features that should be designed with channel characteristics in mind.

During the design process, the use of accurate channel models can aid in design decisions regarding the use of mitigating measures for combating channel effects. Many of these measures are well known, and include the use of multiple antennas, forward error correction (FEC) coding and interleaving, and equalization. Specification of these techniques requires accurate channel knowledge.

The channel model typically forms one "block" in a sequence of blocks that represents the entire communication system model. These block-based models are useful for both analysis and computer simulations. Modern communication system design relies extensively on such simulations for "trade studies" and performance prediction, and channel models in simulation form are of great value. One can even use purely "stored" channel data in simulations, where this stored data may be obtained from measurements.

Even though all current and future wireless communication systems are adaptive, design is never done in the absence of good channel knowledge. Systems may adapt to changes in channel conditions themselves, or to changes in user requirements or changes in local interference conditions; the channel changes are often the most difficult conditions to which systems must adapt. Channel-induced degradations have been studied extensively (Stuber, 2001). One significant effect that can result from inaccurate channel modeling is a "floor" in the bit error ratio (BER), wherein regardless of any increase in received signal power, the BER reaches a lower limit; this limit may be unacceptable to a user if it is large enough. Another significant consequence of inaccurate channel modeling can be latency—a delay caused by failure to meet some communication system performance requirement. A deep and lengthy channel fade could cause the communication link to exceed its BER requirement, and this in turn may require re-transmissions at the MAC layer, which could yield delay that is unacceptable to the system user, both objectively and subjectively, depending upon the application. In summary, accurate channel characteristics are important for system design and evaluation at multiple layers of the communications protocol stack.

In Table 1 we list a number of key channel parameters and the PHY and MAC design parameters they affect (Matolak, Wu, & Sen, 2010). We define these parameters in subsequent sections.

Table 1. Channel parameters and corresponding signal/system parameters they affect (Matolak, Wu, & Sen, 2010)

Channel Parameters	Affected Signal/System Design Parameters
Multipath delay spread T_M & coherence bandwidth B_c	Signal and subcarrier bandwidths, symbol rate, cyclic prefix or equalizer length
Channel attenuation α	Transmit power P_r, link range, modulation & FEC & detection algorithms, data rate R_b
Doppler spread f_D & coherence time t_c	Data packet size, signal and subcarrier bandwidths, FEC type/strength, transceiver adaptation rates, duplexing method
Spatial/temporal correlations ρ_s, ρ_t	Diversity method, FEC type, multiplexing method, antenna design

STATISTICAL CHANNEL CHARACTERIZATION REVIEW

Random Process Preliminaries

Although in principle one can model the wireless channel deterministically, for most cases of interest, the environment is complex enough to render this approach impractical. For an accurate deterministic channel model, one would need a large amount of information on the local environment between and around Tx and Rx. This includes dimensions of all objects, Tx to Rx distance, antenna characteristics, and the electrical properties of all objects in the environment (permittivity, conductivity, and permeability). In mobile cases, in particular, tracking the channel can become impractical as distances and geometry changes rapidly. Nonetheless, some work on deterministic (and "quasi-deterministic") models has been done for the V2V channel, e.g., (Maurer, 2005). These models typically use ray-tracing as a high frequency approximation to Maxwell's equations, but are still computationally intensive, and site specific in general. Hence, stochastic models are more widely used for their convenience, and for their ability to accurately represent channel effects.

The V2V channel is generally a linear, time-varying (LTV) system. As such, it is completely characterized by the channel impulse response (CIR), or equivalently, the Fourier transform of this response, the channel transfer function (CTF). For stochastic models, the CIR (and hence CTF)

is a random function. A complete description of the random processes constituting this function consists of the probability density functions of all the processes, of all orders, over all time. In practice, this is never available, but fortunately, is not necessary. For second-order processes (roughly, with finite second moment) (Pursley, 2002), the first order mean function and the second order autocorrelation function provide most of what is needed in practice.

For a random process $X(t)$, we will denote its density function of order m as $f_{X,m}(\vec{x}_m; \vec{t}_m)$, where $\vec{x}_m = (x_1, x_2, \ldots x_m)$, and an analogous definition holds for the vector $\vec{t}_m$; the random variable x_i is implicitly paired with the time instant t_i. The mean function $\mu(t) = E[X(t)]$, and the autocorrelation function is $R_{XX}(t_1, t_2) = E[X(t_1)X^*(t_2)]$ where E denotes expectation, and the asterisk denotes complex conjugation. When we deal with vectors, the notation will be as above for $\vec{x}_m$.

Small Scale, Large Scale, and Medium Scale Fading

Since V2V link distances will typically be short, transmit powers need not be large, even for the 5 GHz frequency band. Large scale channel effects refer to those that change over many wavelengths, hundreds or more. The term "fading" generally refers to fluctuation of signal amplitude, and although some authors reserve this term for what is more precisely termed "small-scale" fading, the term has more general application. For all wireless systems, signals are attenuated with distance d due to the spreading of electromagnetic waves; in free-space, power density decays as $1/d^n = 1/d^2$. In this case, the path loss exponent $n=2$. In built-up or cluttered environments, this exponent can take values from 3-5, or even larger (Rappaport, 2002). For roadways, the simple "two-ray" (or, "plane-earth") model (Parsons, 2000) has shown to apply (Cheng, 2007) reasonably well. Other researchers (Karedal, 2009), (Kunisch, 2008) have found some path loss exponents less than 2, which indicates possible waveguiding effects, or in the case of open highways, inclusion of multiple MPCs in representing a single MPC. More complicated path loss models are also available, e.g., (Konstantinou, 2008). For the short link distances of anticipated V2V applications, these path loss models can be used to help determine link budget parameters such as transmit power, receiver noise temperature, antenna gains, etc. In any case, large scale path losses will only change slowly, even at highway speeds, and are thus relatively easy to compensate for in V2V systems with data rates exceeding tens of kilobits/second. Our treatment of this channel effect thus ends here.

The other large scale effect most commonly addressed in conventional mobile radio systems is shadowing, or obstruction. This is caused primarily by buildings or terrain, and this effect may also occur in V2V systems, for example when the Tx or Rx vehicle turns a corner in an urban area and the LOS is blocked by large buildings. Terrain blockage can also occur, but this would likely be on longer links when a vehicle goes beyond a hill crest. Thus, these large scale effects are not as common in V2V settings, so at present, there is little to no research on explicit models for such effects.

Small scale fading is traditionally caused by multipath propagation, and this occurs on spatial scales of approximately one-half wavelength, $\lambda/2$. For the upper end of the WAVE band at 5.925 GHz, this half-wavelength distance is approximately 2.5 cm. Hence even for small or moderate velocities, this effect can occur fairly rapidly (hence small-scale fading is sometimes termed "fast fading," despite the imprecision and limited applicability of this term). This small scale fading has also been studied for decades, e.g., (Stein, 1987), and for narrowband conditions—where the channel is well-modeled via an amplitude and phase—or for MPCs composed of a number of unresolved components, multiple statistical models have been used to describe the amplitude distributions. Table 2 (adapted from (Matolak, 2006) lists the most common distributions. Once sufficient power is provided to a receiver, small-scale fading is typically the most important channel impairment.

Finally, we make brief mention of medium-scale fading. This type of fading occurs on spatial scales between those of large- and small-scale, and has generally been neglected for conventional mobile radio. A recent exception is in (Calcev, 2008), where the authors term this "meso-scale" fading. For V2V cases, this medium-scale effect is attributable to large vehicles such as trucks or buses, which can move rapidly near or between Tx and Rx.

Medium scale fading was modeled in (Sen, 2006), and (Matolak, 2008), and can also be accounted for in geometry-based stochastic (GBS) models (Karedal, 2009). Our focus in the rest of this chapter will be on small-scale fading effects, with brief treatment of medium scale fading.

Channel Impulse Response (CIR) and Channel Transfer Function (CTF)

Since the wireless V2V channel is well-modeled as linear, it is completely specified by its CIR (or CTF). Although the CIR is strictly a continuous function—since even if the channel multipath components are well modeled as discrete, analog filters and antennas at Tx and Rx yield continuous functions—the CIR is most often modeled as being a sum of discrete impulses (Proakis, 2001). This form is given as

Table 2. Commonly used fading amplitude (r) probability density functions. Variable $\Omega=E(r^2)$.

Distribution	Probability Density Function	Comments
Rayleigh	$$p_R(r) = \frac{2r}{\Omega}\exp\left[-\left(\frac{r^2}{\Omega}\right)\right]$$	• Widely used for ease of analysis • Derived from Central Limit Theorem
Ricean	$$p_{Ri}(r,K) = \frac{2r(1+10^{K/10})}{\Omega}\exp\left[\frac{-r^2(1+10^{K/10})}{\Omega}-10^{K/10}\right]$$ $$I_0\left(2r10^{K/20}\sqrt{\frac{1+10^{K/10}}{\Omega}}\right)$$	• Ricean "K-factor" $k=(LOS\ power)\div(Scattered\ power)$, $K=10log_{10}(k)$ (dB) • For $k\rightarrow0$, pdf $\rightarrow$ Rayleigh • For $k\rightarrow$large, pdf $\rightarrow$non-fading • $I_0 = 0^{th}$-order modified Bessel function of 1st kind
Nakagami-m	$$p_N(r,m) = \frac{2m^m r^{2m-1}}{\Gamma(m)\Omega^m}\exp\left[\frac{-mr^2}{\Omega}\right]$$	• $m\geq0.5$ • For $m=2$, equals the Rayleigh pdf • $\Gamma=Gamma$ function
Weibull	$$p_w(r) = \frac{b}{a^b}r^{b-1}\exp\left[-\left(\frac{r}{a}\right)^b\right]$$	• b = shape factor, determines fading severity (b similar to Ricean k, Nakagami m)
Lognormal	$$p_L(r,\mu,\sigma) = \frac{10}{r\ln(10)\sqrt{2\pi\sigma^2}}e$$ $$xp\left\{-[10\log(r)-\mu]^2/(2\sigma^2)\right\}$$	• For $r=$ received power, $w=$ power in dBW, pdf of w is Gaussian, with mean = μ, standard deviation = σ.

$$h(\tau;t) = \sum_{k=0}^{L(t)-1} z_k(t)\alpha_k(t)\exp\{j[\omega_{D,k}(t)(t-\tau_k(t))-\omega_c(t)\tau_k(t)]\}\delta[\tau-\tau_k(t)]$$
$$= \sum_{k=0}^{L(t)-1} z_k(t)\alpha_k(t)e^{j\varphi_k(t)}\delta[\tau-\tau_k(t)]$$

(1)

where the CIR $h(\tau;t)$ is in complex baseband (or, "lowpass equivalent") form. This CIR is defined as the response of the channel at time t to an impulse input τ seconds earlier. The Dirac deltas denote the discrete impulses, and these mean that the channel produces component-specific attenuations, phase shifts, and delays for any signal sent into the channel. The discrete approximation is quite good for signal bandwidths up to tens of MHz or more (Qiu, 2002).

The terms in (1) are defined as follows: $\alpha_k(t)$ is the amplitude of the kth resolved multipath component (MPC) at time t; the kth resolved phase is $\phi_k(t)$; τ_k is the kth path's delay; the radian carrier frequency is $\omega_c(t)$; and, the kth resolved Doppler frequency is $\omega_{D,k}(t)=2\pi v(t)f_c(t)cos[\theta_k(t)]/c$, where $v(t)$ is the relative Tx-Rx velocity, c is the speed of light, and $\theta_k(t)$ is the aggregate phase angle of all components arriving in the kth delay "bin." The carrier frequency in Hz is $f_c=\omega_c/(2\pi)$. The "resolution" of this CIR is determined by the signal bandwidth, hence tacitly implying that empirical channel models of this form are in general signal-bandwidth-specific. The resolution in the delay domain is approximately equal to the reciprocal of the signal bandwidth, e.g., for a 20 MHz signal, the resolution "bin" width is 50 nanoseconds, which means that components separated in delay by an amount smaller than 50 nanoseconds are "unresolvable," and are in effect "smeared" together via convolution of the CIR with bandlimiting Tx and Rx filters.

The CIR in (1) is generalized from those most commonly seen in texts, e.g., (Stuber, 2001), by virtue of the following three features: a time-varying number of MPCs $L(t)$; a "persistence process" $z(t)$ that accounts for the MPC finite "lifetime"; and explicit time variation of carrier frequency $\omega_c(t)$, which allows for modeling of Tx/Rx oscillator variations and/or carrier frequency hopping. The time-varying number of MPCs can in general be subsumed into the persistence processes.

The CTF for the CIR in (1) is

$$H(f;t) = \sum_{k=0}^{L(t)-1} z_k(t)\alpha_k(t)e^{j2\pi f_{D,k}(t)[t-\tau_k(t)]}e^{-j2\pi f_c\tau_k(t)}e^{-j2\pi f\tau_k(t)}$$

$$(2)$$

where we have assumed the carrier frequency $f_c(t) = f_c$ is constant. Since the Doppler frequencies are typically much smaller than the carrier frequency, the first exponential term contains slow time variation associated with $f_{D,k}$. The second exponential dominates small scale fading because f_c is usually *much* larger than $f_{D,k}$, (for example, if f_c=5.8 GHz, a relative velocity of 200 km/hr yields a maximum Doppler of only f_D=1070 Hz, yielding $f_c/f_D \cong 5.4 \times 10^6$). This second exponential can change substantially when delay $\tau_k(t)$ changes by small amounts, e.g., fractional nanosecond delay changes (corresponding to path length changes of centimeters) can cause 2π shifts in this exponential argument when f_c=5 GHz. The last exponential in (2) contains the frequency dependence of $H(f;t)$.

Equation (1) indicates that the CIR is a function of both delay τ and time t. In his classic treatment of random channels (Bello, 1963), Bello termed this CIR function the input delay spread function. Figure 2 shows a conceptual version of this CIR (Matolak, 2008) that illustrates fading in time and variation of MPC amplitude (| α_k |) as a function of delay. This CIR form is based upon (1), and is useful for analysis, simulations, and hardware design via the popular tapped-delay line (TDL) model. The TDL is a linear, finite impulse response filter, illustrated in Figure 3. In this figure, the digital input symbols are denoted xk, the output symbols are yk, and the kth MPC is given by $h_k(t) = z_k(t)\alpha_k(t)e^{j\varphi_k(t)}$. The multipath persistence (or "birth/death") processes zk(t) are indicated in Figure 3 as dashed-line boxes; these processes take values in the set {0,1}

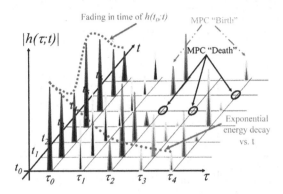

Figure 2. Conceptual illustration of (magnitude of) time-varying CIR (adapted from Matolak, 2008)

and multiply the conventional CIR amplitude and phase process product $\alpha_k(t)e^{j\varphi_k(t)}$. When the CIR is modeled as random, α, z, and ϕ are random processes. For GBS models we discuss later, the random phase quantities are obtained from the desired carrier frequency, model velocities, and delays, the latter two of which can be randomly generated.

CIR and CTF Correlation Functions

Assuming the CIR and CTF are second-order processes, we are interested in their mean and autocorrelation functions. Our brief discussion here follows the conventions developed by Bello (Bello, 1963). In most cases, the CIR mean is determined by the strongest MPC, which is usually also the MPC with the smallest delay. If this strongest MPC consists of a LOS, or non-fading component, it will have a non-zero mean that is typically slowly varying, while all the other MPCs that consist of at least one reflection[2] are well-modeled as zero-mean, due to the typically uniform phase distribution of $\phi(t)$. If a non-fading or LOS component is present, the fading amplitude statistics of this MPC are commonly modeled as Ricean (see Table 2), and in this case, the autocovariance function can be obtained by subtraction of the mean function $\mu(t)$ from the autocorrelation

Figure 3. Tapped-delay line model for time-varying CIR of (1)

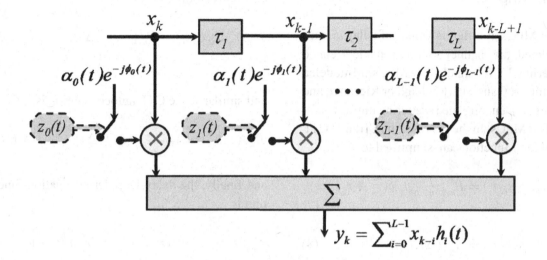

function. When $\mu(t)$ is zero, the autocovariance and autocorrelation functions are the same.

For the CIR, the correlation function is[3]

$$R_{hh}(\tau_0, \tau_1; t_0, t_1) = E[h(\tau_0; t_0)h * (\tau_1; t_1)] \quad (3)$$

Equation (3) indicates that R_{hh} quantifies the correlation of the resolved MPC at delay/time pair (τ_{00}, t_0) with that of the MPC at delay/time pair (τ_1, t_1) (see Figure 2). When the delay difference $|\tau_0 - \tau_1|$ is large, this generally yields a low correlation value since MPCs at disparate delays will most likely correspond to physically distinct propagation paths that are well approximated as independent.

The CTF correlation function is found analogously:

$$R_{HH}(f_0, f_1; t_0, t_1) = E[H(f_0; t_0)H * (f_1; t_1)] \quad (4)$$

Here, R_{HH} measures the correlation between the CTF evaluated at frequency/time pairs (f_0, t_0) and (f_1, t_1). The correlation functions of the CIR and CTF are related by a double Fourier transform (F):

$$R_{HH}(f_0, f_1; t_0, t_1) = \int \int R_{hh}(\tau_0, \tau_1; t_0, t_1)e^{-j2\pi f_0\tau_0}e^{-j2\pi f_1\tau_1}d\tau_0 d\tau_1 \quad (5)$$

A third correlation function of interest defined by Bello is the delay-Doppler correlation function

$$R_{SS}(\tau_0, \tau_1; \nu_0, \nu_1) = \int \int R_{hh}(\tau_0, \tau_1; t_0, t_1)e^{-j2\pi \nu_0 t_0}e^{-j2\pi \nu_1 t_1}dt_0 dt_1$$
$$= F\{F[R_{hh}(\tau_0, \tau_1; t_0, t_1)]\} \quad (6)$$

where the two transforms are with respect to t_0 and t_1. The delay-Doppler correlation function quantifies correlation between MPCs at delay/ Doppler shift pairs (τ_0, ν_0) and (τ_1, ν_1).

The fourth and final correlation function of Bello is denoted $R_{DD}(f_0, f_1, \nu_0, \nu_1) = F\{F\{R_{SS}\}\}$ (with transforms with respect to τ_0, τ_1). This is also equal to $F\{F\{R_{HH}\}\}$ (with transforms with respect to t_{00}, t_1). The function R_{DD} is the correlation function of the output Doppler-spread function $H_O(f, \nu)$, but since neither H_O or R_{DD} is very widely used, we omit further mention of these functions.

Correlated and Uncorrelated Scattering

When MPCs at different values of delay are uncorrelated, the channel is termed an uncorrelated scattering (US) channel. If the MPCs are modeled as complex Gaussian (Rayleigh or Ricean α, and uniform ϕ), uncorrelated scattering implies *independent* MPCs. In the US case, the CIR and CTF correlation functions are simplified to

$$R_{hh}(\tau_0, \tau_1, t_0, t_1) = R_{hh}(\tau_0, t_0, t_1)\delta(\tau_0 - \tau_1) \tag{7}$$

$$R_{HH}(f_0, f_1, t_0, t_1) = R_{HH}(\Delta f, t_0, t_1) \tag{8}$$

which means that R_{hh} is non-zero only when $\tau_0 = \tau_1$. The term $\Delta f = |f_0 - f_1|$, and (8) means that the CTF correlation function depends only upon the *difference* between f_0 and f_1 and not upon absolute frequency values. This result for the CTF is called wide-sense stationarity (WSS) in frequency, so we have the equivalence relation US (delay)⇔WSS(frequency). When scattering is uncorrelated, the delay-Doppler correlation function simplifies to $R_{SS}(\tau_0, \nu_0, \nu_1)\delta(\tau_0 - \tau_1)$.

Even though one does not always find US in practice, particularly for MPCs that are close in delay (e.g., two components from two equal-velocity vehicles moving in the same direction), the US assumption is often invoked for simplifying the CIR correlation function. Also worth note is that in many cases, MPCs may not be complex Gaussian, and hence even US will not in general yield independent MPCs.

Wide Sense Stationary and Non-Stationary Modeling

In general terms, a stochastic process $X(t)$ is wide-sense stationary (WSS) if its mean $\mu(t)$ is constant, and if its autocorrelation $R_{XX}(t_0, t_1)$ depends only on the time difference $\Delta t = |t_0 - t_1|$, and not on absolute times (Papoulis, 2001). A WSS CIR simplifies the CIR correlation function to

$$R_{hh}(\tau_0, \tau_1, t_0, t_1) = R_{hh}(\tau_0, \tau_1, \Delta t), \tag{9}$$

and similarly, the CTF autocorrelation is,

$$R_{HH}(f_0, f_1, t_0, t_1) = R_{HH}(f_0, f_1, \Delta t) \tag{10}$$

and finally, the delay-Doppler correlation function is

$$R_{SS}(\tau_0, \tau_1, \nu_0, \nu_1) = P_S(\tau_0, \tau_1, \nu_0)\delta(\nu_0 - \nu_1) \tag{11}$$

where $P_S(\tau_0, \tau_1, \nu)$ is the delay-Doppler cross power spectral density. Analogous to US, (11) means that if scatterers have different Doppler shifts, their contributions to the CIR are uncorrelated. This can be expressed as WSS (time)⇔US(Doppler).

Clearly for small enough time differences Δt, WSS can be invoked, but for practical purposes this duration must be at least as long as a transmitted symbol duration (to allow coherent detection). More often, this duration (sometimes termed the "stationarity time") is many symbols or frames in duration, in which case the channel is denoted slowly fading. Conversely, if one allows Δt to become large enough, eventually the CIR statistics will vary, so that strict-sense stationarity will never apply in mobile channels. In mobile cases WSS will be violated if mobility is over a wide area.

As implied, one reason for the appeal of the WSS (and WSSUS) assumption(s) is their relative mathematical simplicity, but they must be used with care. Even established models for cellular (COST, 2007), LANs (IEEE, 2007), (Medbo, 1999), and metropolitan area networks (IEEE, 2005a), (IEEE, 2005b) incorporate non-stationarity (NS) without explicitly stating so, through the use of distributions for channel delay spreads. Some currently existing NS models are the COST 259 model (Correia, 2001), and the UMTS model (ETSI, 1997), the latter of which employs a pair of two separate models that are switched between, as also used in (Schafhuber, 2005). NS models for the V2V case appear in (Sen, 2008), (Matolak, Wu, & Sen, 2010), and work on the topic of NS modeling is growing (Matz, 2005). For the purpose of channel modeling, models should incorporate NS characteristics to a degree sufficient to capture the most significant effects, yet balance this without increasing model complexity too much. More will be stated subsequently on the NS topic, but for this section, we conclude our comments on NS by noting that NS models for effects at layers other than the PHY are also being investigated (Konrad, 2003). Finally here, we note that measured instances of correlated scattering have not been documented as widely as NS conditions (Matolak, 2007). In most studies thus far, correlated scattering has been found to be less significant to the performance of communication systems than non-stationary.

When both US (delay) and WSS (time) hold, we arrive at the most commonly assumed condition, the WSSUS channel. The WSSUS condition simplifies the correlation functions even further:

$$R_{hh}(\tau_0, \tau_1, t_0, t_1) = R_{hh}(\tau_0, \Delta t)\delta(\tau_0 - \tau_1)$$
(12)

$$R_{HH}(f_0, f_1, t_0, t_1) = R_{HH}(\Delta f, \Delta t)$$
(13)

$$R_{SS}(\tau_0, \tau_1, \nu_0, \nu_1) = P_S(\tau_0, \nu_0)\delta(\tau_0 - \tau_1)\delta(\nu_0 - \nu_1)$$
(14)

In (13) the two-dimensional function R_{HH} is called the spaced-frequency, spaced-time (SFST) correlation function, and in (14), $P_S(\tau, v)$ is the scattering function. The WSSUS case has been analyzed extensively, in part because it yields the simplest functions, but also because assuming WSSUS enables additional simplified functions

to be defined, and these functions can correspond directly to measured quantities and single channel-characterizing parameters.

Specifically, if we set $\Delta t=0$, $R_{hh}(\tau,0)=\psi_h(\tau)$, which is known as the power delay profile (PDP). The PDP is defined as the channel's average power output versus delay (with an impulse input), and this function is frequently measured. With $\Delta t=0$, $F\{R_{hh}(\tau,0)\}=R_{HH}(\Delta f,0)=\psi_{Hf}(\Delta f)$, which is the spaced-frequency correlation function. This function quantifies the correlation between channel effects at frequencies separated by Δf. The width of $\psi_h(\tau)$ is termed the multipath delay spread T_M, and via the Fourier transform, this delay spread is reciprocally related to the width of $\psi_{Hf}(\Delta f)$, the coherence, or correlation bandwidth B_c.

For the "dual" condition, we set $\Delta f=0$, then the SFST becomes $R_{HH}(0,\Delta t)=\psi_{Ht}(\Delta t)$, the spaced-time correlation function, which analogously quantifies the correlation between channel effects separated by Δt in time. The scattering function for the WSSUS case is given by $P_S(\tau,v)=F\{F\{R_{HH}(\Delta f,\Delta t)\}\}$, and $P_S(0,v)=P_S(v)$ is the Doppler spectrum, whose width is termed the Doppler spread f_D. The Doppler spread is (via Fourier) reciprocally related to the width of $\psi_{Ht}(\Delta t)$, and this width is called the coherence, or correlation time t_c.

In summary, for the WSSUS case, we have T_M=width$\{\psi_h(\tau)\}\sim 1/B_c$, and f_D=width$\{P_S(v)\}\sim 1/t_c$. The multipath delay spread T_M quantifies the amount by which the channel spreads an input impulse in delay, and analogously, the Doppler spread f_D quantifies the amount by which the channel spreads an input tone in frequency. The coherence bandwidth B_c is said to quantify the channel's frequency selectivity, and similarly, the coherence time t_c quantifies the channel's time selectivity, or the rate of time variation. The most commonly used measure for T_M is the root-mean-square delay spread (RMS-DS) σ_τ, but other measures are also used (ITU, 1999): two of these are the delay window $W_{\tau,P}$, which measures the duration in delay of the average CIR that contains the central p% of the total CIR energy (with $p/2$%

on each side outside the window); and the delay interval I_Y, which is the duration in delay of the average CIR that contains all MPCs within Y dB of the strongest MPC. By "average CIR" is meant the average of all CIRs taken (measured) over the stationary time.

TYPES OF V2V CHANNEL MODELS

General Remarks on Channel Modeling

Just like the famous quote by Albert Einstein regarding a theory, a channel model should be as simple as possible—but no simpler. That is, the model should contain all features necessary to represent the actual channel, but not be more complex than it needs to be. This falls into the area of "engineering judgment" somewhat, because the model's sufficiency depends upon how it is compared to the actual channel: one can compare various statistics of modeled and measured CIRs (or CTFs), or one can use the model and measured data within a more comprehensive simulation that uses a performance criterion such as BER to assess model fidelity. In any case, the closest we can get to the "actual channel" is usually some filtered version of the CIR, and this should be accounted for in designing the final model.

Channel models can be bandwidth-specific, but they need not be. In fact, some research (Papazian, 2005) has shown that delay spreads are neither a strong function of bandwidth, nor a strong function of center frequency. Yet, channel models are typically defined with some system, or channel bandwidth in mind. This may help in making the model more convenient to use, for example to make MPC delays correspond to multiples of the underlying system sample period.

Real wireless channels have been widely measured, and the WSSUS parameters of delay spread and Doppler spread are often used to help create models. Channel correlation functions

R_{hh} and R_{HH}, or scattering function $P(\tau,v)$, can also be estimated, but gathering comprehensive measurements for these throughout an environment of interest can be both time-consuming and expensive, thus researchers usually aim to capture representative CIRs or CTFs for the environment, and from these, the various WSSUS functions are estimated; often these CIRs (CTFs) and the functions computed from them represent averages or occasionally, expected worst-case conditions.

Channel models may also be provided in either the time or frequency domains, with the latter being convenient for some modulation schemes such as OFDM. Most models are time-domain models that represent the CIR, even if measurements of the CTF were actually made. Standards setting bodies also usually specify a time domain model for system performance evaluation, such as the Stanford University Interim models (IEEE, 2001) for non-mobile applications of the IEEE standard 802.16. The time domain is chosen because most engineers are more familiar with time domain models, and also because they are easiest to use in time domain based analyses and simulations. If the time-domain channel models have a small number of MPCs, an equivalent frequency domain channel model may require a very large number of coefficients when the number of frequency points of interest is large. Finally, channel models usually do not explicitly model characteristics associated with equipment imperfections, such as frequency & time offsets, although for both TDL and GBS models, frequency offsets due to Doppler shift can be easily incorporated.

Theoretical Statistical Models

The earliest V2V channel models were theoretical statistical models (Akki, 1986), (Akki, 1994). Any theoretical model that attempts to apply to a complicated environment must employ some simplifying assumptions. The models by Akki assume perfect isotropic scattering about the mobile receiver, and complex Gaussian MPCs, and they provide the spaced-time autocorrelation function $\psi_{Ht}(\Delta t)$ and corresponding Doppler spectrum $P_S(v)$. These functions clearly show the faster time variation expected of the V2V case, resulting from a wider Doppler spectrum. Even if not widely applicable in practice, these functions—which are actually extensions of the well-known cellular model by Jakes and Clarke (Jakes, 1993)—provide means to check limiting cases of more practical models. These models also assume WSSUS. The spaced-time correlation function for this model is a product of two Bessel functions (a logical extension of the cellular channel result of a single Bessel function):

$$\psi_{Ht}(\Delta t) = J_0(2\pi f_1 \Delta t) J_0(2\pi f_2 \Delta t) \qquad (15)$$

where here, f_i is the maximum Doppler shift due to motion of the ith mobile, i=1 or 2, and J_0 is the ordinary Bessel function of the first kind, order zero. The Doppler shift is $f_{Di} = v_i/\lambda$, with v_i the velocity, and λ the wavelength (constant velocity is required for the WSS assumption). The Doppler spectrum for this case is a complicated function expressed in terms of the complete elliptic integral of the first kind.

In (Vatalaro, 1997) the authors generalized the two-dimensional scattering model to a three-dimensional case. By doing so, they derived expressions for spaced-time autocorrelation function and Doppler spectrum, but these too are complicated integral equations that require antenna patterns and angle of arrival distributions and so in general must be numerically evaluated.

Another recent theoretical V2V result appears in (Zheng, 2006), in which non-isotropic scattering was modeled. The author employed a von Mises probability density function for angle of arrival, and obtained the following closed-form expression for the spaced-time autocorrelation function

$$\psi_{Ht}(\Delta t) = \prod_{i=1}^{2} \frac{I_0[\sqrt{\kappa_i^2 - 4\pi^2 f_i^2 \Delta t^2 + j4\pi\kappa_i f_i \Delta t \cos(\mu_i)}]}{I_0(\kappa_i)}. \qquad (16)$$

In (16), f_i is the maximum Doppler shift due to motion of mobile i, μ_i is the mean angle of arrival of plane waves for vehicle i, and κ_i is a parameter of the von Mises probability density function. This parameter quantifies the spread of the angle of arrival. Function I_0 is the zero-order modified Bessel function of the first kind. The corresponding Doppler spectrum must be found numerically from the Fourier transform of (16).

To this author's knowledge, there are no well established theoretical models for the V2V channel PDP $\psi_h(\tau)$ or its transform, the SF correlation function $\psi_{Hf}(\Delta f)$. This pertains equally well to the cellular channel, and other common channels (e.g., indoor), primarily because a large variety of PDP shapes are known to exist in practice. Many researchers call on two forms of PDP for analyses, the uniform and the exponentially decaying. The exponential profile is generally more realistic, and is expressed as

$$E_h(k) = a_1 e^{-a_2 k} + a_3, \qquad (17)$$

where $E_h(k)$ denotes the energy of the kth MPC, k=1,2, …, is the MPC index and the a's ($a_1, a_2 \geq 0$) are appropriate constants derived from measurements. In principle, the MPC delays corresponding to the indices can take any positive real value, but in practice, they are often quantified to be some multiple of a minimum delay (often the reciprocal of the signal or channel bandwidth).

Some of the GBS models—at least those that assume regular geometries—can also yield some analytical expressions. For example, (Zajic, 2008) provides an approximate analytical model for the V2V ST correlation function in three spatial dimensions. This function is based upon an assumed cylindrical distribution of scatterers about both Tx and Rx, and also employs the von

Mises angle pdf for the angle of arrival and angle of departure. This approximate function is still a fairly complex expression composed of trigonometric and zero-order modified Bessel functions, and derives from two integrals over the elevation angles of arrival and departure.

Deterministic Models

In very simple situations, one can use deterministic models. The "plane-earth" model (Parsons, 2000), also known as the 2-ray model, assumes a LOS path and one ground-reflected path between Tx and Rx. This model can pertain to the V2V channel between two cars on a level road (Gallagher, 2006), but if omni-directional Tx and/or Rx antennas are used, nearby obstacles will almost certainly yield more than just these two MPCs. In addition, if inter-vehicle distances change it may be challenging to track the channel variations. If other parameters such as antenna gains for the two rays or ground reflection coefficients are not accurately specified, the plane-earth model accuracy degrades. Also, the condition of having only two vehicles in the area has limited applicability, especially when vehicular networking is of interest.

The most common deterministic models use ray tracing. Ray tracing is a high-frequency approximation that assumes all obstacles in the environment are large with respect to wavelength. Thus, ray tracing cannot model diffuse scattering. The ray tracing model is created by employing local environment data to build a geometric approximation to the environment. In addition to object dimensions, the electrical properties of all objects must also be approximated. In the high frequency approximation, plane waves are represented by rays, which are "traced" from Tx to Rx, via any direct, reflected, or diffracted paths. For these types of models to be accurate, in addition to accurate environment data, a large number of rays must be used.

Several recent V2V ray tracing models appear in (Maurer, 2001), (Maurer, 2004). The authors

included typical roadside structures and vehicles in the simulations, and found reasonably good agreement with measurements. When accurate local environment data is available, ray tracing can produce accurate results. In addition, the site-specific nature of ray tracing can be circumvented through the use of random obstacle generation, and this is exactly what is done by some GBS models (hence making these initially deterministic models "quasi-deterministic"). Despite this, ray tracing models are generally computationally intensive, and their accuracy is degraded if complexity is reduced, e.g, by inclusion of fewer rays, or exclusion of diffraction calculations.

Empirical Statistical Model: Tapped Delay Line (TDL)

The TDL channel model consists of (i) the number of MPCs, (ii) a statistical model for the MPC amplitude random processes[4], and, (iii) the MPCs' time rate of change (or equivalently, their Doppler spectra). The number of MPCs, L, is obtainable from T_M (or B_c), typically by employing the mean value of RMS delay spread multiplied by the channel bandwidth. The time rate of change is based upon the Doppler spread f_D (equivalently, on t_c). We also require the relative energy of each MPC, usually obtained from an average PDP, and often given by the exponentially-decaying energy vs. delay of (17). All these parameters are obtained from measurements.

In most models, we employ a normalized CIR, in which the average channel energy is set to unity: $\sum_{k=0}^{L-1} E(|h_k(t)|^2) = 1$, with $E(\cdot)$ again denoting expectation; this normalization may not be used at all times in NS models. The TDL model then appears as in Figure 3, and can be specified in tabular form. For each MPC, the table includes the MPC amplitude distribution type (Table 2) and the parameters required to completely specify the distribution, the MPC energy (or fraction of energy for the normalized case), and the MPC's Doppler spectrum shape and/or bandwidth. Some example models appear in (Acosta-Marum, 2007) and (Sen, 2008).

Empirical Statistical Models: Geometry Based (GB)

The GBS models are not inherently empirical—in fact they were initially developed as analytical models. Some recent work on GBS models appears in (Zajic, 2008), (Zajic, 2009), (Patzold, 2008), and (Cheng, 2009). These models may be termed "conventional" GBS models in that they employ *regular* geometries, and do not impose amplitude fading on the MPCs associated with discrete scatterers. The regular geometries typically use circles, ellipses, or cylinders, or combinations of these shapes to represent the locations of discrete scatterers in the Tx to Rx local environment. Ray tracing is used to identify MPCs that go from Tx to Rx via zero, one, or sometimes more scatterers, but what makes these models statistical is that various probability distributions are used to specify model parameters. These include the angle of departure (AoD) of rays from the Tx and the angle of arrival (AoA) at the Rx, elevation AoA and AoD, and sometimes ray amplitudes. If the geometric object dimensions and vehicle velocities are constant, the GBS model may be WSSUS.

Sometimes researchers compare their analytical GBS results with those of a "reference model." This model is usually a sum of sinusoids CIR that has an infinite number of terms, and is invoked solely for comparison with the analytical functions (typically ST correlation or SF correlation). In practice, a finite, but still often large number of sinusoids must be used (e.g., greater than 60) for the "reference" model. Hence employing these models means substantial simulation complexity. In addition, setting up the models requires a fairly comprehensive geometric description of the environment, and this is also complex, although once set up for an environment of interest, the set-up complexity does not affect the model's

"run complexity" in the generation of CIRs, other than that ray tracing from Tx to object to Rx must be completed for all scatterers "in view" of the antenna gain patterns.

These models are empirical only because the distributions of angles, objects, and other parameters are extracted from measurements; otherwise they could be viewed as quasi-deterministic. A more rigorous empirical model is that of (Karedal, 2009). The highway version of this model is illustrated in Figure 4. For simplicity of presentation, the various angles between rays have not been shown on the figure. This GBS is a simplified ray-tracing model, with three classes of scatterers included: mobile discrete (other vehicles), static discrete (roadside or median-strip obstacles), and diffuse. An LOS component can also be present. The CIR for this model is of the usual form, with some additional spatial functions:

$$h(\tau;t) = \sum_{k=0}^{L-1} \alpha_k(t) e^{j2\pi d_k(t)} \delta(t - \tau_k(t))$$
$$\delta(\theta_R - \theta_{R,k}(t)) \delta(\theta_T - \theta_{T,k}(t)) g_R(\theta_R) g_T(\theta_T)$$

$$(18)$$

where α is MPC amplitude, $d_k(t)$ is the distance from Tx to scatterer to Rx, θ_R is the AoA, θ_T the AoD, and g_R and g_T are the antenna gain patterns at receiver and transmitter, respectively. Based upon measurements, (Karedal, 2009) found that the amplitudes should be modeled as fading, and that over time, MPCs "appeared and disappeared" just as in the "birth-death" TDL persistence processes models. Obstacles in the environment are randomly distributed, with the distributions again based upon measurements. More detail will be provided on this GBS in the next section.

Figure 4. GBS model layout for highway environment (Karedal, 2009)

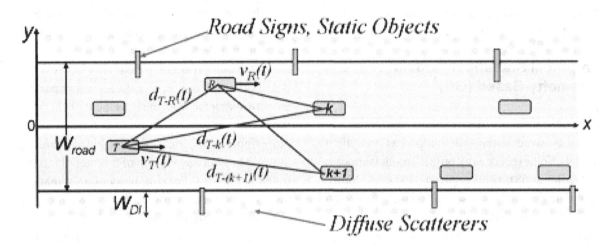

REFINEMENTS AND EXAMPLE V2V CHANNEL MODELS

Non-Stationary Model Considerations

As noted, V2V channels will vary more rapidly than conventional cellular channels, thus even if the WSSUS approximation is used, the V2V channel may be WSS for much shorter durations. More papers that cite NS conditions in V2V channels are appearing regularly. In addition to those already cited, (Paier, 2009) and (Renaudin, 2010) have also attempted to quantify non-stationarities in V2V channels. An obvious "large scale non-stationarity" is that of propagation region transitions, for example as vehicles move from an urban to a highway environment. These channels may be significantly different, and hence if an analysis or simulation spans these different channel classes, the channel characteristics would need to change accordingly. In the case of TDL models, this would mean that the number of MPCs and their statistics could change, and some method of smoothly transitioning from one TDL to another would be required. One way of doing this is to gradually "fade in" or "fade out" the selected MPCs and switch their Doppler spectra during the period

when the relative MPC energy is small. For GBS models, an entirely new geometric environment would need to be created, with a corresponding transition environment. In the GBS case, the obstacle distributions or their parameters would need to be switched during the transition period.

The MPC persistence processes can model medium scale appearance and disappearance of MPCs, but the time scale of this needs to be calibrated depending upon velocity. While abrupt appearance/disappearance of MPCs is not generally realistic, when these are low-energy MPCs this will not change channel statistics appreciably. In addition, if needed, a "fade-in/fade-out" transition could also be applied to the persistence processes to avoid the abrupt "on/off" behavior. One other comment on persistence is that in the case of short packet transmissions, e.g., the 10 ms packet duration of WiMAX or LTE, a transient MPC may be very well modeled by a persistence process.

In (Matz, 2005), the author developed a mathematical framework to analyze non-WSSUS channels. Here the term "non-WSSUS" means both non-WSS in time (implying time varying Doppler spectra) and non-US, or correlated scattering (implying non-WSS in frequency). The system functions in (Matz, 2005) are four-dimensional (as are Bello's), and the WSSUS model is a special case of this generalized non-WSSUS model that can apply if the time and frequency intervals are small enough. The general case falls under the category of time-frequency analysis (Cohen, 1995), and this complicates the mathematics substantially, and requires that the 4D functions be specially processed to obtain familiar quantities such as the scattering function. Thus, although these generalized functions provide insight and are an elegant topic of investigation, due to their complexity they are not convenient for practical use in their current form.

Example TDL Model

Some example TDL V2V models for a 20 MHz channel bandwidth are listed in Table 3 (Matolak, Wu, & Sen, 2010). All MPC delays are multiples of 50 ns (1/20 MHz), so for example, the kth MPC occurs at delay $(k-1)50$ ns. Models for five different channel classes are provided: Urban, with antennas outside the car (UOC); Small City; Open, with high traffic density (OHT); Open, with low traffic density (OLT); and Urban, with antennas inside the cars (UIC). The open areas are highways. The Markov steady-state and transition probabilities for the MPC persistence processes are included in the last three columns. The steady-state probabilities are the probability of the MPC being "on" (P_1) or "off" $(P_0=1-P_1)$. The transition probabilities P_{ij} denote the probabilities of switching between these states, e.g., $P_{01}=Pr(off{\to}on)=Pr("birth")$ in one time step. These transition probabilities satisfy the following equations: $P_{00}=1-P_{01}$ and $P_{11}=1-P_{10}$.

The amplitude fading for all MPCs is modeled using the Weibull probability density function (Papoulis, 2001). The Weibull distribution is equal to the Rayleigh distribution when the Weibull β parameter is 2, and fading is worse than Rayleigh when $\beta<2$. As Table 3 indicates, worse than Rayleigh fading (as also found in (Cheng, 2007)) occurs on a number of MPCs. Rationales for such severe fading include multiple scattering (Gesbert, 2002), Central Limit Theorem violation due to a

small number of unresolvable multipath components in each delay bin, and frequent channel transitions (Sen, 2006), which in effect re-distribute MPC energy among components. Correlation matrices for correlations between the MPCs are also provided in (Matolak, Wu, & Sen, 2010).

Example GB Stochastic Model

We summarize here the model of (Karedal, 2009) for the highway environment. As shown in Figure 4, and as previously described, the CIR consists of MPCs from four types of scatterers: mobile discrete (MD), static discrete (SD), diffuse (DI), and LOS. Prior to use, the model user must extract the number P of MD scatters, the number Q of SD scatterers, and the number R of DI scatterers based upon the assumed scatterer probability distributions. These are uniform in both x- and y-dimensions for the MD and DI scatterers, and for the x-dimension of the SD scatterers. The y-coordinates of the SD scatterers are selected from (truncated) Gaussian distributions. The highway dimensions (width, length, number of lanes) must also be specified.

The path loss exponent n is fixed at 1.8 for the LOS component, 5.4 for the DI components, and drawn from a uniform distribution once for each of the MD and SD components. Path gains are relative to a reference path gain G_0 specified for each scatterer type, and for the MD and SD components, G_0 is a linear function of n. MPC fading is modeled via correlated lognormal random variables with correlation distance found (from measurements) to follow a Gaussian distribution. Specifically, except for the diffuse components, path gain for the ith MPC is given by

$$\alpha_i(d_i) = g_i e^{j\varphi_i} \sqrt{G_{0,i}} \left(\frac{d_{ref}}{d_i} \right)^{n_i/2} \qquad (19)$$

Table 3. TDL channel parameters for 20 MHz bandwidth V2V channels (from (Matolak, Wu, & Sen, 2010), ©2010 IEEE, used with permission)

Tap Index k	Energy	Weibull Factor (β_k)	$P_{00,k}$	$P_{11,k}$	P_1
UOC					
1	0.8090	3.17	na	1.0000	1.0000
2	0.0882	1.69	0.2523	0.9287	0.9129
3	0.0398	1.70	0.3538	0.8615	0.8236
4	0.0237	1.69	0.4919	0.7911	0.7088
5	0.0162	1.68	0.5768	0.7172	0.5995
6	0.0132	1.71	0.6219	0.7176	0.5724
7	0.0100	1.74	0.6719	0.6732	0.5012
Small City					
1	0.8111	4.11	na	1.0000	1.0000
2	0.1033	2.00	0.1364	0.9396	0.9315
3	0.0513	1.72	0.375	0.8897	0.8505
4	0.0230	2.00	0.3790	0.7378	0.7041
5	0.0113	2.24	0.5091	0.7476	0.6573
OHT					
1	0.9073	4.49	na	1.0000	1.0000
2	0.0642	1.64	0.2239	0.8853	0.8713
3	0.0178	2.00	0.5188	0.7330	0.6429
4	0.0107	2.00	0.6084	0.6161	0.5048
OLT					
1	0.9196	4.97	na	1.0000	1.0000
2	0.0635	1.63	0.2293	0.8839	0.8693
3	0.0170	1.69	0.5057	0.7145	0.6344
UIC					
1	0.6498	2.73	na	1.0000	1.0000
2	0.1109	1.75	0.0952	0.9717	0.9697
3	0.0619	1.79	0.1800	0.9362	0.9280
4	0.0381	1.79	0.3486	0.8784	0.8429
5	0.0284	2.00	0.3986	0.8367	0.7867
6	0.0238	2.00	0.4885	0.8304	0.7493
7	0.0218	1.79	0.4219	0.7804	0.7233
8	0.0178	1.76	0.5221	0.7687	0.6744
9	0.0132	1.59	0.5933	0.6921	0.5677
10	0.0114	1.77	0.6767	0.7072	0.5231
11	0.0093	1.59	0.6963	0.6302	0.4496
12	0.0079	2.00	0.6939	0.6338	0.4539
13	0.0056	2.00	0.7512	0.6030	0.3862

where d_i is the sum of distance from Tx to scatterer plus distance from scatterer to Rx, d_{ref} is a reference distance, $G_{0,i}$ is the reference power gain, phase ϕ_i is uniform, and gain g_i is a lowpass filtered lognormal random variable with spatial correlation function given by a Gaussian function with coherence distance d_c specified as the distance where the Gaussian function reaches relative value 0.5. This correlation function can be viewed as the spatial translation of the ST correlation function (translation via $d=v\Delta t$, with v the mobile velocity). Path gain for the diffuse components is given by a similar function with $g_i e^{j\varphi_i}$ replaced by a zero-mean, unit-variance complex Gaussian. The LOS path gain also follows (19).

Thus, once the geometry is defined, along with antenna gain patterns, the various random variables are drawn from their respective distributions, and the CIR is constructed according to (18), where $L=P+Q+R$, or one larger than this value if an LOS component is present. The velocities of all mobiles must be tracked, and at each time step the new CIR is constructed. Note that to implement this GBS model within a digital communication system simulation, convolution with any Tx and Rx filters must be done, and this implies that a very fine quantization may be required in the delay domain. For a given channel bandwidth, MPCs are also combined within the delay bin resolution. At the end of the cascade of Tx+channel+Rx CIRs, the resulting composite CIR may then be "re-sampled" to yield symbol-spaced samples (or ½ -symbol spaced), for use in the remaining processing of the simulation (note that this then yields in effect a TDL!). Alternatively, for some modulation schemes, e.g., OFDM, a frequency-domain channel may be more appropriate. This can be obtained via Fourier transform of the composite CIR, and subsequent multiplication of the three transfer functions; zero-padding of the CIR (and/or Tx and Rx filter IRs) would likely be required to obtain the same number of frequency-aligned samples in the final CTF.

MIMO and Multi-Band V2V Models

As with conventional (e.g., cellular) systems, multiple-input/multiple-output (MIMO) schemes, manifested through the use of Tx and Rx antenna arrays, are growing in popularity. This is because of the performance advantages they offer, in terms of diversity gain, increased throughput, or both. The use of MIMO comes at some cost in terms of complexity, primarily due to multiple radio frequency components such as filters and mixers, and the control processing required to implement various MIMO algorithms.

We do not go into any detail on MIMO schemes here, but rather discuss the impact on modeling V2V MIMO channels. As noted, for each additional antenna beyond the first Tx and first Rx antenna, an additional CIR must be generated. Thus, for N_T Tx antennas and N_R Rx antennas, there is a total of $N_T N_R$ CIRs. For GBS models, CIR generation can be done in the same manner as for the single-input/single-output (SISO) CIR. Any correlation or mutual coupling between antennas must be added separately, and this too should be based upon measurements. All this pertains to the conventional GBS models with regular geometries as well.

For the TDL models, similar comments apply regarding the number of additional CIRs. If measurements of MPC correlations among antenna pairs are available, correlated MPCs can be generated using established algorithms, e.g., the one in (Matolak, Sen, & Xiong, 2008) for correlated Weibull random variables. Independence or uncorrelatedness among $N_T N_R$ pairwise CIRs is difficult to achieve in practice. In general, the MIMO channel model is expressed by a matrix extension of the CIR in (1), with $h_{ji}(\tau;t)$ denoting the CIR between Tx antenna $i\in\{1, 2, ...N_T\}$ and Rx antenna $j\in\{1, 2, ...N_R\}$.

By "multiband" channels, we mean channels that are used for simultaneous communications in multiple, non-contiguous blocks of spectrum. These are being researched for cellular (Hara,

2005), (Zhang, 2008) systems, and so may also be of use for future V2V systems, for the excellent diversity they offer. In principle, even for bands that are widely separated in frequency, CIRs can be generated using either the TDL or GBS approach. Different large- and small-scale and fading characteristics may be required for the disparate bands, but if obtained from measurements, just as with the MIMO case, generation of multiband CIRs is in principle a straightforward extension.

V2V Networks and Relays

Future V2V communications may take place via ad hoc networks (sometimes termed VANETs, for vehicular ad hoc networks). In this case, there are multiple V2V channels between the multiple vehicles that constitute the network. Each of these channels can be modeled via the techniques already described, but in terms of network simulation, the correlations between the multiple channels would be of use. For this, GBS models might be preferable, at least initially, until multi-vehicle measurements that quantify correlations are available for developing correlated TDL models.

In some cases, vehicles relay messages over multiple links. To the author's knowledge, there are no available measured results for this type of relay channel yet, and results for the overall, or composite channel, would also depend upon the relaying approach (e.g., amplify and forward, decode and forward, etc.). One analytical result in this area appears in (Talha, 2009), where the authors assume complex Gaussian CIR statistics for each link, and derive analytical expressions for resultant amplitude probability density functions, and the second-order statistical functions of level crossing rate and average fade durations. As with other analytical models, despite the elegance of the mathematics, these functions are likely of use primarily as "boundary conditions" for limiting cases of practical conditions.

Remarks on Channel Estimation

There are two types of channel estimation: the first is when channels are measured specifically for the purpose of gathering channel statistics and developing models, and the second is when channels are estimated during communication. We briefly discuss both here.

For estimating the CIR, one can use pulsed waveforms or wideband direct-sequence spread spectrum signals. The CTF can be estimated via multitone techniques (Molisch, 2009). In either case, one has limited bandwidth and this yields finite resolution in the delay domain. Deconvolution techniques can be employed on the measured responses to more closely approximate the actual CIR, but often this is not viewed as necessary, particularly when the measurement bandwidth is larger than any anticipated signal bandwidth. One must also ensure that the CIR estimate is obtained before the actual channel can change, hence, one must know at least the maximum expected Doppler shift (and minimum coherence time) that will be encountered. This is usually easily accomplished if one knows the maximum relative vehicle velocity.

Channel estimation has a long history (Parsons, 2000), and for the V2V case, delay spreads will typically be smaller than those in cellular. In contrast, the more rapid time variation of the V2V channel may require faster processing than is needed for estimating cellular channels.

In terms of channel estimation during signal transmission, this too is well established, and most existing system standards have in place methods for intermittent (often, periodic) channel estimation. The most common method is the use of some known data symbols (approximating "pulses"); the receiver correlates with the received waveform for these known symbols, and in essences "builds" an estimate of the CIR periodically. For OFDM systems, these known symbols are distributed in both frequency and time, whereas in single-carrier systems, the symbols are time multiplexed.

Specifically for OFDM, samples of the CTF $H(f;t)$ are estimated, and these samples form a discrete vector $\vec{H}_M = (H_1, H_2, ... H_M)$, where H_i is the response at the ith (of M) frequencies in the discrete Fourier transform. The known (pilot) symbols are distributed in both time and frequency among some K symbols in time and M subcarriers across frequency. These pilot symbols should be close enough in the frequency domain to enable good estimates of the CTF samples H_i between those pilot subcarriers; similarly, the pilot symbols should be frequent enough in the time domain to ensure that multiple pilots are received within the channel coherence time. This yields sampling at the Nyquist rate in both the time and frequency domains. For OFDM systems, the receiver first extracts the channel-corrupted pilot symbols, then performs some filtering. The channel-corrupted pilot symbols are given by the matrix equation

$$\vec{R} = H\vec{X} + \vec{W} \qquad (20)$$

where H is a diagonal matrix with elements H_i, vector $\vec{X} = (X0, X1, ... XM\text{-}1)T$ is the transmitted data symbol vector in one OFDM symbol, and $\vec{W}$ is the noise vector for the M subcarriers. Then to find the channel estimate for the kth frequency (subcarrier), we can divide by the known pilot symbol Xk: $\hat{H}_k = R_k / X_k = H_k + W_k / X_k$. Two-dimensional Wiener filtering of these estimates is optimal for estimating the remaining channel coefficients on the data subcarriers (Molisch, 2001), but due to the enormous complexity of this approach, separate time- and frequency-domain techniques, such as averaging, interpolation, or minimum mean-square error filtering, are often used. Details on these approaches appear in (Li, 2006).

SUMMARY, CONCLUSION, AND AREAS FOR FUTURE WORK

In this chapter, we provided an overview of V2V channel characterization. After reviewing some of the unique features of V2V channels, we noted applications, likely frequency bands of operation, and initial V2V system standards. After noting the importance of accurate channel modeling, we reviewed fundamentals of statistical channel modeling, as applied to the channel impulse response and transfer function. We then described various types of V2V channel models, including deterministic, and the more empirically based tapped delay line and geometry-based stochastic models. Example tapped delay line and geometry-based stochastic models were described. A brief discussion of MIMO and multiband models, of V2V relaying, and of channel estimation, completed the chapter.

The most significant conclusion we offer is that V2V channels can be substantially different from the conventional cellular channel: they can change (fade) more rapidly, and incur more severe fading. These characteristics must be incorporated into accurate V2V channel models, and both the TDL and GBS models may be used for multiple classes of V2V channels. The GBS model is in general substantially more complex, but can inherently include MIMO systems. Channel estimation for V2V channels will generally need to be done faster than in conventional channels.

Future work on V2V channel modeling is still required. There is no GBS model equivalent to the one in (Karedal, 2009) for urban or suburban cases. Additional quantification of the time scales of NS processes is needed, particularly for TDL models. Measurements in other frequency bands may also be of interest in the future, and as V2V networks are deployed, models for relay channels will also be required.

REFERENCES

Acosta-Marum, G., & Ingram, M. (2007). Six time- and frequency-selective empirical channel models for vehicular wireless LANs. *IEEE Vehicular Technology Magazine, 2*(4), 4–11. doi:10.1109/MVT.2008.917435

Aggelou, G. (2005). *Mobile ad hoc networks: From wireless LANS to 4G networks*. New York, NY: McGraw-Hill.

Akki, A. (1994). Statistical properties of mobile-to-mobile land communication channels. *IEEE Transactions on Vehicular Technology, 43*(4), 826–831. doi:10.1109/25.330143

Akki, A., & Haber, F. (1986). A statistical model of mobile-to-mobile land communication channel. *IEEE Transactions on Vehicular Technology, 35*(1), 2–7. doi:10.1109/T-VT.1986.24062

American Society for Testing and Materials. (2008). *ASTM E2213: Standard specification for telecommunications and information exchange between roadside and vehicle systems—5 GHz band dedicated short range communications (DSRC)-Medium access control (MAC) and physical layer (PHY) specifications*. Retrieved 22 September, 2008, from http://www.astm.org.

Andrews, J., Ghosh, A., & Muhamed, R. (2007). *Fundamentals of WiMAX: Understanding broadband wireless networking*. Upper Saddle River, NJ: Prentice-Hall.

Bai, F., & Krishnamachari, B. (2010). Exploiting the wisdom of the crowd: Localized, distributed information-centric VANETS. *IEEE Communications Magazine, 48*(5), 138–146. doi:10.1109/MCOM.2010.5458375

Belanovic, P., Valerio, D., Paier, A., Zemen, T., Ricciato, F., & Mecklenbrauker, C. (2010). On wireless links for vehicle-to-infrastructure communications. *IEEE Transactions on Vehicular Technology, 59*(1), 269–282. doi:10.1109/TVT.2009.2029119

Bello, P. (1963). Characterization of random time-variant linear channels. *IEEE Transactions on Communications, 11*(12), 360–393. doi:10.1109/TCOM.1963.1088793

Calcev, G., Chizhik, D., Goransson, B., Howard, S., Huang, H., & Kogiantis, A. (2007). A wideband spatial channel model for system-wide simulations. *IEEE Transactions on Vehicular Technology, 56*(2), 389–403. doi:10.1109/TVT.2007.891463

Cheng, L., Henty, B., Stancil, D., Bai, F., & Mudalige, P. (2007). Mobile vehicle-to-vehicle narrow-band channel measurement and characterization of the 5.9 GHz dedicated short range communication (DSRC) frequency band. *IEEE Journal on Selected Areas in Communications, 25*(8), 1501–1516. doi:10.1109/JSAC.2007.071002

Cheng, X., Wang, C., Laurenson, D., Salous, S., & Vasilakos, A. (2009). An adaptive geometry-based stochastic model for non-isotropic MIMO mobile-to-mobile channels. *IEEE Transactions on Wireless Communications, 8*(9), 4824–4835. doi:10.1109/TWC.2009.081560

Cohen, L. (1995). *Time-frequency analysis*. Upper Saddle River, NJ: Prentice-Hall.

Correia, L. (Ed.). (2001). *Wireless flexible personalised communications. COST 259 Final Report*. Chichester, UK: Wiley.

COST. 231. (2007). *Final report*. Retrieved 19 April, 2007, from http://www.lx.it.pt/cost231/final_report.htm.

European Telecommunications Standards Institute (ETSI). (1997). *Universal mobile telecommunications system (UMTS): Selection procedures for the choice of radio transmission technologies of the UMTS.* (ETSI document UMTS 30.03, ver. 3.1.0, TR 101 112, v3.1.0, Section B.1.4.2).

Gallagher, B., Akatsuka, H., & Suzuki, H. (2006). Wireless communications for vehicle safety: Radio link performance & wireless connectivity methods. *IEEE Vehicular Technology Magazine*, *1*(4), 4–24. doi:10.1109/MVT.2006.343641

Gesbert, D., Bolcskei, H., Gore, D., & Paulraj, A. (2002). Outdoor MIMO wireless channels: Models and performance prediction. *IEEE Transactions on Communications*, *50*(12), 1926–1934. doi:10.1109/TCOMM.2002.806555

Hara, Y., & Taira, A. (2005). System configuration for multiband MC-CDM systems. *Proceedings Fall Vehicular Tech. Conf.*, Dallas, TX.

Institute of Electrical and Electronics Engineers. (2001). *Channel models for fixed wireless applications.* (IEEE Broadband Wireless Access Working Group document IEEE 802.163c-01/29). Retrieved 11 September, 2009, from http://wirelessman.org/tg3/contrib/802163c-01_29r4.pdf.

Institute of Electrical and Electronics Engineers. (2005a). *Channel models for IEEE 802.20 MBWA system simulations.* (IEEE document 802.20-03/48). Retrieved 28 March, 2005, from http://grouper.ieee.org/groups/802//20/Contribs/C802.20-03-48.pdf.

Institute of Electrical and Electronics Engineers. (2005b). *IEEE 802.20 channel models (V1.0), IEEE 802.20 PD-08.* Retrieved 28 March, 2005, from http://grouper.ieee.org/groups/802//20/P_Docs/IEEE_802.20-PD-08.doc.

Institute of Electrical and Electronics Engineers. (2007). *Channel models for fixed wireless applications.* (IEEE document 802.16.3c-01/29r4).

Institute of Electrical and Electronics Engineers. (2008). *IEEE wireless access in vehicular environments website.* Retrieved 23 September, 2008, from http://grouper.ieee.org/groups/802/11/Reports/tgp_update.htm.

Institute of Electrical and Electronics Engineers. (2010). *IEEE wireless local area networks working group website.* Retrieved 20 October, 2010, from http://ieee802.org/11/.

International Telecommunications Union (ITU). (1999). *Document ITU-R P.1407-1: Multipath propagation and parameterization of its characteristics.*

Jakes, W. (1993). *Microwave mobile communication.* New York, NY: IEEE Press.

Jiang, D., & Delgrossi, L. (2008). IEEE 802.11p: Towards an international standard for wireless access in vehicular environments. *IEEE International Symposium on Wireless Vehicular Communications (WiVec)*, Calgary, CA.

Jiang, D., Taliwal, V., Meier, A., Holfelder, W., & Herrtwich, R. (2006). Design of 5.9 GHz DSRC-based vehicular safety communication. *IEEE Communications Magazine*, *44*(10), 36–43.

Karedal, J., Tufvesson, F., Czink, N., Paier, A., Dumard, C., & Zemen, F. (2009). A geometry-based stochastic MIMO model for vehicle-to-vehicle communications. *IEEE Transactions on Wireless Communications*, *8*(7), 3646–3657. doi:10.1109/TWC.2009.080753

Kaul, S., Ramachandran, K., Shankar, P., Oh, S., Gruteser, M., Seskar, I., & Nadeem, T. (2007). *Effect of antenna placement and diversity on vehicular network communications.* IEEE Conference on Sensor, Mesh, & Ad Hoc Networks, San Diego, CA.

Konrad, A., Zhao, B., Joseph, A., & Ludwig, R. (2003). A Markov-based model algorithm for wireless networks. *Wireless Networks, 9*, 189–199. doi:10.1023/A:1022869025953

Konstantinou, K., Kang, S., & Tzaras, C. (2008). A measurement-based model for mobile-to-mobile UMTS links. *Proceedings IEEE Spring Vehicular Technology Conference*, Singapore.

Kunisch, J., & Pamp, J. (2008). Wideband car-to-car radio channel measurements and model at 5.9 GHz. *Proceedings of the IEEE Fall Vehicular Technology Conference*, Calgary, Canada.

Li, Y., & Stuber, G. (2006). *Orthogonal frequency division multiplexing for wireless communications.* New York, NY: Springer. doi:10.1007/0-387-30235-2

Matolak, D. (2006). *Wireless channel characterization in the 5 GHz microwave landing system extension band for airport surface areas.* Final Project Report for NASA ACAST Project, Grant Number NNC04GB45G, May 2006.

Matolak, D. (2008). Channel modeling for vehicle-to-vehicle communications. *IEEE Communications Magazine, 46*(5), 76–83. doi:10.1109/MCOM.2008.4511653

Matolak, D. (2010). *Wireless channel modeling: Fundamentals, quantification, and high-fidelity models for future communication systems.* University of Malaga Spring/Summer session School of Telecommunications short course, Malaga Spain, 14 & 23 June 2010.

Matolak, D., Sen, I., & Xiong, W. (2008). On the generation of multivariate Weibull random variates. *IET Communications Journal, 2*(4), 523–527. doi:10.1049/iet-com:20070133

Matolak, D., Sen, I., Xiong, W., & Apaza, R. (2007). Channel measurement/modeling for airport surface communications: Mobile and fixed platform results. *IEEE Aerospace & Electronics Magazine, 22*(10), 25–30. doi:10.1109/MAES.2007.4376108

Matolak, D., Wu, W., & Sen, I. (2010). 5 GHz band vehicle-to-vehicle channels: Models for multiple values of channel bandwidth. *IEEE Transactions on Vehicular Technology, 59*(5), 2620–2625. doi:10.1109/TVT.2010.2043455

Matz, G. (2005). On non-WSSUS wireless fading channels. *IEEE Transactions on Wireless Communications, 4*(5), 2465–2478. doi:10.1109/TWC.2005.853905

Maurer, J., Fugen, T., Schafer, T., & Wiesbeck, W. (2004). A new inter-vehicle communications (IVC) channel model. *Proceedings of the IEEE Vehicular Technology Conference*, (pp. 9-13).

Maurer, J., Schafer, T., & Wiesbeck, W. (2001). A realistic description of the environment for inter-vehicle wave propagation modeling. *Proceedings of the IEEE Vehicular Technology Conference*, (pp. 1437-1441).

Maurer, J., Schafer, T., & Wiesbeck, W. (2005). Physical layer simulations of IEEE 802.11a for vehicle-vehicle communications. *Proceedings of the IEEE Vehicular Technology Conference*, Dallas, TX.

Medbo, J., Hallenberg, H., & Berg, J. (1999). Propagation characteristics at 5 GHz in typical radio-LAN scenarios. *Proceedings of IEEE Vehicular Technology Conference*, (vol. 1, pp. 185-189).

Molisch, A. (Ed.). (2001). *Wideband wireless digital communications.* Upper Saddle River, NJ: Prentice Hall.

Molisch, A., Tufvesson, F., Karedal, J., & Mecklenbrauker, C. (2009). A survey on vehicle-to-vehicle propagation channels. *IEEE Wireless Communication Magazine, 16*(6), 12–22. doi:10.1109/MWC.2009.5361174

Paier, A., Karedal, J., Czink, N., Dumard, C., Zemen, T., & Tufvesson, F. (2009). Characterization of vehicle-to-vehicle radio channels from measurements at 5.2 GHz. *Wireless Personal Communications, 50,* 19–32. doi:10.1007/s11277-008-9546-6

Papadimitratos, P., de la Fortelle, A., Evenssen, K., Brignolo, R., & Cosenza, S. (2009). Vehicular communication systems: Enabling technologies, applications, and future outlook on intelligent transportation. *IEEE Communications Magazine, 47*(11), 84–95. doi:10.1109/MCOM.2009.5307471

Papazian, P. (2005). Basic transmission loss and delay spread measurements for frequencies between 430 and 5750 MHz. *IEEE Transactions on Antennas and Propagation, 53*(2), 694–701. doi:10.1109/TAP.2004.841391

Papoulis, A., & Pillai, U. (2001). *Probability, random variables, and stochastic processes* (4th ed.). New York, NY: McGraw-Hill.

Parsons, J. D. (2000). *The mobile radio propagation channel* (2nd ed.). New York, NY: John Wiley & Sons. doi:10.1002/0470841524

Patzold, M., Hogstad, B., & Youssef, N. (2008). Modeling, analysis, and simulation of MIMO mobile-to-mobile fading channels. *IEEE Transactions on Wireless Communications, 7*(2), 510–520. doi:10.1109/TWC.2008.05913

Proakis, J. (2010). *Digital communications* (4th ed.). Boston, MA: McGraw-Hill.

Pursley, M. (2002). *Random processes in linear systems.* Upper Saddle River, NJ: Prentice-Hall.

Qiu, R. (2002). A study of the ultra-wideband wireless propagation channel and optimum UWB receiver design. *IEEE Journal on Selected Areas in Communications, 20*(9), 1628–1637. doi:10.1109/JSAC.2002.805249

Rappaport, T. (2002). *Wireless communications: Principles and practice* (2nd ed.). Upper Saddle River, NJ: Prentice-Hall.

Reichardt, L., Fugen, T., & Zwick, T. (2010). Influence of antennas placement on car to car communications channel. *Proceedings of European Conference on Antennas & Propagation 2010,* Berlin, Germany.

Renaudin, O., Kolmonen, V., Vainikainen, P., & Oestges, C. (2010). Non-stationary narrowband MIMO inter-vehicle channel characterization in the 5 GHz band. *IEEE Transactions on Vehicular Technology, 59*(4), 2007–2015. doi:10.1109/TVT.2010.2040851

Renaudin, O., Kolmonen, V., Vainikainen, P., & Oestges, C. (2011). Wideband measurement-based modeling of inter-vehicle channels in the 5 GHz band. *Proceedings of European Conference on Antennas & Propagation 2011,* Rome, Italy.

Sai, S., Niwa, E., Mase, K., Nishibori, M., Inoue, J., & Obuchi, M. (2009). Field evaluation of UHF radio propagation for an ITS safety system in an urban environment. *IEEE Communications Magazine, 47*(11), 120–127. doi:10.1109/MCOM.2009.5307475

Schafhuber, D., & Matz, G. (2005). MMSE and adaptive prediction of time-varying channels for OFDM systems. *IEEE Transactions on Wireless Communications, 4*(2), 593–602. doi:10.1109/TWC.2004.843055

Sen, I., & Matolak, D. (2008). Vehicle-vehicle channel models for the 5 GHz band. *IEEE Transactions on Intelligent Transportation Systems, 9*(2), 235–245. doi:10.1109/TITS.2008.922881

Sen, I., Matolak, D., & Xiong, W. (2006). Wireless channels that exhibit "worse than Rayleigh" fading: Analytical and measurement results. *Proceedings of MILCOM 2006,* Washington, DC.

Sesia, S., Toufik, I., & Baker, M. (Eds.). (2009). *LTE: The UMTS long term evolution: From theory to practice.* West Sussex, UK: John Wiley & Sons. doi:10.1002/9780470742891

Stein, S. (1987). Fading channel issues in system engineering. *IEEE Journal on Selected Areas in Communications,* 5(2), 68–89. doi:10.1109/JSAC.1987.1146536

Stuber, G. L. (2001). *Principles of mobile communication* (2nd ed.). Boston, MA: Kluwer Academic Publishers.

Talha, B., & Patzold, M. (2009). Statistical modeling and analysis of mobile-to-mobile fading channels in cooperative networks under line-of-sight conditions. *Wireless Personal Communications,* 50, 1–17.

Tank, T., & Linnartz, J.-P. (1997). Vehicle-to-vehicle communications for AVCS platooning. *IEEE Transactions on Vehicular Technology,* 46(2), 528–536. doi:10.1109/25.580791

US Department of Transportation. (2010). *Intelligent transportation systems.* Retrieved 16 November, 2010, from http://www.its.dot.gov/index.htm.

Uzcategui, R., & Acosta-Marum, G. (2009). WAVE: A tutorial. *IEEE Communications Magazine,* 47(5), 126–133. doi:10.1109/MCOM.2009.4939288

Vatalaro, F., & Forcella, A. (1997). Doppler spectrum in mobile-to-mobile communications in the presence of three-dimensional multipath scattering. *IEEE Transactions on Vehicular Technology,* 46(1), 213–219. doi:10.1109/25.554754

Wada, T., Maeda, M., Okada, M., Tsukamoto, K., & Komaki, S. (1998). Theoretical analysis of propagation characteristics in millimeter-wave intervehicle communication system. *IEICE Transactions in Communication,* 83(11), 1116–1125.

Zajic, A., & Stuber, G. (2008). Three-dimensional modeling, simulation, and capacity analysis of space-time correlated mobile-to-mobile channels. *IEEE Transactions on Vehicular Technology,* 57(4), 2042–2054. doi:10.1109/TVT.2007.912150

Zajic, A., Stuber, G., & Pratt, T. (2009). Wideband MIMO mobile-to-mobile channels: Geometry-based statistical modeling with experimental verification. *IEEE Transactions on Vehicular Technology,* 58(2), 517–534. doi:10.1109/TVT.2008.928001

Zhang, J., & Matolak, D. (2008). FG-*MC-CDMA system performance in multi-band channels.* IEEE Communication Networks & Services Research Conference, Halifax, Nova Scotia, CA.

Zheng, Y. R. (2006). A non-isotropic model for mobile to mobile fading channel simulations. *Proceedings of MILCOM '06,* Washington, DC.

Zhu, J., & Roy, S. (2003). MAC for dedicated short range communications in intelligent transport system. *IEEE Communications Magazine,* 43(12), 60–67.

KEY TERMS AND DEFINITIONS

Channel Impulse Response (CIR): Response of the channel to an ideal impulse input, typically the response at time t to an impulse input at time $t-\tau$.

Channel Transfer Function (CTF): Fourier transform of the channel impulse response; magnitude and phase of the channel at a specific frequency f, time t.

Delay Spread: Extent, in delay, of the channel impulse response; typically quantified via the root-mean-square value.

Geometry-Based Stochastic (GBS): Randomized, simplified ray-tracing model for the wireless channel, in which environment geometry is specified, with objects distributed according to probability distributions.

Non-Stationary: Statistically non-stationary, i.e., statistics of phenomena change over time/space.

Tapped Delay Line (TDL): Linear, finite impulse response filter used to model the time-varying wireless channel; consists of a delay line, with outputs weighted via random processes that model multipath components.

Wireless Channel: Complete set of communication system (linear system) parameters for all electromagnetic wave components that travel from transmitter to receiver, in frequency band and spatial volume of interest.

ENDNOTES

[1] V2V communication will certainly be used in "off-road" conditions, and propagation and channel modeling are certainly of interest for this case, but we restrict our attention here to V2V systems on roadways in urban, suburban, highway, and rural areas.

[2] We use the term "reflection" loosely, to encompass actual reflection, diffraction, or scattering.

[3] Note that for complex baseband functions, a factor ½ multiplies the expectation for complex envelope scaling (Proakis, 2001). Since this does not affect the most important feature—autocorrelation shape—we ignore this factor here.

[4] MPC phases are almost always assumed to be uniformly distributed on $[0, 2\pi)$, except in the case of an LOS or dominant component, in which case that particular MPC's phase is modeled as having a narrow (sometimes Gaussian) distribution about its mean phase..

Chapter 3
Modulation and Coding Techniques for Inter-Vehicular Communications

Corneliu Eugen D. Sterian
Polytechnic University of Bucharest, Romania

ABSTRACT

Direct inter-vehicular communications are presumably more difficult to perform than communications within a cellular network or between a moving vehicle and the roadside, where there is a large fixed infrastructure. It is assumed in this chapter that the mobile channel between the two vehicles is so rapidly variable that it is not possible to measure it in real-time. The authors therefore selected and considered only modulation and coding techniques for which the knowledge of the channel state was not necessary at both the transmitter and the receiver, that is, differential and noncoherent communications. To be realistic, only space-time coding communication systems with two transmit antennas were considered. The authors have purposely avoided too much theoretical development, with the intent of making clear that the implementation of all the techniques mentioned in this chapter, it should not be a too difficult task for the electronic technology of today. Future research directions are also suggested to conclude the chapter.

INTRODUCTION

The science of intelligent transportation systems (ITS) cleverly exploits the achievements of other technical disciplines like electronics, telecommu-nications, computer science, automatic control, information technology and so on to improve the quality and safety of the traffic. Direct vehicle-to-vehicle (V2V) communication has recently received considerable attention from both the academia and the car industry. This is certainly a bit bumpier to realize than the communication

DOI: 10.4018/978-1-4666-0209-0.ch003

within a cellular network, since both vehicles are supposed to be on the move and thus, the wireless channel between them is strongly time variable. Moreover, the requirements for the reliability of a V2V communication link are more stringent: avoidance of collisions may closely depend on it. In this chapter, we thus try to select and recommend for use only those modulation and coding techniques that are known to be less exigent with the quality of the mobile radio channel. But while such techniques are robust and work well on a poor channel, their data rate performance is accordingly lower. This clearly puts a constraint on the amount of information that can be transmitted on a V2V digital link. On the other side, we see at the present stage of the technology no urgent reason to offer two drivers running on a highway the possibility to directly transmit to each other large computer files, music or movies, or to play chess. Vital information as measured in bits should be short.

The literature on V2V is abundant. However, most papers and articles dedicated to this important topic give little consideration to the physical layer, assuming more or less that this technical problem has already been solved. However, as witnessed by the incessant flow of new papers dealing with transmission techniques that could support V2V communications, it is not so. Let us start by noting that textbooks describing wireless communications have hundreds of pages. In this chapter, we take the realistic approach to review the modulation and coding techniques that do not require the knowledge of the wireless channel. The simplest such modulation is *frequency-shift keying* (FSK); it is robust and naturally noncoherent, but unfortunately allows for a rather low data rate. The *phase-shift keying* (PSK) is a coherent modulation requiring the recovery of the carrier frequency at the receiver; however, its differential version needs no such operation, which makes it fit for V2V direct communication. Fortunately, differential PSK can be combined with *trellis coded modulation* (TCM) in order to improve

the transmission performance. Another powerful means to improve the performance of a wireless digital link is the transmit antenna diversity. In this chapter, we consider only communication systems with two transmit antennas, but more than two can be used. There are two reasons for this choice: the first one is the limited editorial space. The second one, maybe more important, is that, according to the mathematical theory of orthogonal designs, square orthogonal matrices with complex-valued entries do not exist for a size larger than 2×2. This technique is known as space-time block coding. It generally requires the acquisition of *channel state information* (CSI) at the receiver. However, a version of it called *unitary space-time modulation* was devised for which CSI is not necessary. A differential encoding of space-time block codes is also possible; it can be viewed as a generalization for two transmit antennas of the differential PSK. We then present in some detail *super-orthogonal space-time trellis coded differential* PSK. The actual trend is, of course, to increase the transmission data rate for which wireless channels with larger bandwidth are needed. But broadband channels require adaptive equalization. All the techniques mentioned above are narrowband single-carrier coding and/or modulation methods for which equalization is not an issue. They can be used for broadband channels as well, but the equalization in this case is difficult to perform. To avoid the equalization of broadband channels, multicarrier modulation is usually preferred. For wireless channels, it is known as *orthogonal frequency division multiplexing* (OFDM). Instead of using a single-carrier, OFDM uses a rather large set of frequencies between which harmonic relations exist. Therefore, OFDM is a highly synchronous and coherent transmission technology. In order to apply it to V2V communications, OFDM must be somehow transformed into a noncoherent technique. We summarize a possibility of doing this from the open literature but certainly the research will continue in this direction.

Toward the end of the chapter, we try to sketch future research directions. We conclude with some final remarks.

REQUIREMENTS FOR A VEHICLE-TO- VEHICLE DIGITAL LINK

Classification

Following recent survey articles (Sichitiu 2008, Dar 2010), we can divide the ITS applications into *safety applications* (collision avoidance, road sign notifications, incident management), *efficiency applications* (management applications, monitoring applications) and *comfort applications* (entertainment applications, contextual applications). Different ITS applications have different requirements. Vehicular communications (VC) can be divided into inter-vehicle communications (IVC), roadside-vehicle communications (RVC) and hybrid- vehicle communications (HVC). RVC has fundamental similarities with cellular telecommunication networks, both of them having a powerful infrastructure. Roadside equipment consists of access points like the base stations in the cellular networks. They are connected through fiber optic cables having enormous channel capacity. Many useful ITS applications, including mobile Internet access, can be based on RVC. IVC systems, instead, have no infrastructure at all; of course, the cars are equipped with *onboard units* (OBUs). There can be separate OBUs for IVC and RVC, or the same OBU can be designed to work with both IVC and RVC. The specificity of IVC and RVC makes them useful for rather different ITS applications. While the IVC systems have the advantage of possessing a much lower transmission delay over the RVC systems, their drawback is that they have a much smaller data rate. HVC systems extend the range of RVC systems by using other vehicles as relays, or mobile routers.

Restrictions and Limitations

While a vehicle can communicate in a variety of ways, we are interested in this chapter only in these transmission techniques that can be considered as safe and reliable in a highly variable mobile channel such that the receiver cannot acquire CSI. This drastically reduces our possible choice to differential and noncoherent transmission techniques. We are forced to do so, since they have inferior performance compared to synchronous techniques. For narrowband transmission systems, each synchronous technique has a differential or noncoherent counterpart. For broadband transmission systems, a multi-carrier method called *orthogonal frequency-division multiplexing* (OFDM) is generally used; it is synchronous and, what is a much serious drawback for a V2V communication, the CSI is very difficult if not impossible to acquire by the receiver in real time, making necessary a noncoherent demodulation or the use of some form of differential modulation on each subcarrier. Any could be the particular solution. Importantly, however, it certainly will be very signal-processing intensive and thus require novel algorithms. This remains, therefore, an open research topic.

FREQUENCY-SHIFT KEYING (FSK)

Binary Frequency-Shift Keying (BFSK)

To transmit a string of bits $b_0, b_1, b_2, \ldots, b_n, b_{n+1}, \ldots$ over a bandpass channel, two waveforms are needed. For binary FSK, these waveforms are:

$$s_0(t) = A\cos\left(2\pi f_0 t + \varphi_0\right), nT \leq t < (n+1)T,$$
for 0

and

$$s_1(t) = A\cos\left(2\pi f_1 t + \varphi_1\right), nT \le t < (n+1)T,$$
for 1.

where f_0 and f_1 are two frequencies called *characteristic* frequencies, φ_0 and φ_1 are initial phases, and T is the bit duration. The parameter A, called *amplitude*, is established by the transmit amplifier of the data modem. Generally, there is no relation between the periods of the sinusoids $T_0 = 1 / f_0$ and $T_1 = 1 / f_1$, and the bit duration T. This modulation format is therefore *noncoherent*. It is simple and robust, a good reason why it was the earliest type of digital modulation having been used on both wireline and wireless channels. However, it has a limitation. If we define the bit rate by $R = 1/T$, then the maximum bit rate for binary FSK is:

$$R_{max} = \frac{3}{2}\left|f_0 - f_1\right|.$$

The transmission by BFSK is naturally *asynchronous*. To make it into a *synchronous* one, a bit synchronization block (synchrobit for short) should be included in the receiver.

A coherent type of FSK can be constructed by imposing a particular relation between T_0, T_1 and T. For instance, under the constraint that the two signals $s_0(t)$ and $s_1(t)$ are orthogonal, we have

$$T = \frac{2n+m}{4}T_0 = \frac{2n-m}{4}T_1.$$

where n and m are integers.

Phase jumps are known to broaden the signal bandwidth. To avoid this, continuous phase FSK (CPFSK) can be used. The continuity of the phase requires memory, and a transmission system using such modulation format is by far more complex than one using simple FSK. It is important to mention that a particular form of CPFSK called Gaussian minimum shift keying (GMSK) is used by mobile cellular networks that apply the European standard known as GSM (global system for mobile) and also in the Bluetooth networks.

Details of all forms of FSK are very well covered in any textbook on digital communications; see for instance Fuqin Xiong: Digital Modulation Techniques, Artech House 2000.

M-ary Frequency-Shift Keying (MFSK)

More than only two characteristic frequencies can be used to digitally transmit information. Let M be a power of two: $M = 2^m$. The binary data stream generated by the information source is divided into *m*-tuples of m bits called *messages* such that each message has a duration of $T = mT_b$, where T_b is the bit duration. To each one of the M messages we assign a waveform

$$s_i(t) = A\cos\left(2\pi f_i t + \varphi_i\right), nT \le t < (n+1)T$$

for $i = 1,..., M$. Indeed, this modulation format is used in such an important application as *frequency-hop spread spectrum*, or *code division multiple access* (CDMA) with frequency hop (FH). Various developments of it can be found in the literature. We suggest to the reader (Atkin 1989), where a given message selects more than a single frequency to simultaneously convey it. Other good examples are (Luo 2005), where a class of multitone FSK schemes for noncoherent communications in wideband Rayleigh-fading channels is introduced, and (Ghareeb 2005), where similar transmission is considered over slow nonselective Nakagami-*m* fading channels.

DIFFERENTIAL PHASE-SHIFT KEYING (DPSK)

In order to improve the bandwidth efficiency, defined as the number of bits transmitted per second in a frequency bandwidth of one Hertz, let us divide the binary data stream generated by the information source into m-tuples as we have done in the case of MFSK. To each one of the $M = 2^m$ messages we then assign a waveform

$$s_i(t) = A\cos\left(2\pi f_c t + \varphi_i\right), \; nT \leq t < (n+1)T \tag{1}$$

for $i = 0,..., M-1$, where the amplitude A and the carrier frequency f_c are constant parameters, and the information is carried by the phase φ_i. This defines the M-ary phase-shift keying (MPSK). The phase φ_i has the expression:

$$\varphi_i = \frac{2i\pi}{M} + \theta_0, \; i = 0,..., M-1 \tag{2}$$

where θ_0 can be taken as 0 or π/M. In practice, M can take only the values 2, 4, and 8. Sometimes, $M = 16$ is considered in the research literature but, as far as we know, we cannot mention even a single actual communication system using it. With trigonometry, we can write (1) as

$$s_i(t) = A\cos\varphi_i \cos\left(2\pi f_c t\right) - A\sin\varphi_i \sin\left(2\pi f_c t\right)$$

The baseband equivalent of $s_i(t)$ is

$$s_i = A\left(\cos\varphi_i + j\sin\varphi_i\right).$$

For $A = 1$, we can represent all the M messages as signal points on a circle centered in the origin and with unit radius. It results in a figure called *signal constellation*. The signal constellations for $M = 4$ and $M = 8$ are shown in Figure 1 (a) and (b), respectively. For $M = 2$, only the two points on the abscissa axe are used. In Figure 1, the signal points are labeled in natural order, that is, the message corresponding to the binary value of i is assigned the phase φ_i as given in (7). Another possible assignment is the *Gray coding*, where neighboring points are assigned to messages differing in a single bit.

Actually, we are not interested in the MPSK modulation format, for the coherent demodulation of which carrier phase recovery is required, but in the differential version of it, DMPSK. Indeed,

Figure 1. Circular signal constellations for MPSK: (a) QPSK; (b) 8PSK

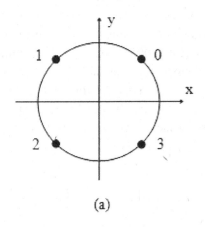

(a)

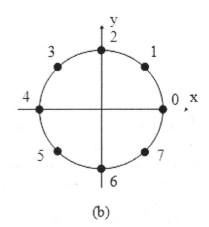

(b)

differential encoding is used in order to eliminate the phase ambiguity in the carrier recovery process.

For $M = 2$, we have *differential binary phase-shift keying* (DBPSK). It does not require a coherent reference signal for demodulation. The phase of the cosine wave transmitted over the channel is not the absolute phase corresponding to the input bit, but this phase referenced to the phase of the signal transmitted in the previous bit interval. In other words, if the bit b_n is to be transmitted in the nth bit interval, the bit selecting the signal phase is

$$d_n = b_n \oplus d_{n-1}.$$

The bit d_0, actually not sent and carrying no information, is conveniently chosen as zero.

For $M = 4$, we have *differential quadruple phase-shift keying* (DQPSK). The message is comprised of two bits to be transmitted in the nth symbol interval, say b_{2n} and b_{2n+1}. With natural labeling, they determine the absolute phase φ_{i_n} according to Equation (2), where the decimal integer i_n is given by

$$i_n = 2b_{2n+1} + b_{2n}. \tag{3}$$

However, the signal waveform transmitted over the channel has not this phase, but the relative phase ψ_{ℓ_n}, such that

$$\psi_{\ell_n} = \left(\varphi_{i_n} + \psi_{\ell_{n-1}}\right) \bmod 2\pi \tag{4}$$

where

$$\ell_n = 2d_{2n+1} + d_{2n}. \tag{5}$$

We derive easily that

$$\ell_n = \left(i_n + \ell_{n-1}\right) \bmod 4. \tag{6}$$

From (3)-(6), we obtain

$$d_{2n} = b_{2n} \oplus d_{2n-2}$$

$$d_{2n+1} = b_{2n+1} \oplus d_{2n-1} \oplus \left(b_{2n} \cdot d_{2n-2}\right).$$

The demodulator recovers the differential bits $d_{2n-2}, d_{2n-1}, d_{2n}$, and d_{2n+1}. From them, the message bits are derived as

$$b_{2n} = d_{2n} \oplus d_{2n-2}$$

$$b_{2n+1} = d_{2n+1} \oplus d_{2n-1} \oplus \left(\overline{d}_{2n} \cdot d_{2n-2}\right).$$

For $M = 8$, we have *differential eight phase-shift keying* (D8PSK). The message is comprised of three bits b_{3n}, b_{3n+1}, and b_{3n+2}. Similar to the case $M = 4$, we have:

$$i_n = 4b_{3n+2} + 2b_{3n+1} + b_{3n}$$

and

$$\ell_n = 4d_{3n+2} + 2d_{3n+1} + d_{3n}.$$

We have

$$d_{3n} = b_{3n} \oplus d_{3n-3}$$

$$d_{3n+1} = b_{3n+1} \oplus d_{3n-2} \oplus \left(b_{3n} \cdot d_{3n-3}\right)$$

$$d_{3n+2} = b_{3n+2} \oplus d_{3n-1} \oplus \left[b_{3n+1} \cdot d_{3n-2} + \left(b_{3n+1} \oplus d_{3n-2}\right)b_{3n} \cdot d_{3n-3}\right].$$

The message bits result from the differential bits as follows:

$$b_{3n} = d_{3n} \oplus d_{3n-3}$$

$$b_{3n+1} = d_{3n+1} \oplus d_{3n-2} \oplus \left(\overline{d}_{3n} \cdot d_{3n-3} \right)$$

$$b_{3n+2} = d_{3n+2} \oplus d_{3n-1} \oplus \left[\left(d_{3n+1} \oplus \left(\overline{\overline{d}_{3n} \cdot d_{3n-3}} \right) \right) d_{3n-2} + \overline{d}_{3n+1} \cdot \overline{d}_{3n} \cdot d_{3n-3} \right]$$

While differential PSK needs no carrier recovery for demodulation, it requires a signal-to-noise power ratio 3 dB higher than its coherent counterpart for the same bit error rate (BER) performance. Moreover, its performance depends on the quality of the transmission channel. It would be naive to believe that it will work well on a poor channel. In a deep fade, it will definitely break down if no forward error correction is used as well.

TRELLIS-CODED DIFFERENTIAL 8PSK MODULATION

Let us consider a *single-input single-output* (SISO) wireless communication system having a bandwidth efficiency of 2 bits/s/Hz. We suppose that CSI is not available to both the transmitter and the receiver. Such a system can use a simple modulation format, like differential QPSK. However, the performance can be improved considerably by *trellis-coded modulation* (TCM) (Edbauer 1989). TCM was introduced by G. Ungerboeck in 1982 in his seminal paper entitled "Channel coding with multilevel/phase signals" and as early as 1984 a rotationally invariant TCM scheme devised by Lee-Fang Wei was adopted in the V.32 Recommendation of CCITT (nowadays ITU-T) for a data modem transmitting 9600 bits/s over switched telephone lines. TCM is indeed an advanced modulation and coding technique very well documented in the literature and thus we assume that the reader has at least some notions of it.

Ungerboeck stated the following principle: the TCM system must use a signal constellation which is double-sized as compared to that used by the uncoded system taken as reference. Therefore, a TCM system with bandwidth efficiency of 2 bits/s/Hz will use the 8PSK signal constellation as il-

lustrated in Figure 1 (b). The information source generates a string of bits that enter a serial-to-parallel converter such that two consecutive input bits simultaneously appear at the output in parallel. Denote them as $b1_n$ and $b2_n$. The couple of bits $b1_n$ and $b2_n$ enter a rate 2/3 systematic feedback convolutional encoder that outputs three bits: $c0_n$, $c1_n = b1_n$ and $c2_n = b2_n$. If no differential encoding is used, the three bits $c0_n$, $c1_n$ and $c2_n$ select one out of the eight points of the 8PSK signal constellation, and this point is then transmitted over the channel. Two mappings of the set of groups of three bits into the signal constellation are frequently used: the natural and the Grey coding. We choose to use the natural coding: the signal point numbered by c_n ($c_n = 0, \ldots, 7$) is selected by the three bits $c0_n$, $c1_n$ and $c2_n$ such that:

$$c_n = 4c2_n + 2c1_n + c0_n.$$

When using PSK, this signal point is transmitted as the phase angle $\varphi_n = c_n \cdot \pi / 4$ of the cosine carrier waveform. However, when DPSK is used instead, the signal point actually transmitted over the channel is determined by three bits $d0_n$, $d1_n$ and $d2_n$ such that, forming with them the decimal integer

$$d_n = 4d2_n + 2d1_n + d0_n$$

we have the following differential encoding:

$$d_n = \left(c_n + d_{n-1} \right) \bmod 8. \tag{7}$$

The differential encoding Equation (7) expresses the fact that the information is not carried by the absolute phase angle $c_n \cdot \pi / 4$, but by the phase in the current symbol interval relative to the phase in the previous symbol interval. The phase angle of the carrier waveform is thus no more φ_n, as in absolute PSK, but $\psi_n = d_n \cdot \pi / 4$ such that

$$\psi_n = \left(\varphi_n + \psi_{n-1}\right) \bmod 2\pi . \tag{8}$$

Ignoring the filtering operation and for unitary amplitude, the transmit waveform is the real-valued function of time

$$s_n\left(t\right) = \cos\left(2\pi f_c t + \psi_n\right),\ nT \leq t < \left(n+1\right)T \tag{9}$$

where T is the symbol duration and f_c is the carrier frequency. Using trigonometry, (9) can be written as

$$s_n\left(t\right) = \left(\cos\psi_n\right)\cos\left(2\pi f_c t\right) - \left(\sin\psi_n\right)\sin\left(2\pi f_c t\right),\ nT \leq t < \left(n+1\right)T$$

It is a common practice when analyzing digital transmission systems to formally ignore the modulation-demodulation by introducing the *equivalent low-pass* signal

$$s_n = \cos\psi_n + j\sin\psi_n .$$

Clearly, the real and the imaginary parts of s_n are the abscissa and the ordinate, respectively, of the signal point transmitted over the channel at discrete time n. It can be seen that

$$s_n\left(t\right) = \mathrm{Re}\left[s_n \cdot e^{j2\pi f_c t}\right]$$

where Re denotes the real part of the complex-valued quantity within the brackets. By the same token, we introduce

$$u_n = \cos\varphi_n + j\sin\varphi_n .$$

As mentioned in (Edbauer 1989), a block interleaver can be used to improve the performance of the transmission system over fading channels, but we ignore it here just to simplify the descrip-

tion. The operation of a convolutional encoder is conveniently described with the help of a trellis diagram. Let us consider two binary variables $\sigma 1_n$ and $\sigma 2_n$ that determine the inner state of the convolutional encoder at discrete time n. Then, the inner state can be expressed as a decimal integer as follows:

$$\sigma_n = 2\sigma 2_n + \sigma 1_n .$$

Partition the 8PSK signal constellation into four subsets as follows:

$$S_0 = \left\{0, 4\right\} \tag{10}$$

$$S_1 = \left\{1, 5\right\} \tag{11}$$

$$S_2 = \left\{2, 6\right\} \tag{12}$$

$$S_3 = \left\{3, 7\right\} . \tag{13}$$

Define also two families F_0 and F_1 such that:

$$F_0 = S_0 \cup S_2$$

and

$$F_1 = S_1 \cup S_3 .$$

The partition is such that the minimum squared Euclidian distance (MSED) between the points within a given family, denoted as δ_1^2, equals the MSED between the points of the QPSK signal constellation taken as reference, which is 2. Note that the MSED within any subset defined in (10)-(13) is $\delta_2^2 = 4$, and the MSED of 8PSK is $\delta_0^2 = 2 - \sqrt{2}$, such that we have $\delta_0 < \delta_1 < \delta_2$.

Let the second input bit $b2_n$ remain uncoded such that it will appear unmodified at the mapper and rename it as $c2_n$. The first input bit $b1_n$ instead enters a rate 1/2, four-state, systematic feedback convolutional encoder that outputs two bits: $c0_n$ and $c1_n = b1_n$. The operation of the convolutional encoder is best described with the help of a trellis diagram shown in Figure 2.

The state transitions have been labeled according to the rules stated by Ungerboeck as follows:

1. Transitions originating in the same current state are labeled with different signal point subsets belonging to the same family, be it F_0 or F_1.
2. Transitions reaching the same next state are labeled with different signal point subsets belonging to the same family, be it F_0 or F_1
3. All the signals are used equally often.

The value 0 of the input bit $b1_n$ selects the upper transition, while the value 1 selects the lower transition originating in the current state, and thus, one out of the four subsets S_0, S_1, S_2 and S_3 will be selected according to the bit $b1_n$ and the current state σ_n. The uncoded bit $b2_n$ then picks the point within the selected subset for transmission over the wireless channel. Using the rules of Ungerboeck mentioned above results in the logical diagram of the TCM encoder shown in Figure 3. It includes a rate 2/3, 4-state, convo-

lutional encoder and a mapper of the three output bits $c0_n$, $c1_n$, and $c2_n$ into the 8PSK signal constellation. For differential encoding, the output of the mapper, denoted by u_n, is transformed into the transmit signal s_n according to the Equation (8).

The performance of the transmission system can be improved by enlarging the number of states from 4 to 8 or to 16. In such a case, both input bits $b1_n$ and $b2_n$ are convolutionally encoded. However, it should be mentioned that the complexity grows high, while the additional returns from this complexity are diminishing.

We assume a narrow-band wireless channel, such that the channel gain between the transmit antenna and the receive antenna, denoted here by h, is frequency-independent but time-variable; moreover, we assume that this h is constant at least on two consecutive symbol intervals, and changes randomly otherwise. The decoder performs sequence decoding by using the Viterbi algorithm with soft decision. We need a suitable branch metric. For differential decoding, the receiver is based on the following measured quantities:

$$r_{n-1} = h \cdot s_{n-1} + z_{n-1} \tag{14}$$

$$r_n = h \cdot s_n + z_n \tag{15}$$

where z_{n-1} and z_n are noise components. Define the decision variable

Figure 2. Trellis diagram of a four-state TCM encoder for 2D 8PSK

Figure 3. Four-state rate 2/3 TCM encoder

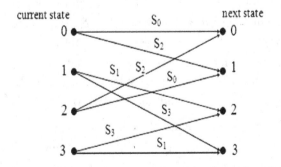

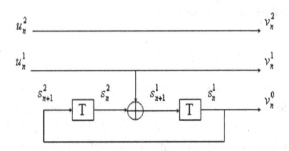

$$R = r_n \cdot r_{n-1}^*.$$

Substituting (14) and (15) in this expression, we obtain:

$$R = |h|^2 \cdot s_n \cdot s_{n-1}^* + \text{noise terms}$$
$$= |h|^2 \cdot u_n + \text{noise terms}.$$

The quantized version of R is used in the Viterbi algorithm.

SPACE-TIME BLOCK CODING

As explained in a previous chapter of this book, the wireless channel is strongly time- and frequency-variable. An adverse phenomenon encountered on this channel is the fading caused by the multipath propagation of radio waves. The fading can be viewed as a random, severe attenuation making challenging the task of the receiver to recover the transmitted signal. To combat this, receive antenna diversity, that is, using more than a single antenna at the receiving site, has been successfully used for many years. However, this method, while very effective, is difficult if not impossible to apply with small handheld transceivers. Motivated by this fact, Alamouti introduced an ingenious scheme for two transmit antennas (Alamouti 1998). It is by now very well known. We describe it in our own notation and using the baseband representation of signals.

Let us consider a communication system with two transmit antennas and a single receive antenna. It has to transmit a string of 2D (complex-valued) symbols taken from the signal constellation of a digital modulation like PSK or QAM: $s_0, s_1, s_2, s_3, \ldots, s_{2n}, s_{2n+1}, \ldots$. The first transmit antenna just transmits this string of symbols as such. The second transmit antenna sends the same information, but in a different order and form: when the first transmit antenna sends the symbol s_{2n}, the second transmit antenna sends the symbol $-s_{2n+1}^*$, and in the next symbol interval, while the first transmit antenna sends s_{2n+1}, the second antenna sends s_{2n}^*. This scheme can be conveniently represented by the transmit matrix

$$\mathrm{M}_n = \begin{pmatrix} s_{2n} & -s_{2n+1}^* \\ s_{2n+1} & s_{2n}^* \end{pmatrix}. \tag{16}$$

It is easy to check that the two columns (as well as the two rows) are orthogonal. This fact is essential for the separate decision made on s_{2n} and s_{2n+1}. Let us denote the (complex-valued) gains from the first and the second transmit antennas to the receiver by h_1 and h_2, respectively. The observations are the complex-valued output signals of a 2D demodulator, denoted by r_{2n} and r_{2n+1}. We then have

$$r_{2n} = h_1 \cdot s_{2n} - h_2 \cdot s_{2n+1}^* + z_{2n} \tag{17}$$

and

$$r_{2n+1} = h_1 \cdot s_{2n+1} + h_2 \cdot s_{2n}^* + z_{2n+1}. \tag{18}$$

The maximum likelihood detector uses the following two combined signals:

$$\tilde{s}_{2n} = h_1^* \cdot r_{2n} + h_2 \cdot r_{2n+1}^* \tag{19}$$

$$\tilde{s}_{2n+1} = h_1^* \cdot r_{2n+1} - h_2 \cdot r_{2n}^*. \tag{20}$$

Substituting (17) and (18) in (19) and (20), we get

$$\tilde{s}_{2n} = \left(|h_1|^2 + |h_2|^2 \right) s_{2n} + h_1^* \cdot z_{2n} + h_2 \cdot z_{2n+1}^* \tag{21}$$

$$\tilde{s}_{2n+1} = \left(|h_1|^2 + |h_2|^2 \right) s_{2n+1} + h_1^* \cdot z_{2n+1} - h_2 \cdot z_{2n}^* \tag{22}$$

The assumption often made is that the receiver can acquire channel state information (CSI), that is, the receiver can measure in real time the values of h_1 and h_2, considered as constant on the symbol intervals of s_{2n} and s_{2n+1}. Having CSI, the receiver will make a decision symbol by symbol based on the Equations (20) and (21).

Note that, for direct inter-vehicular communications, this assumption is not realistic. However, the Alamouti's scheme remains important since it allows for developments not requiring the knowledge of CSI.

UNITARY SPACE-TIME MODULATION

By definition, a $k \times k$ unitary matrix is a matrix **U** such that

$$\mathbf{U} \cdot \mathbf{U}^H = \mathbf{U}^H \cdot \mathbf{U} = \mathbf{I}_k. \qquad (23)$$

In (23), the index H denotes the Hermitian, that is, complex conjugate transpose of the matrix. A familiar instance of unitary matrix for $k = 2$ is the Alamouti's matrix. Unitary matrices have been proposed for space-time coding as applied to *multiple-input multiple-output* (MIMO) communication systems having no need of CSI at both the transmitter and the receiver in (Hochwald 2000a) and (Hochwald 2000b). Let us consider a communication system with k transmit antennas. With symbols taken from an MPSK signal constellation, we form a collection of P distinct $k \times k$ unitary signal matrices $\mathbf{U}_0, \mathbf{U}_1, \mathbf{U}_2, \ldots, \mathbf{U}_{P-1}$. At the discrete time n, the input bits select a unitary matrix $\mathbf{U}_{i_n}$, where the index $i_n \in Q$, where $Q = \{0, 1, 2, \ldots, P\text{-}1\}$. Actually, for transmission over the channel the differential matrix $\mathbf{D}_n$ is used such that

$$\mathbf{D}_n = \mathbf{D}_{n-1} \cdot \mathbf{U}_{i_n}.$$

The transmission starts with the identity matrix $\mathbf{D}_0 = \mathbf{I}_k$. For differential demodulation, we make the usual assumption that the fading coefficients are constant across every two consecutive transmission blocks. Let the receiver be equipped with r receive antennas; then, the $r \times k$ receive matrix at discrete time n is given by

$$\mathbf{R}_n = \mathbf{H} \cdot \mathbf{D}_n + \mathbf{Z}_n$$

where **H** is an $r \times k$ channel matrix and $\mathbf{Z}_n$ is an $r \times k$ noise matrix whose entries are independent complex noise samples with zero mean and variance σ_z^2. It follows that

$$
\begin{aligned}
\mathbf{R}_n &= \mathbf{H} \cdot \mathbf{D}_{n-1} \cdot \mathbf{U}_{i_n} + \mathbf{Z}_n \\
&= \left(\mathbf{R}_{n-1} - \mathbf{Z}_{n-1} \right) \mathbf{U}_{i_n} + \mathbf{Z}_n \\
&= \mathbf{R}_{n-1} \cdot \mathbf{U}_{i_n} + \mathbf{Z}_n - \mathbf{Z}_{n-1} \cdot \mathbf{U}_{i_n}.
\end{aligned}
$$

Then

$$\mathbf{Z}_n' = \mathbf{Z}_n - \mathbf{Z}_{n-1} \cdot \mathbf{U}_{i_n}$$

is an $r \times k$ noise matrix whose entries are independent complex noise samples with variance $2\sigma_z^2$.

The maximum-likelihood differential demodulation rule is

$$\hat{i}_n = \arg \max_{q \in Q} \left\| \mathbf{R}_{n-1} + \mathbf{R}_n \cdot \mathbf{U}_q^H \right\|.$$

The symbol $\|\cdot\|$ denotes the Frobenius norm of a matrix, that is, the sum of the norms of all the entries of the matrix.

The doubling of the noise variance entails for the differential demodulation a loss of 3 dB compared to the coherent one that is performed if CSI is available to the receiver.

A similar idea can be found in (Hughes 2000). Let N be an integer larger than the number of transmit antennas k and form a group of $N \times N$ unitary matrices:

$$G^H \cdot G = G \cdot G^H = I_N.$$

The main assumption made here is that an $k \times N$ matrix D exists such that for any unitary matrix G in the group DG generates an $k \times N$ matrix whose entries belong to the signal constellation. The set of all DG matrices forms a space-time group code.

Using the concept of concatenated codes, unitary space-time codes can be easily combined with TCM or Turbo-codes, as suggested in the open literature.

DIFFERENTIAL SPACE-TIME BLOCK CODING

Differential space-time block coding has been introduced in (Tarokh 2000) as a generalization of the DMPSK for more than a single transmit antenna. Let us consider the 2×2 transmit matrix defined by Equation (16). Its elements are transmitted over the channel from the two transmit antennas in two consecutive symbol intervals. The symbols are taken from an MPSK signal constellation. However, the $2m$ input bits select another matrix, called *encoding matrix*, namely:

$$ME_n = \begin{pmatrix} u_{2n} & -u_{2n+1}^* \\ u_{2n+1} & u_{2n}^* \end{pmatrix}.$$

Then, the matrix encoding equation is:

$$M_n = ME_n^T \cdot M_{n-1}.$$

The rationale behind this operation is as follows. Remember that the transmit matrix is orthogonal and thus its rows are orthogonal vectors. They can form a basis. Therefore, any two-dimensional vector $\left(s_{2n}, -s_{2n+1}^*\right)$ can be uniquely represented in the orthogonal basis given by $\left(s_{2n-2}, -s_{2n-1}^*\right)$ and $\left(s_{2n-1}, s_{2n-2}^*\right)$. So we can write:

$$\left(s_{2n}, -s_{2n+1}^*\right) = u_{2n}\left(s_{2n-2}, -s_{2n-1}^*\right) + u_{2n+1}\left(s_{2n-1}, s_{2n-2}^*\right)$$

This can be rewritten on components:

$$s_{2n} = u_{2n} \cdot s_{2n-2} + u_{2n+1} \cdot s_{2n-1} \quad (24)$$

$$s_{2n+1} = u_{2n}^* \cdot s_{2n-1} - u_{2n+1}^* \cdot s_{2n-2}. \quad (25)$$

From (24) and (25), we have:

$$u_{2n} = s_{2n-2}^* \cdot s_{2n} + s_{2n-1} \cdot s_{2n+1}^*$$

$$u_{2n+1} = s_{2n-1}^* \cdot s_{2n} - s_{2n-2} \cdot s_{2n+1}^*$$

Let us consider a communication system with two transmit antennas and a single receive antenna. In order to equally distribute the transmitter energy between the two antennas, the symbols s_{2n} and s_{2n+1} are taken from a circular constellation with radius $1/\sqrt{2}$. All the MPSK signal constellations, BPSK, QPSK and 8PSK, include the point $(1/\sqrt{2}, 0)$. The transmission can start by sending $s_0 = s_1 = 1/\sqrt{2}$. The first $2m$ input bits then select $\left(u_2, u_3\right)$ and the symbols actually transmitted over the channel, s_2 and s_3, result according to Equations (24) and (25). This procedure goes on until the end of the session. Assuming that the fading coefficients are constant across four consecutive symbol intervals, the receiver is based on the following measured quantities:

$$r_{2n-2} = h_1 \cdot s_{2n-2} - h_2 \cdot s_{2n-1}^* + z_{2n-2} \quad (26)$$

$$r_{2n-1} = h_1 \cdot s_{2n-1} + h_2 \cdot s_{2n-2}^* + z_{2n-1} \quad (27)$$

$$r_{2n} = h_1 \cdot s_{2n} - h_2 \cdot s_{2n+1}^* + z_{2n} \quad (28)$$

$$r_{2n+1} = h_1 \cdot s_{2n+1} + h_2 \cdot s_{2n}^* + z_{2n+1} \quad (29)$$

where $z_{2n-2}, z_{2n-1}, z_{2n}$, and z_{2n+1} are noise components. Define the following decision quantities:

$$R_1 = r_{2n-2}^* \cdot r_{2n} + r_{2n-1} \cdot r_{2n+1}^*$$

$$R_2 = r_{2n-1}^* \cdot r_{2n} - r_{2n-2} \cdot r_{2n+1}^*.$$

Introducing (26)–(29) in these expressions, we obtain:

$$R_1 = \left(|h_1|^2 + |h_2|^2\right) u_{2n} + \text{noise terms} \tag{30}$$

$$R_2 = \left(|h_1|^2 + |h_2|^2\right) u_{2n+1} + \text{noise terms}. \tag{31}$$

The receiver computes the vector $\left(u_{2n}, u_{2n+1}\right)$ that is closest to $\left(R_1, R_2\right)$ and makes the decision that u_{2n} and u_{2n+1} are the message symbols selected at the transmit site for transmission over the channel. By inverse mapping, the message bits result.

The same penalty of around 3 dB is incurred by this differential space-time block coding as in the case of DMPSK with single transmit antenna.

From Equations (30)-(31), the benefit of using two transmit antennas is obvious: while the random variables h_1 and h_2 can vanish sometimes, if they are independent, the probability that both of them are simultaneously small is very low and thus almost all the time nonzero quantities on which to base its decisions are available to the receiver.

DIFFERENTIAL SUPER-ORTHOGONAL SPACE-TIME TRELLIS CODING

Space-time block codes can provide diversity advantage, but no coding gain. They can be concatenated with outer codes that are known to contribute a coding gain. For instance, unitary space-time modulation combined with TCM results in trellis-coded unitary space-time modulation. In this section, we follow the approach in (Zhu 2006) but further developed in (Sterian 2011). Let us consider a point-to-point noncoherent wireless communication link with two transmit antennas

and one receive antenna. The signal constellation used for transmission out of each antenna is MPSK, that is, BPSK, QPSK or 8PSK. For the average power of the received signal at the receive antenna to be 1, the average energy of the symbols transmitted from each antenna is normalized to be 1/2. Denote the 2D symbol interval by T. A 4D symbol is transmitted in two consecutive time intervals of duration T and thus its duration equals $2T$. We number the 4D symbol intervals by n, $n = 0, 1, 2,\ldots$, and denote the first and the second half of the generic 4D symbol interval by $2n$ and $2n + 1$, respectively.

The transmission unit is a *frame*, that is, a block of N 4D consecutive symbols that are decoded together by maximum likelihood sequence estimation using Viterbi algorithm. The nth 4D symbol of the frame comprises two consecutive 2D symbols denoted as s_{2n} and s_{2n+1}; they are transmitted by the first antenna in two successive 2D symbol intervals $2n$ and $2n + 1$. The second antenna is fully redundant, that is, it transmits the same information as the first one, but in a different order and form. Let us introduce the binary variable a_n that can assume the values $+1$ and -1 as shown later. Then, the transmission matrix is:

$$M_n = \begin{pmatrix} s_{2n} & -a_n \cdot s_{2n+1}^* \\ s_{2n+1} & a_n \cdot s_{2n}^* \end{pmatrix}.$$

For a particular value of a_n, this is simply an Alamouti's matrix, or an orthogonal design. All the matrices for a_n fixed and entries from a given MPSK signal constellation form a family, F_0 for $a_n = +1$ and F_1 for $a_n = -1$. Similar to what we have done in the previous section, let us consider the two orthogonal vectors $\left(s_{2n-2}, -a_{n-1} \cdot s_{2n-1}^*\right)$ and $\left(s_{2n-1}, a_{n-1} \cdot s_{2n-2}^*\right)$. Any vector $\left(s_{2n}, -a_n \cdot s_{2n+1}^*\right)$ can be uniquely represented in the orthogonal basis given by these vectors. Define the encoding matrix as

$$ME_n = \begin{pmatrix} u_{2n} & -a_{n-1} \cdot a_n \cdot u_{2n+1}^* \\ u_{2n+1} & a_{n-1} \cdot a_n \cdot u_{2n}^* \end{pmatrix}.$$

The differential encoding equation can be written as

$$M_n = ME_n^T \cdot M_{n-1}.$$

This is equivalent to:

$$s_{2n} = u_{2n} \cdot s_{2n-2} + u_{2n+1} \cdot s_{2n-1}$$

$$s_{2n+1} = a_{n-1} \cdot a_n \left(u_{2n}^* \cdot s_{2n-1} - u_{2n+1}^* \cdot s_{2n-2} \right).$$

Solving for u_{2n} and u_{2n+1}, we get:

$$u_{2n} = s_{2n-2}^* \cdot s_{2n} + a_{n-1} \cdot a_n \cdot s_{2n-1} \cdot s_{2n+1}^*$$

and

$$u_{2n+1} = s_{2n-1}^* \cdot s_{2n} - a_{n-1} \cdot a_n \cdot s_{2n-2} \cdot s_{2n+1}^*.$$

The general structure of the transmission system is depicted in Figure 4.

The signal constellation has $M = 2^m$ points. At each interval of $2T$ seconds, $2m$ bits are gathered at the input of the transmitter. Half of these bits enter a rate-$m/(m+1)$ systematic feedback convolutional encoder whose output is composed of the m input bits and a single new bit denoted by $c0_n$. All the encoding matrices with $a_{n-1} \cdot a_n = 1$ form the family F_0, while the family F_1 comprises all encoding matrices with $a_{n-1} \cdot a_n = -1$. The selected matrix belongs to F_0 if $c0_n = 0$ and to F_1 if $c0_n = 1$. Together, the $m+1$ output bits of the convolutional encoder select a subset of 2^m encoding matrices. Then, the second half of m input bits select one of these encoding matrices to be differentially encoded. To better explain the operation of the transmitter, let us focus on the case of QPSK. As shown in Figure 1(a), it has four 2D signal points, labeled as 0, 1, 2, and 3. By grouping these 2D points into 4D points, we obtain 16 points from (0, 0) to (3, 3). We form with them the following 4D subsets:

$$S_0 = \left\{ (0,0),(1,1),(2,2),(3,3) \right\}$$

$$S_1 = \left\{ (0,1),(1,2),(2,3),(3,0) \right\}$$

$$S_2 = \left\{ (0,2),(1,3),(2,0),(3,1) \right\}$$

$$S_3 = \left\{ (0,3),(1,0),(2,1),(3,2) \right\}.$$

The grouping was done in such a way as to maximize the intra-subset Hamming distance to $d_H = 2$. To select one out of the four subsets S_i, $i = 0, \dots, 3$, two bits are required, say, $c1_n$

Figure 4. Transceiver structure of super-orthogonal space-time trellis encoded DMPSK for fading channels

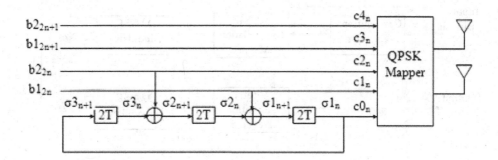

and $c2_n$, such that the index i can be written as $i = 2c2_n + c1_n$.

In two consecutive signaling intervals $2n$ and $2n + 1$, four bits are gathered at the input of the transmitter, denoted by $b1_{2n}, b2_{2n}, b1_{2n+1}, b2_{2n+1}$. The first two bits, $b1_{2n}$ and $b2_{2n}$, enter a rate-2/3 systematic feedback convolutional encoder, while the next two bits, $b1_{2n+1}$ and $b2_{2n+1}$, remain uncoded. The three output bits of the rate-2/3 convolutional encoder are $c0_n$, $c1_n$, and $c2_n$ such that $c1_n = b1_{2n}$ and $c2_n = b2_{2n}$. The index of a matrix subset SM_p is given by

$$p = 4c2_n + 2c1_n + c0_n.$$

To select a point from a 2D QPSK constellation, constituent of a 4D constellation, two bits are required, denoted by $w1_\ell, w2_\ell$, where $\ell \in \{2n, 2n+1\}$. The two convolutionally encoded bits $c1_n$ and $c2_n$ select a 4D subset that is the set of all 4D signal points for which the following two equations hold true:

$$w1_{2n+1} = c1_n \oplus w1_{2n}$$

$$w2_{2n+1} = c2_n \oplus w2_{2n} \oplus \left(c1_n \cdot w1_{2n}\right).$$

The two uncoded input bits, $b1_{2n+1}$ and $b2_{2n+1}$, determine the 4D signal point within the already selected 4D subset such that $w1_{2n} = b1_{2n+1}$ and $w2_{2n} = b2_{2n+1}$.

In the context of space-time trellis coding, the TCM rules stated by Ungerboeck sound as follows:

1. The state transitions originating in even-numbered states are assigned transmission matrices belonging to the family F_0 and the state transitions originating in odd-numbered states are assigned transmission matrices belonging to the family F_1.

2. The state transitions reaching the same next state are assigned transmission matrices from the same family, be it F_0 or F_1.

Using these rules, we can derive the logic diagram shown in Figure 5.

This logic diagram is also valid for coherent demodulation. To reflect the differential encoding, two-tuples $\left(u_{2n}, u_{2n+1}\right)$ are assigned to state transitions of a topological trellis.

For differential decoding, the receiver is based on the following measured quantities:

$$r_{2n-2} = h_1 \cdot s_{2n-2} - h_2 \cdot a_{n-1} \cdot s_{2n-1}^* + z_{2n-2} \quad (32)$$

Figure 5. Super-orthogonal space-time trellis encoder for QPSK signal constellation

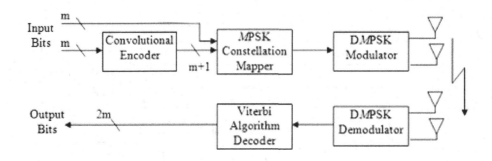

$$r_{2n-1} = h_1 \cdot s_{2n-1} + h_2 \cdot a_{n-1} \cdot s_{2n-2}^* + z_{2n-1}$$

$$(33)$$

$$r_{2n} = h_1 \cdot s_{2n} - h_2 \cdot a_n \cdot s_{2n+1}^* + z_{2n} \qquad (34)$$

$$r_{2n+1} = h_1 \cdot s_{2n+1} + h_2 \cdot a_n \cdot s_{2n}^* + z_{2n+1} \qquad (35)$$

where z_{2n-2}, z_{2n-1}, z_{2n}, and z_{2n+1} are noise components. Define the following decision quantities:

$$R_1 = r_{2n-2}^* \cdot r_{2n} + a_{n-1} \cdot a_n \cdot r_{2n-1} \cdot r_{2n+1}^*$$

$$R_2 = r_{2n-1}^* \cdot r_{2n} - a_{n-1} \cdot a_n \cdot r_{2n-2} \cdot r_{2n+1}^*.$$

Introducing (32)–(35) in these expressions, we get:

$$R_1 = \left(|h_1|^2 + |h_2|^2 \right) u_{2n} + \text{noise terms}$$

$$R_2 = \left(|h_1|^2 + |h_2|^2 \right) u_{2n+1} + \text{noise terms}.$$

Assuming that a_{n-1} is known, the receiver computes the vector $\left(u_{2n}, u_{2n+1} \right)$ that is closest to $\left(R_1, R_2 \right)$ for both $a_n = +1$ and $a_n = -1$ in order to make a hard decision. For soft decision, the quantized version of $\left(R_1, R_2 \right)$ is used in the Viterbi algorithm.

A second decoding strategy is possible. For the Viterbi algorithm, we can write the branch metric as

$$BM_n = \left| r_{2n} - h_1 \cdot s_{2n} + h_2 \cdot s_{2n+1}^* \right|^2 + \left| r_{2n+1} - h_1 \cdot s_{2n+1} - h_2 \cdot s_{2n}^* \right|^2$$

Developing this expression, we obtain:

$$BM_n = \left| r_{2n} \right|^2 + \left| r_{2n+1} \right|^2 + \left(|h_1|^2 + |h_2|^2 \right)\left(|s_{2n}|^2 + |s_{2n+1}|^2 \right)$$
$$+ 2\,\text{Re}\left\{ \left(-h_1^* \cdot s_{2n}^* + h_2^* \cdot a_n \cdot s_{2n+1} \right) r_{2n} - \left(h_1^* \cdot s_{2n+1}^* + h_2^* \cdot a_n \cdot s_{2n} \right) r_{2n+1} \right\}.$$

Note that the first terms are positive and common to all state transitions of a trellis section and only the last term depends on the signal being actually transmitted. We are thus motivated to define a reduced metric

$$RM_n = +2\,\text{Re}\left\{ \left(-h_1^* \cdot s_{2n}^* + h_2^* \cdot a_n \cdot s_{2n+1} \right) r_{2n} - \left(h_1^* \cdot s_{2n+1}^* + h_2^* \cdot a_n \cdot s_{2n} \right) r_{2n+1} \right\}$$

The branch metric BM_n is minimized by the most negative value of the reduced metric RM_n. Using the differential encoding and neglecting the noise term, we get:

$$RM_n = -2\,\text{Re}\left\{ \left(r_{2n-2} \cdot r_{2n}^* + a_{n-1} \cdot a_n \cdot r_{2n-1}^* \cdot r_{2n+1} \right) u_n + \right.$$
$$\left. + \left(r_{2n-1} \cdot r_{2n}^* - a_{n-1} \cdot a_n \cdot r_{2n-2}^* \cdot r_{2n+1} \right) u_{2n+1} \right\}.$$

For each state transition, the receiver knows all the quantities from this expression. The survivor is selected as that transition entering a given next state that makes RM_n to be the most negative one. It is evident that the knowledge of the fading coefficients h_1 and h_2 is not required. In (Sterian 2011) it is claimed that the second decoding algorithm can provide the same performance compared with the first one, while reducing the decoding complexity by around 30%.

OTHER TRANSMISSION TECHNOLOGIES

Infrared (IR) light is familiar to us as it is used for the remote control of home appliances like the TV set or the DVD player. It is highly directional and allows for high data rate with a range less than 100 m. Consequently, it can be used for lane-specific communication.

Millimeter-wave (MMWAVE) technology operates in the frequency band 60–64 GHz and has various advantages over IR (Dam 2010). It can be useful for infotainment purpose.

Different other wireless communication technologies like *Bluetooth* and *Zigbee* are also mentioned in the literature and can be useful for particular ITS applications.

NONCOHERENT SPACE-FREQUENCY CODED MIMO-OFDM

The modulation and coding techniques considered to this point can be applied to narrowband wireless transmission systems. We say that a transmission system is narrowband if the bandwidth of the available channel is much smaller than the carrier frequency. The narrowness of the bandwidth allows us to assume that the transfer function of the transmission system is frequency-independent. The maximum possible data rate depends practically linearly on the channel bandwidth. Therefore, for higher and higher data rates, larger and larger bandwidths are needed. But broadband channels require equalization, a signal processing operation which is generally difficult to perform and sometimes even impossible. Fortunately, less processing intensive channel equalization methods in the frequency domain are known for single carrier transmission systems. Nevertheless, by far more popular is another approach, namely, the multi-carrier communication (Fazel 2003). For instance, OFDM is stipulated in the important WiMAX standard. Simply put, the large available bandwidth is divided into N much smaller subbands and the high data rate input stream is demultiplexed into N much lower data rate strings, each one of which being transmitted over a narrowband subchannel. Equalization is still required on each subband, but it is a very simple one – actually, it is an *automatic gain control* (AGC). On wireless channels, this multi-carrier technique is known as *orthogonal frequency division multiplexing* (OFDM). It is a synchronous modulation technique and is rather easily implemented using *inverse discrete Fourier transform* (IDFT) at the transmit side and the *discrete Fourier transform* (DFT) at the receive side. The problem with it is that it requires channel estimation.

There are noteworthy attempts to circumvent this problem. An instructive paper in this respect is (Borgmann 2005). We make an attempt to re-sume it here as follows. We consider only frequency-selective fading environments with purely Rayleigh-fading channels. There are M_T transmit antennas and M_R receive antennas. The channel consists of L matrix-valued taps H_ℓ of dimension $M_R \times M_T$, $\ell = 0, 1, \cdots, L - 1$. The matrix-valued transfer function of the channel is given by

$$H\left(e^{j2\pi\theta}\right) = \sum_{\ell=0}^{L-1} H_\ell e^{-j2\pi\ell\theta}, \ 0 \le \theta < 1.$$

Each one of the M_T transmit antennas sends an OFDM frame. Let N denote the number of subcarriers. As usual for OFDM systems, the transmitter applies an N-point inverse fast Fourier transform (IFFT) to N consecutive data symbols and prepends a cyclic prefix of length $L_{CP} \ge L$ to the parallel-to-serial converted OFDM symbol. The receiver discards the cyclic prefix and applies an N-point FFT to each of the M_R received signals. Denote by $c_{k,m}$ the data symbol transmitted from the mth antenna on the kth subcarrier. With the transmitted data symbols form the vectors $c_k = \left[c_{k,0} \ c_{k,1} \cdots c_{k,M_T-1}\right]^T$ $\left(k = 0, 1, \cdots, N - 1\right)$. The received signal vectors are given by $r_k = \sqrt{E_s} H\left(e^{j2\pi k/N}\right) c_k + z_k, \ k = 0, 1, \cdots, N - 1$ where E_s is an energy scaling factor and z_k is complex-valued circularly symmetric white Gaussian zero-mean noise. Define $y_k = \sqrt{E_s} H\left(e^{j2\pi k/N}\right) c_k$ and $Y = \left[y_0 \ y_1 \cdots y_{N-1}\right]^T$. Then the transmission of an entire OFDM symbol is written as $R = Y + Z$. Here $R = \left[r_0 \ r_1 \cdots r_{N-1}\right]^T$ is the $N \times M_R$ matrix of received signals, $Z = \left[z_0 \ z_1 \cdots z_{N-1}\right]^T$ is the $N \times M_R$ additive noise matrix and the transmitted signal is represented by the $N \times M_T$ matrix $C = \left[c_0 \ c_1 \cdots c_{N-1}\right]^T$. Skipping some developments, the following maximum likelihood (ML) rule is introduced in (Borgmann 2005):

$$\hat{C}_{ML} = \arg \min_{C_i \in \mathcal{C}} \left(tr\left(R^H \Sigma_i^{-1} R \right) + M_R \ln \det \Sigma_i \right)$$

Under some assumptions, this formula is further simplified and pragmatic design criteria are introduced. We jump on the noncoherent space-frequency codes construction given in (Borgmann 2005). Let have $M_T = 2$ transmit antennas and $L = 2$ taps. The codeword matrices $C_i \left(i = 0, 1, \cdots, K-1 \right)$ are chosen as $C_i = \Phi^i \left[f_p \; f_{p'} \right], i = 0, 1, \cdots, K-1$ where f_p denotes the pth column of the $N \times N$ FFT matrix F and $\Phi = \mathrm{diag}_{k=0}^{N-1} \left\{ e^{j\frac{2\pi}{K} u_k} \right\}$, where $0 \leq u_k \leq K-1$ for $k = 0, 1, \ldots, N-1$. Various examples are given in tabular form in (Borgmann 2005). As clearly stated in the CONCLUSION section of this reference, the decoding complexity of the given construction is exponential in the code rate and thus designing noncoherent space-frequency codes with reduced complexity algorithms remains a challenge for the future research.

FUTURE RESEARCH DIRECTIONS

Wireless communications are based on the existence of electromagnetic waves, including light. It is highly improbable that a new transmission medium will be discovered. As exotic alternatives, we are left for the time being with acoustic waves and telepathy!

There is also little hope of inventing new digital modulations. We thus expect that the main research effort will be focused on the discovery of novel signal processing algorithms to be applied in the receiver design. Designing broadband V2V direct communication systems is a big challenge. An idea to be better explored would be differential OFDM, as an extension of differential PSK from single-carrier to multi-carrier transmission systems. Again, this can be done for multiple transmission antennas. Of similar complexity could be the use of *code division multiple access* (CDMA) in a mobile ad hoc network (MANET). While a firm effort directed towards improving known methods and techniques is easy to anticipate, let us not forget that nowhere is *serendipity* more at home than in scientific research. Indeed, to make discoveries, one has to work hard on known ground, but with an open mind as to see what is there to be seen.

CONCLUSION

In this chapter, we made an inventory of differential and non-coherent modulation and coding techniques for possible use in direct vehicle-to-vehicle communications. We bluntly assumed that the wireless channel between two cars on the move is generally too rapidly variable to baffle any attempt to measure it in real time. This is not to say that such measurement is not possible in rather particular cases, for instance, if a car closely follows the other car traveling at the same speed. What is frustrating is the penalty in the signal-to-noise ratio incurred by the differential and non-coherent techniques compared to their coherent versions. It is probable that in order to improve performance, novel signal-processing techniques will be developed in the future. Scientific research is not a deterministic process, the outcome is negative sometimes but can be unexpectedly lucky as well. Indeed, nowhere is the concept of *serendipity* more at home than in the scientific research. Discoveries can be wanted, but not anticipated. All we can say is that direct vehicle-to-vehicle communication is a field of intense research today and this justifies us to expect great results.

REFERENCES

Alamouti, S. M. (1999). A simple transmit diversity technique for wireless communications. *IEEE Journal on Selected Areas in Communications, 16*(8), 1451–1458. doi:10.1109/49.730453

Atkin, G. E., & Corrales, H. P. (1989). An efficient modulation/coding scheme for MFSK systems on bandwidth constrained channels. *IEEE Journal on Selected Areas in Communications, 7*(9), 1396–1401. doi:10.1109/49.44578

Borgmann, M., & Bölcsei, H. (2005). Noncoherent space-frequency coded MIMO-OFDM. *IEEE Journal on Selected Areas in Communications, 23*(9), 1799–1810. doi:10.1109/JSAC.2005.853800

Dar, K., Bakhouya, M., Gaber, J., & Wack, M. (2010). Wireless communication technologies for ITS applications. *IEEE Communications Magazine, 48*(5), 156–162. doi:10.1109/MCOM.2010.5458377

Edbauer, F. (1989). Performance of interleaved trellis-coded differential 8-PSK modulation over fading channels. *IEEE Journal on Selected Areas in Communications, 7*(9), 1340–1346. doi:10.1109/49.44579

Fazel, K., & Kaiser, S. (2003). *Multi-carrier and spread spectrum systems*. Chichester, UK: Wiley. doi:10.1002/0470871385

Ghareeb, I. (2005). Noncoherent MT-MFSK signals with diversity reception in arbitrary correlated and unbalanced Nakagami-*m* fading channels. *IEEE Journal on Selected Areas in Communications, 23*(9), 1839–1850. doi:10.1109/JSAC.2005.853877

Hochwald, B. M., & Marzetta, T. L. (2000a). Unitary space-time modulation for multiple antenna communications in Rayleigh flat fading. *IEEE Transactions on Information Theory, 46*(2), 543–564. doi:10.1109/18.825818

Hochwald, B. M., & Sweldens, W. (2000b). Differential unitary space-time modulation. *IEEE Transactions on Communications, 48*(12), 2041–2052. doi:10.1109/26.891215

Hughes, B. L. (2000). Differential space-time modulation. *IEEE Transactions on Information Theory, 46*(7), 2567–2578. doi:10.1109/18.887864

Luo, C., Médard, M., & Zheng, L. (2005). On approaching wideband capacity using multitone FSK. *IEEE Journal on Selected Areas in Communications, 23*(9), 1830–1838. doi:10.1109/JSAC.2005.853803

Sichitiu, L. M., & Kihl, M. (2008). Inter-vehicle communication systems: A survey. *IEEE Communications Surveys, 10*(2), 88–105. doi:10.1109/COMST.2008.4564481

Sterian, C. E. D., Ma, Y., Pätzold, M., Bănică, I., & He, H. (2011). New super-orthogonal space-time trellis codes using differential M-PSK for noncoherent mobile communication systems with two transmit antennas. *Annales des Télécommunications, 66*(3/4), 257–273. doi:10.1007/s12243-010-0191-1

Tarokh, V., & Jafarkhani, H. (2000). A differential detection scheme for transmit diversity. *IEEE Journal on Selected Areas in Communications, 18*(7), 1169–1174. doi:10.1109/49.857917

Zhu, Y., & Jafarkhani, H. (2006). Differential super-orthogonal space-time trellis codes. *IEEE Transactions on Wireless Communications, 5*(12), 3634–3643. doi:10.1109/TWC.2006.256986

ADDITIONAL READING

Alexiou, A., & Falconer, D. (2006). Challenges and trends in the design of a new air interface. *IEEE Vehicular Technology Magazine*, *1*(2), 16–23. doi:10.1109/MVT.2006.283571

Bahai, A. R. H., Saltzberg, I. B. R., & Ergen, I. M. (2004). *Multi-carrier digital communications theory and applications of OFDM*. New York, NY: Springer.

Biglieri, E. (2005). *Coding for wireless channels*. New York, NY: Springer.

Colavolpe, G., Barbieri, A., & Caire, G. (2005). Algorithms for iterative decoding in the presence of strong phase noise. *IEEE Journal on Selected Areas in Communications*, *23*(9), 1748–1757. doi:10.1109/JSAC.2005.853813

Duman, M. D., & Ghrayeb, A. (2007). *Coding for MIMO communication systems*. Chichester, England: Wiley. doi:10.1002/9780470724347

Fettweis, G., Zimmermann, E., Jungnickel, V., & Jorswieck, E. A. (2006). Challenges in future short range wireless systems. *IEEE Vehicular Technology Magazine*, *1*(2), 24–31. doi:10.1109/MVT.2006.283582

Gallagher, B., & Akatsuka, H. (2006). Wireless communications for vehicle safety: Radio link performance and wireless connectivity methods. *IEEE Vehicular Technology Magazine*, *1*(4), 4–16. doi:10.1109/MVT.2006.343641

Goldsmith, A. (2005). *Wireless communications*. Cambridge, UK: Cambridge University Press.

Haykin, S. (2001). *Communications systems*. New York, NY: Wiley.

Jafarkhani, H. (2005). *Space-time coding: theory and practice*. Cambridge, UK: Cambridge University Press. doi:10.1017/CBO9780511536779

Jiang, D., Taliwal, V., Meier, A., Holfelder, W., & Herrtwich, R. (2006). Design of 5.9 GHz DSRC-based vehicular safety communication. *IEEE Wireless Communications*, *13*(5), 36–43. doi:10.1109/WC-M.2006.250356

Krishnamoorthy, A., & Anastasopoulos, A. (2005). Code and receiver design for the noncoherent fast-fading channel. *IEEE Journal on Selected Areas in Communications*, *23*(9), 1769–1778. doi:10.1109/JSAC.2005.853802

Lee, K. C., Lee, U., & Gerla, M. (2010). Geo-opportunistic routing for vehicular networks. *IEEE Communications Magazine*, *48*(4), 164–170. doi:10.1109/MCOM.2010.5458378

Li, Y., McLaughlin, S., Cruickshank, D. G. M., & Wei, X. (2006). Towards multi-mode terminals. *IEEE Vehicular Technology Magazine*, *1*(4), 17–24. doi:10.1109/MVT.2006.343628

Oestges, C., & Clercckx, C. (2007). *MIMO wireless communications*. Academic Press.

Orozco-Lugo, A. G., Galván-Tejada, G. M., Lara, M., & Kontorovitch, V. (2007). Noncoherent channel equalization for DDPSK. *IEEE Transactions on Wireless Communications*, *6*(1), 269–281. doi:10.1109/TWC.2007.05166

Palazzi, C. E., Roccetti, M., & Ferretti, S. (2010). An intervehicular communication architecture for safety and entertainment. *IEEE Transactions on Intelligent Transportation Systems*, *11*(1), 90–99. doi:10.1109/TITS.2009.2029078

Proakis, J. G. (2001). *Digital communications*. New York, NY: McGraw-Hill.

Riediger, M. L. B., & Ho, P. K. M. (2005). An eigen-assisted noncoherent receiver for Alamouti-type space-time modulation. *IEEE Journal on Selected Areas in Communications*, *23*(9), 1811–1820. doi:10.1109/JSAC.2005.853811

Song, L.-Y., & Burr, A. G. (2007). Differential quasi-orthogonal space-time block codes. *IEEE Transactions on Wireless Communications, 6*(1), 64–68. doi:10.1109/TWC.2007.05188

Stüber, G. L. (2001). *Principles of mobile communication* (2nd ed.). Boston, USA: Kluwer Academic Publishers.

Stübing, H., Bechler, M., Heussner, D., May, T., Radusch, I., Rechner, H., & Vogel, P. (2010). sim^TD: A car-to-X system architecture for field operational tests. *IEEE Communications Magazine, 48*(4), 148–154. doi:10.1109/MCOM.2010.5458376

Tao, M. (2006). High rate trellis coded differential unitary space-time modulation via super unitarity. *IEEE Transactions on Wireless Communications, 5*(12), 3350–3354. doi:10.1109/TWC.2006.256954

Tse, D., & Viswanath, P. (2005). *Fundamentals of wireless communication*. Cambridge, UK: Cambridge University Press.

Valenti, M. C., & Cheng, S. (2005). Iterative demodulation and decoding of Turbo-coded M-ary noncoherent orthogonal modulation. *IEEE Journal on Selected Areas in Communications, 23*(9), 1739–1747. doi:10.1109/JSAC.2005.853794

Vucetic, B., & Yuan, J. (2004). *Space-time coding*. Chichester, UK: Wiley.

Wang, D., & Xia, X.-G. (2005). Super-orthogonal differential space-time trellis coding and decoding. *IEEE Journal on Selected Areas in Communications, 23*(9), 1788–1798. doi:10.1109/JSAC.2005.853810

Wang, J., Wang, X., & Madhian, M. (2005). Design of minimum error-rate Cayley differential unitary space-time codes. *IEEE Journal on Selected Areas in Communications, 23*(9), 1779–1787. doi:10.1109/JSAC.2005.853799

Yuen, C., Guan, Y. L., & Tjhung, T. T. (2006). Single-symbol-decodable differential space-time modulation based on QO-STBC. *IEEE Transactions on Wireless Communications, 5*(12), 3329–3334. doi:10.1109/TWC.2006.256950

KEY TERMS AND DEFINITIONS

Asynchronous: An operation is said to be asynchronous if it is performed without the use of fixed time intervals. An information source emits digital symbols asynchronously without the help of a clock signal. In still another words, the transition from a symbol to the next one occurs not necessarily at regular time points.

Coherent Communication: In a coherent transmission, the waves maintain a fixed and predictable phase relationship with each other over a period of time. A modulated signal is coherent if the carrier frequency period and the symbol duration are in a ratio of small integers. Both the carrier frequency and the symbol timing must be recovered in the receiver for coherent demodulation.

Coded Modulation: Until Ungerboeck, modulation and forward error-correction coding were performed separately and were designed by different people with little concern for the other operation. Coded modulation organically integrates modulation and channel coding into a single operation, under common designing criteria. It is divided in block-coded modulation and trellis-coded modulation. A trellis-coded modulator includes a convolutional encoder and a mapper into a signal constellation whose number of points is double compared with the uncoded system taken as reference. The term "trellis" comes from the trellis diagram, which is a directed graph illustrating the state transitions of the convolutional encoder.

Differential Encoding: Instead of transmitting the string of absolute values of the information symbols $a_1, a_2, \ldots, a_n, \ldots$, one transmits over the channel a string of differential symbols $d_1, d_2, \ldots, d_n, \ldots$, such that, at discrete time n, we have $d_n = a_n + d_{n-1}$. The initial value d_0, known to the receiver and thus actually not sent, is conveniently chosen in particular cases.

Multiple-Input Multiple-Output (MIMO): In the theory of systems, this is a system with many inputs and many outputs. In the context of communication theory, this is just another name for antenna diversity at both the transmitter and the receiver. In still another words, it is to be understood as space-time coding.

Noncoherent Communication: The receiver of a noncoherent communication system cannot acquire CSI and thus it cannot perform maximum likelihood decoding. Generally, the transmitter is the same as for a coherent communication system. Since the receiver doesn't know the channel, the decision rule of Bayes is not applicable and so it must be replaced by another, ad hoc, decision rule.

For instance, the receiver can estimate the channel from the previously received and decided data.

Space-Time and Space-Frequency Coding: We can view the classical error detection and correction codes as a form of time diversity in the sense that the information is spread over the bits of a codeword, and these bits are serially transmitted one after the other. In multi-carrier modulation, the information is spread over the frequency band of the transmission system. Using more than a single transmit antenna ads a spatial dimension to such coding.

Synchronous Transmission: A synchronous operation is performed under the control of a clock, or timing signal. This one is a periodic train of dc pulses, commonly generated by a crystal-controlled electronic oscillator. In a synchronous transmission system, the symbols emitted by an information source are read out under the control of a timing signal. The receiver has usually to recover this timing signal from the transmitted symbols with the help of a phase-locked loop (PLL).

Chapter 4

PHY/MAC Layer Design in Vehicular Ad Hoc Networks:
Challenges, Standard Approaches, and Alternative Solutions

Claudia Campolo
Università Mediterranea di Reggio Calabria, Italy

Hector Agustin Cozzetti
Istituto Superiore Mario Boella, Italy

Antonella Molinaro
Università Mediterranea di Reggio Calabria, Italy

Riccardo Maria Scopigno
Istituto Superiore Mario Boella, Italy

ABSTRACT

Peculiarities of the vehicular environment make the design of the Physical (PHY) and Medium Access Control (MAC) layers for Vehicular Ad-hoc Networks (VANETs) very challenging. Technical solutions should carefully cope with (i) quickly changing network topologies caused by vehicles mobility, (ii) short connection lifetimes, (iii) multi-hop vehicle-to-vehicle communications, (iv) hostile environments for radio signal propagation, and (v) heterogeneous nature and quality requirements of various types of applications. The main aim of this chapter is to serve as an introduction for readers interested in vehicular network design, with a special focus on the MAC layer. It includes a detailed description of the major features and operating principles provided by PHY and MAC layers of the IEEE 802.11p and IEEE 1609 standard suites to support Wireless Access in Vehicular Environments (WAVE). The last part of the chapter contains a brief survey of some relevant MAC proposals in the scientific literature that try to cope with the challenges of vehicular networks. Most of them follow the contention-based channel access idea of the standard and propose extensions to the 802.11p MAC layer in order to achieve higher throughput and fairness; others capitalize on a centralized access to achieve deterministic service quality.

DOI: 10.4018/978-1-4666-0209-0.ch004

1. INTRODUCTION

In the last few years, vehicular ad hoc networks (VANETs), which provide connectivity among vehicles and between vehicles and the roadside infrastructure, have aroused the increasing interest of the research community (Huang, 2010), (Olariu & Weigle, 2009), (Watfa, 2010). The reasons of such an interest come from the fact that VANETs can be considered as a viable solution for improving road safety and transport efficiency, and also as an enabling technology to provide value-added services to travelers on the road.

Past and ongoing research projects, supported by car manufacturers and electronic industries, governments and academia, have obtained allocation of frequency spectrum and are specifying standards, designing applications, and running field trials for VANETs (Papadimitratos et al., 2009).

Based on their targets, potential applications for VANETs can be arranged into the following classes: *on-the-road safety*, *transport efficiency*, and *information/entertainment (infotainment)* applications (Hossain et al., 2010).

Safety-related applications distribute information about hazards and obstacles on the road with the primary aim of limiting the risk of car accidents and making the driving more efficient and safe (Biswas et al., 2006). Due to their critical nature, these applications have real-time constraints, with a maximum allowed latency of 100 ms (CAMP, 2005); they typically rely on one-hop broadcasting and multi-hop vehicle-to-vehicle (V2V) or vehicle-to-roadside (V2R) communications.

Transport efficiency is pursued by traffic management applications that focus on optimizing flows of vehicles to reduce the travel time and avoid traffic jam situations (e.g., enhanced route guidance/navigation, traffic light optimal scheduling, lane merging assistance), or they focus on vehicle monitoring and urban sensing (e.g., pollution, forensic). These applications, by making the transportation systems more efficient,

are also environmental friendly. In fact, by optimizing routes, gas emission can be reduced and fuel consumption can be decreased. Transport efficiency applications do not have stringent delay requirements; their quality gracefully degrades with the increase in packet loss and delay; and they can rely on V2R or V2V communications.

Also referred to as *non-safety* applications, *comfort* applications aim to provide the road traveler with information support and *entertainment* that makes the journey more pleasant (e.g., audio-video streaming, data download, information advertisements). Most of these applications rely on V2R communications; they often exploit the presence of roadside units acting as gateways towards the Internet.

The successful, reliable and efficient delivery of the aforementioned set of applications strongly relies on the design of a medium access control (MAC) layer able to cope with the challenges of the vehicular environment and with the various kinds of service requirements.

The main challenges for an effective and efficient MAC layer design for VANETs are summarized in the following list.

- **Heterogeneous applications.** VANETs have their own set of applications, specifically designed for the road environment, which mainly differ for the quality of service (QoS) requirements. On the one hand, safety-related applications have obvious real-time and reliability constraints, e.g., collision warnings must be timely distributed among all potentially involved vehicles. On the other hand, comfort/entertainment applications exhibit very different requirements, from the no special delivery requirements of information support applications (e.g., point of interest advertisements, map download, parking payment, automatic tolling service) to the guaranteed quality needs of entertainment applications (e.g., media streaming, voice over IP, multiplayer gaming, web browsing). Moreover, non-safety and safety applications need to be concurrently supported without adversely affecting the performances. Therefore, efficient *traffic prioritization* shall be provided by the MAC layer.

- **Node mobility**. Vehicles move at high speed: from 0 to 40 m/s, even doubled when considering the speed difference of vehicles moving in opposite directions. This results in quickly changing network topologies and in short V2V and V2R connection lifetime, which strongly hinders the establishment of stable and durable end-to-end paths. Therefore, *low-latency, highly reactive and efficient communication establishment and channel access procedures* are required.

- **Infrastructureless and infrastructure-based communications**. Some applications for VANETs rely on V2V communications, while others require the support of roadside infrastructure with the installation of wireless nodes (located along the highways, in gas stations, or in urban crossroads) that offer connectivity to vehicles and, potentially, control the access to the shared channel. Given the large deployment costs of a ubiquitous roadside infrastructure, only a few roadside nodes will be installed in the near future. Therefore, it is crucial for a MAC protocol to be able to *support both V2V communications* (not centrally controlled) *and V2R communications*, by letting vehicles efficiently utilize the scarce and precious roadside units' resources.

- **Variable node density**. Vehicular networks can be characterized by variable traffic density. Sparse traffic conditions characterize off-peak hours for example, or the initial VANET deployment phase due to a limited market penetration rate.

High traffic conditions with several cars concentrated in a small area characterize, for instance, urban crossroads in peak hours. Since the number of vehicles cannot be easily estimated in advance, MAC protocols have *to scale well with the number of potentially active nodes*, while ensuring high channel access opportunities and without increasing congestion.

- **Hostile propagation environment**. Propagation environments can be highly heterogeneous in VANETs. Highway scenarios are typically free of obstacles and buildings; they are normally characterized by Line-Of-Sight (LOS) conditions. Urban grids, conversely, are generally dominated by Non-LOS (NLOS) communications, with multiple reflecting objects that degrade the received signal quality and strength. In both environments, due to the relatively low elevation of vehicle antennas, it is reasonable to expect that vehicles themselves act as obstacles to the signal propagation. Moreover, the mobility of transmitter and receiver, and also the mobility of surrounding objects, can exacerbate the multipath fading adverse consequences and create the Doppler effect. Physical and MAC layers have to counteract the effects of a hostile propagation channel through proper frequency/bandwidth allocation schemes and robust transmission procedures.

- **Node capabilities**. VANETs should take power constraints and time synchronization problems less into consideration when compared with other resource-constrained wireless ad hoc networks. Vehicles can enjoy a practically unlimited power supply; moreover, VANET nodes can be equipped with navigation receivers and on board sensors that provide information about time coordinates, node position, speed, and direction. This paves the way for position-aware and synchronous MAC solutions at low cost and complexity. This aspect will be analyzed in the last part of the chapter.

The main focus of research communities and standardization bodies today is on using the IEEE 802.11 Carrier Sense Multiple Access with Collision Avoidance (CSMA/CA) as a MAC protocol for VANETs. IEEE 802.11 technology is a mature, high-bandwidth and low-cost technology with the capability to well fit the multi-hop, distributed, unstable and ad hoc nature of vehicular environments. To this aim, the IEEE 802.11p (IEEE 802.11p, 2010) standard has been recently published as an amendment to IEEE 802.11 (IEEE 802.11, 2007); it is intended to operate with the IEEE 1609 protocol suite (IEEE P1609.0, 2009) to provide the Wireless Access in Vehicular Environments (WAVE) protocol stack (in Figure 1). The IEEE 802.11p physical and MAC layers and the IEEE 1609 standards will be extensively described in Sections 2, 3 and 4 of the chapter.

The 802.11p MAC protocol well handles high mobility and topology changes, but it makes successful and time-bounded data delivery very hard ensure. Therefore, the feasibility of new approaches, currently under investigation by the research community, will be presented in Section 5. Adaptive distributed CSMA/CA mechanisms, deterministic time-division multiple access (TDMA) mechanisms deployed on top of the

Figure 1. The IEEE 802.11p/WAVE protocol stack

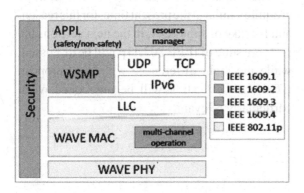

802.11p MAC layer and hybrid MAC solutions combining the benefits of distributed and deterministic approaches, will be discussed. In Section 6, conclusive remarks will be summarized.

2. THE IEEE 802.11P/WAVE PROTOCOL SUITE

2.1. IEEE 802.11p/1609 Standards Family: An Overview

The history leading to the development of current Dedicated Short Range Communications (DSRC) goes back in the early 1990s, when the U.S. Department of Transportation (DOT) and the Intelligent Transportation Society of America (ITSA) - a non-profit organization whose members come from industry and academia - developed a plan for Intelligent Transportation System (ITS) services. From the beginning, this framework recognized wireless communications as a cornerstone for the implementation of many ITS services.

At that time, some vehicular applications, such as road toll collection, used the spectrum between 902 and 928 MHz; but this band was too small and crowded to enable the envisioned evolution of ITS services. In 1997 ITSA petitioned the Federal Communications Commission (FCC) for 75 MHz of bandwidth in the 5.9 GHz band, and in 1999 the FCC granted the request by allocating the spectrum in the 5.85-5.925 GHz range to DSRC-based ITS radio services. The primary purpose was to enable public safety applications to save lives and improve vehicular traffic flow. Private services were also permitted in order to lower the network deployment and maintenance costs to encourage DSRC development and adoption.

The ITSA recommended the adoption of a single standard for the physical (PHY) and MAC layers of the architecture and proposed the one developed by the American Society for Testing and Materials (ASTM) based on IEEE 802.11a. In 2004, an IEEE task group (task group *p* of the

IEEE 802.11 working group) assumed the role initiated by the ASTM and started developing an amendment to the IEEE 802.11 standard. The document is known as IEEE 802.11p (IEEE 802.11p, 2010) and ratified in July 2010.

The IEEE 802.11p PHY layer is an amended version of the 802.11a specifications, based on Orthogonal Frequency-Division Multiplexing (OFDM) with proper modifications introduced to cope with the hostile mobile environment for radio propagation. At the MAC layer, IEEE 802.11p inherits the main rules of the baseline 802.11 standard (IEEE 802.11, 2007) with its prioritized channel access, but it simplifies the MAC operations for authentication and association, which were considered too time-consuming to be adopted in short-lived vehicular communications.

802.11p is intended to cooperate with the IEEE 1609 standard family, which is developing specifications covering higher layers (above PHY and MAC) in the protocol suite, by collectively making the WAVE stack in Figure 1.

The IEEE 1609 standards currently consist of five documents:

- **IEEE 1609.0**. It is still a draft version (IEEE P1609.0, 2009), referred to as the *WAVE architecture*, and defines the overall IEEE 1609 framework.
- **IEEE 1609.1**. It defines services, interfaces and data flows corresponding to the *WAVE Resource Manager* (IEEE P1609.1, 2009).
- **IEEE 1609.2**. It covers the format of secure messages and their processing, to protect WAVE communications from attacks, such as eavesdropping, spoofing, alteration and replay, and to provide privacy to its users (IEEE P1609.2, 2009).
- **IEEE 1609.3**. It defines the addressing and routing functions associated with the Link Layer Control (LLC), the network and transport layers of the ISO/OSI model; the standard calls them *WAVE networking*

services. They are divided into two sets: *data-plane* services whose function is to deliver data, and *management-plane* services used to configure and maintain the system. In the data plane, WAVE supports both the traditional TCP/UDP/IP protocol stack and a new lightweight protocol for the exchange of small packets carrying high-priority and time-sensitive safety or road messages. Management-plane services include, among the others, application registration, channel usage monitoring, and Basic Service Set (BSS) management (IEEE P1609.3, 2010).

- **IEEE 1609.4**. It provides enhancements to 802.11p MAC layer to support multichannel operation and it mainly specifies the following functions: channel routing, user priority, MAC service data unit (MSDU) data transfer, and channel coordination, as extensively detailed in (IEEE P1609.4, 2010).

At this time, the IEEE 1609 working group is also developing new standards: 1609.5 (Communications Management), 1609.6 (Facilities), and 1609.11 (Electronic Payment Service).

The regulatory landscape in Europe is more complex and involves more players than in the United States. The main role is played by the European Telecommunication Standardization Institute (ETSI), which created a Technical Committee for ITSs at the end of 2007.

The standardization paths of USA and Europe are quite similar at the present time; for this reason, and for sake of simplicity, in the next sections the protocol suite of IEEE 802.11p will be discussed, while the main differences with the European ETSI standardization will be mentioned when particularly relevant.

Figure 2. DSRC spectrum allocation in US

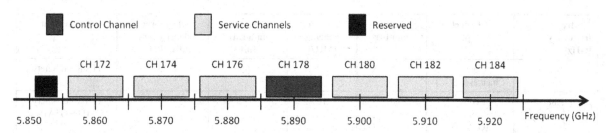

2.2. Spectrum Allocation for VANETs

The 75 MHz DSRC frequency band in the U.S at 5.9 GHz is divided into seven 10 MHz wide channels (Figure 2). The lower 5 MHz band is reserved as a guard band, Channel 178 is the so-called *control channel* (CCH), which is restricted to safety communications only; the rest can be used as *service channels* (SCH) available for both safety and non-safety usage.

In Europe, an overall 50 MHz band, still around 5.9 GHz, was allocated for ITS (ETSI ES 202 663 V1.1.0, 2010): it is subdivided into five channels, one of which is the so-called Control Channel (G5CC); the four others are Service Channels, named G5SC4, G5SC3, G5SC1 and G5SC2 (with central frequencies spanning from 5.86 GHz to 5.89 GHz). The numbering shows an inversion between G5SC1 and G5SC2 to reflect the concept of *guard-zone* channel explained below. An additional channel, Service Channel 5 (G5SC5), is located in the 5.47 – 5.725 GHz band for Radio Local Area Network (RLAN) applications. Finally, the High Availability Low Latency (HALL) channel - 5905 to 5925 MHZ – is left for future use.

A guard zone channel, G5SC2, is introduced between control and service channel in order to avoid potential interference on the control channel (G5CC) or service channel G5SC1: here the allowed transmission power is further lowered. The G5SC2 use will be restricted only to low-priority messages.

Table 1 summarizes the European channel allocation and its main characteristics, as well as the bond between ITS frequency ranges and the vehicular applications in the 5 GHz European bands for DSRC.

Summing up, the differences between the American and the European regulations for multichannel management in VANETs span from the control channel location around the 5.89 GHz (channel 178) in the U.S. and around 5.9 GHz (channel 180) in Europe to the number of available channels.

At this stage of standardization, the advantage of the American DSRC seems to be flexibility coming from the availability of multiple service channels: this should facilitate new business cases and attract service providers, especially in urban areas – while reserving control channel for safety messages. On the contrary, the point of strength of the European approach would be resiliency, coming from the strictly safety-oriented design of the multichannel environment.

This is further reflected by the way the multichannel is managed: while the American approach involves single-radio devices switching between CCH and SCH, as suggested in IEEE 1609.4 specifications described in the following, in Europe two radios will be required to fulfill the requirement of being continuously connected to the CCH. The former solution is cheaper; the latter is more safety-oriented but, on the other hand, it involves possible issues rising from adjacent and non-adjacent channel interference.

Table 1. European channel allocation

Centre frequency [GHz]	Channel type	Channel number	Channel spacing [MHz]	Default data rate [Mbit/s]	Tx power density limit [dBm/GHz]	Application
5.9	Control Channel (G5CC)	180	10	6	23	ITS Road Safety
5.88	Service Channel 1 (G5SC1)	176	10	6	23	ITS Road Safety (ITS G5A)
5.89	Service Channel 2 (G5SC2)	178	10	12	13	ITS Road Safety (ITS G5A)
5.87	Service Channel 3 (G5SC3)	174	10	6	13	ITS Non-Safety Applications (ITS G5B)
5.86	Service Channel 4 (G5SC4)	172	10	6	-10	ITS Non-Safety Applications (ITS G5B)
5.47 to 5.725 (RLAN band)	Service Channel 5 (G5SC5)		Several	depending on channel spacing	17	BRAN / RLAN / WLAN

As a final remark, the DSRC band constitutes a free but licensed spectrum both in USA and EU. Consequently both the FCC in USA and CEPT (Conférence Européenne des Administrations des Postes et des Télécommunications) in Europe do not charge a fee for the spectrum usage.

Conversely, this band is more restricted in terms of constraints and technologies: for instance, FCC regulates the usage within certain channels and limits all radios to be compliant to a standard.

3. IEEE 802.11P: THE PHYSICAL LAYER

3.1. OFDM General Concepts

OFDM-based techniques have mushroomed in telecommunications, both in the area of wired and wireless communications. The main reason for this success is that very high data rates can be mapped onto low symbol-rate modulation schemes: the symbols can be relatively long compared to the channel time characteristics, thus increasing robustness against inter-symbol interference – as caused by multipath propagation. In other words, by adapting to the highly variable environment OFDM can boost the available rate from the about 0.5 Mbps of the old DSRC up to 27 Mbps. Everything being taken into account, it is advantageous to transmit a number of low-rate data streams in parallel instead of a single high-rate data stream.

In a traditional FDM system, many carriers are spaced apart in such a way that the signals can be received by using conventional filters and demodulators. Conversely, OFDM systems overcome the simplistic paradigm of conventional techniques involving non-overlapping carriers: multiple overlapping orthogonal carriers are exploited, almost doubling the available bandwidth or, from another perspective, further squeezing the channel capacity to its upper bound.

The word *orthogonal* refers to a precise mathematical relationship between the carrier frequencies: the carriers are all synchronous and are arranged so that the sidebands of the individual carriers overlap but, despite this, signals

Figure 3. OFDM frequency multiplexing

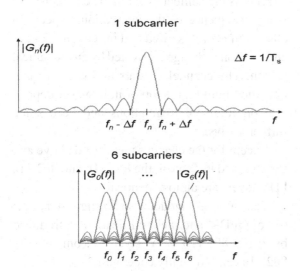

are received without adjacent carrier interference: cross-talk between the sub-channels is eliminated and inter-carrier guard bands are not required (see Figure 3). Basically, the orthogonal property corresponds, in the time domain, to the phenomenon why frequencies which have a whole number of cycles in the symbol period T, result in zero cross-talk contribution in the integration process subtended by Discrete Fourier Transform (DFT) at the input of an OFDM digital receiver. Thus, the carriers are linearly independent (i.e., orthogonal) if the carrier spacing is a multiple of 1/T.

Also the transmitter and the receiver design of OFDM systems is different from that of other FDM methods: in OFDM receivers a separate filter for each sub-channel is not required and the first logical block is a bank of demodulators, *(i)*

translating each carrier down to DC, *(ii)* with the resulting signal integrated over a symbol period to decode raw data. Additionally, the implementation can be further simplified and the decoding process can be faced in a completely digital implementation, built around fast Fourier transforms.

However, beyond these conceptual ideas, the full transmitting and receiving chains of an OFDM-based transceiver are very complex. This is particularly true for 802.11 OFDM, where several logical blocks are meant to cope with different phenomena and tasks. These are further discussed in subsection 3.3.

3.2. OFDM in IEEE 802.11p and 802.11a

The OFDM technique, implemented in the PHY layer of radio devices based on IEEE 802.11a and 802.11p, is based on 52 orthogonal sub-carriers, modulated by using one of the following digital modulations: Binary Phase Shift Keying (BPSK), Quadrature Phase Shift Keying (QPSK), 16-point Quadrature Amplitude Modulation (16-QAM), and 64-point Quadrature Amplitude Modulation (64-QAM). Convolution coding increases resilience by coding rate of 1/2, 2/3, or 3/4. As a result, the available data rates are determined by the couple coding rate and modulation type, as shown in Table 2.

802.11a is designed for high data rate communications among slow moving devices in indoor environments. To make it work in harsh vehicular environments, in IEEE 802.11p all time-parameters get doubled, compared to the corresponding

Table 2. Data rates and channel spacing

Modulation scheme	BPSK	BPSK	QPSK	QPSK	16-QAM	16-QAM	64-QAM	64-QAM
Coding rate	1/2	3/4	1/2	3/4	1/2	3/4	2/3	3/4
Data rate [Mbit/s] with 10 MHz channel	3	4.5	6	9	12	18	24	27
Data rate [Mbit/s] with 20 MHz channel	6	9	12	18	24	36	48	54

ones in 802.11a. On the one hand, the doubled durations reduce the effect of Doppler spread, due to the movement of vehicles and of their surroundings, by inducing a smaller bandwidth; on the other hand, the doubled guard interval reduces inter-symbol interference (ISI) caused by multi-path propagation. As a consequence, the channel width shrinks from 20 to 10 MHz and the data rates are halved too - compared to 802.11a - as illustrated in Table 2. As on option two adjacent channels in 802.11p may be used as one 20 MHz channel.

Besides the clock rate, the spectrum emission masks and adjacent channel rejection were redefined by 802.11p to fit the requirements of outdoor vehicular environments. Concerning the former, for each bandwidth four different spectrum emission masks (SEM) for four different power classes (A, B, C and D) are defined, as shown in Table 3, with a maximum allowable Effective Isotropic Radiated Power (EIRP) up to 44.8 dBm (30W), to support larger ranges: the largest value is reserved for approaching emergency vehicles. In 802.11p the transmission spectrum mask is defined up to 15 MHz offset from the center frequency; detailed masks are specified in the standard documents.

As for adjacent channel rejection (ACR), devices compliant to the 802.11p amendment will be required to meet more stringent requirement compared to 802.11a: ACR is required to be 12 dB higher for adjacent (and 10 dB higher for non-adjacent) channels, in the respective modulations.

An additional difference between 802.11a and 802.11p is the number of available channels: this is a consequence of the international spectrum allocation plan – as discussed in section 2.2 - not an intentional change motivated by any technical reason. The channel settings and multichannel operation built on the top of it, however depend also on Regional Regulations and need some further analysis.

Except for the changes mentioned above and summarized in Table 4, the 802.11p and 802.11a PHY layers are almost identical.

The analysis conducted so far suggest that the use of OFDM and the modifications introduced by IEEE 802.11p PHY layer as compared to 802.11a can efficiently cope with most of the issues introduced by the high mobility of vehicles. However, it should be mentioned that other physical phenomena are not properly handled by 802.11p, as outlined in (Zang et, al,, 2005). In fact, although the doubled guard interval eliminates ISI, fading can also create some problems to OFDM due to selective attenuation on the distinct subcarriers. Although this effect is counteracted by the equalizer in the receiver, as will be discussed in the following paragraph, refined

Table 3. Power classes in 802.11p

Power class	Max. (reference) transmit power (mW)	Maximum Permitted EIRP (dBm)
Class A	0	23
Class B	10	23
Class C	100	33
Class D	760	33 for *non government* 44.8 for *government*

Table 4. Main differences between 802.11p and 802.11a

Parameter	IEEE 802.11p	IEEE 802.11a
Frequency band	5.85-5.925GHz	5.15-5.35GHz; 5.725-5.835GHz
Data rate	Max 27Mb/s	Max 54Mb/s
Channel bandwidth	10MHz	20MHz
Number of channels	7	12
OFDM signal duration	8.0 µs	4.0 µs
Guard time	1.6 µs	0.8 µs
FFT period	6.4 µs	3.2 µs
Preamble duration	32 µs	16 µs

and effective equalization algorithms are required (Cheng et. al., 2006). In addition, the wireless channel between two vehicles can be affected by Doppler-shift and spread, both depending on the movement of two cars and of their surroundings. However, since 802.11p technology will be used in urban, suburban and highway environments at a variety of speeds, it will face channels with different Doppler spreads and additional research efforts are required to counteract their effects.

3.3. OFDM Transceiver Chains for 802.11a and 802.11p

The encoding/decoding chain of an OFDM transceiver for 802.11 networks is much more complex than the simplistic couple made up by the line encoder and OFDM block: a transceiver involves a plethora of additional mechanisms and blocks, each meant to optimize a specific aspect and/or to counteract a particular physical phenomenon.

In practice, the main processing steps which an OFDM signal must undergo, according to the standard IEEE 802.11a, are depicted in Figure 4.

The transceiver chain is fed by a DATA unit delivered by upper layers. The very first step consists in data *scrambling* (by a 127-long frame scrambler) to prevent long sequences of equal symbols. The same type of scrambler is used to descramble the received data. When transmitting, the initial state of the scrambler will be set to a pseudo-random nonzero state.

Encoding starts after the preliminary scrambling step. Roughly, binary input data is first encoded by a *convolutional encoder* to provide error-correction capability: the coding rate can vary among 1/2, 2/3 and 3/4. Then, *interleaving* takes place: every encoded group of bits is interleaved by an algorithm which maps adjacent bits over non adjacent sub-carriers, and adjacent encoded bits alternatively onto less and more significant bits of the constellation. This leads to the *mapping* onto the selected QAM code-set.

To facilitate coherent reception, 4 pilots are added to the 48 QAM symbols, yielding an overall number of 52 QAM values per OFDM symbol. Such OFDM symbol is modulated onto 52 subcarriers by applying the Inverse Fast Fourier Transform (IFFT) with 64 points. With 52 modulated carriers, the symbols feeding the OFDM modulation are 64 – the additional 12 are *null* carriers that form a guard-band in the frequency domain. All in all, the heart of the chain is indeed the 64-point FFT/IFFT block. These steps are also called *pilot insertion* and *inverse FFT*.

The output is then serialized and the digital-to-analog conversion follows: it is, however, preceded by some operations meant to prevent mismatch between the phase and amplitude of consecutive symbols, which is also known as spectral *re-growth*. IEEE 802.11p accounts re-growth by inserting a prefix and by appending a suffix window (*cyclic extensions* on guard-time) on which the symbols are extrapolated and matched the one to the other, following precise mathematical relationships (*windowing*). This also improves the SEM.

Finally an IQ modulator converts the signal into analog (*digital-to-analog conversion*), which

Figure 4. OFDM transmission chain

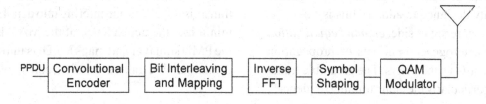

Figure 5. OFDM receiving chain

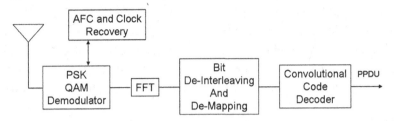

is up-modulated to the 5 GHz band, amplified, and transmitted through the antenna.

Basically, the receiver conversely performs the same operations as the transmitter, but involving some additional non-obvious tasks (Figure 5).

A brief foreground may help understand. In the receiver, unlike the transmitter, the frequency (offset) and symbol timing are not mastered, but need to be estimated from the received signal. Furthermore, frequency and timing are neither stable among different sources (that is among consecutive frames), nor within the same frame (due to physical propagation phenomena). Thus, some additional functions must address, in a continuously fed-back loop, the *time and carrier recovery*.

Considering how much synchronization is critical and how timing can be influenced by propagation, re-synchronization is required at each OFDM symbol: contextually with synchronization, the guard interval can be removed and the useful 52 samples identified.

The same guard interval and cyclic extension adopted against spectral re-growth also help synchronization and the correlation between the symbol and the same one time-shifted is maximum when the guard interval and the symbol end are overlapped.

Synchronization is required also at a frame level and is demanded to a training sequence specifically designed to address this issue.

Finally, at receiver side, *channel equalization* faces the heterogeneous effects of propagation onto the distinct subcarriers. The preamble transmission, particularly the "long training sequence", enables the implementation of a channel equalization algorithm. By using the well-known sequence, built-up by 52 real values, the analytical effect of the channel can be inferred and the appropriate correction coefficients can be computed to minimize fading destructive effects and equalize the processed data.

3.4. The 802.11 PHY Sublayers

The transceiver chain carries out functions which entirely fall in the domain of the PHY layer. However, not all the 802.11p PHY functions have been considered yet. The PHY layer can be split into a *Physical Medium Dependent* (PMD) and a *Physical Layer Convergence Procedure* (PLCP) sublayer. The transceiver chains implement the PMD functions.

The PMD sublayer, in fact, provides transmission and reception of PHY layer data units via the wireless medium. On top of the PMD sublayer, a logical tier is required to adapt the data units from the data-link layer to the PMD format, and vice versa. This is the PLCP sublayer.

The MAC layer communicates with the PLCP sublayer via primitives (a set of fundamental instructions) and a pre-defined logical interface called *service access point* (SAP). When the MAC layer invokes a transmission primitive, the PLCP prepares *MAC protocol data units* (MPDUs) for transmission. Without entering into details, PLCP minimizes the dependence of the MAC layer on the PMD sublayer and maps MPDUs into a frame format suitable for transmission; conversely, it delivers incoming frames from the wireless medium to the MAC layer. This includes the operations of:

- Adding information needed by the transmitter and the receiver to properly encode/decode the frame (such as the data rate, the frame check sequence (FCS), and the frame length);
- Multiplexing information by means of the *Service* field;
- Appending a PHY-specific *preamble* to start synchronization and indicate the beginning of the PHY frame.

The 802.11 standard refers to this composite frame (the MPDU with an additional PLCP preamble and header) as a *PLCP protocol data unit* (PPDU). The MPDU represents the *payload* of the PPDU and is called the *PLCP Service Data Unit* (PSDU). Figure 6 illustrates the PPDU frame format.

The PPDU is unique to the OFDM PHY; it consists of a *PLCP preamble*, a *Signal* and *Data* fields. The *PLCP preamble* is used to acquire the incoming signal, train and synchronize the receiver; the *PLCP Header* (or Signal field) contains information about the rate and the length of the carried PSDU: the *Data* field contains a variable

number of OFDM symbols transmitted at the rate indicated in the PLCP Header.

The PLCP preamble and the Signal fields are always transmitted at the basic rate allowed by 802.11p - 3 Mbps, BPSK with convolutional coding rate ½ - independently of the data rate used to transmit Data.

4. IEEE 802.11P: THE MAC LAYER

4.1. Basic MAC Operations: BSS Setup

IEEE 802.11 networks are built upon the concept of BSS as a set of wireless *stations* (STAs) that agree to exchange data. Two types of BSS are specified by the standard: *infrastructure* and *independent* BSSs. In an infrastructure BSS a group of STAs is anchored by an *Access Point* (AP) that establishes and announces its own BSS by periodically sending *beacon* frames. A STA - listening beacons from an AP - can join the BSS through a number of interactive steps, including synchronization, authentication, and association.

Multiple BSSs can be interconnected through a *Distribution System* (DS) into an *Extended Service Set* (ESS), which appears as a single BSS to the LLC layer.

Figure 6. OFDM PLCP PPDU

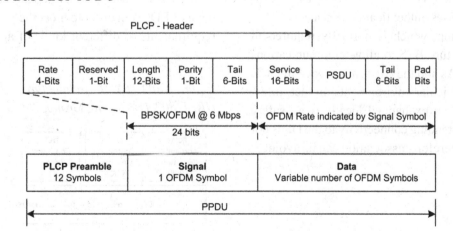

An independent BSS (IBSS), also referred to as an *ad hoc* network, exists without an AP. Communications in an IBSS directly occur among stations. All STAs share the burden of transmitting beacon frames to announce the existence of the IBSS and its parameters and to allow synchronization of STAs.

Both infrastructure and independent BSSs are allowed by IEEE 802.11p, but the synchronization, authentication and association procedures imply excessive latency and overhead to fit the rapidly changing vehicular environment with very short-lived connections. Therefore, a new operational mode has been introduced in 802.11p, referred to as communication *outside the context of a BSS* (OCB), that avoids the latency associated with establishing a BSS. Such a communication mode is activated by setting the *dot11OCBEnabled* flag to true. Differently from baseline 802.11, in OCB mode also STAs which are not member of a BSS are allowed to transmit data without preliminary authentication, and association signaling.

In OCB mode, beacon frames are used neither for BSS advertisement nor for synchronization purposes. Therefore, stations rely either on default parameter values or on information carried out in other frames, like the *timing advertisement* (TA) frame, introduced by 802.11p, mainly for synchronization reasons. Also, in OCB communications, any required authentication service would be provided by the upper layers to mutually identify communicating STAs. In the WAVE stack, IEEE 1609.2 provides authentication services.

Association, which is normally required in an infrastructure BSS to allow communications between STAs and the AP, is not needed in OCB mode. In vehicular environments, in fact, information is often exchanged locally (e.g., safety alerts), so extending connectivity to the DS is not necessary, therefore, association can be avoided.

4.2. IEEE 802.11 MAC Architecture: An Overview

IEEE 802.11p inherits the MAC architecture of the baseline IEEE 802.11 standard, which is illustrated in Figure 7. The main functionalities of the MAC layer are listed in the following, with emphasis on some relevant fallouts of each feature in the VANET scenario.

The *distributed coordination function* (DCF) is the fundamental access method that is mandatory in all STAs; the *point coordination function* (PCF) is a centralized access only optionally usable in an infrastructure network; the *hybrid coordination function* (HCF), which has been introduced to support QoS, combines a contention-based access mechanism, called the *enhanced distributed channel access* (EDCA), and a controlled access mechanism, referred to as the *HCF controlled channel access* (HCCA), for contention-free data transfer.

DCF and EDCA are distributed contention-based channel access schemes, which can be used both in infrastructure and independent BSSs. PCF and HCCA, instead, can be only used in centrally coordinated infrastructure-based networks, since they rely on a polling mechanism managed by a Coordinator, usually co-located with the AP.

Due to the dominant ad hoc nature of vehicular communications, a distributed channel access scheme is the best candidate for IEEE 802.11p, which, consequently, adopts the same core mechanism of EDCA in order to meet the prioritization requirements of different kinds of applications.

Figure 7. 802.11 MAC architecture (Adapted from (IEEE 802.11 Working Group, 2007))

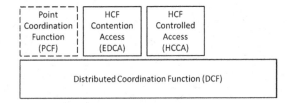

However, for the sake of completeness, in this section we will briefly review the four access mechanisms mentioned above, by underlining their features and arguing their suitability/unsuitability for vehicular communications.

4.3. MAC Layer Design: Challenges and Basic Rules

Distributed channel access schemes (DCF and EDCA) rely on the CSMA/CA technique. The CSMA basic idea is "to listen before talk", i.e., a station that desires to transmit must probe the medium before transmission to determine whether it is busy or not. Channel sensing is not sufficient to guarantee collisionless transmissions in 802.11 networks, especially due to what is called the *hidden terminal* problem. This is a fundamental challenge in 802.11 networks which the MAC layer has to cope with. A potential hidden terminal is any STA which is located out of the range of the transmitting node S, but close enough to the destination D so that it can disturb an ongoing transmission towards D with its own simultaneous transmission towards any node in its coverage area. In Figure 8, node B is hidden to node A and vice versa, since they do not hear each other; therefore, they may seize the channel and transmit

simultaneously, thus causing a collision at node C, which is in the coverage area of both stations.

To fight against the hidden terminal problem, channel probing can exploit both a physical and a *virtual* sensing to determine whether the channel is idle or busy during a given time interval. Physical carrier sensing is done by monitoring any channel activity caused by other sources, in analogy to other CSMA-based networks (like Ethernet). Virtual sensing is instead implemented *(i)* by adding a preliminary (optional) *Request-to-Send* (RTS)/*Clear-to-Send* (CTS) frame handshaking between the sender and the receiver, and *(ii)* by including in all transmitted frames an indication of their expected duration so that the non-destination stations, by overhearing any of these frames, can be aware of the time interval during which the channel will remain busy. A counter, called *Network Allocation Vector* (NAV) will be set accordingly by each STA to keep track of the channel status and it will be decremented by one slot-by-slot regardless of the sensed channel status. Once a station has set its NAV, its transmission is deferred until the channel becomes idle (i.e., the NAV is zero).

Another characteristic of the MAC data exchange in 802.11 networks is that it employs an immediate positive acknowledgment scheme for unicast frames, which allows the sending an STA to realize that the transmission was successful. Upon a successful frame reception, the receiving STA sends back an acknowledgment frame (ACK) to the source. If the ACK is not received, the frame is considered as lost and retransmitted by the source node. Contrarily to unicast frames, broadcast and multicast frames are never acknowledged; hence, they cannot be retransmitted. The same rule holds for RTS/CTS handshake that is optionally implemented only before unicast data exchange.

The 802.11 MAC layer mandates that a gap of a minimum specified duration exist between contiguous frame sequences. The time interval between frames is called the *interframe space* (IFS). Five IFSs are defined to provide different

Figure 8. The hidden terminal problem: A and B are hidden terminals; their simultaneous transmissions cause collisions on C.

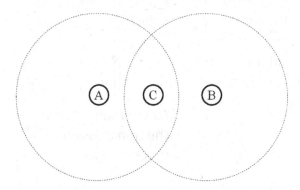

channel access priorities: short interframe space (SIFS), PCF interframe space (PIFS), DCF interframe space (DIFS), arbitration interframe space (AIFS), and extended interframe space (EIFS).

- The SIFS is the shortest of the IFSs; it is used prior to transmission of an ACK frame, a CTS frame, and by a STA responding to any polling request from the Coordinator (in PCF or HCCA scheme).
- The PIFS can be used only by the Coordinator operating under the PCF (or HCCA) to gain priority access to the medium at the start of the contention-free period. A PIFS is equal to a SIFS plus one slot time.
- The DIFS is used by all STAs (included the AP) operating under the DCF to transmit data/management frames after a previous frame has been correctly received and the STA's backoff time has expired. A DIFS is equal to a SIFS plus two slot times.

- The AIFS[i] is used by the traffic belonging to Access Category (AC) *i* in a QoS-enabled STA operating in EDCA mode; it replaces DIFS used in DCF. An AIFS is equal to a SIFS plus AIFSN slot times (with AIFSN greater than or equal to two for a STA, and AIFSN greater than or equal to one for an AP).
- EIFS shall be used instead of a DIFS (or an AIFS[i] if operating in EDCA mode) following an unsuccessful frame reception (e.g., the reception of a frame in error). An EIFS is equal to a SIFS plus a DIFS (or an AIFS[i]) plus the time required to transmit an ACK frame at the lowest PHY mandatory rate.

The IFS values are determined from attributes specified by the PHY layer; they are all fixed (except for the AIFS[i]) and independent of the data rate. The temporal relationships among IFSs are shown in Figure 9.

Figure 9. IFS temporal relationships

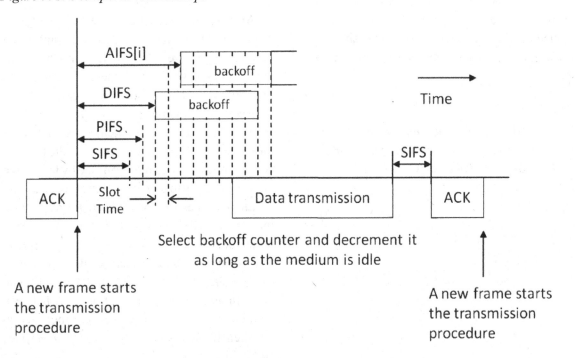

4.4. Distributed Channel Access: DCF and EDCA Schemes

DCF is the fundamental distributed channel access method, which is mandatory in all 802.11 STAs, in both independent BSS and infrastructure network configurations.

According to the DCF rules, a STA shall sense the medium idle for a DIFS before attempting to transmit a frame. If the medium is detected as busy, the STA shall defer its transmission of an additional random *backoff* time to avoid collisions between multiple STAs that have been deferring to the same event.

After deferral following a busy medium condition, or prior to a new frame transmission attempt immediately after a successful transmission, the STA selects the backoff counter value as follows:

Backoff Time = Random()· aSlotTime

where *aSlotTime* is the slot time duration, *Random()* is a pseudo-random integer drawn from a uniform distribution over the interval [0,CW-1], where CW is the *Contention Window* that takes *aCWmin* as an initial minimum value at the first transmission attempt and is doubled (exponential growth) at every failed transmission (with an upper limit equal to the maximum size *aCWmax*).

A failed transmission is characterized by the lack of reception of an expected ACK frame. This may indicate to the sender either that an error has occurred in the transmitted data frame or that an error has occurred in the ACK frame. To the sending STA these two conditions are indistinguishable.

The backoff counter is decremented by one at the end of each idle slot. As soon as the timer reaches zero the STA is allowed to transmit. If the channel is determined to be busy during any slot interval, the backoff timer countdown is frozen; it will be resumed following a DIFS (or an EIFS) period during which the channel is determined to be idle.

The exponential backoff works only for unicast, as further discussed below.

The DCF consists of the above described *basic* access mode, that is also illustrated in Figure 10 (a), as well as the optional RTS/CTS access mode, introduced to counteract the hidden terminal problem. When the RTS/CTS access mode is enabled, a sender first contends for seizing the channel to transmit a RTS frame and then it transmits the data frame only after it has received a CTS frame from the intended destination.

RTS and CTS frames are shorter than normal data frames and they carry information about the upcoming channel occupancy and its duration. Once the RTS/CTS handshaking takes place successfully, the medium reservation information is distributed in the neighborhood. Both the sender's neighbors (by overhearing the RTS frame) and the receiver's neighbors (by overhearing the CTS frame) are informed about the upcoming data transmission and will refrain from accessing the channel, thus avoiding collisions.

The unicast data exchange when the RTS/CTS mechanism is enabled, and the corresponding NAV updating procedure, is depicted in Figure 10 (b).

To reduce the overhead incurred when the RTS/CTS access mode is enabled, the standard specifications allow a STA to use such an exchange for individually addressed data frames only when the data frame size is longer than a given threshold indicated by the *dot11RTSThreshold* attribute. Longer packets are also more prone to channel errors and collisions; therefore, the RTS/CTS mechanism becomes more effective as the packet size increases.

In case the CTS frame is not successfully received, the transmitting node will repeat the procedure in order to retransmit the RTS frame up to a certain number of retries, after performing a new backoff and readjusting the contention window size, as described for the basic access mode. A frame is dropped if the retry counter exceeds the maximum retry limit. The CW value and the retry limits are reset to *aCWmin* and 0, respectively, after every successful frame transmission or when the retry limit is reached.

Unfortunately the RTS/CTS mechanism cannot be used for broadcast/multicast frames, because multiple simultaneous CTS transmissions would cause collisions at the sender. For the same reason, multicast/broadcast data frames are never acknowledged. Since failed broadcast/multicast transmissions cannot be detected, and hence frames are never retransmitted, the size of the CW never changes for this kind of traffic, leading to poor performance due to collisions, especially if several nodes are contending for the channel. To compensate for the inherent unreliability of broadcast transmissions, broadcast frames are often transmitted at the lowest PHY mandatory data rate (that is notoriously the most robust to channel errors and interference).

In a vehicular environment, most traffic is characterized by a broadcast nature (e.g., safety messages, BSS advertisements), thus, even if the RTS/CTS mechanism combats collisions due to hidden terminals, it is not extensively used. Even for unicast data transmissions, a protocol with low overhead is preferred to the use of the RTS/CTS handshaking mechanism: it would better adhere to the requirement of providing real-time delivery of safety services in VANETs.

Based on the DCF rules, all the STAs compete for accessing the channel with the same priority, i.e., they all use a DIFS as the mandatory idle channel period before selecting the random backoff. There is no differentiation mechanism that guarantees better service to traffic with more stringent requirements (such as real-time multimedia traffic), and there is no mechanism that effectively differentiates multiple flows within a STA. To cope with these issues, the EDCA mechanism has been specified and adopted as the core access scheme for 802.11p networks: as

Figure 10. Unicast data exchange in the basic access mode (a) and in the RTS/CTS access mode (b).

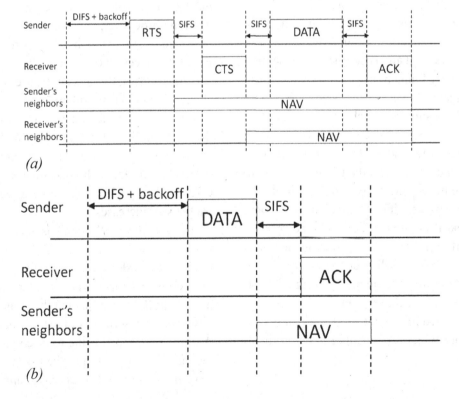

a matter of fact it provides a tool to differentiate traffic while keeping a scalable and distributed approach - unlike PCF and HCCA.

EDCA provides differentiated and distributed channel access to data traffic using eight different user priorities (UPs), in analogy with the IEEE 802.1D priority tags (IEEE Std. 802.1D, 2004). Data from the higher layer tagged with a specific UP value is mapped into an AC at the MAC layer. The four ACs are labeled as AC0, AC1,..., AC3, in increasing priority order, according to their target applications, i.e., background, best effort, video, and voice. AC3 has the highest priority and corresponds to voice traffic.

A STA maintains separate queues for each AC and implements separate EDCA functions for each queue. Traffic differentiation can be achieved by varying the following parameters for each AC:

- the amount of time a STA senses the channel to be idle before randomly extracting the backoff or transmitting the data frame (AIFS[AC]);
- the contention window (CW) size to be used for the backoff (*aCWmin*, *aCWmax*);
- the time interval during which a STA may transmit a series of frames separated by a SIFS, after it has seized the channel, namely the *transmission opportunity (TXOP) limit*.

A STA obtains a TXOP for a given AC if the carrier sensing mechanism determines that the medium is idle at the AIFS [AC] slot boundary, after a correctly received frame, and the backoff time for that AC has expired. The AIFS [AC] is defined as follows:

$$\text{AIFS[AC]} = \text{aSIFSTime} + \text{AIFSN[AC]} \cdot \text{aSlotTime}$$

where AIFSN[AC] is an integer AIFS number assigned to each AC.

If a STA manages several ACs, and the backoff timers associated with more than one AC expire

simultaneously, then internal collisions occur and a virtual resolution function will be used to assign the TXOP to the highest priority class. The other competing frames will be retransmitted (or discarded if exceeding the maximum number of retries) according to the backoff mechanism as if the transmission attempt failed. The values of the main MAC parameters in 802.11p are reported in Table 5. The EDCA parameters set of each AC to be used in baseline 802.11 standard (when *dot11OCBEnabled* is false) is reported in Table 6, while values for 802.11p (when *dot11OCBEnabled* is true) are reported in Table 7. Smaller values of aCWmin, aCWmax, and AIFSN, and larger TXOP limit values are assigned high-priority ACs to achieve better channel access chances. In vehicular networks, when dot11OCBEnabled is true, the TXOP limit is set to zero for each AC, indicating that only one frame can be transmitted after having seized the channel.

4.5. Centralized Channel Access: PCF and HCCA Schemes

The aim of centralized schemes is to ensure time-bounded channel access delays to real-time traffic, especially under heavy load, when the contention-based distributed MAC schemes cannot guarantee an upper bound for the access delay.

When the PCF is enabled, a contention-free period (CFP), which is managed by a Point Coordinator (PC) through a polling-response scheme, alternates with a contention period (CP), during which the DCF controls the access of STAs to the channel.

Table 5. 802.11p MAC parameters

Parameter	Value
aCWmin	15
aCWmax	1023
aSlotTime	13 μs
aSIFSTime	32 μs

Table 6. Default EDCA Parameters Set if dot11OCBEnabled is false

Access category	CWmin	CWmax	AIFSN	TXOP limit
AC0	aCWmin	aCWmax	7	0
AC1	aCWmin	aCWmax	3	0
AC2	(aCWmin+1)/2-1	aCWmin	2	3.008 ms
AC3	(aCWmin+1)/4-1	(aCWmin+1)/2-1	2	1.504 ms

At the nominal beginning of each CFP, the PC senses the medium. When the medium is determined to be idle for one PIFS period, the PC transmits a beacon frame containing the CFP parameter sets (e.g., the CFP repetition interval, the CFP maximum duration and remaining duration). When receiving the beacon, each STA sets its NAV to the advertised CFP duration. By setting the NAV, STAs are prevented from taking control of the medium during the CFP unless they are explicitly polled by the PC. The CFP is explicitly ended by the PC by transmitting an End frame. When receiving this frame, all STAs will reset their NAV.

After the initial beacon frame, the PC waits for one additional SIFS period, and then it cyclically polls the STAs in its polling list, so granting them the right to transmit. A polled STA answers with a data or a null frame after one SIFS period. All unicast data transmissions during the CFP must be acknowledged after one SIFS period. Only in the case in which the SIFS period elapses without receiving any expected frame, the PC may send its next frame one PIFS after its last transmission. The exclusive use of IFSs shorter than DIFS during the CFP reduces the risk of hidden STAs determining the medium to be idle for one DIFS and possibly corrupting a transmission in progress.

Like the PCF scheme, HCCA relies on a polling-based channel access scheme, but unlike PCF, the stations can be polled in given time intervals also during the contention period. At any time during the CP, the QoS-aware coordinator, the Hybrid Coordinator (HC), can take control of the channel and start limited-duration contention-free intervals, called Controlled Access Periods (CAPs).

The HC uses its higher access priority to initiate the frame exchange during the CAP and allocate TXOPs to itself and to other STAs in order to provide contention-free transfer of QoS data. Unlike in PCF, in HCCA a polled STA can transmit multiple frames in an assigned TXOP.

The polling mechanism enforced in PCF and HCCA rules the frame transmissions of the STAs so as to eliminate contention for a limited period of time. Notwithstanding, the two schemes have not gained much interest from the research community, since they are centralized and can be only used in the infrastructure topology. Therefore, they loosely match the requirements of a distributed vehicular environment. In addition, the standard leaves many details unspecified (e.g., the scheduling policy, the admission control algorithm), which could lead to poor QoS performance.

4.6. MAC Frame Types and Formats

Coming to the frame formats, the IEEE 802.11 MAC layer uses three types of frames: *data,*

Table 7. Default EDCA Parameters Set if dot11OCBEnabled is true

Access category	CWmin	CWmax	AIFSN
AC0	aCWmin	aCWmax	9
AC1	aCWmin	aCWmax	6
AC2	(aCWmin+1)/2-1	aCWmin	3
AC3	(aCWmin+1)/4-1	(aCWmin+1)/2-1	2

control, and *management* frames. Data frames carry user data from higher layers. Management frames (e.g., beacon) enable stations to establish and maintain communications; they are not forwarded to the upper layers. Control frames (e.g., RTS, CTS, ACK) assist in the delivery of data and management frames between stations.

MAC frames (whatever kind they are) constitute the data carried by the previously mentioned PLCP layer and consist of the following basic components: a MAC header; a variable length Frame Body; and an FCS.

- The *Frame Body* field consists of the MAC service data unit. The frame body is of variable size; its maximum length is determined by the maximum MSDU size (2304 octets) plus any overhead from security encapsulation.

- *FCS* is a 4-byte field which contains a 32-bit cyclic redundancy code (CRC) used for detecting bit errors in the MAC frame. The CRC is computed over all the fields of the MAC header and the Frame Body.

- The *MAC header* format comprises a set of fields that occur in a fixed order in all frames of a given type.

Figure 11 depicts the most common MAC frame format. In the MAC header:

- The *Frame Control* field consists of the following subfields: Protocol Version, Type, Subtype, To DS, From DS, More Fragments, Retry, Power Management, More Data, Protected Frame, and Order.

The Type and Subtype fields together identify the function of the frame. For each of the three frame types (control, data, and management), there are several defined subtypes. The combinations of the bit To DS and From DS defines if the frame must be exchanged among members of the BSS/IBSS or outside the context of a BSS (To DS=From DS=0), or if the frame involves the DS (To DS=1 or From DS=1 or From/To DS=1).

- The *Duration/Id* field is typically used to update the NAV, since it includes the duration value (in microseconds) required to transmit the current frame, possibly including some overhead for its response, if required, and appropriate IFSs.

- The *Sequence Control* field consists of two subfields, the Sequence Number and the Fragment Number, which are used to identify a given frame and its fragments. Fragmentation is the process of partitioning a MSDU or a MMPDU (MAC Management Protocol Data Unit) into smaller MAC level frames, MPDUs, to meet the maximum allowed size of an MPDU.

- The *QoS Control* field is used to identify the traffic class or traffic stream to which the frame belongs and various other QoS-related information about the frame that varies by frame type and subtype (e.g., ACK policy, TXOP duration, queue size).

- The *four Address Fields* are used to indicate the basic service set identification (BSSID), the source address (SA), the

Figure 11. MAC frame format (Adapted from (IEEE 802.11 Working Group, 2007))

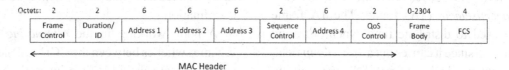

destination address (DA), the transmitting STA address (TA), and the receiving STA address (RA). Certain frames may not contain some of the address fields.

The BSSID field uniquely identifies each BSS. In an infrastructure BSS the value of this field is the MAC address currently in use by the AP. In an independent BSS, instead, it is a locally administered IEEE MAC address formed from a 46-bit random number with the individual/group bit set to 0 and the universal/local bit set to 1. The value of all 1s is used to indicate the wildcard BSSID. A wildcard BSSID can only be used in management frames of subtype probe request. Moreover, according to the 802.11p amendment, data frames with a wildcard BSSID are permitted when the dot11OCBEnabled flag is true and the OCB mode is enabled.

The source address SA is the MAC address of the device that created the MSDU in the frame body. The DA is the MAC address of the device that is the ultimate destination of the MSDU in the frame body, it can be outside the BSS. The RA is the MAC address of the station that receives the frame from the wireless medium. The TA is the MAC address of the station that transmits the frame on the wireless medium.

The first three fields (Frame Control, Duration/ID, and Address 1) and the last field (FCS) in Figure 11 constitute the minimal frame format and are present in all frame types. For instance, the commonly used control frames, i.e., RTS, CTS, ACK frames, include them, without carrying out a frame body.

The 802.11p amendment inherits the same frames defined for baseline 802.11, with the main difference that the beacon frame foreseen in independent and infrastructure modes is replaced in the newly introduced OCB mode by the *Timing Advertisement* (TA) frame. The TA frame can be used to distribute time synchronization information since it carries out a *Timestamp* field, which conveys the local time of the transmitting device, and the *Time Advertisement information element,* which contains data that can be used by recipients to estimate the Coordinated Universal Time (UTC).

4.7. IEEE 1609.4 Multi-Channel Operations

While describing the topic of spectrum allocation, some differences between the American and the European standard in the area of multichannel operations have already been introduced. In this section, for sake of simplicity, the analysis will be focused on IEEE protocol suite.

The 802.11p MAC layer interacts with the IEEE 1609.4 (IEEE P1609.4, 2009) that supports multichannel operation and addresses routing and data transfer from the upper layers to the designated channel and queue at the MAC layer. The 1609.4 specifications define the use of CCH, which is reserved for system control and safety messages, and up to six SCHs used to exchange non-safety data packets (e.g., IP traffic) and WAVE-mode short messages.

WAVE devices are expected to be deployed either as single-radio devices, which operate on one radio channel at a time or as multi-radio devices, which are capable of simultaneous operation on multiple radio channels (at least two).

In a WAVE environment both kinds of devices must have the chance to find each other, i.e. to tune in the same channel at the same time so that they can communicate. Therefore, above the IEEE 802.11p PHY and MAC layers, the 1609.4 specifications define four channel access switching modes: continuous, alternating, immediate, and extended access, as reported in Figure 12.

According to the *continuous* access scheme a node always stays tuned to the CCH to exchange safety-related data; this mode requires no channel coordination.

A node working in the *alternating* access scheme switches between the CCH and the available SCHs at scheduled time intervals. Specifi-

Figure 12. WAVE channel switching modes

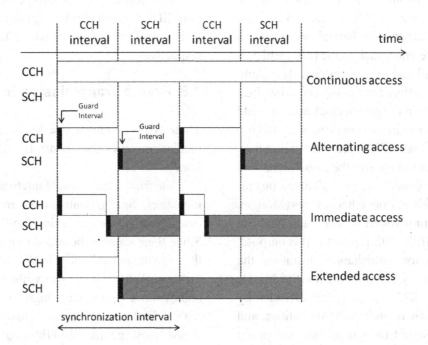

cally, the channel time is divided into synchronization intervals with a fixed length of 100 ms, consisting of a CCH interval and a SCH interval. While the synchronization interval duration is fixed in order to meet the requirements of safety applications which cannot tolerate latencies higher than 100 ms (CAMP, 2005), the IEEE 1609.4 draft states that CCH and SCH interval durations may be adaptable, although they are typically 50 ms-long intervals. Single-radio devices have to monitor the CCH during common time intervals (the CCH intervals), and to (optionally) switch to one SCH during the SCH intervals. For multi-radio devices, the requirement to tune into CCH during the CCH interval can be satisfied by one of the radios, while a second radio could be tuned into one of the SCHs. The described operation allows the safety warning messages to be transmitted on CCH, while non-safety data applications may simultaneously run over SCHs.

The *immediate* access allows immediate communications over the SCH without waiting for the next SCH interval, by avoiding the latency of the residual CCH interval. The *extended* access allows communications over the SCH without pauses for CCH access and is useful for services which require a huge amount of data to be transferred and takes several periods to be delivered.

At the beginning of each channel interval, a 4 ms-long guard interval accounts for the radio switching delay and timing inaccuracies in the devices. During the guard interval, a switching device is not available for communication due to the transition between channels. At the beginning of the guard interval, all MAC activities are suspended and they start (or are resumed) at the end of the guard interval. To prevent multiple switching devices from attempting to transmit simultaneously at the end of a guard interval, the medium is declared as busy during the guard interval, so that all devices extract a random back-off before transmitting. This helps to limit, but it does not prevent, collisions between frames which were queued during the previous channel interval.

All 1609.4 channel access methods, except the continuous access, require time synchronization for switching channels on the channel interval boundaries. The current WAVE standard assumes that coordination between channels may exploit a global time reference, such as the UTC, which is provided by a global navigation satellite system. This approach suffers from being centralized; an attack or failure in the global clock source could lead to wide-spread irrecoverable network failure.

It is likely that WAVE networks will adopt, eventually, a combination of the global signal and some other distributed approaches that rely on timing signals received from other devices (Morgan, 2010). The Timing Advertisement frame has been introduced in IEEE 802.11p just to this purpose.

To account for multichannel operation, the WAVE MAC entity specified in IEEE Std 802.11, as amended by 802.11p, is further extended by IEEE 1609.4. There are two MAC entities, and hence two separate EDCA functions, one for the CCH and one for the SCH, which handle different sets of queues in each STA, as shown in Figure 13.

Each access category has an independent channel access function, with priority access ruled by the appropriate EDCA parameter set values. Default EDCA parameter sets are defined for CCH and SCH intervals, as shown in Table 6 and 7, respectively.

4.8. Frame Transmission in WAVE

Three types of frames can be exchanged in vehicular networks: data, control, and management frames.

Data frames may include safety and non-safety messages. Safety-related data are transmitted (usually broadcasted) during the CCH interval. Since their scope is bounded to a specific area, they can be transmitted as WAVE Short Message Protocol (WSMP) messages without IP overhead and without preliminary signaling. The IEEE 1609.3 draft standard specifies that the maximum WSMP message size is 1400 bytes (IEEE P1609.3, 2009). WSMP packets may be transmitted on any channel, CCH or SCH.

Figure 13. MAC queues in a WAVE device

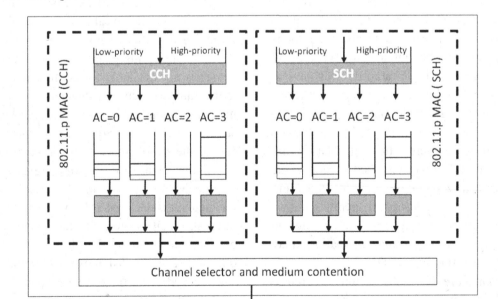

WAVE also supports IP (version 6) traffic; data frames containing IP datagrams may be sent only on SCHs.

The EDCA parameter set specified in IEEE 802.11p for dot11OCBEnabled operation - reported in Table 7- has been optimized for WSMP message transfer (e.g., safety data) and is recommended to be used on CCH. Service providers may announce the EDCA parameters set for the SCHs, which can be different of the default specified in IEEE 802.11p and reported in Table 6.

Concerning *control frames*, they have been specified by IEEE Std 802.11 and are not additionally addressed in the IEEE 1609 family.

Management frames included in 1609 standards are the *Timing Advertisement* (TA) frame, specified in IEEE 802.11p to distribute WAVE time synchronization information, and the *Vendor Specific Action* (VSA) frame, specified in IEEE Std 802.11. The content of VSA frames is specified within IEEE 1609.4 for carrying standardized WAVE management information including *WAVE Service Advertisements* (WSAs). Alternatively, WSAs can be included in TA frames. VSA and TA frames can be transmitted on any channel.

A node that initiates a BSS is called *provider*, while a node that joins a BSS is called *user*. A WAVE node cannot simultaneously create its own BSS and join other node's BSS, this means that a node cannot act as a WAVE user and a provider at the same time.

To establish a BSS on the SCH, the provider has to periodically broadcast announcement messages on the CCH that includes the WSAs. WSAs contain all the information identifying the offered WAVE services and the network parameters necessary to join the BSS, such as the identifier of the BSS, the Provider Service Identifier (PSID), the SCH where a given service is provided for multi-PHY devices, the SCH this BSS will use for single-PHY devices, timing information, the EDCA parameter sets.

A WAVE service can be almost any type of information (with the exception of basic safety messages) offered to either a driver or a passenger, such as traffic alerts, tolling, navigation, entertainment, and Internet access.

The main fields of a WSA frame are depicted in Figure 14. The WSA *Provider Service Table* is a complex field which contains a *Service Info* segment for each service advertised in the WSA. There is a *Channel Info* segment for each SCH on which the advertised service is offered. The *WAVE routing advertisement* (WRA) is used for IPv6-based services to provide information about how to connect to the Internet, e.g., default gateway and domain name server address.

A node should monitor all WSAs on the CCH to learn about the existence and the operational

Figure 14. WSA frame format

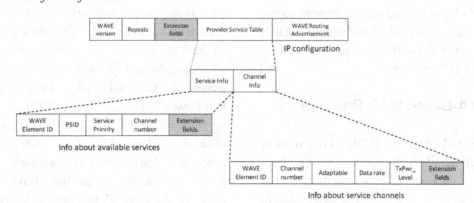

parameters of available BSSs. After that, the node may join the BSS by simply switching to the advertised SCH on the subsequent SCH interval. It is the IEEE 1609.3 network management layer (IEEE P1609.3, 2009) that decides which SCH to tune in when a control interval is over.

The *WAVE Management Entity* (WME) in each node keeps track of SCHs that are in use by nearby WAVE devices, so that it can choose the channel that will be less likely congested. How this is to be done is not specified in the IEEE 1609.3 standard.

Since WSAs are broadcasted by providers without any feedback on their successful reception, sending more WSAs in the CCH interval provides greater reliability. To this purpose, a *repeat rate* parameter is introduced that is the number of times the advertisement is transmitted every five seconds.

5. SHORT SURVEY OF MAC SOLUTIONS FOR VANETS

MAC schemes targeting the VANET scenario can be mainly classified in CSMA-based and TDMA-based solutions (Leng, et al., 2009), (Menouar, et al., 2006). In the next subsections the most representative solutions of each approach will be reviewed. However, since all the emerging solutions proposed by the main standardization bodies (ETSI in Europe and IEEE in USA) that are making decisions on VANET standards in the 5.9 GHz band foresee an amendment to the 802.11 standard fitting WAVE and supporting ITS applications, the focus will be on protocols based on the CSMA/CA scheme.

5.1. CSMA-Based MAC Protocols

Solutions based on the IEEE 802.11 CSMA/CA scheme well handle high mobility and topology changes, but they cannot guarantee traffic flow prioritization mechanisms and a deterministic

upper bound on the channel access delay. These drawbacks make CSMA-based protocols unsuitable for real-time traffic support (such as safety messages or audio/video applications) in VANETs.

Providing different channel access priorities to different application classes, as suggested in the IEEE 802.11p standard, could result in failure due to uncontrollable network collisions. Moreover, although IEEE 802.11p, by inheriting the 802.11e channel access rules, can provide certain QoS support in single-hop networks (Ni, 2005), it does not take into account different channel contention levels, link qualities, variable node densities and high mobility, which are the main features to be considered when designing MAC schemes for VANETs.

Several proposals that enhance the 802.11p MAC protocol have been published in the scientific literature, which adjust the MAC parameters (e.g. contention window CW and channel access priority) *on the fly* based on the environmental changes. These solutions achieve better throughput and fairness performance compared with 802.11p.

In (Wang, 2008) a centralized algorithm has been proposed which adapts the CW size according to the number of nearby vehicles. Specifically, the window is enlarged when the number of competing nodes increases and it is reduced when the number of nodes decreases. However, detecting the number of nearby vehicles is not easy, both if a roadside node collects and relays such information and if vehicles exchange beacons to propagate the information. Therefore, the same authors also propose a distributed solution, where each transmitting node only relies on its local channel information. The number of competing nodes is estimated by counting the amount of time a channel is detected as busy. A similar approach is followed in (Jang & Feng, 2010).

Nodes with different speeds may experience different residence times in the coverage area of a roadside unit in case of V2R communications. As a consequence, they do not have similar chances to access the channel, this leading to unfairness.

In (Alasmary & Ashtiani, 2008) a MAC scheme based on DCF is proposed; the basic idea is to adapt the minimum CW size of each node according to its speed; the higher the speed, the shorter the window. In such a way, fairness among vehicles is guaranteed, and all vehicles have the same chance of communicating with the roadside unit regardless of their speed. The same unfairness issue may exist in V2V communications as stated in (Alasmary & Zhuang, 2010), where two schemes which adapt the channel access parameters have been proposed. The first scheme is a *p*-persistent CSMA/CA-based mechanism where the backoff interval is based on a geometric distribution and set according to the number of neighboring nodes; the second scheme assigns channel access priority, and CWmin/CWmax values, based on the relative speed of vehicles.

Due to its inherent characteristic of random access, the EDCA scheme used by 802.11p could cause unpredictable delays. Moreover, unnecessary backoff procedures waste both time and bandwidth resources. Furthermore, the adaptive scheme described above might fail. Such a behavior could be detrimental both for time-critical safety applications and for real-time multimedia non-safety applications. Therefore, *hybrid* MAC schemes which combine the benefits of both deterministic channel access schemes and contention-based solutions have been recently pursued.

By leveraging on the multi-channel WAVE architecture, a cluster-based communication scheme is presented in (Zhang & Su, 2006), where nearby vehicles moving in the same direction are grouped into a cluster managed by an elected cluster-head. Cluster members access the channel in a contention-free manner, while contention-based communications occur among cluster-heads for inter-cluster communications. Even though cluster-based solutions have some scalability advantages, the signaling overhead required to form and maintain the clusters could be unbearable in a vehicular scenario. Moreover, vehicles are required to be equipped with dual-

transceivers to simultaneously handle intra-cluster and inter-cluster communications, resulting in better utilization of the frequency band. However, the high costs of duplex radios and the *adjacent* and *non-adjacent channel interference* problem (Rai et al., 2007) make the proposed solution not easily deployable.

The WAVE specifications allow single-radio devices to exchange both safety and non-safety data by leveraging on the *alternating* channel switching scheme described in Section 4.7. Such a scheme is strictly followed in (Zang et al., 2007), where a novel MAC protocol, Vehicular Mesh Network (VMESH), has been proposed for V2R communications. In VMESH, SCHs are assigned on a reservation-based TDMA scheme, which allows contention-free channel access for non-safety applications. Reservations are managed through signaling exchange carried over a slotted fraction of the CCH interval, where vehicles periodically broadcast data on their position and receive information on the allocated resources from a roadside unit. The main shortcoming of such an approach is that by fractioning the CCH interval, the transmission opportunities of safety messages are reduced with a consequent additional increase in delivery latency. Moreover, because of the cyclic WAVE scheme, bandwidth demanding applications could starve while waiting for being transmitted over SCH.

Enhanced channel access schemes are proposed in (Liu et al., 2009) and (Wang et al., 2009), which allow a node to stay tuned on a SCH, before switching to CCH, as long as needed to complete the non-safety data exchange. In (Liu et al., 2009) a multi-radio roadside unit is able to simultaneously monitor CCH and SCHs and to promptly broadcast emergency warning messages, which otherwise could be missed as in (Wang, 2009). On every channel, time is divided into a contention-free period, during which vehicles are individually polled by the roadside unit to send safety messages, and a contention-based period, during which nodes can either send control messages on the CCH, or non-safety commercial services on the SCHs. The two solutions mentioned above anticipate the channel switching scheme allowed in the new IEEE 1609.4 standard, i.e., the *extended* access.

A deterministic polling-based MAC placed on top of IEEE 802.11p, which coexists with a contention-based access, is also proposed in (Bohm & Jonsson, 2009). The collision-free channel access scheme, enhanced with a prioritization method based on the vehicles' positions, allows the roadside unit to schedule data traffic and poll the mobile nodes for the delivery of safety messages. Although the authors claim that their solution complements the IEEE 802.11p standard, they do not consider the WAVE multi-channel operation and the availability of several SCHs for delivering non-safety applications. Multichannel operation is instead considered in (Amadeo et al., 2010), where a WAVE-compliant MAC scheme for V2R and V2V communications is proposed to support QoS-sensitive infotainment applications. A node willing to act as a WAVE provider, either a roadside unit or a vehicle, enforces a centralized polling-based channel access scheme, enhanced with position-based information exchanged among nodes and retrieved via positioning systems like GPS/Galileo. Specifically, the provider reserves a contention-free period in the SCH interval, during which it polls only vehicles which are expected to be under its coverage. By doing so, the provider can avoid retransmissions of data packets to those vehicles that have moved out of its coverage. Since the 802.11p standard does not foresee explicit association procedures, vehicles interested in the services offered by the provider enforce a three-way handshaking procedure in order to reserve a contention-free access during the SCH interval. The proposed solution outperforms legacy 802.11p, especially in dense network scenario, by ensuring time-bounded delays and high goodput values.

The multi-channel WAVE capability, which allows multiple transmissions to take place in the neighborhood simultaneously and without interference, is fully exploited in (Mak et al., 2009). The solution relies on a contention-free period for safety data exchange, which is handled by the roadside unit, and a distributed contention period for non-safety services. The main weakness of the proposed scheme is that outside the roadside unit's radio coverage there is no centralized control for the channel access of safety messages.

By strictly following the WAVE user/provider role definition, in (Choi et al., 2007) the authors propose a new solicitation-based operation mode for IEEE 802.11p, where transmissions (and retransmissions) of data frames are initiated only by users sending a new WAVE-poll frame. Such a solution is particularly indicated for scenarios in which the BSS's users continuously change over time due to high vehicular mobility.

5.2. TDMA-Based MAC Protocols

In summary, it can be said that CSMA/CA can intrinsically work in a distributed way, without requiring any centralized coordination; it manages time and space multiplexing; it is simple, scalable, well-known, and several products based on its philosophy are available and proved.

Conversely, CSMA/CA cannot unfortunately guarantee deterministic QoS to any transmissions either *(i)* in terms of access time (CSMA/CA can unpredictably defer also high-priority transmissions) or *(ii)* in terms of collision prevention (especially when the number of stations grows high and for broadcast – unacknowledged transmissions). Moreover, without RTS/CTS mechanisms, this protocol cannot prevent the issue of hidden terminal. Finally, the CSMA/CA overhead, including statistical waiting time from collision avoidance and the time elapsed between consecutive correctly received broadcast frames, are not *a priori* known.

So, despite its strengths CSMA, shows relevant weaknesses which are pushing the scientific community to investigate possible alternatives to the general idea of CSMA/CA scheme.

TDMA offers another channel access philosophy for shared medium networks. It allows several users to share the same channel by dividing it into different time slots, according to a predefined frame structure. The users transmit one after another, each using (theoretically) only its given time slot.

While the approach is intuitive and widely explored in literature, especially for fixed networks, the adaptation to VANET requires several investigations in order to solve several open issues.

TDMA approaches can, in principle, guarantee a deterministic QoS, because each station can be assigned a timeslot on which collisions (by the other stations) are prevented: in this way delays and bandwidth get fixed. On the other hand the construction of a distributed and scalable contention protocol is tricky, in particularly averting scarce spatial resource reuse.

Another possible weakness of TDMA solutions regards the absolute synchronization which needs to be shared among all the nodes in order to let them work. Today, this constitutes one of the very initial challenges in slotted VANET construction (it is supposed to be provided by an external source, such as a GPS or other Global Navigation Satellite System receiver). Since GPS cannot be guaranteed and may not be always available in urban areas, it is mandatory to find solutions to let protocols also work in absence of GPS signal.

Recently some slotted protocols have been demonstrated to also work in a distributed way and in an urban vehicular scenario with encouraging results.

Among TDMA-based channel access protocols, the Reliable R-Aloha (RR-Aloha) in (Borgonovo et al., 2002) is one of the few proposing a slotted solution that is also distributed and hidden terminal-free. This protocol foresees that each station, before transmitting, senses the medium for a frame duration and selects a free slot to be used in subsequent frames; unfortunately the ca-

pability of RR-Aloha to work in VANETs has not been properly investigated. Some recent attempts (Bilstrup et al., 2009), (Lenoble et al., 2009) and (Scopigno & Cozzetti, 2009) specifically addressed the issue of adapting slotted solutions to the case of mobile networks. This represents a challenging research topic and requires solving several open issues: among them a solution to face topology changes due to mobility and new mechanisms to overcome the limited scalability due to scarce slot re-use.

In (Bilstrup et al., 2009) the Self-organizing TDMA (S-TDMA) solution, already utilized in ship collision avoidance systems, has been evaluated in vehicular environments. Differently from the Decentralized-TDMA (DTMA) solution introduced in (Lenoble et al., 2009), where collisions can be experienced if the number of nodes exceeds the number of available slots per frame, a simple slot-reuse is proposed by S-TDMA, where nodes select the slot used by the furthest node.

However, S-TDMA does not address the hidden terminal problem, which is instead intrinsically solved by the Mobile Slotted-Aloha (MS-Aloha) protocol proposed in (Scopigno & Cozzetti, 2009). In MS-Aloha nodes piggyback their view of the status of each slot (busy, free, or subject to a collision) in their data packets, by specifying to which node the slot is allocated: this avoids hidden terminals and undetected collisions. Additionally, thanks to its protocol extensions in the signaling plane, MS-Aloha solves all the issues which can hinder its application to VANETs. In particular its scalability is enforced by slot re-use at two-hop distance and by mechanisms of cross-layer thresholding. Mobility is managed thanks to piggyback signaling and a proper memory refresh.

MS-Aloha and S-TDMA are currently being investigated also in ETSI as a possible next generation MAC solution to be deployed on top of the 802.11p PHY layer.

6. CONCLUSION

In this chapter we have provided a description of the ongoing standardization activities in the field of vehicular networking, with a special focus on IEEE 802.11p and IEEE 1609 standard families, covering, respectively, the PHY/MAC layers and the higher layers of the vehicular protocol stack.

The conducted analysis suggests that the IEEE 802.11p PHY layer can efficiently cope with most of the issues introduced by the high mobility of vehicles, except for the Doppler spread, for which additional research efforts are required.

We have discussed the features and operating principles of the main approaches for MAC layer protocols in VANETs proposed in recent years. Although MAC protocols can rely on a reliable physical layer, both standard and literature solutions cannot be able to simultaneously cope with all the challenging and conflicting issues of scalability, reliability, and QoS in VANETs.

On the one hand, the standard protocol is simple to implement, requires distributed control, and well handles mobility and topology changes, but it cannot guarantee deterministic access delay or reliable data delivery (especially for broadcast traffic). Such weaknesses are pushing the scientific community to investigate possible alternatives.

Among them, the best candidates to be further investigated are some (TDMA-based) slotted protocols that work in a distributed way, some hybrid MAC solutions that combine the benefits of both deterministic and contention-based channel access solutions, and some enhanced CSMA-based approaches which behave adaptively to applications, traffic load and interference, network topology and vehicles' speeds.

REFERENCES

Alasmary, W., & Ashtiani, F. (2008). A modified 802.11-based MAC scheme to assure fair access for vehicle-to-roadside communications. *Computer Communications, 31*(12), 2898–2906. doi:10.1016/j.comcom.2008.01.030

Alasmary, W., & Zhuang, W. (2010). Mobility impact in IEEE 802.11p infrastructureless vehicular networks. *Ad Hoc Networks, 57*(1), 56–63. doi:doi:10.1016/j.adhoc.2010.06.006

Amadeo, M., Campolo, C., & Molinaro, A. (2010). Enhancing IEEE 802.11p/WAVE to provide infotainment applications in VANETs. *Ad Hoc Networks, Special Issue on Recent Advances in Analysis and Deployment of IEEE 802.11e and IEEE 802.11p Protocol Families.* Advance online publication. doi:10.1016/j.adhoc.2010.09.013

Bilstrup, K., Uhlemann, E., Strom, E., & Bilstrup, U. (2009). On the ability of the 802.11p MAC method and stdma to support real-time vehicle-to-vehicle communication. *EURASIP Journal on Wireless Communications and Networking, 2009.* doi:10.1155/2009/902414

Biswas, S., Tatchikou, R., & Dion, F. (2006). Vehicle-to-vehicle wireless communication protocols for enhancing highway traffic safety. *IEEE Communications Magazine, 44*(1), 74–82. doi:10.1109/MCOM.2006.1580935

Bohm, A., & Jonsson, M. (2009). Position-based data traffic prioritization in safety-critical, real-time vehicle-to-infrastructure communication. *IEEE Vehi-Mobi Workshop in IEEE International Conference on Communications (ICC)* (pp. 1-6). Dresden, Germany.

Borgonovo, F., Capone, A., Cesana, M., & Fratta, L. (2002). *RR-ALOHA: A reliable R-ALOHA broadcast channel for ad-hoc inter-vehicle communication networks.* Med-Hoc-Net 2002.

CAMP Vehicle Safety Communications Consortium. (2005). *Vehicle safety communications project. Task 3 Final Report.* Identify Intelligent Vehicle Safety Applications Enabled by DSRC.

Cheng, Y.-H., Lu, Y.-H., & Liu, C.-L. (2006). Adaptive channel equalizer for wireless access in vehicular environments. *International Conference on ITS Telecommunications,* (pp. 1102-1105). Chengdu.

Choi, N., Choi, S., Seok, Y., Kwon, T., & Choi, Y. (2007). A solicitation-based IEEE 802.11p MAC protocol for roadside to vehicular networks. *IEEE Mobile Networking for Vehicular Environments,* (pp. 91-96). Anchorage, AK.

ETSI ES 202 663 V1.1.0, (2010). *Intelligent transport systems (ITS).* European Profile Standard for the Physical and Medium Access Control Layer of Intelligent Transport Systems Operating in the 5 GHz Frequency Band.

Hossain, E., Chow, G., Leung, V., McLeod, B., Misic, J., Wong, V., & Yang, O. (2010). Vehicular telematics over heterogeneous wireless networks: A survey. *Computer Communications, 33*(7), 775–793. doi:10.1016/j.comcom.2009.12.010

Huang, C. M. (Ed.). (2010). *Telematics communication technologies and vehicular networks: Wireless architectures and applications.* Hershey, PA: IGI Global.

IEEE 802.11 Working Group. (2007). *IEEE Std. 802.11-2007: Wireless LAN medium access control (MAC) and physical layer (PHY) specifications.*

IEEE 1609.0/D0.7. (2009). *Draft standard for wireless access in vehicular environments (WAVE) - architecture.*

IEEE P1609.1 SWG. (2009). *IEEE P1609.1/ D0.6, IEEE 1609.1: Trial-use standard for wireless access in vehicular environments (WAVE) – Resource manager.*

IEEE P1609.2 SWG. (2009). *IEEE P1609.2/D0.7, IEEE 1609.2: Trial-use standard for wireless access in vehicular environments (WAVE) – Security services for applications and management messages.*

IEEE 802.11p Working Group. (2010). *IEEE standard 802.11p: Wireless LAN medium access control (MAC) and physical layer (PHY) specifications: Amendment 6- Wireless access in vehicular environments.*

IEEE P1609.3 SWG. (2010). *1609.3-2010: IEEE standard for wireless access in vehicular environments (WAVE) – Networking services.*

IEEE P1609.4 SWG. (2010). *1609.4-2010: IEEE standard for wireless access in vehicular environments (WAVE) – Multi-channel operation.*

Jang, H.-C., & Feng, W.-C. (2010). Network status detection-based dynamic adaptation of contention window in IEEE 802.11p. *IEEE Vehicular Technology Conference (VTC Spring)* (pp. 1-5). Taipei.

Leng, S., Fu, H., Wang, Q., & Zhang Y. (2009). Medium access control in vehicular ad hoc network. *Wireless Communications and Mobile Computing.* Advance online publication. doi:10.1002/wcm.869

Lenoble, M., Ito, K., Tadokoro, Y., Takanashi, M., & Sanda, K. (2009). Header reduction to increase the throughput in decentralized TDMA-based vehicular networks. *IEEE Vehicular Networking Conference (VNC),* (pp. 1-4), Tokyo, Japan.

Liu, K., Guo, J., Lu, N., & Liu, F. (2009). *RAMC: A RSU-assisted multi-channel coordination MAC protocol for VANET* (pp. 1–6). Honolulu, HI: IEEE GLOBECOM Workshops.

Mak, T. K., Laberteaux, K. P., Sengupta, R., & Ergen, M. (2009). Multichannel medium access control for dedicated short-range communications. *IEEE Transactions on Vehicular Technology, 58*(1), 349–366. doi:10.1109/TVT.2008.921625

Menouar, H., Filali, F., & Lenardi, M. (2006). A survey and qualitative analysis of MAC protocols for vehicular ad hoc networks. *IEEE Wireless Communications*, *13*(5), 30–35. doi:10.1109/WC-M.2006.250355

Morgan, Y. L. (2010). Notes on DSRC & WAVE standards suite: Its architecture, design, and characteristics. *IEEE Communications Survey & Tutorials*, *12*(4), 1–15. doi:doi:10.1109/SURV.2010.033010.00024

Ni, Q. (2005). Performance analysis and enhancements for IEEE 802.11 wireless networks. *IEEE Network*, *4*(19), 21–27. doi:doi:10.1109/MNET.2005.1470679

Olariu, S., & Weigle, M. C. (Eds.). (2009). *Vehicular networks: From theory to practice*. CRC Press.

Papadimitratos, P., La Fortelle, A., Evenssen, K., Brignolo, R., & Cosenza, S. (2009). Vehicular communication systems: Enabling technologies, applications and future outlook on intelligent transportation. *IEEE Communications Magazine*, *47*(11), 84–95. doi:10.1109/MCOM.2009.5307471

Rai, V., Bai, F., Kenney, J., & Laberteaux, K. (2007). *IEEE 802.11 11-07-2133-00-000p: Cross-channel interference test results: A report from VSC-A project*.

Scopigno, R., & Cozzetti, H. A. (2009). Mobile slotted Aloha for VANETs. *IEEE Vehicular Technology Conference (VTC Fall)*, (pp. 1-5). Anchorage, AK.

IEEE Std. 802.1D, (2004). Media access control (MAC) bridges.

Wang, S. Y., Chou, C. L., Liu, K. C., Ho, T. W., Hung, W. J., & Huang, C. F. … Lin, C. C. (2009). Improving the channel utilization of IEEE 802.11p/1609 networks. *IEEE Wireless Communications and Networking Conference (WCNC)*, (pp. 1-6), Budapest.

Wang, Y., Ahmed, A., Krishnamachari, B., & Psounis, K. (2008). IEEE 802.11p performance evaluation and protocol enhancement. *IEEE International Conference on Vehicular Electronics and Safety (ICVES)*, (pp. 317-322). Columbus, OH.

Watfa, M. (Ed.). (2010). *Advances in vehicular ad-hoc networks: Developments and challenges*. Hershey, PA: IGI Global. doi:10.4018/978-1-61520-913-2

Wisitpongphan, N., Tonguz, O. K., Parikh, J. S., Mudalige, P., Bai, F., & Sadekar, V. (2007). Broadcast storm mitigation techniques in vehicular ad hoc networks. *IEEE Wireless Communications*, *14*(6), 84–94. doi:10.1109/MWC.2007.4407231

Zang, Y., Stibor, L., Orfanos, G., Guo, S., & Reumerman, H.-J. (2005). *An error model for inter-vehicle communications in highway scenarios at 5.9 GHz*. Montreal: ACM PE-WASUN.

Zang, Y., Stibor, L., Walke, B., Reumerman, H.-J., & Barroso, A. (2007). Towards broadband vehicular ad-hoc networks: The vehicular mesh network (VMESH) MAC protocol. *IEEE Wireless Communications and Networking Conference (WCNC)*, (pp. 417-422). Kowloon.

Zhang, X., & Su, H. (2006). Cluster-based multi-channel communications protocols in vehicle ad hoc networks. *IEEE Wireless Communications*, *13*(5), 44–51. doi:10.1109/WC-M.2006.250357

Chapter 5
The Challenge of a Future Slotted Standard for Vehicular Ad-Hoc Networks

Riccardo Maria Scopigno
Istituto Superiore Mario Boella, Italy

Hector Agustin Cozzetti
Istituto Superiore Mario Boella, Italy

ABSTRACT

This chapter is about alternative MAC solutions for VANETs, based on a synchronous, slotted philosophy. After highlighting the limitation of the incumbent CSMA/CA solution, the chapter explains the rationale for a slotted standard and briefly introduces the three solutions found in literature (namely MS-Aloha, D-TDMA and STDMA). In particular, one of them, MS-Aloha, seems particularly rich in functionalities and solves several open issues, in particular in terms of scalability. Its characteristics are presented and discussed, also by means of simulations and quantitative metrics. The comparative analysis between CSMA/CA and MS-Aloha performances permits to gain a deeper insight and draw conclusions on possible perspectives.

SLOTTED PROTOCOLS FOR VANETS: MOTIVATIONS AND CHALLENGES

So far, the only standardized solution for VANETs relies on collision avoidance as defined in WiFi. As a matter of fact, the American WAVE standard (and European standards as well) is built on the top of IEEE 802.11p, which largely inherits IEEE 802.11a features.

The reasons why IEEE 802.11 met such a unanimous suffrage are manifold and can be deduced by analyzing the intrinsic requirements of VANETs: some of them – unfortunately not all – are simply fulfilled by CSMA/CA. This perspective also highlights, on the other hand, the

DOI: 10.4018/978-1-4666-0209-0.ch005

main limitations of current solutions and explains a certain motivation spread in literature towards possible alternative solutions.

Some emerging synchronous protocols are aimed at this goal and have been recently demonstrated to be theoretically able to satisfy all the requirements subtended by VANETs; as a result, their investigation was further encouraged, specifically addressing some practical open issues.

In order to proceed neatly, first the specific characteristics of vehicular ad hoc networks are shortly recalled in order to highlight the underlying requirements.

In VANETs the number of participating nodes is not always known and, more importantly, cannot be restricted. In addition the number of nodes which can be sensed may strongly vary due to: *(i)* fading, *(ii)* obstruction by buildings (in urban areas) and other vehicles and *(iii)* mutual mobility among cars - which can reach as high as 300 Km/h in highways.

Furthermore, the ad hoc network topology is decentralized, without stationary access points or base stations that regulate access to the shared channel: the so-called infrastructure may be present under certain scenarios but is not mandatory and, consequently, a coordination function cannot be demanded. All in all, the concept of radio-cell and channel reuse, as applied in cellular networks, does not hold for VANETs.

Scalability issues, therefore, become more prominent due to the lack of a central mechanism that has global knowledge of all nodes within the network. The capability to support a certain network load is determined by a number of factors. A desired solution should scale properly both with an increasing number of users and with heavier per-node traffic loads – the two constraints often struggle the one against the other and cannot be simultaneously satisfied.

Notably, in a broadcast environment, traditional methods for delivery control - such as acknowledgements (ACK) - cannot be easily adopted; consequently, reliability in broadcast mode can only be increased by multiple transmissions, which, conversely, impact the network load.

Summing up these considerations, an architecture for broadcasted cooperative awareness messages (CAM) in VANETs, requires a MAC which can satisfy the following requirements (from here onwards referred to as *VANET MAC Requirements*). A MAC should be:

1. *decentralized*, in order to work without any fixed infrastructure;
2. *immune from* the problem of *hidden terminal*;
3. *reactive*, so as to cope with rapid changes in the network topology;
4. properly *scalable* both with traffic and with the number of stations, consequently
5. involving a *low protocol overhead*, for the sake of efficiency.

As a sub case of scalability, the MAC should also boost the effective delivery of urgent messages by mechanisms such as:

6. *priority* (and/or pre-emption) and
7. *prevention of blocking* states.

The MAC method should also be

8. *deterministic*, in order to guarantee a fixed delivery-time for safety messages;
9. *reliable* by providing a high packet-delivery rate (almost ideal);
10. *fair*, giving all nodes at least one opportunity to access the channel within each time period.

Finally a MAC solution would be preferred if:

11. it could be *compatible to* some already *existing solution*s – in order to shorten the time-to-market and rely on existing experience;
12. it provided some additional "awareness tools", such as some kind of *acknowledgement for broadcast packets*– this could

drive some decisions on safety message re-transmissions

13. it included measures to *prevent MAC* Denial-of-Service (*DoS*) *Attacks*;

14. it were *standalone*; in other words the MAC solution should not depend on other blocks - such as a GPS receiver – to work.

The above list of requirements is quite exhaustive and can help quickly analyze CSMA/CA.

CSMA/CA can intrinsically work in a distributed scenario, without requiring any centralized coordination; moreover it manages time and space multiplexing, it is simple, scalable and well-known, and several products based on its philosophy are already available and proved. It also includes also priority mechanisms.

Unfortunately, CSMA/CA cannot guarantee deterministic QoS to any transmissions either *(i)* in terms of access time (CSMA/CA can even unpredictably defer high-priority transmissions) or *(ii)* in terms of collision prevention (especially when the number of stations increases greatly and collision detection for broadcast – unacknowledged - transmissions.

In addition, without RTS-CTS mechanisms (whose overhead would be too heavy) CSMA/CA cannot prevent the issue of hidden terminal. Finally, the protocol overhead of CSMA/CA, including statistical waiting time from collision avoidance and the time elapsed between consecutive correctly received broadcast frames, are not *a priori* known.

Altogether items (2) and (8) are not fulfilled. Requirements (5) and (9) need a deeper insight. Preferences described by item (12) and (13) are not satisfied.

As a result, most of the requirements are met by CSMA and this is the reason for its success. Reversely, some requirements are not satisfied, in particular, the critical requirement on determinism cannot be fulfilled by CSMA/CA. This scientific context motivated the international community to investigate alternative solutions

Time division multiple access (TDMA) is based on another channel access philosophy for shared medium networks. It allows several users to share the same channel by dividing it into different time slots, according to a predefined frame structure. Each user is assigned a distinct slot.

While the approach is intuitive and widely explored in literature, especially for fixed networks, the adaptation to VANETs requires several investigations, to solve several well-known open issues.

The TDMA approach can, in principle, guarantee a deterministic QoS, because each station can be assigned a timeslot in which collisions (by the other stations) are prevented: in this way delays and bandwidth get fixed.

On the other hand, the construction of a distributed and scalable reservation protocol, in particular averting scarce spatial resource reuse presents a tricky problem.

In the following paragraphs some existing solutions are discussed: in particular one, perhaps the most complete one, will be extensively discussed, showing its almost ideal performance and drawing conclusions on its pending open issues.

EXISTING SOLUTIONS FOR SLOTTED VANETS

Quite recently slotted protocols have been shown to work also in a distributed way and in an urban scenario leading to encouraging results. Based on (Borgonovo, et. al., 2002) (Makido, et. al., 2007) the possibility of supporting a distributed synchronous VANET has been envisaged by three different slotted approaches (namely MS-Aloha, D-TDMA and S-TDMA) - currently investigated also in ETSI as possible next generation solutions.

The communication requirements for VANETs have been profusely analyzed in the previous sections. The proposed slotted solutions try to solve some CSMA/CA problems, as, for example, the potential undetermined channel access delay or the low performance when traffic exceeds the

The Challenge of a Future Slotted Standard for Vehicular Ad-Hoc Networks

communication capacity. In fact, the TDMA approach can, in theory, offer fixed and guaranteed access time.

However, synchronous solutions show some potentially critical issues (slot-reuse, overheads and flooding of relevant network information among nodes, synchronization, etc.) that become more relevant in urban congested scenarios and under high mobility. Some TDMA protocols have so far solved most of these points; other are more conceptual and less specified.

In this paragraph S-TDMA and D-TDMA will be shortly introduced. MS-aloha will be presented in the following sections.

The TDMA solution, called Self-organizing Time Division Multiple Access (STDMA) (Mui, et. al., 2002), claims to implement a decentralized MAC scheme with a predictable channel access delay. This algorithm is already utilized in commercial applications, as in a system called Automatic Identification System (AIS), where it focuses on collision avoidance among ships.

In STDMA, all the nodes are supposed to share a common synchronisation source by means of a global navigation satellite system (e.g., GPS/Galileo). The vehicles in the network access the communication channel (divided into slots) and, continuously, send messages giving their own position. This information is used by nodes to choose a free slot in the frame.

In STDMA, as originally defined for ships, four different phases are implemented when a node wants to gain the channel access: *initialization, network entry, first frame*, and *continuous operation*. In the first step (initialization), the vehicles listen to the communications (position messages) during one frame in order to discover slot assignments; a free slot in the frame is selected during the second phase (network entry), following rules which are meant to provide some dynamic changes (for slowly varying environments). Upon selecting the first slot, the vehicle starts the third step (the *first frame* phase) where the station continuously allocates its nominal transmission slots (NTS)

and transmits its position; the NTS is timed-out between 4 and 8 minutes. In the *continuous operation phase*, the station transmits in the allocated NTS's and decrements the slot time-out. When the time-out reaches zero, a new NTS is selected.

Summing up, STDMA performs well in the maritime environment and has been already proved, implemented and applied to ship surveillance.

Conversely, the modifications required to STDMA for its application to VANETs have not been addressed yet. In particular the answers to the following questions should be specified:

1. It seems that no node forwards information about other nodes (the information about node A can be received only by nodes which are one-hop far from A). So the solution does not seem to be robust. Again, the hidden terminal issue seems to be the main issue.

2. Moreover, it is not clear how signalling can work under mobility (the initial reservation requests can get lost). For example, what happens if, due to an urban canyon, the position of a node is not available? What if a station suddenly appears (turning a corner)?

3. How can signalling scalability be ensured? Does signalling work also for multi-hop networks?

4. How can slot re-use based on position be managed? What messages should be forwarded over multiple hops to announce positions? What the protocol overhead caused by such messages? Is slot re-use based on position the best solution, or should it consider the received power (for example, obstructions or line-of-sight in urban settings)?

5. How much is the protocol physical layer compatible to 802.11p?

For these reasons, the protocol remains a good candidate, but it needs a more thorough analysis, mainly addressing the mentioned issues of urban complex environments.

Decentralized-TDMA (DTDMA) (Makido, et. al., 2007) (Tadokoro, et. al., 2008) (Lenoble, et. al., 2009) is another alternative MAC solution proposed for VANETs.

Also in this case, the bandwidth is structured in periodic frames divided into slots (where nodes can transmit their packets). Packets are composed of four components: a *preamble*, a *frame information* (*FI*), a *payload data*, and a *transmission cycle*. The frame information structure is used to notify the status of each slot:

- ACK (ACKnowledgement): received a packet correctly;
- RTC (Request To Change): a packet collision was detected;
- NACK (Negative ACKnowledgement): failed to receive a packet;
- FREE: no received packet.

This information is particularly useful to all the nodes in the VANET: in fact, they can receive "feedback" about the channel status from multiple nodes, preventing hidden terminals and largely increase the immunity from the loss of a single *FI* (thanks to multi-hop propagation of *FI*s). In other words, vehicles continuously share their own view of all the slots, extending the reach of network knowledge.

When a node transmits a packet, the slot status is established as follows:

1. Rule: Analysing the *FI*s received the node searches for a free slot (free-state) from the *N* slots in the frame structure. If there are some available slots, the vehicle randomly selects one for packet transmission;
2. Rule: If the transmitting node *A* does not receive a notification of packet collision (RTC) from the other nodes, this slot is "engaged" by *A*. The vehicle transmits the message using this slot in the next frame, until it receives a RTC notification. In this case (also if one RTC is received), the

node detects the collision and releases the slot. According to the previous rule, a free slot is selected in the next frame and a new transmission is re-attended.

In VANETs collisions may still occur but, thanks to the frame information exchanges, they are detected and resolved (second rule), also in the case of hidden stations. Once a slot has been successfully reserved, it can be used by a node unless a new collision occurs. A node should select a slot that is free, at least within its communication range. But if the number of transmitting nodes exceeds the number of slot/frame N, some vehicles will select the same slot causing collisions and reducing the D-TDMA performance.

Unfortunately, in this situation, the proposed algorithm becomes either blocking or degraded. So D-TDMA's theoretical communication potential depends directly on the available resources. In vehicular environments, where traffic congestion causes a high density of node and information, this aspect becomes a critical weakness to be further analysed, especially in case of safety applications.

MS-Aloha shares the base concept with D-TDMA but seems to have reasonably solved most of its open issues.

MS-ALOHA: A POSSIBLE SOLUTION

Slotted solutions need to address and solve tricky issues in order to become suitable for VANETs. In fact, the signalling strategy must satisfy several mutually hindering features, hopefully optimally trading-off among them.

For this reason, the MS-Aloha protocol, the synchronous VANET protocol which will here be discussed, was defined in several steps. Moving the steps from a previous protocol called RR-Aloha, suitable only for fixed networks (first proposed in (Borgonovo, et. al., 2002)), it was customised for VANET by the RR-Aloha+ extensions (presented in (Cozzetti, et. al., 2009)) which, themselves, represented a novel protocol.

Afterwards, a new version called Mobile Slotted Aloha (MS-Aloha) solved some open issues on scalability, basically facilitating slot re-use and management of mobility (Scopigno, et. al., 2009). Some further features (cross-layer thresholds, pre-emption) were defined in (Scopigno, et. al., 2010) and successive papers.

Here, the most mature version of the protocol will be discussed.

Signalling Rationale and Overview

Before entering into the details of the MS-Aloha frame structure, its signalling will first be discussed. The only subtended concept, here shortly premised, is that a periodic frame structure is supposed to exist, including a certain number of fixed-length slots which represent distinct channels in the wireless medium. The frame is absolutely synchronised by a Coordinated Universal Time (UTC) so that any node which has the same UTC perfectly knows the current position in the frame, independently of received frames.

UTC can be ensured – and is indeed supposed to be provided by – a Global Navigation Satellite System (GNSS) such as GPS: in fact, a GPS receiver is supposed to be on-board, independently of VANET transceiver). Solutions for missing GPS signals are left for future study and introduced in the conclusions.

Hence a *periodic frame structure* and the *absolute synchronization* will be the only two *initial hypotheses* on which the following discussion about MS-Aloha relies on.

A slotted protocol, under a purely conceptual perspective, does not intrinsically subtend the concept of resource reservation and can be either connectionless or connection-oriented. However, the former case would fall in the class of collision avoidance and/or collision detection protocols (as in the case of slotted Aloha – Roberts '72), so it

would not represent a true alternative to IEEE 802.11p.

Conversely, in order to ensure a deterministic behaviour of the MAC, the slotted protocol needs to be connection-oriented. This is the case of MS-Aloha.

Under the hypothesis of a connection-oriented paradigm, the simplest solution is constituted by a protocol involving the classical connection set-up phases of a telephone call, with a reservation request and confirmation, followed by data exchanges up to the final tear-down call.

Unfortunately, this paradigm cannot be applied to VANET for several reasons.

First of all, the approach cannot be easily managed with broadcast transmissions, because reservations cannot be confirmed by all the nodes. Additionally, the hidden station problem holds and the delivery rate of messages in wireless networks (and in particular in VANETs) is affected by strong losses. Consequently, *one-shot* reservation requests and acknowledgments are likely to be lost. Moreover, some tear-down messages might not be received and the corresponding calls would be in a ghost state (until timing-out). Finally, strong mobility and varying channel conditions hamper the possibility of a node knowing the reservations which apply to all the nodes in its radio range.

For these reasons, MS-Aloha adopts the following different approach:

1. All the nodes which are connected continuously (while transmitting their packet) implicitly attempt to reserve the same slot in next frame.

2. All the nodes append a description about the state of all the slots, based on the information either directly or indirectly received.

The first rule is meant to face the issues rising from mobility and packet losses. The second one is aimed at preventing the hidden terminal problem. It is worth highlighting that, as plenty of simulations show, the continuous announcement of channel state in the *FI*s by all the nodes, also improves the stability of VANETs, against phenomena (like fading) which may cause significant message loss.

From a practical point of view, this requires that all the nodes which have already been allocated a slot, broadcast back their view of the frame, specifying for each slot the following information: *(i)* if it is free, busy or affected by collisions; *(ii)* what node is using it and *(iii)* if such information is directly sensed or not.

These announcements are carried by a dedicated trailer of the slots (called "Frame Information" *FI*) which needs to include as many sub-ðelds *FIj* as *N*, the number of slots (*FI0, FI1, ... FIN − 1*).

This may potentially affect the efficiency by causing heavy overheads. However, MS-Aloha manages this potential problem by adopting some tricks which will be discussed while describing MS-Aloha's frame format.

Coming to details, three simple rules have been defined in MS-Aloha.

- **Slot State Announcements**: MS-Aloha has three possible state conditions for a slot: busy, free and collision (without reservation). In each *FIj* subfield the transmitting node has two bits to specify what the STATE of the slot it can perceive is. Said state is based on *(i)* direct sensing and *(ii)* by the other *FI*s received.

  Hidden terminals are detected in the following way: if *A* receives from *B* but not from *C* (i.e. *C* is a hidden terminal for *A*) it knows about *C* from the subfield *FIA* of the *FI* received from *B*.

  For the sake of precision, the following rules are followed by each node while generating their *FI* information:

  1. If all the *FIj* received and direct sensing of slot *j* converge to the *free* state, the slot is announced *free*.
  2. Similarly, if all the *FIj* received and direct sensing of slot *j* converge to its being occupied by node *M* or being

free, then the *busy* state by node *M* is confirmed and forwarded.

  3. In all the other cases, a *collision* is notified in *FIj*.

- **Memory Refresh:** The information related to slot *j's* status must be refreshed to avoid the persistence of expired information. A simple counteraction is that each node flushes the information on slot *j* when the frame has reached the *j* position again (the information on slot allocation expires after a frame-time). Simulations show that this memory refresh-time is long enough to avoid propagating insubstantial information and provides an effective knowledge of wireless channel state.

- **Reservation Procedure:** If a terminal M needs to transmit, it can try to gain access to a slot perceived *free* after sensing the channel for a whole frame-duration – again both by direct sensing and by the aggregation of the information received in the *FI*s. The access attempt is carried out simply by sending a broadcast frame on the chosen slot (say slot *j*). The reservation is confirmed if all the nodes which are in its radio range confirm it in their *FI*s. Notably, due to the rationale behind *FI* aggregation, the received *FI* delivers acknowledgements spanning more than one hop (at least two hops).

Physical Layer, Frame Format and Label Swapping

Following the same approach of its protocol predecessors (RR-Aloha and RR-Aloha+), the physical layer is not speciðed in MS-Aloha: any encoding suitable for the wireless channel could be adoptcd.

In order to facilitate the *VANET MAC Requirement* 11) (backward compatibility), MS-Aloha is supposed to exploit the same physical layer (i.e. line encoding) as 802.11p: this also has the beneficial effect of facilitating comparative analyses between the two.

In principle, the choice of using the same physical layer as 802.11p also allows the coexistence of MS-Aloha and CSMA/CA: the two MACs could drive the same radio block and be housed on different channels (or time-multiplexed in the same way as EDCA and HCCA).

Finally, 802.11p provides PLCP, an effective protocol for frame detection and its correct alignment: MS-Aloha needs it because it represents a tool to recover from imperfect synchronization (caused by propagation delays) which can grow as much as the value specified for *guard-time* (see below).

Concerning the frame format, in a top-down perspective, each slot (as shown in Figure 1) is expected to house 3 sets of information:

- A guard-time *Tg;*
- Physical layer information (*Layer-1*), carrying MAC layer *(Layer-2)* information inside;

- The trailer called *FI* – containing as many *FIj* subfields as the number of overall slots in the frame.

The guard-time *Tg* is meant to manage propagation and computational time (it is typically set at 1 μs). The guard-time, together with the initial hypothesis on absolute synchronization, is meant to counter disruptive effects of delays on the critical time-structure.

In fact, UTC prevents nodes from deriving synchronization from the received frames because this would lead to cumulative delays and circular inconsistencies (Scopigno, et. al., 2009).

The guard time is meant instead to nullify the effects of delays coming from propagations as well as possible minor errors in synchronization (for instance during hold-on periods due to missing GPS signals).

Layer-1 is the same as for 802.11p (including both PMD and PLCP sub-layers).

The nested *Layer-2* information corresponds to the classical 802.11p frame: in MS-Aloha literature

Figure 1. MS-Aloha frame format. From top to bottom: (i) overall MS-Aloha Frame, with N slots (from 0 to N-1), FI trailer and guard-time Tg; (ii) FIj subfields contained in each FI; (iii) the subfield involved in each FIj.

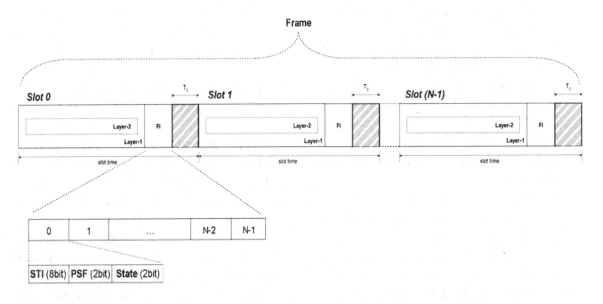

the Layer-2 format is supposed to be exactly the same of 802.11p, but, for sake of precision, the fields MAC Address3 and MAC Address4 could be erased, leading to a saving of 12 Bytes.

The only modification required to either *Layer 1* or *Layer 2*, is the introduction of a field to provide a short (8-bit) identifier (*STI*) of the node, somehow associated to its MAC address, to be used inside the *FI* instead of MAC addresses (typically 48-bit long).

This approach was proposed to achieve a trade-off between the need of a univocal identifier and the need for a reduced frame size. In fact, if one frame has N slots and the *STI* label is k-bit long, this implies that in *each FI*, more than $k \times N$ bits are required; consequently, in a full MS-Aloha period, more than $k \times N^2$ bits constitute an added overhead, required just to identify nodes in the *FI*s.

Wrapping-up: Layer-1/Layer-2 are backward compatible to 802.11p with the exception of the *STI* 8-bit-long field, added to shortly identify the node.

FI, conceptually is a PLCP function. In MS-Aloha, for the sake of simplicity, it is put outside the MAC layer and appended to it.

The *FI*, which includes as many *FIj* sub-ðelds as the number of slots, each describe how the slot is perceived by using the following 12 bits:

- *STI* (source temporary identifier) - 8 bit: the short identifier of the node whose transmission has been received by node M on slot j (it will be further discussed later on). *STI is used only to identify collisions* following MS-Aloha signalling rationale. The *STI* is empty if the slot is unused.
- *PSF* (priority status field) - 2 bit: field indicating the priority of data transmitted in the slot. It is used for pre-emption mechanisms.
- *STATE*: a 2-bit long field indicating jth-slot state in M's view: [00] = *free*; [01] = *busy*; [10] = *collision*.

Consequently, each *FI* is 12 X N-bit long (N is the number of slot in a MS-Aloha period).

This implies that, in order to achieve an acceptable latency and efficiency, the number of slots must be kept under control. For instance, a frame length of 100 ms would be compatible with the use of 224 slots each of less than 500 µs: at a line rate of 12 Mb/s, this would house a 200-byte payload (and the required *FI*s).

These are the settings typically used in literature.

Management of Source Temporary Identifiers: Label Swapping

So far, the only thing which has not been explained yet is how to use the field called *STI* (Short Temporary Identifier).

The *STI* was proposed to achieve a trade-off between the need to identify each node in the *FI*s and the need to have a reduced frame size. However, the 8 bits of *STI* only allow 256 nodes to be distinguished, which can appear to be limiting in an urban context.

However, it is important to add that if two nodes choose the same *STI*, there will be no problem as long as they do not attempt to access the same slot. In fact, *STI* is meant only to determine collisions by the *FI* analysis. If two nodes use the same STI in distinct slots, the identification flow is still ensured by the couple "slot number + *STI*".

Consequently, the only ambiguous case happens for the statistically not-negligible event of two nodes randomly selecting the same STI and free slot. In that case the *STI* would not identify the collision as it is required to do.

The threat was finally solved by introducing a two-way handshake-like *STI* swapping (depicted in Figure 2.), which is specifically meant to resolve the case of two nodes using the same label in the same slot.

In the proposed "label swapping" approach, MS-Aloha does the following:

- It exploits the unused information of the source MAC address to resolve different nodes. Notably, the solutions must consider that a MAC address – for instance the MAC of node A using a given slot *j* - spans only one hop. At the second hop, in fact, only the information summarised by *FI* is broadcasted (this contains A's *STI*, not its MAC addresses).

- Every time a node receives a frame directly from node A, it computes a new *STI'*A, based on some hashing between *STI*A and *MAC*A. All the nodes compute the same *STI'*A. The other nodes just receive *STI'*A and, therefore, no ambiguities take place.

- *STI* assumes a "temporary duration" and *STIs* are swapped at each *(i)* transmission by A and *(ii)* acknowledgment(s) by the others. Consequently, also *STI* are refreshed accordingly to the memory refresh.

In greater detail, two nodes A and B might choose the same *STI*A = *STI*B, but the nodes receiving such information (say node C, D and E) will not just propagate the *STIs* in their *FIs*, but will generate new 8-bit *STI* label, based on a hashing of the STI and of the MAC source (respectively *STI'*A, *STI'*B). C, D and E will compute the same *STI'*A, *STI'*B because they have also received A's and B's MACs.

When the *FI's* are received by node A or by a node one-hop far from A, they will be able to repeat the same hash operation and understand if the *STI* indicates the same node or not (in this case a collision must be announced).

There is still a non-null probability that also the result of the hash function is the same (so that also *STI'*A = *STI'*B), however the process is further carried on in the same way and node A (resp. B). When transmitting in next period, it will indicate its *STI''*A, and so on. This would sooner or later solve this quite unlikely event.

The chosen memory refresh time prevents any potential additional issues, as flushing the memory after an MS-Aloha period synchronizes the label swapping process.

Pre-Emption and Service-Oriented Multiplexing

MS-Aloha is built on the top of a connection-oriented approach. As such, it is potentially exposed to the problem of slot exhaustion, which would cause a blocking state: this represents a particularly harmful situation for the protocol and represents a danger for safety applications carried over it.

In connectionless approaches these cases are bounded by priority (as in the case of EDCA for 802.11p). Two possible solutions may help in connection-oriented protocols:

- An improved resource re-use;
- The introduction of mechanisms to prioritize safety traffic, even with pre-emption over already established and running connections.

Figure 2. Two-way handshake of STI label against an STI shortage

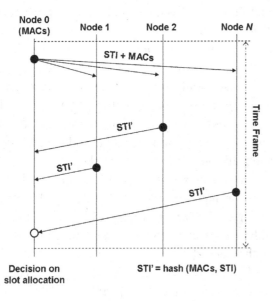

Improved slot re-use will be discussed in the next paragraphs for MS-Aloha, while pre-emption is briefly introduces here. In order to enable pre-emption decisions, each node is required to know the priority of running connections and required reservations. For this purpose, each *FIj* subfield in each *FI* contains not only the indication of the slot state and of the node using it (if it is engaged), but also the priority indication in the Priority State Field (*PSF*). Being 2 bits long, *PSF* admits 4 possible states, in decreasing order of priority: [00, 01, 10, 11].

The way these *PSF* should be used is not specified and different options could be adopted. Here, a possible solution is proposed.

- *PSF* = [00] - *Emergency*. This is for emergency vehicle only. Even if all the slots are engaged, an emergency channel can be set-up by emergency vehicles rejecting any other lower-priority connections.
- *PSF* = [01] - *Safety*. This is for ordinary safety communications among vehicles. Each node may be supposed to have a safety connection set-up while active. Each node can occupy only one slot with *safety* priority.
- *PSF* = [10] – *Auxiliary* and *PSF* = [11] – *Entertainment*. The last two configurations are for statistical multiplexing. As a matter of fact, any connection-oriented approach may cause some stiffness in resource re-use. However, this does not happen if any low-priority connections (*auxiliary* and/ or *entertainment*) can dynamically reserve free slots and, conversely, higher priority connections can force them to leave. Each node can be assigned more than one slot only in the *entertainment* class of priority.

The proposed pre-emption solution would offer the benefit of coupling emergency needs with safety priority and multiplexing, setting up reasonable Service Level Agreement (SLA) scenario for all the services carried by VANET.

Improved Spatial Multiplexing and Soft-Clustering: 2SM

Conceptually, MS-Aloha deployment can still be hindered by its *scalability* in terms of its number of available free slots.

The available slots can be starved primarily by the number of stations attempting to access the channel, but also by a faulty mechanism in the propagation of the channel state as, for example, spanning more than required and consequently blocking more slots than required. In fact, an unconstrained multi-hop announcement of the channel state might extend the slot reservation beyond the bounds of wireless coverage, causing resource waste.

Effectively, so far, MS-Aloha does not foresee a limit to the number of hops over which the information must be forwarded. As a consequence, this can cause the propagation of over multiple hops, unless the *FI* is refreshed; a slot can be managed as *busy* even if it is not in that area, leading to dangerous resource exhaustion.

An opportune protocol extension (*2-hop Spatial Multiplexing* - 2SM) was introduced to assure that the information on channel state (*FI*) is not forwarded more than two hops from the transmitting node. While still avoiding the problem of hidden terminals, this approach keeps a slot busy only where strictly required. This behaviour requires preserving within the *FI* some kind of information about the number of hops which have already been covered.

For this purpose, a free configuration of the STATE bits in the *FI* was used. The STATE field was re-defined in the following way: [00] = *free*; [01] = *busy*; [10] = *collision*, [11] = *2 hops reached*.

In practice, the STATE *2 hops reached* is transmitted by a node in its *FI* when a slot is perceived busy but it is not directly sensed. Conversely, when a node receives STATE = *2 hops reached*, it means that this information third hop has already covered three hops[1]. In this case, the receiving node is required to consider the slot engaged but to propagate the information of *free* slot.

The algorithm of usage of STATE field is called (*2SM*) and is summarised in Figure 3.

Notably, an efficient slot assignment can save precious resources, potentially critical to assure an effective reaction to collision under mobility conditions. Simulations show that MS-Aloha with 2SM provides the following benefits:

- It improves slot re-use and is very effective since it optimizes resource exploitation without affecting protocol resilience.
- It manages slot re-use according to a power-aware paradigm. More explicitly, some protocols (such as STDMA) propose that a slot can be re-used, based on geometrical considerations. Unfortunately, this is hard-

ly manageable because: *(i)* it requires that all the nodes continuously forward heavy protocol overhead to describe the position of all the other nodes; *(ii)* nodes are mobile and dynamic ; *(iii)* the position itself is not meaningful. In fact, due to obstructions (buildings, corners, etc.), heavier interferences may come from farther nodes.

Conversely, 2SN makes decisions based on the received messages; this introduces a power-aware approach which is further exploited by cross-layer thresholds.

- This approach introduces the effect of *soft-clustering*. While some approaches define clustering and, based on this, determine features (such as slot re-use), here, the opposite effect takes place. In fact, 2SM solves the slot re-use issue and induces some clustering. As depicted in Figure 4,

Figure 3. The flowchart diagram of slot state propagation with the 2-hop Spatial Multiplexing feature (2SM)

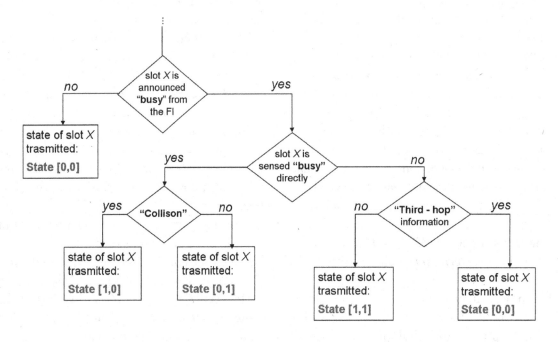

given a certain slot (22 and 33 in the pictures), it can be simultaneously used more than once. So nodes which see it at one hop (orange), at two hops (green) or free (white) constitute themselves clusters. But they are "soft" in that for different slots the clusters have different aspects (the two pictures in Figure 4 refer to the same simulation time).

Cross-Layer Thresholds: 2SMt

Space efficiency is intuitively linked to slot-reuse. Slot selection is a probabilistic event so it is not deterministic that a slot is reused at the minimum possible distance. However, with a large number of nodes and longer periods (and also considering the effects of mobility) the minimum distance occurring between nodes using the same slot on a straight road is likely to be very close to three times the radio range of a node, due to 2SM mechanism.

On the other hand, 2SM introduced the concept of slot re-use based on received power. Based on this idea, MS-Aloha was further extended to force the increase of slot reuse (Scopigno, et. al., 2010), acting on the area where a slot is announced as *busy*.

It is, in fact, possible to introduce adequate thresholds to obtain bigger resource exploitation.

For this purpose, MS-Aloha adds a logical threshold (*Thr*) at the MAC layer; only frames received with a power higher than *Thr* are considered by its MAC. On the contrary, frames with lower power may be received by the upper layer (depending on SNR as usual) but do not contribute to the *FI* of the node (as if they were not received). In this way, the width of soft-clusters is reduced, causing a reduction in the minimum possible distance required to use the same slot. This solution slightly modifies *2 Hop Spatial Multiplexing* (2SM) into *2 Hop Spatial Multiplexing with Thresholds* 2SMt.

Conceptually, 2SMt falls in the area of cross-layer PHY-MAC mechanisms, because it drives MAC decisions based on physical layer parameters.

If excessively prominent, cross-layer thresholds are likely to increase interference (collisions) among nodes using the same slots. In fact, this feature has a lower PDR at the longer distance (around ~150 meters), but unchanged performance in the neighbourhood of the transmission (the main zone of interest). This will be discussed in the section on quantitative results.

Figure 4. Slot re-use in MS-Aloha simulations involving 2SM functionality. The number indicates the slot, the red circle the nodes using it, the orange nodes are those 1-hop away, the green nodes are 2 hops away, the white nodes do not know about the given slot. The grey blocks induce extra attenuation at the corners.

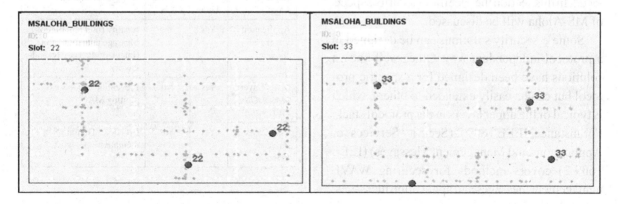

Importantly, given a mechanism with thresholds, it is also possible to make spatial re-use dynamic; for instance, several thresholds can be pre-defined and each station, based on network state (such as network congestion), can change – dynamically and in a distributed way – its thresholds to facilitate slot re-use. This is a further step which is currently under study and is already showing additional advantages.

Perspectives for e-Security and DOS Prevention

The implications of security in vehicular ad-hoc networks are huge for several reasons and, basically, for human safety, although the complex and highly dynamic setting makes the overall problem very challenging.

In VANETs, possible vulnerabilities affecting any node in the network can dramatically lower the security level of the whole network; moreover, the typical characteristics of the wireless medium hamper the effectiveness of the controls of communications.

As a result, security can be managed at different layers of the network stack (e.g. MAC-level WPA2 encryption and authentication, network-layer IPsec, transport-layer TLS, SSL), reflecting the more generally accepted argument that security is a cross-layer topic (Pilosu, et. al., 2010). The most suitable solution not only depends on the characteristics of the application being protected, but also on the kind of the attack which has to be faced. In this section the specific e-security aspects of MS-Aloha will be discussed.

Some e-security solutions can be designed in a protocol independent way. Other well-known solutions have been designed for a specific protocol but can be easily extended to others, which is typical of the upper layers in the protocol stack. For instance, IEEE 1609.2 (Security Services for Applications and Management Messages) (IEEE 1609.2) covers methods for securing WAVE management messages and application messages.

Despite what has been defined for the IEEE 1609 (IEEE 1609 WAVE Standards) stack, they may also apply to slotted approaches, as in case of the Public-Key Infrastructure.

Finally, there are mechanisms which apply only to a specific protocol. This is the case of some controls which are enabled only by MS-Aloha and address the prevention of Denial-of-Service (DoS) attacks by means of consistency checks. This plethora of results is widely discussed in the literature (Pilosu, et. al., 2010); here the unique aspects related to MS-Aloha MAC will be discussed.

The MAC layer of VANETs can be objective for Denial-of-Service (DoS) attacks (pure jamming approaches are neglected because they destroy every kind of radio communications).

For instance, CSMA/CA implies that all the nodes are fair in computing collision-avoidance waiting times. If any station did not follow the CSMA/CA rules, it could gain a higher bandwidth than it should (*unfairness*) or prevent transmission by the other nodes (*pure DoS*). Unfortunately, such behaviours are difficult to discover in CSMA/CA, because each node cannot go beyond its own view of the channel and cannot infer possible violations to the CSMA/CA rules.

In MS-Aloha, violations are more evident and the attack can be twofold: *(i)* a node can either

Table 1. E-security aspects involved by CSMA/CA and MS-Aloha

Logical Layer	MS-Aloha	CSMA/CA	Mechanisms
Application Layer *Full Security*	Yes	Yes	Identity (non repudiation) Message authentication (integrity) Privacy (pseudonym)
MAC Layer *MAC/DOS Prevention*	Yes	No	Prevention of DoS exploiting MAC
Link Layer *Baseline Privacy*	Yes	Yes	Broadcast Domain Segmentation

attempt to access more slots than it should (*unfairness*) or *(ii)* cause logical collisions that block any transmissions (*pure DoS*).

Fortunately, MS-Aloha possesses plenty of redundant information. For each slot, every node can receive up to *N* (number of slots per frame) STATE indications. In the typical configuration, every frame has 224 slots, resulting in redundant information about the channel STATE. So, conceptually, it is possible to leverage on such redundant information to identify and manage nodes trying to disturb/disrupt the communication with fake information about the slot occupation.

The underlying hypothesis is that two nodes that are near each other perceive the channel almost in an identical way. For instance, in an area of about 80 meters around the node (where the Packet Delivery Rate is still about 90%), the involved nodes should receive the same channel status. From this starting point, it is possible to infer possible inconsistent slot allocations. Reversely, depending on the way *FI*s are modified, two kinds of attacks can be driven: *(i)* the *FI*s sent are completely random, inconsistent with the other ones; *(ii)* the *FI*s are generated starting from a genuine *FI*, changing only some fields. Intuitively, the more an *FI* is incoherent with the others, the easier it is to identify malicious behaviour.

An example is shown in Figure 5. Node D wants to unfairly control the full channel so it announces an *FI* containing the sequence "*D,D,D,D,D*", after spoofing node D address and *STI*. In this way the full channel is first freed to then be maliciously engaged by D.

The spatial and temporal correlation of the received *FI* can be exploited to prevent such cases by evaluating the dependability of the *FI* information received.

Figure 5. Example of DoS attack in MS-Aloha

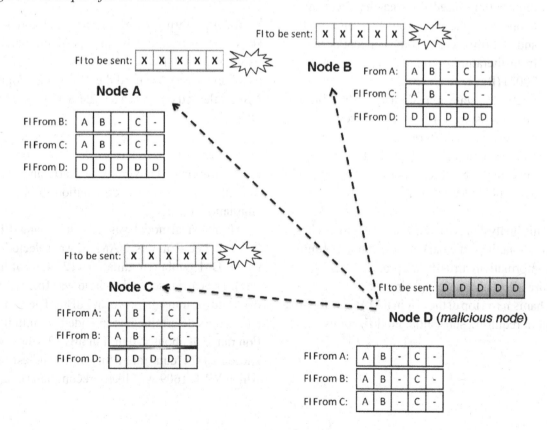

For example, if a single node signals a collision in slot "*i*", MS-Aloha can implement proper controls and discard the notification. In other words, the collision can be validated only if other nodes confirm it by direct sensing.

Additionally, correlation among *FI*s can also take place in the time domain.

The logic can be further refined and summarized in the following way:

- Each *FI* subfield can be evaluated separately;
- Any *FI* information can be "accepted" only if confirmed by a given number of nodes; this also prevents problems due to the sudden appearance of a node, as, for example, a car exiting a garage. Such a node is supposed to accept the FI status of the other nodes (outside the garage) and not disrupt the overall current slot assignment. The correlation can be enriched by weighting information based on what has been announced in the past from the same node and slot (this recalls some concept derived from literature on reputation (Mui, et. al., 2002) (Raya, et. al., 2005);
- Each slot state transition (*e.g.* free-busy, busy-collision, ...) can be assigned a specific evaluation criterion. Here, the novelty and the potential is high and is enabled once more by the redundant information available in MS-Aloha.

This analysis reveals that slotted approaches (MS-Aloha, in particular) can exploit the redundant information carried by the protocol itself. This feature allows MS-Aloha to implement security mechanisms on top of the original MAC protocol, without requiring substantial modifications.

QUANTITATIVE EVALUATION BY SIMULATIONS

This section provides an overview of some simulation results, which are meant to show quantitative figures to better understand the performance achievable by MS-Aloha. In order to gain a more effective understanding of the possible improvements coming from the slotted approach, a comparison analysis between CSMA/CA and MS-Aloha is also carried out.

Results show that TDMA (MS-Aloha in particular) replaces the nondeterministic behaviour of CSMA/CA with a delay-bounded channel access mechanism, which also grants an *a priori* known bandwidth to devices.

Scenarios are defined to test both the CSMA/CA and MS-Aloha protocol under realistic and challenging conditions.

Scenarios and Tools

Protocol performance assessment and comparisons were carried out by means of simulations using the well-known NS-2 (NS-2 Network Simulator Tool). We used the 2.33 version of the NS-2, released on March 31, 2008, to implement all agents.

At physical level, the WiFi model developed by Mercedes-Benz Research and Development North America - University of Karlsruhe (TH), proved to be the best code solution to improve simulation accuracy.

The physical model was set up following IEEE 802.11p specifications. QAM 1/2 was selected for the OFDM symbol modulation (12 Mbps of line rate). The carrier sense threshold was fixed at -96 dBm and the transmit power at 7 dBm. These three parameters determined an intended communication range of about 150 m. Finally, 12 Mbps was chosen as the data rate (this is the highest rate which IEEE 1609 will likely recommend).

Concerning the fading model, Nakagami *m*-distribution (Nakagami, 1960) is commonly considered a good model of the fast fading phenomena; Nakagami's distribution is determined by two parameters, namely Ω and *m*, where Ω is the average power received at any distance *d* from the transmitter and *m* is the Nakagami fading parameter, determining the probability density function's shape (the greater the value for *m*, the more negligible fast fading becomes. *m*=1 turns the Nakagami distribution into a Rayleigh). The simulations here presented borrowed Nakagami's settings where Ω was set as d^2; $m = 3$ for values of $d < 50$ meters (line-of-sight conditions), $m = 1.5$ for middle-range distances and 1 for higher distances ($d > 150$ meters).

The frame structure of MS-Aloha was defined considering a frequency of 10 Hz and a payload of 200 bytes (typical of safety services). Hence, the frame was set for 224 slots, each 446 µs long, resulting in an overall frame duration of 100 ms.

The configuration trace files (mobility, position) were obtained by SUMO (Sub-Urban Mobility Simulator) software.

Only two scenarios are considered here, each with two different goals:

- In the first scenario, for overhead analysis, we simulated two straight roads, each containing two lanes, as shown in Figure 6 (a). The overall number of nodes was fixed at 200 because in this scenario it is easier to compute the overhead of MS-Aloha as each node can be assigned up to 2 or 1 of the 224 slots.

In this situation, the packet generation rate varies in [5, 50] Hz. Both unicast and broadcast traffic is simulated. In the case of unicast, the nodes communicate in couples, with a peer-to-peer distance of about 60 meters. The simulation lasted 50 seconds.

This scenario is exploited to evaluate temporal efficiency (analysis of protocol overheads).

- The second scenario is a bi-dimensional grid topology (Figure 6 (b)). In this case, only broadcast frames are sent at a 10Hz rate. The grid is made up of 5 x 5 blocks, each 150 meter long, with double lane roads (the area is wide 750m). The simulation consisted of 450 nodes moving at 50 km/h in opposite directions. This choice represents a congested urban scenario to analyse the protocol's behaviours. In order to congest the network as much as possible, attenuation by blocks and building, was neglected (Scopigno, et. al., 2010). This scenario is exploited to evaluate spa-

Figure 6. Simulation scenarios for (a) time efficiency in unicast and broadcast, (b) space efficiency in a crowded urban area 750m wide and 450 nodes (224 slots): PDR and slot re-use are computed.

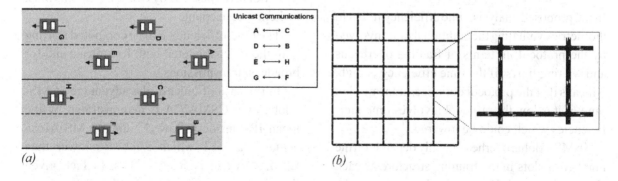

(a)   *(b)*

tial efficiency in terms of slot reuse or, in other words, spatial multiplexing.

The simulations are carried out using the same settings for CSMA/CA and MS-Aloha: separate analyses are meant to discuss the specific characteristics of each of them while a common final discussion is aimed at highlighting the weaknesses and points of strength of the proposed MAC protocols. The selected scenarios help stress the network communications thanks to the involved high density and mobility. In order to quantify results and enable an objective comparative analysis, the following metrics are used:

- **PDR:** Packet Delivery Rate is the function that shows how much a node is likely to receive a packet varying the distance from the transmitting node;
- **IPT:** Inter-Packet Time represents the time between two consecutive correct transmissions. It is computed as the average across all flows and the whole simulation;
- **Mean Collisions:** the average number of collisions over the whole simulation and all the nodes;
- **Slot Re-Use** is number of times a slot is simultaneously used by different nodes.

The last two metrics are suitable only for the slotted protocol.

Analysis of Time Overheads

In the proposed analysis, time efficiency refers to the metric evaluating the additional time involved by the protocol, in terms of framing overheads and waiting times. If the time efficiency is high, it means that the protocol optimizes transmission time; if it is low the protocol involves time inefficiencies which could be lowered.

In MS-Aloha, overhead mainly depends on the number of slots in the framing structure as each slot requires a subfield in the *FI* to announce the state of all the slots. For the slotted protocol, this value is fixed.

Conversely, in CSMA/CA, the main time overhead is due to its collision avoidance mechanism, which implies probabilistic waiting times. Notably, in CSMA/CA, the waiting time differs for unicast and broadcast services as the former preserves an exponential back-off (which prevents collision by widening waiting time), while the latter has fixed contention windows and a higher percentage of collisions (which must be accounted in the computation).

For this reason, the two protocols are compared by means of distinct simulations respectively analysing broadcast and unicast transmissions.

The case of unicast is conceptually more precise because it accounts also for collisions which are counteracted by retransmissions (which are activated thanks to the check on frame acknowledgments) and consequent exponential backoff. On the other hand, these measures affect time efficiency, causing delays.

In the case of unicast for CSMA/CA, the *interpacket time* (IPT) can be computed at the receiver side based on the packets which have been correctly received.

The case of broadcast is somehow less precise because statistics can be extracted only at the transmitter side and need to be calculated based on the collision rate considering the mean packet-delivery rate (PDR) at receiver side. Consequently, the metric (and the comparison) becomes unfair because while collisions are mostly prevented by MS-Aloha, they are not by CSMA/CA. This must be kept into account.

The time-efficiency will be computed starting with the IPT parameter, both for unicast and for broadcast transmissions.

In the case of unicast, the advantage of MS-Aloha over CSMA/CA is demonstrated by the mean IPT inside a flow (Figure 7). MS-Aloha achieves an IPT which is always lower than CSMA/CA and is fixed at 0.1s. In fact, given the periodic frame structure with a 0.1s period, each station can only transmit one packet per 0.1s (despite the growing application rate, the connection-oriented approach provides stability to the network). Notably, MS-Aloha slot re-use is disabled and, for simplicity, each station is assigned a predefined slot. Conversely, the slot re-use enabled by MS-Aloha (2MS, 2MSt), in general, can further improve the protocol's IPT.

The performance of MS-Aloha is highlighted by channel saturation. While the slotted approach can guarantee the same IPT regardless of the application rate, in CSMA/CA, a heavy saturation causes more collisions and retransmissions and longer contention windows, due to back-off. This phenomenon also affects the mean IPT, which increases as high as 0.7 seconds, which is 7 times the value of MS-Aloha.

Finally, while the minimum IPT of CSMA/CA may lower, this value is not deterministic and can be hardly reached, as demonstrated by the mean values.

Unlike MS-Aloha, in CSMA/CA, the IPT varies with the application rate. Intuitively, the region

of "saturation" should be specifically addressed, since it is the operating area which is expected to be used the most and is critical for transmission. Saturation is demonstrated by an increasing IPT despite the increasing application rate (so it starts at about 10 Hz with 200 nodes).

As anticipated, broadcast behaves differently (Figure 8) and saturation is reached later due to lack of retransmissions. The advantages of the slotted solution are initially less prominent. Conversely, when the IPT of CSMA/CA starts to grow, it diverges more severely.

However, in this case, collisions are neither considered nor prevented by any collision avoidance in CSMA/CA, while they do not take place in MS-Aloha. As a result, the IPT figures should be refined.

Following the ideas of (Scopigno, et. al., 2010), based on the IPT, a parameter of efficiency η can be derived, considering also all the protocol overheads. Roughly:

Figure 7. Unicast IPT with 200 nodes and growing application rate

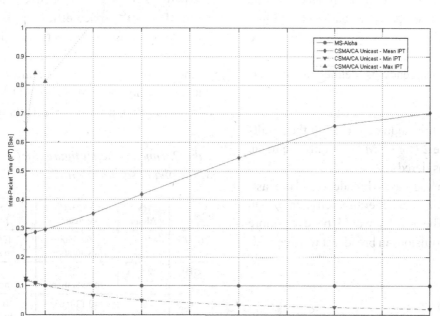

Figure 8. Broadcast IPT with 200 nodes and growing application rate

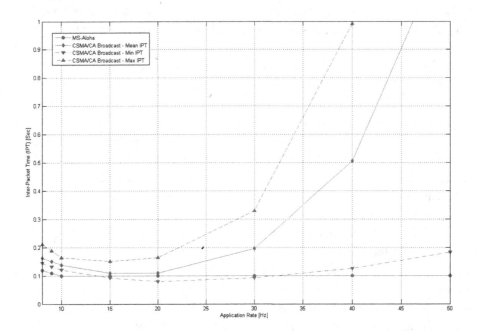

- The overhead OH is given by the difference between the overall transmission time in the air, which is basically given by the IPT divided by the number of nodes N, and the time Pt strictly required to transmit the payload (payload-length divided by line rate); in the proposed scenario, $Pt = 133\,\mu s$;
- The overhead ratio OHr can be computed as the ratio $OHr = (IPT - Pt)/Pt$;
- Finally, efficiency is defined as $\eta = 1/(1+OHr)$.

Altogether this approach leads to the results shown in Table 2 (for CSMA/CA only the mean values are considered):

All in all, in both cases (broadcast and unicast) MS-Aloha achieves a better time-efficiency than CSMA/CA. The results would be even more significant if collisions in broadcast were considered.

Analysis of Spatial-Multiplexing

Moving on to the space domain, the first step required to evaluate space efficiency for different protocols is to define common metrics able to fairly compare the protocols' respective performances.

In MS-Aloha, space efficiency is intuitively linked to slot-reuse. Slot selection is a probabilistic event so it is not deterministic that a slot is reused at the minimum possible distance. However, with larger numbers of nodes and longer periods, taking into account the effects of mobility,

Table 2. Time-efficiency figures for CSMA/CA and MS-Aloha in scenario (a).

	MS-Aloha	CSMA/CA unicast	CSMA/CA broadcast
IPT/N	446 µs	1000-3500+ in saturation	1000-5000+ in saturation
OHr	2.35	6.5-25+ in saturation	6.5-36+ in saturation
η	~0.3	<0.13-0.03 in saturation	<0.13-0-0.28 in saturation

Table 3. Slot re-use in MS-Aloha

Time		Nodes without slot	Unused	Once	Twice	Three times	Four times	Five times	Six times
1	No Thr	65	5	106	71	33	6	3	0
	-86 dBm	55	7	89	85	38	2	3	0
	-80 dBm	15	28	53	75	43	21	4	0
5	No Thr	67	3	124	54	29	11	3	1
	-86 dBm	37	1	109	56	42	14	1	1
	-80 dBm	7	13	63	77	58	12	1	0
15	No Thr	62	3	140	31	22	20	7	1
	-86 dBm	34	1	110	58	36	12	7	0
	-80 dBm	5	13	59	86	52	11	3	0
25	No Thr	79	3	148	36	25	10	5	2
	-86 dBm	44	0	127	44	26	22	4	1
	-80 dBm	3	13	59	85	50	16	1	0
50	No Thr	87	3	159	34	16	12	4	4
	-86 dBm	66	1	130	43	34	13	3	0
	-80 dBm	2	12	59	84	55	13	1	0

the maximum number of times which any slot is reused can provide an effective measurement of spatial multiplexing.

Fortunately, an alternative metric is suitable for both protocols. This metric is the Packet Delivery Ratio (*PDR*) which represents the percentage of nodes at a given distance that correctly receive a given packet. PDR is computed as the mean reception rate across all the transmissions. As such PDR varies in the range [0,1] and depends on distance; usually, it is a strictly decreasing function.

PDR is suitable for both CSMA/CA and MS-Aloha, in fact, spatial coordination works perfectly if the PDR is ideal, that is when packet loss is merely due to signal attenuation, not to collisions or interference.

The two proposed metrics are evaluated in the previously described grid scenario, where congestion is very likely to take place due to the heavy crowding. For the sake precision, car density is not constant. For example, the number of neighbours is greater in the centre of the grid.

Table 3 shows slot distribution at different times of the simulation in the urban scenario. For each time, the results are provided for the pure MS-Aloha (2SM) and for MS-Aloha 2SMt, with the cross-layer threshold set at -86 and -80dbm (for more details see the section: "Improved Spatial Multiplexing and Soft-Clustering: 2SM").

With pure MS-Aloha, only few nodes get blocked compared to the entire density (451 vehicles), which can be interpreted as an effect of slot exhaustion.

No node gets blocked with a threshold (-86dbm). With higher thresholds (-80dbm), collisions are mainly due to mobility (always fewer than 25 collisions) and slot reuse becomes heavier. This is confirmed, for instance, at 50 seconds, when there are 4 blocked nodes and 9 unused slots, which means that the nodes are only temporarily blocked due to collisions attributable to mobility.

With the 2SMt feature, the scenarios becomes so unloaded that, despite the statistical selection of free slots, a number of more than 10 are unused at any moment of the simulation. Conversely, this also means that the maximum number of slots being reused is not fully significant (it could be higher than measured).

The number of collisions in pure MS-Aloha and in MS-Aloha with 2SMt and threshold at -86dbm is somehow related to a critical slot distribution. Roughly speaking, the number of nodes without a slot corresponds to the nodes with a slot used 3-5 times the previous time, as confirmed by a step-by-step analysis. On the other hand, the threshold at -80dbm makes 3-time reuse more stable, also under mobility. This implies that there is margin for scalability (the number of slots used 3 times can grow).

Denser slot reuse is supposed to worsen the signal-to-noise ratio and, consequently, PDR at a given distance. A node is, in fact, likely to suffer some interference from one or more nodes using the same slot. This effect should become particularly relevant for a threshold fixed at least 10 times higher than the sensitivity. This is confirmed by PDR graphs. Figure 9 shows the results of pure MS-Aloha (-96dbm sensitivity) and MS-Aloha with 2SMt. They differ significantly only when the threshold is set at -80dbm. In this case, no node gets blocked and the PDR worsens, however, only at distances greater than 60m.

Figure 9 also shows that the PDR decreases with heavier slot reuse. This demonstrates that

MS-Aloha's performance is, in general, better than CSMA/CA's, thanks to its lower interference among simultaneous transmissions.

On the other hand, MS-Aloha coordinates channel access also over space, avoiding potential collisions in the same slots. This explains the higher PDR achieved by the slotted approach when compared to CSMA/CA. The latter cannot completely prevent collisions and the statistical waiting time is evenly distributed, without any policy based on position. This becomes particularly relevant in the urban grid scenario, where MS-Aloha outperforms CSMA/CA more markedly because of the bi-dimensional contribution to interference.

All in all, also in the spatial domain, MS-Aloha, thanks to the information carried in the FI trailers, can coordinate transmission more effectively than CSMA/CA, especially in congested urban scenarios.

Figure 9. PDR for CSMA/CA, MS-Aloha and MS-Aloha 2MSt

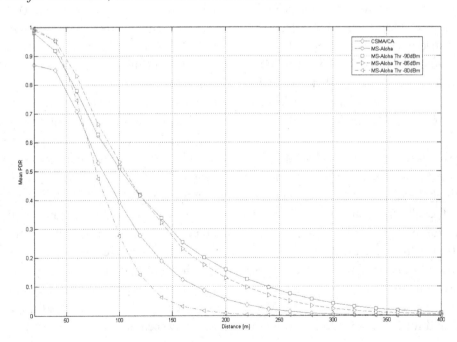

CONCLUSION: PROTOCOL RATING AND OPEN ISSUES

In order to wrap-up the discussion on slotted protocols, here we draw some encouraging conclusions about MS-Aloha, following the guideline of *VANET MAC Requirements* listed at the beginning of the chapter. Afterwards, the main open issues of the protocol will be introduced.

MS-Aloha and D-TDMA share a common idea on slot signaling and reservation, which employs multiple announcements based on a frame indicator to append all the slots and describe their state. These two actions are meant to prevent the hidden terminal issue. Additionally, MS-Aloha proposes specific solutions to improve scalability under several conditions.

So far, with reference to the numbering originally given to *VANET MAC Requirements,* it can be said that MS-Aloha is (8) deterministic (1) decentralized, and (2) immune to the hidden terminal problem posed by constructions.

It is also (3) reactive, thanks to the continuous FI announcement and periodic memory refresh, which works better than the set-up and tear-down mechanisms. Moreover, thanks to the *SM* approach, (4) scalability is achieved and, with *SMt*, (7) blocking states are prevented.

Moreover, MS-Aloha possesses a (6) preemption mechanism which manages priority in connections and some degree of statistical multiplexing of unused bandwidth for entertainment services, while remaining (10) fair.

Quite surprisingly, MS-Aloha showed (5) lower protocol overheads than CSMA/CA and achieved higher packet delivery rates (PDRs), thanks to its effective space-multiplexing. If the PDR data is coupled with the (12) acknowledgment available also for broadcast packets (from the *FI* received back), the (9) reliability of MS-Aloha can be definitely said to be higher than CSMA/CA.

Interestingly, MS-Aloha also revealed a nice potential to provide tools aimed at revealing and nullifying denial-of-service attacks.

Concerning the (11) compatibility to upcoming and/or incumbent solutions, it is only partial and it is limited to most of the IEEE 802.11p physical layer; this, however, could form the basis of building mixed-mode boxes, working in part with CSMA/CA and in part exploiting MS-Aloha MAC.

Finally, and this may be the main weakness of MS-Aloha, the protocol depends on an absolute synchronization, which needs to be shared among all the nodes in order to let them work. This constitutes one of the very initial hypotheses in MS-Aloha's construction and is supposed to be provided by an external source, such as a GPS (or other GNSS) receiver.

Since GPS cannot be guaranteed and may not be available in urban areas (due to urban canyons, for instance), it is necessary to find solutions that permit MS-Aloha to work also in the absence of GPS. Possible solutions include one or more of the following measures: *(i)* extension of guard time *Tg* in order to be compatible with the hold-on achievable by the on-board oscillator; *(ii)* slot selection policy; for instance, a node which is not GPS-looped can select a slot which is in between two *free* slots, so that its plesiochronous time cannot disturb any other slot; *(iii)* the use of previous solutions together with a scheme for distributed synchronization as available from literature to derive it from nodes which receive GPS (Ganeriwal, et. al., 2003) (Schenato, et. al., 2007); *(iv)* other solutions are theoretically possible, such as mechanisms to back-step to CSMA/CA or to use CSMA/CA and MS-Aloha on separate channels (they share a common physical layer) and to use only CSMA/CA when MS-Aloha is not available.

It is worth reminding readers that MS-Aloha, unlike S-TDMA, depends only on absolute time (not also on position) to work. This makes it simpler to identify a workaround solution.

In other words, the issue of synchronization is THE main issue of MS-Aloha (and of other slotted MAC for VANETs), but, hopefully, there are several directions which can be explored to solve it.

Table 4. Comparison between MS-Aloha and CSMA/CA, referred to VANET MAC requirements

VANET MAC Requirements	MS-Aloha	CSMA/CA
1) Decentralized	Yes	Yes
2) Immune from Hidden Terminal	Yes	Only by RTS/CTS (heavy)
3) Reactive	Yes	Yes
4) Scalable	Yes	Yes
5) Low Protocol Overhead	Limited and fixed	Quite heavy due to Collision Avoidance
6) Priority/Preemption	Pre-emption (connection-oriented)	Priority (connectionless)
7) Prevention of Blocking	Yes	Not Applicable
8) Deterministic	Yes	No
9) Reliable	Very High PDR; ACKs available	Medium-High PDR
10) Fair	Yes (non-blocking + preemption)	Yes
11) Backward Compatible	Partially (PHY) with 802.11a/p	Yes with 802.11a
12) Acknowledgments	For Unicast and Broadcast	Only for Unicast
13) DoS Prevention	Possible	Not possible
14) Standalone	No. GNSS receiver required.	Yes

Eventually, the above discussed considerations are collectively gathered in the following table which provides a comparative analysis between CSMA/CA and MS-Aloha.

All in all, the main points of strength of CSMA/CA are its simplicity and its distributed approach. Additionally CSMA/CA can benefit from a long lasting experience on WiFi and does not require any additional component to work.

Conversely, moving on to a comparison of protocols' performances, MS-Aloha shows a stronger potential than CSMA/CA. In fact, MS-Aloha is deterministic, reliable, immune from hidden terminals, fair and decentralized (despite its connection-oriented paradigm).

Moreover, MS-Aloha achieves higher PDR and involves lower protocol overheads than CSMA/CA.

The main weakness of the synchronous protocol, instead, lies in the required synchronization, which must be always guaranteed to let MS-Aloha work.

Altogether, if the issue of synchronization can be solved and MS-Aloha's backward compatibility to IEEE 802.11p can be enforced, the challenge of a future slotted standard for VANETs can be successfully met.

REFRERENCES

Bilstrup, K., Uhlemann, E., Ström, E. G., & Bilstrup, U. (2009). On the ability of the 802.11p MAC method and STDMA to support real-time vehicle-to-vehicle communication. *EURASIP Journal on Wireless Communications and Networking, 2009*. doi:10.1155/2009/902414

Borgonovo, F., Capone, A., Cesana, M., & Fratta, L. (2002). RR-ALOHA: A reliable R-ALOHA broadcast channel for ad-hoc inter-vehicle communication networks. In the *Proceedings of Med-Hoc-Net*.

Cozzetti, H. A., & Scopigno, R. (2009). *RR-Aloha+: A slotted and distributed MAC protocol for vehicular communications*. In First IEEE Vehicular Networking Conference (VNC 2009).

Cozzetti, H. A., Scopigno, R., Casone, L., & Barba, G. (2009). *Comparative analysis of IEEE 802.11p and MS-Aloha in VANETs scenarios.* In the Second IEEE International Workshop on Vehicular Networking (VON 2009).

Ganeriwal, S., Kumar, R., & Srivastava, M. B. (2003). Timing-sync protocol for sensor networks. In the *Proceedings of the 1st ACM International Conference on Embedded Networked Sensor Systems,* (pp. 138–149).

IEEE. (2010). *1609: WAVE standards.* Retrieved from vii.path.berkeley.edu/1609_wave/.

IEEE. (2010). *1609.2: Trial use standard for wireless access in vehicular environments (WAVE) - Security services for applications and management messages.* Retrieved from vii.path.berkeley.edu/1609_wave/.

Lenoble, M., Ito, K., Tadokoro, Y., Takanashi, M., & Sanda, K. (2009). *Header reduction to increase the throughput in decentralized TDMA-based vehicular networks.* In First IEEE Vehicular Networking Conference (VNC 2009).

Makido, S., Suzuki, N., Harada, T., & Muramatsu, J. (2007). Decentralized TDMA protocol for real-time vehcile-to-vehicle communications. *IPSJ Journal, 48*(7), 2257–2266.

Mui, L., Mohtashemi, M., & Halberstadt, A. (2002). A computational model of trust and reputation. In the *Proceedings of the 35th Hawaii International Conference on System Science* (HICSS).

Nakagami, M. (1960). The m-distribution: A general formula of intensity of rapid fading. In *The Statistical Methods in Radio Wave Propagation: Proceedings of the Symposium at the University of California.* Permagon Press.

NS-2. (n.d.). *Network simulator tool.* Retrieved from http://www.isi.edu/nsnam/ns.

Pilosu, L., Cozzetti, H. A., & Scopigno, R. (2010). *Layered and service-dependent security in CSMA/CA and slotted VANETs.* In 7th International ICTS Conference on Heterogeneous Networking for Quality, Reliability, Security and Robustness (QShine 2010).

Raya, M., & Hubaux, J.-P. (2005). The security of vehicular ad hoc networks. In the *Proceedings of the 3rd ACM Workshop on Security of Ad Hoc and Sensor Networks,* (pp. 11-21).

Schenato, L., & Gamba, G. (2007). A distributed consensus protocol for clock synchronization in wireless sensor network. In the *Proceedings of the 46th IEEE Conference on Decision and Control,* (pp. 2289–2294).

Scopigno, R., & Cozzetti, H. A. (2009). *GNSS synchronization in VANETs.* In the Third IEEE International Conference on New Technologies, Mobility and Security (NTMS 2009).

Scopigno, R., & Cozzetti, H. A. (2009). *Mobile slotted Aloha for VANETs.* In IEEE 70th Vehicular Technology Conference (VTC Fall 2009).

Scopigno, R., & Cozzetti, H. A. (2010). *Signal shadowing in simulation of urban vehicular communications.* In the 6th International Conference on Wireless and Mobile Communications (ICWMC 2010).

Scopigno, R., & Cozzetti, H. A. (2010). *Evaluation of time-space efficiency in CSMA/CA and slotted VANETs.* In IEEE 71th Vehicular Technology Conference (VTC Fall 2010).

Shakkottai, S., Rappaport, T. S., & Karlsson, P. C. (2003). Cross-layer design for wireless networks. *IEEE Communications Magazine, 41*(10). doi:10.1109/MCOM.2003.1235598

Standard, I. E. E. E. 802.11p. (2010). *Wireless LAN medium access control (MAC) and physical layer (PHY) specifications: Amendment 6- Wireless access in vehicular environments.*

SUMO. (n.d.). *SUMO vehicles movement simulator*. Retrieved from http://sumo.sourceforge.net.

Tadokoro, Y., Ito, K., Imai, J., Suzuki, N., & Itoh, N. (2008). *Advance transmission cycle control scheme for autonomous decentralized TDMA protocol in safe driving support system*. In the Intelligent Vehicles Symposium.

ENDNOTE

[1]   If another node (say D) receives both the STATE = *two hops reached* [1 1] from a node A and a one- or two-hop busy configuration [1 0] by another, the latter overwrites the former (in order to preserve collision prevention) mechanisms.

Chapter 6
Channel Impairments for V2V Communications in ITS Scenarios

D. Muñoz
ITESM Campus Monterrey, Mexico

R. Rodríguez
UANL Campus Monterrey, Mexico

S. Villarreal Reyes
ITESM Campus Monterrey, Mexico

ABSTRACT

This chapter describes different propagation scenarios in V2V communications based on practical Intelligent Transportation System applications. The intention is the study of propagation impairments for modeling purposes. It is important to consider the environmental characteristics of the scenario in order to choose the proper model to evaluate performance. The intention of this chapter is to explore how well current models fit the scenarios and to identify areas of opportunity for new model design. Many devices including sensors, transponders, and communication radios of different kinds co-exist in a typical urban scene. Interference among these devices and electromagnetic coupling with external waves is possible. Therefore, integration of the various technologies is imperative, and conditions for physical interaction of the radio waves needs to be provided. This is critical for the correct function of automatic systems that control safety sensible information. Very strict standard electromagnetic compatibility restrictions and regulations are applied to vehicles. These emissions and immunity tests need to be reengineered in the near future in order to consider new radio devices for communication among vehicles through sensors and transponders.

DOI: 10.4018/978-1-4666-0209-0.ch006

INTRODUCTION

Car accidents represent a high cost in infrastructure, money, time, etc., but more important human lives. This situation grows in urban scenarios where thousands or millions of persons need, depending of their activities, to drive a vehicle several times during the day. During a trip, a lot of events could provoke a car accident: small distance between cars, crowded roads, mechanical failures, pavement conditions, weather, skills and concentration of the drivers, etc. The main idea behind Intelligent Transportation Systems (ITS) is to provide a safer environment for the drivers (also pedestrian, infrastructure, etc.) and help them to avoid collisions and accidents. But, to develop applications and inter-networking technologies for ITS face several issues: the travel scenario is continually changing; vehicles are moving at different speeds and directions; there are wave propagation limitations, etc. Additionally, a good communication channel is needed to support vehicle interaction.

Nowadays Vehicular Ad-Hoc Networks (VANET´s) deal with the mobility characteristics of vehicles treating them as nodes of a network. The set of VANET´s forms a reconfigurable network because one vehicle can join or leave the network depending on how far it is from the other members. VANET´s present opportunities to develop a variety of communication-based automotive applications that demand the characterization of different models for vehicle channel wireless communication.

The challenges:

- To provide efficient Hybrid Communications between V2V communication and Vehicle to infrastructure communication.
- To analyze different scenarios, like crash security modules and low bridge road crosses.

- To find the relationship between Bit Error Rate (BER) and Signal to noise ratio (SNR).
- To define the access mode usual Frames for vehicular communication.
- To get a simulation for different modulation schemes.
- To investigate about electromagnetic fields' propagation, channel models and antenna configurations within the specific ITS scenarios.

In this chapter, we will focus primarily on three aspects. Initially, we will describe different scenarios in vehicle-to-vehicle communication (V2V) for high added value applications. These scenarios are subject to propagation impairments such as reflection, diffraction, Doppler Effect, among others. These impairments are partially mitigated by modulation and coding techniques. Therefore, different configurations need to be considered and compared, for instance, antenna diversity MIMO (Multiple Input Multiple Output) vs. SISO (Single Input Single Output). For these particular scenarios we will explore the most recent published work dealing with models built to measure performance. Finally, we will identify for the set of described scenarios opportunity areas in the channel models proposed in the literature.

BACKGROUND

Electronic devices and solutions considered to be part of what is called ITS scenarios are currently being developed for Dedicated Short Range Communication (DSRC technology). They support Vehicle to Vehicle and Vehicle to Infrastructure Communication where many applications have been identified for safety, security and commercial orientations. Frequency bands had already been allocated for these technologies and services. The US Federal Communication Commission (FCC) in 1999 allocated 75 MHz of bandwidth of the 5.9 GHz band to DSRC, according to the Institute of Electrical and Electronics Engineers (IEEE) 802.11p standard meant to operate in the 5.85 – 5.925 GHz frequency band supporting high vehicular speeds, while the IEEE 802.11a standard addresses low mobility in door wireless local area networks (WLAN) systems. In coordination with Europe and Japan the FCC has active programs based on DSRC in the 5.8 GHz band. In Japan, a standard for vehicle to infrastructure (V2I) communication was published in 2001, based on time division multiple access (TDMA), and targets a range of about 30m. The primary use is in electronic toll collection and more than 20 million on-board units were deployed with this system by 2008.

In (Popescu-Zeletin, 2010) some unfortunate traffic events are described which could have been prevented by using ITS technology. These are the result of situations described above. Some of the scenarios are hereby summarized:

- Head-on vehicle collisions.
- Rear-end collisions.
- Side collisions.
- Multi-vehicle collisions.

Head on Vehicle Collision

This scenario is the most dangerous collision between vehicles. The relative speed is the sum of both vehicle speeds. This occurs frequently on roads having two traffic lanes with different traveling directions and without a barrier separating them. The drivers need to invade the opposite lane to overtake slow cars. The inexperience of the driver and a mistaken calculation about the distance and acceleration of the vehicle approaching in the opposite direction in the invaded lane produces this type of accident.

Rear-End Vehicle Collision

Collisions of this type occur frequently in highways. When the car in front of us unexpectedly stops, we need to dodge or step on the brake in time. In this scenario the actual speed and distance of the vehicles is important to determine the collision risk factor.

Side Collision at Intersections

This type of collision has many variants. The side impact may not necessarily occur at a perpendicular angle. The collision can occur in a roundabout, curved or perpendicular intersection, even during right or left hand turns. Depending on the speed, these collisions can produce turnovers of cars being impacted in the right spot. The vehicle needs to communicate with infrastructure and other cars to obtain data and determine a free line. For this case it is necessary to be aware of blind spots to determine the position and speed of the vehicle and its neighbors. The V2V system should establish a priority/agreement between vehicles to prevent collisions.

Multi-Vehicle Collision

When a car has an accident and it is blocking the way with no sign of advice, other vehicles can impact it because the drivers may not react in time. The visibility, the speed and the distance are factors which determine a possible collision. This situation is aggravated in the presence of heavy traffic or in high speed lanes.

To implement V2V communications for the previous scenarios it is necessary to know the main characteristics of the propagation medium. The radio channel has several detrimental properties that affect the implementation's performance, like fading, attenuation, diffractions, refractions, coupling loss, absorption, power delays, Doppler effect, etc. These phenomena cause bit error rates, latency, packet errors, frequent retransmissions, signal loss, etc., that lead to less throughput, loss of signal communications, inaccurate results or outdated information.

A good channel model is one which possesses the main characteristics of the propagation medium to handle the inherent limitations in a suitable way for our purposes in the V2V communications. For the models of interest we would like to consider a typical urban scenario such as a group of vehicles circulating in a street or avenue at a time with average traffic. If vehicles are meant to communicate wirelessly among them they need proper antennas (or antenna arrays). Since the antennas are positioned within or outside the vehicle at a regular short height with respect to the ground, the urban landscape will be full of obstacles for the wireless propagation of the waves. At frequencies around 5.9GHz which are the target frequencies for V2V communications, the wavelength is small compared to the distances among vehicles.

To better understand the propagation issues in V2V communication scenarios, some of the main characteristics of the channel model are described next.

Channel Parameters

The wireless channels have, in general, time-variant impulse responses $h(t, \tau)$, which are the sum at the receiver of all the different contributions when the signal travels along the propagation medium (multipath components). When an impulse input is received at a time $t-\tau$ the functions show the response of the channel at time t. All the information about the channel is contained in the impulse response. Some parameters, like path loss, fading statistics, Doppler spread and delay spread can describe the channel in a more compact way.

Path Loss

When a radio signal travels through the medium it is attenuated (loss of strength). The small scale attenuation is called path loss. Absorption, reflec-

tion, refractions, distance between transmitter and receiver, position and height of antennas, etc. are some of the factors causing this impairment. The distance d is usually used to calculate the average path loss in a deterministic way.

Fading Statistics

The power of the signal received at the receptor can present variations even in short distances. These variations can be positive or negative for communications purposes. The variations are a result of the interference between multipath components. These variations are described statistically and are called "small-scale fading". Raleigh distribution is usually used to describe non-line-of-sight (non-LOS) scenarios while Rice distribution is used for line-of-sight (LOS) scenarios.

Power Delay Profile

The power delay profile (PDP) determines how much power arrives between a time τ and a delay $\tau + d\tau$ at a receiver (Ph(τ_y). The averaged magnitude of the impulse response averaged over the small-scale fading is used to obtain the PDP. The PDP gives a description of "how spread out" the received waveform is at the receiver.

Doppler Effect

When a moving transmitter sends a signal over the propagation medium the receptor perceives a change in frequency of the wave as the distance between them changes: a higher frequency is perceived during the approach of the transmitter, and a lower one if the transmitter is leaving behind the receiver.

The equation with the source and receiver moving at the same time is defined as follows:

$$f = \left(\frac{v + v_r}{v + v_s} \right) f_0 \tag{1}$$

Where:

f = is the observed frequency

f_0 = is the emitted frequency

v = velocity of waves in the medium

v_r = velocity of the receiver relative to the medium

v_s = velocity of the source relative to the medium

The above mentioned characteristics need to be considered when modeling propagation channels. Impairments depend heavily on the frequency band of interest and on the environment of the medium. For wireless channels the phenomena of absorption, scattering and refraction depend on the gases or fluids in the medium as well as on the materials of the objects with which the EM fields interact. The increase of the transmitted power can mitigate some of the impairments but in most bands of interest power is regulated. In road environments, for different real scenarios, there is sometimes Line-of-Sight but not always, for this condition the communication is through reflections and diffractions. Models will also depend on frequency and power combinations. If vehicles can communicate directly with each other and also with the infrastructure, important aspects such as high vehicle speeds, compatibility with vehicular positioning, and vehicle sensors communications can be described within a propagation scene. Mobile to Mobile channel models are the basis for the analysis of V2V communication and infrastructure performance. MIMO propagation models in real scenarios for V2V communication constitute an important line of research.

WAVE PROPAGATIONS MODELS

The models available for V2V communications are sometimes the result of experiments and/or measurements in specific scenarios. Other models are based on simulations and only a few are analytical developments. Currently, there are not many specific propositions about channel modeling in V2V communications: a Geometry-based Stochastic Channel Model (GSCM), MIMO and ray-tracing models.

The GSCM model has a group of scatters placed (diffuse or discrete) randomly across the proposed scenario, according to a statistical distribution. Each scatter has certain channel properties (e.g. diffraction and reflection indices). The transmitter and receiver are positioned among the scatters. The radio signal is propagated through a cloud of obstacles or scatters suffering from different kinds of modification in its trajectory and in its intensity. The receiver is hit by several waves coming from multiple obstacles. The total contribution of the scattered waves, LOS and NLOS, sum up at the receiver.

Lund Model

In (Khil, 2010), a path loss model is proposed. The authors call the model "Lund Model" and it is in the GSCM category. The Lund Model was developed taking as a reference the measurements for the highway scenario in (Karedal, 2009).

The Lund Model has two versions, Lund Model 1 and Lund Model 2. Lund Model 1 implements the scenario showed in (Karedal, 2009) to calculate the impulse response depending on scatters' location. Lund Model 2 adapts the path loss model proposed in (Karedal, 2010) that provides a model to calculate path loss depending on the distances between receiver (Rx) and transmitter (TX). Model 1 is more general because calculations are based on the number and positions of the scatters. Model 2 is based on specific conditions during measurements and might be unrealistic in other scenarios.

The Lund Model was implemented in an ns-3 discrete-event network simulator under the GNU GPLv2 license. The authors considered two scenarios for the transmitter and receiver: the first one with LOS between them and the second with an obstruction in the LOS between them. To validate the data they compared their results using Lund Model 1 and 2 with several available propagation loss models in ns-3: Friis, Log-Distance and Nakagami.

In case number one, Lund Model reported very similar values and matched better with the measurement results. Nakagami model is too optimistic; Friis model and Log-Distance model are very pessimistic. For the second case only Lund Model 1 distinguished between obstructed and unobstructed nodes, assigning them quite different path loss values.

The results show that, depending on the model used, there can be significant differences in the system's performance. Lund Model 1 shows a more realistic situation of the environment in V2V communications.

MIMO Model for V2V

In (Karedal, 2009) a new wideband multiple-input-multiple-output (MIMO) model for V2V is introduced. The model was constructed based on the GSMC approach and extensive MIMO channel measurements performed at 5.2 GHz in highway and rural environments in Lund, Sweden. The characteristics of the two scenarios are described as follows:

The highway has a concrete barrier (approximately 0.5m high) between two-line road, few commercial buildings and fields, and scarcely static scattering points along the road. During measurements, the traffic was light to medium density. The rural environment has a one-lane motorway with fields on both sides of the road, some residential and farm houses and few road signs. The traffic was from nothing to little during the measurements.

To implement the transmission between transmitter (TX) point and receiver (RX), point circular antenna arrays were used. The arrays were placed at a height of approximately 2.4m above the street level. For channel measurements a RUSK LUND channel were used. RUSK LUND performs MIMO measurement based on the "switched-array" principle. For recorded positioning data of TX and RX,

a built-in GPS was used. The measurements were performed with TX and RX driving in the same direction (SD) and driving in opposite directions (OD). The test was repeated several times with few variations in speed and distances.

Complex channel impulse responses $h(t,T)$ were obtained using Inverse Fourier Transforming (IDFT) over the recorded frequency responses $H(t,f)$. The analysis using the time-delay function showed some conclusions:

- A strong LoS path is present.
- Discrete components bring significant energy, generally represented by a single tap.
- During measurements the discrete components present many delays bins.
- Mobile and static scattering objects may produce the discrete components.
- A tail of weaker components follows the LoS.

The Doppler-resolved impulse responses, $h(v,T)$, were derived by Fourier transforming $h(t,T)$ with respect to t to analyze the Doppler characteristic of the received signal. The conclusions were:

- The Doppler spectrum changed significantly according to variations of the speed or position of the scatters relative to TX and RX.
- The discrete scatters have a small Doppler spread.
- The tail of weaker components with large Doppler and delay spreads. This part of the channel was called "diffuse".

To track a discrete scatter a separately estimation of the delay T_i and amplitudes α_i of the multipath contributions at each time was made. Later, a tracking of the components over large time scales was performed. The results showed that the signal from a discrete scatter is time variant due to ground reflections. Thus, the standard GSCM is not well suited for this type of reflection because they assume complex path amplitudes as non-fading. The conclusions of the measurements were used to parameterize the proposed geometry-based-stochastic MIMO model.

The model has a two-dimensional geometry and distinguishes between three types of point scatters: mobile discrete, static discrete, and diffuse. For the impulse response, they divided it in to four parts: the LOS component, the discrete components stemming from reflections off mobile scatters, the discrete components stemming from reflections off static scatters and the diffused components. Each mobile scatter was assigned a constant velocity along the x-axis given by a truncated Gaussian distribution. This was performed to avoid negative velocities in the wrong lane as well too high velocities. The spatial distributions of the discrete scatters are greatly simplified. The given scatter densities are based on counting the number of visible scatters along the measured road strips (for static scatters) or coarse traffic statistics. The model adjusts were done based on the measurements. The reference power and path loss were obtained by simulations.

Ray Tracing Model

In (Maurer, 2005) a ray tracing approach for V2V communications is presented. In this research they modeled the environment adjacent to the road more accurately by using stochastic positioning. The authors implemented various morphographic classes, e.g. urban, suburban, highway or motorway with a comprehensive set of typical objects such as buildings, trees, parked cars, bridges, traffic signs, etc. Each class was assigned a different set of probabilities of occurrence for all these objects.

In the construction of the simulation process they placed the objects randomly adjacent to the road lane according to their probability of occurrence. Furthermore, the size and the relative position to the lane of certain objects (e.g. buildings and trees) varied randomly within certain limits.

For the wave propagation model they assumed that the IVC-channel model is a combination of multiple reflections, diffractions and scattering from trees. Modified Fresnel reflection coefficients are used to model the reflections. Diffractions are described by the uniform geometrical theory of diffraction (UTD) and the corresponding coefficients for wedge diffraction. Scattering from trees is considered to be totally incoherent, i.e. no distinct specula component is present. They used ray-tracing to model the multi-path wave propagation in the aforementioned traffic scenarios. Depending on the propagation phenomena, different approaches of ray-tracing exist (the method of image transmitters, Fermat's principle, etc.).

A measurement in a real scenario was performed to verify the proposed model. The authors performed Wide-band V2V propagation measurements at the centre frequency of fc = 5.2 GHz and a RUSK ATM vector channel sounder was used as measurement platform. The reported measurements were performed in an urban environment in the city of Karlsruhe, Germany. In order to verify the absolute behavior of the ray-tracing model, it is reported that the distinct measurement scenarios were reconstructed and simulated in a deterministic way. During the measurement only the receiver is moving. The transmitter is kept stationary as well all the other vehicles. The comparison between measurement and simulation in the work assumes that the implemented ray-tracing model delivers an excellent coincidence with real IVC channels in terms of the narrow-band and wide-band behavior.

Wave Propagation Model

In (Maurer, 2001) a wave propagation model tool is introduced using a ray optical approach and the "Wiedemann" road traffic model. The model was developed using simulation and taking into account individual driving behavior. Each single vehicle gets a statistically generated set of intrinsic parameters, such as acceleration and braking power, driving characteristics and motivation, reaction time and desired speed. These parameters characterize the type of the individual vehicle and its driver. The "Wiedemann-Model" delivers time series of instantaneous positions and velocities of individual vehicles that interact with each other and their environment. Like in ray tracing, a variety of morphographic classes are defined and implemented for different environments, e.g. urban, suburban, rural road, motorway, etc. Each class includes several objects such as buildings, vegetation, parked cars, bridges, tunnels, traffic signs, trees, crash barriers, etc. Different probabilities of occurrence are assigned to each object, depending on the class. The simulation model is composed of two curved and three straight sections; the straight sections have different gradients. Next to the lane, buildings, parked cars and single trees are positioned randomly according to their morphographic class. For the simulation an analysis of relative positions of cars and trucks (with different speeds and directions) over time was made. Ray optics was used to model wave propagations and the method of the image theory for path searching. It was assumed that a transfer function of the corresponding propagation channel is completely defined by the propagation paths. Various channel parameters, such as received power, delay spread, Doppler spread, angular spread, etc. can be derived.

The conclusion was that wideband as well as narrowband analyses are possible. Furthermore, the dynamic character of the model enables it to generate time series of simulations.

Geometrical Two-Ring Model with Diffracting Street Corner

For those scenarios where vehicles need to turn the corner and then incorporate themselves into a street or avenue with regular traffic flow, there is a model proposed in (Wei, 2008), explaining a reference MIMO model for vehicle to vehicle fading channel communication. This model has

several transmit and receive antennas (MIMO) to improve system performance and more capacity in comparison to other communication systems (e.g. SISO). The particular scenario is a street with one corner and two moving cars, one in every side. Each car has a random scatters in form of a ring near to it. No lines of sight are present due the obstructions by buildings, scatters and street corner. The communication between the TX and the RX present many diffractions, caused by the multiple objects found around cars, such as trees, houses, etc.

A geometrical two-ring scattering model is used to model the scattering environment around each car. Because of independent groups of scatters, one for each car, the double-Rayleigh propagation model is used. This creates a model that allows for the angles of arrival and for the departure angles to be represented statistically as a correlation function of angles taking into consideration two antennas (MIMO system).

Consider in Figure 1 a situation where we have two vehicles equipped with two antennas each. The multiple-antennas placed on the surface of the cars, which are surrounded by a ring of scatters are separated by a distance δ_T for the transmitter vehicle and δ_R for the receiver vehicle. Both cars are moving to the same street corner and the communication can be expressed as a function of a double Rayleigh process.

Vehicles are moving at speeds V_T and V_R respectively. The distance of each vehicle to the corner diffractions produced are indicated by D_1 and D_2 and the distance R_R and R_T is respectively the distance to each ring. If one considers S_T^m and S_R^n as the representation of all possible diffractions caused by objects near the cars, the model represents the vehicles considered to be distant independently of their position.

The central idea of this model is to consider the angles formed by the trajectories between the antennas and taking first as a reference the transmitter side. The symbol ϕ_T^m denotes the angle of

Figure 1. Two ring model for corner street diffraction

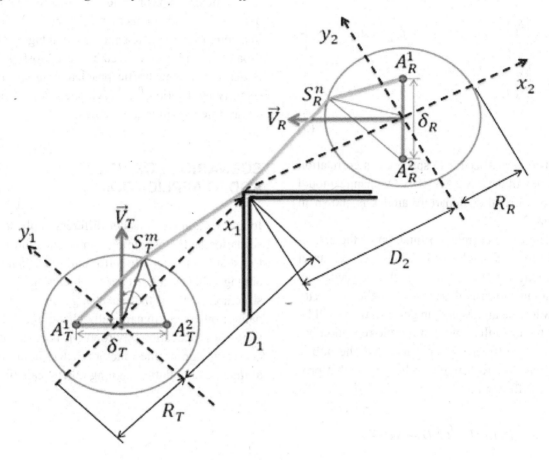

departure; α_T denotes the angle of the direction to the vehicle and β_T the angle of the orientation.

Now, with respect to the receiving side, we have that ϕ_R^n denotes the angle of departure; α_R denotes the angle of the direction to the vehicle and β_R the angle of the orientation.

A stochastic channel matrix, with four diffuse components, is used to express the MIMO V2V frequency-nonselective Rayleigh fading channel:

$$H(t) = \begin{pmatrix} h_{11}(t) & h_{12}(t) \\ h_{21}(t) & h_{22}(t) \end{pmatrix} \tag{2}$$

The correlation between $h_{11}(t)$ and $h_{22}^*(t)$, the diffuse components, is used to define the space time cross-correlation function (CCF) between the links A_T^1 corner A_R^1 and A_T^2 corner A_R^2:

$$\rho_{11,22}(\delta_T, \delta_R, \tau) = E\left[h_{11}(t) h_{22}^*(t+\tau)\right] \tag{3}$$

The 3-D space time CCF has follows:

$$\rho_{11,22}(\delta_T, \delta_R, \tau) = \rho(\delta_T, \tau) \cdot \rho(\delta_R, \tau) \tag{4}$$

As well with a Bessel function, denoted by J_0:

$$\rho_{11,22}\left(\delta_T, \delta_R, \tau\right) = \rho\left(\delta_T, \tau\right) \cdot \rho(\delta_R, \tau) =$$

$$J_0\left(2\pi\sqrt{\left(\frac{\delta_T}{\lambda}\right)^2 + (f_{T\max}\tau)^2 - \frac{k\delta_T}{\pi}f_{T\max}\cos(a_T - \beta_T)\tau}\right) \cdot$$

$$J_0\left(2\pi\sqrt{\left(\frac{\delta_R}{\lambda}\right)^2 + (f_{R\max}\tau)^2 - \frac{k\delta_R}{\pi}f_{R\max}\cos(a_R - \beta_R)\tau}\right).$$

$$(5)$$

The normalized 2-D space cross correlation function of the 2 X 2 MIMO V2V channel model for the arrival at departure angles is shown in Figure 2.

The cross correlation function of the arrival and departure angles shown in the corner street diffraction model concludes that a successful communication is determined by the similarity between the angles and, in general, there will be less losses in the power of mobile reception because any diffracted beam that reaches the mobile will have a street, tree or other object that produces diffraction.

The next section provides some useful cases to discuss the applications of V2V communication in a common urban area and its advantages. The urban scenario was selected because most of the issues concerning traffic problems, safety and security applications are developed in crowded environments within large cities.

SCENARIOS FOR VALUE ADDED APPLICATIONS

In this section we consider different application scenarios and constraining communication factors that limit successful information exchanged among vehicles and between vehicles and infrastructure. Some of these exchanges are of static nature; others are dynamically changing. Either way, the propagation environment is constantly changing. For instance, factors such as humidity, altitude, and pollution, among others, can affect

Figure 2. Normalized 2-D space CCF

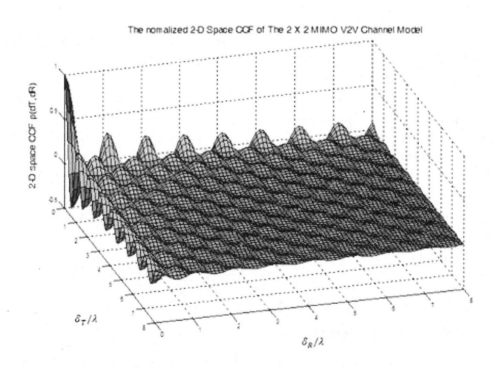

measurements and readings. Therefore, it is important to consider the environmental characteristics of the scenario in order to choose the proper model to evaluate performance. Mathematical models change considerably when dealing with different antenna configurations and digital signal processing algorithms. These factors are influenced by the particular ITS applications.

In order to define what the models of interest for V2V communications are, it is imperative to understand the environment of each application. For instance, vehicles in low crowded high speed highways or in suburban or rural environments are scarce. Applications in these situations are less real time demanding. However, most of the issues concerning traffic problems, safety and security applications are present in crowded environments within large cities where speed is more severely regulated and distances among vehicles are shorter. In these situations the wireless channel presents certain characteristics which have been studied in the past.

This is why our approach starts by considering specific situations and important parameters for modeling are identified from them. In this way,

we can visualize, within the known propagation models, opportunity areas for the characterization of certain ITS scenarios.

Scenario 1: Communication among Vehicles in a Parking Lot

When vehicles are in a parking lot, as shown in Figure 3, communications between them could be present to prevent collisions or indicate the presence of other vehicles inside the parking lot. This scenario shows that communication problems need to be grounded in a wireless sensor network with parked cars. It is important to know about statistics of the moving vehicles in order to predict what the possible paths for the mobile are. In general, the driver´s vision range is limited and is not aware of all objects, so vehicle sensors could make it possible to perform their maneuvers in an assisted way. Proximity sensors are already being used but communication or cooperation among vehicles constitutes a step further.

Collective sensing of the environment is possible if a building or lot infrastructure interacts with parked vehicles in order to provide the new

Figure 3. Parking lot

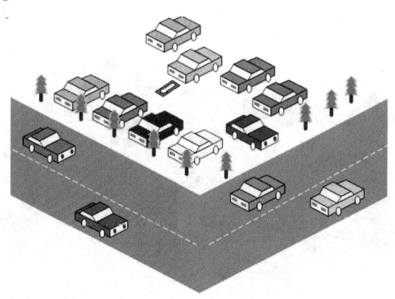

comers with directions and occupancy information to ease their accommodation. A vehicle is a machine which because of its dimensions can carry considerable computation capabilities and battery power. If enough information is given, let us say, from a radio frequency identification (RFID) tag, the vehicle's computer can identify the model and brand of the parked cars and can download dimensions, weight or other pertinent data. This can be used effectively in controlling of movements at short proximity.

The channel between two cars parked one next to each other has essentially a short range wireless, possibly line of sight, and a set of rays or paths. Doppler Effect will be negligible and the communication will require small amounts of power considering that there is no motion. Only the cars that want to leave the parking spot or those arriving will need information from parked cars.

The cars that are circulating outside the park could receive information about free spots, expected leaving time of the parked vehicles or impaired special facilities, this in order to make a decision on whether to access the parking lot or not. With the aid of sensors and communication among vehicles, the car which is coming out of a parking place will have the necessary data to meet

the timing for natural incorporation to the road by accelerating in the proper fashion in a secure and controlled set of movements.

Scenario 2: Street and Parking Exit of Vehicles from Garages

In some cities, crowded areas like downtown or intense commercial zones have reduced spaces for vehicles. There are many vehicles parked on the streets and cars leaving or entering parking places of offices, stores or homes need to deal with the traffic passing through the streets. It is therefore necessary to share information about the obstacles that are blocking the street (parked cars). This scenario illustrated in Figure 4, considers sharing information such as speed, distance, and the approximation of the cars that are in motion with the vehicles which are trying to come out of a parking place. These variables are essential for the car that is reversing out of a garage. The communication will allow the driver to accurately check the position while going backwards without having to be turning his neck. The information from parked cars will effectively prevent a collision. The vehicle circulating close to an area with parking places may also send warning messages

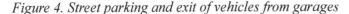

Figure 4. Street parking and exit of vehicles from garages

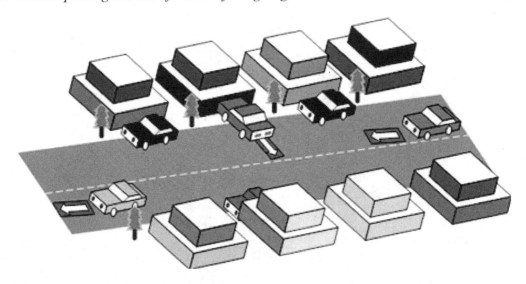

through a sensor network to cars that are going to exit. The speed from vehicles that are in motion cannot be controlled easily, that is why the V2V Communication models are for the most part a structure of different scenarios that take into account mobile fading channels.

Scenario 3: Opposite Direction and Corner in a Street Scenario

This scenario is illustrated in Figure 5. If two cars are moving in opposite directions, their speed, path trajectory and relative distance between one another form a set of useful parameter vector information which can be processed to prevent accidents. The Doppler Effect doubles because it accumulates proportionally according to the speeds of the cars traveling towards each other. This situation dominates a channel where cars share information by sending messages to prevent collisions.

The car in the corner wants to join the two-way traffic flow and needs to communicate with the vehicles in opposite directions. The car may be hampered by other parked cars complicating the situation. Therefore it is desirable for those parked cars to have the ability to send information about the existence of cars circulating on the same street so the car can safely incorporate itself into the lane. The models that can be used for this V2V communication must contain a study of the diffraction caused by the corner of the car that will be incorporated into the lane.

Scenario 4: Same Direction in Highway

Taking into consideration the propagation models that evaluate the Vehicle to Vehicle communication of cars traveling in the same direction on a high speed road, this scenario gives an explanation about the problem when vehicles try to change

Figure 5. Communication in opposite direction

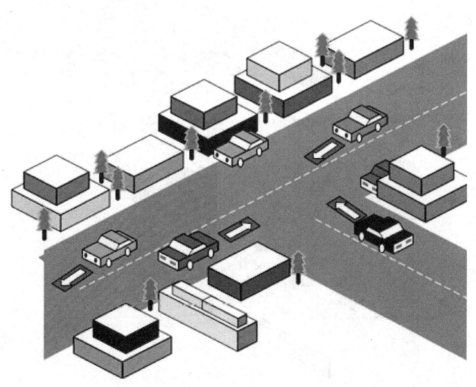

from the lateral slow speed lane into the central high speed one in high-speed roads. The scenario suggests essentially share information for measuring the variables of speed, distance, acceleration, among cars and to calculate the proper time for vehicles to come to a correct incorporation into the lane. Certain speed needs to be gained in order to merge safely but the lateral lane is sometimes crowded, preventing smooth incorporation, even with the proper information available. Cooperation is needed from vehicles traveling in the lane closest to the lateral. Speed reduction is not always desirable but a temporal change of lanes might.

It is a problem for the driver when he/she cannot continue his/her way to the central lanes of the road. Therefore, communication with the cars that are approaching at high speed over the immediate lane

can be useful to coordinate temporal lane change in order to ease incorporation of other vehicles. It is important to allow the transmission of messages that somehow provide a kind permission request to enter the road in an efficient manner. This scenario is illustrated in Figure 6.

Danger messages sent by cars that are ahead on the road will have a direct impact on traffic behavior. These applications require proper adjustment of communication parameters by using propagation models of a channel which considers transmission of information of mobiles traveling in the same direction and which are continuously providing data traffic information to regulate speed.

Figure 6. Communication in the same direction

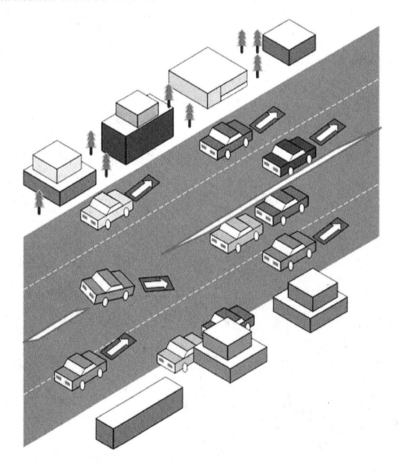

Scenario 5: Incorporate Into the Side of a High Speed Highway

In this scenario, illustrated in Figure 7, we can see that there must be communications between vehicles for drivers who want to merge into the side of a high-speed highway. Vehicles are continuously parked on the curb which hinders the entry of cars instead of providing information about how traffic is on the low-speed road. When a vehicle enters the high-speed highway's side, it should slow down and does not get direct information about vehicles that are circulating. It is complicated for the driver to just look back to see cars that are approaching, instead of having a direct communication with the cars that are circulating on the low- speed road and prevent a collision.

Scenario 6: Cruise Ship Communication Street

On a cruise ship we must analyze what will be the communication of vehicles going in the same direction, opposite direction and the vehicles that are crossing the streets. Sometimes drivers do not respect road signs and speed limits. To avoid collisions between them road signs need to be interpreted not only by the driver but also by the vehicle in order to inform opportunely the situation. Not all crossroads have semaphores. Sometimes there are only stop signs in both directions, which is very confusing. It is assumed that the vehicle arriving at this intersection will make a full stop and perhaps let the other vehicle pass. However it is not always clear who arrived at the intersection first or which street has the right of way. Decisions can be made more quickly and in a more secure way if infrastructure interacts with the vehicles coordinating who goes first making

Figure 7. Incorporation to a high speed highway

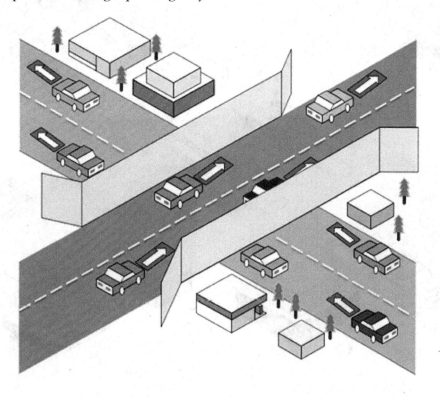

vehicle circulation smoother. Figure 8 illustrates this scenario.

MODEL CORRESPONDENCE WITH THE PROPOSED SCENARIOS

In urban scenarios it is a common practice to consider ray tracing models to characterize the channel. The signal at the receiver antenna is a linear combination of attenuated, delayed and frequency shifted components derived from a multipath scenario. In other words, the transmitting antenna is assumed to emit rays which in turn hit the surface of several obstacles, reflect or diffract, and decompose into multiple rays. The receiver antenna captures these rays but at different times since each ray takes different paths. Since the ray represents a sinusoidal wave, the difference in time of arrival causes it to arrive with a different phase relative to other rays. Furthermore, the difference in distance and the nature of the surfaces hit during propagation attenuates each ray in a different way. In addition the direction

Figure 8. Cruise ship communication

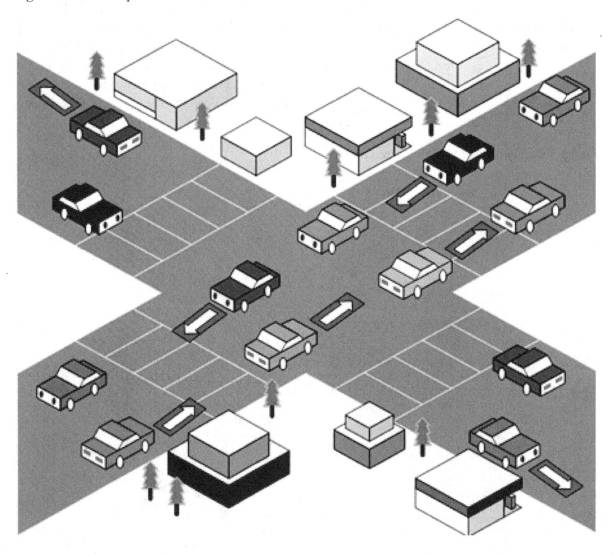

of arrival is different; therefore, the horizontal component of velocity is the projection of the vector representing the ray but with respect to a different angle. This causes a variation in the Doppler frequency shift of the signal with each ray. The phenomenon just described is represented with an impulse response function.

$$h(\tau;t) = \sum_{k=0}^{L} \alpha_k(t)\delta\left[t - \tau_k(t)\right]\exp\{j\left[\omega_c\left(t - \tau_k(t)\right) + \omega_{D,k}(t)t\right]\} \tag{6}$$

$$h(\tau;t) = \sum_{k=0}^{L} \alpha_k(t)\delta\left[t - \tau_k(t)\right]e^{j\varphi_k(t)} \tag{7}$$

This expression represents the channel output when a single impulse is transmitted through it. In Equation 1, the Greek letter α represents attenuation, τ represents delay and ω_D represents the frequency shift. Equation 2 is a compact form of Equation 1 where φ is a combination of the carrier frequency and the Doppler shift ω_D. These three parameters are random variables which have been plenty characterized in the literature. In order to calculate performance, an expected value of the power arriving to the receiver must be estimated by integrating the corresponding probability of error over the joint probability density function of all three random variables. This error probability is different for the digital modulation scheme used in the communications system. Additionally, diversity could be considered in which case the expression for the probability density function changes. Some analytical expressions are found in (Simon 2005). Sometimes the numerical integral should be calculated in order to have a figure of the performance in terms of error probability versus signal to noise ratio. Despite the fact that this methodology is formal, what is still a challenge is to characterize the nature of the random variables. The stochastic process is not necessarily stationary and may differ from scenario to scenario. The

wireless sensor networks and their integration to other communication networks require dynamic adjustments of the configuration settings. Intelligent devices require, in turn, adequate models which change with time and environment.

In our proposed scenarios, the obstacles have to be considered for propagation model and analysis, as well as the corner and roundabout intersections. Since the number of obstacles and reflections is large and the obstacles are close, as well as at long distances from the antennas, the number of signals depends on the number of scatters in the vicinity of the receiver antenna producing resolvable pulses. Actually, no one of the analyzed models represents V2V communication and the propagation wave in the channel in a reliable way.

In urban scenarios, such as the ones proposed in this chapter, a combination of the advantages of every model would be a better approach. The combination should be dynamic in a state machine fashion and every state could be triggered by a parameter indicating the delay spread of the channel and the proximity of obstacles. Outside information from the infrastructure could be very useful in changing the propagation model.

SOLUTIONS AND RECOMMENDATIONS

In (Khil, 2010), Lund Models returns the received power based on the transmitted power and the environment. It takes into consideration the position of all the scatters surrounding the transmitter and the receiver to calculate the real received power. But, in the experiment of the second scenario with obstacles between transmitter and receiver, the results were no so good comparing the other nodes and their path loss (e.g. node S4 and RX, or S4, S1 and S6, or S2 and S11). The better results in simulations with Lund Models 1 and 2 are very clear because they compared them against three models already implemented in the ns-3 simulator. It is necessary to remember that the ns-3 was designed principally to model Internet systems, thus the other models were not constructed by taking into account the obstacles and power loss in the communication between transmitter and receiver.

In (Karedal, 2009) all the measurements were realized with transmitter and receiver at constant distances (for vehicles in the same direction) and speeds.

Based on the documentation of the measurement conditions, it is concluded that the experiment has several flaws:

- During each measuring the velocity of TX and RX were fixed to equal value. The speed value was changed for each new measurement
- The distance between TX and RX was kept approximately constant during the SD scenario.
- They did not include the effects of a concrete barrier (approximately 0.5m high) that was separating the direction of travel in the highway use section.
- The LOS path is always strong. This is an ideal case and cannot be applied in urban scenarios.
- The scenario environment does not mention the presence of curves, turns, corners, etc. during the measurements.

The main drawback is that the model was developed to be in agreement with the measurement results and only applies for specific scenarios. Furthermore, the suggested model is better suited for SISO modeling than MIMO.

In (Maurer, 2005) the main difference with the other work is that the ray-tracing approach first develops the model with several morphographic classes of objects. First the simulation was made and then the real scenario was constructed to compare the results. We can conclude the following:

- During the measurements only the receiver is moving. The transmitter remains static and the other vehicles are stopped as well. Because there are no variations in environment conditions the model shows a very important simplification of the reality in an urban scenario with multiple vehicles in movement.
- The velocity of the receiver is 10 km/h. This velocity is very slow and constant, and does not reflect the driving characteristics in a real urban scenario with traffic, braking, accelerations and stops.
- The receiver travels a straight route with no variations, e.g. turns, line changing, etc.
- For one of the measurements the LoS between the TX and the RX is always clear and strong, because no other vehicles were present. This is not always true because new cars can incorporate or leave randomly to the line.
- Despite the simulated model, to take into account the path loss in corners only reflects an ideal case in an urban city with no traffic in movement, constant speed at the receiver and a strong LoS. Obviously, this is not the common situation in an urban scenario.

In (Maurer, 2001) a new wave propagation tool was implemented using the "Wiedemann-Model" to generate realistic traffic. Driving behavior, moving vehicles (trucks and cars) and a better environment description are the main characteristics of this tool. Ray-optical methods were used to model wave propagation within the constructed scenario. In this model we can note:

- The diffraction effects were discarded.
- Only single and multiple reflections are used for the first calculations.
- It is assumed that parameter gathering is possible. Parameters such as delay spread, average fading, and level crossing rate

are considered but no simulation was performed to validate the tool and the model.

In (Wei, 2008) a V2V communications model with street corners was introduced. Despite the urban scenario was modeled in a more realistic way, taking to account communications between vehicles with presence of obstacles and corner streets, we can note:

- Only 2x2 antenna configuration was used. With MIMO more complex arrays can be built.
- The scatters around the cars are assumed to be infinite.
- All of the scatters are static. In a real urban scenario, this is not always the case.
- It is assumed that all the waves arrive with the same power level at receiver.
- Several equations are mentioned, but do not give examples of their application.

FUTURE RESEARCH DIRECTIONS

One of the most important applications of V2V communications is active and passive safety and security for the vehicles circulating on the road. Approximately about 80% of traffic accidents occur in good weather conditions (Popescu-Zeletin, 2010). The safety of the persons in a vehicle depends on the experience of the driver and his/her capacity to react to sudden events, such as traffic jams, pedestrian crossing, lack of visibility, bad weather, etc.

Future research involves design of a proper communication channel for V2V using MIMO and an information decision system to help the drivers during their travels in different scenarios. Development of a system able to display fundamental information about the environment and traffic conditions in real time is desirable. This system, through data mining, sensors and GPS, should be capable to analyze the actual information and determine the best option according to circumstances. The desired actions could be:

- Provide visual alerts with or without sound, depending on the importance of the event.
- Offer safety options to avoid vehicle collisions with different objects, e.g. other cars, pedestrian, pot holes, etc.
- Carry out automatic emergency maneuvers, like brake pressure.
- Improve traffic flow.
- Determine the desirable speed according to traffic in order to economize resources, like fuel consumption, time, etc.
- Use RFID tags in vehicles to obtain relevant information to be used in the decision making system (like main status of the vehicle, percentage of collisions, driver infractions, etc.).
- Control movements at short distances, e.g. in a parking lot. RFID can provide information for the parked cars and help in the maneuvers; for instance, if a free space is available or the dimensions of the car fits well on the parking space.
- Employ sensors to analyze the correctness state of the main parts of the vehicle. If a mechanical failure can happen the system will alert the driver or implement an emergency countermeasure. The information decision system could share this information via V2V to alert other drivers to take precautions and reduce the risk.

CONCLUSION

In V2V communications the transmitter and the receiver are moving constantly at different speeds and directions. The antennas' height is short with limited radio coverage since no fixed access points are present. Current models get their statistical parameters of the stochastic processes through extensive measurements and simulations. Otherwise, they are obtained for particular scenarios under valid assumptions. The common assumption of the WSSUS model is violated in V2V communication because it assumes a fixed Doppler spectrum for every delay and does not represent the non-stationary channel responses reported in the measurements. The standard GSCM is not well suited for this type of reflections because they assume the complex path amplitudes as non-fading.

For the model of interest, an urban scenario such as a group of vehicles circulating in a street or avenue at a time with average traffic intensity, we introduce several useful cases compatible with the most common activities and the advantages to the drivers. Most of the analyzed models do not adapt very well to the proposed scenarios because the urban landscape is full of obstacles that hinder wave propagation. At frequencies around 5.9GHz, which are the target frequencies for V2V communications, the wavelength is small compared to the distances among vehicles, the Line of Sight (LOS) is not always present and the statistics of the process present bigger delay spreads. The MIMO antennas are small with a limited radio wave reception.

The actual channel models represent a simplification of the reality. Most of the cases were under an ideal scenario with no traffic, turns or obstructions between transmitter and receiver. Moreover diffractions are not considered in the calculations.

In conclusion, regarding the useful cases proposed in this work, a more realistic model needs to be proposed for V2V communication. Before developing a new model, it is important to analyze the inherent medium characteristics (propagation channels) and the role of the elements that can be found in real urban scenario. Some of the desirable variables to be considered during the design of the model are: mobile transmitters and receivers,

variable distant between vehicles, vehicles in the same and opposite directions, vehicles at different speeds, high Doppler shifts, path loss, power delay, obstruction of the communication link (fading), non-line-of-sight (NLOS), diffractions, diversity of scatters distributed randomly across the road (vehicles, trees, buildings, road signals, pedestrian, etc.), weather, and road characteristics (number of lines, width lines, bridges, intersections, roundabout intersections, etc.).

The models may have different purposes. Analytical abstractions such as the ones presented by Maurer may be intended for average performance calculations. Commercially, the manufacturers of communication equipment for vehicles would like to fabricate devices with an average performance criteria meeting the bounds presented in the models. For better efficiency, we believe that a finite state machine which can jump among several modes could provide a dynamic mechanism to select device settings in order to tune the communication parameters, modulations and antenna arrays in different situations to optimize performance.

REFERENCES

Karedal, J., Paier, A., & Zemen, T. (2009). A geometry-based stochastic MIMO model for vehicle-to-vehicle communications. *IEEE, 8*(7), 3646-3657. Retrieved December 10, 2010, from http://ieeexplore.ieee.org/.

Khil, M., Bür, K., Tufvesson, F., & Aparicio, J. (2010). Simulation modeling and analysis of a realistic radio channel model for V2V communications. *IEEE ASNC 2010,* (pp. 981-988). Retrieved January 12, 2011, from http://ieeexplore.ieee.org/.

Maurer, J., Schäfer, M., & Wiesbeck, W. (2001). A realistic description of the environment for inter-vehicle wave propagation modeling. *IEEE Vehicular Technology Conference,* (vol. 3, pp. 1437-1441). Retrieved November 8, 2010, from http://ieeexplore.ieee.org/.

Maurer, J., Sörgel, W., & Wiesbeck, W. (2005). Ray-tracing for vehicle to vehicle communications. *Proceedings of the International Union of Radio Science.* Retrieved November 24, 2010, from http://www.ursi.org/Proceedings/ProcGA05.

Popescu-Zeletin, R., Radusch, I., & Rigani, M. (2010). *Vehicular-2-X communication: State-of-the-art and research in mobile vehicular ad hoc networks.* New York, NY: Springer.

Wei, C., Zhiyi, H., & Tianren, Y. (2008). A street reference model of MIMO vehicle-to-vehicle fading channel. *IEEE Conference on Industrial Electronics and Application,* (pp. 275-278). Retrieved January 7, 2011, from http://ieeexplore.ieee.org/.

KEY TERMS AND DEFINITIONS

Line-of-Sight (LOS): Direct path without obstacles between transmitter and receiver.

Multiple Input and Multiple Output (MIMO): The MIMO systems use a multi antenna implementation at the transmitter and receiver to improve communication performance sending multiple streams through the antennas.

Non-Line-of-Sight (NLOS): When scatters block the path between transmitter and receiver.

Scatter: Any object in a street or road (trees, boxes, lamppost, etc). The scatters can block, reflect, and diffract, etc., the wave signal.

Single Input and Single Output (SISO): The SISO systems only use one antenna to in the transmitter and the receiver. SISO systems are less complex and slower than MIMO systems.

Section 2
Theory and Application of the Network Layer

Chapter 7
Reactive Location–Based Routing Algorithm with Cluster–Based Flooding

Raul Aquino Santos
University of Colima, Mexico

ABSTRACT

Location-Based Routing Algorithm with Cluster-Based Flooding (LORA-CBF) employs two location services: Simple and Reactive. A Simple Location Service has been implemented for neighbors nodes, and for faraway nodes, a Reactive Location Service is employed. In LORA-CBF, the source node includes the location of its destination in each packet. The packet moves hop by hop through the network, forwarded along via cooperating intermediates nodes. At each node, a purely local decision is made to forward the packet to the neighbor that is geographically closest to the destination. However, location information by itself does not guarantee the transmission between neighboring nodes in vehicular ad-hoc networks. Mobility and contention of wireless media may cause loss of packets being transferred, and this is very important aspect to consider in the development of wireless routing algorithms. Here, the authors have addressed this problem by including a predictive algorithm in LORA-CBF.

INTRODUCTION

The idea of using geographical information in highly mobile nodes is to improve packet forwarding decisions (Käsemann, et. al., 2002). Before forwarding a packet, a node using location information only needs information about the immediate neighbourhood and the position of the destination. However, as an essential prerequisite for location-based routing, a location service is needed from which a node can learn the current position of its desired communication partner. To preserve location information on other nodes in

DOI: 10.4018/978-1-4666-0209-0.ch007

the network, each mobile node maintains a location table. This table contains an entry for every node in the network whose location information is known, including the node's own location information. Three location services have been described in (Camp, Boleng & Wilcox, 2002): DREAM Location Service (DLS), Simple Location Service (SLS) and Reactive Location Service (RLS).

DREAM Location Service (DLS)

In the DREAM location service, each location packet updates the location tables containing the coordinates of the source node based on some reference system, the source node's position, and the time the location packet was transmitted. Each mobile node in the ad hoc network transmits a location packet to nearby nodes at a given rate and to faraway nodes at another, lower rate. The rate a mobile node transmits location packets adapt according to when the mobile node has moved a specified distance from its last update location. Since faraway nodes appear to move more slowly than nearby mobiles nodes, it is not necessary for a mobile node to maintain up-to-date location information on them. Thus, by differentiating between nearby and faraway nodes, the overhead of location packets can be reduced.

Simple Location Service (SLS)

A node using the Simple Location Service transmits a location packet to its neighbours at a given rate. The rate a mobile node transmits location packets adapts according to location change, via a similar procedure used for nearby nodes in DLS. Each location packet in SLS contains up to E entries from the node's location table and the E entries are chosen from the table in a round robin fashion. As multiple location packets are transmitted, all the location information a node contains is shared with its neighbours.

A node using SLS will also periodically receive a location packet from one of its neighbours. The

node will then update its location table, based on the received table entries, in such a manner that location information with the most recent time is maintained.

Reactive Location Service (RLS)

In the Reactive Location Service (RLS), when a mobile node requires a location for another node and the location information is either unknown or expired, the requesting node will first ask its neighbours for the requested location information. If the node's neighbours do not respond to the requested location information within a timeout period, the node will flood a location request packet in the entire network.

When a node receives a location request packet and does not know the requested location information, the node propagates the flood location request. If, however, a node receives a location request packet and the node's location table contains the requested location information, the node returns a location reply packet via the reverse source route obtained in the location request packet. In other words, each location request packet carries the full route (a sequential list of nodes) that a location reply packet should be able to traverse in its header.

ROUTING OF PACKETS USING LOCATION INFORMATION

The advantage of using positional information in vehicular ad-hoc wireless networks (VANET) is that routing can be fully dynamic and distributed and the number of flooding packets observed in dynamic ad-hoc networks compared to non-positional algorithms is reduced.

In non-positional based routing algorithms, link failures or link changes may lead to the transmission of route error packets. In this case, either local route error correction is required or the route error has to travel back to the source. The source then sends a fresh route request looking for a new route to the destination. If the nodes in the network are mobile with constantly changing links, the probability of communications failures increases, causing the source not to be able to send data packets to the destination. However, with positional-based routing algorithms, routing can be done without the use of route error packets. A source node using geographic forwarding includes the location of its destination in each packet. The packet moves, hop by hop, through the network, forwarded along via cooperating intermediates nodes. At each node, a purely local decision is made to forward the packet to the neighbour that is geographically closest to the destination. The fact that forwarding does not involve any global information helps geographic routing scale and cope well with highly mobile nodes.

In this chapter, we propose a reactive location routing algorithm with cluster-based flooding for inter-vehicle communication (LORA-CBF) because of the increasing number of vehicles in circulation. In 1950 the number of vehicles registered in United Sates was around 50 million and for 2000 it was around 150 million. This tendency motivates us to design an algorithm that functions well in dense and highly mobile networks.

Reactive Location Routing Algorithm with Cluster-Based Flooding (LORA-CBF)

This algorithm inherits the properties of reactive and hierarchical routing algorithms and has the advantages of acquiring routing information only when a route is needed. First of all, LORA-CBF improves the traditional routing algorithms based on non-positional routing by making use of location information provided by GPS, and secondly, it minimizes flooding of its Location Request (LREQ) packets. Flooding, therefore, is directive for traffic control by using only the selected nodes, called gateway nodes, to diffuse LREQ messages. The purpose of gateway nodes is to minimize the flooding of broadcast messages in the network by reducing duplicate retransmission in the same region.

Member nodes are converted to gateways when they receive messages from more than one cluster-head. All the members in the cluster read and process the packet but do not retransmit the broadcast message. This technique significantly reduces the number of retransmissions in a flooding or broadcast procedure in dense networks. Therefore, only the gateway nodes retransmit packets between clusters (hierarchical organization). Moreover, gateways only retransmit a packet from one gateway to another in order to minimize unnecessary retransmissions, and only if the gateway belongs to a different cluster-head. To avoid synchronization of neighbours' transmissions, as observed in (Jacquet, et al., 2002), (Floyd & Jacobson, 1994), we have delayed each packet transmission randomly.

Some Cluster-Based Flooding strategies for routing in wireless ad-hoc networks have been reported in the literature (Mitelman & Zaslavsky, 1999), (Krishna, et al., 1997), (Das, Sivakumar & Bharghavan, 1997), (Sivakumar, Das & Bharghavan, 1998), (Chiang, et al., 1997). The main contribution in this work is the re-broadcast and gateway selection mechanism. The cluster formation in (Mitelman & Zaslavsky, 1999) is based on the Link Cluster Algorithm (LCA) (Baker, Ephremides & Flynn, 1984) and the algorithm is based on the Link State Routing protocol, where all nodes in the cluster are expected to acknowledge the Link State Update (LSU). If one of the nodes does not send an acknowledgement, the cluster-head retransmits the LSU to that particular node. Flooding is transmitted from source to a destination via cluster-heads and gateways. In (Krishna, et al., 1997), and (Das, Sivakumar & Bharghavan, 1997), the re-broadcast is carried out only by the boundary nodes. Nodes other than boundary nodes just listen and update their tables. In (Sivakumar, Das & Bharghavan, 1998), there are two types of routing strategies: Optimal Spine Routing (OSR) and Partial-knowledge Spine Routing (PSR). OSR uses full and up-to-date knowledge of the network topology, thus the source can determine the route to the destination. On the other hand, PSR uses partial knowledge of the network topology and takes a greedy approach to compute the shortest path from the source to the destination. In (Chiang, et al., 1997), the authors use a cluster-head controlled token protocol (like polling) to allocate the channel among competing nodes. We have implemented a re-broadcast strategy, where only gateways that belong to a different cluster-head re-broadcast the location request packets, improving the routing overhead in dense networks.

Apart from normal Hello messages, LORA-CBF does not generate extra control traffic in response to link failures and additions. Thus, it is suitable for networks with high rates of geographical changes. As the protocol keeps only the location information of the [source, destination] pairs in the network, the protocol is particularly suitable for large and dense networks with very high mobility. LORA-CBF is designed to work in a completely distributed manner and thus does not depend upon any central entity. In addition, it does not require a reliable transmission for its control messages. Each node sends its control messages periodically, and can therefore sustain some packet loss. This is, of course, important in radio networks like the one being considered here, where deep fades are possible.

LORA-CBF does not operate in a source routing manner (Johnson, Maltz & Hu, 2004). Instead it performs hop by hop routing: each node uses its most recent location information of its neighbour nodes to route a packet. Hence, when a node is moving, its position should be registered in a routing table such that the movements can be predicted to correctly route the packets to the next hop to the destination.

PROTOCOL FUNCTIONING

The Reactive Location Routing Algorithm with Cluster-Based Flooding (LORA-CBF) carries out different functions that are required to perform the task of routing. Here we discuss some functionalities of the protocol.

Neighbour Sensing

Each node must detect the neighbouring nodes with which it has a direct link. To accomplish this, each node periodically broadcasts a Hello message, containing its location information, address and its status. These control messages are transmitted in broadcast mode and are received by all one-hop neighbours, but they are not relayed to further nodes. A Hello message contains:

- Node Address.
- Type of node (Undecided, Member, Gateway or Cluster-head).
- Location (Latitude and Longitude).

Operation of Reactive Location Routing Algorithm with Cluster-Based Flooding (LORA-CBF)

LORA-CBF is formed with one cluster-head, zero or more members in every cluster and one or more gateways to communicate with other cluster-heads. Each cluster-head maintains a "Cluster Table." A "Cluster Table" is defined as a table that contains the addresses and geographic locations of the member and gateway nodes. We have assumed that all nodes can gather their positions via GPS or some local coordinate system.

When a source attempts to send data to a destination, it first checks its routing table to determine if it knows the location of the destination. If it does, it sends the packet to the closest neighbour to the destination (Figure 1). Otherwise, the source stores the data packet in its buffer, starts a timer and broadcasts Location Request (LREQ) packets.

Figure 1. Flow diagram for LORA-CBF

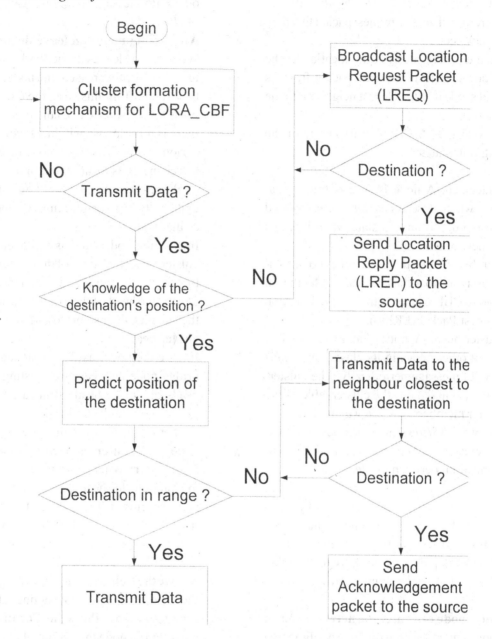

Only gateways and cluster-heads can retransmit the LREQ packet. Gateways only retransmit a packet from one gateway to another in order to minimize unnecessary retransmissions, and only if the gateway belongs to a different cluster-head.

Upon receiving a location request, each cluster-head checks to see if the destination is a member of its cluster. Success triggers a Location Reply (LREP) packet that returns to the sender using geographic routing, because each node knows the position of the source and the closest neighbour based on the information from the LREQ received and the Simple Location Service (SLS). Failure triggers retransmissions by the cluster-head to adjacent cluster-heads (Reactive Location Service, RLS). The destination address is recorded in the packet. Cluster-heads and gateways, therefore, discard a request packet that they have already seen.

Once the source receives the location of the destination, it retrieves the data packet from its buffer and sends it to the closest neighbour to the destination.

A node in LORA-CBF can be in any of the following four states:

- Undecided: A node is in this transitional state when it searches for a cluster-head and is initially in this state when it enters the network or wakes up.
- Member: A node that is a member of a cluster assigned to a cluster-head. A Member in LORA-CBF cannot retransmit a Location Request Packet (LREQ).
- Cluster-head: A node that is responsible for all other nodes in its cluster and sends a Hello message periodically. The cluster-head also maintains the cluster table of the cluster members and gateway nodes.
- Gateway: A node that is member of at least two cluster-heads that can be used for communication between clusters.

Because ad-hoc wireless networks have no static nodes, there will be frequent link breaks between nodes, due to the dynamic nature of these types of networks. Four events may happen that can lead to making or breaking network links:

1. **A new node can enter the network:** When a node enters the network, it can follow two paths; it either joins an existing cluster-head or forms a cluster choosing itself as the cluster-head. Being in Undecided state, it transmits a Hello message searching for an existing cluster-head. If the node receives a response, it joins the cluster-head and changes from Undecided to Member. Otherwise, it elects itself as the cluster-head and sends

out Hello message assigning itself the role of cluster-head.

2. **An existing node can leave the network:** When a node leaves the network due to failure or some other reason, the node is said to be turned off. In this case, the cluster-head waits for a response from the failed node. If there is no response within a specified time period, the node is either considered off or has changed its location out of the range of its cluster-head. In this case, the cluster-head updates its cluster table removing the details of that node.

In case the node that has switched off is a cluster-head, the nodes of the cluster change to an undecided state and search for a different cluster-head. If they find a cluster-head, they change their status to a Member of that cluster-head.

In case the node that has switched off is a bridge node between two existing cluster-heads, the cluster-head will update its Cluster Table when the cluster-head does not receive further messages from the gateway.

3. **A node can enter the vicinity of an existing cluster:** When a node belonging to an existing cluster-head enters the vicinity of another cluster-head, its status becomes that of a Member and it changes its status to gateway before rebroadcasting its Hello message. In this case, when the cluster-heads receive the Hello message from the gateway, they simply update their routing table.

4. **A node can leave the vicinity of an existing cluster:** If a node moves out of the vicinity of an existing cluster X and makes its way to a new cluster Y, the cluster head of X updates its routing table so that the node is no longer a member and the cluster-head of Y updates its routing table to include the node to as a Member by transmitting Hello messages between cluster-head X and Y. If the node moves out of a cluster and cannot

find a new cluster-head, it elects itself as the cluster-head.

Basically, the algorithm consists of four stages:

1. Cluster formation.
2. Location discovery (LREQ and LREP).
3. Routing of data packets.
4. Maintenance of location information.

Cluster Formation

To enable cluster formation and maintenance, all nodes keep the information about their neighbours in their neighbour table.

Let t be the period of time between the Hello broadcasts. When a node first switches on, it first listens to Hello packets on the broadcast channel.

If any other node on the broadcast channel is already advertising itself as a cluster-head (status of node = cluster-head), the new node saves the heard cluster-head ID in its cluster-head ID field and changes its status to member. At any point in time, a node in the mobile network can associate itself with a cluster-head. The cluster-heads are identified by the cluster-head ID. Otherwise, the new node becomes cluster-head, which becomes responsible for cluster maintenance and periodically sending a Hello Message (Figure 2).

When one member receives the Hello message, it registers the cluster-head and responds with a reply Hello message. The cluster-head then updates the Cluster Table with the address and position (longitude and latitude) of every member in the cluster.

Figure 2. Cluster formation mechanism for reactive location routing algorithm with cluster-based flooding (LORA-CBF)

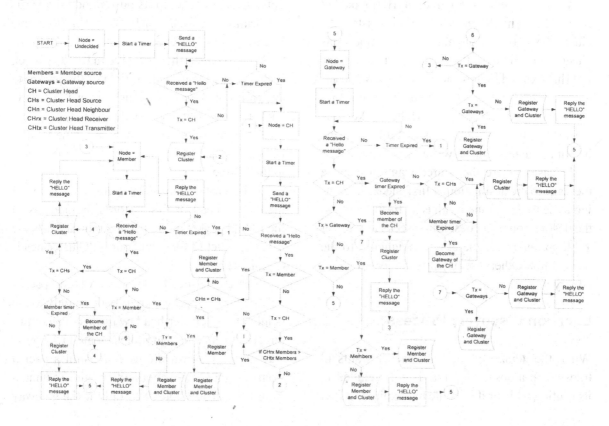

Figure 3. Gateway node in LORA-CBF algorithm

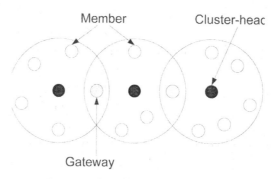

Figure 4. Location request packet (LREQ)

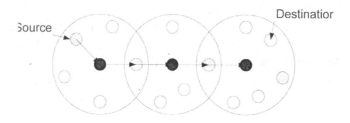

When a member receives a Hello packet from a different cluster-head, it first registers the cluster-head, but the member does not modify its cluster-head ID until the expiration time for the field has expired. Before the member rebroadcasts the new information, it changes its status to a gateway. After receiving the Hello packet, the cluster-heads update the Cluster Table with the information about the new gateway (Figure 3).

In cases where the source wants to send a message to the destination, it first checks its routing table to determine if it has a "fresh" route to the destination. If it does, it first seeks its Cluster Table to determine the closest neighbour to the destination. Otherwise, it starts the location discovery process.

Location Discovery Process

When the source of the data packet wants to transmit to a destination that is not included in its routing table or if its route has expired, it first puts the data packet in its buffer and broadcasts a Location Request (LREQ) packet (Reactive Location Service, RLS).

When a cluster-head receives a LREQ packet, it checks the identification field of the packet to determine if it has previously seen the LREQ packet. If it has, it discards the packet; however, if the destination node is a member of the cluster-head, it unicasts the Location Reply (LREP) packet to the source node.

If the destination node is not a member of the cluster-head, it first records the address of the LREQ packet in the list and rebroadcasts the LREQ packet to its neighbouring Cluster-heads (Figure 4).

Each cluster-head node forwards the packet only once. The packets are broadcast only to the neighbouring cluster-head by means of an omni-directional antenna that routes them via the gateway nodes. Gateways only retransmit a packet from one gateway to another to minimize unnecessary retransmissions, and only if the gateway

Figure 5. Location reply packet (LREP)

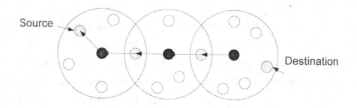

Figure 6. Data and acknowledgement packets being forwarding in LORA-CBF

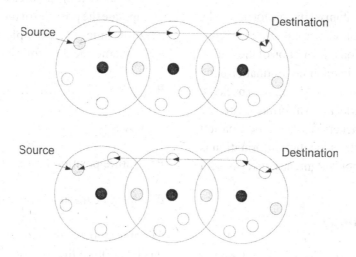

belongs to a different cluster-head. When the cluster-head destination receives the LREQ packet, it records the source address and location. From this, the destination's cluster-head determines the location of the source node. The destination then transmits a LREP message back to the source via its closest neighbour (Figure 5).

Finally, the packet reaches the source node that originated the request packet. If the source node does not receive any LREP after sending out a LREQ for a set period of time, it goes into an exponential back off before re-transmitting the LREQ. Hence, only one packet is transmitted back to the source node. The reply packet does not have to maintain a routing path from the source to the destination. The path is determined from the location information provided by the source node, and the path traversed by the LREQ may be different from that traversed by the LREP.

Routing of Data Packets

The actual routing of data packets is then based on the location of source, destination and neighbours (Figure 6).

Since the protocol is not based on source routing, packets travel the path from the source to a destination based on their relative locations. The packets find paths to the destinations individually each time they are transmitted between the source and the destination. Packets are transmitted based on the fact that the two nodes know their positions relative to each other. Moreover, since the transmission is in the direction of the destination node, the path found will be shorter than other routing mechanisms (non-positional-based). In non-positional-based routing strategies, the shortest path is measured in hops. Therefore, the path found may not be the shortest. However, the path found using location information will be significantly shorter. If the source of the data packet does not receive the acknowledgement packet before its timer expires, it will retransmit the data packet again. This situation might occur during loss of packets due to drop out or network disconnection.

Maintenance of Location Information

The LORA-CBF algorithm is suitable for networks with very fast mobile nodes because it maintains and updates the location information of the source and destination every time source/destination pairs send or receive data and acknowledgment packets. The source updates its location information before sending each data packet. When the destination receives a data packet, its location information is updated and an acknowledgment packet is sent to the source.

Forwarding Strategy

LORA-CBF uses MFR (Most forward within radius) as its forwarding strategy. In MFR the packet is sent to the neighbours that best reduce the distance to the destination. The advantage of this method is that it decreases the probability of collision and end-to-end delay between the source and the destination (Giordano, Stojmenovic & Blazevic, 2003).

SHORT-TERM PREDICTIVE ALGORITHM

In highly mobile environments, having the correct knowledge of neighbour positions is fundamental in the routing efficiency of any algorithm. LORA-CBF predicts the next position (geographical location) of every neighbour node, based on its short-term predictive algorithm (Vilalta et al., 2002). After predicting the position of all neighbour nodes, LORA-CBF sends the packet to the

neighbour node which has the best position (MFR). The best position means that it can reach the node that is closest to the destination.

Mobility and contention of the wireless media may cause the loss of packets being transferred, and this is a very important aspect to consider in the development of predictive algorithms. We address this problem, including the gap between packets being received (Figure 7).

The short-term predictive algorithm tries to extrapolate the position of the next hop k positions ahead in time. For example, a simple technique is to assume the data follows a linear trend.

$$P_{j+k} = P_j + \Delta P * e \dots \dots \dots \quad (1)$$

Where:

P_{j+k} future position of the next hop.

P_j current position of the next hop.

ΔP interval between current position and previous position of the next hop.

e factor indicating the gap between packets received.

The predictive algorithm is useful in networks with very high mobility and which are contention-based. In LORA-CBF, a Hello message is broadcast periodically. Every node keeps the location information of every neighbour from which it has received Hello messages. When one node receives a packet for transmission to a particular destination, it first checks its routing table to determine if it knows the location of the destination node. If it does, it triggers the short-term predictive algorithm to calculate the future position of the destination. If the node can reach the destination, it sends the packet directly. Otherwise, before retransmitting it, the node predicts the locations of the neighbour nodes, based on previous positions, and sends the

Figure 7. Sort-term predictive algorithm used in LORA-CBF

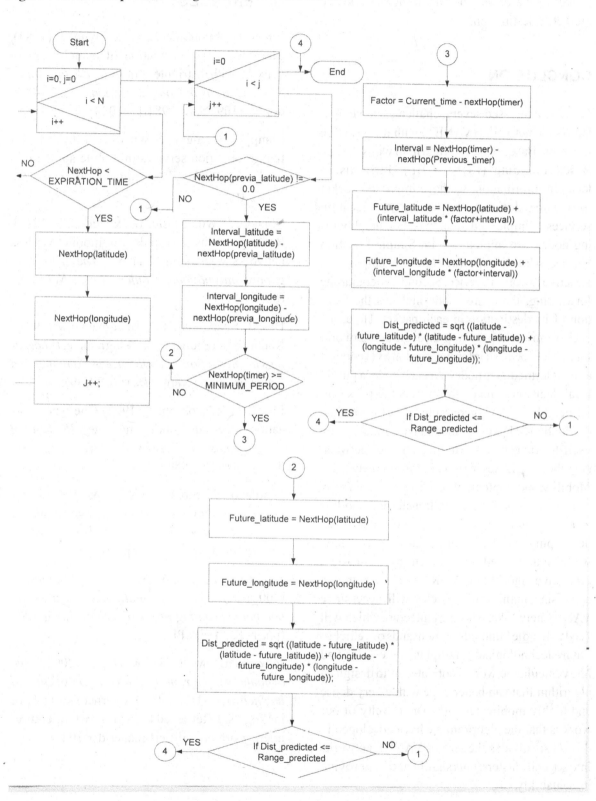

packet to the closest neighbouring node to the predicted destination.

CONCLUSION

We have addressed several challenges in vehicular ad-hoc networks (VANET) with the Reactive Location-Based Routing Algorithm with Cluster-Based Flooding (LORA-CBF). First, using location information, we have improved packet forwarding decisions employing two location services: Simple and Reactive. For neighbouring nodes, we implemented a Simple Location Service, while for faraway nodes; we employed a Reactive Location Service. Second, in geographic forwarding, the source node includes the location of its destination in each packet. Here, the packet moves hop by hop through the network, forwarded location information along via cooperating intermediates nodes. At each node, a purely local decision is made to forward the packet to the neighbour that is geographically closest to the destination. However, location information by itself does not guarantee the transmission between neighbouring nodes in vehicular ad-hoc networks. Mobility and contention of wireless media may cause loss of packets being transferred, and this is a very important aspect to consider when developing wireless routing algorithms. Here, we have addressed this problem by including a predictive algorithm in LORA-CBF. In sum, the increasing number of vehicles will necessitate VANET networks, whose architecture which will need to handle hundreds or thousands of vehicles. Future technological paradigms in the area of ad hoc vehicular networks motivated us to design an algorithm that can better cope with a very dense and highly mobile network. The novelty of our work is that the algorithm we have developed in this thesis divides the size of VANET networks into several clusters, thus significantly improving its scalability.

REFERENCES

Baker, D., Ephremides, A., & Flynn, J. (1984). The design and simulation of a mobile radio network with distribute control. *IEEE Journal on Selected Areas in Communications, 2*, 226–237. doi:10.1109/JSAC.1984.1146043

Camp, T., Boleng, J., & Wilcox, L. (2002). Location information services in mobile ad hoc networks. *International Communication Conference* (ICC), (pp. 1-7).

Chiang, C., Wu, H., Liu, W., & Gerla, M. (1997). Routing in clustered multihop, mobile wireless networks with fading channel. *The IEEE Singapore International Conference on Networks*, (pp. 197-211).

Das, B., Sivakumar, R., & Bharghavan, V. (1997). Routing in ad hoc networks using a spine. *Proceedings in International Conference in Computer and Communication Networks*, (pp. 34-39).

Floyd, S., & Jacobson, V. (1994). The synchronization of periodic routing messages. *IEEE/ACM Transactions on Networking, 2*(2), 122–136. doi:10.1109/90.298431

Giordano, S., Stojmenovic, I., & Blazevic, L. (2003). Position based routing algorithms for ad hoc networks: A taxonomy. *Ad Hoc Wireless Networking Conference*, (pp. 103-136).

Jacquet, P., Laouiti, A., Minet, P., & Viennot, L. (2002). *Performance of multipoint relaying in ad hoc mobile routing protocols. Networking 2002* (pp. 1–12). Italy: Pise.

Johnson, D., Maltz, D., & Hu, Y. (2004). *The dynamic source routing protocol for mobile ad hoc networks* (DSR). IETF Internet Draft (Work in Progress). Retrieved from http://www.ietf.org/internet-drafts/draft-ietf-manet-dsr-10.txt.

Käsemann, M., Hartenstein, H., Fübler, H., & Mauve, M. (2002). Analysis of a location service for position-based routing in mobile ad hoc networks. *Proceedings of the 1st German Workshop on Mobile Ad Hoc Networks,* (pp. 1-13).

Krishna, P., Vaidya, N., Chatterjee, M., & Pradhan, D. (1997). A cluster-based approach for routing in dynamic networks. *ACM SIGCOMM. Computer Communication Review, 27*(2), 49–65. doi:10.1145/263876.263885

Mitelman, B., & Zaslavsky, A. (1999). Link state routing protocol with cluster based flooding for mobile ad-hoc computer networks. *Proceedings of the Workshop on Computer Science and Information Technologies CSIT'99*, (pp. 28-35).

Sivakumar, R., Das, B., & Bharghavan, V. (1998). Spine routing in ad hoc networks. *ACM/Baltzer Cluster. The Computer Journal, 1*, 237–248.

Vilalta, R., Apte, C., Hellerstein, J., Ma, S., & Weiss, S. (2002). Predictive algorithms in the management of computer systems. *IBM Systems Journal, 41*(3). doi:10.1147/sj.413.0461

Chapter 8
Evaluation of the LORA– CBF Routing Algorithm with Selective Gateway in an Ad Hoc WiMAX Network

Alejandro Galaviz-Mosqueda
Centro de Investigación Científica y Educación Superior de Ensenada, México

ABSTRACT

Vehicular Ad-Hoc Networks (VANETs) are characterized by their high mobility, where wireless links between vehicles unpredictably can change. This mobility makes it very challenging to establish and maintain a communication link in vehicular networks; therefore, networking in these kinds of networks has become a very intense area of study. Consequently, research of ad hoc routing and medium access control strategies has become an intensive part of current study. The research community has expressed considerable interest in introducing WiMAX as medium access technology and geographic strategies for routing algorithms. This work presents an evaluation of the LORA-CBF geographic routing algorithm that permits seamless communication in an ad-hoc WiMAX network.

INTRODUCTION

Vehicles are an important tool in everyday life. In fact, in major cities, people spend an important part of each day in their vehicles, either driving or stuck in traffic jams. Today, there are many existing technologies designed to make vehicular road travel safer, easier and more enjoyable (e.g. geographical positioning system, proximity sensors, multimedia communication). Despite these advances, however, the impact of these devices in the areas of comfort and safety is somewhat limited because the information gathered by

DOI: 10.4018/978-1-4666-0209-0.ch008

these cannot be share among vehicles, due to a lack of network connectivity. Therefore, the great challenge for these kinds of networks is to meet the issues placed on both the medium access and routing algorithms.

In order to share data more effectively and dynamically in applications, thus improving passenger safety, convenience, and comfort, protocols and network devices must provide both timely and reliable data transfer among vehicles. Deploying network devices in vehicular scenarios represents a huge technical challenge that involves every layer of the communication model; however, this is particularly important for the lowest three layers (i.e. physical, medium access and network). This is primarily due to the highly dynamic network environment, characterized by the constant entry and exit of nodes, and the difficulty of handling highly dense vehicular networks (Aquino, Gonzalez, Villaseñor, &Crespo, 2009; Aquino, Gonzalez& Villaseñor, 2008; Aquino, Rangel & Edwards, 2008; Aquino & Edwards, 2006).

According to Briesemeister,Schäfers & Hommel, (2000), the highly dynamic nature and multiple demands imposed on vehicular networks means that participating nodes must:

- Have radio transceiver technology that provides omni-directional coverage
- Be capable of rapid vehicle-to-vehicle communications to keep track of dynamic topology changes
- Possess highly efficient routing algorithms that fully exploit network bandwidth.

However, unlike other scenarios, nodes in vehicular networks undergo constant and rapid change. In conventional networks, nodes can move slowly or even be static, however, in vehicular scenarios, the network topology can change in a fraction of a second. For example a car accident can turn a highway scenario where vehicles are free to move from lane to lane at speeds exceeding 90km/h to a city scenario where travel speeds can

be extremely restricted and movement between lanes is impossible.

This chapter presents the challenges of incorporating WiMAX and geographic routing (i.e. LORA-CBF) in vehicle-to-vehicle multi-hop networks. We believe that a mixture of geographic routing algorithm that is supported by a WiMAX layer can outperform proposals explored until now in vehicle-to-vehicle networks.

This chapter also compares Ad hoc On-demand Distance Vector (AODV) and Location Routing Algorithm with cluster based flooding (LORA-CBF) in a static, dense scenario in WiMAX-mesh mode as the first step in order to develop a fully mobile communication subsystem.

The rest of this chapter is organized as follows, Section 2 is an overview of the literature of VANETs and WiMAX related proposals as well as a brief review of routing protocols in VANETs, Section 3 presents LORA-CBF algorithm, in Section 4 the simulation setup is described, Section5 shows the analysis of the gathered results and finally in Section 6 the chapter conclude.

LITERATURE REVIEW

Multi-Hop Vehicular Networks under WiMAX

Numerous researchers have worked to overcome issues related to vehicular communications (e.g. Brown, Cullen, Brackstone, Gunton & McDonald, 2000; Rajamani& Shladover, 2001;Varaiya, 1993;Yang, Liu & Zhao,2004;Yin, et al. 2004;Car-2car Communication Consortium, 2010; Communication for eSaftey, 2010; SAFESPOT Integrated Project, 2010). In 2004, the IEEE group created the IEEE 802.11p (WAVE) task force; the workforce established a new standard that essentially employs the same PHY layer of the IEEE 802.11a standard, but uses the 10 MHz bandwidth channel instead of the 20 MHz bandwidth of IEEE 802.11a. With respect to the MAC layer, WAVE is based on a contention method (i.e. CSMA/CA), similar to other standards in this group.

The MAC layer in IEEE 802.11p suffers from several significant drawbacks. For example, in vehicular scenarios, WAVE drops over 53% of packets sent, according to simulation results (Bilstrup K., Uhlemann, Strom, &Bilstrup U., 2008). WAVE also has a limited transmission range. Simulations carried out by Ahmed, Krishnamachari& Psounis, (2008) show that only 1% of communication attempts at 750m are successful in a highway scenario presenting multipath shadowing. Furthermore, results gathered by Stibor, Zang& Reumerman, (2007) show that throughput decays as the number of vehicles increases. In fact, throughput decreases to almost zero with 20 concurrent transmissions. Stibor et al (2007) argue, based in their results, that WAVE is not scalable. Additionally, IEEE 802.11p does not support QoS, which is essential in Vehicular Ad hoc Networks (VANETs).

Recently, the IEEE 802.16 taskforce (IEEE Std. 802.11e, 2005, 2005; IEEE std. 802.16j, 2009) actualized this standard to better permit it to handle QoS, mobility, and multihop relay communications. Networks using the WiMAX MAC layer can now potentially meet a wider range of demands, including VCN.

Worldwide Interoperability for Microwave Access (WiMAX) is a nonprofit consortium supported by over 400 companies dedicated to creating profiles based on the IEEE 802.16 standard.

The first IEEE 802.16 standard considers fixed nodes in a straight line with line of sight between the base station and each fixed remote node (IEEE std 802.16, 2004). Later, the IEEE 802.16e task force (TF) amended the original standard to provide mobility to end users in non-line-of-sight conditions (Peters & Heath, 2009). The most recent modification to IEEE 802.16e was in March, 2007. This modification, 802.16j-2009, allows multihop relay communications.

IEEE 802.16j operates in both transparent and non-transparent modes. In transparent mode, mobile stations (MS) must decode the control messages relayed from the base station (BS). In other words, they must operate within the physical coverage radius of the BS. In non-transparent mode, one of the relay stations (RS) provides the control messages to the MS. The main difference between the transparent and the non-transparent mode architecture is that in transparent mode, RS increases network capacity while in non-transparent mode, the RS extends the BS range. Additionally, the RS can be classified according to mobility and can be fixed (FRS), nomads (NRS) or mobiles (MRS) (Peters & Heath, 2009).

WiMAX in Multi-hop Vehicular Communication Networks is now a hot topic in research, mainly because the WiMAX concept tends to adapt well to vehicular network technology. However, despite recent progress in implementing vehicular networks with WiMAX, much work has yet to be done.

This section presents proposals that employ IEEE 802.16 as their underlying technology for multi-hop vehicular communication networks.

CEPEC

Authors Yang, Ou, Chen, & He, (2007) propose a cluster based routing protocol for multihop vehicular communication based on the IEEE 802.16-2004 mesh standard with a centralized scheduler. Coordinated External Peer Communications (CEPEC) divides networks into segments and each segment represents a cluster. In order to accomplish this task, CEPEC needs to determine the geographic position of every vehicle; therefore, all vehicles must be equipped with GPS. The main objective of the protocol described in Yeng et al., (2007) is to provide fair Internet access to every participating node in the network.

The centralized scheduler used in Yeng et al., (2007) can be an important development, because it needs a highly stable network. If a node suddenly changes its direction and enters a new network, its transmission schedule could not be valid anymore. The latter situation can be very common in vehicular scenarios and implies that network performance could suffer significant deterioration in terms of packet loss, latency, etc.

Yang et al., (2007) obtained their results using a proprietary development simulation tool, their results shows that all segments have fair access to the Internet, but it is very important to mention that CEPEC was tested in a two lane straight highway with a limited length. Important variables such as direction change or delays caused by segment restructuring were not presented in the paper.

VFHS

The authors Chiu, Hwang, &Chen, (2009), developed a handover mechanism called "vehicular fast handover scheme (VFHS)". Chiu et al. (2009) developed a hybrid architecture using the IEEE 802.16e and IEEE 802.16j standards. The proposal is quite interesting because they employ vehicle-to-vehicle communication to directly exchange control information. The authors Chiu et al. (2009) classify the participating nodes in the network as follows:

- Relay Vehicles (RV) act as mobile relay stations that use the IEEE 802.16j standard. The authors suggest that this role can be assigned to a public transportation bus.
- Broken Vehicles (BV) are cars that are temporally outside of the coverage of any RV
- Oncoming Small-size Vehicles (OSV) are small vehicles driving in the opposite direction of the RV.

OSVs directly transmit the information maintained in layers 2 and 3 to the BVs approaching the coverage area of the RV which the OSV is leaving. The information passed from OSV to BV is necessary to synchronize communications between the oncoming vehicles and the network. VFHS uses an explicit cross layer design approach

(Srivastava & Motani, 2005). The NS-2 simulator tool was used to simulate Srivastava & Motani, (2005) proposal and the results show that the handoff mechanism developed helped to reduce the handoff latency between relay vehicles.

In the topology described in Chiu et al., (2009), the relay vehicles are equipped with IEEE 802.16j, which is used to register the buses at a base station that functions according to IEEE 802.16e. This proposal does not provide a communications solution for vehicles beyond the RV coverage. Additionally, it does not consider a routing mechanism to assist nodes select the optimal RV for overlapping coverage areas.

An Interference and QOS Aware Distributed Scheduling

Amin, Wang& Ramanathan, (2008) presents a scheduling mechanism called "An interference and QOS aware distributed scheduling approach for hybrid IEEE 802.16e mesh networks", Amin, Wang& Ramanathan, (2008) study their protocol in a network configuration with military potential that is organized hierarchically into three levels: satellite for backhaul, IEEE 802.16-204 in mesh mode, and IEEE 802.16e for mobile stations. The portable base stations can be further classified as MBSs (with backhaul) and the moving units as MSSs (without backhaul). It is important to note that the latter (MSs) can be served by a MSS or MBS. Each MBS communicates with the different segments of the network through a dedicated interface. Consequently, MBS have three interfaces and MSS have only two. Finally, MSs only have one IEEE 802.16e-2005 interface. Each BS (MSS or MBS) is a gateway to the cluster, which is a collection of MSs served by a BS. To send packets between clusters, MSs employ an intra-gateway protocol Mobility-Aware Intra Gateway Routing (Amin & Wang, 2007). Basically, the scheduling algorithm developed by Amin, Wang, & Ramanathan, (2008) focuses on managing the tunnel between the point to multipoint (PMP) and mesh interfaces in each BS, prioritizing the PMP link.

A significant drawback in (Amin, Wang, & Ramanathan, 2008) is the lack of an ad-hoc mode. As a result, MSs can be served only within the radio coverage of a MBS or MSS. Vehicles outside the coverage of a BS, but within the radio range of an MS, cannot be registered in the network. Furthermore, if the PMP link capacity is surpassed, the transmission request is discarded. Therefore, if there is a way to transmit in an ad-hoc fashion, transmissions between neighbor vehicles are allowed without wasting BS resources.

802.16j Proposals

The authors Ge, Wen, Ang, & Liang, (2010) use an architecture based on IEEE 802.16j. They suggest a method for mobile stations to select an optimal relay station where the radio coverage areas of RSs overlap. The proposed method is only described mathematically and is based on non-linear optimization. Their mathematical results show that network capacity can significantly increase. However, Ge et al. (2010) do not perform simulations or implementations of their proposal.

In (Fei, Yang, Ou, Zhong & Gao, 2009), the authors propose a dynamic bandwidth allocation algorithm with a QoS guarantee for IEEE 802.16j-enabled vehicular networks. The strategy works as follows: bandwidth requests corresponding to different types of services are allocated to each relay station in a centralized way, based on the minimal average queuing delay of total network. Fei et al. (2009) suggest employing an optimization application that uses Lagrange multipliers. Simulation results in Fei et al. (2009) were obtained by using Mathlab and the shows that the mathematical optimization applied to the type of service minimizes queue delay. A significant drawback in this proposal is that Fei et al. (2009) assume that the primary link is the downlink, based on a basic internet connection. However, in vehicular networks, both the downlink and uplink connections are equally important. For example, a user can be making a video call or relaying it in both directions because the user requires significant resources from the uplink while sending the video to the Internet.

Table 1 summarizes the main characteristics of the proposals described.

The analyzed proposals reveal that there is currently no dynamic fully distributed routing mechanism that satisfies the demands of vehicular networks. However, our review shows that WiMAX is a viable alternative for vehicular communications (VC). Also, researchers are currently interested in integrating this technology

Table 1. A comparative table of proposals of WiMAX for vehicular networks

Reference	Modificated Layer				Simulation	Standard	Publication Year
	Ad-Hoc	PHY	MAC	RED			
CEPEC	Yes	Yes	Yes	Yes	Propietary	2004	2007
A Cross Layer Fast Handover	No	Yes	Yes	No	NS2/NIST	e,j	2009
An interference QoS aware distributed schedulin	No	No	Yes	Nyes	NS2/NIST	e,2004	2008
Optimal relay selection in 16j MHR vehicular Networks	No	No	Yes	Yes	No	j	2010
Bandwidth allocation algorithm with QoS guarantee for 6j vehiclar networks	No	No	Yes	No	Matlab	j	2009

into vehicular ad hoc networks. Nevertheless, a lot of work has to be done before WiMAX can be deployed in communications systems. How to most effectively provide inter-vehicular communication in VC is still a contentious topic. Also important are issues related to the network architecture, particularly regarding how to form groups in the absence of the BS (ad-hoc domain) that can still interact with the BS upon demand. Equally important is how to provide access control in coverage area boundaries and determine which routing mechanism best optimizes network bandwidth. To the best of our knowledge, any proposal that involves WiMAX and VC can form an ad-hoc domain without a BS or RS.

Routing in Mobile Ad-Hoc Networks

An infrastructure network is formed by a set of nodes managed by a central entity. On the other hand, an ad-hoc network is defined as a set of nodes that has no single coordinating point. Finding an optimal route according to the parameters established (e.g. distance, hops, etc) from a source node to a destination is known as the routing protocol, which is of vital importance to network function. A routing protocol consists of a routing decision algorithm (Popescu-Zeletin, Radusch & Rigani, 2010). This routing decision algorithm is based on the information available in actualized tables of specific nodes and their capacity to forward information from one node to another, based on a specific set of rules that are established in the algorithm. Popescu-Zeletin et al. (2010) propose evaluating the performance of a routing algorithm according to the following metrics:

- **Packet delivery ratio:** the ratio between received and sent data packets
- **Latency:** the delay in data packets from source to destination
- **Routing over-head:** the relation between protocol control packets per payload data

- **Fault tolerance:** the process of detection and recovery of broken links

The abovementioned metrics are highly interdependent, which means that there is a tradeoff between them. For example, improving fault tolerance leads to decreased routing information. This, in turn, decreases routing overhead due to the reduction of routing information being sent. This is important because decreased routing information optimizes bandwidth and increases data transmission.

Routing a packet in a conventional network is not a particularly challenging task because a central entity identifies each node in the neighborhood and these nodes can forward the message from a network node to an access point. This research, however, focuses on routing algorithms for ad-hoc networks, where their infrastructure-less nature does not permit such stable or preset routing.

MANET Routing

Mobile ad-hoc networks or MANETs represent a challenging area of research in which new aspects need to be constantly studied because of new technologies. Routing in ad-hoc networks is a much more difficult task. It becomes even more complicated when it involves mobility. Consequently, the handoff mechanism in MANETs is vital when choosing a routing strategy.

MANET routing algorithms can be classified as either being source routing, topology-based or geographical. Source routing algorithms define the route from the source to the destination, based on the source node decision. Topology-based routing algorithms locate the destination node through their neighbors or routes already established by their neighbors. Finally, in geographic routing, each node decides the next relay hop based on geographical information.

Topology-based routing algorithms can be further classified as proactive, reactive or hybrid, which is a combination of the former two. Proactive routing uses a similar strategy to that used of a conventional cabled network. Participating nodes in a proactive protocol establish the routes in advance, based on information exchanged with their neighbor nodes. Proactive routing minimizes the delay in data information because routes are immediately available; however, in a highly dynamic network, this approach causes significant overhead. Important examples of proactive protocols are: Optimized Link State Routing or OLSR (Clausen & Jacquet, 2003) and Destination Sequenced Distance Vector or DSDV, based on Dijkstra´s (Dijkstra, 1959) and Bellmand-Ford's (Bellman, 1958) shortest path routing strategies.

Reactive routing strategies gather routes on demand, meaning that they only find a route if some application needs it. This strategy introduce less overhead in the network, but the transmission delay increases because the route discovery process floods the network with Hello messages to find the destination. The Ad-hoc On-Demand Distance Vector, AODV (Perkins, Belding-Royer & Das, 2003) is an important protocol in this category, which uses a set of control messages to discover a route. When a node needs to transmit along a specific route, it sends out a route request (RREQ), which is flooded along the potential route to the destination node in broadcast mode. The major problem with this protocol is that the subsequent flooding introduces a lot overhead, especially in dense networks.

Each of the previous described strategies (proactive and reactive) has its respective advantages and disadvantages. As we mentioned previously, the performance of a protocol greatly depends on the specific scenario. For example, when a scenario is static or has very low mobility with a high data load, a reactive strategy introduces more overhead than a proactive routing strategy. This is the case because the transmitting node has to launch a route discovery several times, which involves

many nodes in a flooding process. Meanwhile, proactive approaches only launch their flooding process at the beginning of the transmission cycle or if there is a sudden change. Because the number of scenarios in ad-hoc networks can vary greatly, choosing a routing protocol involves carefully characterizing the network scenario.

VANET Routing

Vehicular ad-hoc networks (VANETs) represent a very special type of MANET. The major demand of a VANET, however, is the speed necessary for it to provide the timely security sensitive information it must handle. The speed of VANET nodes requires researchers to develop a routing strategy that can handle the very dynamic nature of a VANET, where vehicles confront many physical obstacles, do not maintain steady speeds, and have vehicles entering and exiting the network in great numbers at irregular intervals. Because of these three major demands, existing MANET routing approaches cannot be directly implemented in VANETs (Olariu & Weigel 2010). For example, in source routing, the set of relay nodes along a specific trajectory must decide upon a route a priori, which is provided by the source node. In a VANET, however, the location of relay nodes cannot be predicted based on simple geographic or traffic rules. Consequently, a second group of geographic protocols must be developed to provide a more promising routing strategy for VANETs (Popescu-Zeletin et al. 2010). A detailed performance evaluation of MANET routing protocols in VANETs conditions can be observed in Jiancai L., Feng C. & Jiakai X., (2010) and in Liu N., Qian H., Yan J. & Xu Y. (2009).

AODV is still a very common routing protocol, both in both MANET and VANET studies (e.g. Jiancai et al. (2010), Liu et. al. (2009)). For this reason, AODV is presented in detail before geographic routing in this chapter.

AODV

The Ad hoc On-demand Distance Vector (AODV) (Perkins, Belding-Royer, & Das, 2003) is perhaps the most used and studied ad-hoc routing protocol. This routing protocol is based on a reactive strategy and uses a set of control messages to establish a route between mobile nodes. The most important control messages are: Route Request (RREQ), Route Replay (RREP) and Hello.

In AODV, as in other reactive routing protocols, a route is only established when a node wishes to share information with another node, and does not already have a valid route to the destination.

In order to define a specific route, a RREQ message is broadcast, then each intermediate node receiving the RREQ records the reverse path to the source node and verifies if it is the destination node or if its own routing table has a valid route to the destination node. If it has a valid route to destination node in its routing table, it will send a RREP (Route Reply packet) along the reverse path; if not, it will re-broadcast RREQ. This mechanism is applied until the RREQ reaches the destination node or reaches the node which contains the routing information of the destination node. If a route fails during data packet forwarding, the intermediate node, where the failure occurs, launches a RREQ process to solve the failure.

AODV has several issues concerning its use in vehicle-to-vehicle multihop networks. For example, the initial flooding may cause significant overhead in dense scenarios. Another drawback is when the destination node sends the RREP through the reverse path that is prone to failures due to the high mobility of the vehicles. However, proposals based on AODV for vehicular networks still are a research topic. An important example of research in this area is the approach presented in Li, Liu & Chu, (2010), which improves the recovery strategy when a link breaks. The improvement consists in broadcast in addition to the recovery of RREQ data packets. Their simulation AODV performs well with their improvement; however,

they perform simulations with only 40 vehicles and in the scenario with higher velocities (30m/s), the data frequency is low (2.5 p/s), and in the scenario with higher data frequency (4.5 p/s), the velocity is low (15 m/s).

Geographic Routing in VANETs

A Geographic routing strategy means that a packet will be forward based on the geographical position of the destination, instead of an IP address. In geographic routing approaches a node knows its own location, generally with a GPS on-board system, and shares it among its neighbors (i.e. nodes within their radio range). Nodes can broadcast their position through periodic beacons, which also are used for neighborhood maintenance.

A geographic strategy can be divided into two steps: first, the source node needs to acquire the physical position of a destination. The second step is to employ a data dissemination algorithm. Obtaining the position is done through a localization acquisition service which can be carried out by the routing algorithm (e.g. Aquino & Edwards, 2006) or through a localization service (e.g. Mo, Zhu, Makki, Pissinou & Karimi, 2009) that performs the task independently (e.g. Zhao & Cao, 2006; Mo, Zhu, Makki & Pissinou, 2006). Data dissemination forwards the data packets from source to destination. In this step, a node only needs local information because it knows the position of the destination node. Making the forwarding decision is a process made on a hopper-hop basis.

Geographic routing algorithms are widely used in existing VANET protocols (e.g. Popescu-Zeletin, Radusch, & Rigani, 2010) and can be classified in several ways. Lee K., Lee U. & Gerla M., (2010) divides the geographic routing protocols according to delay restrictions in Delay-Tolerant Networks (i.e. networks that support important delays), non-delay tolerant networks and a mixture of the former two; Bernsen & Manivannan, (2009) uses a wide set of criteria to classify routing algorithms. As the purpose of this chapter is not a routing survey, we will describe some outstanding routing strategies in the following paragraphs. Readers especially interested in the subject should refer to the former references.

OCTOPUS

Melamed, Keidar & Barel, (2005) presents a geographic routing protocol called Octopus. As in almost all geographic algorithms, the authors assume that each node can determine its own location through triangulation or GPS devices. In Octopus, space is divided into a lattice of horizontal and vertical strips. Nodes called location servers store the location of each node located in the same strip by means of periodic diffusion of strip update packets (SUP). SUP initiate at one end of strip and travel along the length of the strip. In the SUP trajectory, each node adds its own location and transmits it both vertically and horizontally. Octopus is formed by three sub-protocols:

- **Location Update**, which maintains the location table
- **Location discovery**, which performs the location discovery process that consists of search through the strips to obtain the location of a specific destination.
- **Forwarding**, which delivers the data throughout the network from source to destination, estimating the position of the target with the two most immediate locations received.

Results gathered by Melamed et al. (2005) using the NS-2 simulator shows that Octopus supports different dynamic scenarios and is scalable. Because the protocol was originally developed for MANETs, there are some unresolved issues regarding its deployment in vehicular networks. For example, the location update service is initiated by border nodes in the grid. As this marks the end

of the grid, there is no need to transmit beyond this point. However, it is important to note that vehicular networks have no fixed geographical area. Contrary to previous studies, this work uses a random way point mobility model (Bettstetter, Hartenstein& Pérez-Costa, 2002) which does not represent authentic node behavior in VANETs.

VADD

Zhao & Cao,(2006) present the Vehicle-Assisted Data Delivery (VADD) protocol. The protocol, developed especially for VANETs, is based on a store and forward approach, which depends on digital maps maintained in a GPS navigator. VADD consists of two stages: the first stage selects the next street to take and the second stage determines the following street that will be chosen by the next hop node. In order to carry out this process, the authors assume the following:

- Vehicles know their location by either triangulation or a GPS device.
- Vehicles are equipped with pre-loaded digital maps
- Vehicles have detailed traffic statistics immediately available (i.e. density, maximum speed, mean vehicle speed)

The VADD protocol introduces the above information in a mathematical formula to estimate the expected delivery delay of each street. After this, the node that is carrying a packet decides whether or not to forward the packet or continue carrying it until it reaches a plausible relay node. The authors propose three solutions to select a next hop: 1) select the node closest to the next intersection; 2) choose a node that drives towards the relative position of the next intersection selected and 3) select more than one relay.

The authors of VADD present results gathered in the well-known NS-2 simulator that demonstrate that VADD outperforms other MANET protocols (i.e. GPSR and DSR) with regards to packet delivery ratio and latency. However, VADD has the severe limitation that it is suitable only for delay tolerant networks (Jain, Fall& Patra, 2004). The authors Zhao &Cao, (2006) do not explain how vehicles discover the localization of destinations, which is a very important factor because the localization process can consume significant resources.

GPSR with Predictive Mode

Wang, Wu, Lee & Ke, (2010) propose a routing strategy which consists of four blocks: beaconing, routing strategy in straight roads, at the intersections and the recovery strategy.

The beaconing block consists of sending periodic broadcast messages to broadcast basic information such as position, direction and speed to its neighbors (i.e. nodes within its radio range). The second block is the routing strategy selected to choose the next hop to forward data packets to on straight roads. This is based on a greedy forwarding (i.e. choose the next hop closest to the destination).

The third block is about routing at the intersections, where nodes change to a predictive mode, where they must calculate the future position of the neighboring nodes. The prediction of future position is made through a mathematical formula also provided in Wang, et al. (2010). Finally, the recovery strategy is the fourth block and consists of using the right-hand rule (karp & Kung, 2000) when the routing algorithm fails.

Wang et al., (2010) uses the NS-2 simulation environment to perform their simulations. Results gathered from simulations show that their geographic routing strategy is well suited to urban vehicular scenarios. However, there are unresolved issues in their investigation. For example, the routing strategy still must deal with the local maximum problem. More extensive simulations to test their protocol in different vehicle densities need to be run.

CBDRP

Song, Xia & Shen, (2010) present a design of a cluster-based directional routing protocol (CBDRP). The main idea of CBR is to divide the geographical area in grids of at least 350 m (considering the radio range of IEEE 802.11p standard). The division is fixed and is based on digital maps or GPS, with each grid having its own cluster head.

The main process is to select the cluster head, which is based on beacon interchange. The process is as follows: first each node waits for a T1 period of time, if it does not receive a cluster beacon, then it sends a regular beacon (called APPLY) and waits for a period of time T2. The purpose of this APPLY messages is to find the node closest to the grid's center. If the node does not receive an APPLY message or a cluster message before the T2 period has elapsed, it will elect itself as cluster head.

When the cluster head is leaving its own grid, it will broadcast a LEAVE message. The remaining nodes in the grid will then elect a new cluster head according to the above procedure.

For data dissemination, CBDRP performs a 4-step procedure. The first and the second steps are devoted to route establishment in a very similar way to the AODV route discovery process. The third step is a link failure strategy, consisting of a carry and forward approach. Finally, the fourth step disconnects the link after the transmission ends.

In order to evaluate CBDRP, Song et al., (2010) performs simulations in the well-known NS2 simulator. The scenario consists of 60 nodes moving uniformly from 25 m/s to 35 m/s in a 20m x 3200 m straight highway. They conclude that CBDRP outperforms the AODV and GPSR algorithms. Their conclusion is based on the simplicity of the CBDRP algorithm and that they require less information than GPSR and AODV to maintain the neighborhood updated.

CONCLUSION

According to the proposals analyzed in this work, we can conclude the following:

Because of the several differences between vehicular and mobile ad-hoc networks (e.g. mobility, computing power, battery constraints, etc.) routing algorithms developed for MANETs cannot be directly deployed in vehicular networks. Therefore, new routing algorithms focusing on strengths and weaknesses of VANETs are necessary.

Geographic routing is very desirable in VANETs because protocols that apply this strategy have greater scalability. In addition, clustering is a very suitable technique for routing protocols in VANETs because it also improves resource utilization. However, the overhead in cluster position-based protocols can be an important issue that must be carefully studied in order to minimize the overhead caused by the control information necessary for cluster formation and maintenance.

LORA-CBF

Location Routing Algorithm with cluster based flooding (LORA-CBF) is a position-based routing algorithm that also uses a clustering algorithm to achieve routing scalability. In addition, LORA-CBF is fully independent of roadside units because it implements its own location service in a fully distributed manner. The following paragraphs will explain the different stages of the LORA algorithm in greater detail.

Clustering

LORA-CBF organizes the vehicles in groups using its cluster formation algorithm. A node that is within a cluster may have one of the following roles:

- *Undecided:* a node that is beginning the clustering process.

- *Member:* cluster nodes that only demand services (e.g. route discovery).
- *Gateway:* nodes that have the ability to forward packets between clusters.
- *Cluster Head:* the node that manages the cluster so that they can more efficiently communicate with others clusters.

The clustering algorithm consists of 6 basic conditions:

1. All nodes start a random T1 timer and send a beacon with the undecided status (U).
2. If T1 expires and the node does not receive a cluster head (CH) beacon, it becomes a CH, initiates a random timer T2 and sends a beacon with CH status.
3. If CH1 receives a beacon from CH2 which has more members, CH1 changes its status to Member of CH2
4. If a Member (M) of a CH1 receives a beacon from CH2, it registers the CH2 and changes its status to gateway (G).
5. If a G node receives a beacon from a member belonging to another CH, it registers the M node and its cluster.
6. If a node with M status receives one beacon from a node with G status that belongs to another cluster, the M node changes its status to G.

The main objective of clustering is to control the overhead caused by the flooding process. Hence, the cluster organization algorithm of LORA-CBF improves the scalability of the routing algorithm because only nodes with the correct status (i.e. G and CH) can forward the route request messages.

Location Service

When a packet from a higher layer arrives at the network layer and the route to the destination is unknown, LORA_CBF starts the location discovery process (ldp). The first step of ldp is flooding, which consists of sending the location request packet (LREQ) to obtain the location of the desired destination node. This flooding process is controlled via a cluster hierarchy, which means that only G and CH nodes can forward the LREQ packet. However, in very dense scenarios like the one chosen for this simulation, many gateways can retransmit the LREQ, increasing the overhead. Consequently, we have modified the location discovery algorithm. Cluster-based flooding employs a selective gateway forwarding approach in which only the gateway closest to the cluster head forwards the LREQ.

Once the LREQ reaches a cluster of the destination node, the destination's cluster head returns a location replay packet (LREP) to the source node by unicast. Because the source position is known at this point, the LREP packet can travel geographically, i.e. each node can select the most forward within radius (MFR) neighbor closest to the source.

Data Dissemination

When the LREP packet reaches the source, the data can now begin forwarding to the destination node geographically, the same way as in the MFR strategy.

The Table 2 shows the main characteristics of the routing protocols described above.

Simulation Design and Results

The OPNET modeler package v16.0 was used to simulate the performance of both AODV and LORA-CBF. The scenario presented in this work is a circular road model (see Figure 1). This scenario does not present nodes entering or exiting the system. Furthermore, all vehicles are fixed and preserve a constant vehicular density and distribution. The circular scenario represents a 6-lane highway with lane separations of 10 meters. Additionally, the external lane has a 3 km radius, meaning it has an approximated length of 19 km.

The scenario includes a total of 120 vehicles, each of the six lanes containing 20 vehicles. The separation between any two vehicles in any one of the six lanes is 18° or approximately 942m. We conservatively assume 1000 meters as the radio range of WiMAX stations; however Yang et al. suggest 2.4km as the transmission range. Every node has only two neighbors in its own lane. On the other hand, horizontally, the separation, as previously mentioned, is 10 meters. Consequently, each node has 5 radial neighbors (i.e. from the center to the outside circle). Therefore, each node in our scenario has 17 neighbors.

Table 2. VANET Routing Protocol

	Improved AODV	Octopus	VADD	GPSR	CBDRP	LORA-CBF
Vehicle to vehicle	*	*	x	*	*	*
Positioin Based	x	*	*	*	x	*
Predictive	x	x	*	*	x	*
street Aware	x	x	*	*	x	x
Position System required	x	*	*	*	*	*
Map required	x	x	*	x	x	x
Location service Required	x	x	*	*	x	x
Clustering	x	x	x	x	*	*

Figure 1. Graphic description of the implemented scenario in OPNET

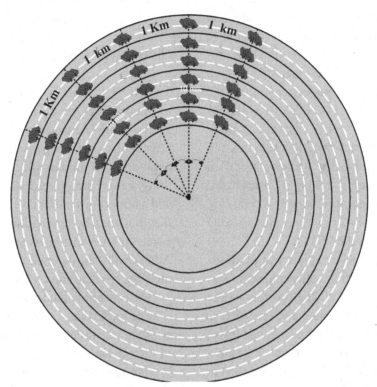

We positioned the first node at the center of the first lane on the eastern side of the east-west axis. From this point, nodes were added at 18° intervals along all of the 6 lanes in a clockwise fashion. The precise location of each node was calculated with (1) which is the parametric equation of the circumference with the parameter x= ρ•cos Ω, where ρ is the radius of the corresponding lane and Ω is an angle that increases from 0° to 360°. Finally, (x,y) are the coordinates of the node.

$$x \cdot exp(2) + y \cdot exp(2) = \rho \cdot exp(2) \qquad (1)$$

Simulation Metrics

We chose important metrics that according to Popescu-Zeletin et al.(2010), permit us to measure the scalability of the network. The metrics considered are listed below:

- Packet delivery ratio (PDR): the number of packets received by the destination divided by the number of packets sent.
- Routing load: the total number of control data transmitted by all nodes. The transmission at each hop is counted once for both routing and data packets.
- WiMAX delay: measured at the MAC layer, it only measures the medium access delay.
- WiMAX load: the total load (in bits/sec) submitted to the WiMAX layer by all higher layers of all network WiMAX nodes.
- WiMAX throughput: the total data traffic (in packets/sec) forwarded from WiMAX layers to higher layers in all network WiMAX nodes.

SIMULATION SETUP

WiMAX

The PMP mode of the IEEE 802.16e-2005 standard was modified to allow nodes to communicate with each other in an ad-hoc fashion, without a Base Station (BS). The main modification is generating one flow per neighbor with a corresponding CID. This means that each node can have as many flows as it has nodes within its radio range. Each flow is generated through the DSA process defined in the standard.

Once the flows are initiated in the node, the LORA_CBF routing protocol organizes the network hierarchically with the above cluster algorithm. The cluster head then handles the responsibility of assigning the bandwidth grants to each neighbor. Presently, a scheduling algorithm between clusters is not within the scope of this chapter.

Table 3 shows the mainly parameters of our simulation

Results

We simulated a total of 103 seconds using the LORA-CBF algorithm, which was initiated on second four to allow for cluster formation. On second 4, LORA-CBF began transmitting ip datagrams of 1024 bits at rate of one packet per second using 4 hops. We also simulated AODV for 60 seconds to compare the load generated by each protocol in the MAC layer.

Figure presents LORA-CBF's routing load expressed in packets per seconds.

It is important to note that the major routing load occurs during the initial phase of cluster formation, during the first second. When the first packet was sent, the route discovery process was launched. LORA-CBF required only 35 routing packets to carry out its route discovery process. This, we believe, is a small number of packets, considering the highly dense scenario chosen for

this simulation. After the route is set, each node only sent the periodic beacon. This represented a total of 120 packets transmitted per second. Figure 3 is the routing load expressed in bits per second. It shows that LORA-CBF, once the cluster algorithm sets up the cluster, generates a very low amount of traffic. Each node only generates 0.384 Kb/s (corresponding to the hello packet). This means that the 120 nodes only inject 46.08 Kb/s to the network layer.

The maximum delay for a WiMAX packet is 5 ms. this delay is calculated per hop, meaning that it only represents the delay from one station to its most immediate neighbor. For packets transmitted 4 hops, the delay from the source to the destination is always less than 20 ms.

Figure 4 shows the total load in bits per second, which is introduced by the network and application layers. The gray line corresponds to the first 60 seconds of LORA-CBF. The initial load the first three seconds is due to LORA-CBF's cluster formation stage. After the cluster is formed, the overhead is minimized. Beginning at second 4, the information forwarded by nodes consists of 1024-bit ip packets and the 384 bits, if it is a hello packet. Importantly, the graphic shows the total load introduced through the 4 hops in order to reach the final destination packets (i.e. 1024x4 bits). AODV does not show significant initial activity during the first 3 seconds because AODV does not form clusters. Although this initial delay can be interpreted as a drawback for LORA-CBF, AODV uses significantly more resources beginning at second 4. This is primarily true because AODV does not possess a hierarchical structure to limit its network nodes from simultaneously retransmitting packets. LORA-CBF, on the other hand, only selects cluster heads to retransmit the route request packet.

Figure 5 presents WiMAX throughput, which is significantly higher in the cluster formation stage. Following the cluster formation stage, network throughput decreases. Again, AODV has less traffic than LORA-CBF in the first three

Figure 2. Routing load offered by the 120 nodes participating depicted in packets per second

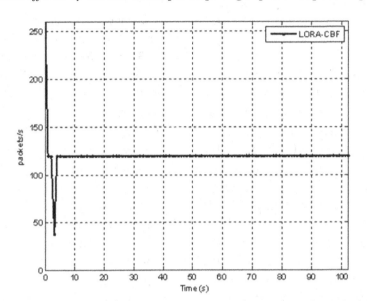

Figure 3. Total amount of routing traffic generated by the 120 nodes running LORA

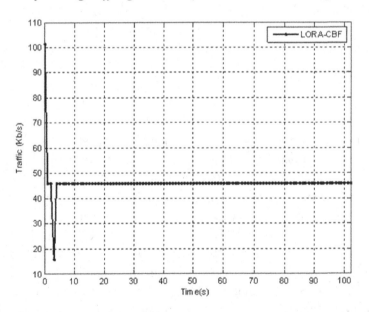

seconds. However, AODV must flood packets after the initial 4 seconds, causing network traffic to remain high. On the other hand, once LORA-CBF forms its clusters, only cluster heads or selected gateways retransmit the RREQ; therefore, the traffic after the route discovery stage is limited exclusively to the transmission of IP packets.

CONCLUSION AND FUTURE WORK

The LORA-CBF algorithm and WiMAX have potential in high-density scenarios because the LORA clustering algorithm allows for scalability. Furthermore, the WiMAX contention free medium access and the NLOS property are well

Table 3. Simulation settings

PHY		
Parameters	Values	
Base Frequency	5 GHz	
Channel Bandwidth	5 MHz	
FFT Size	512	
Subcarrier Spacing (Df)	10.94khz	
Simbol Duration (T_s)	102.9ms	
Transmission Power	.9 w	
Transmission Range	1000m	
Network		
Parameters	AODV	LORA
Hello Interval	Uniform(1,1.1)	Uniform(1,1.1)
Allowed Hello Loss	3	3
Active Route Timeout	5s	5s
TTL Parameters — Start	1	20
TTL Parameters — Increment	2	N/A
TTL Parameters — Threshold	7	N/A
Addresing Mode	IPv4	IPv4/Geographical
Simulation Scenario		
Simulation Plataform	OpNET v16.0	
Model	Static Circular Road	
Simulation Time	101 seconds	
Averaged Runs	5	
Total Vehicles	20	
Horizontal Gap between Vehicles	1000m	
Vertical Gap between Vehicles	10m	

Figure 4. WiMAX Load (bits/sec) introduced by each routing algorithm simulated

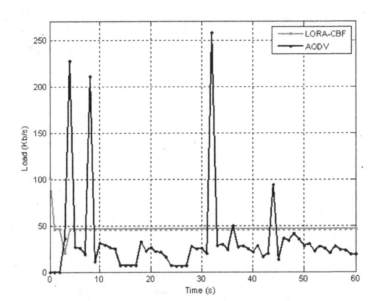

Figure 5. WiMAX throughput (Kbits/sec) gathered in our simulation

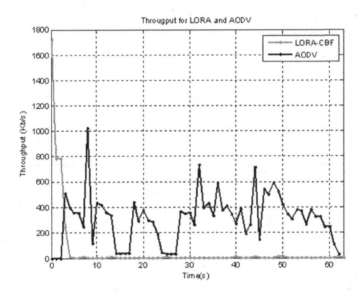

suited for scenarios with heavy traffic load and a high-density of wireless signal interference (e.g. buildings and vehicles). Clustering is a promising strategy, especially in dense scenarios like in highway with heavy traffic or in urban scenarios, where WiMAX has important potential because it is specially developed for NLOS conditions.

Significantly, the route discovery process of a four-hop route only required an overhead of 35 packets. A comparison between LORA-CBF and AODV in the same scenario shows that LORA_CBF's hierarchical architecture and selective gateway forwarding approach results in improved use of bandwidth than AODV. Future research will focus on improving the WiMAX ad-hoc mode that we developed. The goal expected is to achieve better performance than contention based medium access layer and test the LORA protocol in a more realistic scenario. Finally, future work will implement a predictive algorithm for the LORA-CBF protocol to improve its overall performance in highly mobile scenarios.

REFERENCES

80216-2004I.S. (2004). *IEEE standard for Local and metropolitan area networks-Part 16: Air interface for fixed broadband wireless access systems*. Retrieved from http://www.ncbi.nlm.nih.gov/pubmed/20715964.

80216e. (2005). *I.S. Part 16: Air interface for fixed and mobile broadband wireless access systems*.

80216j. (2009). *I.S. IEEE standard for local and metropolitan area networks--Part 16: Air interface for broadband wireless access systems--Amendment 1: Multihop relay specification*.

Ahmed, A., Krishnamachari, B., & Psounis, K. (2008). IEEE 802.11p performance evaluation and protocol enhancement. *2008 IEEE International Conference on Vehicular Electronics and Safety*, (pp. 317-322).

Amin, R., & Wang, K. C. (2007). An integrated routing and scheduling approach for persistent vehicle communication in mobile wimax mesh networks. *Military Communications Conference*, (pp. 1-7).

Amin, R., Wang, K. C., & Ramanathan, P. (2008). An interference and QOS aware distributed scheduling approach for hybrid IEEE 802.16E mesh networks. *MILCOM 2008 IEEE Military Communications Conference*, (pp. 1-7).

Aquino, R., Apolinar, V., Luis, A., & Crespo, A. J. (2009). Simulación de algoritmos para regular el flujo vehicular y la comunicación entre vehículos móviles autónomos utilizando redes Ad Hoc. *Revista Iberoamericana de Automatica e Informatica Industrial, 6*, 75–83.

Aquino, R., Potes, A., & Villaseñor, L. A. (2008). *Un nuevo algoritmo de enrutamiento para redes ad hoc vehiculares (A novel routing algorithm for vehicular ad hoc networks)* (pp. 120–131). Revista Facultad de Ingenieria Universidad de Antioquia.

Aquino, R., Rangel-Licea, V., & Edwards, A. (2008). Inter-vehicular communications using wireless ad hoc networks. *Ingeniería. Investigación y Tecnología, 9*, 319–328.

Aquino, S. R., & Edwards, B. A. (2006). A reactive location routing algorithm with cluster-based flooding for inter-vehicle communication. *Computación y Sistemas, 9*, 297–313.

Bellman, R. (1958). On a routing problem. *Quarterly of Applied Mathematics, 16*, 87–90.

Bettstetter, C., Hartenstein, H., & Pérez-Costa, X. (2002). Stochastic properties of the random waypoint mobility model: Epoch time, direction distribution, and cell change rate. *Proceedings of the 5th International Workshop on Modeling Analysis and Simulation of Wireless and Mobile Systems*, (pp. 7-14).

Bilstrup, K., Uhlemann, E., Strom, E. G., & Bilstrup, U. (2008). Evaluation of the IEEE 802.11p MAC method for vehicle-to-vehicle communication. *2008 IEEE 68th Vehicular Technology Conference*, (pp. 1-5).

Briesemeister, L., Schäfers, L., & Hommel, G. (2000). Disseminating messages among highly mobile hosts based on inter-vehicle communication. *IEEE Intelligent Vehicle Symposium*, (pp. 522-527).

Brown, A. C., Cullen, E. J., Wu, J., Brackstone, M., Gunton, D. J., & McDonald, M. (2000). Vehicle to vehicle communication outage and its impact on convoy driving. *Proceedings of the IEEE Intelligent Vehicles Symposium 2000*, (pp. 528-533).

Car2car Communication Consortium. (2010). Retrieved from http://www.car-to-car.org/.

Chiu, K. L., Hwang, R. H., & Chen, Y. S. (2009). A cross layer fast handover scheme in VANET. *IEEE International Conference on Communications* (pp. 1-5).

Clausen, T., & Jacquet, P. (2003). *RFC3626: Optimized link state routing protocol (OLSR)*. RFC Editor United States.

Communication for eSafety. (2010). Retrieved from http://www.comesafety.org.

Dijkstra, E. (1959). A note on two problems in connexion with graphs. *Numerischemathematik*, 269-271.

Fei, R., Yang, K., Ou, S., Zhong, S., & Gao, L. (2009). *International Conference on Scalable Computing and Communications; Eighth International Conference on Embedded Computing 2009*, (pp. 200-205).

Ge, Y., Wen, S., Ang, Y. H., & Liang, Y. C. (2010). Optimal relay selection in IEEE 802.16j multihop relay vehicular networks. *IEEE Transactions on Vehicular Technology*, 2198–2206. doi:10.1109/TVT.2010.2044822

Jain, S., Fall, K., & Patra, R. (2004). Routing in a delay tolerant network. *ACM SIGCOMM Computer Communication Review*, *34*(4), 145. doi:10.1145/1030194.1015484

Melamed, R., Keidar, I., & Barel, Y. (n.d.). Octopus: A fault-tolerant and efficient ad-hoc routing protocol. *24th IEEE Symposium on Reliable Distributed Systems (SRDS'05)*, (pp. 39-49).

Olariu, S., & Weigle, M. (2010). *Vehicular networks from theory to practice*. Florida: Chapman & Hall/CRC Computer & Information Science Series.

Perkins, C., Belding-Royer, E., & Das, S. (2003). *RFC3561: Ad hoc on-demand distance vector (AODV) routing*. Retrieved from http://portal.acm.org/citation.cfm?id=RFC3561.

Peters, S. W., & Heath, R. W. (2009). The future of WiMAX: Multihop relaying with IEEE 802.16j. *IEEE Communications Magazine*, *47*(1), 104–111. doi:10.1109/MCOM.2009.4752686

Popescu-Zeletin, R., Radusch, I., & Rigani, M. (2010). *Vehicular-2-X communication: State-of-the-art and research in mobile vehicular ad hoc networks* (pp. 67–83). Berlin, Germany: Springer Verlag.

Rajamani, R., & Shladover, S. (2001). An experimental comparative study of autonomous and co-operative vehicle-follower control systems. *Transportation Research Part C, Emerging Technologies*, *9*(1), 15–31. doi:10.1016/S0968-090X(00)00021-8

SAFESPOT Integrated Project. (2010). Retrieved from http://www.safespot-eu.org/.

Srivastava, V., & Motani, M. (2005). Cross-layer design: A survey and the road ahead. *Communications Magazine, IEEE*, *43*, 112–119. doi:10.1109/MCOM.2005.1561928

Stibor, L., Zang, Y., & Reumerman, H. J. (2007). Evaluation of communication distance of broadcast messages in a vehicular ad-hoc network using IEEE 802.11p. *IEEE Wireless Communications and Networking Conference*, (pp. 254-257).

Varaiya, P. (1993). Smart cars on smart roads: Problems of control. *IEEE Transactions on Automatic Control*, *38*(2), 195–207. doi:10.1109/9.250509

Wang, Y., Wu, T. Y., Lee, W., & Ke, C. (2010) A novel geographic routing strategy over VANET. In *Proceedings of AINA Workshops*, (pp. 873-879).

Yang, K., Ou, S., Chen, H., & He, J. (2007). *A multihop peer-communication protocol with fairness guarantee for IEEE 802.16-based vehicular networks. Vehicular Technology* (pp. 3358–3370). IEEE.

Yang, X. Liu, J., Zhao, F., & Vaidya, N. (2004). A vehicle-to-vehicle communication protocol for cooperative collision warning. *The First Annual International Conference on Mobile and Ubiquitous Systems: Networking and Services*, (pp. 114-123).

Yin, J., ElBatt, T., Yeung, G., Ryu, B., Habermas, S., Krishnan, H., & Talty, T. (2004). Performance evaluation of safety applications over DSRC vehicular ad hoc networks. *Proceedings of the first ACM Workshop on Vehicular Ad Hoc Networks*, (pp. 1-9).

Zhao, J., & Cao, G. (2006). VADD: Vehicle-assisted data delivery in vehicular ad hoc networks. *Proceedings IEEE INFOCOM 2006. 25TH IEEE International Conference on Computer Communications*, (pp. 1-12).

KEY TERMS AND DEFINITIONS

AODV: A routing algorithm designed for MANETs. It's a reactive routing protocol.

Cluster-Based Routing: It is a routing strategy that forms sets of nodes and establish hierarchies inside these sets.

Geographic Routing: It's a routing algorithm where the packets are forwarded according with geographical position of the nodes.

LORA-CBF: It's a position based algorithm designed for VANETs that minimize the overhead of flooding with a cluster based strategy.

Mobile Ad-Hoc Networks (MANET): It is a self-configuring network that has no infrastructure.

OPNET Modeler: Is an event driven network simulation platform.

Routing Protocol: Set of rules to guarantee that source packets reach the final destination.

Vehicular Ad-Hoc Networks (VANETs): It is a special case of MANETs where all participating nodes are vehicles the main characteristic of VANETs is the high speed and non uniform density.

Worldwide Interoperability for Microwave Access (WiMAX): It's a last mile wireless broadband standard.

Section 3
Theory and Application of Higher Layers

Chapter 9
Development of Applications for Vehicular Communication Network Environments:
Challenges and Opportunities

JA Guerrero-Ibáñez
University of Colima, México

C Flores-Cortés
University of Colima, México

P Damián-Reyes
University of Colima, México

ABSTRACT

Nowadays, modern society faces serious problems with transportation systems. There are more traffic jams, accidents, and fatalities, and CO_2 emissions are increasing fast. Thus, improving the safety and efficiency of transportation systems is imperative. Developing a sustainable transportation system requires a better usage of the existing infrastructure, the adoption of emerging technologies (e.g. embedded devices, sensors, and short range radio transmitters), and the development of applications capable of operating in wireless and spontaneous networks. This chapter gives readers a global vision of the issues related to the development of applications for vehicular ad-hoc networks(VANET). It also presents a classification and an overview of the top-level application domain. In addition, it investigates the importance of information in vehicular networks and analyses the requirements for different types of vehicular applications. Finally, the communication schemes that underpin the operation of VANET applications, as well as the security threats they are exposed to, are studied.

DOI: 10.4018/978-1-4666-0209-0.ch009

INTRODUCTION

Modern society is facing serious problems with the transportation systems. In the last years the levels of traffic congestion, fatalities, accidents and pollution have increased significantly. To improve the safety, security and efficiency of the transportation systems and enable the development of novel vehicular applications *Intelligent Transportation Systems* (ITS) have been developed (Qian & Moayeri, 2008). These systems are characterized for utilizing communication and information technologies in vehicles and transportation infrastructures. Different countries or regions have defined their own vision and definition for ITS:

- **ERTICO – ITS Europe** defines ITS as the new application that information and communication technologies are finding in urban transport and it is also referred as "*Transport Telematics*" (ERTICO-a, 1998).
- **ITS America** defines ITS as a broad range of different technologies which hold the answer to many of the existing transportation problems. ITS is comprised of a number of technologies including information processing, communications, control, and electronics. With the integration of all these technologies into existing transportation systems, lives, time and money will be saved (America, 2009).
- **ITS Australia** defines ITS as a broad term which is used to describe developments in communication and computing technologies applied to transport services in general. (Australia, 2009).
- **ITS Japan** states that ITS offer a fundamental solution to various issues that concern to transportation systems, including traffic accidents, congestion and environmental pollution. ITS deals with these issues using the most advanced communi-

cation and control technologies (Japan, 2009).
- **ITS Canada** defines ITS as the application of advanced and emerging technologies (e.g. computers, sensors, control, communications and electronic devices) in transportation to save lives, time, money, energy and the environment. (Canada, 2009)

As read, different regions of the world share a same vision of *ITS*: the usage of emerging technologies to solve issues concerning to transportation systems. One of the most important components of ITS is the *vehicular ad-hoc network* (VANET). A VANET is an upcoming type of wireless ad-hoc network designed to provide support to a wide variety of applications with the aim of bringing modern society a series of benefits in areas such as vehicular safety, entertainment and traffic control among others.

Providing vehicles with relevant information about other vehicles or environmental data may improve the safety, efficiency and effectiveness of existing transportation systems. With the development of wireless and cellular networks several innovative vehicular applications for security, traffic control, and entertainment can be developed. Although some vehicular application requirements have already been investigated in the *Mobile Ad-hoc Network* (MANET) environment, there still exist important challenges to be studied for correctly exploiting vehicle and traffic information (e.g. the knowledge of the dynamics of a vehicle) to improve inter-vehicular communication. In this sense, several factors can influence the development and adoption of applications for vehicular networks and they must be considered for the successfull development of applications. Some of these factors include: i) low latency requirements for different applications, ii) extensive growth of interactive and multimedia applications and iii) the emergence of different security and privacy concerns.

This chapter gives readers a global vision of the traffic and transportation issues and how the use of communication and information technologies contribute to the solution of different transportation challenges. In specific, the chapter focuses on VANET applications and the related development issues. The chapter provides an overall view of the top-level application domain, showing a classification based on the usage of applications in this complex communication environment. Also, a review that shows the importance of information in vehicular networks and an analysis of the requirements for different types of applications is presented. Finally, a review of different vehicle communication regimes is presented. The analysis includes different communication schemes (e.g. broadcast and position based) and architectures (i.e. vehicle-to-vehicle and vehicle-to-infrastructure).

BACKGROUND

Modern society is facing more traffic jams, higher levels of fatalities and accidents, higher fuel bills and the increase of CO_2 emissions due to the lack of control in the growth of vehicles and high concentrations of people in urban zones. The technical report of the *United Nations Population Fund* showed that for the first time, more than half of the world's population, around 3.3 billion people live in urban areas. By 2030, this number is expected to swell to almost 5 billion (UNFPA, 2007). It is well known that in urban areas travelers can spend a large percentage of their day stuck in traffic. This has caused an important increase on traffic congestion. Traffic congestion in urban areas is a serious problem that has a huge economical, environmental and road safety impact. An earlier study estimated the cost of traffic congestion for the US economy in 2009 in $90bn (Lomax & Schrank, 2005) and for the European Union economy another study esti-

mated this cost for 2010 in approximately 1% of its Gross Domestic Product (GDP) (EEA, 2006).

Building additional or extending existing roads cannot solve the traffic congestion problem due to the high costs and the environmental and geographical limitations. The environmental cost has been documented in different technical reports. For example, the technical report of the European Environment Agency (EEA) revealed that in 2004 the European Union road transport accounted for 26% of greenhouse gas emissions (EEA, 2006). Even though the economic costs are significant; a major concern is the human cost in vehicular accidents. A technical report of the Commission for Global Road Safety indicateed that road crashes kill at least 1.3 million people each year and injure 50 million. Importantly, 90% of these road casualties occur in developing countries. Each year 260,000 children die on the road and another million are seriously injured. By 2015 road crashes are predicted to be the leading cause of premature death and disability for children aged five and above (Safety, 2009). This hidden road injury epidemic is a crisis for public health and a major contributor to the causes of poverty. Nonetheless, aid agencies, development non-governmental organizations (NGO), philanthropic foundations and key international institutions continue to neglect or ignore this rapidly growing problem. Road transport is a necessity for our mobility; however, new measures are required to make it safer and more efficient.

Emerging technologies should be established as basic elements of transportation systems. Increasing capacity and flexibility of emerging technologies could make possible a real development of cooperative automotive systems decreasing investment, operational costs and accidents and making more efficient the transport systems. Emerging technologies must guarantee the required demands of transportation systems. Communication technologies should be used to build vehicular networks to improve safety and reduce traffic congestion. The safety and efficiency of roads can be substantially improved with the deployment of intelligent systems such as adaptive traffic control, incident detection and management systems in cities and highways. Vehicular systems should improve road safety, in particular in the pre-crash phase when an accident can potentially be avoided or at least its severity significantly reduced. To enable VANETs vehicles must be equipped with at laest one wireless radio and deployment of numerous roadside units may be necessary. Roadside units can be utilized to extend the network coverage, enabling communication between distant vehicles (i.e. beyond its radio range), supporting a high-speed, and low-latency network and providing services to both public and private companies. Research groups are focusing their efforts on defining and prototyping communications systems and defining standards to support *Vehicle-to-Infrastructure* (V2I) and *Vehicle-to-Vehicle* (V2V) communication.

Even tough VANETs are a subclass of ad-hoc networks; a number of important differences exist with other types of ad-hoc networks such as MANETs and *Wireless Sensor Networks* (WSNs). Thus, for the successful development of protocols and applications, the characteristics of VANETs must be taken into consideration. The following are some of the characteristics that make different VANETs from other types of networks (Li & Wang, 2007):

- **Topology:** VANETs are characterized by highly dynamic topologies where participating nodes move at high speeds, compared with other ad-hoc networks such as MANETs, resulting in different rates of connection and disconnection of nodes. For example, when two vehicles encounter each other and are traveling in opposite directions, a rapid change in the topology of the network may occur because of the short period of time these two vehicles are able to establish a direct communication link. In contrast, a group of vehicles travelling on

a highway on a same direction may be able to maintain their communication for longer periods of time.

- **Energy, storage, and processing power:** VANET's nodes are vehicles such as cars and buses equipped with sources of unlimited energy power. Even tough these nodes are mobile, size constrains are not as restrictive as in MANET environments where devices must be handheld or pocket size, thus, higher processing power and larger storage capacity can be supported.

- **Geographical information:** Geographical information plays an important role in VANETs for setting up the ad-hoc network and disseminating routing and application information. For example, information about a road accident may be only of interest for vehicles travelling on a given lane and direction, thus such information must be routed using node's geographical information.

- **Mobility model:** Even tough VANET's nodes are highly mobile; predictions on their movement can be accomplished using known information such as highways, roads and streets layouts and direction, position and speed of vehicles.

- **Communication environments:** VANET's communication environments can be classified into two groups: i) *a highway environment*, where simple unidirectional movement patterns can be observed and ii) *a city environment*, where environmental elements such as buildings, trees and other obstacles may block radio communication making inter-vehicle communication more restrictive and complex.

- **Delay constraints:** In many VANET applications meeting with hard delay constraints is a crucial requirement. In particular, safety applications must communicate alert messages within short periods of time (refer to Table 1) to prevent drivers and/or systems from possible accidents.

- **Sensors:** Vehicles participating within a VANET environment are equipped with different on-board sensors. These sensors generate information that can be utilized to route messages and provide applications of relevant information. Examples of on-board sensors include global positioning systems (GPS), proximity sensor, engine failure and vehicle speed sensors.

APPLICATIONS FOR VEHICULAR COMMUNICATION NETWORKS

The introduction of reactive and proactive applications is necessary in the transportation systems. Applications for vehicular networks can be classified in different ways. For example, according to their penetration rate they can be divided into two categories: behavior and warning applications (Popescu-Zeleti, Radusch & Rigani, 2010). Cooperative behavior applications utilize communication technologies for supporting inter-vehicular cooperation schemes for gathering other vehicles information. These applications enhance the perception of the environment through the usage of different on-board sensors. On the other hand, warning applications are focused on the dissemination of traffic conditions and alerts of on-road incidents to improve traffic fluency and safety by preventing and avoiding accidents.

Another classification is based on the application area. According to this classification, applications for vehicular networks are divided into three major groups: safety, infotainment and traffic control. The first category, safety applications, groups all applications designed for increasing vehicles and people safety both on roads and in urban zones. The second group of application is called infotainment. This category refers to applications that provide both drivers and passengers added-value services. For example, entertainment or relevant information about traffic conditions. Finally, applications that increase traffic fluency are called traffic control. This type of applications attempt to improve traffic efficiency reducing congestion and fuel consumption and promoting a positive environmental and economic impact.

Safety Applications

One of the most promising and critical application of vehicular communications is the improvement of road traffic safety. Millions of traffic accidents occur world- wide, resulting in tens of thousands of casualties and billions of dollars in direct economic costs.

In this sense, goverments and departments of transportation have been establishing agresive goals to increase road safety through the implementation of different intelligent transportation system initiatives. On one hand, the European Transport Policy is targeting a reduction of 40% of road fatalities from 2010 to 2020 (European Transport Safety Council, 2008). On the other hand, in 2008 the U.S. Department of Transportation's Research and Innovative Technology Administration challenged the industry to reduce 90 percent of traffic crashes by 2030 (Research and Innovative Technology Administration, 2008). To achieve the future road safety vision, time-sensitive and safety-critical applications for vehicular communication networks are necessary. Safety applications and systems attempt to increase the protection of pedestrians, people inside the vehicle and the vehicle itself. These systems and applications will help to save lives by avoiding or minimizing the effects of accidents.

Different efforts have been made to decrease the number of accidents, however with today's technology it is still very difficult to achieve this objective. In the last years, research and development work has been carried out to overcome road safety problems by developing driver assistance systems that use technologies such as sensor networks, radio-frequency identification (RFID) readers, video cameras, among others to model the traffic state that surrounds the vehicle in order to warn the driver in case of a potential dangerous situation (Doshi, Shinko, & Trivedi, 2009) (Bertolazzi, Biral, Da Lio, Saroldi, & Tango, 2010).

According to the usage, saefty applications can be classified into three categories: i) active safety, ii) proactive safety and iii) warning applications. The active safety category, groups applications designed for detecting danger and avoiding accidents in situations where, for example, the driver's eyes stray from the road or visibility is poor. They are intended to prevent accidents through coordination between the driver and the vehicle. Existing active systems, asist drivers in critical situations to avoid accidents or mitigate the impact. Some examples of active safety applications are:

- **The Adaptive Cruise Control(ACC) system** uses headway sensors to continuously measure the distance with other vehicles to automatically adjust the speed ensuring that the vehicle does not get too close to the one in front. The driver activates the cruise control by setting the desired maximum speed and then selecting the time gap with the vehicles ahead. The ACC system then adjusts the vehicle's speed to match that of the preceding vehicle as necessary.

- **The Forward Collision Warning (FCW) system** can help to avoid rear-end impacts or minimize the effects of these type of collisions. A radar mechanism continuously scans the area in front of the vehicle. If the vehicle approaches too close to another one, then, the driver is alerted via sound and light signals. If the risk of a collision increases despite the warnings, the brakes are pre-charged and prepared for an efficient braking when required by the driver. When a collision is imminent and the driver does not react, the car automatically activates the brakes to reduce the impact of the accident. Existing implementations of

the FCW system varies from one vehicle or manufacturer to another.

- **The Speed Regulation system** helps to maintain the speed limit according to the road where a vehicle is currently traveling.

- **The Blind Spot Information system** uses small cameras fitted on each side-mirror to detect when a car or motorcycle has entered in the driver's blind spot area. To alert the driver, a warning light is activated. The system is capable of recognizing and ignoring the car's own shadow, and also works at night.

- **The Lane Departure Warning (LDW) application**, assists the driver in maintaining his/her lane position, giving a warning if the vehicle crosses lane markings unintentionally. The warning can be acoustic or haptical (e.g. a vibration or small torque on the steering wheel or driver's seat). The system maintains the vehicle position by detecting lane markings or street boundaries via a video sensor. A warning only occurs when driving above a certain minimum speed.

- **Safe Human Machine Interaction (HMI) – Navigation** is an in-vehicle information and communication system intended to be used by the driver while the vehicle is in motion, for example, to deliver navigation and traffic information. For its development, essential security and usability aspects for the human/machine interface need to be taken into account. The navigation system provides location and route guidance information to the driver. Different types of systems (e.g. OEM fitment, after-market solution) with different display positions and technologies (e.g. central information display, head-up, or separate detachable display) are already available in the market.

It is important to note that active safety applications do not use inter-vehicular communication. To further reduce injuries and fatalities, vehicle safety systems require going beyond active safety applications; therefore, it is necesary to develop intelligent safety systems that support inter-vehicular and vehicle-to-infrastructure communications.

The proactive safety applications enable vehicles to communicate and coordinate responses with other vehicles to prevent and avoid accidents. These systems provide an extended information horizon to warn the driver or on board systems of dangerous situations in a much earlier phase. This kind of applications anticipate critical situations and take preventive actions to deal with them. Proactive applications are mainly based on frequent beacon messages that contain safety-relevant parameters such as position, speed, distance, among others.

Finally, warning applications represent a temporal message condition. In this kind of applications warning messages have to be disseminated in order to increase the number of vehicles receiving the traffic warning information. Warning messages can be sub-divided into normal alert messages and quick alert messages. Quick alert messages are alerts that must be sent as soon as possible. Commonly, quick alerts are triggered by an event. The main requirement for this type of applications is a low latency. On the other hand, normal alert messages are sent to disseminate relevant information about traffic conditions such as information of congestion at a given intersection, for example.

Infotainment Applications

The time a person spends in a vehicle (e.g. a car or bus) has increased in the last few years, mainly due to the growth of cities and the resulting increase in vehicular traffic. This issue obliges automobile manufacturing companies to include in their vehicles elements that help their occupants being more productive and comfortable during the time they spend inside the vehicle. To achieve this goal automotive infotainment has emerged. This is an area that includes a set of technological solutions for vehicles that range from traditional AM / FM radios to powerful wireless technologies that enable Internet access and modern communication and location systems. The main idea is to combine entertainment, navigation and telecommunications in an easy to use interface.

Infotainment is supported by a wide variety of existing technologies, some of which focus on entertainment aspects where important companies dedicated to creating audio solutions for vehicles can be found. For instance, technology specifically designed for automobile sound systems. This technology re-defines noise compensation in vehicles, it measures both the music volume and unwanted noise to automatically adjust on real-time the music output so listeners can hear most of the music; Additionally, it helps in creating a balanced sound field of 360 degrees on each seat, allowing passengers to feel like if they were in the middle of the music. Other technologies are designed to minimize driver's distractions. These solutions are based on the usage of wireless technologies like Bluetooth and Wi-Fi, which are already integrated in the car. This technology allows a complete and seamless integration with smart phones, making possible to access automotive-certified smartphone content from a driver-optimized interface helping drivers to stay focused on their driving task, but at the same time remain connected. Some of the technologies that enable this optimization include voice recognition, text-to-speech, speech-to-text, large reconfigurable displays and touch screens.

Traffic Control Applications

Private and government initiatives such as *ERTICO* (ERTICO, 2010) and *ITS America* (RITA, 2010): among others investigate systems that guarantee security, comfort and satisfaction of both drivers and passengers while in the vehicle. The following are some examples of traffic control applications that have been developed within the beforementioned initiatives:

- **Freeway and arterial management:** These systems are designed to manage traffic along arterial roadways employing traffic detectors, traffic signals, and various means for communicating information to travelers. These systems make use of information collected by traffic surveillance devices to smooth the flow of traffic along travel corridors. They also disseminate important information about travel conditions to travelers via technologies such as dynamic message signs (DMS) or highway advisory radio (HAR), in-vehicle signing, or specialized information transmitted only to a specific set of vehicles.

- **Crash prevention and safety systems:** These systems detect unsafe conditions and provide warnings to travelers to take action to avoid crashes. These systems provide alerts to vehicles approaching at dangerous curves, off ramps, restricted overpasses, highway-rail crossings, high-volume intersections, and also inform of the presence of pedestrians, bicyclists, and even animals on the roadway. Crash prevention and safety systems typically employ sensors to monitor the speed and characteristics of approaching vehicles and also include environmental sensors to monitor roadway conditions and visibility. These systems may be either permanent or temporary. Some systems simply provide a general warning of the recommended speed for prevailing roadway conditions. Other systems provide more specific warning by taking into account each vehicle characteristics (e.g it is a truck or car). In

some cases manual systems are employed, for example, where pedestrians or bicyclists manually set the system to provide warnings of their presence to travelers.

- **Road weather management activities:** This development refers to road weather information systems, winter maintenance technologies, and coordination of operations within and between state departments of transportation (DOTs). ITS applications assist drivers with the monitoring and forecasting of roadway and atmospheric conditions, disseminating weather-related information, weather-related traffic control measures such as variable speed limits, and both fixed and mobile winter maintenance activities.

- **Traveler information applications:** These applications use a variety of technologies, including internet websites, telephone hotlines, as well as television and radio, to allow users to make more informed decisions regarding trip departures, routes, and mode of travel. The ongoing implementation of the designated 511 telephone number will improve access to traveler information across the United States.

- **Incident management systems:** These systems can reduce the effects of incident-related congestion by decreasing the time to detect incidents, the time for responding vehicles (such as ambulances, police car, fire trucks, among others) to arrive, and the time required for traffic to return to normal conditions. Incident management systems make use of a variety of surveillance technologies, often shared with freeway and arterial management systems, as well as enhanced communications and other technologies that facilitate a coordinated response in case of a traffic incident.

CHALLENGES IN VEHICULAR NETWORKS

Successful operation of applications for vehicular networks depend on the information that both vehicles and base stations exchange. Information that vehicles and base stations exchange can be classified into three categories. The first category, common information, refers to the dissemination of general information that can be used by any application. This information can be included in the header of the message. Thu, the header can be composed by: a message identifier used for control, a node identifier that allows applications identifying the node that generated the information, and a node type identifier to indicate weather the node is a vehicle or a roadside device.

The second category, permanent information, is related to information that needs to be transmitted repeatedly within the vehicular network. At the most basic level, this type of information refers to shared data of the environment such as vehicle position, speed, and acceleration, among others. Finally, the specific information category groups all application specific information, for example, information required by the navigation, alert, and safety systems among others.

Irrespectively of the supported applications, vehicles usually broadcast periodically a beacon message that includes speed, location, and in some cases the vehicle status (e.g. fuel level, temperature, oil level, etc). The broadcast frequency of beacon messages varies from one application to another, for example in safety applications, beacon messages are broadcasted between 3 and 10 times per second. On the other hand, non-safety applications are different in nature, this type of applications is focused in transmitting large data files, supporting multi-hop communications and internet service provision, nevertheless, latency is less important.

To protect private information transmitted in VANETs of users including drivers, passengers, manufacturers, component suppliers and service providers strong security and privacy schemes are necessary. For example, safety applications must be protected to avoid malicious manipulation of data, which could potentially harm vehicle drivers with incorrect information. Also for commercial applications, the information must be protected to prevent loss of revenue (CAMP Vehicle Safety Communications Consortium, 2005).

Application Requirements in Vehicular Networks

As mentioned before, an important requirement for enabling inter-vehicular communication is the rapid and efficient exchange of important messages. Applications for vehicular networks have different requirements and face different technical issues. In essence, vehicles in a VANET must receive and send data quickly. However, each application will have its own needs. These reasons make necessary the implementation of quality of service (QoS) management in vehicular communication.

Applications that can be deployed on VANETs range from highly critical applications that require high levels of guaranties of QoS from the underlying communication schemes to non-critical applications where different QoS parameters can be relaxed. For example, a safety application designed to notify vehicles about possible in front collisions (e.g. a forwarding collision warning application) requires messages to be delivered within a short interval of time (see Table 1) otherwise the information received may be useless and consequently the application may fail in preventing the driver from a serious accident. On the other hand, for an infotainment application (e.g. a music and video entertainment application) the delivery of messages may not be as critical as it is for the safety application. QoS is usually defined as a set of service requirements in terms of data latency, bandwidth utilization, and probability of packet delivery ratio.

Table 1. Requirements for vehicular communications applications

Application	Communication Type	Rate	Maximum latency	Data transmitted	Range
Traffic signal violation	V2I	10 Hz	100 ms	Signal phase, timing, position, direction, road geometry.	250 m
Curve speed warning	V2I	1 Hz	1000 ms	Curve location, curvature, slope, speed limit, surface.	200 m
Emergency brake lights	V2V	10 Hz	100 ms	Position, heading, velocity, acceleration.	200 m
Pre-crash sensing	V2V	50 Hz	20 ms	Vehicle type, position, heading, velocity, acceleration, yaw rate.	50 m
Forward collision	V2V	10 Hz	100 ms	Vehicle type, position, heading, velocity, acceleration, yaw rate.	150 m
Left turn assist	V2I or V2V	10 Hz	100 ms	Signal phase, timing, position, direction	300 m
Lane-change warning	V2V	10 Hz	100 ms	Position, heading, velocity, acceleration, turn signal status.	150 m
Stop sign assist	V2I or V2V	10 Hz	100 ms	Position, velocity, heading.	300 m
Electronic Toll Collection	V2I	10 Hz	50 ms.		15 m
Internet Access	V2I	10 Hz	500 ms		300 m
Automatic parking	V2I	10 Hz	500 ms	Position, distance	300 m
Roadside service finder	V2I or V2V	10 Hz	500 ms	Position, velocity	300 m

The time transcurred between the emission and recepcion of a message from a vehicle or infrastructure is termed as data latency. This parameter has been used in several works for evaluating and optimizing different routing mechanisms (Skordylis & Trogoni). On the other hand, bandwidth utilization refers to the amount of data that can be carried out from one point (which could be a vehicle or a base station) to another in an interval of time of one second. This parameter is very relevant for determining the system performance and has been utilized to estimate the bandwidth consumption based on factors such as the interference range between nodes (Huang, Chuang, Chen, Yang, & Chen). Finally, packet delivery ratio refers to the result of dividing the number of data packets that are sent by a node and the number of packets received by the destination node. This parameter is mainly utilized for determining reliable routes.

Based on these parameters or metrics, applications for vehicular networks can be divided into two categories: safety applications and non-safety applications. In safety applications inter-vehicle communication is usually achieved utilizing a broadcast mechanism for disseminating information whereas in non-safety applications an on-demand communication is utilized (i.e. a message is only sent when a request is received). Table 1 shows the requirements for both safety and non-safey applications (CAMP Vehicle Safety Communications Consortium, 2005).

VANET Architectures

So far, two primary VANET architectures have been proposed: i) vehicle-to-vehicle communication (V2V) and ii) vehicle-to-infrastructure communication (V2I) (Figure 1). In the V2V architecture, vehicles are equipped with an OnBoard Unit (OBU), which is fitted with at list one short-range wireless ad-hoc radio such as 802.11p. Thus, as vehicles come into proximity to other vehicles they join to the ad-hoc network. To disseminate information such as traffic and alerts, different multi-hop communication schemes are utilized (e.g. broadcast and geocast). To communicate in a V2I architecture, RoadSide Units (RSUs) are deployed at different points along highways, roads, cities, etc. RSUs are equipped with wireless radios that can provide a larger ratio of coverage and may relay on some network infrastructure to enable RSU-to-RSU communication. Thus in a V2I, OBUs interact with RSUs and vice versa.

Network Access Technologies for VANET

Different VANET applications have different requirements in terms of bandwidth, latency, error rate, area of coverage, among others. These requirements must be satisfyed at any time and any place. In this sense, it is necessary to evaluate the properties of different existing network access technologies such as wireless LANS, WiMAX, cellular networks, satellite communications, among others. Thus the challenges is to chose the access technology that better satisfyies the service requirements of the different VANET applications. The 802.11-based Wireless LAN has achieved a great acceptance in the market. This technology provides support for high-speed data transmission

Figure 1. VANET architectures: (a) vehicle-to-vehicle communication and (b) vehicle-to-infrastructure communication.

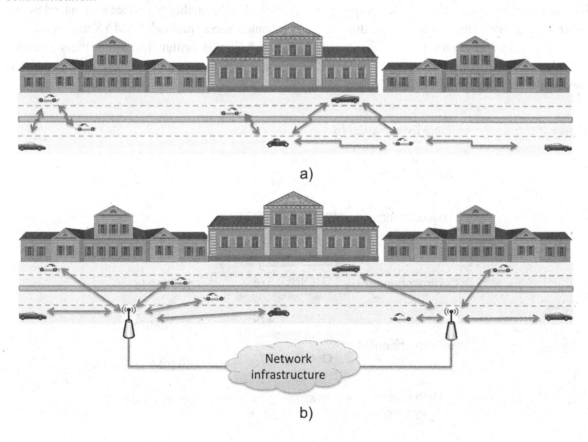

a)

b)

but its area of coverage is limited. Even though this technology can reach a data rate of 100Mbps, its short transmission range leads to frequent interruptions of communications particularly when the speed of vehicles is high making necessary to deploy many access points along the road.

The 802.11 task force group has been working in the development of a new communication standard, which is known as IEEE 802.11p. This new standard is based on the 802.11a technology and is also referred to as the dedicated short-range communications (DSRC) standard. This standard provides support to ITS applications for this frequency spectrum has been divided in seven channels (10MHz each): one control channel (CCH) and six service channels (SCHs) as shown in Figure 2 (Wang, Chou, & Lin, 2010). Nodes use control channel to exchange network control messages and use service channels to exchange data packets and WAVE short messages. The link bandwidth of these channels is further divided into transmission cycles. Each cycle comprises a control and a service frame. The draft of this standard suggest a frame duration of 50 milliseconds for either a control or a service frame. The DSRC supports a very high data rate (6-27Mbps) with

a maximum coverage of 1000m. Some studies have investigated the performance of DSRC for the different VANET applications. The results of these investigations have shown that the reliability of DSRC in vehicle-to-vehicle communication is satisfactory for it usage in vehicular safety applications (Bai & Krishnan, 2006; Ma, Chen, & Refai, 2009).

WiMAX is a technology based on the IEEE 802.16 standard that supports a large geographical coverage (up to 50 km), and offers an important bandwidth to end-users (up to 72 Mbps theoretically). Even though the IEEE 802.16 standard only supports fixed broadband wireless communication, other versions of the 802.16 standard (such as the IEEE 802.16e/802.16j/ mobile WiMAX standards) support speeds up to 160 km/h and classify the information in several classes of service. In terms of quality of service, WiMAX defines 5 categories of service as shown in Table 2 (IEEE-SA Standards Board, 2009). In WiMAX the quality of service is managed by the channel access method. WIMAX makes use of a scheduling algorithm for which the subscriber station needs to compete only once for initial

Figure 2. Channels available for the 802.11p

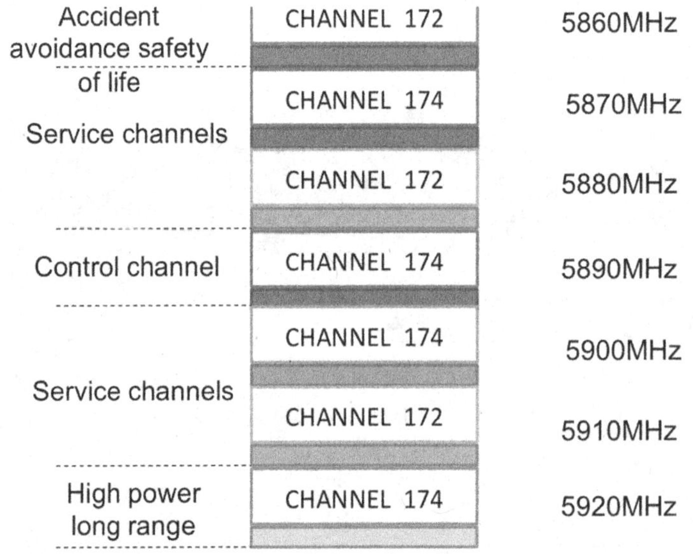

Accident avoidance safety of life	CHANNEL 172	5860MHz
Service channels	CHANNEL 174	5870MHz
	CHANNEL 172	5880MHz
Control channel	CHANNEL 174	5890MHz
Service channels	CHANNEL 174	5900MHz
	CHANNEL 172	5910MHz
High power long range	CHANNEL 174	5920MHz

entry into the network. After that, it is allocated an access slot by the basestation.

Different comparative analysis of the 802.11p versus the 802.16 have reported that the 802.16-based technology offers a wider radio of coverage and higher data rates than the 802.11p. The obtained results also showed that the latency of 802.16 is significantly larger when the communication distant is short (e.g. less than 100m). However, the results revealed the great competitiveness of the 802.16-based technology in the context of vehicle to infrastructure communication (Msadda, Cataldi, & Filali, 2010), (Chou, Li, Chien, & Lan, 2009).

3G cellular wireless technology supports a very broad area of coverage and high-mobility. Current 3G networks deliver a data rate that ranges from 384 kbps to 2 Mbps for fixed nodes. 3G systems deliver smoother handoffs compared to WLAN and WiMAX systems, however, their main weakness is their latency. 3G technology usually obtains delays values in the order of several hundreds of milliseconds which are too high

for critical applications. However, as it has been studied, cellular networks are able to maintain a regular behaviour in latency times (Landman & Kritzinger, 2005).

Satellite communication is another technology available for supporting vehicular communications because its provides ubiquitous coverage at any location. However, the main problems of networks that utilize this technology are the high costs and large propagation delays. The design of a global platform for vehicular communications is an important challenge. The design of the global platform should be on the basis of intelligent integration of readily available technologies in order to minimize the deployment cost and to make the deployment fast. However, the design should also support new emerging technologies. Research work have been carried out in two directions: heterogeneous architectures and multi-interface mobile nodes. The first direction proposes the design of integrated architectures composed by different technologies interconnected using an ad-hoc communication model (Yang, Ou, Chen,

Table 2. QoS categories for 802.16 standard

QoS class	Description	QoS specifications
Unsolicited grant service (UGS)	This class supports real-time service flows with periodic transmissions of fixed-size data packets such as T1/E1 and VoIP without silence suppression.	• Maximum sustained rate. • Maximum latency. • Tolerance. • Jitter tolerance.
Real-time polling service (rtPS)	This class supports real-time service flows with periodic transmissions of variable-size data packets, such as MPEG video.	• Minimun reserved rate. • Maximum sustained rate. • Maximum latency tolerance. • Traffic priority.
Extended real-time polling service (ertPS)	Real-time service flows that generate variable-sized data packets on a periodic basis.	• Minimum reserved rate. • Maximum sustanined rate. • Maximum latency tolerance. • Jitter tolerance. • Traffic priority.
Non-real-time polling service (nrtPS)	This type of service offers regular unicast polls from BS to SS so as to ensure that each service flow can receive bandwidth request opportunities even during network congestion.	• Minimum reserved rate. • Maximum sustained rate. • Traffic priority.
Best effort (BE)	This type of service is intended to provide efficient service for BE traffic such as web surfing. Generally, a bandwidth contention mechanism is used to request bandwidth from BS for each service flow.	• Maximum sustained rate. • Traffic priority.

& He, 2007; Pack, Rutagemwa, Shen, Mark, & Park, 2007). The second direction stuies the usage of several radios in the OBU of vehicle in order to enhance the performance of the network.

Data Dissemination Schemes

Given the complexities of VANETs in terms of, for example, their dynamic topology, mobility models, hard delay constrains, etc. and the different system architectures utilized, transporting information from one vehicle to another or to all vehicles within a given region or area is a highly challenging task. A lot of research has been carried out to develop protocols and mechanisms that can provide network services (e.g. routing) to applications in a VANET environment. Next, a classification of the different protocols for transporting information that have been proposed is presented and briefly analyzed (Li & Wang, 2007; Maihofer, 2004; Nundloll, Blair, & Grace, 2009; Zeadally, Ray, Yuh-Shyan, Angela, & Aamir, 2010; Mauve, 2010):

- **Broadcast:** This routing method is generally utilized for disseminating information such as traffic, weather, emergency, road conditions, etc to other vehicles. This communication scheme sends packets to all nodes in the network using flooding. When messages need to be disseminated beyond the radio transmission range, a multi-hop mechanism is utilized. Thus, in a naive broadcast implementation, all receiving nodes simply rebroadcast received messages. To limit duplication of messages, nodes broadcast messages only once and a time to live parameter can be utilized to limit messages' area of distribution. Using this routing scheme, delivery of messages to all nodes is guaranteed, however, a large amount of bandwidth is consumed, this is why this routing scheme only performs well when a small number of nodes is par-

ticipating within the VANET and its performance drops quickly when the size of the network increases.

- **Geocast:** It is a multicast routing service that delivers messages to nodes located within a given geographical region. These routing protocols generally define a forwarding zone that limits flooding of messages. Using this routing scheme it is possible to, for instance, report an accident to vehicles located within a given region or alert a driver when driving on a motorway in the wrong-way.
- **Forwarding:** The purpose of this routing scheme is to transport messages between two nodes via multiple hops. This mechanism is useful when the requested information is only of interest of a few nodes. For example, a node may request information to a nearby car parking about free car parking spaces and fees. When a node is requesting information, a unicast message is sent. To forward the message to its destination a route is reactively constructed, for example, by looking at local routing tables or by asking to nearby nodes whether they know about the destination node.
- **Clustering:** The cluster-based approach consists on grouping nodes located within a given region (e.g. nodes with direct link with each other). For each cluster, a cluster head node is elected which is responsible for managing inter and intra-cluster communication. The cluster-based structure functions as a virtual network infrastructure whose scalability favors routing and media access protocols although an overhead cost is paid when forming clusters in highly mobile network environments and network delays may occur on large networks.
- **Beaconing:** This routing mechanism is suitable for applications that require sharing information with other vehicles

periodically (e.g. exchange of local traffic information). In this routing scheme a node announces information periodically. Receiving nodes, do not re-broadcast the received message immediately, instead, they integrate and store received information on its local information cache. On receiver's next beacon a message is constructed using both local and received information and broadcasted to neighboring nodes.

- **Position-based:** For this routing scheme to work, information on the location of each node is fundamental. To decide how to route messages, nodes utilize geographical location information obtained from sources such as street maps, traffic models and on-board navigational systems. Routing decisions at each node are done taking into consideration the position of the destination node and each node's location information. As routing tables are not required, no overhead is incurred on maintaining and establishing routes.

- **Delay-tolerant:** There exist scenarios where density of vehicles can be really low and consequently establishing end-to-end routes is not possible. For example at nights, traffic in cities can be really low and available vehicles may not be close enough to receive and forward messages. Also, in rural areas vehicles density may be low. In sparse networks like those described before, a delay-tolerant protocol can be utilized. This routing mechanism is based on the concept of carry and forward, where a node carries messages and these are only forwarded when another node moves into its vicinity, otherwise, they are simply carried.

- **Ad-hoc (address-based/topology-based):** This category groups routing protocols initially designed to operate in MANET environments. With the emergence of VANETs

attempts to test these routing protocols in such new environments have been carried out. However, requirements on these address-based and topology-based mechanisms such as unique address identification among others make these protocols less suitable for VANETs.

Security and Privacy Threats

VANETs' architectures and communication schemes provide developers an environment for deployment of a wide variety of applications. However, major concern and still open issues of such environments are security and privacy. On one side, strong security mechanisms are required to protect both applications and users from possible attacks, and on the other hand, robust schemes are needed to protect users' private information. VANETs' security is highly important as their vulnerabilities could lead to disastrous accidents where people's integrity may be put at risk. Similarly, secrecy of personal data transmitted through the network including but not limited to identity, location, must be guaranteed. Next, some of the possible security and privacy threats for VANETs are listed ((Stampoulis & Chai, 2007) (Parno & Perrig, 2005) (Qian & Moayeri, 2008) (Raya & Hubaux, 2007)):

- **Denial of Service:** An attacker may intentionally prevent communication of vehicles located within its communication range by overwhelming nodes' resources or jamming their communication by, for instance, generating interfering transmissions or selectively erasing messages. This attack may prevent delivery of important information to its destination. For instance, on a denial of service attack, vehicles may not be able to receive messages from a vehicle alerting of an accident ahead.

- **Impersonation:** A vehicle within a VANET may pretend to be or act as a special type of vehicle (e.g. ambulance or patrol car) or infrastructure (e.g. roadside unit) spoofing traffic or safety messages. Examples of techniques that can be utilized towards impersonation include message fabrication, alteration and replay. An attacker impersonating a roadside unit, for instance, may contaminate the network fabricating false safety alarms.

- **Privacy Violation:** To prevent spoofing attacks (e.g. Sybil) a mechanism to bind each vehicle driver within the VANET to a single identity could be utilized. A strong authentication scheme like this could be utilized to provide forensic evidence to traditional law enforcement mechanisms and prevent attacks on vehicular networks. However, a system like this may also result in drivers abandoning their anonymity and exposing valuable information to attackers. The frequent exchange of messages containing sensitive personal data such as location, trip details, vehicle identification and e-payment information among others pose a highly important risk to privacy violations, as attackers can potentially overhear messages and misuse listened information.

- **On-board and In-transit Traffic Tampering:** On board units are susceptible to attacks from outsiders whom may attempt to alter sensed data such as speed or location. Similarly, attackers may manipulate critical in-transit traffic information corrupting or dropping overheard messages.

Security and Privacy Challenges

Due to unique characteristics of VANETs including fast mobility of nodes, frequent changes in topology, self-organization of nodes and user requirements, guarantying security and privacy is extremely hard. As surveyed before, this style of network is highly susceptible to different types of attacks and adversaries (e.g. greedy drivers, snoops and pranksters). Thus, to support VANET applications a number of security and privacy challenges must be addressed. To address these security and privacy challenges the following design principles have been proposed (Qian & Moayeri, 2008; Parno & Perrig, 2005):

- **Default Network Access:** Messages broadcasted should be accessible to all nodes that can receive them, and, all nodes must assist in enabling multi-hop communication.

- **Authenticated Localization of Message Origin:** Vehicular applications must be able to determine the origin of a message at a given location. With exception of the originator, nodes should not be able to modify messages and receivers must corroborate the message's sender.

- **Visibility of Events:** In distributed protocols, events that trigger joint computations or actions must be visible to or attested by all participating nodes (e.g. neighboring nodes). To attest messages, a node is either responsible of the generated event or has locality and timeliness privileges such as reception of the message within a given interval of seconds from its generation.

- **Mandated (non-circumventable) Mediation:** All actions that impact on the security state of the network (e.g. nodes identification scheme and authentication mechanism) must be mediated by a network authority and should not be bypassed or avoided by any node.

- **Accountability:** Protocol executions and messages that have an impact in substantial functions of the network (e.g. an alert message notifying of a vehicle failure) should be subject to auditions.

- **Vehicle Autonomy:** With exception of mediated messages and protocols (see mandated meditation) VANET applications can be autonomous with respect of other nodes. For example, messages from other nodes can be rejected.

- **Separation of Privilege:** Security, privacy and fault-tolerance systems must be distributed among multiple authorities. The roles of authorities and infrastructure should be separated.

- **Liability and Faulty Behavior:** A node causing deliberate or accidental actions that disrupt the operation of the VANET (e.g. iteration of other nodes or systems) must be legally responsible for its actions and therefore authorities should be able of identifying it. As the faulty behavior could be intentional or as a result of network or nodes' failures authorities could utilize a staged response mechanism where penalties may range from a warning notification on the first stage to an eviction from the system on the last stage.

- **Privacy:** Personal data such as identity of the driver and vehicle, location, speed and traveling routes must be protected. Nevertheless, as mentioned in the liability and faulty behavior principle, authorities must be capable of identifying messages' senders in case of an accident or violation to legal regulations.

- **Availability:** Regardless of faults or malicious conditions the network and applications must remain operational. This implies that design of protocols and applications should be secure, fault-tolerant and resilient to attacks.

Development Platforms

Testing, and evaluating the protocols and mechanisms required by VANET applications in real scenarios is not always feasible. Thus, development platforms such as simulators and testbeds are very important. Investigating the performace of VANET applications by deploy-

ing it on a real environment could be ideal as the complexity of such environments is very difficult to model. However, to date it is very difficult to find a geographical region or environment where a significant number of vehicles are already equipped with the technology necessary for these purposes. In addition, there exist important limitations for managing an environment like this to, for instance, study the applications using different environmental settings. Therefore, to design and evaluate VANET applications different simulators an testbeds have been proposed. These virtual and experimental environments allow developers to configure the environment according to their specific needs. For example, to evaluate scalability an environment can be populated with a large number of nodes, similarly, to asses latency, message dissemination, transmission delay or packet communication overhead different environments can be configured. Modeling nodes dynamicity and mobility and radio capabilities are examples of the challenges that existing simulators and testbeds still need to overcome. NoW (Festag, et al., 2008), DRIVE (Pinart, Lequerica, Barona, Sanz, García, & Sánchez-Aparisi, 2008) and COM2REACT (C2R Consortium, 2011) are examples of projects investigating the development of testbeds whereas NCTUNS (EstiNet Technologies Inc., 2011), NS-3 (The ns-3 Project, 2011) and OMNET (Omnet++ project, 2011) are instances of simulators that provide support for VANETs.

FUTURE RESEARCH DIRECTIONS

To successfully develop and deploy applications in vehicular networks there still extist different challenges that require been studied further. In particular, in the security and socio-economic domains there still exist various issues that have not been fully addressed.

Security Aspects for Future Research

Security is a very important challenge that must be solved. Vehicular communication networks pose some of the most challenging problems in the wireless communication research. The unique features of the vehicular networks, such as high-speed, high mobility and the large number of nodes that potentially can participate in the network add complexity to the challenge of security in vehicular networks. In this sense vehicular applications must satisfy several requirements before they can be deployed. It is essential to make sure that "life-critical safety" information cannot be inserted or modified by an attacker; likewise, the system should be able to help establishing the liability of drivers; but at the same time, it should protect as far as possible the privacy of the drivers and passengers. It is obvious that any malicious behavior of users, such as a modification and replay attack with respect to the disseminated messages could be fatal to other users. Performance and real-time delivery is also an issue for security in vehicular communication applications. All vehicles must transmit safety messages with frequencies between 100 to 300 ms. This implies that, for instance, future cryptographic techniques should perform with low traffic and processing overheads. Research on security aspects in vehicular communication networks has just started and some works have are available in the literature (Raya & Hubaux, 2007), (Leinmuller, Schoch, & Maihofer, 2007). In general terms, some of the security aspects that still require further research include user authentication, data authentication and integrity, privacy, data confidentiality, availability, liability and secure communications.

Socio-Economic Aspects for Future Research

From the socio-economic perspective, there are several key challenges that need to be investigated furhter. To succeed in the development and implementation of applications for vehicular networks a much higher penetration rate is necessary. Inter-vehicular communication has the potential of improving roads and urban areas safety, however the development of a strategy that defines the mechanisms necessary for introducing this technology into the market and exploiting it economically is necessary. The benefits of vehicular communications for traffic safety and transport efficiency must be analyzed and quantified. In this sense, little work has been done to evaluate the impact of vehicular communications as a new source of information on driving behavior. It is necessary to model the human factor aspects. Another important point is to examine and enumerate the cost-benefit relationship of vehicular communications. Designing deployment strategies for dissemination of vehicular communication into modern society. Owing to the network effect, there is the challenge of convincing early adopters to buy vehicular communication equipment when they will find a communication partner. Finally, vehicular networks will have being an important part of an intelligent transportation system. Vehicular networks will have been integrated into ITS.

CONCLUSION

In the last few years a suite of systems and applications for VANETs has emerged. This suite includes applications that can be utilized for improving vehicular safety, enhancing traffic control, and making more efficient the driver task and comfortable the time passengers expend inside the car while traveling. With system like these, it is possible to develop transport systems that are capable of optimizing fuel consumption, minimizing traffic congestion, reducing CO_2 emmisions and more importantly reducing humang casualties. In addition, there exist an important number of private and public initiatives that have been created and are dedicated to the development and research of vehicular systems. Still, because of the characteristics of VANETs in terms of, for example, its dynamic network topology, mobility patterns, low latency, etc, development and deployment of vehicular applications is still very challenging. What is more, to correctly operate, most VANET applications require support of some infrastructure (i.e. RSU) to extend vehicles short range communication coverage enabling and extending data dissemination. Unfortunatelly, the number of availables RSUs and OBUs in today's scenarios is still very limited and this condition limits and makes difficult deployment and evaluation of existing applications. Succesfull development of VANETs and the related applications are conditioned to the definition of stantards that facilitate the integration of heterogeneous systems. Similarly, the creation of strategies for increasing users aceptability and accessibility to vehicular applications and technologies is necesary. Finally, to guaranty privacy and security of users, data and applications novel mechanisms need to be developed.

REFERENCES

C2R Consortium official website. (2011). *The COM2REACT project*. Retrieved April 15, 2011, from http://www.com2react-project.org/.

America, I. T. (2009). *Intelligent Transportation Society of America*. Retrieved from http://www.itsa.org/.

Bai, F., & Krishnan, H. (2006). Reliability analysis of DSRC wireless communication for vehicle safety applications. *IEEE Intelligent Transportation Systems Conference 2006* (pp. 355-362). Toronto. doi: 10.1109/ITSC.2006.1706767

Bertolazzi, E., Biral, F., Da Lio, M., Saroldi, A., & Tango, F. (2010). Supporting drivers in keeping safe speed and safe distance: The SASPENCESubproject Within the European Framework Programme 6 Integrating Project PReVENT. *IEEE Transactions on Intelligent Transportation Systems*, *11*(3), 525–538. doi:10.1109/TITS.2009.2035925

CAMP Vehicle Safety Communications Consortium. (2005). DOT HS 809 859 [online] *Vehicle Safety Communications project task 3 final report: Identify intelligent vehicle safety applications enabled by DSRC*. Washington, DC: U.S. Department of Transportation. Retrieved from http://www.nhtsa.gov/DOT/NHTSA/NRD/Multimedia/PDFs/Crash%20Avoidance/2005/CAMP3scr.pdf.

Canada, I. (2009). *Intelligent Transportation Systems Society of Canada*. Retrieved from http://www.itscanada.ca.

Chou, C., Li, C., Chien, W., & Lan, K. (2009). *A feasibility study on vehicle-to-infrastructure communication: WiFi vs. WiMAX*. Tenth International Conference on Mobile Data Management: Systems, Services and Middleware. Washington, DC: IEEE Computer Society. doi: 10.1109/MDM.2009.127

Doshi, A., Shinko Yuanhsien, C., & Trivedi, M. M. (2009). A novel active heads-up display for driver assistance. *IEEE Transactions on Systems, Man, and Cybernetics. Part B, Cybernetics*, *39*(1), 85–93. doi:10.1109/TSMCB.2008.923527

EEA. (2006). *Technical report 9: Urban sprawl in Europe - The ignored challenge*. Copenhagen, Denmark: European Environmental Agency.

ERTICO-a. (1998). *Intelligent city transport: A guidebook to intelligent transport systems*. Brussels, Belgium: ITS City Pioneers Consortium.

ERTICO ITS EUROPE. (2010). *ITS Europe project activities*. Retrieved June 15, 2010, from http://www.ertico.com/activities/.

EstiNet website. (2011). *Estinet network simulator and emulator*. Retrieved February 14, 2011, from http://www.estinet.com/products.php.

European Transport Safety Council. (2008). *Road safety as a right and responsibility for all*. Brussels, Belgium: European Transport Safety Council (ETSC).

Festag, A., Noecker, G., Strassberger, M., Lubke, A., Bochow, B., & Torrent-Moreno, M. ... Kunisch, J. (2008). NoW - Network on Wheels: Project objectives, technology and achievements. *Proceedings of 5rd International Workshop on Intelligent Transportation* (pp. 211 – 216). Hamburg, Germany.

Huang, C.-J., Chuang, Y.-T., Chen, Y.-J., Yang, D.-X., & Chen, I.-F. (n.d.). QoS-aware roadside base station assisted routing in vehicular networks. *The Engineering Applications of Artificial Intelligence, 22*(8), 1292-1301. New York, NY. *ACM*. doi:10.1016/j.engappai.2009.04.003

IEEE-SA Standards Board. (2009). *IEEE standard for local and metropolitan area networks part 16: Air interface for broadband wireless access systems. IEEE Computer Society and the IEEE Microwave Theory and Techniques Society*. New York, NY: IEEE.

Japan, I. (2009). *ITS Japan*. Retrieved from http://www.its-jp.org/english/.

Landman, J., & Kritzinger, P. (2005). Delay analysis of downlink IP traffic on UMTS mobile networks. *Journal Performance Evaluation, 62*(1), 68–82. doi:10.1016/j.peva.2005.07.007

Leinmuller, T., Schoch, E., & Maihofer, C. (2007). Security requirements and solution concepts in vehicular ad-hoc networks. *Forth Annual Conference on Wireless on Demand Network Systems and Services*, (pp. 84-91). Obergurgl. doi: 10.1109/WONS.2007.340489

Li, F., & Wang, Y. (2007, June). Routing in vehicular ad hoc networks: A survey. *IEEE Vehicular Technology Magazine, 2*(2), 12–22. doi:10.1109/MVT.2007.912927

Lomax, T., & Schrank, D. (2005). *Urban mobility study*. Texas: Texas Transportation Institute. Retrieved from http://mobility.tamu.edu/ums/report/

Ma, X., Chen, X., & Refai, H. (2009). *Performance and reliability of DSRC vehicular safety communication: A formal analysis*. EURASIP Journal on Wireless Communications and Networking - Special Issue on Wireless Access in Vehicular Environments.

Maihofer, C. (2004). A survey of geocast routing protocols. *IEEE Communications Surveys and Tutorials, 6*(2), 32–42. doi:10.1109/COMST.2004.5342238

Mauve, M. (2010). Information dissemination in VANETs. In Hartenstein, H., & Laberteaux, K. (Eds.), *VANET vehicular applications and inter-networking technologies* (pp. 49–80). Wiley&Sons Ltd.

Msadda, I., Cataldi, P., & Filali, F. (2010). A comparative study between 802.11p and mobile WiMAX-based V2I communication networks. *2010 Fourth International Conference on Next Generation Mobile Applications, Services and Technologies* (pp. 186-191). Washington, DC: IEEE Computer Society. doi: 10.1109/NGMAST.2010.45

NS-3 Project. (2011). *The NS-3 network simulator*. Retrieved April 10, 2011, from http://www.nsnam.org/.

Nundloll, V., Blair, G., & Grace, P. (2009, December). A component-based approach for (re)configurable routing in VANETs. *Proceedings of the 8th International Workshop on Adaptive and Reflective Middleware*. Illinous: USA. doi: 10.1145/1658185.1658187

Omnet Community. (2011). *Omnet++ event simulation environment*. Retrieved April 5, 2011, from http://www.omnetpp.org.

Pack, S., Rutagemwa, H., Shen, X., Mark, J., & Park, K. (2007). Efficient data access algorithms for ITS-bsed networks with multihop wireless link. *IEEE International Conference on Communications* (pp. 4785 - 4790). Glasgow, UK: IEEE. doi: 10.1109/ICC.2007.790

Parno, B., & Perrig, A. (2005). Challenges in securing vehicular networks. *Proceedings of the Workshop on Hot Topics in Networks*.

Pinart, C., Lequerica, I., Barona, I., Sanz, P., García, D., & Sánchez-Aparisi, D. (2008). DRIVE: A reconfigurable testbed for advanced vehicular services and communications. *Proceedings of the 4th International Conference on Testbeds and Research Infrastructures for Development of Networks and Communities*. Brussels, Belgium: ICST.

Popescu-Zeleti, R., Radusch, I., & Rigani, M. (2010). *Vehicular-2-X communication*. Berlin, Germany: Springer. doi:10.1007/978-3-540-77143-2

Qian, Y., & Moayeri, N. (2008). Design of secure and application-oriented VANETs. *Vehicular Technology Conference* (2794-2799). Singapore: IEEE. doi: 10.1109/VETECS.2008.610

Raya, M., & Hubaux, J.-P. (2007). Securing vehicular ad hoc networks. [Amsterdam, The Netherlands: IOS Press.]. *Journal of Computer Security*, *15*(1), 39–68.

Research and Innovative Technology Administration. (2008). *Transportation vision for 2030*. U.S. Department of Transportation. Retrieved from http://www.rita.dot.gov/publications/transportation_vision_2030/.

Safety, C. F. (2009). *Make roads safe, a decade of action for road safety*. Commission for Global Road Safety. Retrieved from http://www.makeroadssafe.org/publications/Pages/homepage.aspx.

Skordylis, A., & Trogoni, N. (n.d.). Delay-bounded routing in vehicular ad-hoc networks. *9th ACM International Symposium on Mobile Ad Hoc Networking and Computing* (pp. 341-350). New York, NY: ACM. doi: 10.1145/1374618.1374664

Stampoulis, A., & Chai, Z. (2007). *A survey of security in vehicular networks*. Retrieved from http://zoo.cs.yale.edu/~ams257/projects/wireless-survey.pdf.

UNFPA. (2007). *Technical report: State of world population 2007: Unleashing the potential of urban growth*. New York, NY: United Nations Population Fundation. Retrieved from http://www.unfpa.org/swp/2007/english/introduction.html.

Wang, S., Chou, C., & Lin, Ç. (2010). *The GUI user manual for the NCTUns 6.0 network simulator and emulator. Network and System Laboratory, Department of Computer Science*. Taiwan: National Chiao Tung University.

Website, R. I. T. A. (2010). *Department of Transportation research programs*. Retrieved October 13, 2010 from http://www.rita.dot.gov/rdt/dot_research_programs.html.

Yang, K., Ou, S., Chen, H., & He, J. (2007). A multihop peer-communication protocol with fairness garantee for IEEE 802.16-based vehicular networks. *IEEE Transactions on Vehicular Technology*, *56*(6), 3358–3370. doi:10.1109/TVT.2007.906875

Zeadally, S., Ray, H., Yuh-Shyan, C., Angela, I., & Aamir, H. (2010, December 9). *Vehicular ad hoc networks (VANETS): Status, results, and challenges*. Telecommunication Systems. Springer Science+Business Media. doi: 10.1007/s11235-010-9400-5

APPENDIX: ACRONYMS USED

ACC: Adaptive Cruise Control.
ADAS: Advanced Driver Assistance Service.
DOT: Department Of Transportation.
EEA: European Environment Agency.
FCW: Forwarding Collision Warning.
GDP: Gross Domestic Product.
GPS: Global Positioning System.
ITS: Intelligent Transportation Systems.
LDW: Lane Departure Warning.
LEO: Low-Earth Orbit.
GPRS: General Packet Radio Service.
GSM: Global System for Mobile communications.
MANET: Mobile Ad-hoc Network.
HMI: Human Machine Interaction.
NGO: Non-Governmental Organization.
OBU: OnBoard Unit.
OEM: Original Equipment Manufacturer.
QOS: Quality Of Service.
RFID: Radio-Frequency Identification.
RSU: RoadSide Unit.
RWIS: Road Weather Information System.
V2I: Vehicle-to-Infrastructure.
V2V: Vehicle-to-Vehicle.
VANET: Vehicular Ad-Hoc Network.
WSN: Wireless Sensor Network.

Chapter 10
Communication Architectures and Services for Intelligent Transport Systems

Marina Aguado
University of the Basque Country, Spain

Nerea Toledo
University of the Basque Country, Spain

Marion Berbineau
IFSTTAR, Institut Français des Sciences et Technologies des Transports, de l'Aménagement et des Réseaux, France

Eduardo Jacob
University of the Basque Country, Spain

ABSTRACT

Current challenges in mobility and sustainable development are closely related to increasing travel safety, optimizing the use of transport infrastructure, reducing operating and maintenance costs and making public transport more attractive. The proposed solutions to these major challenges depend to a high extent, on political decisions, development of good practices, and also on the innovation and technology introduced through on-going Intelligent Transport Systems (ITS) programs and initiatives. This chapter provides an overview on the communication architectures able to support these ITS programs. In order to do so, this chapter presents the current standardization initiatives in the vehicular environment, a description from the telecom point of view of the different ITS services, and finally, a survey on the radio access technologies capable of dealing with such a demanding scenario.

DOI: 10.4018/978-1-4666-0209-0.ch010

INTRODUCTION

Current challenges in mobility and sustainable development are closely related to increasing travel safety, optimizing the use of transport infrastructure, reducing operating and maintenance costs and making public transport more attractive. The proposed solutions to these major challenges depend at a high extend, on political decisions, development of good practices and also on the innovation and technology introduced through on-going Intelligent Transport Systems (ITS) programs and initiatives.

Intelligent Transport Systems refers to those efforts to devise how to involve information and communication technologies (ICT) to improve safety, efficiency and competitiveness in cars, buses, railways and mass transportation systems (goods & persons).

These Intelligent Transport Systems rely on communication architectures, computation, databases and geo-location information. This chapter covers a taxonomy of these Intelligent Transport Systems and their communication architectures underneath. In order to do so, this chapter is structured as follows.

The second section presents an overview on the most relevant communication frameworks for the vehicular environment. It introduces the current standardization initiatives (Communication Access for Land Mobiles from International Organization for Standardization, ISO CALM, the Intelligent Transport Systems initiative from the European Standard Institute, ETSI ITS and the Wireless Access in Vehicular Environment initiative from the Institute of Electrical Electronic Engineers, IEEE WAVE) and other innovative ones.

The third section provides a taxonomy on Intelligent Transport Services and introduces for each service its key performance indicators. The fourth section describes the current telecom context. It provides a survey and comparison on current radio access technologies able to cope with the extremely demanding vehicular scenario and the high mobility scenario with regard to vehicular to infrastructure communications.

To conclude, the fifth section presents a thorough survey of the current radio access technologies to be applied in vehicle-to-infrastructure communications.

COMMUNICATION ARCHITECTURES FOR THE VEHICULAR SCENARIO

Standardization Initiatives

One of the most significant characteristic of the ITS context is the amount of agents that have to cooperate in the definition of a communication architecture. These agents embrace vehicle manufacturers; ISPs (Internet Service Providers) with a large heterogeneity in the access network; Internet mobility operators that aim at managing the mobility of the ongoing communications; governmental organizations that are expected to legislate the infrastructure deployment and its utilization; and standardization bodies who are in charge of defining standardized protocols and procedures. Having such a variety, the introduction of Information and Communication Technology (ICT) in the ITS context requires strong mutual effort for decision taking and best solution design.

Due to its major role in the design of communication architectures, this section focuses on the standardization initiatives that have been undertaken throughout standardization organizations like the ISO, ETSI or the IEEE. It is worth pointing that having detected that ITS is an essential technology, standardization organizations have established ad-hoc working groups between the ETSI, IEEE, IETF (Internet Engineering Task Force), ISO and ITU (International Telecommunication Union) for joint development of specifications. We next describe the communication architectures that are currently being standardized.

THE ISO CALM ARCHITECTURE

Standardization on ITS started in 2001 in ISO, who first named ITS to an evolved transportation scenario where technologies like ICT are introduced. The aim of ISO was to define a basic set of ITS communication standards.

Currently, the definition of a communication architecture for the ITS scenario is going ahead in the Working Group 16 of the ISO Technical Committee 204, which is defining the CALM (Communication Access for Land Mobiles) architecture ([ISO], 2010). CALM defines a framework to enable efficient ITS communication services and applications. The architecture is open and with room for future functionalities considering the difference between the communication technologies and the vehicle lifetimes.

CALM defines a set of air interface protocols and parameters, networking protocols and upper layer protocols for wireless data communications holding up current communication technologies and also enabling future ones. The architecture has been designed to support heterogeneous networking through dedicated convergence layers between multiple access technologies like IEEE802, 3GPP, 3GPP2 or IMT-Advanced (International Mobile Telecommunications).

Although agents involved in the vehicular scenario where at first reluctant to accept IPv6 as the networking protocol, currently they are convinced that there is no serious long term networking alternative for ITS other than IPv6. Consequently, communication architectures like CALM have adopted IPv6 as the networking protocol, but a non-IP connectivity and routing solution named CALM FAST designed for safety applications is also defined in the CALM architecture. This CALM FAST protocol comes into play in fast ad-hoc communication scenarios. The IP networking layer of CALM comprises the following protocols: IPv6 and its mobility extensions, Network Mobility Basic Support (NEMO BS), GeoNetworking and CALM FAST. However, being an open and evolving architecture, there is room for future networking protocols.

Besides common architecture layers, CALM also defines a Management Plane where the Interface Management Entity (IME), the Network Management Entity (NME) and the CALM/Application Management Entity (CME) are specified. This plane is where the *intelligence* of the architecture resides. Applications interact with the Management Plane to give their requirements. These requirements are utilized to select the networking layer and manage the interface selection. It is worth mentioning that although in the ITS context the killer applications are related to safety, thanks to the Internet connectivity, CALM can support a wide scope of applications, which will use the traditional protocol stack over IPv6.

With the goal of covering all the possible communication scenarios in a vehicular context, CALM defines three communication modes: Vehicle-to-Vehicle (V2V), Vehicle-to-Infrastructure (V2I) and Infrastructure-to-Infrastructure (I2I). By doing so, all the interactions that are necessary to have a safe and efficient ITS context are addressed.

The first deployment of the CALM architecture has been worked out in the CVIS (Cooperative Vehicle-to-Infrastructure Systems) European project (CVIS, 2006). In this project two CALM capable devices have been developed: a CALM Router, which is responsible for managing the connectivity continuity of V2V and V2I communications; and a CALM Host, which is an on board equipment that implements a simple version of the CALM architecture with indispensable functions.

THE ETSI ITS ARCHITECTURE

Following the results of the ISO, work on standardizing a communication architecture for the ITS scenario began in the ETSI in 2007. This work is being carried out by the Technical Committee for

Figure 1. Overview of the ISO CALM architecture

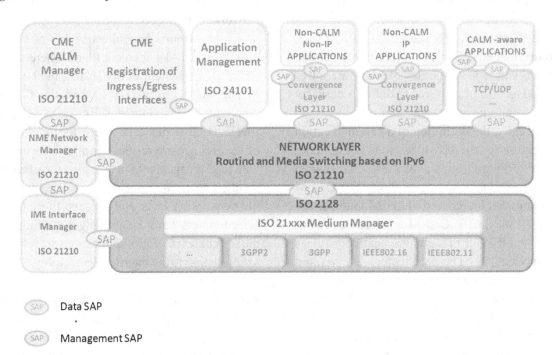

ITS (ETSI TC ITS) whose founding was pushed by the ISO.

The goal of defining an European-centric architecture was twofold: convert the ISO CALM standard in European Norms (EN); and develop the necessary test suites for conformance and interoperability testing. Therefore, the ETSI ITS architecture can be regarded as a sub-set of functionalities of the ISO CALM architecture. Notice that the ISO CALM aims at defining an open, fully operational framework, while the ETSI ITS architecture aims at having an interoperable basic set of functionalities enabling different implementations. However, both architectures are almost identical.

Due to its implementation-oriented nature of the ETSI ITS architecture, several European Projects have been developed lately. The most outstanding ones are the following: Communication for eSafety (COMeSafety, 2006), CVIS, Geo-addressing and geo-routing for vehicular communications (GeoNet, 2008), Secure vehicle communication (SEVECOM, 2006), Co-operative networks for intelligent road safety (COOPERS, 2006), Extended framework architecture for co-operative systems (E-FRAME, 2008), Pre-drive (Pre-Drive C2X, 2008), An integrated wireless and traffic platform for real-time road traffic management solutions (iTETRIS, 2008) and SAFESPOT (SAFESPOT, 2008). It is also worth pointing the work carried out by the industry driven consortium: C2C-CC (Car-to-Car Communication Consortium). The results of these projects have been a valuable input in the definition of the ETSI ITS architecture and have fed the specification of its functionalities.

As an important part of the architecture, the basic set of applications and services and functional and operational requirements have been defined based on the results of the Pre-Drive C2X, CVIS, SAFESPOT and Coopers projects. Regarding the transport and network layers, the ETSI ITS

Figure 2. Overview of the ETSI ITS architecture

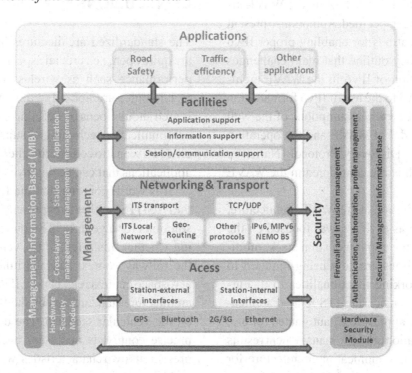

architecture supports the same networking protocols specified by the ISO CALM architecture. However, unlike CALM, the ETSI ITS architecture defines the interoperability with legacy IPv4 systems. In addition, specific dedicated transport protocols may be introduced to the already existing TCP and UDP protocols. A Data Link Layer and a Physical Layer are also defined in the ETSI ITS architecture, where different wireless access technologies like the 5.9 GHz European Profile of the DSRC standard based on IEEE802.11p can be adopted.

Notice that unlike the ISO CALM architecture, the ETSI ITS architecture is a more layered model and more details of each level of the stack are provided.

It has not been until September 2010 when the ETSI included in a very succinct way Internet connectivity provisioning in the specification of the architecture ([ETSI], 2010). Thus, further work is ongoing through all the agents involved.

THE IEEE WAVE ARCHITECTURE

The IEEE is also designing a communication architecture for the vehicular scenario named WAVE (Wireless Access in the Vehicular Environment) ([IEEE], 2010). This architecture is mainly focused on specifying the use of an amendment to the IEEE802.11 standard: IEEE802.11p.

In WAVE, the management structure, security mechanisms and the physical access for up to 27 Mbps and a range of up to 1 Km for low latency wireless communications are defined. Two different entities are specified in the WAVE architecture to support V2V and V2I communications: the OBU (On-Board Unit) and the RSU (Roadside Unit). It is worth pointing that in the first versions of the architecture no routing features have been defined for the OBU, so no heterogeneous networking was considered.

Although the IPv6 protocol has been lately adopted by the WAVE architecture, Clausen *et al.* (2010) analyzed in a research report that the requirements to introduce IPv6 in the WAVE architecture are underspecified. Authors also present a set of specifications for enabling proper IPv6 over WAVE. They outline that main challenges of the introduction of IPv6 in the WAVE architecture are related to the use of IPv6 formats, non compatibility of certain assumptions of the well defined link model of WAVE and the operation of the Neighbor Discovery Protocol (Narten *et al.,* 2007) which is not considered in the WAVE architecture.

From the evolution of the WAVE architecture, we observe that as at first it was focused on the lower layers of the communication stack, modifications or add-ons are now being required to introduce networking functionalities to it. Furthermore, only considering ITS related applications like safety applications, automated tolling, enhanced navigation or traffic management results in not having a communication architecture for other type of demanding services that may request different performance requirements.

CONCLUSIONS

The standardized architectures here introduced are quite open, i.e., crucial aspects for application performance such as wireless communication technologies are not defined. Consequently, research should focus on defining specific wireless communication technologies suitable for the specific ITS scenario considering the heterogeneity of applications that can be deployed in this context.

It is worth pointing that the ISO CALM and the ETSI ITS architectures present communication solutions for a generic ITS context, not specifying whether this refers to the vehicular context, the railway context, the maritime context, the aerospace context, etc. Unlike ISO and ETSI, the architecture standardized by the IEEE is focused on the vehicular scenario. The definition of the precise context is necessary because each one presents its own characteristics, which a generalist architecture may not address. Therefore, research should also focus designing a specific architecture for each ITS scenario. At the same time, the different communication architectures should converge

Figure 3. Overview of the IEEE WAVE architecture

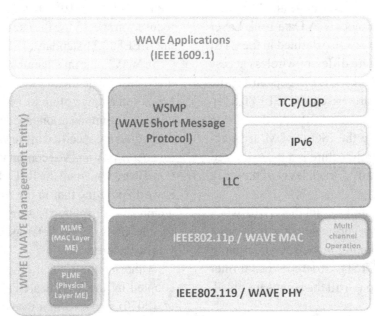

and be interoperable to ensure people's safety and tackle the connectivity necessities to the always moving globalized world.

In order to contribute to this research area, next sections firstly describe the ITS most common services and then we introduce a survey on communication technologies for the specific vehicular to infrastructure/railway scenario.

INTELLIGENT TRANSPORT SERVICES TAXONOMY AND THEIR CORRESPONDING KEY PERFORMANCE INDICATORS (KPIS)

As previously stated, Intelligent Transport Systems or Services are designed to increase transport and travel safety, productivity and transport efficiency through the use of information and communication technologies. These services use a wide range of electronic and wired or wireless communication systems that are integrated at infrastructure and vehicle level. They also require a close cooperation between the infrastructure all along the vehicle route (motorway, railway, tram, metro line,etc.) and the vehicles.

These Intelligent Transport Services use different communication technologies in accordance to the existent communication flows, the communication tiers or entities involved.

This section provides an overview on the currently identified envisaged main Intelligent Transport Services. It offers a taxonomy of all these services and finally concludes identifying, when possible, their expected key performance indicators from the quality of service point of view. Not under all circumstances are the specific KPIs for each ITS application clearly defined.

Intelligent Transport Services Taxonomy

Current Intelligent Transport Services may be classified according to the estimated communication range. We can find then *short range and long range ITS services.*

Figure 4. ITS taxonomy

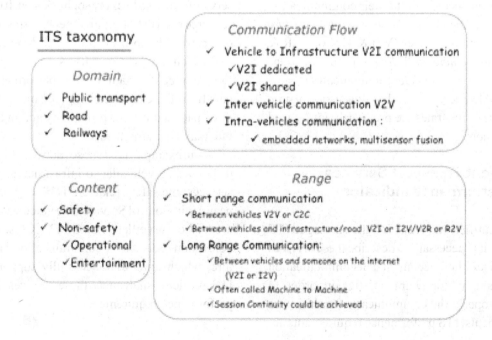

Table 1. Additional parameters needed in addition to traffic class (ITU-R, 2006)

Traffic Class	CBR	VBR	ABR	UBR
Information Required	QoS Average bit rate Delay requirement	QoS Average bit rate Peak bit rate	QoS Average bit rate Minimum bit rate (or maximum delay)	None

Short range ITS are those existing services between vehicles (V2V) or between vehicles and infrastructure/ road or railway (V2I or I2V/ V2R or R2V).

Regarding long range ITS services, we can find communication services between vehicles and specific entities or information servers on the Internet. They are often named as Machine to Machine communication services and the key challenge point is to keep session continuity in the high mobility context and with a high handover rate.

If we take into consideration the information content, ITS services may also be classified into *safety and non-safety* related ITS services.

Having into account the specific domain those ITS services aim to cover, we can find *public transport, road and railway* ITS services.

Last but not least, ITS services may also be classified in accordance to their communication flow. We can then find *Vehicular to Infrastructure* communication services (V2I & I2V or V2R & R2V) and *Vehicle to Vehicle* communications (V2V) and *Intra Vehicle* communications such as embedded networks and multisensory fusion.

Figure 4 illustrates the previously introduced ITS taxonomy.

Intelligent Transport Services Key Performance Indicators

Once identified and classified the envisaged ITS services, it is necessary to describe these services in terms of their technical telecommunication profile and major characteristics in order to match properly the communication architecture requirements. ITS performance requirements are expressed through their expected Key Performance Indicators (KPIs).

According to ITU-R Report M.2072 (ITU-R, 2006), the different information services can be classified as: Constant Bit Rate (CBR), Variable Bit Rate (VBR), Available Bit Rate (ABR), Unspecified Bit Rate (UBR). The VBR has two subclasses according to its real-time nature: rtVBR (real-time VBR) and nrtVBR (non real-time VBR). Table 1 describes the parameters that are necessary to define when characterizing each different type of traffic classes.

It is worthy to point out that, traditionally, in the field of circuit-switched telecom networks, the traffic engineering term quality of service refers to "achieved" service quality.

On the contrary, in the field of computer networking and packet-switched telecommunication networks, the traffic engineering term quality of service (QoS) is a bit more sophisticated. It refers to resource reservation control mechanisms. Quality of service is the ability to provide different priority to different applications, users, or data flows, or to guarantee a certain level of performance to a data flow. For example, a required bit rate, delay, jitter, packet dropping probability and/or bit error rate may be guaranteed.

As an example, next subsection describes three different ITS vehicular to infrastructure/railway services: the safety related ETCS service (European Train Control Service), the voice service and the Video Surveillance or CCTV (Close Circuit Television) service. A communication architecture, which aims to successfully support these ITS services, shall meet these services specific performance requirements.

Performance Requirements for ETCS Service

Following the decision to adopt GSM, Global System for Mobile Communication, in 1992, the Union Internationale des Chemins de Fer (UIC), the European Union and several railway companies launched a project named EIRENE (European Integrated Radio Enhanced Network). Its aim was to specify the functional and technical requirements for mobile networks which could both fulfill the railway needs and ensure cross-border interoperability. The EIRENE specification identifies the GSM-R necessary requirements to cope with the ETCS traffic needs, with special emphasis in the QoS parameters demanded. This specification defines the functional and systems requirements specifications necessary to ensure that core railway functionality is provided.

The EIRENE specification also defines the requirements for an EIRENE network and the performance levels which are to be achieved. The aim is to provide interoperability between networks and a consistent level of service. The definition of an EIRENE network is a railway telecommunication network, based on the GSM standard, which complies with all related mandatory requirements as specified in the EIRENE (UIC,2006)(UIC,2006A). The difference between an EIRENE network and an EIRENE system is that the EIRENE system includes terminals.

The EIRENE System Requirements Specification defines a radio system satisfying the mobile communications requirements of the European railways. It encompasses ground-train voice and data communications, together with the ground based mobile communications needs of trackside workers, station and depot staff and railway administrative and managerial personnel.

Table 2 presents the performance requirements in terms of quality of service parameters for the ETCS service supported under an EIRENE network (UIC,2007):

Table 2. ETCS QoS parameters

ETCS QoS Parameter (KPIs)	Requirement
Connection establishment delay (CED)	< 8.5 s (95%) ≤ 10 s (100%)
Maximum end-to-end transfer delay (30 byte data block) (TED) Average end-to-end transfer delay	≤ 0.5 s (99%) ≤ 400 to 500 ms
Network registration delay (NRD)	≤ 30 s (95%), ≤ 35 s (99%), ≤ 40 s (100%)
Handover effective time (between BSs)	< 300 ms
Transmission Data Rate	≥ 2.4 kbps

Connection Establishment Delay (CED)

This is the value of the elapsed time between the connection establishment request and the indication of successful connection establishment on the requesting side. This parameter is successfully validated if the 95th-percentile is less than 8.5s. This parameter represents the necessary time to perform the connection establishment routine.

Maximum End-to-End Transfer Delay (of 30 Byte Data Block) (TED)

TED definition is the value of the elapsed time between the request for transfer of a data frame and the indication of successfully transferred end-to-end data frame. The length of data frame shall be 30 bytes. It has been created within the simulation tool a specific statistic to record this KPI.

Average End-to-End Transfer Delay

The average transfer delay is calculated having into account the full set of message communication exchange in the simulation run. The average is between 120 and 130 ms. This parameter is successfully validated if its value is lower than the 400-500 ms demanded for GSM-R deployment.

Table 3. Voice service QoS requirements for EIRENE networks supporting voice applications

Voice service QoS Parameter (KPIs)	Requirement
Connection establishment delay (CED)	< 8.5 s (95%) ≤10 s (100%)
Maximum end-to-end transfer delay Average end-to-end transfer delay	≤ 0.5 s (99%) ≤ 400 to 500 ms
Handover effective time (between BSs)	> 300 ms

Table 4. CCTV demanded KPIs

CCTV QoS Parameter (KPIs)	Requirement
Average Throughput	> 384 kbps
End-to-end transfer delay	< 60 ms
Packet delay variation within a flow	< 20 ms
Information Loss PER (Packet Error Rate)	< 1%
One way Radio Access Network Transfer Delay	< 25 ms
Handover delay	< 50 ms
Bounded Packet loss during handover	< 1%

Transmission Data Rate

In accordance with EIRENE specifications, the transmission data rate has to be higher or equal to 2.4 kbps.

Performance Requirements for Voice Services

In the railway domain the voice service or voice communication between the train driver and the operational control centre and also with other machine drivers and shunting staff is still a highly demanded and prioritized service.

A railway communication architecture, when providing voice services, shall meet the specific EIRENE QoS requirements related to voice service application (UIC,2007). Table 3 details these requirements.

Performance Requirements for Video Surveillance Service

The use of surveillance systems has long been pointed out as a means of improving public security. Increasing fear of global terrorism has brought renewed developments in this sector.

Enhanced surveillance systems can automatically spot suspicious behaviour and raise an alarm. These surveillance applications consist generally of video monitoring of specific areas (corridors, stations, platforms…) and video transmission to a control centre. These applications are one of the key challenging services from a telecommunica-

tion point of view. They require high data rate and performance in order that the video content can be on-time processed by the security teams.

Deploying this application in uplink stream in the public transport domain represents great technical challenge and research effort. In this section the surveillance application, also named CCTV (Close Circuit Television) service is characterized. The Key Performance Indicators (KPI) are also identified. For security applications the video quality must allow specific image processing at control centre for event detection. Due to the nature of the information source, special attention to the client playout delay has to be considered. This playout delay depends on jitter, a specific QoS KPI.

As an example, commercial surveillance application demonstration from SIEMENS uses to transmit real-time 2 Video stream 704 x 576 frame format at 12fps and encoded MPEG-4. The average flow was in this case 1.5 Mbps. (Lardenoisse, 2005)

There are not QoS requirements currently defined for the CCTV application in the railway domain. The approach taken was to identify the QoS requirements expected when this application is supported in networks that meet the IMT-Advanced requirements as reported in ITU-T Rec Y.1541 and ITU-T Rec. G.114 (05/2003).

The proposed requirements specified in Table 4 are been proposed taking into account the requirements for Class 2 (Voice and Video Conferencing, low to moderate bit rate, real-time, synchronous, and symmetric) and Class 3 (Streaming Media high bit rate).

SURVEY OF CURRENT RADIO ACCESS TECHNOLOGIES FOR V2I SERVICES

In the last few years, Wireless Mobile Networks are facing the long term challenge to properly address the air link channel limitations together with the growing demand on services, fast mobility and wide coverage. In fact the traffic profile in Wireless Mobile Networks has changed abruptly. Data services are the key service driving the bandwidth demands in Wireless Mobile Networks. It is foreseen that the development of IMT-2000, the ITU global standard for third generation wireless communication, will reach a limit of around 30 Mbps. In the vision of the ITU, ITU-R Report M.2072, there may be a need for new wireless access technologies capable of supporting even higher data rates.

The ITU-R has recently proposed the International Mobile Telecommunications – Advanced (IMT-Advanced) technical requirements; one of the most demanding and challenging scenarios covered by the IMT-Advanced is the high speed scenario. The new capabilities of these IMT-Advanced systems are envisaged to handle a wide range of supported data rates according to economic and service demands in multi-user environments. Target peak data rates are up to approximately 100Mbit/s for high mobility, such as mobile access, and up to approximately 1 Gbit/s for low mobility such as nomadic local wireless access. However, it is necessary to take into account that IMT-Advanced is a long term endeavour. The specification of IMT-Advanced

technologies will probably not be completed until at least 2010.

Until recently, there was a technological gap regarding access techniques which could offer high transmission data rates and high interactivity (low latency) able to support real time applications in high mobility environments such as the vehicular environment. However, research community efforts are underway to develop new generation wireless mobile networks that provide broadband data communication in this high speed vehicular scenario and new technologies capable of fulfilling the aforementioned technology gap have been developed. Currently, there are a number of initiatives that aim to provide ubiquitous connectivity at different mobility profiles.

The standard based broadband wireless technologies able to support the vehicular mobility profile while offering a high transmission data rate are:

- IEEE802.11p or Wireless Access for the Vehicular Environment (WAVE),
- IEEE802.20 or Mobile Broadband Wireless Access (MBWA),
- IEEE802.16,
- Third Generation Partnership Project (3GPP) Long Term Evolution (LTE)

These emerging broadband and mobile access wireless technologies have some common features such as QoS support, low latency and advanced security mechanisms. They are also designed to support QoS and real-time applications such as voice-over-Internet protocol (VoIP), video, etc. They also may offer deployment bandwidth on the order of 40 to 100Mbps per base station.

OFDM and higher order MIMO antenna configurations are the core enabler for scaling throughput of these wireless mobile technologies. All the three 4G (4th Mobile Communication Generation) candidates are based on OFDM and MIMO, consequently their major features are similar on the physical layer.

Figure 5. The vehicular to infrastructure network reference model (V2INRM)

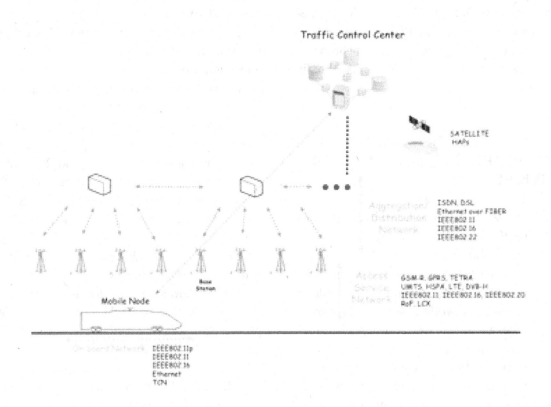

The IEEE802.16.m specification and the Third Generation Partnership Project (3GPP) Long Term Evolution (LTE) specification are currently the only two candidates to cover the IMT-Advanced requirements.

The Vehicular to Infrastructure Network Reference Model (V2INRM)

A general Vehicular to Infrastructure Architecture Reference Model (V2INRM) is represented in Figure 5. The mobile node communicates with the traffic control centre or railway information service provider through the access network all along the rail net and the aggregation or distribution network. This section provides an overview on the different technologies commonly used in these identified types of networks.

Most of the train to ground communication architectures fits this Reference Model but for the architectures based on satellite communication and on High Altitude Platforms (HAPs).

The architecture of a satellite based communication network is different from a terrestrial one. The satellite is considered as a central node and receives several communications coming from several transmitters on the ground. Therefore, satellite communication does not fit this reference architecture; there are not aggregation or base stations nodes all along the motorway net.

Radio Access Technologies for the Access Service Network

This section is structured as follows: first satellite solutions are introduced, then wireless terrestrial systems identifying separately the cellular technologies and then wireless area network technologies. This section partly uses the results obtained in study carried out within the Train IPSAT French

National Research Project for Innovation on Transport (Berbineau, 2006) and Kuran's survey (Kuran, 2007).

Satellite Systems

On the contrary to their common use in maritime and aeronautical scenarios, satellite technology for communication with terrestrial mobiles is not intensively used. The major drawbacks when considered its application in the railway domain are related to the bandwidth price (1-3M€ approximately. per year for a 36MHz transponder) and the existence of areas where the satellite signal is not received on the train (stations, tunnels, cuttings, urban canyons, mountain areas, etc).

Besides that, the big distance between the different nodes involved in the architecture of a satellite based communication network leads to significant transmission delays that can reach 500ms. Furthermore, the satellite tracking performed by the antenna sets up technical requirements that also increase system complexity and cost also in the context of railway applications (vicinity of catenaries, EMC potential problems, space available, etc.) (Berbineau, 2006). Another issue is that satellite based communication systems are generally non symmetrical. They allow information transfer at high data rate in the downlink direction and only a low data rate in the uplink direction. The advantages of satellite solutions, particularly with geostationary satellites, are mainly the wide geographical coverage and the immediate availability of communication infrastructures for deployment of services.

There are currently numerous implementations of satellite communication for signalling purposes in most of the Latin American large heavy haul railway companies using Omnisat satellite and Autotrac equipment from Qualcomm.

There are also currently deployed industrial solutions or pre-tested solutions oriented towards passenger services and internet on-board. These solutions are provided by Point Shot Wireless (Canada) and IComera (Sweden). They are normally a multi-segmented architecture composed of satellite network, a cellular network and wireless area network. 21Net is testing a bidirectional satellite solution with Thalys in SNCF (French state-owned company which operates freight and passenger trains). Acorde is also deploying a testbed for Renfe (Spanish state-owned rail operator).

Focused on broadband internet access to passengers, there is also the "FIFTH" (Fast Internet for Fast Train Hosts) project. The passengers reach on-board servers using 802.11b/g cards and an on-board gateway is connected via satellite link to the outer (Internet) world. Similarly, the MOWGLY project, MObile Wideband Global Link sYstem, promotes a broadband access satellite architecture for collective mobile vehicles (aircraft, trains and vessels). (MOWGLY, 2006)

Terrestrial Systems

This section introduces the different terrestrial access technologies grouped into cellular systems and wireless area network access technologies.

Cellular Technologies

GSM-R (2nd Generation Mobile Communication Technology)

Most of the European high speed train to ground architectures uses GSM-R technology in the access network. However there is some concern on GSM-R limitations derived from being a second generation mobile communication technology. These limitations have been stated in the motivations section in the introduction chapter. It is becoming clearer that with its limited data throughput and limited spectrum (2x4MHz) available, it will not be able to cover the needs of all emerging and future communication applications for the railway domain. (INTEGRAIL, 2008).

First steps towards a packet switched approach for train control system have been suggested in (Ruesche et al, 2008). Under a similar approach, the authors identified that GSM-R as a circuit switched technology considerably limits the possible number of voice and data connections in each ccll at the same time. In order to save the high capital investment already performed of railway operators, they propose to use the so-called general packet radio services (GPRS). Although, the authors proposed an enhanced solution when compared to GSM-R that could make use of GMS-R deployments, GPRS is still a 2.5G mobile communication technology with very low data rate support.

UMTS (3rd Generation Mobile Communication Technology) and UMTS evolutions (HSDPA, HSUPA and HSOPA)

Universal Mobile Telecommunication System (UMTS) is a third generation mobile telecommunication technology successor of GSM. One of its major drawbacks is its mandatory interoperability with 2nd generation technology systems and particularly GSM.

From the point of view of meeting the railway scenario demands, UMTS technology provides support for full mobility and voice security mechanisms However the theoretical rate if 384 kbps is available only for one user at a time in one small cell size. UMTS bandwidth performance is also more dependent on radio conditions than in GSM-R.

UMTS evolutions are expected to achieve higher downlink data rates from 385 kbps to 10Mbps. However, it is also worthy to point out that these 3G or UMTS evolutions from W-CDMA (Wideband Code Division Multiple Access) to HSPA (High Speed Packet Access) have been achieved via upgrades to operators' existing 3G networks. These networks do not have the scaling capability to address future data traffic patterns

associated with mobile broadband use. They are all technologies based upon CDMA (Code Division Multiple Access) and its support for higher order MIMO (multiple-input and multiple-output) is not efficient. (WiMAX Forum, 2008)

Another constraint comes from the fact that currently, telecom operators offer high data rate only in dense urban areas. No UMTS is available, or planned to be available, in low dense scenario such as the railway scenario, and a new UMTS-R approach is out of the scope due to economic reasons.

The German railway company Deutsche Bahn is currently offering broadband Internet connection in their high speed trains. Several wireless technologies such as UMTS (T-Mobile) and proprietary WLAN from CISCO are involved.

LTE

The Third Generation Partnership Project (3GPP) long term evolution, commonly named as LTE technology is the 4th generation mobile communication technology been proposed by the 3GPP group. LTE meets the requirements of next generation networks specified in IMT-ADV profile. LTE requirements specifies high speed vehicular mobility support, useful data rate between 75 and 37.5 Mbps and round-trip times of less than 30 ms. LTE also supports flexible carrier bandwidths, from 1.4MHz up to 20MHz as well as both FDD (Frequency Division Duplex) and TDD (Time Division Duplex). As a next generation network, the LTE network is based upon core internet protocol TCP/IP.

There are, however, some constraints such as it is not considered a license exempt profile operation and currently it is still in specification stage. Until the time of this writing, its specification does not consider mesh support. It is expected that LTE in Europe shall occupy 900/1800 MHz, 2100 MHz. It is also been considered that it may make use of the digital dividend band (700 MHz).

PMR Professional Mobile Radio

These standardized and mature systems (TETRA and TETRAPOL) are digital private radios dedicated to professional uses and mainly deployed in domains such as police, metro, buses... etc. They are able to provide direct mobile to mobile communication. Their major drawback is related to their support to data services. The highest data rate is close to 7.2 kbps.

Nevertheless, these type of systems have been recently deployed in metropolitan bus services (Asenjo, 2006) and also for train control applications. In (Vieira, 2009), the author describe a full commercial operation of a train control system which equates to ETCS level 2 that uses as telecom infrastructure the data network provided by a TETRA architecture.

DVB-H

The DVB-H standard is an extension to the DVB-T standard for terrestrial digital television, with additional features to meet the specific requirements of handheld, battery-powered receivers. The letter "H", which stands for handheld, stresses that the focus is on delivering multimedia contents to small, mobile devices. The interactivity is not covered by this standard, however there are already commercially available in Europe dual mode terminals employing UMTS as the return channel.

There are already implemented some initiatives (Zhang, 2008) using DVB-H for deploying TV services on the ongoing Chinese High Speed Railway. This solution is successful as a unidirectional multicast services technology, however the uplink channel represents the same drawbacks as the previously identified for UMTS technology.

Wireless Area Networks Technologies

WLAN or IEEE802.11

Wireless digital technologies represented by the IEEE802.11b/g standard provide high data rate (up to 54Mbps) but not vehicular support. Last speci-fication IEEE802.11n adds MIMO techniques and manages to attain 190Mbit/s. However the support for full mobility is still uncovered.

The full or vehicular support within the IEEE802.11 family is achieved in the IEEE802.11p or WAVE initiative (Wireless Access in Vehicular Environments). WAVE initiative seems quite a promising technology since it has been chosen for V2I and V2V networks and there are solid and important investments from the automotive sector. However the maximum cell range supported is lower than 400m. A recent tutorial can be found in (Uzcátegui, 2009).

In a parallel approach to the UIC ERTMS Project, in the urban guided transport domain is currently been standardized the UGMTS (Urban Guided Transport Management System) specification. European Research Project MODURBAN (Modular Urban Guided Rail System) is defining the telecom technology to support control and command applications. In this case, GSM is not the choice. The most representative companies in this industry sector (ALSTOM, SIEMENS, Thales...) are trying to propose as standard their proprietary versions based on modified versions of the IEEE802.11.

Alstom has deployed its radio based system URBALIS based on IEEE802.11 in Shangai and Singapore lines. Alcatel deployed its radio based CBTC system using IEEE802.11 Frequency Hopping Spread Spectrum (FHSS) standard with overlapping radio coverage in Las Vegas Monorail, Hong Kong and Metro Paris. (Kuun,2004). Another radio based CBTC project is installed in NYCT Canarsie Line where SIEMENS has installed its 2.4 GHz spread-spectrum radios with discrete antennas. (Lardennois, 2003)

Another project, TEBATREN by InfoGLOBAL for Metro Madrid, consists of a CISCO proprietary solution based on IEEE802.11 that also incorporates radio systems such as band translators and radiating cable systems.

In 2008, Robotiker Tecnalia Technology Center in Zamudio used IEEE802.11a technology to bring traffic light information inside a car. Their test consisted of a 500m straight track without any obstacles and in the light of sight. They reached broadcast ranges from 95m up to 430m and a data transmitting success rate from 65% to 95%. (Iglesias et al, 2008).

Last but not least, (Schweiger et al., 2011) presents the results of initial tests and measurements perfomed in the testbed ElisaTM (Efficient Light Signal Adaptation Testbed Munich). The chosen communication technology is IEEE802.11p and the testbed consists of four intersections in a mostly residential area in Munich, Germany. The performance results report a reliable message reception at 300m distance and a maximum range of 500m. 86,7% of all exchanged message were correct.

WMAN: IEEE802.16

The scope of the IEEE 802.16 family is to develop the air interface technology for Wireless Metropolitan Area Networks (WirelessMAN), by specifying the medium access control layer (MAC) and the physical layer (PHY), of combined fixed and mobile broadband wireless access system providing multiple services. The IEEE 802.16 standard has evolved from a fixed scenario IEEE802.16d towards a mobile typical vehicular (up to 120km/h) with IEEE802.16e. The group has just released the IEEE802.16 2009 standard. This release, previously known under draft title P802.16Rev2 [P80216REV22008], consolidates IEEE 802.16-2004, 802.16e-2005 and 802.16-2004/Cor1-2005, 802.16f-2005, and 802.16g-2007. WiBRO, the WMAN South Korean initiative, began to align itself with the WiMAX Forum implementation in 2004. Currently both approaches are harmonized in current WiMAX profile.

The IEEE 802.16 is focused on filling the existent gap between very high data rate wireless local area networks and very high mobility cellular systems. The next standardization effort in which the IEEE 802 is involved, the IEEE 802.16m

project, follows this line. The IEEE 802.16m amends the IEEE 802.16 WirelessMAN-OFDMA specification providing an advanced air interface that meets the requirements of next generation mobile networks targeted by the cellular layer of IMT-Advanced. The purpose of this standard is to provide performance improvements necessary to support future advanced services and applications, such as those described by the ITU in Report ITU-R M.2072

IEEE 802.16m specification supports the mobility classes and scenarios supported by the cellular systems IMT-Advanced, including high speed vehicular scenario (up to 350km/h or even up to 500km/h).

Regarding the economic viability of IEEE 802.16, the proposed amendment is done within the framework of international standardization, which will further enhance the economic viability of the standard. Because IMT-Advanced is intended to be a globally deployed system, it is expected that cost effective performance can be achieved through large economies of scale. IEEE 802.16e was first released in December 2005. Currently, the standard and its certification programs have clearly demonstrated its maturity.

IEEE802.16 specification provides mobile to mobile infrastructure-less communication. IEEE802.16j specification (to be included in next IEEE802.16 release) expands IEEE802.16 current deployment alternatives PTP(Point to Point), PTMP (Point to Multipoint) and mesh topologies by supporting a relay topology, this way enhancing the IEEE802.16 support for backhaul and last mile deployments. It specifies multi-hop relay capabilities and functionalities of interoperable relay stations and base stations.

IEEE802.16 standard supports license exempt profile operation. Additionally, it is currently working in the P802.16H/D8a proposal. This amendment provides measures to increase the efficiency and robustness of license exempt operation, specifies improved mechanisms as policies and medium access control enhancements and facilitate the coexistence of such systems with primary users.

The IEEE802.16 supports public safety first responders, military and emergency services such as call-prioritization, pre-emption and push-to-talk. The involved tools to obtain this feature are the contention-based and the allocation-based radio resources.

Currently, WiMAX Forum plots a mobile profile in the 700 MHz band, the recently identified by the ITU as the digital dividend spectrum; this spectrum is starting to be abandoned by TV broadcasters moving to all digital delivery, all around the world. WiMAX-700 specifications are already concluded, as reported in IEEE Mobile WiMAX 2007. There are several interesting technical considerations from the railway low density context point of view regarding the 700 MHz UHF frequency band:

- Lower path loss (26.5 dB lower than in the 2.5 GHz or 3.5 GHz bands)
- Lower Doppler Shift
- The enhanced signal processing reach (up to 65 km) leads to the fact that the number of base stations necessary to cover the same area is about 10% of those at 3.5 GHz profile. This represents an enhanced cost effective deployment when compared with 3.5 GHz deployments.
- A 700 MHz PHY profile can compliment 2.5GHz and 3.5GHz networks. In dense environments such as the busy junctions situations, with higher subscriber density and high capacity demand small cells are necessary. In this case the optimal recommended deployment proposed is to deploy 700 MHz umbrella cells for coverage and compliment then with 2.5 GHz and 3.5 GHz macro or micro cells to meet capacity requirements.

Most of the current implementations of IEEE802.16 in the access network are pre-WiMAX versions, such as the internet access provided along the 96km London-Brighton route with T-Mobile and Nomad Digital initiatives (Judge, 2005). There are also other research initiatives considering IEEE802.16 technology in the access network such as the European Research projects BOSS and also early studies like the one found in (Ritesh Kumar, 2008).

WMAN (Wireless Metropolitan Area Network) HAPs or High Altitude Platforms

High Altitude Platforms fill in the gap between WMANs and WWANs. In HAP systems, floating platforms (or air vehicles) serve as the BS over wide areas. HAPS merge several advantages of both terrestrial and satellite systems. Located at the stratosphere, the end-to-end delay introduced is compared to terrestrial networks. Also similar to satellite systems, HAP platforms have a LOS (Line of Sight) connectivity with most terrestrial user terminals in its coverage area. They may reach virtually all the railnet within the LOS, but for stations, tunnels, cuttings, urban canyons. In the European Research Project Capanina (Grace, 2010), the primary scenario considered has been broadband connection to high-speeds trains. The HAP system proposed in this research project aims to serve fixed users as well as mobile users with speeds up to 300kmh. A HAP provides a data rate of 120Mbps for an area of 60km wide.

WRAN (Wireless Regional Area Network): the IEEE802.22 specification

The IEEE 802.22 working group is currently working on developing a standard cognitive radio-based PHY/MAC/air interface for use by license-exempt devices on a non-interfering basis in the TV Broadcast Service spectrum. WRAN utilizes white spaces in the TV frequency spectrum on a non-interference basis. The television spectrum was selected for this application due to its propagation characteristics. Cognitive radios reuse fallow TV spectrum in an opportunistic way by detecting if the channel is occupied before using it. This technology targets to provide only fixed broadband access in rural and remote areas with performance comparable to DSL (Digital Subscriber Line) and cable modems. The standard was expected to be finalized by 2008 but it is still in draft version.

WWAN(Wireless Wide Area Region): the IEEE802.20 specification

In the process of bringing mobility support to IEEE802.16, some experts argued that it would be better to design a special standard for mobility support. Based on this idea, IEEE approved Task Group 20 to develop a standard based on mobile user support. So IEEE802.20 or MBWA Mobile Broadband Access was born in December 2002. However, the activity of the working group was suspended in the third quarter of 2006. Currently IEEE802.16 and IEEE802.20 seem share the same goal and market. In accordance to some companies only one of the two technologies will achieve wide market availability. Due to the fact that IEEE802.16 is an older and more complete technology than IEEE802.20 and future IEEE802.16m will cover the high mobility scenario; IEEE802.20 future is currently quite difficult. In 2004, Vodafone tested pre-certified IEEE802.20 commercial equipment Flash-OFDM from Flarion in Metro Tokyo.

SURVEY OUTCOMES

Nowadays, the most commonly used technologies are 2nd generation cellular-based (trackside) and satellite solutions. 2nd generation cellular systems, PMR included, and satellite solutions cannot be considered as an appropriate solution because either they are quite limited in bandwidth or suffer from an unacceptable delay and high cost. IEEE802.11 proposal for high speed vehicular scenario, IEEE802.11p, has a too limited coverage. Apart from that it is no mature enough. RoF and LCX solutions demand quite of an extended wired deployment. IEEE802.22 is not intended to provide support to mobile end users. HAPs do not support handover capability. The three technologies to be considered for the access network in the vehicle to infrastructure network reference model (V2INRM) are HSPA, LTE and IEEE802.16.

4G technologies, LTE and IEEE802.16, are a step forward from HSPA technology when comparing data rate and latency features (Krapichler, 2007)(Arthur,2007). Then, when considering LTE and IEEE802.16, mainly IEEE802.16m, both PHY layers are similar, OFDM and MIMO support and consequently there is no doubt about their capacity to cover the data rate and low latency needs of all emerging and future communication applications for the railway domain. Nevertheless, while IEEE802.16e rollouts initiated in late 2007, LTE rollout is not expected until 2011. Major LTE constraints are related to LTE maturity, cost and LTE operators' interest in low density, and consequently low return of investment, deployments.

There are some other identified features in the IEEE802.16 specification (mobile to mobile support, license exempt operation, public emergency services support and 700 MHz profile), that currently contribute to consider the IEEE802.16 access technology as one of the currently best competitive access technology in the vehicular to ground network reference model (V2INRM).

CONCLUSION

The industry and the research community are actively contributing to the definition of a communication architecture for the ITS context that standardization bodies aim to bring into agreement. However, the standards are in continuous evolution. This denotes that ITS is still a non exploited research field and that efforts should be channeled into providing input to the standardization organizations.

In this chapter we have presented the communication architectures for the ITS context that are being defined by the standardization bodies. We have found that due to the complexity derived from the ITS context characteristics, the architectures are open and let room for further introduction of new protocols and procedures. This results in having underspecified several protocols and functionalities. Consequently, further specification and add-ons may be required to have the demanded services.

In fact, the standardized architectures do not define important aspects such as wireless communication technologies that directly contribute to ITS services' KPI. Based on this gap in the definition of the communication architectures and being aware of the challenges it presents, we have provided a thorough survey of the different radio access technologies for V2I communications.

The analysis on radio access technologies presented herein should be considered as the basis to define an integral architecture that considers the specific particularities of the different ITS contexts: vehicular, railway, maritime or aerospace, also considering demanded services in each scenario. At the same time, the different communication architectures should converge and be interoperable to ensure people's safety and tackle their connectivity necessities.

Besides, research should be channeled into providing valuable feedback to the standardization bodies and defining an efficient work framework for cooperation of the involved agents. Strong mutual efforts of the research community, industry, standardization bodies and governmental institutions will turn ITS into reality.

REFERENCES

C2C-CC. (n.d.). Retrieved from http://www.car-to-car.org.

Arthur, D. (2007). *HSPA and mobile WiMAX for mobile broadband wireless access- An independent report prepared for the GSM Association.*

Asenjo, A., & Gonzalez, E. (2006). Voz y datos digitales en el bus. Transportes Metropolitanos de Barcelona. *Comunicaciones World, 211*, 58.

Baldessari, R., Festag, A.. & Lenardi, M. (2007). *C2C-C consortium requirements for NEMO route optimization*. IETF Draft draft-baldessari-c2ccc-nemo-req-01.

Berbineau, M., et al. (2006). *High data rate transmission for high speed trains. Dream or reality? Technical state of the art and user requirements.* Train-IPSAT Project - WP1 PREDIT 3 - CAL-FRANCE (Synthèse INRETS N° 51).

Clausen, T., Baccelli, E., & Wakikawa, R. (2010). *IPv6 operation for WAVE – Wireless access in vehicular environments*. (Tech. Rep. N°7383).

COMeSafety Project. (n.d.). Retrieved from http://www.comesafety.org/.

COOPERS Project. (n.d.). Retrieved from http://www.coopers-ip.eu.

CVIS Project. (n.d.). Retrieved from http://www.cvisproject.org.

ETSI EN 302 665. (2010). *Intelligent transport systems (ITS): Communications architecture.*

FRAME Project. (n.d.). Retrieved from http://frame-online.net/.

GeoNet Project. (n.d.). Retrieved from http://www.geonet-project.eu/.

Grace, D., & Mohorcic, M. (2010). *Broadband communications via high-altitude platforms*. John Wiley & Sons, 2010.

IEEE P1609.4/D9. (2010). IEEE draft standard for wireless access in vehicular environments (WAVE) - Multi-channel operation.

INTEGRAIL Project. (2008). Retrieved from http://www.integrail.info.

ISO-21217-CALM-Architecture. (2010). *Intelligent transport systems - Communications access for land mobiles (CALM) - Architecture.*

iTETRIS Project. (n.d.). Retrieved from www. ict-itetris.eu.

ITU-R Report M.2072. (2006). *World mobile telecommunication market forecast.* Question ITU-R 229/8.

ITU-T Rec Y.154. (2008). *Network performance objectives for IP-based services amendment 3: Revised appendix VIII – Effects of IP network performance on digital television transmission QoS.*

Judge, P. (2005). *100 mph WiMAX hits the rails to Brighton.* Retrieved from Techworld.com.

Krapichler, C. (2007). LTE, HSPA and mobile WiMAX: A comparison of technical performance. *Hot Topics Forum: LTE vs WiMAX and Next Generation Internet, 2007 Institution of Engineering and Technology,* (pp. 1-31).

Kuran, M. S. (2007). A survey on emerging broadband wireless access technologies. *Computer Networks, 51*(11), 3013–3046. doi:10.1016/j. comnet.2006.12.009

Kuun, E., & Richard, W. (2004). Open standards for CCTC and CCTV radio-based communication. *Alcatel Telecommunications Review,* 243-252.

Lardennois, R. (2005). *Wireless communication for signalling in mass transit.*

MOWGLY Project. (2006). *Mobile wideband global link system.* Retrieved from http://www. mowgly.org.

Narten, T., Nordmark, E., Simpson, W.. & Soliman, H. (2007). *Neighbor discovery for IP version 6 (IPv6).* IETF RFC 4861.

Pre-Drive C2X Project. (n.d.). Retrieved from http://www.pre-drive-c2x.eu.

ITU-T Rec. G.114. (2003). *One way transmission time.* ITU-T Recommendation G.114. 2003.

Ritesh Kumar, K., Angolkar, P., Das, D., & Ramalingam, R. (2008). *SWiFT: A novel architecture for seamless wireless internet for fast trains.* Vehicular Technology Conference, 2008.VTC-2008 Singapore IEEE 67th. 10.1109/VETECS.2008.322.

Ruesche, S. F., Steuer, J., & Jobmann, K. (2008). The European switch: A Packet-switched approach to a train control system. *IEEE Vehicular Technology Magazine, 3*(3), 37-46. ISSN: 1556-6072.

SAFESPOT Project. (n.d.). Retrieved from http:// www.safespot-eu.org.

SEVECOM Project. (n.d.). Retrieved from http:// www.sevecom.org.

Union Internationale des Chemins de Fer (UIC). (2006). *UIC Project EIRENE: Functional requirements specification.* Reference PSA167D005 v.7.0. UIC. EIRENE User Group. 2006.

Union Internationale des Chemins de Fer (UIC). (2006A). *UIC Project EIRENE: System requirements specification.* Reference: PSA167D006 Version:15.0. UIC. EIRENE Project Team. 2006.

Union Internationale des Chemins de Fer (UIC). (2007). *ERTMS/GSM-R quality of service specification reference O-2475 3.0.* UIC, QoS Working Group. UIC ERTMS/GSM-R Operators Group. 2007.

Vieira, P. (2009). *MRS logística switches to CBTC.* Railway Gazette, Marzo.

WiMAX Forum Report. (2008). *Deployment of mobile WiMAX networks by operators with existing 2G & 3G networks.*

Zhang, W., Gui, L., Ma, W., Liu, B., & Xiong, J. (2008). The television broadcasting network of Chinese High Speed Railway. *IEEE International Symposium on Broadband Multimedia Systems and Broadcasting*, (pp. 1-4).

Chapter 11
Analyzing the Trade-Offs Between Security and Performance in VANETs

Jetzabel Serna
Universitat Politécnica de Catalunya (UPC), Spain

Jesus Luna
Technische Universitaet Darmstadt, Germany

Roberto Morales
Universitat Politécnica de Catalunya (UPC), Spain

Manel Medina
Universitat Politécnica de Catalunya (UPC), Spain

ABSTRACT

Vehicular Ad-hoc NETworks (VANETs) currently provide a prominent field of research, which aims at improving everyday road safety and comfort. To achieve this, the deployment of several potential applications is envisioned, promising to provide extraordinary benefits, but will also represent important security challenges due to the unique characteristics of VANETs. In this chapter, VANET's security issues are addressed, and the most outstanding security approaches are discussed. As a proof of concept, a PKI -based protocol, able to cope with the interoperability issues among untrusted CA domains is presented, and the trade-offs between security and performance are empirically analyzed and stressed.

INTRODUCTION

Vehicular Ad Hoc Networks (VANETs) are a subgroup of Mobile Ad hoc Networks (MANETs) and the technical basis of Intelligent Transportation Systems (ITS). The basic architecture of a

DOI: 10.4018/978-1-4666-0209-0.ch011

VANET consists of vehicles and Road Side Units (RSUs), and the communications among them are classified as vehicle-to-vehicle (v2v) and vehicle-to-infrastructure (v2i). In VANET communication, the information exchanged among vehicles plays a fundamental role; the timely and accurate exchange of safety-related information could prevent a great number of fatal road accidents. In any safety-related vehicular application, the information transmitted among vehicles is considered critical; thus, without security, an attacker could manipulate the information and potentially cause harm. Therefore, security is of utmost importance in order to prevent potential security attacks. Moreover, since vehicles in a VANET also benefit from accessing a wide number of infotainment applications offered by different Service Providers (SPs), confidentiality and privacy should also be provided by the infrastructure, which also plays an important role in any VANETs' architectural solution.

The adoption of Public Key Infrastructure (PKI) technology, which has been proven to be a suitable solution in other distributed environments, will enable the establishment of secure communication channels, by providing services needed to prevent a wide range of security attacks. Current PKI systems consist of a Central Authority (CA) responsible for registering users and issuing credentials (containing the corresponding private and public key-pair). In VANETs, it is envisioned that vehicles will be registered with their own regional CA, and therefore a common architecture will require a wide range of CAs within regional scopes. Thus, when a vehicle travels to a different geographical region or domain, it is assumed that mutual authentication and trusted communication will be achieved thanks to previous cross-certification agreements (mostly manual). However, since certificate revocation is also the responsibility of the issuing CA, a disadvantage of cross-certification is that it is not possible to obtain up-to-date revocation information, which opens a vulnerability window for the relying party that must be considered.

Apart from the revocation issues just mentioned, and despite the benefits of enabling the use of PKI technologies in VANETs, due to the high mobility of vehicles, the system introduces different network constraints that should be taken into account for the overall security design. A successful deployment must process and transmit the information within the timing and communications parameters limited by the network, thus, the need of carefully designing a suitable security solution, able to meet the VANET's performance requirements, especially those related to the bandwidth usage and the processing overhead.

The aim of this chapter is to provide an overview of VANETs' authentication and interoperability challenges related with the use of several and possibly untrusted Certification Authorities. Via a set of empirical results, this chapter further analyzes the trade-offs between security and performance on the use of a PKI-based protocol, proposed by our research in order to cope with these security problems.

BACKGROUND

VANETs represent the most relevant form of MANETs and their successful deployment will allow the implementation of several interesting applications, primarily aimed at improving road's overall safety and also capable of enhancing driver comfort. In this section we will first briefly introduce VANETs' basic components and applications, and discuss the reasons why despite their potential benefits, VANETs also raise important security implications that must be solved. An extensive review of the literature focusing on VANETs' authentication is then presented in the second part of this section.

VANET's Components and Applications

In the VANET's basic architecture, mobile nodes are represented by vehicles and fixed nodes by the infrastructure's RSUs. Vehicles in a VANET are assumed to be equipped with processing, recording and communication features, capable of processing and storing a great amount of information. According to the Dedicated Short Range Communications - DSRC standard (Lee Armstrong),

(J. Guo, 2006), vehicular communications will allow data rates from 6-27Mbps at a maximum transmission range of 1000m, thus, enabling nodes to exchange all kinds of application-related information.

VANETs share similar characteristics with other ad-hoc networks, but also posses' unique features that can influence positively the deployment of several applications. These special features also represent an interesting challenge when designing any architectural solution. The most challenging features inherent to a VANET system include the dynamic topology and the mobility models (vehicles moving at a variable and high speed and in different trajectories). On the other hand, thanks to a vehicle's geo-localization functionality and its "infinite" energy supply, VANETs are an enabler for a set of potential applications that can be classified as:

- Warning: Applications aimed to detect risky situations, such as the propagation of alerts in case of accidents.
- Traffic management: aimed at distributing information related to traffic issues, such a traffic congestion, road conditions, etc.
- Infotainment: aimed at providing a wide range of services such a location based services, Internet access, etc.

As it can be inferred by the aforementioned applications, VANETs will be capable of offering a wide range of valuable services. However, along with the rise of VANETs, a set of security issues has also appeared; nevertheless, several research proposals are presently aiming to properly identify and address them. A compromised VANET may disrupt the whole technology's applicability and acceptance, by, for example, causing life-threatening situations (i.e. false warnings that could results on road accidents).

Thus, an important challenge in VANET deployment is just finding the proper techniques and architectural solutions to enforce security and, in particular, authentication, even in the presence of nodes (vehicles) belonging to different "authentication realms" (usually linked with more than one geographical area). A review of the main VANET security approaches found in the literature is presented next.

VANET Security

In recent years, security in VANETs has attracted the interest of a wider research community. An extensive study of security issues in vehicular networks has been presented by (Parno & Perrig, 2005), (Raya & Hubaux, 2005), (Gerlach, Festag, Leinmüller, Goldacker, & Harsch, 2007) and (Raya & Hubaux, 2007). Since, in VANETs, access is granted by default, in order to be able to prevent any generic attack, the system should rely on a secure and trusted communication infrastructure able to satisfy a set of security requirements that include *i)* authentication, *ii)* integrity, *iii)* confidentiality, *iv)* availability, *v)* non-repudiation and *vi)* privacy.

According to current state of the art research, to implement a secure service access in vehicular networks the Wireless Access in Vehicular Environments (WAVE) standard (ITS Committee, 2007) assumes that vehicles will be capable of running cryptographic protocols. Thus, the use of Public Key Infrastructures (PKI) and X.509v3 (Housley, Polk, Ford, & Solo, 2002) digital certificates have been proposed as suitable solutions to overcome the authentication and authorization challenges in VANETs.

Another issue worth mentioning is that the sole use of PKI does not provide privacy. Authors of (Doetzer, 2005) presented an extensive study on the implications of missing privacy and have especially highlighted the importance of privacy preservation for the public acceptance of VANET technology. Since, in general, digital certificates include information regarding the node's identity; the author proposes an approach based on digital pseudonyms. However, the use of long-term credentials, even if combined with a pseudonym approach, opens up the possibility of linking a pseudonym with the vehicle's real identifier (e.g. an attacker overhearing the communications for a long period in parking lot). Thus, the concept of short-term certificates with pseudo-identifiers was exploited by other authors (K. Sampigethaya, 2005) (Gerlach M., 2006), who have introduced several approaches that focus on mechanisms to identify the most suitable time to change a pseudonym. Finally, authors of (E. Fonseca, 2007) presented a study of pseudonymity and its applicability, where they identified a set of open issues to be solved. Certificate revocation has then been identified as one of these important issues, mainly due to *i)* the large number of certificates to be issued for a single vehicle, and *ii)* the need of "fresh" revocation information, which has led to the need of implementing additional mechanisms.

Authors of (Fischer L, 2006) proposed an authentication protocol based on anonymous messages, with quorum-based blinded certificate issuance. The main drawback of the proposed revocation model is that when a vehicle is detected as malicious, it cannot be immediately isolated because of the number of certificates previously stored in its On Board Unit (OBU), which will still be valid for some arbitrary time. A more complex approach was proposed by authors of (Kargl, et al., 2008), which consisted of three different protocols: *(i)* Revocation using Compressed Certificate Revocation Lists (RC2RL), *(ii)* Revocation of the Tamper-Proof Device – RTPD, and *(iii)* Distributed Revocation Protocol – DRP. The main disadvantage of this proposal is the existence of collusion attacks, in particular within the DRP protocol. Finally, authors of (Jason J. Haas, 2009) proposed a mechanism based on bloom filters, and consisting of two main mechanisms, one to reduce the size of the CRLs and the second one to organize and distribute the updates on the CRLs instead of the full CRL itself. However, the use of CRLs represents two major problems. First, is that static lists are difficult to handle, and second is that in

distributed environments involving different CA domains; the management of trust relationships with CRLs could become cumbersome.

In "traditional" PKI environments OCSP-based protocols have been proven to be a secure alternative to CRLs; however, in VANETs, this option has been discarded with the common argument that if communication failures occurred, the OCSP revocation information would be hard to manage. Authors of (Papapanagiotou, Marias, & Panagiotis, 2008), presented a certificate validation scheme based on a distributed version of OCSP for authorization and authentication in VANETs. Their approach focused on distributing cached OCSP responses, thus avoiding the exchange of extended certificate status lists. We believe this is an interesting approach that could be complementary to our contributed solution, to be further discussed in the next sections.

In order to reduce the number of exchanged keys in VANETs, the idea of group signatures emerged as an alternative to traditional PKI approaches, and was initially introduced by (Guo J, 2007). Following a similar idea, authors of (Lin, S., Ho, & Xuemin, 2007) presented a group-based approach where vehicles own a group signing keys issued by a trusted group leader. As an alternative to the aforementioned proposals, a hybrid approach has been presented by the authors of (Hui Liu, 2010). Their proposal consists of a combination of group-based signatures and identity based signatures, where the former are used for authentication among private vehicles and, the latter for public vehicles and RSUs. Nevertheless, the main drawbacks of group-based approaches include: 1) that vehicles must trust a group leader that is responsible for issuing the corresponding signing keys; 2) due to the speed and trajectories of vehicles, group members should be considered volatile rather than permanent and, therefore, using a regular vehicle as a group leader might comprimise the communications availability and 3) a large number of members in a group could increase the computational complexity, the total number of exchanged messages and thus severely impact the overall system performance. Finally, to overcome the trust issues originated due to the group leader being a regular vehicle, authors of (Xiaoping Xue, 2011) present a new group-based certificate solution. The main difference among other group-based solutions is that in the latter, the group certificates are issued by the RSU's, which are assumed be trusted by following a top authority approach (however, note that RSUs are also considered vulnerable to different security attacks, and, therefore, can not be completely trusted).

On the other hand, non-PKI approaches have mostly focused in identity-based cryptography. The concept of identity-based cryptography was introduced by (Franklin, 2003) to ease the deployment of the PKI by simplifying the management of a large number of public keys. However, it is important to mention that it is based on an underlying public key cryptosystem and the issuance and utilization processes are very similar to those used in a traditional PKI domain. In VANETs, this idea was first adopted by authors of (Lin, S., Ho, & Xuemin, 2007), who proposed an approach based on group-based signatures (as discussed above), and this idea was followed by authors of (M. Al-Qutayri, 2010). However, their approach although interesting, lacks many implementation details, specifically on the certificate revocation process Moreover, neither the interoperability issues among different domains nor the impact on performance are discussed.

In summary, up to now, research proposals by (Plossl, Nowey, & Mletzko, 2006), (Raya & Hubaux, 2007), (Liu, Fang, & Shi, 2007), and (Papadimitratos P., et al., 2008) have envisioned a wide range of certification authorities (CAs) acting as trusted third parties within regional scopes, which in turn, result in the implementation of inter-domain authentication protocols and the establishment of trust issues among them (e.g. a German vehicle requesting services in a French infrastructure). In our previous research (Casola, Luna, Mazzeo, Medina, Rak, & Serna,

2010), we have analyzed the security implications derived from the VANETs' inter-PKI authentication process. In particular, we have placed special emphasis on the importance of trust when authenticating among different domains. This, on the other hand, has been mostly overlooked by the aforementioned research works by assuming explicit cross-certification agreements, which, in turn, are based on a static approach and have been proven to be hard to manage. In order to provide VANET interoperability among untrusted PKI domains, we have proposed a PKI-based authentication protocol capable of dynamically establishing trust relationships among unknown domains, just as introduced next.

PKI-BASED AUTHENTICATION FOR VANETS

Authentication protocols based on Public Key Infrastructure technologies (PKI) have proved useful for VANETs, mostly thanks to the security several features these solutions offer. Take, for example, the use of encryption to query a VANET's service provider while avoiding eavesdropping. Also, the use of PKI and digital certificates enable the use of digital signatures, in order to provide more guarantees to, for example, emergency messages being exchanged among vehicles in the case road accidents.

Unfortunately, the sole use of PKI on a VANET scenario comes with a couple of security challenges:

- Lack of real-time revocation: in its current version the ITU-T X509.v3 standard (RFC:3820 - Internet X.509 Public Key Infrastructure (PKI), 2004) only considers the use of Certificate Revocation Lists. These might not be appropriate to VANET environments, where in many cases, the different entities require "fresh" (updated) status information about the drivers' and vehicles' digital certificates.

- Interoperability: as mentioned at the beginning of this chapter, the use of several Certification Authorities (CAs) in VANETs conveys several interoperability challenges. The big question here is: how to assess the "trust level" of a CA, in order to decide if it is "trusted enough"?

In order to contribute to a solution for these challenges, the rest of this section will describe the architecture and associated protocols of an interoperability system for VANETs.

Architecture

Taking into account the unique features of a VANET and our previous research (Casola, Luna, Mazzeo, Medina, Rak, & Serna, 2010), the architecture proposed in Figure 1 contains a set of basic functionalities that allow:

1. The use of near real-time revocation information for multi-CA VANET environments,

based on the Online Certificate Status Protocol –OCSP- (Myers, 1999).
2. The use of a security metric able to compute the "security level" associated with a digital certificate, also in near-real time, in order to decide if the VANET nodes should trust it or not.

As will be demonstrated later in this chapter, the proposed architecture offers a fair balance between security and performance, just as expected from a VANET system.

The core components of this architecture (the Authentication System and the Multi-CA OCSP) will be further analyzed next.

The Authentication System

The Authentication System (AS) has a twofold objective:

1. To apply the *basic path validation* on VANET digital certificates and,
2. To perform the *extended path validation* on VANET digital certificates.

Figure 1. Proposed VANET security architecture

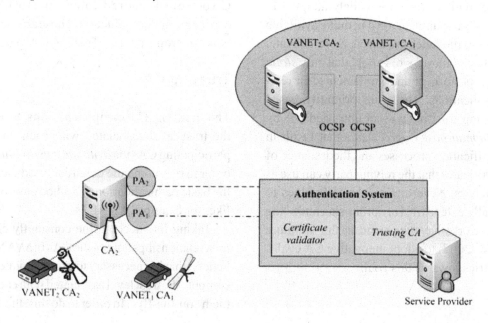

Basic Path Validation, according to the x.509 v3 standard (RFC:3820 - Internet X.509 Public Key Infrastructure (PKI), 2004) and (Housley, Polk, Ford, & Solo, 2002), is the process that determines if a digital certificate is "trusted," according to the following criteria: 1) the verifier has to verify the digital signature, 2) the information within the certificate (expiration date, certificate version, etc), 3) the suspension/revocation status and 4) the validity of all certificates in the certification path until a trust anchor.

It is easy to observe that the "basic path validation" process does not include any check to assess the trust level of the issuing CA, and even more importantly, does not perform any real-time lookup on the certificate's statue, thus opening a vulnerability window for the whole system. Due to the previous restrictions, our research also has proposed the "extended path validation", where if the CA is not trusted, the verifier has to perform basic path validation *and additionally* has to evaluate if a trust relationship can be created with the otherwise untrusted CA.

In the proposed architecture the "Certificate Validator" block is in charge of performing the basic path validation, while the "Trusting CA" performs the extended path validation. While the former validation process is widely adopted in the literature and implemented in many available applications, the latter process is more delicate. Present state of the art works hold that only *static checks* are performed and implemented in real-world applications. These are primarily based on extending trust links to an untrusted CA by *explicit human-based agreements* that result in cross-certification processes and the issuance of cross-certificates that the relying party can use as Trust-Anchors. Nevertheless, the techniques to dynamically extend trust are promising and some scientific works have appeared in the literature (Casola V., 2007) to adopt innovative CA evaluation metrics towards this goal.

Certificate Validator

This module is in charge of performing the basic path validation process, just as defined by (Housley, Polk, Ford, & Solo, 2002). The primary goal of a Basic Path Validation process is to verify the binding between a subject's distinguished name or a subject's alternative name and the subject's public key, as represented in the end entity certificate, based on the public key of the trust anchor (i.e. a Certification Authority). This process requires obtaining a sequence of certificates that support that binding. To meet this goal, the path validation process verifies, among other things, that a prospective certification path (a sequence of n certificates) satisfies the following conditions:

- For all x in $\{1, ..., n-1\}$, the subject of certificate x is the issuer of certificate $x+1$;
- certificate 1 is issued by the trust anchor;
- certificate n is the certificate to be validated; and
- for all x in $\{1, ..., n\}$, the certificate was valid at the time in question.

As mentioned before, the Certificate Validator by itself cannot decide the trust level of the issuing CA or the real-time revocation status of the digital certificate under evaluation. These are the reasons why we proposed the "Trusting CA" subsystem.

Trusting CA

The *Trusting CA* component aims to evaluate the trust level associated with each one of the participating CAs via *dynamic trust evaluation*, in order to overcome the potential disadvantages of the basic path validation in ad-hoc environments, like, for example, VANETs.

Taking into account the constantly changing trust relationships among the CAs in a VANET, our belief is that it is necessary to use techniques able to compute the trust level associated with each one of them "on-the-fly". In order to do this, the Trusting

CA subsystem implements two mechanisms. For evaluating the CA's security level and generating the dynamic trust relationship, we propose using the Reference Evaluation Methodology –REM- (Casola V., 2007), whose main goal is to provide an automatic mean to compute the security level of a digital certificate. This methodology has been widely adopted to dynamically build CA federations (Casola, Luna, Oscar, Mazzocca, Medina, & Rak, 2007). A more detailed explanation of our previous research with the use of REM and VANETs can be found in (Casola, Luna, Mazzeo, Medina, Rak, & Serna, 2010).

The second core component of the Trusting CA subsystem is the Online Certificate Status Protocol, which is implemented as an interface between the Authentication System and the Multi-CA OCSP, just as explained next.

Multi-CA OCSP Module

To complete the Basic Path Validation process, our proposal introduces the notion of near-real time validation via the Online Certificate Status Protocol – OCSP (Myers, 1999). OCSP was created to be used instead of or –as in most cases- in conjunction with other mechanisms like *local* Certificate Revocation Lists (CRL), to provide timely information regarding the revocation status of a digital certificate. Even though it was initially designed for applications carrying highly sensitive and valuable information, nowadays it is being used in a wide variety of systems.

When deploying a PKI, certificate validation using OCSP may be preferred over the use of CRLs, because OCSP can provide more timely information regarding the revocation status of a certificate.

OCSP is based on a request-response scheme, in which an OCSP Client issues a certificate status query to an OCSP Responder which includes the following data:

- Target certificate identifier, consisting of an unordered list of certificate identifiers formed with the issuer's distinguish name hash, issuer's public key hash and finally the serial number of the certificate whose status is being requested.
- Optional extensions which may be processed by the OCSP Responder; for example, to demand information about the Certificate Authority quality.

The OCSP request itself may be secured if the client uses a nonce (protection against replay attacks) and digitally signs it. Once received by the OCSP Responder, this request is verified (i.e. digital signature), processed and a definitive response message is produced. For each one of the certificates in an OCSP Request, the OCSP Response message will contain any of the following status: *Good*, *Revoked* (either permanently or temporarily) and *Unknown*.

The signing key of the OCSP Responder is a very sensitive issue in a PKI environment and, in fact, depending on the certificate being used to sign the responses, we can define three different operation modes:

- Authorized OCSP Responder mode
- Transponder OCSP Responder mode
- Trusted OCSP Responder mode

For the proposal presented in this chapter, the *Trusted* mode (Figure 2) is used to centrally provide a single OCSP service connected to several VANETs' PKI hierarchies. In Figure 2 we can observe that the OCSP signing certificate (subject *T*) belongs to a hierarchy that differs from that of the certificates being requested (neither of *A*, *Y* or *W*). For example, the OCSP service has to be explicitly trusted by the user with subject *X*-. In practice, OCSP Responders working under such centralized models, implement a response cache (the "OCSP cache" from Figure 2) to increase

Figure 2. Typical OCSP architecture in trusted mode

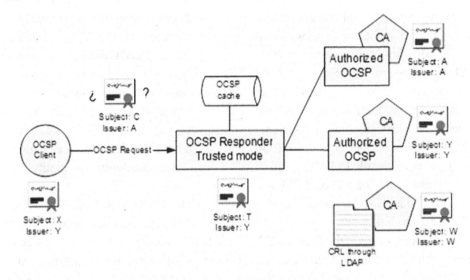

their performance while reducing the number of queries to external *Authorized OCSP Responders* and other revocation sources (like CRLs through HTTP).

Scenarios for VANETs' Authentication

The architecture proposed in Figure 1 enables authentication in any distributed infrastructure with multiple Certification Authorities, nonetheless for VANETs it must deal with the communication failures that are inherent in these systems due to their dynamic, ad-hoc nature (i.e. mobile nodes).

Dealing with a VANET's communication failures is an important issue that has been addressed by our design, assuming that *(i)* the communication is among vehicles and infrastructure (*v2i*) is asynchronous, and *(ii)* that a "Personal Agent" (PA) is associated with each vehicle. This PA is in charge of creating *stateful* connections, so it might be possible to keep track of a vehicle's authentication requests despite the possible disconnections that could take place.

Despite the contributed architecture either *v2v* or *v2i* scenarios can be used. As a proof of concept,

the following section focuses on our explanation of the *v2v2i* scenario which contains all of the constructions being used by the proposed protocol.

Authentication on Vehicular Communications

In order for VANET vehicles to communicate with infrastructures (e.g. multimedia services) from different PKI domains (thus untrusted), the proposed protocol requires a registration process in the new domain so a new temporary certificate can be issued by the foreign CA. Thanks to this temporary certificate, it is possible to validate and be validated by other vehicles in the foreign PKI domain, even if no infrastructure is available.

In order to *fully validate* a temporary certificate (basic and extended path validation -as presented in previous sections), it is necessary for the requestor to contact the proposed authentication service using the protocol shown in Figure 3.

During the protocol's design, one of our most important criteria was to introduce maintain a low overhead in the VANET. For this reason, we decided to use a unique certificate identifier for the certificate (*Cert_id* in Figure 3), instead of trans-

Figure 3. The proposed v2v2i communication protocol

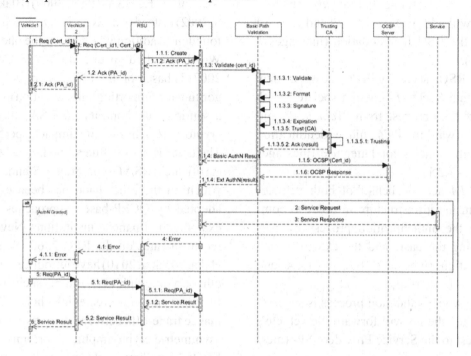

mitting the whole digital certificate in the exchanged messages. The proposed *Cert_id* can be created via an approach like the one used by RCF 2560 (Myers, 1999), just as shown in Table 1.

Where:
- *issuerNameHash* is the hash of the Issuer CA's distinguishing name.
- *issuerKeyHash* is the hash of the Issuer CA's public key.
- The hash algorithm used for both of these hashes, is identified in *hashAlgorithm*.

- And *serialNumber* is the serial number of the vehicle's certificate for which the status is being requested.

Figure 3 shows the proposed authentication protocol in a *v2v2i* scenario, where *"Vehicle 1"* requests a service from the infrastructure (RSU) via a second vehicle (*"Vehicle 2"*). In this case, both *"Vehicle 2"* and the Infrastructure are on a PKI domain different from that of *"Vehicle 1"*. Broadly speaking, the following interactions will occur:

- When *"Vehicle 1"* requests a service from the RSU, it will send a signed message to

Table 1. Proposed Cert_id in ASN.1

```
Cert_id ::=    SEQUENCE {
                   hashAlgorithm AlgorithmIdentifier,
                   issuerNameHash OCTET STRING, -- Hash of Issuer's DN
                   issuerKeyHash OCTET STRING, -- Hash of Issuers public key
                   serialNumber CertificateSerialNumber }
```

"Vehicle 2" (adding its *Cert_id*), which in turn will add its own *Cert_id* and forward it to the RSU for validation (messages 1 – 1.1).

- The RSU server will requests a new Personal Agent –*PA*-, will associate it with the service request from *"Vehicle 2"* and will forward the PA's unique identification to both vehicles for latter use (messages 1.1.1 – 1.2.1).

- This *PA* acts on behalf of both vehicles within the infrastructure in order to complete the authentication process by performing the basic and the extended path validation (messages 1.1.3 – 1.1.4 and 1.1.5 – 1.1.6, respectively).

- If the whole validation process is successful, then the PA will forward the vehicle's request to the Service Provider –SP- (messages 2 – 3).

- Finally, the *PA* will store the results of the original request, even if the connection was lost. In subsequent messages, communicating vehicles and the RSU will include their PA_{id}, which can be verified by the VANET infrastructure without the need to repeat the authentication protocol (messages 5 – 6).

The following section presents the experimental evaluation of the proposed protocol.

SECURITY AND PERFORMANCE ANALYSIS

One of the main concerns when designing a new security protocol for VANETs is precisely the trade-off versus the expected performance, because, despite their advantages, the use of public key algorithms requires more processing time. In order to cope with such performance issues, different proposals implementing PKI in VANETs have used the *Elliptic Curve* Digital Signature Algorithm –ECDSA- (Petit, 2009) (Blake-Wilson S, 2002) instead of the RSA cryptosystem typically found in "traditional" PKIs. On the one hand, the WAVE standard specification (ITS Committee, 2007) is based on the ECDSA cryptographic algorithm for supporting authentication in VANETs, assuming that contrary to RSA, the ECDSA cryptosystem minimally impacts performance. The latter is mainly due to the large size of RSA certificates (RSA Cryptography Standard, 2002), which on the other hand has been extensively adopted by OCSP-based approaches used, for example, by financial institutions. Nevertheless, recent updates on the RFC 2560 (Santesson & Hallam-Baker, 2010) have introduced support for other cryptographic algorithms such as ECDSA. In order to provide greater insight into the performance trade-offs between these two widely used asymmetric cryptographic algorithms (RSA and ECDSA), we have performed a set of experiments consisting of: *i)* measuring a message's signature generation and verification times, *ii)* performing a VANET certificate validation process with the protocol proposed in the previous section, using the basic and extended path mechanisms, and *iii)* performing a set of simulations to determine the transmission delays introduced by the security overhead. Next, we will present the most representative outcomes obtained.

Cryptographic Overhead

The performance of cryptographic algorithms can be strongly affected by the hardware capabilities and the library used to perform them. Over the past few years, different researches have attempted to demonstrate the performance impact of the two well-known cryptographic algorithms RSA and ECDSA (Petit, 2009), (G. Martínez-Silva, 2007), concluding that ECDSA outperforms RSA, thus making it more suitable for resource constraint scenarios. Taking into consideration that currently there is no agreement about VANETs' on-board hardware capabilities, we present illustrative

Table 2. Signature generation and verification times

eSigning algorithm	Signature generation (hash + crypt) time T_s	Signature verification time T_v	Signature size	% security overhead
RSA	0.009s	0.007 s	128 bytes	64%
ECDSA	0.011s	0.011 s	55 bytes	27.5%

measures taken from an experiment done with a Core II Duo 2Ghz processor and 2GB RAM. All messages, signatures and certificates were generated and verified with the OpenSSL 0.9.8o library (OpenSSL, 2010) using RSA with a key length of 1024bits and an ECDSA with a key length of 192bits. In both cases, the SHA-1 hash function was used. Finally, the percentage of the security overhead is represented assuming that typically, in a VANET, the exchanged messages will be of around 200 bytes (U.S Department of Transportation, 2006)

In Table 2, we can observe that for the obtained times (T_s and T_v), there is no considerable difference between both algorithms (in fact, it was approximately 37.5%). *Taking into account the total number of messages exchanged by the protocols, our belief is that the generation and verification times will not severely impact the overall performance of the VANET.* Moreover, even though RSA slightly outperformed ECDSA, this is probably due to the impact of the cryptographic protocols on the size of the signed messages. ECDSA performs better overall because the security overhead introduced represents only 27,5% of a 200 byte message (whereas in RSA, it represented the 64% of it).

Additionally, in order to quantify the validation time required to perform either the basic or the extended path validation (as described in previous sections), we h measured the time required to cryptographically validate a certificate (basic path validation) and the time required by the OCSP Responder to validate a certificate (as required by the extended path validation) (EJBCA OCSP, 2011). Obtained results are shown in Table 3.

Transmission Overhead

To determine the security overhead, we have measured the transmission times introduced by the different cryptographic protocols in order to provide a more realistic perspective of the security-performance trade-off on a VANET system. We configured an experimental simulation with the widely adopted Network Simulator tool (NS2, 2010). The experimental setup was based on an urban scenario similar to the Eixample district of the city of Barcelona. The scenario consisted of 100 vehicles distributed in a 1km² grid map. The map included traffic lanes and lights, and vehicles with variable speeds between 5-55km/hr, including accelerations and decelerations and a maximum pause time of 2s. The simulation time was setup to 1000s and, during this time, the nodes followed different trajectories in a reflective mode (once the destination was reached, vehicles followed a different trajectory). The nodes' mobility pattern was generated using the Manhattan model with the MobiSim (Mousavi, Rabiee, Moshref, & Dabirmoghaddam, 2007) and the SUMO tool (D. Krajzewicz, 2008). We changed the number of nodes that simultaneously transmitted information to traffic loads of 15, 25, 35, and 45, with a

Table 3. Certificate validation execution times

Basic path validation	
eSigning	Validation time (T_u)
RSA	0.006s
ECDSA	0.007s
Extended path validation	
OCSP responder	0.002s

transmission range of 250m, an a transmission rate of 4pckts/s and a data rate of 6Mb. We also changed the packet size according to each scenario in relation to the security overhead; we considered 55 bytes for an ECDSA signature (using key length of 192 bits), 128 bytes for a RSA signature (using a key length of 1024 bits), 38 bytes for the ID of the certificate *Cert_ID* (as defined in *Table 1*) and 600 bytes, considering a X.509v3 standard certificate with ECDSA signature (generated with the OpenSSL library). Table 4 summarizes the set of parameters used for the NS2 setup.

The initial distribution of nodes was randomly assigned and the number of connection links was selected according to the different traffic loads. During the simulation time, transmitting nodes where not always in direct communication range with destination nodes (therefore, most packets were delivered via multi-hop).

Figure 4, shows the results of the incurred transmission delays for both types of signatures. It can be observed that with messages of 55 bytes corresponding to the ECDSA Signature, the performance was slightly better than with the 128 bytes of the RSA signature (7ms and 8ms respectively, considering a traffic load of 35 nodes). On the other hand, if we consider that in a VANET all exchanged messages will be signed,

Table 4. NS2 configuration parameters

Simulation area	1km²
Simulation time	1000s
Type of area	Urban
Routing protocol	AODV
Max queue length	50
Bandwidth	6Mb/s
Node density	100 vehicles
Speed range	5-55km
Transmission range	250m
Message size	{38, 55, 128 and 600} bytes
Transmission rate	4pckt/s =0.25 interval

we can easily conclude that ECDSA implies a better transmission performance. Moreover, the traffic load is an additional factor that will affect the communications. As shown in Figure 4, the transmission delays achieved in a VANET with a traffic load of 40 nodes is almost the double those achieved while transmitting 25 nodes; therefore, the need to minimize the security information to be included in each packet. Let us, for example, compare the transmission delays of 21 ms corresponding to the 600 byte packets of a full X.509v3 certificate with ECDSA and the transmission delay of 6.8ms incurred by the certificate identifier (Cert_Id), which consists of a 38 bytes packet (according to *Table 1*), both with a traffic load of 35 nodes. In this case, we emphasize, once again, the importance of carefully designing the contents of each authentication message (e.g. using a Cert_ID instead of the full certificate inside the transmitted message).

Figure 5 shows that if up to 45 vehicles simultaneously transmit information, the packet delivery rate remains above the 95% for a 600 byte message size, which is suitable enough for a VANET environment. However, this can be improved to 98% considering solely the use of a Cert_ID. As for the size of the different signatures, we can conclude that since the size of the packet remains relatively, low there is no significant difference between them and the overall PDR for both is above the 98%. On the other hand, for a traffic load of 45 or more transmitting nodes, we noticed that as the packet size increased, the packet delivery rate decreased. If we consider a congested scenario (more than 50 vehicles transmitting within transmission range), large packet sizes will drastically impact the number of packets being delivered. Thus, the sole use of identifiers in a message will significantly reduce the packet size (in approximately 93.6% when compared with those messages containing a full X.509v3 certificate attached).

Figure 4. Transmission delay

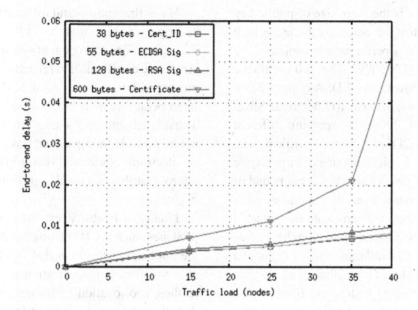

Figure 5. Packet delivery rate

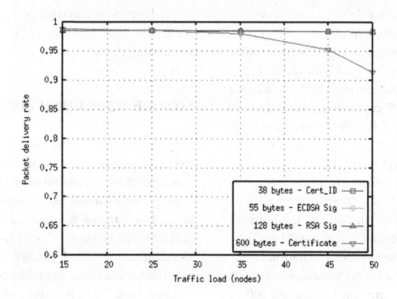

Discussion and Recommendations

Even though PKI-based solutions have been identified as a viable solution (Papadimitratos P., Buttyan, Hubaux, Kargl, Kung, & Raya, 2007) (Gerlach, Festag, Leinmüller, Goldacker, & Harsch, 2007) (Parno & Perrig, 2005) (Raya & Hubaux, 2007) (Raya & Hubaux, 2007) and is recommended in emerging standards (ITS Committee, 2007), new approaches which are not based on PKI (Lin, S., Ho, & Xuemin, 2007), (M. Al-Qutayri, 2010) argue that the main drawback of the latter is the large size of public key certificates exchanged among vehicles, which significantly affects performance. Typically, the size of a standard X.509v3 RSA full certificate is around 1024 bytes and ECDSA is around 600 bytes, however, as explained in (G. Martínez-Silva, 2007) and (Petit, 2009), by applying different techniques an ECDSA X.509v3 certificate can be reduced. Nevertheless, in our experiments, we have considered 600 bytes as the upper bound of an ECDSA in order to measure the transmission delays incurred from the certificate exchange.

In summary, performed simulations have demonstrated that the overall transmission delay of a certificate of 600 bytes is of 10ms, with a traffic load of 25 transmitting nodes, and 20ms, with a traffic load of 35 nodes, which does not represent a major impact in non-congested scenarios. However, considering that increasing traffic loads will result in increasing delays, to minimize the impact, we propos the use of Cert_ IDs. Looking back to the graph in Figure 4, with a traffic load of 35 nodes, the Cert_ID has a transmission delay that represents less than 50% of the one incurred by the full certificate (9ms and 20ms respectively). Therefore, our design decision of issuing messages with a Cert_id just as used by the OCSP standard (Myers, 1999).

Moreover, if we consider two vehicles travelling in opposite directions at the maximum allowed speed (55km/h) in urban regions, the minimal potential communication duration will be of 10s. During those 10s, the vehicles will transmit messages every 300ms, thus the transmission time of a Cert_ID will only represent 3.33% of the 300ms that a vehicle has to spend in order to process a single message. Note that, during the potential communication period, vehicles are assumed to be in each other's direct transmission range (300m). This means that outside the direct transmission range, the potential duration of communication

will increase if intermediate nodes are available to deliver messages via multi hop.

Note that non-standard certificates such as originally proposed in (U.S Department of Transportation, 2006), could also reduce the total size of the certificate and related communication messages, but as highlighted by the authors, no interoperability will be provided among PKIs. Thus, in EU member states, this solution might not be feasible to implement (take, for example, the electronic National ID cards in the EU, where interoperability was a design criteria from the beginning).

Finally, it is also worth mentioning that approaches such as (D. Borsetti, 2009) work at the application level, so that vehicles might be able to select communication nodes according to their geo-location and trajectories (position, direction and speed). This strategy improves the overall protocol's performance by disallowing communication with vehicles travelling in opposite direction and in which the communication duration is considered lower than those sharing similar trajectories

FUTURE RESEARCH DIRECTIONS

Future research directions will include different mechanisms to enforce v2v authentication validation, especially when no infrastructure is available. In particular, we would like to further investigate a policy-based approach, which consist of assigning different trust levels to vehicles and information.

Another interesting challenge in vehicular communication arises from the necessity of providing at least the same degree of privacy that is currently achieved without vehicular networks. Privacy is an important issue, which also brings us to a discussion the trade-offs derived from achieving a desirable degree of privacy and limiting the application's functionality (e.g. location privacy might limit location based services - LBS- functionality).

Finally, as mentioned by authors of (J. M. de Fuentes, 2010), we also believe that due to the lack of a real VANET implementation, security approaches are generally evaluated via simulations that are often in very controlled and heterogeneous scenarios, thus the need of establishing a common framework to accurately evaluate and compare different security solutions.

CONCLUSION

This chapter presented an overview of current security approaches for VANETs, with a special focus on the authentication and interoperability issues that are inherent in vehicular communications.

We have analyzed PKI-based solutions to provide mutual authentication and have presented an OCSP-based authentication protocol that thanks to the use of a Personal Agent –PA-, is capable of dealing with the issues that derive from the connections failures. Additionally, we have empirically analyzed the security overhead of the proposed protocol and, in order to reduce the overall performance impact, we have proposed the use of a Cert_ID identifier instead of transmitting the full certificate. With the inclusion of the trusting CA component, we cope with the inter-operability problems caused by multiple CAs, thus by avoiding the use of explicit cross-certification schemes which have been proven to be cumbersome to manage. Finally, we have seen that the security provided by PKI-based solutions is leveraged with the effects on VANET performance. Thus, this chapter also provided an extensive analysis of the involved trade-offs.

REFERENCES

Al-Qutayri, M., & Yuen, C. (2010). Security and privacy of intelligent VANETs. In Ali, A.-D. (Ed.), *Computational intelligence and modern heuristics*. InTech.

Armstrong, L. (n.d.). *Dedicated short range communications (DSRC)*. Retrieved from http://www. leearmstrong.com/DSRC/DSRCHomeset.htm.

Blake-Wilson, S., & Brown, D. (2002). *RFC 3278*. Retrieved from http://www.ietf.org/rfc/rfc3278.txt.

Borsetti, D., & Fiore, M. (2009). *Cooperative support for localized services in VANETs*. International Symposium on Modeling Analysis and Simulation of Wireless and Mobile Systems. Tenerife, Spain: ACM.

Casola, V., Luna, J., Mazzeo, A., Medina, M., Rak, M., & Serna, J. (2010). An interoperability system for authentication and authorisation in VANETs. *International Journal of Autonomous and Adaptive Communications Systems, 3*(2), 115–135. doi:10.1504/IJAACS.2010.031087

Casola, V., Luna, J., Oscar, M., Mazzocca, N., Medina, M., & Rak, M. (2007). Lecture Notes in Computer Science: *Vol. 4459. Interoperable grid PKIs among untrusted domains: architectural proposal*. New York, NY: Springer Verlag.

Casola, V., & Mazzeo, A. (2007). A security metric for Public Key Infrastructures. *Journal of Computer Security, 15*(2).

Casola, V., & Mazzoca, N. (2007). Static evaluation of certificate policies for GRID PKIs interoperability. *International Conference on Availability, Reliability and Security* (pp. 391-399). IEEE Computer Society.

Committee, I. T. S. (2007). *IEEE Std 1609.3 - IEEE Trial-Use Standard for Wireless Access in Vehicular Environments*. IEEE Vehicular Technology Society.

Dang, Q., & Santesson, S. (2009). *From Internet X.509 public key infrastructure: Additional algorithms and identifiers for DSA and ECDSA*. Retrieved from http://tools.ietf.org/html/draft-ietf-pkix-sha2-dsa-ecdsa-06.

de Fuentes, J. M., & Gonzalez-Tablas, A. I. (2010). Overview of security issues in vehicular ad-hoc networks. In Cruz-Cunha, M. M. (Ed.), *Handbook of reseach on mobility and computing*. Hershey, PA: IGI Global. doi:10.4018/978-1-60960-042-6.ch056

Doetzer, F. (2005). *Privacy issues in vehicular ad hoc networks. Privacy Enhacing Technologies* (pp. 197–209). Lecture Notes in Computer Science Springer.

EJBCA OCSP. (2011). Retrieved from http://www.primekey.se/Products/EJBCA+PKI/EJBCA+OCSP/.

Fischer, L., & Aijaz, A. (2006). *Secure revocable anonymous authenticated*. Workshop on Embedded Security in Cars.

Fonseca, E., & Festag, A. (2007). *Support of anonymity in VANETs - Putting pseudonymity into practice* (pp. 3400–3405). Hong Kong: WCNC.

Franklin, D. B. (2003). Identity based encryption from the Weil pairing. *SIAM Journal on Computing, 32*(3), 586–615. doi:10.1137/S0097539701398521

Gerlach, M. (2006). *Assesing and improving privacy in VANETs*. Berlin: ESCAR.

Gerlach, M., Festag, A., Leinmüller, T., Goldacker, G., & Harsch, C. (2007). Security architecture for vehicular communication. In *Proceedings of the 5th International Workshop on Intelligent Transportation (WIT)*.

Guo, J., & Balon, N. (2006). *Vehicular ad hoc networks and dedicated short-range communication*. Universty of Michigan - Dearborn School Projects.

Guo, J., & Baugh, J. (2007). *A group signature based secure and privacy-preserving vehicular communication framework. Mobile Networking for Vehicular Environments* (pp. 103–108). MOVE.

Haas, J. J., & Hu, Y.-C. (2009). Design an analysis of a lightweight certificate revocation mechanism for VANET. *Proceedings of the 6th International Conference on VANETs*. Beijing, China: ACM.

Housley, R., Polk, W., Ford, W., & Solo, D. (2002). *RFC3280: Internet X. 509 public key infrastructure certificate and certificate revocation list (CRL) profile*. Retrieved from http://tools.ietf.org/html/rfc3280.

Hui Liu, H. L. (2010). *Efficient and secure authentication protocol for VANET*. International Conference on Computational Intelligence and Security.

Kargl, F., Papadimitratos, P., Buttyan, L., Muter, M., Schoch, E., & Wiedersheim, B. (2008). Secure vehicular communication systems: Implementation, performance, and research challenges. *IEEE Communications Magazine, 46*(11), 110–118. doi:10.1109/MCOM.2008.4689253

Krajzewicz, D. (2008). *SUMO: From simulation of urban mobility*. Retrieved from http://sourceforge.net/apps/mediawiki/sumo/index.php?title=Main_Page.

Lin, X., Sun, X., Ho, P., & Xuemin, S. (2007). GSIS: A secure and privacy-preserving protocol for vehicular communications. *IEEE Transactions on Vehicular Technology, 56*(6), 3442–3456. doi:10.1109/TVT.2007.906878

Liu, X., Fang, Z., & Shi, L. (2007). Securing vehicular ad hoc networks. *2nd International Conference on Pervasive Computing and Applications*, (pp. 424-429).

Martínez-Silva, G., & Rodriguez-Henriquez, F. (2007). On the generation of X.509v3 certificates with biometric information. In H. R. Selim Aissi (Ed.), *International Conference on Security & Management* (pp. 52-57). Las Vegas, NV: CSREA Press.

Mousavi, S. M., Rabiee, H. R., Moshref, M., & Dabirmoghaddam, A. (2007). *MobiSim: A framework for simulation of mobility models in mobile ad-hoc networks.* The 3rd IEEE International Conference on Wireless and Mobile Computing, Networking and Communications.

Myers, M. (1999). *X.509 Internet public key infrastructure online certificate status protocol - OCSP.* Retrieved from http://www.ietf.org/rfc/rfc2560.txt.

NS2. (2010). *The network simulator - NS2.* Retrieved from http://www.isi.edu/nsnam/ns/.

OpenSSL. (2010). *The OpenSSL project.* From www.openssl.org/.

Papadimitratos, P., Buttyan, L., Holczer, T., Schoch, E., Freudiger, J., & Raya, M. (2008). Secure vehicular communication systems: Design and architecture. *IEEE Communications Magazine, 46*(11), 100–109. doi:10.1109/MCOM.2008.4689252

Papadimitratos, P., Buttyan, L., Hubaux, J., Kargl, F., Kung, A., & Raya, M. (2007). Architecture for secure and private vehicular communications. *The 7th International Conference on ITS,* (pp. 1-6).

Papapanagiotou, K., Marias, G., & Panagiotis, G. (2008). A certificate validation protocol for VANETs. *IEEE Globecom Workshop,* (pp. 1 - 9).

Park, Y., & Sur, C. (2010). An efficient anonymous authentication protocol. *Journal of Information Science and Engineering, 800*(3), 785–800.

Parno, B., & Perrig, A. (2005). *Challenges in securing vehicular networks.* Workshop on Hot Topics in Networks (HotNets-IV).

Petit, J. (2009). Analysis of ECDSA authentication processing in VANETs. *The 3rd International Conference on New Technologies, Mobility and Security (NTMS),* (pp. 1-5).

Plossl, K., Nowey, T., & Mletzko, C. (2006). Towards a security architecture for vehicular ad hoc networks. *Proceedings of The First International Conference on Availability, Reliability and Security,* (p. 8).

Raya, M., & Hubaux, J.-P. (2005). The security of vehicular ad hoc networks. *Proceedings of the 3rd ACM Workshop on Security of Ad Hoc and Sensor Networks.*

Raya, M., & Hubaux, J.-P. (2007). Securing vehicular ad hoc networks. *Journal of Compputer Security, Special Issue on Security of Ad Hoc and Sensor Networks,* 39-68.

RFC. 3820 - Internet X.509 Public Key Infrastructure (PKI). (2004). *RFC:3820 - Internet X.509 public key infrastructure (PKI) proxy certificate profile.* Retrieved from http://www.ietf.org/rfc/rfc3820.txt.

RSA Cryptography Standard. (2002). Retrieved from www.rsa.com.

Sampigethaya, K., & Huang, L. (2005). CARA-VAN: Providing location privacy for VANET. *Proceedings of ESCAR.*

Santesson, S., & Hallam-Baker, P. (2010). *OCSP algorithm agility.* Retrieved from http://tools.ietf.org/html/draft-ietf-pkix-ocspagility-09#page-4.

U.S Department of Transportation. (2006). *Vehicle safety communications project. Final Report.* National Highway Traffic Safety Administration, U.S Department of Transportation.

Xiaoping Xue, J. D. (2011). LPA: A new location-based privacy-preserving authentication protocol in VANET. *Security and Communication Networks,* online version before print.

KEY TERMS AND DEFINITIONS

Authentication: The process of verifying someone's identity.

Authorization: The process of determining someone's access rights. Who has access to what? and, in which circumstances?

Interoperability: The ability of different organizations or domains to work together.

On-Board Unit (OBU): A computing platform with processing and networking capabilities, integrated in smart vehicles.

Road-Side Unit (RSU): Base stations situated along the roads, which enable communication between vehicles and infrastructure.

Trust Evaluation: A metric to assess if two or more entities can interact with enough security guarantees.

VANETs: Vehicular Ad-hoc Networks, a form of mobile network, consisting in smart vehicles and base stations situated along the road.

Chapter 12
Cooperative Positioning in Vehicular Networks

Mahmoud Efatmaneshnik
University of New South Wales, Australia

Nima Alam
University of New South Wales, Australia

Asghar T. Balaei
University of New South Wales, Australia

Allison Kealy
University of Melbourne, Australia

Andrew G. Dempster
University of New South Wales, Australia

ABSTRACT

This chapter introduces the concept of Cooperative Positioning (CP) for vehicular networks, or more precisely, VANETs (Vehicular Adhoc NETworks), as an application of DSRC (Dedicated Short Range Communication). It includes a comprehensive review of available and hypothetical vehicular positioning technologies. Amongst these, the importance of CP for Location Based Services using DSRC is emphasized, and some important issues are addressed that need to be resolved in order to implement CP successfully with standard DSRC infrastructure. The performance bounds of CP are derived. Ranging between vehicles is identified as the main hurdle to be overcome. Time-based techniques of ranging are introduced, and the bandwidth requirements are investigated. The robustness of CP to inter-node connection failure as well as GPS (Global Positioning System) dropout is demonstrated via simulation. Kalman Filter performance for CP is evaluated, and proven to be efficient under conditions such as the consistency of GPS signal availability ranging between vehicles. CP has, however, shown to increase the positioning accuracy to 1-meter level, even in the deep urban valleys where vehicles frequently become invisible to navigation. Overall, CP is proven to be a viable concept and worthy of development as a DSRC application.

DOI: 10.4018/978-1-4666-0209-0.ch012

INTRODUCTION

Research and development of technologies using DSRC comprise three different domains:

1. Application domain: the interface with drivers/pedestrians, e.g. the type of applications, the forms of warning and recommendation/assistance messages, etc.
2. Communication domain: DSRC boards, related electronic devices, and hardware/software are considered in this domain, using three layers of the ISO model: the application, physical, and MAC (or communication protocol) layers.
3. Positioning domain: Accurate and reliable positioning technologies are the first and foremost requirement of all DSRC Location-based services such as collision avoidance systems.

This chapter focuses on positioning, with special emphasis on reliable positioning for safety purposes, where three issues must be addressed:

1. Position availability
2. Position accuracy
3. Position frequency

Vehicular navigation is generally assumed to operate based on Global Navigation Satellite Systems (GNSS), mostly GPS (Kaplan & Hegarty, 2006). Using 24 to 32 satellites, GPS signals are available globally and GPS receivers can determine the 3D position of the user in an Earth Centered Earth Fixed (ECEF) coordinate system (Kaplan & Hegarty, 2006). The only condition for this 3D positioning is the visibility of at least four satellites at any time. The case where a receiver is capable of positioning itself based only on the GPS signals as input data, we term *Individual Positioning*. This method suffers from phenomena such as interference, multipath and other sources of errors including unknown delays through the ionosphere and troposphere, which result in a positioning accuracy of about *10 m* (Kaplan & Hegarty, 2006).

The unavailability of GPS signals for covered or dense urban areas and the slow update frequency of the position information (at about *1 Hz*) are factors negatively influencing the suitability of GPS-based positioning for some applications such as Intelligent Transport Systems (ITS), Locations Based Services (LBS), and safety systems. For example, safety systems, such as collision avoidance which needs accuracy of *1 m*, cannot rely solely on GPS-based position data (Shladover & Tan, 2006). Inertial Navigation Systems (INS) (Farrell, 1998) can be used for GPS-positioning accuracy enhancement and temporary GPS outage compensation (Ciurana, Lopez, & Barcelo-Arroyo, 2009; Godha & Cannon, 2007; Hide, Moore, & Smith, 2003; Kaygisiz, Erkmen, & Erkmen, 2004; J. H. Wang & Gao, 2004). Low cost INS suitable for vehicular positioning does not improve positioning accuracy, and its benefits are during poor satellite visibility in which case the GPS accuracy can be maintained for short periods of time.

An innovative approach to achieving more accurate and reliable positioning relies on incorporating data from the sources independent of GNSS into the process of positioning; this is called *Cooperative Positioning (CP)*. Basically, a CP system requires data communication among the participating nodes, users and servers, in a CP process. The focus of this chapter is in the context of DSRC applications. In such a scenario, the most important issue concerning CP is the ranging technique between the vehicles. After discussing this, the performance bounds of CP and its robustness in the context of static and mobile networks is evaluated. The CP algorithm as a localization algorithm is the subject of the last section.

DSRC Applications

DSRC applications can be assigned to two general categories: safety related and non-safety applications. In a report by Crash Avoidance Metric Consortium (CAMP-Vehicle-Safety-Communications-Consortium, 2005) safety applications predominantly are subcategorized into:

- Collision Avoidance applications such as Traffic Signal Violation Warning, Left Turn Assistance and Intersection Collision Warning
- Public Safety applications such as Approaching Emergency Vehicle Warning and Post Crash Warning
- Sign Extension applications such as Curve Speed Warning and Low Bridge Warning
- Vehicle Diagnostics and Maintenance applications such as Just-In-Time Repair Notification
- Cooperative Applications use information from other vehicles such as Cooperative Adaptive Cruise Control, Cooperative Collision Warning, Lane Change Warning, Blind Spot Warning etc.

All safety related Cooperative Applications rely on accurate position information, both of the vehicle's location and the relative location of other vehicles. For example, the Cooperative Collision Warning System (CCWS) is an important application of DSRC. In CCWS "the vehicle receives data regarding the position, velocity, heading, yaw rate, and acceleration of other vehicles in the vicinity. Using this information, along with its own position, dynamics, and roadway information (map data), the vehicle will determine whether a collision with any vehicle is likely. In addition, the vehicle will transmit its position, velocity, acceleration, heading, and yaw rate to other vehicles" (CAMP-Vehicle-Safety-Communications-Consortium, 2005, pp. 26-27). In (Shladover & Tan, 2006),

the baseline positioning requirement for CCWS in a simulation study was *0.5 m*.

Non-safety Applications of DSRC include Traffic Management and Cooperative applications. As an example, Intelligent Traffic Flow Control is a Traffic Management application adjusting traffic light signal phasing based on real-time traffic flow. Cooperative non-safety applications include Cooperative Glare Reduction and CP. These applications tend not to have as strict requirements for positional accuracy, so it is the safety applications which are driving the work discussed here.

CP refers to any method which combines different positioning tools and sensor data in order to improve the quality of positioning for different purposes. The fundamental elements of CP are communication and data fusion. CP methods can be classified into conventional and modern CP.

Conventional CP

If data communication is considered to be the key aspect for CP, the term Conventional CP can be applied to Differential GPS (DGPS) (Kaplan & Hegarty, 2006), Real Time Kinematic (RTK) positioning (Hofmann-Wellenhof, Lichtenegger, & Collins, 2001), and Assisted GPS (A-GPS) (Diggelen, 2009). More recent methods based on data communication plus ranging or range-rating between the nodes and data from other resources, we term Modern CP methods. These are discussed in the next section.

In DGPS, positioning errors (actually errors in the measurements of satellite range) calculated at a nearby base station, or interpolated in a network, are broadcast to users, enabling them to correct their estimates. Using DGPS, positioning accuracy of about *1 m* is possible, because the expected multipath and receiver errors are very low. This situation is not achievable in dense urban areas, as satellite visibility is poor and (uncorrectable) multipath errors are high.

RTK, designed for positioning accuracy of centimeters, is a technique based on satellite signal carrier phase measurements and relies on communication between the user (rover) and a reference node (base). This technique requires that at least five GPS satellites be commonly visible for the base station and rover. This technique is not viable in dense urban areas due to its technical requirements, such as requiring the receiver tracking loops not to incur "cycle slips". Multipath and poor signal levels again prevent this system from operating in urban areas.

A-GPS is based on data communication between the user's receiver and a support system. Assistance servers are used to provide information that i) speeds up satellite acquisition, and ii) avoids to decode the full satellite data message at the receiver, saving at least 30 seconds, and allowing weaker signals to be used for measurement. However, visibility of four GPS satellites is still needed and the ultimately achievable accuracy is of the same order as GPS. If weak signals are used in the solution that could not be acquired with a GPS receiver without assistance, positioning accuracy is likely to be poor due to the weakness of those signals. Figure *1* shows the information flow of these methods in general (Hofmann-Wellenhof, et al., 2001; Kaplan & Hegarty, 2006).

Considering the constraints and requirements of the conventional CP methods, none can be a viable solution for vehicular position–based applications, which need high accuracy and availability of positioning. Table 1 shows the concerns for conventional CP methods if considered for vehicular applications other than navigation.

Figure 1. Conventional CP methods and their required data communications

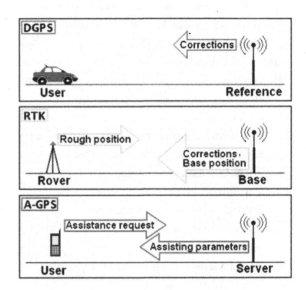

These methods all have shortcomings when it comes to vehicular applications, especially in urban areas. Because of these concerns, the necessity to provide innovative approaches such as CP in vehicular applications is evident. Modern cooperative techniques such as integrating GPS with INS, odometer, digital compass and digital map information have been introduced, but they also have their own shortcomings often related to the cost (Bonnifait, Bouron, Crubille, & Meizel, 2001; Stephen, 2000). Note that any positioning technology using DSRC needs to be extremely cost effective for mass production. This eliminates the possibility of using highly accurate MEMS (Micro Electrical and Mechanical Sensors) INS because these are currently very expensive.

Table 1. Conventional CP concerns for vehicular applications

Conventional CP	Concerns for vehicular applications
DGPS	Updates rate, multipath, GPS coverage,
A-GPS	Updates rate, GPS accuracy
RTK	Updates rate, continuous communication, cost, GPS coverage

Modern CP

Modern CP is based on three fundamentals: data resources, data communication, and data fusion. We differentiate this Modern CP from Conventional CP, in the following ways: i) the communication system may also be involved in the creation of required data, ii) communication is more sophisticated than a broadcast (DGPS, RTK) or request/response (AGPS), iii) participating nodes may have non-homogenous data. Figure 2 is a scheme for a modern CP system. In this figure, nodes represent vehicles and the roadside infrastructure nodes are called anchors.

According to Figure 2, the nodes do not necessarily have the same knowledge about the outside world and data fusion is performed by each node. It is possible to transfer all data to a reference node, with higher processing capabilities and return the results to other nodes through the network. This implies the possibility of both centralized and distributed CP algorithms, and a significant use of the communications bandwidth.

In Figure 2, all of the nodes communicate with each other. This topology is not necessarily viable due to the limited communication bandwidth. In (Boukerche, Oliveira, Nakamura, & Loureiro, 2008; Wymeersch, Lien, & Win, 2009), an overview of modern CP techniques with regard to dynamic networks, time varying topologies, centralized and distributed algorithms, and range-based algorithms is presented.

A variety of modern CP techniques for different situations are proposed in (Benslimane, 2005; Chen, Martins, Huang, So, & Sezaki, 2008; Dao, Leung, Clark, & Huissoon, 2007; K. Jo, Lee, & Kim, 2007; K. H. Jo & Lee, 2007; Karam, Chausse, Aufrere, & Chapuis, 2006a, 2006b; Parker & Valaee, 2006, 2007b; Patwari et al., 2005; Patwari, Hero, Perkins, Correal, & O'Dea, 2003). All of the CP methods presented in these articles are based on estimated distance between the network nodes. The distance between each pair of nodes is assumed to be supplied by some radio ranging method. However, the constraints and limits of radio ranging techniques imposed

Figure 2. Modern CP system architecture, as a data fusion approach to several information sources and with tolerance towards information source variability in each node

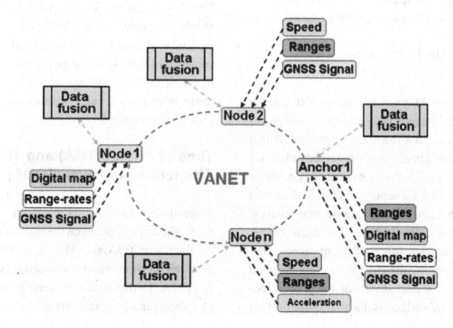

by the communication medium and the impacts on the CP algorithm are not well acknowledged in the literature.

Raw DSRC Range Measurements for cP

There are several different methods of radio ranging, including Received Signal Strength (RSS), Time of Arrival (TOA), Time Difference of Arrival (TDOA), Round Trip Time (RTT), and Carrier Frequency Offset (CFO). Angle of Arrival (AOA) is a technique to determine the bearing of an arriving signal. It is not considered for CP due to high levels of error caused by multipath channels in urban areas, which induce much greater errors in AOA systems than the others, and the extra size and complexity required of the antenna (Sakagami, Aoyama, Kuboi, Shirota, & Akeyama, 1992).

Received Signal Strength (RSS)

Ranging with RSS is very popular due to its simplicity and lower deployment costs compared to other methods, but it is very inaccurate. The following equation, or a variant, is mostly used for modeling the channel loss and the basis for RSS technique (Rappaport, 1996):

$$P(r) = K - 10\alpha \log(r) \quad dBm \tag{1}$$

In Equation (1), r is the distance between the transmitter and the receiver, P is the received power at the receiver, and K is a known constant, which can be calculated based on the received power for a known distance. The path loss exponent, α, varies between around *2,* for suburban areas, and around *4,* for urban canyons with dense construction (Barclay, 2003). The exponential characteristic of the term scaled by this coefficient causes large errors in estimating distance if it is not assigned properly. This model does not adequately account for fading variations due to multipath. This

manifests itself in a vehicular environment as α varying randomly due to the changing relative locations of reflecting obstacles and objects. In a stochastic system Cramer-Rao Lower Bound (CRLB) sets the lower bound of the variance for any unbiased estimator, under the normality assumption of all random variables (Trees, 2003). Assuming a normal distribution for the path loss exponent, $N(m, \sigma^2)$, it has been shown in (Alam, Balaei, & Dempster, 2009) that CRLB for the RSS-based distance estimation error is:

$$\sigma_r^2 = \frac{\sigma^2 (r \ln(r))^2}{m^2 + 2\sigma^2} \tag{2}$$

More explicitly, in (Malaney, 2007; Weiss, 2003), the effect of path loss exponent uncertainty on positioning accuracy is investigated. Dynamic estimation of α in a vehicular network is inevitable for RSS-based ranging. In (Alam, Balaei, & Dempster, 2010a; Hata, 1980; Li, 2006; Mao, Anderson, & Fidan, 2007; Mazuelas et al., 2008; Shirahama & Ohtsuki, 2008) a variety of techniques are presented for path loss exponent estimation. The achieved accuracy for path loss exponent estimates in these works confirms that RSS-based ranging is not suitable for CP. For example, according to Eq. (2), for a distance of *100 m,* a typical path loss exponent estimation error variance of *0.09* in the suburbs and *α=2,* results in a ranging error of around *68 m.* This would result in an even greater position error, which is clearly unacceptable.

Time of Arrival (TOA) and Time Difference of Arrival (TDOA)

Time-based techniques measure signal the propagation time between the transmitter and the receiver. For TOA and TDOA, synchronization between the transmitter and receiver is necessary. In TDOA, the difference between the arrival times at a receiver of signals from two synchronized transmitters is considered for distance estimation. Also, the difference between the arrival times of a signal in different synchronized receivers from a single source can be used for TDOA. Time-based methods are more complex and expensive than RSS because of this synchronization requirement. In (Alsindi, Alavi, & Pahlavan, 2009; Falsi, Dardari, Mucchi, & Win, 2006; Smith & Abel, 1987; Venkatraman, Caffery Jr, & You, 2004; X. Wang, Wang, & O'Dea, 2003; A. Y. Z. Xu, Au, Wong, & Wang, 2009) techniques are proposed to estimate TOA and TDOA in different circumstances. The performance of time-based techniques is related to Signal to Noise ratio (SNR), signal duration, and signal bandwidth (Deleuze, Martret, Ciblat, & Serpedin, 2004; Patwari, et al., 2005; Sieskul & Kaiser, 2005). The following bound for TOA error in a multipath-free channel is presented in (McCrady, Doyle, Forstrom, Dempsey, & Martorana, 2000; Patwari, et al., 2005):

$$\sigma^2_{TOA} \geq \frac{1}{8\pi^2 f^2 BT\gamma} \tag{3}$$

where T is the coherent integration (i.e. observation) time, B is the signal bandwidth, $f \approx 0.4\,B$ is the rms spanned bandwidth (Zensus, Diamond, & Napier, 1995), and γ is Signal to Noise Ratio (SNR) at the receiver. For TDOA, assuming independent estimates of the arrival time of the received signals, ranging variance will be twice that of the TOA-based technique. Equation (3) implies that for more accurate time-based ranging, higher SNR and wider bandwidth is required. It also indicates that ranging accuracy of lower than *1 m* is achievable if the nodes are adequately synchronized. However, for DSRC-based vehicular communication, the three main challenges are synchronization, limited bandwidth, and environmental noise.

Round Trip Time (RTT)

In a vehicular network, providing synchronization between nodes may be technically difficult and expensive. Avoiding the necessity of synchronization, RTT is a solution for ranging between transmitter and receiver based on round trip signal propagation time. In this method, one node, say node 1, transmits a packet at time t_1 to another one, say node 2, and waits for acknowledgement, which is received at time t_2. So:

$$RTT = t_2 - t_1 = \tau_{TX1} + \tau + \tau_{P2} + \tau + \tau_{RX1} \tag{4}$$

In Eq. (4), τ_{TX1} is the transmission delay at node 1, τ is the signal flight time from node 1 to node 2 and vice versa, τ_{P2} is the processing time in node 2, and τ_{RX1} is the receiver delay when receiving the acknowledge from node 2. It is assumed that the distance between the nodes does not change significantly over RTT, so τ is the same for two signal trips. Figure 3 indicates the RTT timing. Regarding Eq. (4), there is:

$$\tau = 0.5(RTT - \tau_{TX1} + \tau_{P2} + \tau_{RX1}) \tag{5}$$

Having τ, the distance between two nodes can be estimated. τ_{TX1}, τ_{P2}, and τ_{RX1}, can be calculated for a known distance between transmitter and receiver in a calibration process if all the delays are constant. Note that τ_{TX1} and τ_{RX1} depend on factors such as packet size and transmission rate whereas τ_{P2} depends on the processing speed. However, the distance between the nodes has no effect

Table 2. Latency and accuracy of RTT-based ranging

Number of RTTs	1000	500	300	100
Latency (s)	1	0.5	0.3	0.1
Average error (m)	1.70	4.72	6.64	9.03

Figure 3. Concept of RTT between two nodes and demonstration of delays

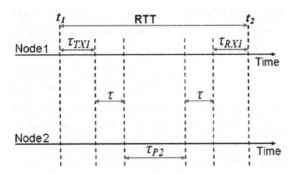

on the delays. In (Bahillo et al., 2009; Ciurana, Barcelo-Arroyo, & Cugno, 2009; Ciurana, Lopez, et al., 2009; Gunther & Hoene, 2005; McCrady, et al., 2000; Prieto Tejedor et al., 2009), different techniques are presented for RTT estimation. The main drawback of these methods are:

- The necessity of the numerous measurements for achieving better ranging resolutions.
- Channel congestion due to all nodes willing to make measurements at once.
- Synchronicity of all range measurements that must be measured one at a time, by some additional computational algorithm.

This results in latency of the distance estimates and significantly more bandwidth occupation. The first leads to the ranging error for mobile

nodes and the other reduces the number of nodes which can use a common channel. Table 2 shows some test results for relation of latency and ranging accuracy (Ciurana, Lopez, et al., 2009).

Carrier Frequency Offset (CFO)

Although range-rate is not often considered in CP algorithms, it is a parameter which can be used for positioning. TRANSIT, the original satellite-based positioning system, which was operational from the 1960s to the 1990s, is an example of range-rate-based positioning, (Danchik, 1998; Seeber, 2003). Further positioning methods based on range-rate are proposed in (Amar & Weiss, 2008; Amundson, Koutsoukos, & Sallai, 2008; Chan & Towers, 1992; Czarnecki, Johnson, Gray, Ver-Wys, & Gerst, 1999; B. Xu, Shen, & Yan, 2009). Range-rate between a transmitter and receiver can be estimated based on Doppler shift or integrated carrier phase difference between transmitter and receiver (Hofmann-Wellenhof, et al., 2001; Seeber, 2003). If r is the distance between transmitter and receiver, the Doppler Effect implies:

$$f_r = f_s(1 - \frac{1}{c}\frac{dr}{dt}) \qquad (6)$$

where f_r is the received frequency, f_s is the transmitted frequency, and c is the speed of light. Knowing the transmitted frequency and measuring the received frequency, one can estimate range-rate by

Table 3. Radio ranging and range-rating concerns in the vehicular networks

	Accuracy	Complexity	Concern
RSS	Very low	Low	Unknown path loss model
TOA	High	Very high	Synchronization required
TDOA	High	Very high	Synchronization required
RTT	Fair	Fair	Latency
CFO	High	High	Clock drift ambiguity

Equation (6). CFO between receivers, operating with commercial crystal clocks, is not simply a result of the Doppler Effect. The clock drift in the receiver and transmitter cause a deviation from the nominal carrier frequency. For this reason, the CFO of the received signal is a combination of Doppler shift and clock drift. For the velocities in a vehicular environment, the frequency deviation due to Doppler is much less than clock drift. The main challenge for CFO-based range-rating is extraction of Doppler shift from the CFO. This clock-offset estimation is the counterpart in TOA and TDOA of clock synchronization. There is a variety of methods to estimate CFO, including those proposed in (Chiavaccini & Vitetta, 2004; Cui & Tellambura, 2007; Lv, Li, & Chen, 2005; Schmidl & Cox, 1997; Tao, Wu, & Xiao, 2009; Tureli, Liu, & Zoltowski, 2000), which focus on CFO estimation for OFDM.

Bandwidth, signal integration time, and SNR are the parameters which affect the accuracy of CFO estimation. Carrier phase-based conventional CP methods such as RTK, which can achieve mm levels of accuracy, cannot be implemented within the VANET because they need to continually track the received signal carrier phase. For a VANET, using packet-based communication, such carrier phase tracking is not possible. Thus, carrier phase estimation for highly accurate positioning, similar to RTK, is a significant and open challenge for modern CP.

An analysis of ranging and range-rating techniques shows that there are limited feasible choices for radio ranging in a vehicular environment. Table 3 summarizes the related issues for each method. Referring to this table, RTT seems to be a potential method for radio ranging for vehicular CP. Range-rating with CFO estimation can also be a component of CP algorithm. Both of these methods impose some constraints on the number of participating nodes in CP algorithms because of the latency and required bandwidth.

RSS cannot be used for vehicular CP due to uncertainties in the path loss model and its high level of error. TOA and TDOA are technically very difficult to implement in VANETs, unless GPS synchronisation is required of DSRC equipment. This result implies that the viability of a

Figure 4. Modern CP for different situations, where all vehicles have sufficient satellite visibility (a), some vehicles have sufficient satellite visibility (b), vehicles have partial satellite visibility (c), no vehicle has satellite visibility (d)

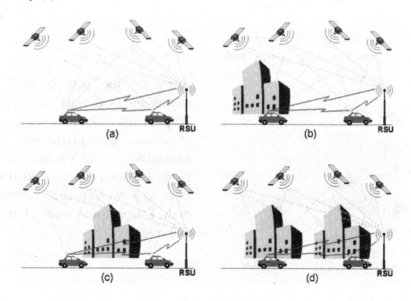

majority of proposed CP algorithms in the literature is under question due to the failure to account for radio ranging concerns and constraints.

CP PERFORMANCE

The main difference between what conventional CP methods provide and the objective set for modern CP is the availability of GNSS signals. Conventional CP methods are functional if enough GNSS signals are available and data communication is possible between the user and infrastructure. In modern CP, GNSS signal availability is not guaranteed but other information sources such as distance or distance-rate between the nodes are taken into account for positioning and positioning enhancement. Figure *4* shows different situations where modern CP can be used.

The reliability and accuracy required of positioning for some crucial applications such as collision avoidance is a serious challenge for modern CP. The quality and availability of data sources are determining factors for achievable quality through data fusion for different applications. The harsh and mobile environment of VANET and the limited bandwidth of DSRC impose many challenges on data communication, ranging, and range-rating, the main components of modern CP.

The achievable positioning performance through modern CP depends on the quality and

amount of available data, which are fused by a CP algorithm. As a rule of thumb, incorporating more data into a CP algorithm leads to improved performance, but the communication constraints and processing capacity of the nodes are dominant factors preventing the achievement of high performance real-time algorithms, suitable for crucial applications such as collision avoidance.

To investigate the achievable enhancement by a modern CP over GPS-based positioning, a range-based CP, with two network topologies, is considered and the CRLB of CP-based positioning error with regard to ranging and GPS accuracy is derived. For the first scenario, assume a cluster of n vehicles, all communicating with each other, where all of the ranges among them are estimated through a radio ranging technique. Figure *5* shows the situation for *5* vehicles. In a cluster topology any given node can initiate the CP by communicating the measured ranges to its surrounding vehicles.

Considering GPS-based measured *2D* position of the vehicles, measured ranges between them with some sort of radio ranging technique, and a Gaussian error for all of the measurements, Equation (7) represents the conditional joint Probability Density Function (PDF) of measurements

$$f(Z|W) = \frac{(2\pi)^{-N/2}}{\sqrt{\det(\Sigma)}} \exp\left\{-\frac{1}{2}(Z-\eta)^T \Sigma^{-1}(Z-\eta)\right\}$$
(7)

where Z is the vector of random variables of measurements, W is the vector containing the real 2D positions of the vehicles, Σ is the covariance of measurements, η is the vector of the means of measurements, and N is the size of the vector Z. Using Equation (7), the CRLB of the position estimation error for each vehicle is the inverse of the Fischer Information Matrix (FIM) (Trees, 2003) F:

Figure 5. A cluster of vehicles, all linked together

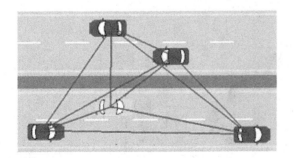

$$F = -E\left\{\frac{\partial^2 \ln(f(Z|W))}{\partial W^2}\right\} \qquad (8)$$

Assuming independency of all measurements, σ_p as the STD of GPS positioning along the axes X and Y, σ_{ij} as the STD of range measurement error between the vehicle i and j, and using Equations (7) and (8), the FIM is:

$$F_{kk} = \begin{cases} \frac{1}{\sigma_p^2} + \sum\limits_{\substack{i=1 \\ i\neq j}}^{n} \frac{(x_i - x_j)^2}{\sigma_{ij}^2 r_{ij}^2} & , k = 2i-1 \\[3em] \frac{1}{\sigma_p^2} + \sum\limits_{\substack{i=1 \\ i\neq j}}^{n} \frac{(y_i - y_j)^2}{\sigma_{ij}^2 r_{ij}^2} & , k = 2i \end{cases} \qquad (9)$$

$$F_{kl} = F_{lk} = \begin{cases} -\frac{(x_i - x_j)^2}{\sigma_{ij}^2 r_{ij}^2} & , k = 2j-1, l = 2i-1, i \neq j \\[1.5em] -\frac{(y_i - y_j)^2}{\sigma_{ij}^2 r_{ij}^2} & , k = 2j, l = 2i, i \neq j \\[1.5em] -\frac{(x_i - x_j)(y_i - y_j)}{\sigma_{ij}^2 r_{ij}^2} & , k = 2i-1, l = 2j, i \neq j \\[1.5em] \sum\limits_{\substack{j=1 \\ j\neq i}}^{n} \frac{(x_i - x_j)(y_i - y_j)}{\sigma_{ij}^2 r_{ij}^2} & , k = 2i-1, l = 2i \end{cases} \qquad (10)$$

Figure 6. CRLB of drms of CP-based positioning incorporating all distances between the vehicles

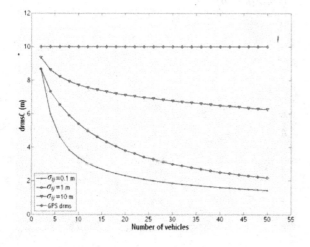

where $i,j=1,...,n$, x_i and y_i are coordinates of the vehicle i, and r_{ij} is the distance between the vehicles i and j. The CRLB for CP-based positioning error is:

$$C = F^{-1} \qquad (11)$$

Now, for vehicle i, the $drmsC_i$ is distance root mean square (Kaplan & Hegarty, 2006) for CRLB and there is:

$$drmsC_i = \sqrt{C(2i-1, 2i-1) + C(2i, 2i)} \qquad (12)$$

To investigate the effect of n and ranging error, σ_{ij} on achievable accuracy of CP for the scenario depicted in Figure 5, the following simulation is run. For each simulation run, the nodes are randomly allocated on the centre lines of lanes in a *300 m* segment of a road with four lanes, each *4 m* wide. The DSRC effective range is set at *300 m*, therefore all generated nodes are effectively in each other's neighbourhood. Note that the network is regarded as a static network in this simulation, which means that the computations are performed for snapshots of the real traffic flow. It is assumed that *drms* (Direct Root Mean Square) of the GPS error is *10 m* and $drmsC_i$ for one of the vehicles, called the target vehicle, is calculated. Here, it is assumed that σ_{ij} is the same for all of the links in the cluster. Figure *6* shows the average of $drmsC$ over *5000* trials for different n and σ_{ij}. As a general rule, the number of trials for CRLB analysis must be high enough so that running the whole test again will almost surely lead to the same results as in Figure *6*.

As can be observed in Figure *6*, the positioning accuracy limit improves when the number of vehicles and ranging accuracy increases. Also, it can be concluded that increasing the number of participating vehicles above about *15* does not improve performance significantly, which is important for saving bandwidth. Of course, for

Figure 7. A target vehicle within a group with star topology

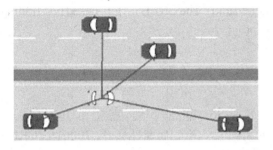

the considered topology, even for *15* vehicles, we need at least *105* links, almost simultaneously at each epoch, in order to implement CP algorithms for a cluster of vehicles similar to that shown in Figure *5*. This is technically very difficult to achieve when considering the limited DSRC bandwidth and communication latency.

In order to improve the viability of CP methods, an alternative topology may be considered. Figure *7* shows a group of vehicles with a star topology with the links only between the target vehicle and its neighbors. A star topology does not require the communication of the measured ranges with surrounding vehicles. For a quick comparison, a cluster of *15* vehicles has *14* links with this topology, which is much fewer than that of previous topology.

Although this approach can increase the viability of CP methods, it has lower performance. Investigating the achievable performance with the star topology, the variances of the links that are absent in the star topology must be set to an infinitely large number in Equations (9) and (10) to compute the FIM and CRLB. In order to implement the star topology in these equations, the STD of ranging, σ_{ij}, for the missed links is assumed to be infinity. This is equivalent to considering no link or no range information between the neighbor vehicles. Applying this rule and considering the same parameters of the previous simulation, Figure *8* shows the achievable performance through CP. As can be seen, the accuracy improvement is lower than in the first scenario. This is expected due to the smaller amount of information incorporated into the CP algorithm to save bandwidth and step towards practicability. The other important point is the limited performance improvement with more accurate ranging. Regarding Figure *8*, the achievable performance with *1 m* and *0.1 m* ranging STD is almost equal. This implies the dominance of the GPS error of the neighbors, which is not compensated by accurate ranging between the target vehicle and its neighbors.

Figure 8. CRLB of drms of CP-based positioning with star topology

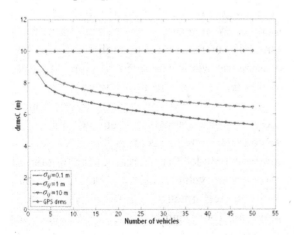

Figure 9. Performance of CP for cluster and star topologies ($\sigma_{ij} = 1$ m)

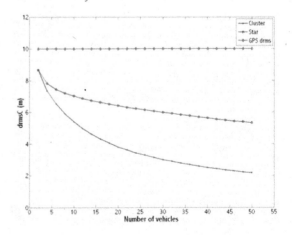

Figure 10. CP performance and bandwidth trade off based on star and cluster topologies

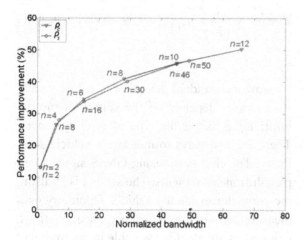

Comparing the performance of CP for cluster and star topologies, Figure *9* shows the achievable accuracies for two methods when the ranging error STD is *1 m*. Although CP with a cluster topology outperforms the star topology, the required bandwidth, which is proportional to the number of links, dramatically increases with the number of vehicles for cluster topologies.

Bandwidth Effect

For a better idea of bandwidth effects on achievable performance for different methods, let *BWS(n)* and *BWC(n)* be the required bandwidths for participating nodes in a star and cluster topology, respectively. Assuming that bandwidth is shared equally among the participating nodes, the required bandwidth for CP can be considered proportional to the number of participating nodes (*n*):

$$\begin{cases} BWC(n) = Kn(n-1)/2 \\ BWS(n) = K(n-1) \end{cases} \tag{13}$$

Where *K* is a known constant. In Equation (13), it is assumed that in the star topology, the neighbors talk to the target vehicle only. According to Equation (13), for a group of *10* to *20*

vehicles, cluster-based CP needs a bandwidth *5* to *10* times that required for star-based CP. To better understand the trade-off between bandwidth and achievable performance, an improvement factor, ρ (%), is defined for the different topologies:

$$\begin{cases} \rho_c = (1 - \dfrac{drmsCPc}{drmsGPS}) \times 100 \\ \rho_s = (1 - \dfrac{drmsCPs}{drmsGPS}) \times 100 \end{cases} \tag{14}$$

where drms has a similar definition to Equation (12), *CPc* refers to CP with cluster topology and *CPs* refers to CP with start topology. Figure *10* shows achievable performance with regard to required normalized bandwidth (*K=1*), when the ranging error STD is *1 m* and *drmsGPS* is *10 m*. As can be seen, although the performance of the CP with a cluster topology is higher than that with a star topology for the same number of nodes, in terms of required bandwidth, the achievable performance improvement is effectively the same for both situations.

CP Information Fusion with Velocity Sensor

For node localization in mobile networks, the motion information of the nodes and their likely routes can be used to refine the position estimates. A computational algorithm that facilitates tracking and fusion of spatial information across time is referred to as a filter. By using a filtering mechanism, the position estimation at each instant *k* in time is refined by the estimation at instant *k-1* based on a mobility model. Assume the velocity-based mobility:

$$\begin{cases} x_i^{k+1} = x_i^k + t^k u_i^k + t^k \xi_x \\ y_i^{k+1} = y_i^k + t^k v_i^k + t^k \xi_y \end{cases} \tag{15}$$

where u and v are the velocity components in X and Y directions. T_k is the time interval between measurements. ξ_x and ξ_y are standard errors with zero mean and variances of σ_u and σ_v, respectively. A sort of hybrid CRLB for mobile networks can be derived according to the above formulation of motion information and the FIM in Equation (11):

$$C_{k+1} = \left(\left(C_k + T_k \Sigma_v \right) + F_{k+1} \right) \qquad (16)$$

where C_{k+1} and C_k are the hybrid CRLB matrices at instants $k+1$ and k respectively, T_k is the scalar elapsed time, Σ_v is the diagonal covariance matrix of the measured velocity of vehicles in directions X and Y, and F_{k+1} is the FIM of the network positions from Equations (9) and (10) at time $k+1$. From Equation (16) it is clear that noisier velocity measurements, thus larger σ_v, lead to a smaller contribution from the previous instant's position information and if this effect is too large, filtering has no effect on the accuracy. An indicator of cooperative positioning error for node i over a period of time (K) can be readily obtained based on $drmsC_i$ in Equation (12) averaged over time:

$$drmsC_i = \left(\frac{1}{K} \sum_{k=1}^{K} C_k \left(2i-1, 2i-1 \right) + C_k \left(2i, 2i \right) \right)^{\frac{1}{2}} \qquad (17)$$

Now the standard deviation of velocity measurement σ_v depends on the source of motion information that is the type of velocity sensor. There are two ways to measure a vehicle's velocity. The first is by using GNSS signal Doppler shift measurements. The second is by using the odometer inside the vehicle. Odometry uses measurements of the elementary wheel rotations. Odometers are already available in the front and rear wheels of vehicles equipped with an Antilock Breaking Systems (ABS). The accuracy of the ABS velocity measurements is about *0.1 m/s,* but requires digital conversion (Bonnifait, et al., 2001; El Najjar & Bonnifait, 2005). Because the speed derived from ABS does not indicate heading, a heading solution is required that can be readily extracted from GPS or other means such as a digital compass, low cost gyros or a digital map, in order to produce a velocity vector.

A digital compass is a very cheap solution for heading. It provides accuracy of *0.5°,* but might

Figure 11. The interface of the traffic simulation software developed with Netlogo agent based programming language

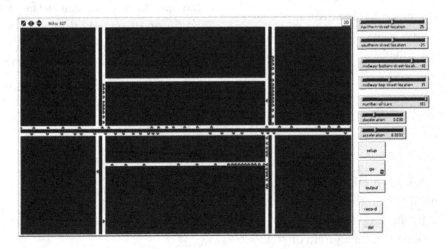

not prove cost worthy. Digital maps are already available in all GPS vehicle navigation systems. The mechanism of extracting heading information from a digital map is based on the fact that the heading of a vehicle is determined by the curvature of the road being travelled. In other words the approximate position of the vehicle can give the heading with simple map matching to determine the position of the vehicle on the road segment.

A simulation study was conducted to demonstrate the performance of CP with the cluster topology when fused with a velocity sensor. By Netlogo™, an agent-based and Java-based programming platform, a street traffic network was simulated. Figure *11* is a snapshot of the Netlogo traffic network. The length of the horizontal road was set at *2 km*. From this simulation, only the ground truth values of the vehicles' positions were obtained. The rest of the calculations, such the noisy GPS measurements and DSRC range measurements were performed in the Matlab™ environment. Four traffic conditions were considered that were controlled by the total number of vehicles in the traffic simulation street network. The considered traffic rates were *300 vehicles/hour* (*v/h*) in the main streets for sparse/fast traffic, *600 v/h*, *900 v/h* and *1200 v/h* for heavy/slow traffic. In all four cases a target vehicle was set to travel

a particular path of about *2 km*. The simulation time in each case thus depends on traffic conditions; for example, for sparse traffic, it takes a shorter time than for heavy traffic to travel the same distance. The DSRC range was set at *250 m*. The underlying assumptions for this test and all the following tests are that the inter-node ranging error has a mean of zero and variance of σ_{ij}, which was changed from *1 m* to *10 m*. The drmsGPS was again set at *10 m*.

Figure *12 (a)* shows the expected error for CP based on CRLB analysis for heavy traffic conditions. The errors are averaged over the simulation run time (roughly around *200 s* for sparse traffic condition). The ranging STD varied between *1 m* and *10 m* as shown on the curves; the standard deviation of velocity measurements varied from *0.1 m/s* to *2.1 m/s*. It can be seen that CP error is highly sensitivity to velocity error. Better than *1 m* accuracies are typical when the velocity measurement has an error standard deviation of about *0.1 m/s*. Note that this velocity error margin can be met with ABS-based odometers (Bonnifait, et al., 2001; Stephen, 2000). Figure *12 (b)* shows the typical CP error in all types of traffic conditions. This figure shows that the velocity measurement accuracy contributes more to the CP accuracy than heavier traffic conditions.

Figure 12. Error bounds for heavy traffic conditions with several range measurements error standard deviation (from 1 to 10) and velocity error standard deviation (a). The range errors are indicated on the error curves. Average CRLB based error over the simulation run for $\sigma_R=3m$. The traffic conditions in terms of rate of vehicles/hour (v/h) are indicated on the error curves (b).

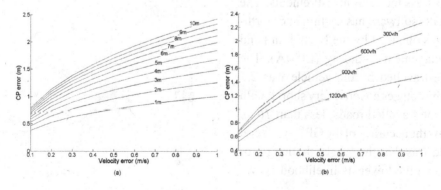

Figure 13. The increase in CP error for ranging STD of 3 m due to 10 outages of between 15m to 35m in every kilometre of the road and for various traffic rates as printed on the curves.

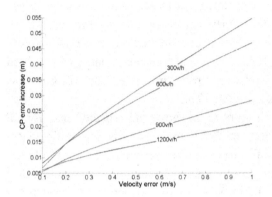

CP Robustness to GPS Outage

As mentioned earlier, GNSS is not a robust system in urban areas where high-rise buildings determine satellite visibility and the level of signal degradation due to multipath. The urban structure and shape of high-rise and other buildings lead to time-dependent masked areas where some or all of GNSS satellites are invisible in particular time slots, making impossible a robust position estimation. In a test in the City of Sydney Central District Area (CBD) on 25/11/2009, using a typical GPS navigation receiver Ublox™, ten significant masked areas of lengths between *15 m* to *35 m* were observed in every kilometer (Mahmoud Efatmaneshnik, Kealy, Lim, & Dempster, 2010). Geographic Information System (GIS) software was used to assess the GPS measurements. The map in this GIS software has easting and northing coordinates obtained by the NSW Land and Property Management Authority (LPMA). The total distance travelled by the vehicle was *2.7 km*. Most of the outages covered very short length segments of the travelled roads, less than *10 m*, which is below the accuracy of the GPS. A general observed rule was that the longer the length of the masked area the lower its likelihood is. We

built on the results of this test to set up the next simulation to demonstrate the capacity of CP to bridge the GPS outages.

In this simulation, twenty outages of *15 m* to *35 m* lengths were randomly allocated throughout the simulated street network. If a vehicle entered the outage zones, its position error deviation was set at infinity (or a very large number), which literally means the absence of position information in those zones. Figure *13* shows the results in terms of the increase in average CP error relative to the no-outage, as shown in Figure *12* for the previous test. From Figure *13* it is evident that even for sparse traffic, the GPS outages do not have a significant effect on the CP error in terms of *drmsC_i*, as long as ranges can be measured between vehicles. The CP error increase of less than *6 cm* in the worst case indicates that CP is a systematic solution to the GPS outage problem in the urban areas, and that CP is a competent bridging mechanism of short GPS outages.

In Figure *14*, the error bounds for two cases as well as the GPS drop out times (i.e. times in which the vehicle has been travelling in an outage zone) are shown. Case 1 is the worst-case sce-

Figure 14. CP error for two cases. Both cases are for heavy traffic condition and σ_R=10m. The velocity error for Case 1 (red) is σ_v=1m/s and for Case 2 (blue) is σ_v=0.1m/s. The green dashed lines show the outages. A value of 1 indicates GPS availability and 0 the GPS unavailability.

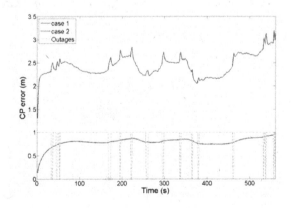

nario for CP performance where traffic conditions are very heavy. Also, the ranging and velocity errors are set at their highest, σ_{ij}=10 m and σ_v=1 m/s. Case 2 has the same traffic conditions and ranging error but better velocity measurements σ_v=0.1 m/s. This figure shows that in case 1, CP error has some sensitivity in the form of sharp short spikes to the outages. However, case 2 has a very smooth error pattern, even during the outages. The smoothness is due, in particular, to better velocity measurements. This figure illustrates the important positive impact of velocity accuracies on both smoothness of the CP solution, its accuracy and most importantly, on the seamless bridging of the GPS outages by CP.

CP ALGORITHMS

A localization algorithm is a computational procedure or an estimation engine that addresses the problem formulation, robustness, estimation accuracy, coordination and computational complexity, given some measurement information. Monte Carlo Localization (Dellaert, Fox, Burgard, & Thrun, 1999), Convex Optimization (Doherty, Pister, & Ghaoui, 2001), Iterative Multilateration (Tay, Chandrasekhar, & Seah, 2006), Multidimensional Scaling (MDS) (Cox & Cox, 1994) and Kalman Filter (KF) for mobile networks (Parker & Valaee, 2007a) are the most popular network localization algorithms. A perfectly efficient CP algorithm is one that has the same errors as CRLB over many trials. In reality, such an algorithm does not exist, but optimal algorithms can deliver estimates with errors very close to CRLB. As is the case for a general estimation problem, these algorithms differ in their cost function that must be optimized and also differ from the method used to optimize the cost function. A simple least squares cost function for a vehicular network with range measurements is:

$$C_{LS} = \sum_{i=1}^{n} \sum_{j=1}^{n} \left(d_{i,j} - \sqrt{\left(x_i - x_j\right)^2 + \left(y_i - y_j\right)^2} \right)^2$$

(18)

where n is the number of vehicles in the cluster or neighborhood of a target vehicle, $d_{i,j}$ is the measured distance between vehicles i and j, and x_i, y_i, x_j, y_j are the estimated coordinates of i and j. This cost function must be minimized with a search algorithm such as a gradient descent algorithm within the neighborhood of the initial nodes' positions that are obtained from GPS measurements (Parker & Valaee, 2006). Similarly, the iterative linear least squares adjustment technique can be applied. Another cost function is maximum a posteriori (MAP) cost function:

$$C_{MAP} = \sum_{i=1}^{n} \left[\frac{\left(x_i - x_{Ti}\right)^2 + \left(y_i - y_j\right)^2}{\sigma_{GPS}^2} \right] + \sum_{i=1}^{n} \sum_{j=1}^{n} \left(\frac{d_{i,j} - \sqrt{\left(x_i - x_j\right)^2 + \left(y_i - y_j\right)^2}}{\sigma_{i,j}^2} \right)^2$$

(19)

Multidimensional scaling (MDS) provides an analytical yet iterative solution that minimizes this cost function. The MDS algorithm can be modified to accommodate the mobility information of the vehicles over time into the estimation process (M. Efatmaneshnik, Balaei, Alam, & Dempster, 2009). The Kalman Filter (KF), however, is an estimation algorithm that considers the dynamics of the systems for more efficient estimation.

Kalman Filter for CP

KF is an optimal state least squares recursive estimation process applied to a stochastic dynamic system such as a vehicular network. KF is a linear, unbiased, and minimum error variance recursive estimation algorithm for the state of a dynamic system that uses noisy measurements taken at discrete real-time intervals. The KF algorithm outperforms a number of other estimation algorithms including the least squares algorithm, and also has very close performance to the hybrid CRLB

(Parker & Valaee, 2007b). The KF process is as follows. Consider the velocity mobility model in Equation (15) as the dynamic state model. The range measurements then are considered in a measurement model:

$$\begin{cases} X_{k+1} = A_k X_k + \Gamma_k \xi_k \\ Z_k = g(X_k) + \eta_k \end{cases} \qquad (20)$$

where X_k is a vector containing the position coordinates of all nodes in a cluster and Z_k is the vector of measured ranges at instant k. The process noise ξ_k and measurement noise η_k are independent zero mean Gaussian white noise with covariance matrices respectively, described by Q_k and R_k. Since for CP the relationship between Z_k and X_k is not linear, a linear Taylor transformation is required:

$$C_k = \frac{\partial g}{\partial X_k}(X_{k|k-1}) \qquad (21)$$

The Kalman then solution is:

$$\begin{aligned} X_{k|k-1} &= A_{k-1} X_{k-1|k-1} \\ P_{k|k-1} &= A_{k-1} P_{k-1|k-1} A_{k-1}^T + \Gamma_{k-1} Q_{k-1} \Gamma_{k-1}^T \\ G_k &= A_{k-1} C_k^T (C_k P_{k|k-1} C_k^T + R_k)^{-1} \qquad (22) \\ X_{k|k} &= X_{k|k-1} + G_k(v_k - C_k X_{k|k-1}) \\ P_{k|k} &= (I - G_k C_k) P_{k|k-1} \end{aligned}$$

Equation 15 can be rewritten in vector form:

$$X_{k+1} = X_k + tV_k + t\xi_k \qquad (23)$$

Which indicates that A_k and Γ_k are the unity matrices. The process noise Q_k, In this case, becomes a diagonal matrix with variances of velocity measurements on its diagonal. If we consider two sources of measurement (the GPS and DSRC ranges), the measurement vector contains the GPS positions of all vehicles, and the measured ranges

between pairs of vehicles. The measurement noise matrix R_k is then a diagonal matrix with variance of GPS measurements and ranges on its diagonal. The heading of the vehicles obtainable from the digital map of the vehicles' navigators is, however, another source of information that can be added to the measurement vector. Additionally, the outcome of the KF, $X_{k|k}$, can be adjusted to make sure it locates within the road boundaries.

Map Information Fusion

Map matching algorithms themselves commonly fall into two categories, termed geometric and topological (Kealy, Scott-Young, & Collier, 2004). The two main map-matching rules are the more commonly used one based on the geometry of the road (Bétaille & Bonnifait, 2000; Taylor, Blewitt, Steup, Corbett, & Car, 2001) and the other based on the heading or bearing of the road (Bernstein & Kornhauser, 1996; Greenfeld, 2002). The first rule makes the assumption that the vehicle is travelling on a road (which is typically the case) and adjusts the position to the center-line of the road (or lane). This simple constraint immediately improves the accuracy of the computed position of the vehicle. The simple algorithm is effective when the nearest road/lane to the estimated position (from GPS or other sources) is, in fact, the road being travelled. However, when approaching intersections or when two roads are close to each other, the nearest road may not be the road being travelled. In these situations, searching for the nearest road can downgrade the position solution. To overcome this problem, a second map-matching rule applied in parallel takes into account the direction of the road on which the vehicle is travelling. This second rule requires that the nearest road to which the vehicle's position is corrected (using the first map matching rule) must have a similar bearing to the direction of travel that is available from GPS, meaning the heading of the vehicle must be the same as the bearing of the road.

Applying the first rule to the estimated state $X_{k|k}$ requires adjustment of the estimated covariance of the state $P_{k|k}$, which will be used in KF equations in the next instance, $k+1$. Here, a scaling diagonal matrix is required to put the one-sigma errors ellipses within the road boundaries. The scaling matrix must have the sine and cosine of the heading of the vehicles on its diagonal. With this scaling, the estimated covariance of vehicle i, σ_i is adjusted to τ_i as follows:

$$\begin{cases} \tau_{x_i}^k = \sigma_{x_i}^k \sin(h_i^k) \\ \tau_{y_i}^k = \sigma_{y_i}^k \cos(h_i^k) \end{cases} \tag{24}$$

Applying the second rule to the KF is achieved by adding a third set of measurements, the headings, to the measurement vector, knowing that the heading of node i at instant k is related to the position of the vehicle at moments k and $k-1$:

$$h_i^k = a\tan\left(\frac{y_i^k - y_i^{k-1}}{x_i^k - x_i^{k-1}}\right) \tag{25}$$

The variance associated with this measure-

Figure 15. The performance of three Kalman Filters compared to the hybrid CRLB

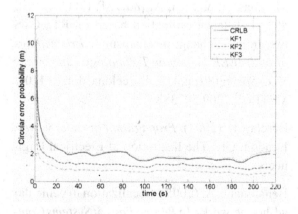

ment must be considered as a very small number

close to zero, since the heading measured from the digital map is very accurate.

KF Performance

A simulation study was carried out to demonstrate the performance of the presented KF. The Netlogo traffic simulation for *1200 v/h* traffic rate was used. Figure *15* shows the performance of KF without any of the map matching rules (KF1), and KF with only the first map matching rule (KF2), snap-to-the-centerline, and KF with both map-matching algorithms (KF3). The simulations ran for about *220 s*. The ranging standard deviation was set at *3 m* and that of GPS (in terms of CEP) was *10 m*. The average of *drmsCi* over the number of simulation runs was used as the overall estimation error. The simulation was repeated *500 times,* at which point the increase of number of iterations did not have any effect on the outcome. One can argue that the simulation trail number is dependent on many subtle characteristics such the topography of the road network, the maximum and minimum velocity of nodes, etc. The performance of KF1, KF2 and KF3 were compared together and with the hybrid CRLB. KF1 performs slightly above the hybrid CRLB that shows the superior performance of KF for cooperative positioning. The performance of KF2 and KF3 are well below (better than) the hybrid CRLB, because the map matching adds more information to the estimation process than was used in the CRLB evaluation. Thus, the accuracy of the final estimation is much better than hybrid CRLB.

FUTURE RESEARCH DIRECTIONS

The CP analyzed in this chapter was only one possible type of CP. Other CP techniques can, however, be envisaged. A simpler approach to CP using DSRC is to use conventional CP without a ranging or range-rating requirement (Alam, Balaei, & Dempster, 2010b), that is similar to the Real Time Kinematic (RTK) technique. Another approach to CP comprises tight GNSS and DSRC network integration in which the vehicles exchange the Satellite pseudoranges rather than GPS positions through the DSRC channel. In this case, positioning with fewer than four visible satellites should be possible.

CONCLUSION

The emergence of infrastructure such as DSRC allows us to establish ad hoc vehicular networks in which range measurements between the moving vehicles can be quantified and included as part of the integrated positioning solution. This new information source, together with GNSS system, forms a platform for robust position estimation that can meet the strict performance requirements of a range of road safety systems and services. CP is an important application of DSRC that has a crucial role for the reliability of safety-related applications; because it can provide consistent below-meter positioning accuracy. A range-based CP was analyzed and proved competent and reliable for the position information in vehicular environments. CP is a positioning solution with no additional cost and with no major implications to DSRC system developers. CP can potentially lead to reliable and consistent below 1-meter positioning accuracy. There are, of course, challenges with ranging such as Synchronization of DSRC boards that need further research.

REFERENCES

Alam, N., Balaei, A. T., & Dempster, A. G. (2009). *Range and range-rate measurements using DSRC: Facts and challenges.* Paper presented at the IGNSS Symposium 2009, Surfers Paradise, Australia.

Alam, N., Balaei, A. T., & Dempster, A. G. (2010a). *Proceedings of the 72nd IEEE Vehicular Technology Conference Fall VTC 2010-Fall* (pp. 1-5). Ottawa. doi:10.1109/VETECF.2010.5594457

Alam, N., Balaei, A. T., & Dempster, A. G. (2010b). *Positioning enhancement with double differencing and DSRC*. Paper presented at the ION GNSS 2010, Portland, USA.

Alsindi, N. A., Alavi, B., & Pahlavan, K. (2009). Measurement and modeling of ultrawideband TOA-based ranging in indoor multipath environments. *IEEE Transactions on Vehicular Technology, 58*(3), 1046–1058. doi:10.1109/TVT.2008.926071

Amar, A., & Weiss, A. J. (2008). Localization of narrowband radio emitters based on doppler frequency shifts. *IEEE Transactions on Signal Processing, 56*(11), 5500–5508. doi:10.1109/TSP.2008.929655

Amundson, I., Koutsoukos, X., & Sallai, J. (2008). Mobile sensor localization and navigation using RF doppler shifts. In *Proceedings of the First ACM International Workshop on Mobile Entity Localization and Tracking in GPS-less Environments* (pp. 97-102). San Francisco, CA. doi:10.1145/1410012.1410034

Bahillo, A., Prieto, J., Mazuelas, S., Lorenzo, R. M., Blas, J., & Fern, Ã. ¡ndez, P. (2009). IEEE 802.11 distance estimation based on RTS/CTS two-frame exchange mechanism. In *Proceedings of 69th IEEE Vehicular Technology Conference VTC-Spring09* (pp. 1-5). Barcelona. doi:10.1109/VETECS.2009.5073583

Barclay, L. (2003). *Propagation of radio waves*. London, UK: The Institution of Electrical Engineers.

Benslimane, A. (2005). Localization in vehicular ad-hoc networks. In *Proceedings of Systems Communications Conference,* Montreal, Canada. doi:10.1109/ICW.2005.54

Bernstein, D., & Kornhauser, A. (1996). *An introduction to map matching for personal navigation assistants*. Newark, NJ: TIDE Center.

Bétaille, D., & Bonnifait, P. (2000). *Road maintenance vehicles Location using DGPS, mapmatching and dead-reckoning: Experimental results of a smoothed EKF.* Paper presented at the IAIN World Congress in Association with the U.S. ION 56th Annual Meeting, San Diego.

Bonnifait, P., Bouron, P., Crubille, P., & Meizel, D. (2001). Data fusion of four ABS sensors and GPS for an enhanced localization of car-like vehicles. In *Proceedings of IEEE International Conference on the Robotics and Automation* (pp. 1597-1602). Seoul. *Korea & World Affairs*. doi:10.1109/ROBOT.2001.932839

Boukerche, A., Oliveira, H. A. B. F., Nakamura, E. F., & Loureiro, A. A. F. (2008). Vehicular ad hoc networks: A new challenge for localization-based systems. *Computer Communications, 31*(12), 2838–2849. doi:10.1016/j.comcom.2007.12.004

CAMP-Vehicle-Safety-Communications-Consortium. (2005). *Vehicle safety communications project task 3 final report: Identify intelligent vehicle safety applications enabled by DSRC. U.S. Depatment of Transporation*. National Highway Traffic Safety Administration.

Chan, Y. T., & Towers, J. J. (1992). Passive localization from Doppler-shifted frequency measurements. *IEEE Transactions on Signal Processing, 40*(10), 2594–2598. doi:10.1109/78.157301

Chen, H., Martins, M. H. T., Huang, P., So, H. C., & Sezaki, K. (2008). Cooperative node localization for mobile sensor networks. In *Proceedings of The 5th International Conference on Embedded and Ubiquitous Computing EUC08* (pp. 302-308). Shanghai. doi: 10.1109/EUC.2008.166

Chiavaccini, E., & Vitetta, G. M. (2004). Maximum-likelihood frequency recovery for OFDM signals transmitted over multipath fading channels. *IEEE Transactions on Communications, 52*(2), 244–251. doi:10.1109/TCOMM.2003.822706

Ciurana, M., Barcelo-Arroyo, F., & Cugno, S. (2009). A robust to multi-path ranging technique over IEEE 802.11 networks. *Wireless Networks, 16*(4), 1–11. doi:10.1007/s11276-009-0180-3

Ciurana, M., Lopez, D., & Barcelo-Arroyo, F. (2009). Lecture Notes in Computer Science: *Vol. 5561. SofTOA: Software ranging for toa-based positioning of WLAN terminals* (pp. 207–221). Tokyo.

Cox, T., & Cox, M. (1994). *Multidimensional scaling*. Chapman & Hall.

Cui, T., & Tellambura, C. (2007). Joint frequency offset and channel estimation for OFDM systems using pilot symbols and virtual carriers. *IEEE Transactions on Wireless Communications, 6*(4), 1193–1202. doi:10.1109/TWC.2007.348312

Czarnecki, S. V., Johnson, J. A., Gray, C. M., Ver-Wys, G., & Gerst, C. (1999). *International Patent No. 5982164*, USA.

Danchik, R. J. (1998). An overview of transit development. *Johns Hopkins APL Technical Digest, 19*(1), 18–26.

Dao, T. S., Leung, K. Y. K., Clark, C. M., & Huissoon, J. P. (2007). Markov-based lane positioning using intervehicle communication. *IEEE Transactions on Intelligent Transportation Systems, 8*(4), 641–650. doi:10.1109/TITS.2007.908574

Deleuze, A. L., Martret, C. L., Ciblat, P., & Serpedin, E. (2004). Cramer-Rao bound for channel parameters in ultra-wide band based system. In *Proceedings of IEEE 5th Workshop on Signal Processing Advances in Wireless Communications* (pp. 140–144). Lisbon, Portugal. doi:10.1109/SPAWC.2004.1439220

Dellaert, F., Fox, D., Burgard, W., & Thrun, S. (1999). Monte Carlo localization for mobile robots. In *Proceedings of IEEE International Conference Robotics and Automation* (pp. 1322-1328). Detroit, Michigan. doi:10.1109/ROBOT.1999.772544

Diggelen, F. V. (2009). *A-GPS: Assisted GPS, GNSS, and SBAS*. Boston, MA: Artech House.

Doherty, L., Pister, K. S. J., & Ghaoui, L. E. (2001). Convex position estimation in wireless sensor networks. In *Proceedings of Twentieth Annual Joint Conference of the IEEE Computer and Communications Societies* (pp. 1655-1663). INFOCOM2001. doi:10.1109/INFCOM.2001.916662

Efatmaneshnik, M., Balaei, A. T., Alam, N., & Dempster, A. (2009). A modified multidimensional scaling with embedded particle filter algorithm for cooperative positioning of vehicular networks. In *Proceedings of IEEE International Conference on Vehicular Electronics and Safety* (pp. 7-12). India. doi: 10.1109/ICVES.2009.5400202

Efatmaneshnik, M., Kealy, A., Lim, S., & Dempster, A. G. (2010). *Analysis of information fusion for low cost, precise and reliable vehicular cooperative positioning with DSRC*. Paper presented at the DSRC Workshop on the side of ICST QShine 2010, Houston, Texas.

El Najjar, M. E., & Bonnifait, P. (2005). A road-matching method for precise vehicle localization using belief theory and Kalman filtering. *Autonomous Robots*, *19*(2), 173–191. doi:10.1007/s10514-005-0609-1

Falsi, C., Dardari, D., Mucchi, L., & Win, M. Z. (2006). Time of arrival estimation for UWB localizers in realistic environments. *EURASIP Journal on Applied Signal Processing*, *2006*. doi:10.1155/ASP/2006/32082

Farrell, J. A. (1998). *The global positioning system & inertial navigation*. New York, NY: McGraw-Hill.

Godha, S., & Cannon, M. E. (2007). GPS/MEMS INS integrated system for navigation in urban areas. *GPS Solutions*, *11*(3), 193–203. doi:10.1007/s10291-006-0050-8

Greenfeld, J. S. (2002). *Matching GPS observations to locations on a digital map*. Newark, NJ: Department of Civil and Environmental Engineering, New Jersey Institute of Technology.

Gunther, A., & Hoene, C. (2005). Measuring round trip times to determine the distance between WLAN nodes. In *Proceedings of NETWORKING 2005, Lecture Notes in Computer Science vol. 3462/2005*, (pp. 303-319). Waterloo, Canada. doi:10.1007/11422778_62

Hata, M. (1980). Empirical formula for propagation loss in land mobile radio services. *IEEE Transactions on Vehicular Technology*, *VT-29*(3), 317–325. doi:10.1109/T-VT.1980.23859

Hide, C., Moore, T., & Smith, M. (2003). Adaptive Kalman filtering for low-cost INS/GPS. *Journal of Navigation*, *56*(1), 143–152. doi:10.1017/S0373463302002151

Hofmann-Wellenhof, B., Lichtenegger, H., & Collins, J. (2001). *Global positioning system theory and practice* (5th ed.). New York, NY: Springer Wien. doi:10.1007/978-3-7091-6199-9

Jo, K., Lee, J., & Kim, J. (2007). Cooperative multi-robot localization using differential position data. In *Proceedings of IEEE/ASME International Conference on Advanced Intelligent Mechatronics* (pp. 1-6). Zurich. doi:10.1109/AIM.2007.4412548

Jo, K. H., & Lee, J. (2007). Multi-robot cooperative localization with optimally fused information of odometer and GPS. In *Proceedings of International Conference on Control, Automation and Systems ICCAS 2007* (pp. 601-605). Seoul. doi:10.1109/ICCAS.2007.4407094

Kaplan, E. D., & Hegarty, C. J. (2006). *Understanding GPS principles and applications* (2nd ed.). Norwood, MA: Artech House Inc.

Karam, N., Chausse, F., Aufrere, R., & Chapuis, R. (2006a). Cooperative multi-vehicle localization. In *Proceedings of IEEE Intelligent Vehicles Symposium* (pp. 564-570). Tokyo. doi:10.1109/IVS.2006.1689688

Karam, N., Chausse, F., Aufrere, R., & Chapuis, R. (2006b). Localization of a group of communicating vehicles by state exchange. In *Proceedings of IEEE/RSJ International Conference on Intelligent Robots and Systems* (pp. 519–524). Beijing. doi:10.1109/IROS.2006.282028

Kaygisiz, B. H., Erkmen, I., & Erkmen, A. M. (2004). GPS/INS enhancement for land navigation using neural network. *Journal of Navigation, 57*(2), 297–310. doi:10.1017/S037346330400267X

Kealy, A., Scott-Young, A., & Collier, P. (2004). *Improving land vehicle safety using augmented reality technologies*. Paper presented at the 4th International Symposium on Mobile Mapping Technology, Kunming, China.

Li, X. (2006). RSS-based location estimation with unknown pathloss model. *IEEE Transactions on Wireless Communications, 5*(12), 3626–3633. doi:10.1109/TWC.2006.256985

Lv, T., Li, H., & Chen, J. (2005). Joint estimation of symbol timing and carrier frequency offset of OFDM signals over fast time-varying multipath channels. *IEEE Transactions on Signal Processing, 53*(12), 4526–4535. doi:10.1109/TSP.2005.859233

Malaney, R. A. (2007). Nuisance parameters and location accuracy in log-normal fading models. *IEEE Transactions on Wireless Communications, 6*(3), 937–947. doi:10.1109/TWC.2007.05247

Mao, G., Anderson, B. D. O., & Fidan, B. (2007). Path loss exponent estimation for wireless sensor network localization. *Computer Networks, 51*(10), 2467–2483. doi:10.1016/j.comnet.2006.11.007

Mazuelas, S., Lago, F. A., Gonzalez, D., Bahillo, A., Blas, J., & Fernandez, P. (2008). Dynamic estimation of optimum path loss model in a RSS positioning system. In *Proceedings of IEEE/ION Position, Location and Navigation Symposium 2008* (pp. 679-684). Monterey, CA. doi:10.1109/PLANS.2008.4569988

McCrady, D. D., Doyle, L., Forstrom, H., Dempsey, T., & Martorana, M. (2000). Mobile ranging using low-accuracy clocks. *IEEE Transactions on Microwave Theory and Techniques, 48*(6), 951–957. doi:10.1109/22.846721

Parker, R., & Valaee, S. (2006). Vehicle localization in vehicular networks. In *Proceedings of IEEE Vehicular Technology Conference* (pp. 679), Montreal, QC. doi:10.1109/VTCF.2006.557

Parker, R., & Valaee, S. (2007a). Vehicular node localization using received-signal-strength indicator. *IEEE Transactions on Vehicular Technology, 56*(6-I), 3371–3380. doi:10.1109/TVT.2007.907687

Parker, R., & Valaee, S. (2007b). Vehicular node localization using received-signal-strength indicator. *IEEE Transactions on Vehicular Technology, 56*(6), 3371–3380. doi:10.1109/TVT.2007.907687

Patwari, N., Ash, J. N., & Kyperountas, S. III, A. O. H., Moses, R. L., & Correal, N. S. (2005). Locating the nodes, cooperative localization in wireless sensor networks. *IEEE Signal Processing Magazine, 22*(4), 54–69. doi:10.1109/MSP.2005.1458287

Patwari, N., Hero, A. O., Perkins, M., Correal, N. S., & O'Dea, R. J. (2003). Relative location estimation in wireless sensor networks. *IEEE Transactions on Signal Processing, 51*(8), 2137–2148. doi:10.1109/TSP.2003.814469

Prieto Tejedor, J., Bahillo Martinez, A., Mazuelas Franco, S., Lorenzo Toledo, R. M., Fernandez Reguero, P., & Abril, E. J. (2009). Characterization and mitigation of range estimation errors for an RTT-based IEEE 802.11 indoor location system. *Progress in Electromagnetics Research B, 15*, 217–244. doi:10.2528/PIERB09050502

Rappaport, T. S. (1996). *Wireless communications: Principle and practice*. New Jersey: Prentice Hall.

Sakagami, S., Aoyama, S., Kuboi, K., Shirota, S., & Akeyama, A. (1992). Vehicle position estimates by multibeam antennas in multipath environments. *IEEE Transactions on Vehicular Technology, 41*(1), 63–68. doi:10.1109/25.120146

Schmidl, T. M., & Cox, D. C. (1997). Robust frequency and timing synchronization for OFDM. *IEEE Transactions on Communications, 45*(12), 1613–1621. doi:10.1109/26.650240

Seeber, G. (2003). *Satellite geodesy: Foundations, methods, and applications*. Berlin, Germany: Walter de Gruyter GmbH & Co.

Shirahama, J., & Ohtsuki, T. (2008). RSS-based localization in environments with different path loss exponent for each link. In *Proceedings of IEEE Vehicular Technology Conference* (pp. 1509-1513). Singapore. doi:10.1109/VETECS.2008.353

Shladover, S. E., & Tan, S. K. (2006). Analysis of vehicle positioning accuracy requirements for communication-based cooperative collision warning. *Journal of Intelligent Transportation Systems: Technology, Planning, and Operations, 10*(3), 131–140. doi:10.1080/15472450600793610

Sieskul, B. T., & Kaiser, T. (2005). Cramer-Rao bound for TOA estimations in UWB positioning systems. In *Proceedings of IEEE International Conference on Ultra-Wideband,* Zurich, Switzerland. doi:10.1109/ICU.2005.1570022

Smith, J. O., & Abel, J. S. (1987). Closed-form least-squares source location estimation from range-difference measurements. *IEEE Transactions on Acoustics, Speech, and Signal Processing, ASSP-35*(12), 1661–1669. doi:10.1109/TASSP.1987.1165089

Stephen, J. E. (2000). *Development of a GNSS-based multi-sensor vehicle navigation system*. University of Calgary.

Tao, J., Wu, J., & Xiao, C. (2009). Estimation of channel transfer function and carrier frequency offset for OFDM systems with phase noise. *IEEE Transactions on Vehicular Technology, 58*(8), 4380–4387. doi:10.1109/TVT.2009.2020066

Tay, J. H., Chandrasekhar, V. R., & Seah, W. K. (2006). Selective iterative multilateration for hop count-based localization in wireless sensor networks. *In Proceedings of 7th International Conference on Mobile Data Management* (pp. 152 - 152). doi:10.1109/MDM.2006.139

Taylor, G., Blewitt, G., Steup, D., Corbett, S., & Car, A. (2001). Road reduction filtering for GPS-GIS navigation. *Transactions in GIS, 5*(3), 193–207. doi:10.1111/1467-9671.00077

Trees, H. L. V. (2003). *Detection, estimation, and modulation theory*. New York, NY: Wiley-IEEE.

Tureli, U., Liu, H., & Zoltowski, M. D. (2000). OFDM blind carrier offset estimation: ESPRIT. *IEEE Transactions on Communications, 48*(9), 1459–1461. doi:10.1109/26.870011

Venkatraman, S., Caffery, J. Jr, & You, H. R. (2004). A novel ToA location algorithm using LoS range estimation for NLoS environments. *IEEE Transactions on Vehicular Technology, 53*(5), 1515–1524. doi:10.1109/TVT.2004.832384

Wang, J. H., & Gao, Y. (2004). GPS-based land vehicle navigation system assisted by a low-cost gyro-free INS using neural network. *Journal of Navigation, 57*(3), 417–428. doi:10.1017/S037346330400284X

Wang, X., Wang, Z., & O'Dea, B. (2003). A TOA-based location algorithm reducing the errors due to non-line-of-sight (NLOS) propagation. *IEEE Transactions on Vehicular Technology, 52*(1), 112–116. doi:10.1109/TVT.2002.807158

Weiss, A. J. (2003). On the accuracy of a cellular location system based on RSS measurements. *IEEE Transactions on Vehicular Technology, 52*(6), 1508–1518. doi:10.1109/TVT.2003.819613

Wymeersch, H., Lien, J., & Win, M. Z. (2009). Cooperative localization in wireless networks. *Proceedings of the IEEE, 97*(2), 427–450. doi:10.1109/JPROC.2008.2008853

Xu, A. Y. Z., Au, E. K. S., Wong, A. K. S., & Wang, Q. (2009). A novel threshold-based coherent TOA estimation for IR-UWB systems. *IEEE Transactions on Vehicular Technology, 58*(8), 4675–4681. doi:10.1109/TVT.2009.2020990

Xu, B., Shen, L., & Yan, F. (2009). Vehicular node positioning based on Doppler-shifted frequency measurement on highway. *Journal of Electronics, 26*(2), 265–269. doi:doi:10.1007/s11767-008-0110-z

Zensus, J. A., Diamond, P. J., & Napier, P. J. (1995). *Very long baseline interferometry and the VLBA*. Orem, UT: Astronomical Society of the Pacific.

ADDITIONAL READING

Abdulhamid, H., Tepe, K. E., & Abdel-Raheem, E. (2007). Performance of DSRC systems using conventional channel estimation at high velocities. *AEÜ. International Journal of Electronics and Communications, 61*(8), 556–561. doi:10.1016/j.aeue.2006.10.005

Bachrach, J., Nagpal, R., Salib, M., & Shrobe, H. E. (2004). Experimental Results for and Theoretical Analysis of a Self-Organizing Global Coordinate System for Ad Hoc Sensor Networks. *Telecommunication Systems, 26*(2-4), 213–233. doi:10.1023/B:TELS.0000029040.85449.7b

Balon, N., & Guo, J. (2006). Increasing broadcast reliability in vehicular ad hoc networks. *In Proceedings of the 3rd international workshop on Vehicular ad hoc networks* (pp. 104-105). Los Angeles, CA, USA. doi:10.1145/1161064.1161088

Benslimane, A. (2004). Optimized Dissemination of Alarm messages in Vehicular Ad-Hoc Networks (VANET). *In Proceedings High Speed Networks and Multimedia Communications HSNMC, Lecture Notes in Computer Science* (Vol. 3079/2004, pp. 655-666), Toulouse, France. doi:10.1007/978-3-540-25969-5_59

Bing Wei, W. C. Xiaoli Ding. (2008). *Inter-Vehicle Positioning System Based on Ad Hoc Wireless Network*. Paper presented at the Symposium on GPS/GNSS, Tokyo.

Blum, J. J., Eskandarian, A., & Huffman, L. J. (2004). Challenges of intervehicle Ad Hoc networks. *IEEE Transactions on Intelligent Transportation Systems, 5*(4), 347–351. doi:10.1109/TITS.2004.838218

Capkun, S., Hamdi, M., & Hubaux, J. P. (2001). GPS-free positioning in mobile ad-hoc networks. Paper presented at the System Sciences. *In Proceedings of 34th Annual Hawaii International Conference on System Sciences* (pp. 10). Proceedings of the the 34th Annual Hawaii International Conference on. doi:10.1109/HICSS.2001.927202

Chang, X. W., & Paige, C. C. (2003). An algorithm for combined code and carrier phase based GPS positioning. *BIT Numerical Mathematics, 43*(5), 915–927. doi:10.1023/B:BITN.0000014566.23457.85

Cheung, K. W., & So, H. C. (2005). A Multi-dimensional Scaling Framework for Mobile Location Using Time-of-Arrival Measurements. *IEEE Transactions on Signal Processing, 53*(1), 460–470. doi:10.1109/TSP.2004.840721

Costa, J. A., Patwari, N., & Alfred, O. Hero, I. (2006). Distributed weighted-multidimensional scaling for node localization in sensor networks. *ACM Trans. Sen. Netw., 2*(1), 39-64. doi: http://doi.acm.org/10.1145/1138127.1138129

Deleuze, A. L., Le Martret, C., Ciblat, P., & Serpedin, E. (2004). Cramer-Rao bound for channel parameters in Ultra-Wide Band based system. *In Proceedings of IEEE Workshop on Signal Processing Advances in Wireless Communications, SPAWC* (pp. 140). Lisbon. doi:10.1109/SPAWC.2004.1439220

Efatmaneshnik, M., Balaei, A. T., & Dempster, A. G. (2009). *A Channel Capacity Perspective on Cooperative Positioning Algorithms for VANET.* Paper presented at the ION GNSS, Savannah, Georgia.

Eichler, S., & Schroth, C. (2007, March). *A Multi-Layer Approach for Improving Scalability of Vehicular Ad-Hoc Networks.* Paper presented at the 4th Workshop on Mobile Ad-Hoc Netzwerke (WMAN), Bern, Switzerland.

Eren, T., Goldenberg, D. K., Whiteley, W., Yang, Y. R., Morse, A. S., & Anderson, B. D. O. (2004). Rigidity, Computation, and Randomization in Network Localization. *In Proceedings of Twenty-third Annual Joint Conference of the IEEE Computer and Communications Societies INFOCOM 2004* (Vol. 4, pp. 2673). Hong Kong. *China.* doi:doi:10.1109/INFCOM.2004.1354686

Gustafsson, F. (2009). Automotive safety systems: Replacing costly sensors with software algorithms. *IEEE Signal Processing Magazine, 26*(4), 32–47. doi:10.1109/MSP.2009.932618

Haykin, S., & Moher, M. (2007). *Introduction to Analog & Digital Communications* (2nd ed.). Hoboken, NJ: John Wiley & Sons Inc.

Hekmat, R. (2006). *Ad-hoc Networks: Fundamental Properties and Network Topologies.* Springer.

Hwang, S. S., & Speyer, J. L. (2009). Collision detection system based on differential carrier-phase Global Positioning System broadcasts. *Journal of Aircraft, 46*(6), 2077–2089. doi:10.2514/1.43517

Savvides, A., Garber, W., Adlakha, S., Moses, R., & Srivastava, M. B. (2003). On the error characteristics of multihop node localization in ad-hoc sensor networks. *In Proceedings of IPSN'03 the 2nd international conference on Information processing in sensor networks, Lecture Notes in Computer Science* (Vol. 2634, pp. 317-332). doi:10.1007/3-540-36978-3_21

Savvides, A., Han, C.-C., & Strivastava, M. B. (2001). Dynamic fine-grained localization in Ad-Hoc networks of sensors. *In Proceedings of the 7th annual international conference on Mobile computing and networking* (pp. 166-179). Rome, Italy. doi:10.1145/381677.381693

Shang, Y., Ruml, W., Zhang, Y., & Fromherz, M. (2004). Localization from connectivity in sensor networks. *IEEE Transactions on Parallel and Distributed Systems, 15*(11), 961–974. doi:10.1109/TPDS.2004.67

Tang, L., Hong, X., & Bradford, P. (2006). Secure Relative Location Determination in Vehicular Network. *In Proceedings of Mobile Ad-Hoc and Sensor Networks, Lecture Notes in Computer Science* (Vol. 4325/2006, 543-554). Hong Kong, China. doi:10.1007/11943952_46

Weiss, A. J., & Picard, J. (2008). Maximum-likelihood position estimation of network nodes using range measurements. *Signal Processing, IET, 2*(4), 394–404. doi:10.1049/iet-spr:20070161

Chapter 13
Data Dissemination in Vehicular Networks:
Challenges and Issues

Nitin Maslekar
IRSEEM-ESIGELEC, France

Mounir Boussedjra
IRSEEM-ESIGELEC, France

Houda Labiod
Telecom ParisTech, France

Joseph Mouzna
IRSEEM-ESIGELEC, France

ABSTRACT

Vehicular ad hoc networks (VANETs) represent an important component necessary to develop Intelligent Transportation Systems. Recent advances in communications systems have created significant opportunities for a wide variety of applications and services to be implement in vehicles. Most of these applications require a certain dissemination performance to work satisfactorily. Although a variety of optimizations are possible, the basic idea for any dissemination scheme is to facilitate the acquisition of the knowledge about the surrounding vehicles. However, the dynamic nature of vehicular networks makes it difficult to achieve an effective dissemination among vehicles. This chapter provides an overview on those challenges and presents various approaches to disseminate data in vehicular networks.

INTRODUCTION

Every year, millions of traffic accidents occur worldwide, resulting in many casualties and billions of dollars in direct economic costs. To combat this problem, for many years now, transportation planners have been pursuing an aggressive agenda to increase road safety. In 2001 the European Transport Policy set the goal of reducing road fatalities by 50% by 2010. Similarly, in 2008 the US DOT's Research and Innovative Technology Administration (RITA) challenged the industry to reduce traffic crashes by 90% by 2030. To achieve

DOI: 10.4018/978-1-4666-0209-0.ch013

this vision, new applications are proposed to assist drivers which will help avoid traffic collisions and increase the road safety. One technology which has drawn a lot of attention of industries and academia to establish intelligent transportation systems and to reduce traffic causalities is Vehicular Adhoc Networks (VANETs).

Simply put, VANETs can be described as wireless platforms that allow vehicles to exchange information for safety and non safety requirements. In this context, VANETs use different technologies to ensure the implementation of Intelligent Transportation System (ITS). Today, among all existing technologies, Dedicated Short Range Communications (DSRC) and IEEE 802.11p Wireless Access for Vehicular Environment (WAVE) have been approved as standards for PHY and MAC layers for vehicular networks. The IEEE 802.11p WAVE standardization process originates from the allocation of the DSRC spectrum band of 5.9 GHz with a bandwidth of 75 MHz and approximate range of 1000m. Morgan (2010) presents a detailed survey of the architecture, design, and characteristics of DSRC & WAVE standards.

The main aim of DSRC and the IEEE 802.11p WAVE standard is to define rules for low connection setup delay, fast network recognition and the differentiation of applications for normal and emergency use. They allow a high throughput communication with low delay among vehicles. This leads to efficient emergency communications. For example, in the case of accidents, an alerting message transmitted among vehicles can be faster and, thus, well-timed, rather than communications sent through an infrastructure network (such as cellular systems).

Although safety has been the prime impetus for the inception of VANETs, they also provide a promising platform for a much broader range of efficiency and comfort applications. Safety refers to applications that render protection to the people in the vehicle as well as the vehicle itself. Efficiency applications are focused on increasing the productivity of road resources by managing traffic flow and monitoring the road conditions. Lastly, comfort services provide entertainment or information to drivers and passengers which make driving more comfortable.

For each class of applications, exchanging data among vehicles is one of the key technological enablers. However, due to inherent properties and limitations of VANETs, distributing information among the vehicles is a very challenging task. The fundamental property of vehicular networks is inconsistent topology which changes rapidly due to the movement of vehicles. Under such circumstances, maintaining connectivity between vehicles is difficult. Secondly, the density of vehicles keeps on varying. In high density scenarios, if all vehicles participate in dissemination, the available bandwidth will be wasted due to redundancy of data. However, on the contrary, for low density scenarios to increase the reliability multiple copies of the same data has to maintained and exchanged when vehicles come within the communication range of each other. Thus, the dissemination technique should be scalable to compensate for varying vehicle densities.

In order to address these limitations, various works for data dissemination in VANETs have been proposed e.g. Little and Agarwal (2005), Nadeem et al. (2006), Leontiadis & Mascolo (2007a), Yu & Heijenk (2008), Maslekar et al. (2010). This chapter classifies these existing works into three major techniques, namely geocast, cluster based and opportunistic. Through this classification, an overview is provided for how each method addresses the various issues relevant in VANETs. The rest of the chapter is organised as follows. First the various requirements of data dissemination in VANETs are discussed. Then the classification of the dissemination techniques is presented, followed by the description and various works related to each method. The chapter ends with a brief summary and future perspective of how DSRC can be of advantage in the field of data dissemination.

DATA DISSEMINATION REQUIRMENTS

The requirement for disseminating information varies depending on the type of application. Some applications require high reliability where as some have stringent delay requirements. Simultaneously, since there is limited bandwidth, the dissemination protocol should not allow redundant packets so that maximum data can be disseminated over the network. According to Strassberger et al. (2009), the dissemination of messages in VANETs need to,

- **Provide low-latency communications** – In VANETs the information for safety applications have to be disseminated quickly among a group of vehicles. Hence, the disseminating protocol should have a low processing time and minimal communication delays. Also, the lifetime of information is quite small. This is especially true for efficiency applications. In such cases, if the information is not transmitted within a short period, the data loses its relevance and is reduced to simple network congestion. Hence, because data is time sensitive, it should be disseminated within a very precise time frame.

- **Provide reliable communications** - In vehicular networks, most of the information is intended for a group of vehicles. Therefore, the data is generally broadcasted by the source onto the network. It is impractical to send acknowledgment packets for such broadcast messages. Hence, the reliability of packet delivery cannot be guaranteed. Moreover, because of the dynamic nature of the network, even at MAC layer, it is not feasible to implement the RTS/CTS schemes. Hence, the issue of reliable transmission has to be handled by the disseminating protocol.

- **Keep signalling, routing, and packet forwarding overhead low** - In VANETs every vehicle transmits and receives data packets into/from a shared medium. This medium is utilized to exchange safety messages as well all other data. Thus, the disseminating protocol should limit the load resulting from beaconing and signalling so that the available bandwidth is not wasted and is accessible for the safety applications.

- **Be fair with respect to vehicular bandwidth usage** - The designed protocol should not lead to starvation for other vehicles trying to access the channel. It is also important to note that the vehicular network is designed with the specific goal of increasing road safety. Hence, messages comprising safety critical information should be able to access the channel with high priority.

- **Be able to work in low and high density scenarios** - In VANETs, the density of vehicles can vary greatly from moment to moment. In high density scenarios, if all the vehicles participate in packet dissemination, the available bandwidth is wasted due to redundancy of data. On the contrary, for low density scenarios, to increase reliability, multiple copies of the same data have to be maintained and exchanged. Thus, the dissemination technique should be scalable to varying densities of vehicles.

Thus, it is evident from the above mentioned requirements that the design of dissemination protocols has to adhere to specific requirements in terms of delay, reliability and scalability. However, in order to achieve these goals, the protocol should not lead to additional network overhead which might prohibit vehicles from accessing the channel. Hence, based on the application, a trade off has to be achieved between all the requirements which will lead to an effective dissemination technique.

DATA DISSEMINATION MODES AND TECHNIQUES

Formally, data dissemination is defined as the transportation of data to the intended recipients while satisfying certain requirements such as delay and reliability. These requirements vary, depending upon the application for which the data is to be disseminated. As such, there can be a classification hierarchy that can exist based on dissemination modes and techniques. Dissemination mode relates to how the data exchange is initiated, whereas the dissemination techniques refer to how the data exchange can take place among the vehicles.

In the literature, according to their transmission modes, the dissemination strategies can be classified into push and pull approaches. The push approach is a proactive method in which the vehicle which has any information to be shared will disseminate it without being probed. Such an approach is useful for safety and efficiency applications, e.g. traffic alerts, weather information, parking space availability, etc. Since this approach relies on broadcasting, it has the inevitable drawback of flooding the network. The pull approach is based on a request response strategy where the data exchange is initiated by request from the vehicles. Such an approach is useful for infotainment applications like web browsing or email services. This approach suffers from contention, interference and collision problems introduced due to simultaneous user requests.

Driven by the unique characteristics and functioning of applications in vehicular networks each dissemination mode can be classified into different techniques. In this chapter, the solutions described in the literature are classified into geocast, cluster or opportunistic techniques (Figure 1).

In vehicular networks most of the messages are relevant only in a specified geographic region. To perform data dissemination under this condition, geocast techniques are proposed by Leontiadis and Mascolo (2007a), Yu and Heijenk (2008). Cluster based dissemination, relates to formation of a group amongst vehicles of similar interests and then exchanging data amongst them. Some of them are defined by Little and Agarwal (2005), Souza et al. (2010). By forming clusters of similar interests, the broadcast storm is reduced and contention is also avoided. Finally, opportunistic data dissemination techniques are proposed to handle the partitioning problem in vehicular networks. Such approaches increase reliability in terms of packet delivery ratio in sparsely connected networks (Nadeem et al. (2010))

In the following sections, fundamentals of the different dissemination techniques, along with the issues and problems pertaining to each of the techniques are discussed. Also, the various existing solutions addressing them are elaborated.

Geocast Dissemination

The geographical importance of the disseminated messages has pioneered the evolution of a dissemination technique termed as geocast. Geocast is a family of network protocols based on the use of geographical positioning of vehicles for disseminating the required data. Originally, it was proposed for mobile ad hoc networks (MANETs) (Festag et al. (2009)). Since then, other variants of geocast have been proposed for other network types, such as vehicular ad hoc networks

Figure 1. Data dissemination techniques

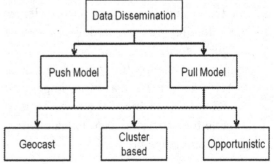

(VANETs), (Zhuang et al. (2011), Delot et al. (2010))

Vehicular communications have specific characteristics and requirements, including intermittent access to a communication infrastructure and the need for self-organization, high node mobility, and scalability. Also, the most information dissemination has importance only within particular geographical regions. These specific requirements of vehicular environments can be addressed using geocast dissemination techniques (Festag et al. (2009)).

Fundamentals of Geocast

In general, the geocast offers a best effort packet delivery between source and destination. The communication is usually dependent on the source because it selects the route through which the packet is to be delivered. Also, the source determines the destination address in terms of a geographical location or a vehicle position. However, the traditional geocast methods do not assure any service quality in terms of packet delivery delay, sequence of packet delivery, or packet loss. In principle, geocast assumes that every vehicle knows its geographical position through GPS or some other positioning system and maintains a location table to store the geographical positions of other vehicles.

The core components of any geocast protocol are beaconing, location server, and forwarding. With beacons, all vehicles periodically broadcast short packets with their IDs, current geographical positions, speeds and direction. Upon receiving a beacon, the vehicles store the information in their location table. This information helps disseminate information to the desired nodes at different geographic positions. If the position information of the nodes is not available in the local location table, the vehicle issues a location query packet to the location server. The location server maintains the position of all the nodes in the neighbourhood. Upon reception of the location reply from the server, the vehicle updates the local location table for further usage. These three concepts form the basis of various geocast protocols.

Geocast Protocols

Since geocast-based applications are concerned about information which is spatially important, the method most commonly used by these applications is based on push approach. One such method is proposed by Zhuang et al. (2011) for time and location critical (TLC) emergency messages where multiple deadlines for different locations are taken into account before delivering the message. Specifically, vehicles near the accident site (or the point-of-interest location) receive a guaranteed and detailed messages to take proper precautions immediately (e.g. slow down or change lanes), and vehicles further away have a high probability of being informed and make location-aware decisions accordingly (e.g. detour or reroute).

To achieve this goal, the authors use the scalable modulation and coding (SMC) scheme proposed by Lin et al. (2010). By redefining the bit-to-symbol mapping in the modulation constellation, SMC encodes information in function of their relative importance at the same time. With carefully designed mappings, nodes closer to the transmitter and with greater signal-to-interference and noise ratio (SINR) can decode more information of both high and low importance (i.e., more detailed information). On the other hand, nodes further away or with lower SINR decode less information from the same broadcast transmission. The SMC scheme fits very well with the TLC framework for emergency message broadcasts, as nearby vehicles (often with high SINR) need guaranteed and detailed information for quick manoeuvring, while more distant vehicles can have an early warning first and then obtain more detailed information as they approach the point-of-interest (POI). Besides using the SMC framework, the authors also obtain the size of the connected vehicle clusters accurately with a simple approach and give a close approximation to its distribution, using the inter-vehicle distances revealed by the latest highway traffic measurement studies by Bai & Krishnamachari (2009). Secondly, the authors also analyze how to use reverse traffic opportunistically to further extend the cluster size and meet the requirement of the TLC framework.

Figure 2 depicts the scenario for a time/location-critical emergency message dissemination framework. The x-axis shows the distance from the POI at 0. For example, a vehicle has an accident at time 0 and broadcasts an emergency message with SMC, which allows the message to be delivered over a short distance with more details (SDMD) and over long distance with fewer details (LDLD) at the same time. The short and long transmission distances are marked as d1 and d2, respectively. The distance d1 is greater than a distance threshold representing the reaction deadline D1, which depends on the vehicle stopping distance which is given based on the human/vehicle reaction time and travel speed. That is, any vehicles within D1 from the POI must be notified immediately to avoid a pileup. The y-axis shows the time deadline at different locations, and the slope of "reaction deadline" is equal to 1/vmax, where vmax is the speed limit.

To ensure all vehicles receive the SDMD message before the time-location dependent deadline, the POI rebroadcasts the SDMD message periodically every τ seconds, with d1 ≥ D1 + τvmax to accommodate the rebroadcast interval. In this work, the authors limit d1 > 200 m, which is reasonable under the IEEE 802.11p DSRC framework.

On the other hand, the LDLD message should be rebroadcast further to reach as many vehicles as possible. In Figure 2, vehicle b receives both the SDMD and LDLD messages, and c receives only the LDLD message from the POI. The vehicle c will rebroadcast the LDLD message after a very small delay whose value is more than the POI's rebroadcast interval τ, assuming all vehicles know their location and all messages contain location information. The same process repeats at vehicle d. However, when d rebroadcasts, the following vehicle g in the same direction is not close enough (i.e., the inter-vehicle distance is beyond d2), but e in the opposite direction is in the transmission range of d. Therefore, d will broadcast it to e which, in turn, will rebroadcast the message to reach f. The opportunistic use of reverse traffic effectively extends the range of LDLD messages to reach more vehicles in the forward direction, when possible and necessary.

The SMC scheme, allows messages of different importance to be broadcasted to different distances

Figure 2. Time-location critical emergency message dissemination scenario

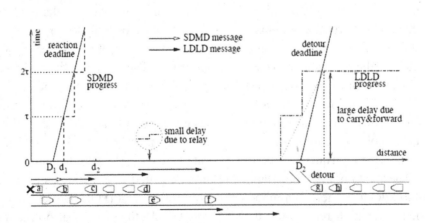

simultaneously. This unique feature fits well with the requirement of instant collision avoidance and advanced travel planning in VANETs. However, it still has the limitation related to the density of vehicles. In sparsely populated scenarios the message will experience very high delays, making the message irrelevant for more distant vehicles.

Delot et al. (2010) present a system for data sharing in vehicular networks called Vehicular Event Sharing with a mobile Peer-to-peer Architecture (VESPA). In this system, a technique based on the concept of Encounter Probability is proposed for vehicles to share information using vehicle-to-vehicle communications. The objective is to facilitate the dissemination of information between vehicles when they meet each other, taking into account the relevance of the data to the drivers.

In this work the authors classify inter-vehicle network events in four categories: stationary non-direction-dependent events, stationary direction dependent events, mobile non-direction-dependent events, and mobile direction-dependent events. According to this classification, direction-dependent events are events that are not relevant for all nearby vehicles, but only for the vehicles travelling in a particular direction towards the event. On the other hand, mobile events are events whose locations change with respect to time. For example, available parking spaces correspond to stationary non-direction-dependent events, since they are static and may interest all vehicles close to that resource independently of their direction of movement. A warning about an accident is a stationary direction-dependent event because its location is fixed and only those vehicles that are expected to encounter the accident will find the message relevant, not the vehicles close to the accident but moving in the opposite direction. This classification, according to mobility and direction features enables the computation of the Encounter Probability (EP).

The Encounter Probability is based on the following four elements:

- The minimal geographical distance between the vehicle and the event over time (Δd).
- The difference between the current time and the time when the vehicle will be closest to the event (Δt).
- The difference between the time when the event is generated and the moment when the vehicle will be closest to the event (Δg).
- The angle between the direction vector of the vehicle and the direction vector of the event (represented by a co-linearity coefficient c).

Based on these parameters EP is given as

$$EP = \frac{100}{\propto *\Delta d + \beta * \Delta t + \gamma * \Delta g + \zeta * c + 1}$$

where $\propto, \beta, \gamma \; and \; \zeta$ are penalty coefficients with non-negative values which are used to balance the relative importance of the Δd, Δt, Δg, and c values. The greater the coefficient, the more penalized the associated valued is when computing the Encounter Probability. Thus, the greater is the α value, the shorter is the spatial range where the event is relevant; β and γ are used to consider only the most recent information and the information about events that will be encountered quickly; finally, ζ is used to weigh the importance of the co-linearity of the direction vectors for direction-dependent events.

The use of the EP ensures that the information about an event is maintained, during the dissemination phase, close enough to the source to be relevant. For instance, the information about an available parking space would not be interesting for persons driving several kilometres away from it. Therefore, in the proposed dissemination solution, each time a vehicle receives a message; it computes the EP for the corresponding event. If the value obtained is above a certain threshold, it has to rebroadcast the message. Otherwise, it does not consider the message. Thus, while the event is considered relevant by a vehicle in a particular area, it is relayed to the neighbouring vehicles, and so on. Moreover, the EP also avoids the dissemination of obsolete events. The information diffused for events such as a parking space or emergency braking is only relevant for a short period of time. For events with a longer lifetime (e.g., an accident), it is possible to adapt the value of the corresponding penalty coefficient c in order not to penalize the EP too much with the age of the event.

The analysis shows the usefulness of the Encounter Probability to estimate the relevance of an event which helps reduce the over head in the system (Figure 3). It also shows that the performance of the protocol remains the same in both dense and sparse scenarios. Hence, the drivers can receive the relevant events well in advance without adding an extra burden on the dissemination protocol.

In other various works, Sormani and Turconi (2006) define a message propagation function which encodes the data with the information about both the target areas and preferred routes, which helps to increase the packet delivery ratio. This is achieved because the function allows vehicles to route the messages through zones characterized by a sufficiently high density of vehicles, thereby increasing their chances of reaching their intended destinations. However, this reliability comes at a cost of overhead in terms of route calculation. Moreover, the vehicular networks are plagued with frequent topology changes; hence, selecting an appropriate route is not an easy task for the propagation function.

Leontiadis and Mascolo (2007a) argue that to achieve reliable dissemination in vehicular networks, a geographical and delay tolerant approach is required. In their work, instead of opting for a function based on target areas, they define a function which selects a route based on minimum estimated time of delivery for the packet. Here, each vehicle periodically broadcasts the destinations region of the packet. The one-hop neighbours calculate the Minimum Estimated Time of Delivery (METD) required for delivering this packet to the destination region and send this value back to the enquiring vehicle. Once the METD value is received by the enquiring vehicle, it either keeps the packet (if it has the lowest METD) or forwards it to the neighbour with the lowest value. This process is repeated until the packet arrives to its destination. The results show that the packets are disseminated reliably with a low delay to the required destination. However, the performance of this algorithm improves with the increase in the

Figure 3. Number of messages disseminated in dense and sparse scenarios

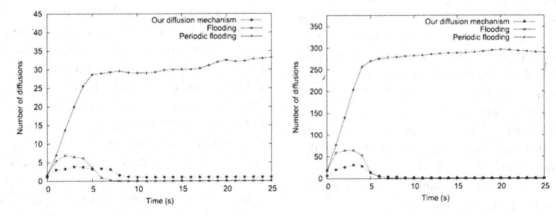

density of vehicles, hence making it vulnerable to sparse network scenarios.

An abiding geocast protocol for disseminating warning message is defined by Yu and Heijenk (2008). This algorithm assumes that only one vehicle will be responsible for detecting the incident and inform the other vehicles in the vicinity. To improve the system efficiency and to overcome fragmentation in the network, the vehicles travelling in the opposite direction are used as relays. In this system vehicles on a stretch of road carry safety messages to vehicles driving in the opposite direction, so as to warn them regarding a dangerous situation ahead. The objective is to disseminate the message to all relevant vehicles before they reach the warning line employing the minimum number of broadcasts. Vehicles moving in the opposite direction are preferred as relays to reduce broadcast overhead. This strategy also helps in message delivery for upstream traffic. However, there is only one initiator of the message and rest all act as relays, making it application specific and vulnerable to single point failure. Also, it does not account for the density of vehicles. Consequently, if there are few or no vehicles travelling in the opposite direction, the information will not be disseminated in a wider area.

Wischhof et al. (2005) discuss a segment oriented data abstraction and dissemination protocol (SODAD). SODAD is based on a subdivision of longer roads into segments. These segments represent a geographic region which are predefined and are fixed with a unique ID. Locally, individual measurements such as speed and/or direction are exchanged between the vehicles, so that a typical vehicle will be able to collect multiple samples of the required information from its immediate vicinity. For disseminating information to further away network areas, vehicles combine the samples that they have for the road segment they are currently driving on. Here, by making use of the defined segments the dissemination area is restricted by position of the sender but within the segment it

still follows a broadcast approach thus wasting the bandwidth.

Shibata et al. (2006) describe a geocast dissemination method where bandwidth utilization is limited by prioritizing the data to be sent. In their approach, the authors divide the given map of a locality into different regions and then compute the density of vehicles in each region. For an efficient convergence of traffic information, the data related to a dense region is propagated among the vehicles with a higher priority. This algorithm facilitates fast relaying of traffic jam information. This is allowed because the traffic information is computed for smaller regions and then aggregated together. However, as with any priority based algorithms, this protocol also suffers from starvation of low priority data.

From the presented geocast techniques it is evident that geocast methods restrict the data to a particular geographic region. This helps in increasing the overall knowledge percentage in the network and also to utilize the available bandwidth in an effective way. Such approaches render a low latency performance; hence they are effective for safety and efficiency applications. It also helps to quicken the transmission of messages in larger areas. They allow for faster convergence of the information making it suitable for efficiency and safety applications. Thus, geocast with its optimizations and extensions provide a strong technical basis to bring VANETs into the real world.

Cluster Based Dissemination

Cluster based dissemination relates to formation of a group among vehicles of similar interests and then exchanging data among them. According to (Fan et. al (2008)) clustering provides three basic benefits: (1) spatial reuse of resources, (2) emergence of a virtual backbone, 3) improved network stability and scalability from the viewpoint of a regular member. By forming clusters of similar interests, the broadcast storm is reduced and thus reduces MAC layer collisions. Since clustering emerges as a backbone network it presents several advantages like providing path for exchanging information at the network layer as well (Hou and Tsai (2001)). In addition to this, clustering also helps in faster aggregation of topology information since the number of vehicles of a cluster is smaller than the number of vehicles of the entire network. Therefore, each vehicle only needs to store a fraction of the total network routing information (Er and Seah (2004).)

Fundamentals of Clustering

The purpose of a clustering algorithm is to produce and maintain a connected cluster which will ascertain a better dissemination of the data. In most clustering techniques vehicles are selected to play different roles. In general, three types of vehicles are defined: Ordinary vehicles, Gateway vehicles and Clusterheads.

Ordinary vehicles are members of a cluster which do not have neighbours belonging to a different cluster. Gateways are vehicles in a non-clusterhead state located at the periphery of a cluster. These types of vehicles are called gateways because they are able to listen to transmissions from another vehicle which is in a different cluster. To accomplish this, a gateway must have at least one neighbour that is a member of another cluster. In any clustering technique the burden of dissemination is on a vehicle called the clusterhead. To exchange information, the clusterheads of different clusters communicate directly or through gateway vehicles. Since clusterheads must perform extra work with respect to ordinary vehicles, they can easily become a single point of failure within a cluster. For this reason, the clusterhead election process should consider for the clusterhead role, those vehicles with a higher degree of relative stability.

Clustering Protocols

Though clustering provides a lot of advantages in terms of being a back bone network, the highly dynamic topology of VANETS presents challenges for cluster formation and reconfiguration, thus increasing cluster instability. Therefore, any clustering algorithm designed for VANETs must strive to maintain cluster stability for as long as possible, otherwise the frequent disconnections will result in degraded performance. As described by Souza et al. (2010), among the basic clustering techniques, namely Lowest ID, Highest degree and Beacon-Based, the first two are inconvenient in vehicular environments. Lowest and Highest degree assumes that one-hop neighbour information is already available and does not consider vehicle connectivity during cluster formation. Also, the cluster head election policy is based on the vehicle ID. In the lowest-ID algorithm, vehicle with the lowest ID within its closed neighbourhood is selected as a cluster-head. On the contrary, in the highest degree algorithm, vehicle with the highest degree in its closed neighbourhood is selected. Hence, most of the techniques in VANETs are beacon based, where flexibility is provided for cluster formation and election of the clusterhead.

In the literature, it is found that such approaches are mostly based on the push model. One such model is proposed by Little and Agarwal (2005), which is an extension of the algorithm proposed for MANETs by Basu et al. (2001). Similar to the initial proposal in the extended version, clusters are formed based on mobility metrics which include the speed and the direction of the vehicle and the signal power detected at the receiving vehicles on the same directed pathway. The received signal strength (RSS) is used as a criteria to assign weights to vehicles. A vehicle with the highest RSS is assigned the highest weight and is elected as the clusterhead. Although this protocol helps in forming stable clusters, it does not consider the losses prevalent in the wireless channel. In practical scenarios the effects of multipath fading are bound to affect the cluster formation method and, thus, the stability

The effects of multipath fading are taken into account in the density based clustering algorithm described by Kuklinski and Wolny (2009). In this approach, cluster formation is based on the weight metric which takes into consideration the radio link quality and the traffic conditions like vehicle density. Results show improved performance in terms of stability as compared to the protocol mentioned in Little and Agarwal (2005).

Souza et al. (2010) present a new aggregate local mobility (ALM) clustering algorithm. In this mechanism, instead of received signal strength, the position of the vehicle is used to calculate the weight associated with it. The weight is assigned to the vehicle based on the relative local mobility. Thus, the vehicle with least relative mobility is assigned the highest weight. This method helps in better election of the cluster head. This algorithm is beacon based and its goal is to prolong the cluster lifetime in VANETs. It performs better in terms of stability as compared to the method proposed by Kuklinski and Wolny (2009). However, since the vehicles are highly dynamic in nature, the position of the vehicles changes very fast. Due to this, the weights are recomputed frequently, which may induce a computational overhead in calculating the weight associated with the vehicles.

Another weight-based clustering method suitable for highway scenarios is proposed by Daeinabi et al. (2010). The main contributions of this work are the proposal of three algorithms. The first being vehicular clustering based on a weighted (VWCA) technique that uses different parameters like the direction, distrust, entropy and the transmission range to select cluster heads so that the stability, connectivity, and security performances of VANET can be improved. Secondly, the authors design an adaptive allocation of transmission range (AATR) technique that uses hello messages and considers the density of traffic around vehicles. This technique guarantees connectivity and ensures that other vehicles can receive messages.

Moreover, AATR is useful in assigning weights to vehicles which helps select the cluster head. Lastly, VWCA defines an algorithm to monitor behaviour of vehicles in the network in order detect abnormal vehicles in the system.

In VWCA, firstly, each vehicle announces itself as a clusterhead by putting its own ID in a beacon. After receiving beacons from its neighbours, each vehicle has complete information about its current neighbours, and it can decide whether to change its current clusterhead status or not. For this purpose, each vehicle executes VWCA in order to select their clusterheads. The VWCA chooses its required parameters in five steps. At first, each vehicle determines its neighbourhood. For this purpose, each vehicle broadcasts a hello message. Each hello message has the Node ID, speed, position, distrust value of the vehicle, and one lifetime. When a vehicle receives hello messages from other vehicles, it can create its neighbourhood list. If a vehicle cannot find any neighbours in its transmission range, it introduces itself as a clusterhead. However, a cluster with one vehicle reduces connectivity in network. Hence, to prevent this eventuality, a vehicle can increase its transmission range dynamically, based on the density of vehicles, to find its appropriate neighbours. Hence, allowing for greater network connectivity. With respect to the DSRC standard, the increased transmission range value should be lower than or equal to 1000 m. Once the vehicles in the neighbourhood are detected, each vehicle assigns priority to the vehicles in the neighbourhood list based on their distrust values. Along with the priority, based on the position information the direction of each vehicle is computed. The authors also adopt the WCA (Wang and Bao, 2007) technique to assign entropy to each vehicle.

After obtaining enough information about the network and creating its neighbourhood tables, vehicle V can calculate its weighted sum. Parameters considered in VWCA to assign weights are as follows:

1. $M_{u,v}$: Direction measure of vehicle V that means either vehicle u is nearing V or u is increasing its distance from V
2. T_d: distrust value of vehicle V.
3. H_v: Entropy value of vehicle V.
4. D_v: Number of neighbours of vehicle V based on dynamic transmission range.

Based on these parameters, the weighted sum of vehicle V is calculated as

$$Wv = w1(Td) + w2(-Hv) + w3(-Dv) + w4(-Mu, v)$$

Where, w1, w2, w3, and w4 are the corresponding weighing factors. Here, the authors assume that w1, w2, w3, w4 > 0 and w1+w2+w3+w4=1. The Parameter W_v is exchanged among neighbourhood vehicles and then the vehicle with the minimum W_v in neighbourhood table is chosen to be the cluster-head. This is because VWCA is based on WCA and the vehicle with the minimum weighted sum is selected as the clusterhead in WCA (Chatterjee et al. (2002)). If there are two or more vehicles with the same W_v, a vehicle with higher entropy or lower distrust value is elected as the cluster head amongst the vehicles.

The performance analysis in Figure 4 shows that VWCA has a better average membership time and CH duration compared to the other clustering techniques. This is because VWCA is based on weights and the vehicle with the minimum weighted sum is selected as the cluster head. However, the graphs show a decline in performance when the density of vehicles increases. This is because by increasing the number of vehicles, the number of cluster heads goes up. Therefore, average CH duration decreases. Moreover, by increasing the number of cluster heads, the probability of leaving the old cluster and joining to a new cluster increases for a member. Therefore, average membership duration reduces.

The performance of the clustering algorithm is better once the clusters are in place. However, the authors do not mention the time required to form a cluster and to stabilize it. This is particularly important when the method is used to deploy safety and efficiency applications.

Ros et al. (2010) describe an acknowledgement-based broadcast protocol (ABSM) to disseminate information in VANETs. In this protocol the beacon messages, along with the position information, also contain the acknowledgments for the circulated broadcast messages. Piggybacking the acknowledgements along with the beacons helps to achieve high reliability within the network. Secondly, to minimize the total

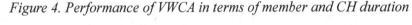

Figure 4. Performance of VWCA in terms of member and CH duration

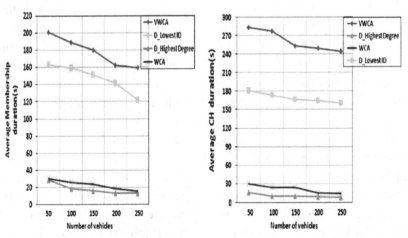

number of retransmissions, a car that receives a broadcast message does not retransmit it immediately. Instead, it waits to check if retransmissions from other neighbours already cover its whole neighbourhood. To acquire 1-hop neighbourhood position information, periodic beacons contain the position of the sender. Such information suffices to compute a cluster called a connected dominating set (CDS).

As mentioned before, beacons also include identifiers of the recently received broadcast messages, which serve as acknowledgments of reception. This way, nodes can check whether all their neighbours successfully receive a message. If this is not the case, a retransmission is scheduled upon the expiry of timeout duration. Hence, the use of acknowledgments makes the protocol more robust to transmission failures while, at the same time, saves redundant retransmissions. For example, as shown in Figure 5, vehicle *a* generates a broadcast message which is first buffered by *a*, and then received by *b, c, d*. Receivers set up a waiting timeout which is shorter if the vehicle belongs to the computed CDS. If *d* is in the CDS, it retransmits first. Vehicles *b* and *c* cancel their retransmission because all their neighbours have been covered by *d's* forwarding. Also, vehicles *e* and *f* receive the message. However, none of them have uncovered neighbours, so the retransmission does not take place.

Over a period of time, vehicle *a* speeds up and overtakes vehicles *b* − *f*. In the case of normal broadcasts, new transmissions would occur because new neighbours *e* and *f* must be covered by *a* and vice versa. However, they are redundant because all the vehicles already received the mes-

sage. The proposed protocol saves these redundant transmissions because the beacons contain the acknowledgment of the message. Consequently, the message is not rebroadcast to the newly discovered neighbours.

ABSM automatically adjusts its behaviour without keeping track of the degree of mobility sensed by the vehicle. Each node independently decides whether or not to forward a received broadcast message. This decision is solely based on the local information that vehicles acquire from their neighbourhood by means of periodic beacon messages. This guarantees ultimate scalability regardless of the size of the VANET. The set of parameters in ABSM is minimal and consists only of few natural choices. Temporary disconnection incurs delivery delay to any protocol. Although the described protocol inherently uses the store-carry-forward paradigm, ABSM does not incur large delivery latencies. Nodes connected to the source will receive the message with small delay, due to propagation via CDS. Under realistic IEEE 802.11p models, ABSM is shown to outperform the traditional broadcast approaches in VANETs. However, the case of simultaneous broadcast has not been addressed in the presented solution.

A position-based clustering technique is proposed by Wang et al. (2008), where the cluster structure is determined by the geographic position of the vehicle and the clusterhead is elected, based on the priorities associated with each vehicle. This priority value validates the time period for existence of a vehicle on the road. A hash function, based on the estimated travel time of the vehicle to the destination, is used to generate this priority for the vehicle. Thus, a hash value representing a

Figure 5. Vehicular scenario for ASBM

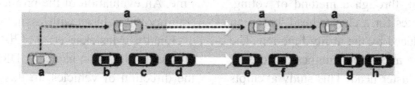

higher value indicates a longer existence for vehicles in the network. The stability of the system is improved by electing the vehicles having a longer trip on the road as the clusterheads. Although this solution provides a stable cluster structure, its performance has not been tested in sparse and jammed traffic conditions, which are very frequent in traffic scenarios. A similar approach is defined by Jerbi et al. (2007), where a cluster of vehicles is formed based on their position on the road. This algorithm does not address cluster maintenance or the header election scheme, making its performance vulnerable to these factors. Another position based clustering algorithm is proposed by Salhi et al. (2007). This is a cross layer protocol, based on hierarchical and geographical data collection and its dissemination mechanism. The cluster formation in this protocol is based on the division of the road segment. The size of this segment is equal to the radio range of the infrastructure. The infrastructures are spread along the road without gaps. Each segment is further divided into equal parts which represent the size of the cluster. In this way, the authors account for the position of the vehicles at a particular segment instead of the individual positions. Though such approach helps in attaining stability, the performance of the algorithm is however affected based on the availability of the infrastructure.

A variation of the position-based approach is described by Fan et al. (2005). Here a utility-based cluster formation technique is used. The utility function uses the closest position and closest velocity to a threshold as a parameter. This threshold is computed based on the previously available traffic statistics which defines the average velocity among the vehicles. A status message which contains the position and the velocity is periodically sent by all the neighbouring vehicles. After receiving this information, through a method of voting, each vehicle votes for a cluster head, based on the results produced by the utility function. The vehicle with the maximum number of votes is elected as the cluster head. This study attempts

to enhance the classical clustering algorithms by taking into consideration the characteristics of VANETs. However, it still applies many fixed weight parameters that fail to adapt to traffic dynamics. For example, the cluster formation interval is fixed, which implies a synchronous formation of clusters. This does not allow for effective cluster reorganization.

A modified version of the MANET Distributed and Mobility Adaptive Clustering (DMAC) algorithm (Basagni (1999)) is proposed for VANETs by Wolny.G (2008). The modified algorithm can adapt to the changes in the network topology caused by the mobility of the vehicles. As with the previous algorithms like Wag et al., a generic weight is allocated to each vehicle. However, this weight is not just based on the position, but on any set of vehicle parameters like connectivity, mobility, etc. The vehicle with the highest weight is elected as the cluster head among the neighbours. The main idea here is to avoid re-clustering when vehicles move in different directions. Instead of any lower level service that would be responsible to link creations, a hello message is periodically exchanged between the vehicles. This is used to link creations and predict the freshness of the vehicle information as well as the time for which the vehicles might be in contact with the cluster head. The results of the analysis show that the proposed modification to DMAC renders stability of the clusters in VANET scenarios. However, compared to the original proposal, the modifications to the DMAC algorithm increases network overhead.

Fan et al. (2008) describe a theoretical analysis of directional based clustering algorithm. The clusters in this algorithm are based on the following mobility metrics (a) moving direction (b) leadership duration and (c) projected distance variation of all the neighbouring vehicles over time. An evaluation of the protocol showed the stability of the cluster with less network overhead.

Finally, Maslekar et al. (2010) propose a clustering algorithm named C-DRIVE, based on the direction of vehicles. In this approach, the clusters are formed based on the direction that a vehicle takes after crossing an intersection. Using this information, C-DRIVE forms clusters in a particular lane. Within each cluster, it is the responsibility of the elected cluster head (CH), which is, the first vehicle travelling in a particular direction, to maintain the cluster and compute vehicle density. During cluster formation, not all information exchanged may be useful in the formation of the clusters. In order to overcome this, in C-DRIVE, a direction-based propagation function is proposed. Results show that C-DRIVE helps reduce the number of broadcasts, thus enabling better channel utilization. From the point of view of efficiency, it is found that the number of overhead during cluster formation is considerably less during cluster formation, leading to an effective formation of the cluster among the vehicles approaching the intersection.

From the presented solutions it is apparent that stability is one of the major factors to be considered in designing the clustering algorithm for vehicular environments. If stability cannot be guaranteed in clustering algorithm, it is vulnerable for safety and efficiency applications in urban environments. Moreover, the application requirement influences the clustering technique and hence based on the application requirement the dissemination protocol can be designed for low latency, overhead, etc.

Opportunistic Dissemination

At the onset, a low penetration ratio is one of the early challenges that VANET will have to handle. VANETs are not only highly dynamic, but they are highly partitioned as well. Hence, continuous connectivity may not be assumed in any protocol design. To allow for long-range data dissemination, concepts from delay-tolerant networking can be applied in vehicular networks (Vasilakos (2011)). In particular, store-and-forward approaches for information transport are a common approach for VANET dissemination protocols. In this approach, vehicles do not immediately forward messages, but carry the information along with them until they come in contact with other vehicles. When opportunities arise, e.g., meeting other vehicles, the information is transmitted to forward it further. In the simplest case, it is spread epidemically by beaconing, but more elaborate schemes have also been discussed (Leontiadis and Mascolo(2007b)).

Fundamentals of Opportunistic Dissemination

The opportunistic dissemination paradigm provides connectivity among vehicles in partitioned wireless networks though opportunistic contacts between vehicles. The opportunistic class exploits both the temporal diversity and the broadcast nature of the wireless propagation to provide connectivity in the presence of hostile wireless propagation conditions. Opportunistic dissemination is usually asynchronous with an emphasis on reliable information dissemination. Communications typically happen when two vehicles are within communication range and are always a one-hop communication. The core components of the opportunistic approach are:

- **Mobile Vehicle** generates the data which is to be disseminated. In this case, the vehicle is the source of information and is responsible for delivering the data to the destination through opportunistic contacts.
- **Opportunistic Network Vehicle** carries the information which is to be disseminated. It acts as the forwarder and uses a data sharing protocol (Leburn et al. (2005)) for data dissemination. The data sharing protocol uses vehicle discovery and one-hop message exchange to disseminate the data.
- **Information Sprinkler** is a fixed opportunistic network vehicle within the network. It is a device placed at a dedicated loca-

tion, thus it is not mobile. The Information Sprinkler uses the same data sharing protocol as other opportunistic network vehicles.

These three core components are necessary for any opportunistic approach. Some of the major research works for opportunistic dissemination in VANETs are discussed in the following section.

Opportunistic Protocols

Leburn et al. (2005) propose a knowledge-based opportunistic approach. This approach is based on the relative velocity of the closest vehicle in terms of its predicted angle and the packet is forwarded to that particular vehicle. This vehicle acts as an opportunistic contact to effectively forward the data. Though the delay is compared more to a traditional broadcast scheme, a vast improvement is observed in the channel utilization and packet delivery ratio. However, in this work, the destination vehicle is considered to be static, which is not practical in vehicular networks.

Another opportunistic technique using the direction vehicles travel (same, opposite or bi-direction) is presented by Nadeem et al. (2006). Depending on its direction, the vehicle may either forward the packet or store it until it encounters a vehicle. Depending on the model, a vehicle will opportunistically transmit the packet when it comes in contact with a vehicle travelling in either the same or opposite direction. Along with packet reliability, this model is validated for latency time and knowledge percentage. Analyses show that opposite direction and bi-directional models have better knowledge than the same-direction model. The bi-directional model shows better knowledge percentage than the opposite direction models, but has a higher error rate. Hence it is observed that, in this algorithm, the opposite direction model used for dissemination of the data shows an improved performance in many scenarios. Although there is significant improvement in dissemination performance in terms of reliability, in each model

all cars participate in the broadcast process which increases bandwidth consumption.

An opportunistic pull approach based on a message's spatio-temporal importance is discussed by Leontiadis and Mascolo (2007b). This protocol dispatches the data to the subscribers which are the vehicles interested in receiving the data. Furthermore, it uses opportunistic cache and replay mechanisms to deliver the notifications with high reliability to the new subscribers in the area throughout the interval during which the data is valid. The authors state that the mobility patterns of the vehicles and their subscriptions are actually linked. They take advantage of this observation to efficiently disseminate events only in areas where this is relevant i.e., in areas where there are hosts that are interested in receiving the notification to which they have subscribed. Simulation results indicate that this algorithm can efficiently deliver the notification in the area. Finally, this algorithm can achieve an almost 100% delivery ratio with fewer overhead than epidemic algorithms that follows a normal broadcast approach (Nekovee.M (2009).) because it a) disseminates the notification mainly to subscribers b) informs multiple subscribers per broadcast and c) has less polling overhead.

One of the recent works on opportunistic approach is mentioned by Ding and Xiao (2010), where static nodes at the intersections are used as relays to improve the performance in terms of data delivery. The core concept of this work revolves around the deployment of static nodes at the intersections which will store the packet at the intersection until the optimal path is available. In this context the optimal path is defined as the path with minimum data delivery delay. As illustrated in Figure 6 a path may not be available at the moment when a packet reaches an intersection, hence, under such scenarios, a static node at each intersection can assist in the packet delivery by storing the packet until the shortest delay path becomes available.

For example, in Figure 6, suppose a packet is sent from A to a remote location. Once the packet is relayed from A to B, B needs to determine the next vehicle to forward the packet to. At the intersection, using the algorithm, the shortest delay path to deliver the packet is computed to be northward. However, there is no vehicle within the communication range of B that can deliver the packet along that direction. Thus, B relays the packet to the static node. The static node stores the packet and forwards it to C when it passes the intersection and goes in a northward direction. The importance of the static node can be noted from the fact that if it were not present, the packet would have been carried by B eastward, which could have led to a much longer packet-delivery path. To accomplish this procedure of communication, authors propose a dissemination protocol which consists of three modules: static-node assisted routing (SNAR), link delay update (LDU), and multipath data dissemination (MPDD).

SNAR handles packet-delivery services by relaying the packets through the intermediate vehicles along the road and static nodes at intersections. It is composed of three modes: vehicle in-road mode, vehicle intersection mode, and static node mode. When a data packet is in a vehicle that is not within wireless transmission of the static node, the SNAR stack on the vehicle works in the vehicle in-road mode. In this mode, the packet will be relayed to other vehicles towards the next intersection. When a data packet is in a vehicle that reaches within the wireless communication range of the static node, the SNAR stack on the vehicle works in the vehicle intersection mode. In this mode, the packet may be delivered to another vehicle in the intersection area, delivered to the static node, or still carried by the vehicle instead of being delivered. The SNAR stack on the static node works in the static-node mode. In this mode it will forward the packet to an appropriate vehicle only if available, or else it will store it in its buffer. In static mode, the node will deliver the packet along the optimal path when there are vehicles available to carry the packet in that direction. Figure 7 shows the state-transition diagram of the static-node mode.

The static node knows its neighbouring vehicles by listening to their periodic beacon messages. Upon arrival of new packets, SNAR enters the scanning state. It looks for the vehicles that can carry the packet along the optimal path in its neighbour set. If there are such vehicles, it will deliver the packet to the vehicle that is farthest in the optimal direction. Otherwise, it will enter the waiting state and return to the scanning state when the neighbour set gets updated because of newly entering vehicles. If the buffer at the vehicle becomes full, it enters the buffer management state and starts eliminating the packets according to

Figure 6. Static node assisted routing in VANETs

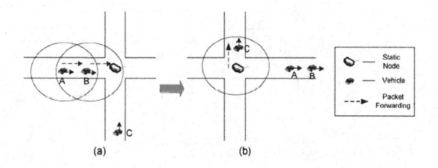

Figure 7. State transition diagram for intersection mode

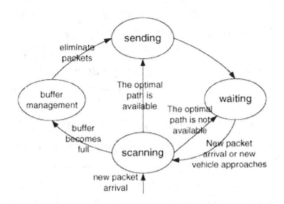

FCFS algorithm. Then it attempts to send the newly arrived packet onto the network.

To better estimate the delay of forwarding packets along each road, the static nodes are designed to measure the packet-forwarding delay and propagate the link delay information. Therefore, the routing decision in each static node can adapt to the changing vehicle densities. The link delay is estimated by the LDU module by piggybacking timestamp information in the data packets between two static nodes. Once the data arrives at the static node for further delivery, it records the current time stamp and then computes the delay. To further decrease the packet-delivery delay without an exponential increase in the protocol overhead, a multipath routing algorithm is implemented at the MPDD module. While this is going on, a priority vector is implemented to help send the packet through the best and second best path.

The performance analysis (Figure 8) shows that SADV works better than VADD in terms of delay and with acceptable convergence of the LDU and moderate network overhead. Multihop data dissemination technique with the use of static nodes at the intersection improves packet delivery in terms of delay.

Furthermore, intelligent partial deployment strategies of static nodes presented by the authors allows for a more generalised outlook to the solution. However, the buffer capacity at the static nodes is not addressed properly. If the buffers are

Figure 8. Performance of SADV in terms of mean delay, optimal path delay, and data size

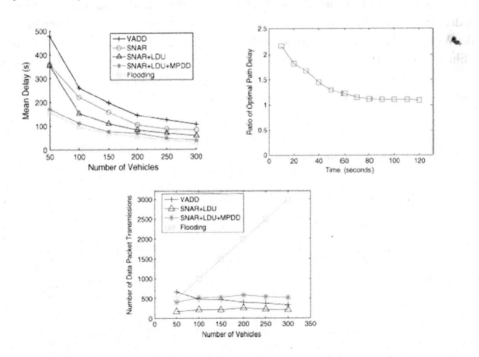

full, the nodes will drop the packets which will affect the reliability of the dissemination technique. The computation of the delay is dependent on the distribution of the vehicles on the road; consequently, the delay incurred in the packet delivery is highly dependent on the mobility and arrivals of the vehicles for a given direction. In the presented scenario, the arrival rate is assumed to be constant, which is not true in practical scenarios. Also, for a particular direction, the volume of vehicles dynamically varies at the intersection and is not considered in the simulations. Due to varying vehicular traffic flow, there is a possibility of starvation for the packets present at the static nodes. The authors do not explain any counter measures to handle this. Hence, in spite of the gains attained by the proposed protocol, there is a scope for improvement in the solution to make it deployable in practical scenarios.

An opportunistic approach for comfort applications is proposed by Mina and Faramarz (2011) to disseminate a large amount of commercial data in urban areas from roadside units. In this work, the data traffic is the advertisement which is generated by roadside advertising units (RSAU). Each RSAU is equipped with a short range wireless broadcast point which broadcasts the advertisements to the vehicles (r2v). Vehicles collect these data when they are travelling towards the RSAU and distribute the collected data when they are moving away from them. To achieve this, the authors extend the DMRC approach proposed by Sardari et al. (2009), where coding schemes

referred as rateless codes are utilised for reliable and efficient data dissemination in VANETs. In this strategy, each RSAU packages its message into smaller data packets of the same size. These packets are then encoded into a set of a slightly larger size using rateless coding. Then the RSAU broadcasts the set of encoded packets.

Based on the role of the vehicles, they are divided in two groups: collectors and carriers. Collector vehicles approaching to the specific RSAU collect the packets and decode them to obtain the message of the RSAU. Once they cross the RSAU, collector vehicles apply rateless coding on the received message and from this point, they act as carriers and keep packets in their buffer and broadcast them periodically. In this scheme, each carrier node can potentially carry packets from several RSAUs simultaneously. Thus, they can act as carriers and collectors for different RSAUs at the same time. In the DMRC scheme, the basic network model is considered with RSAUs placed uniformly along the road at distance d from each other. The space between two consecutive RASUs is named as the segment with φ_i representing the ith source on the road. If a vehicle is located in j^{th} segment from source φ_i, then it is in segment φ_{ij}.

The main performance metric considered is $P_{success}$, which is the probability that a random message is generated at a (random) source φ_i available at node v before it enters the communication range of φ_i. Figure 9 shows the success of the protocol at varying velocities (v) and inter arrival rate (λ).

Figure 9. $P_{success}$ for different velocity and λ

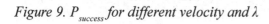

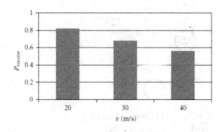
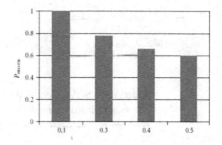

It is obvious that the performance is better at lower velocities and at higher arrival rates. However, the knowledge percentage at a received node might deteriorate when the arrival rate is further lowered, hence making the protocol less significant in sparse and disconnected networks. Also, it is assumed that the RSU are deployed uniformly along the road, which is not practical in vehicular networks. Nevertheless, the concept can be utilised for many other comfort applications in vehicular networks where the delay in packet delivery will not affect the performance.

One opportunistic approach is described by Huang et al. (2010), where an intelligent information dissemination scheme for heterogeneous vehicular networks to deliver real-time services over an IP-based network is defined. This approach assures interoperability, roaming, and end-to-end session management. The core idea of this work is to implement an adaptive vehicle infotainment system, in which cache relay nodes are intelligently determined to cache the infotainment data streams and distribute them to different peers through a service-oriented architecture. In the presented algorithm, when a node asks for a service, it will inquire the management servers to provide the cache relay node list for it. The management servers, which include a cluster head, local cache relay node management server, and global cache relay node management server, provide the information about the relay based on the demand of the request.

Once the requestor node acquires the relay list, it employs a cache relay node determination algorithm to determine the appropriate content server and cache relay nodes. After the content server and cache relay nodes are chosen, the request node will request the content server to provide the requested service. A bandwidth resource reserving mechanism is used in this work to reserve bandwidth resource at each base station in order to reduce the dropping probability. After the requestor has started to receive the infotainment data streams, this requestor will be evaluated whether it is suitable to serve as a cache relay node for other requestors in the HVN by using the cache node suitability decision algorithm.

As shown in Figure 10, when the requestor requests a service, the management servers first provide the list of the candidate cache relay nodes, and the request node sends the query messages to all the cache relay nodes on the list. After receiving the confirmation messages from the candidate cache relay nodes, the request node determines

Figure 10. Paths of querying message and receiving data in an example network

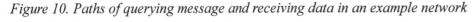

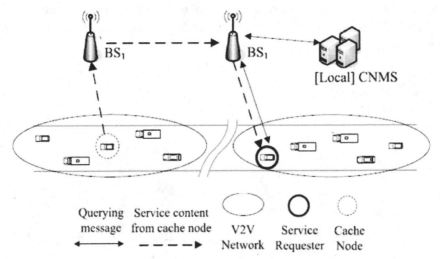

the most appropriate cache relay nodes by using a fuzzy-logic based cache relay node determination algorithm and then ask the chosen cache relay nodes to forward the infotainment data stream. If no appropriate cache relay node is found, the request node directly receives the data from the service content server in the wired environment instead. If all channels of the content server are occupied, the request will wait for the service until its preset timeout expires.

In this work three possible cases in vehicular networks are considered to find the locations of the cache relay nodes. First being, when the cache relay nodes and the requestor are located in the same cluster, which is a simple intra-cluster V2V network. The requestor simply asks the cluster head to provide a candidate cache relay node list, which contains the cache relay nodes' ID. Each vehicle that serves as the cluster head can collect and deliver infotainment data as well as control packets within this cluster. The second case is when the cache relay nodes and the requestor are separated in the different V2V network clusters that are located in the same wide area network. The requestor asks the local cache relay node management server (LCNMS) to provide a cache relay node list. After the cache relay nodes are determined, the infotainment data stream is sent to the requestor via a roadside base station. Finally, when the cache relay nodes and the requestor are distributed in a heterogeneous wide-area network, the requestor asks the global cache relay node management server (GCNMS) to provide a cache relay. The simulation results show that the algorithm has a better throughput and almost negligible delay for the data packets. However, the probability of dropping packets is comparatively greater than the unicast scheme. This is because the required bandwidth cannot be guaranteed during the initial request stages. Though the proposed solution is able to adhere to the QoS requirement of infotainment applications, there is no validated proof for the functioning of the relaying mechanism. The authors do

not explain the probability of finding a cache relay within the network. This factor is important because if the delay experienced during the initial communication setup is high, the users may not be interested in accessing the service. Also, the use of resource reservation in distributed environments like vehicular networks is not a practical proposition because it might lead to a waste of the available resources along with the starvation for other interested nodes.

It is apparent from the presented systems that opportunistic approaches help achieve a better delivery ratio irrespective of the density of networks. This is because the dissemination is done only when two vehicles come in contact with each other. However, this increase in reliability is achieved at the expense of increased latency. Hence, it is not suitable for safety or efficiency applications

CONCLUSION

Data dissemination is one crucial issue that needs to be considered in proposing safety and not-safety applications over VANETs; the requirement for disseminating the information varies depending on the type of the application. Some applications require high reliability whereas some have stringent delay requirements. Simultaneously, since there is limited bandwidth, the dissemination protocol should not allow redundant packets so that the maximum amount data can be disseminated over the network.

A variety of approaches have been proposed over the last years to resolve issues related to data dissemination in VANETs. Based on the mode of operation, dissemination methods can either employ either a push or pull model. The choice of model depends on the application which is to be developed (Table 1). Furthermore, most of the approaches can be classified into geocast, cluster or opportunistic technique. This chapter presented these classifications and discussed their issues.

Table 1. Summary of dissemination models

Dissemination Model	Advantage	Disadvantage
Push	Suitable for popular data	Flooding of the network
Pull	Suitable for user specific data	Cross traffic incurs heavy interference and Collisions

To summarize, in vehicular networks, geocast techniques help reduce the broadcast storm, thus enhancing channel utilization. The second technique, cluster based dissemination, reduces the broadcast storm and contention. Finally, opportunistic data dissemination techniques increase reliability in terms of packet delivery ratio in sparse networks.

An overview of this classification stating the advantages and disadvantages pertaining to each method is provided in Table 1 and Table 2.

There could be further classifications of dissemination techniques. But most of this work fits into aforementioned techniques. All approaches try to address some of the unique features of VANETs. Also, the approach and the technique to be adopted for dissemination are highly dependent on the application for which the protocol is designed. Thus, a particular technique cannot be termed as best or worst in a vehicular environment. The design of the dissemination technique depends on the features and requirement of the applications. In this chapter we observe that each of the dissemination techniques can be applied to different application scenarios in VANETs. How-

ever, to obtain optimum performance, a combination of one or more techniques needs to be applied that are specifically based on the application requirement.

FURTHER DIRECTION

Most of the studied dissemination techniques were not based on the DSRC standard which has been approved as a standard medium for vehicular communications. So, in future studies, it is important to understand the requirements of DSRC and to analyse how it can add value to the mentioned dissemination techniques.

In DSRC the basic link-layer behaviour of communications in the control channel can be defined as single-hop, uncoordinated, broadcast messaging in an unbounded system consisting of all neighbouring equipped vehicles in a dedicated channel. DSRC is seen as the main candidate for safety, short-range applications, subscription free services, road toll services, and other similar localized applications. The US-FCC assigned the 5.850 to 5.925 GHz band range as a freely licensed spectrum utilizing DSRC to enhance road safety. DSRC is capable of delivering a 27 Mbps data-rate by using a two way line-of-sight short-range radio, which is significantly lower cost compared to cellular, WiMax or satellite communications. DSRC operates in stringent environments that require:

- Fast communications to maintain the connection with speeding vehicles at all times.

Table 2. Summary of dissemination techniques

Dissemination Technique	Advantage	Disadvantage
Geocast	Limits the information to a geographic region, helps reduce overhead and transmits data with a low delay	Lack of reliability in severely affected in sparse networks
Cluster Based	Permits more effective dissemination among vehicle of similar interest and helps achieve a better knowledge percentage	Clusterhead election and cluster maintenance is a difficult task
Opportunistic	Is highly reliable communication in partitioned networks	Latency is high in such type of networks

- Strict quality of service committed to predefined threshold delays for safety messages.
- Minimal use of transmission power and provisions to maintain privacy.
- Anonymity of roaming users in addition to many other environmental challenges.

All traditional networks, both wired and wireless, use fixed addresses. However, for many VANET applications, it is not practical to use fixed addresses. First, it may be difficult for a node to know the address of another node due to the third constraint mentioned above. Second, in many applications the intended destination is not a particular node, but rather a group of nodes that happen to be at a certain location. Therefore, geographical addresses may be used in a VANET. Geocast is attractive in DSRC for two reasons. First, it works well in highly mobile networks where network topology changes frequently. Secondly, it offers flexible support for heterogeneous application requirements, including applications for road safety, traffic efficiency and infotainment. In particular, it provides periodic transmission of safety status messages at a high rate, rapid multi-hop dissemination of packets in geographical regions for emergency warnings, and unicast packet transport.

For cluster based dissemination, DSRC can allow for contention-based approaches for Intra-Cluster and Inter-Cluster communications, respectively. DSRC interface uses 7 non-overlapping 10 MHz channels with a communication range of the control channel of 1000 meters and a range of 30 to 400 meters for the service channels. This particular feature of DSRC related to the variation in communication ranges of service and control channels can be of great advantage such that, the control channel can be used to deliver safety data and advertisements across neighbouring clusters, and a service channel can be used to exchange safety and non- safety data within the cluster. This will help increase the throughput of the system

and better disseminate the information to a larger audience with greater efficiency. A larger radio range will also facilitate having more opportunistic contacts between the vehicles. This is of particular importance in sparsely populated areas where opportunistic contacts can contribute to having a better packet delivery ratio.

DSRC will be the base technology for future dissemination of messages in vehicular environments. Currently, DSRC is gaining popularity among researchers and most know that the technical issues are resolvable. Parallel efforts on the business, legal and legislative fronts will shape the business models, address distractive concerns, and build up the case for gradual deployment.

REFERENCES

Bai, F., & Krishnamachari, B. (2009). Spatio-temporal variations of vehicle traffic in VANETs: Facts and implications. In *Proceedings of 6th ACM International Workshop on VehiculAr InterNETworking* (pp. 43- 52). Bejing China.

Basagni, S. (1999). Distributed clustering for ad hoc networks. In *Proceedings of 4th International symposium on Parallel Architectures, Algorithms and Networks* (pp. 310-315).

Basu, K. N., & Little, T. (2001). A mobility based metric for clustering in mobile ad hoc networks. In *Proceedings of Conference on Distributed Computing Systems* (p. 413).

Chatterjee, M., Das, S. K., & Turgut, D. (2002). WCA: A weighted clustering algorithm for mobile ad hoc networks. *Journal of Clustering Computing, 5*, 193–204. doi:10.1023/A:1013941929408

Daeinabi, A., Pour Rahbar, A. G., & Khademzadeh, A. (2010). VWCA: An efficient clustering algorithm in vehicular ad-hoc networks. *Journal of Network and Computer Applications, 34*, 207–222. doi:10.1016/j.jnca.2010.07.016

Delot, T., Cenerario, N., & Ilarri, S. (2010). Vehicular event sharing with a mobile peer-to-peer architecture. *Elsevier Transportation Research Part C: Emerging Technologies, 18,* 584–598. doi:10.1016/j.trc.2009.12.003

Ding, Y., & Xiao, L. (2010). SADV: Static-node-assisted adaptive data dissemination in vehicular networks. *IEEE Transactions on Vehicular Technology, 59,* 2445–2455. doi:10.1109/TVT.2010.2045234

Er, I., & Seah, W. (2004). Mobility-based d-hop clustering algorithm for mobile ad hoc networks. In *Proceedings of IEEE Wireless Communications and Networking Conference* (pp. 2359-2364).

Fan, P., Haran, J., Dillenburg, J., & Nelson, P. (2005). Cluster based framework in vehicular ad- hoc networks. *Lecture Notes in Computer Science, 3738,* 32–42. doi:10.1007/11561354_5

Fan, P., Sistla, P., & Nelson, P. (2008). Theoretical analysis of directional stability-based clustering algorithm for VANET. In *Proceedings of ACM VANET* (pp. 80- 81).

Festag, A., Zhang, W., Le, L., & Baldessari, R. (2009). Geocast in vehicular networks. In Moustafa, H., & Zhang, Y. (Eds.), *Vehicular networks techniques, standards, and applications* (pp. 378–404). CRC Press.

Hou, T., & Tsai, T. (2001). An access-based clustering protocol for multihop wireless ad hoc networks. *IEEE Journal on Selected Areas in Communications, 19,* 1201–1210. doi:10.1109/49.932689

Huang, C. J., Chen, Y. J., & Chen, I. (2009). An intelligent infotainment dissemination scheme for heterogeneous vehicular networks. *Expert Systems with Applications, 36,* 12472–12479. doi:10.1016/j.eswa.2009.04.035

Jerbi, M., Senouci, S., Rasheed, T., & Doudane, Y. (2007). An infrastructure- free traffic information system for vehicular networks. In *Proceedings of 66th IEEE Vehicular Technology Conference* (pp. 2086-2090).

Kuklinski, S., & Wolny, G. (2009). Density based clustering algorithm for VANETs. In. *International Journal of Internet Protocol Technology, 4,* 149–157. doi:10.1504/IJIPT.2009.028654

Lebrun, J., Chuah, C., Ghosal, D., & Zhang, M. (2005). Knowledge- based opportunistic forwarding in vehicular wireless ad hoc networks. In *Proceedings of 61st IEEE Vehicular Technology Conference-Spring,* Vol. 4 (pp. 2289-2293).

Leontiadis, I., & Mascolo, C. (2007a). GeOpps: Geographical opportunistic routing for vehicular networks. In *Proceedings of IEEE International Symposium on World of Wireless, Mobile and Multimedia Networks* (pp. 1-6). Finland.

Leontiadis, I., & Mascolo, C. (2007b). Opportunistic spatio-temporal dissemination system for vehicular networks. In *Proceedings of 1st International MobiSys Workshop on Mobile Opportunistic Networking* (pp. 39-46). San Juan, Puerto Rico.

Lin, C., Yuanqian, L., Siyuan, X., & Jianping, P. (2010). Scalable modulation for scalable wireless videocast. In *Proceedings of 29th IEEE International Conference on Computer Communications* (pp. 1-5). San Diego USA.

Little, T., & Agarwal, A. (2005). An information propagation scheme for VANETS. In *Proceedings of 8th International Conference on Intelligent Transportation System* (pp. 155-160).

Maslekar, N., Boussedjra, M., Houda, L., & Mouzna, J. (2011). C-DRIVE: Clustering based on direction in vehicular environment. In *Proceedings of 4th IFIP New Technologies, Mobility and Security,* Paris.

Mina, T., & Faramarz, H. (2011). Disseminating a large amount of data to vehicular network in an urban area. *International Journal of Vehicular Technology*, 2010.

Morgan, Y. L. (2010). Notes on DSRC & WAVE standards suite: Its architecture, design, and characteristics. *IEEE Communications Surveys & Tutorials, 12*(4), 504–518. doi:10.1109/SURV.2010.033010.00024

Nadeem, T., Shankar, P., & Iftode, L. (2006). A comparative study of data dissemination models for VANETs. In *Proceedings of 3rd Annual Conference on Mobile and Ubiquitous Systems: Networking & Services* (pp. 1-10). San Jose.

Nekovee, M. (2009). Epidemic algorithms for reliable and efficient information dissemination in vehicular. *IET Journal Intelligent Transport Systems, 2*(3), 104–110. doi:10.1049/iet-its:20070061

Ros, F. J., Ruiz, P. M., & Stojmenovic, I. (2010). Acknowledgment-based broadcast protocol for reliable and efficient data dissemination in vehicular ad-hoc networks. *IEEE Transactions on Mobile Computing, 11*(1).

Saha, A., Park, G. L., Ahn, K. J., Kim, C., Lee, B., & Rhee, Y. J. (2009). Data distribution of road-side information station in vehicular ad hoc networks (VANETs). *Proceedings of the International Conference on Computational Science and its Applications,* (pp. 503-512).

Salhi, I., Cherif, M., & Senouci, S. (2007). Data collection in vehicular networks. In *Proceedings of ASN Symposium*.

Sardari, M., Hendessi, F., & Fekri, F. (2009). DMRC: Dissemination of multimedia in vehicular networks using rateless codes. In *Proceedings of the IEEE International Conference on Computer Communications (INFOCOM '09),* (pp. 1–6).

Shibata, N., Terauchi, T., Kitani, T., Yasumoto, K., Ito, M., & Higashino, T. (2006). A method for sharing traffic information using inter-vehicle communication. In *Proceedings of 3rd Annual Conference on Mobile and Ubiquitous Systems: Networking & Services* (pp. 1-7). San Jose.

Sormani, D., & Turconi, G. (2006). Towards lightweight information dissemination in inter-vehicular networks. In *Proceedings of 3rd International Workshop on Vehicular Ad Hoc Networks* (pp. 20-29). Los Angeles.

Souza, E., Nikolaidis, I., & Gburzynski, P. (2010). A new aggregate local mobility (ALM) clustering algorithm for VANETs. In *Proceedings of IEEE International Conference on Communication* (pp 1-5). South Africa.

Strassberger, M., Schroth, C., & Lasowski, R. (2009). Data dissemination in vehicular networks. In Moustafa, H., & Zhang, Y. (Eds.), *Vehicular networks techniques, standards, and applications* (pp. 181–220). CRC Press.

Vasilakos, A. (2011). *Delay tolerant networks: Protocols and applications (Wireless Networks and Mobile Communications)*. CRC Press.

Wang, Y. X., & Bao, F. S. (2007). An entropy-based weighted clustering algorithm and its optimization for ad hoc networks. In *Proceedings of IEEE 3rd International Conference on Wireless and Mobility, Networksing and Communications,* (p. 56). New York, USA.

Wang, Z., Liu, L., Zhou, M., & Ansari, N. (2008). A position based clustering technique for ad hoc intervehicle communication. *IEEE Transactions on Systems, Man and Cybernetics- Applications and Reviews, 38*, 201-208.

Wischhof, L., Ebner, A., & Rohling, H. (2005). Information dissemination in self- organizing intervehicle networks. *IEEE Transactions on Intelligent Transportation Systems, 6*, 90–101. doi:10.1109/TITS.2004.842407

Wolny, G. (2008). Modified DMAC clustering algorithm for VANETs. In *Proceedings of 3rd IEEE International Conference on Systems and Networks Communication* (pp. 268- 273).

Xu, B., Ouksel, A., & Wolfson, O. (2004).Opportunistic resource exchange in intervehicle ad-hoc networks. In *Proceedings of IEEE International Conference of Mobile Data Management* (pp. 4-12).

Yu, Q., & Heijenk, G. (2008). Abiding geocast for warning message dissemination in vehicular ad hoc networks. In *Proceedings of IEEE Vehicular Networks and Applications Workshop (Vehi-Mobi)* (pp. 400-404). Beijing.

Zhuang, Y., Pan, J., Luo, Y., & Cai, L. (2011). Time and location-critical emergency message dissemination for vehicular ad-hoc networks. *IEEE Journal on Selected Areas in Communications*, *29*, 187–196. doi:10.1109/JSAC.2011.110118

ADDITIONAL READING

Adler, C., Eichler, S., Kosch, T., Schroth, C., & Strassberger, M. (2006) Self-organized and context adaptive information diffusion in vehicular ad hoc networks. In Proceedings of, *3rd International Symposium on Wireless Communication Systems* (pp. 307–311).

Adler, C., Eigner, R., Schroth, C., & Strassberger, M. (2006) Context-adaptive information diffusion in VANETs: Maximizing the global benefit. In Proceedings of, *5th IASTED International Conference on Communication Systems and Networks*.

Briesemeister L, Schafers L & Hommel (2000) Disseminating messages among highly mobile hosts based on inter-vehicle communication. In Proceedings of, *IEEE Intelligent Vehicles Symposium*, (pp. 522–527).

Chang, W. R., Lin, H. T., & Chen, B. X. (2008). Trafficgather: An efficient and scalable data collection protocol for vehicular ad hoc networks. In Proceedings of, *5th IEEE Consumer Communications and Networking Conference* (pp. 365–369).

Dornbush, S., & Joshi, A. (2007). StreetSmart Traffic: Discovering and disseminating automobile congestion using VANET's. In Proceedings of, *65th IEEE Vehicular Technology Conference* (pp. 11–15).

Fujiki, T., Kirimura, M., Umedu, T., & Higashino, T. (2007). Efficient acquisition of local traffic information using inter-vehicle communication with queries. In Proceedings of, *10th International IEEE Conference on Intelligent Transportation Systems*, (pp. 241–246).

Kosch, T., Schwingenschlogl, C., & Ai, L. (2002). Information dissemination in multihop intervehicle networks. In Proceedings of, *5th International IEEE Conference on Intelligent Transportation Systems* (pp. 685–690).

Little, T. D. C., & Agarwal, A. (2005). An information propagation scheme for VANETs. In Proceedings of, *8th International IEEE Conference on Intelligent Transportation Systems* (pp. 155–160).

Lochert, C., Scheuermann, B., Caliskan, M., & Mauve, M. (2007). The feasibility of information dissemination in vehicular ad-hoc networks. In Proceedings of, *4th Annual onference on Wireless On-demand Network Systems and Services* (pp. 92–99).

Lochert, C., Scheuermann, B., & Mauve, M. (2010). Information Dissemination in VANETs In (Ed Hartenstein & Laberteaux) *Vehicular Applications and Inter-Networking Technologies* (pp 49 – 80). WILEY Publications.

Sago, H., Shinohara, M., Hara, T., & Nishio, S. (2007). A data dissemination method for information sharing based on inter-vehicle communication. In the Proceedings of, *21st International Conference on Advanced Information Networking and Applications Workshops*, vol. 2,(pp. 743–748).

Zhao, J., & Cao, G. (2008). VADD: Vehicle-assisted data delivery in vehicular ad hoc networks. *IEEE Transactions on Vehicular Technology, 57*, 1910–1922. doi:10.1109/TVT.2007.901869

KEY TERMS AND DEFINITIONS

Cluster Based Dissemination: This relates to dissemination of data to a group of vehicles sharing common interests.

Data Dissemination: Formally data dissemination is defined as the transportation of data to the intended recipients while satisfying certain requirements such as delays, reliability etc.

Geocast Dissemination: Geocast dissemination refers to the delivery of information to a group of destinations in a network identified by their geographical locations.

Opportunistic Dissemination: Opportunistic dissemination is extended form delay tolerant networks is where network communication opportunities appear opportunistic, an end-to-end path between source and destination may have never existed, and disconnection and reconnection is common in the network.

Pull Model: It is a request response strategy for data exchange where the data exchange is initiated by request from the vehicles.

Push Model: A proactive dissemination method in which the vehicle which has any information to be shared will disseminate it without being probed.

VANETs: Vehicular Ad-Hoc Network or VANETs, is a class of Mobile Ad-hoc Network (MANETs) to provide communications within a group of vehicles to and between vehicles and road side stationary units.

Chapter 14
Experience Developing a Vehicular Network Based on Heterogeneous Communication Technologies

Pedro J. Fernández
University of Murcia, Spain

Cristian A. Nieto
University of Murcia, Spain

José Santa
University of Murcia, Spain

Antonio F. Gómez-Skarmeta
University of Murcia, Spain

Johann Márquez-Barja
Polytechnic University of Valencia, Spain

Pietro Manzoni
Polytechnic University of Valencia, Spain

ABSTRACT

This chapter describes the experiences and findings deploying a vehicular network architecture supporting different communication technologies. This approach has been developed taking into account key issues regarding mobility and security. These two aspects have been provided by means of the NEMO and IKEv2 protocols, respectively. In addition, thanks to the EAP protocol, transported by IKEv2, an extensible authentication method can be used to implement an access control mechanism. This work also focuses on how the terminal is aware of the surrounding environment in order to boost the handoff processes among heterogeneous networks using the IEEE 802.21 protocol. Apart from the description of the on-board system architecture, a WiMAX/WiFi deployment has been set up at the infrastructure side to validate the development of the mobility and security environment designed for vehicular networks.

DOI: 10.4018/978-1-4666-0209-0.ch014

INTRODUCTION

The world of wireless communications has undergone exponential evolution in recent years. The "wireless" concept is growing in importance day by day, together with new mobility and security needs which arise in this context. Wireless communication devices move within a determined coverage range and communicate my means of an air medium, which is exposed to any other terminal in the surroundings. This is the reason why extended security mechanisms are needed. Moreover, these devices are usually provided with extended network capabilities using several technologies simultaneously, such as WiFi, Bluetooth, 3G, Wi-MAX, etc., each one covering a range of scenarios determined by its particular features regarding communication range, latency, throughput or jitter. Vehicular networks present a challenging field where mobility and security through several communication mediums are key issues.

In this kind of heterogeneous scenario in which more than one technology is present, deciding when to switch from one communication technology to another (i.e. inter-technology or vertical handover) is quite complex, even more so considering high mobility vehicular scenarios. To make the best decision each time, the information gathered from the surrounding wireless infrastructure must be evaluated, taking into account many parameters obtained from the different information sources, i.e. network layer, communication transceivers, and user preferences. Here is where the 802.21 (IEEE Std. 802.21, 2008) protocol can be greatly useful, supporting the handoff process between two communication technologies. Cross-layer multi-parameters can be used together with techniques such as fuzzy logic, neural networks, and pattern recognition, among others, to decide the feasibility of the handover.

Apart from link-level issues, a change in the (physical) point of attachment to a network may cause changes at network-layer level if a new IP address is assigned (inter-domain handover). Mobility at network layer is one of the main aspects to take into account in vehicular networks (Stephan & Michele, 2009). In this work, NEMO (Network Mobility) (Devarapalli, Wakikawa, Petrescu, & Thubert, 2005) is used to cope with this requirement. This protocol is an evolution of MIPv6 (Johnson, Perkins, & Arkko, 2004), where the new concept of "mobile router" is introduced. By using NEMO, a mobile equipment acts as router for a mobile network and allow mobile network nodes to maintain their IP address despite changing the mobile router attachment point in visited networks. As explained in the rest of the chapter, NEMO is used to support network mobility in the proposed vehicular network.

Among the various technologies applicable for medium-range communications, the IEEE 802.16 standard (IEEE Std. 802.16, 2004) presents a communication media that can be quite useful in vehicular networks. Commonly known as WiMAX, it was originally devised for point-to-point scenarios to provide connectivity to small isolated populations or buildings belonging to the same company. But nowadays, the appearance of the 802.16e extension (IEEE Std. 802.16e, 2005) allows deploying wide-range wireless infrastructures for mobile scenarios. 802.16e is placed midway between WiFi (IEEE Std. 802.11g. 2003) and 3G (3G/UMTS Evolution, 2006), with coverage ranges in the order of several kilometers. This kind of wireless infrastructure can be more suitable for vehicular networks than common WiFi, due to the large distances a vehicle can travel in a short period of time.

Operators have considered WiMAX technology as a business opportunity, using licensed frequency bands. However, it is possible to use license-free frequency bands for WiMAX-based infrastructures. As a proof of concept, a pilot WiMAX infrastructure has been deployed at the University of Murcia using these license-free bands. The Espinardo Campus has been chosen as a testbed area within the University of Murcia for deploying our wireless infrastructure, using both WiFi and WiMAX technologies.

Moreover, one of the main aspects to take into account in wireless and, of course, vehicular communications is security (Fang-Yie, Huang, & Chiu, 2010) (Samara, Al-Salihy, & Sures, 2010). Wireless networks are exposed to different threats and vulnerabilities that encourage malicious users to disclose the transmitted information. As discussed in (Raya, Papadimitratos, & Hubaux, 2006) and (Hubaux, Capkun, & Luo, 2004), there are many vulnerabilities that have to be taken into account in vehicular networks and (Matthias, 2005) describes key security concepts for vehicular networks. In (Parno & Perrig, 2005), the authors discuss the challenges and some attacks encountered in vehicular networks. Some proposals develop these concepts, such as (Raya & Hubaux, 2005), who describe a full security and privacy framework for vehicular networks with simulated evaluations of the security overhead, or (Blum & Eskandarian, 2004), who describe a PKI-based security architecture. In (Hubaux, Capkun & Luo, 2004), authors even take a different perspective of vehicular network security and focus on location privacy. As can be seen, although network security can be provided at different levels in the OSI stack, e.g. at the application level (IEEE 1609.2, 2006), the approach proposed in this work integrates the security support at the network-layer by using Internet Protocol Security (IPsec) (Kent & Atkinson, 1998) and Internet Key Exchange (IKE) (Kaufman, 2006). IKE version 2 (IKEv2) is used to provide the necessary support to IPsec to offer confidentiality and authenticity to transmitted information. In addition, an access control mechanism has been implemented to authorize terminals to access the network. Thanks to the Extensible Authentication Protocol (EAP) (Aboba, Blunk, Vollbrecht, Carlson, & Levkowetz, 2004), IKEv2 can use a set of authentication methods for this purpose. OpenIKEv2 (Pérez, et al., 2008) implements the IKEv2 protocol in the work presented in this chapter. This is an open

source implementation that is being developed at the University of Murcia.

The outline of the rest of the chapter is as follows. The following section describes different types of handover scenarios and their requirements, which is followed by an overview of the IEEE 802.21 and the different phases of the handover process. A detailed explanation of the deployed testbed can be found after that, focusing on mobility and security aspects. Then the main points concerned with designing the on-board unit installed in the vehicle are described. We conclude this chapter with the future challenges to be considered in our architecture and some final conclusions.

HANDOVER SCENARIOS

Mobility is one of the main research topics in the study of wireless networks, due to the benefits offered to end users. Since a vehicle can move at high speeds, it is necessary to count on a wireless infrastructure which can support mobility along the road without losing connectivity. Another requisite in such a mobile environment is security (Sun, Lin, Chen, & Shen, 2007) (Zhou, Qin, Xu, Guan, & Zhang, 2010). Confidentiality and authenticity are mandatory in this kind of scenario (Habib & Ahmad, 2010) because wireless networks are exposed to different threats and vulnerabilities that let any user access and possibly manipulate the transmitted information.

In order to research the kinds of networks mentioned above, we propose a test scenario in which a vehicle connected to a wireless network can move freely, using different access points that are available along its path. These access points could belong to different domains and different wireless technologies, like WiFi, WiMAX and 3G (Yi & Miao, 2010). As a consequence of employing these different technologies, several types of handovers must be taken into account (also outlined in Figure 1):

Figure 1. Different types of handovers in a heterogeneous infrastructure

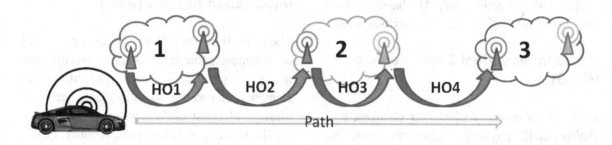

- **Intra-domain and intra-technology handover (HO1 in Figure 1):** This is the least complex type of handover because only the link-layer is involved. The IP address does not change and no mobility or authentication mechanisms are needed in this case.
- **Inter-domain and intra-technology handover (HO2 in Figure 1):** A domain change usually implies an IP address reassignment. For this to happen, both the link-layer and network-layer are involved. Mobility and security mechanisms have to be used in this case.
- **Intra-domain and inter-technology handover (HO3 in Figure 1):** In this case, changing technology implies a more complex interaction, since more than one interface has to be used at the same time. However, the IP address does not change.
- **Inter-domain and inter-technology handover (HO4 in Figure 1):** This is the most complex type of handover, and all the mobility and security processes are involved.

Each type of handover has its particular complexity level. Our approach is to research these handover challenges gradually, starting with the least complex and dealing with advances that allow us to reach the most complex one. The time spent on handovers is greater as the complexity increases. Our goal is to minimize this time by improving processes that take more time, such as the authentication method.

IEEE 802.21 OVERVIEW

As aforementioned, the IEEE 802.21 standard has been designed to provide homogeneous services and mechanisms in order to perform enhanced handovers among heterogeneous networks. The main purpose of this standard is to improve the user experience of mobile devices by facilitating the handover process among IEEE 802 networks and cellular networks.

The Media Independent Handover Function (MIHF) protocol defined by the IEEE 802.21 standard establishes the messages exchanged between peer MIH entities for handover, offering a common message payload across different media (802.3, 802.11, 802.16, Cellular). The standard considers the technology dependent components as *lower layers* and the requesting modules as *upper layers*. These lower layers can be accessed by different functions to retrieve information to detect, prepare and execute the vertical handover (Lee, Sriram, Kim, Kim, & Golmie, 2009), while the upper layers demand that information; therefore, the latter are also referred to as Media Independent Handover Users (MIHU). The MIHF offers both lower and upper layers a Service Access Point (SAP) in order to exchange the service messages. Figure 2 shows the basic 802.21 architecture. The basic services offered by the MIHF are briefly described below:

Media Independent Event Service (MIES)

This service detects lower layer changes, e.g. changes on the physical and data link layer. The MIHF notifies events occurring in the lower layers to the MIHUs as requested. The MIES covers events such as:

- State change events (link up, link down, link parameter changes).
- Predictive events (link going down).
- Network initiated events (load balancing, operator preferences).

Figure 2. IEEE 802.21 architecture

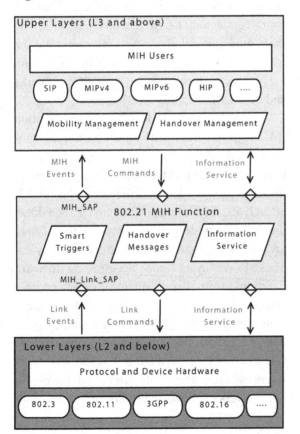

Media Independent Information Service (MIIS)

The MIIS allows the MIHF to discover its network environment, gathering information that the upper layers use to make decisions. The information elements refer to the list of available networks, location of Point of Attachment (PoA), operator ID, roaming partners, cost, security, quality of service (QoS), PoA capabilities, and vendor specific information, among others.

Media Independent Command Service (MICS)

The MICS allows the MIHU to take control over the lower layers through a set of commands. With the information gathered by the MIES and MIIS, the MIHU decides to switch from one PoA to another. Depending on which entity has the handover control, some services are defined as being more useful than others. The following commands are typically used by the MICS:

- MIH Handover Initiate. Used between the network and the mobile device.
- MIH Handover Prepare. Used between the old network (PoA) and the new network.
- MIH Handover Commit. Used between the network and the mobile device.
- MIH Handover Complete. Used between the network and the mobile device, and network to network.

Amendments

In order to fully provide handover services, the 802.21 standard must be implemented in both network and mobile devices. Figure 3 shows the MIHF relationship among network elements.

The media specific amendments required by MIHF are defined as follows:

Figure 3. MIHF relationship

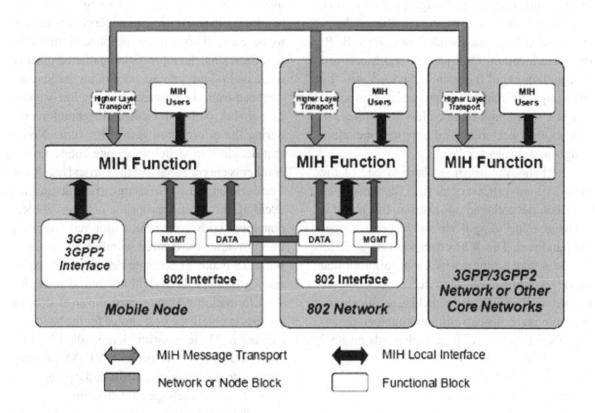

- Container for MIH messages for 802.11, defined in the 802.11u (IEEE P802.11u)
- Container for MIH messages for 802.16, defined in the 802.16g (IEEE P802.11g).
- The 3GPP-SAE (System Architecture Evolution) for 3GPP (3GPP-SAE).
- The IEFT MIPSHOP (Mobility for IP: Performance, Signaling and Handoff Optimization) has defined the Transport for MIH Protocol (MIPSHOP)
- 802.3 is desired.

HANDOVER-RELATED PROCESSES

An accurate handover process should take into account and care about service continuity, network discovery, network selection, security, the device's power-management and QoS issues (Yu Chen, Ja Hsia, & Yi Lia, 2009), focusing mostly on the latter. Several proposals split the whole handover process into three parts:

- Handover information gathering
- Handover decision
- Handover execution

Figure 4 shows the interactions among the three phases required to implement handover in heterogeneous networks. Each part of this diagram is briefly described next.

The handover information gathering phase collects not only network information, but also information about the rest of the components of the system such as network properties, mobile devices, access points, and user preferences. In this phase, the information is collected to be used and processed to make decisions in the handover decision phase. The information typically collected is the availability of neighbouring network links, by offering information such as throughput, cost, packet loss ratio, handoff rate, RSS, BER, distance, location, QoS parameters. Moreover, information about the mobile device's state by gathering information about battery status, resources, speed, and service class is required, as well as user preference information, including budget and services.

The handover decision phase is one of the most critical processes during the handover. Based on the gathered information, this phase is in charge of deciding *When* and *Where* to trigger the handover. The *When* decision refers to the precise instant in time in which to make an optimal handover, while the *Where* refers to selecting the best network fulfilling the switching requirements. In a homogeneous network environment, deciding *When* to handover usually depends on RSS

values, while the *Where* is not an issue since we use the same networking technology (horizontal handover). In heterogeneous networks, the answer to these questions is quite complex. To make the best decisions, the information gathered must be evaluated taking into account many parameters obtained from the different information sources, i.e. network, mobile devices, and user preferences during the information gathering phase. Notice that deciding to switch from one connection to another is the core phase of the vertical handover. The decision phase is in charge of evaluating and deciding the most appropriate network choices that meet both system and user requirements, thus providing the desired seamless communications. To make an accurate decision, this phase takes advantage of algorithms that, considering the information available, carry out an evaluation process to obtain the best choice for the handover execution. These algorithms are called Vertical Handover Decision Algorithms (VHDA) and they are used to weight up and evaluate the parameters involved under each specific criterion.

In the literature, we can find several VHDA proposals. Some of them take into account only the lower layer information given by the media independent information service, and most of the proposals combine the metrics and parameters of the different components to build an accurate cross-layer handover algorithm. It is important to point out that these algorithms may be used for both inter-domain and inter-technology handovers.

The handover decision process basically consists of three phases (Marquez-Barja, Calafate, Cano, & Manzoni, 2010): parameter selection, parameter processing, and parameter aggregation. The parameter selection phase only takes into account the relevant parameters to evaluate and weight a candidate connection. The parameter processing phase allows us to normalize all the parameters, allowing us and to merge them using several techniques such as fuzzy logic, neural networks and specific functions, to extract relevant data. Finally, to make a decision, an algorithm

Figure 4. Handover phases

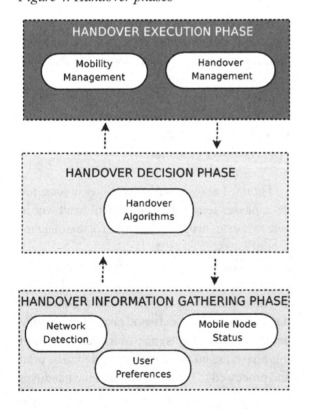

aggregates and evaluates the weight of each parameter and, based on some decision criteria, selects the best candidate. Although the process described applies to most proposals, authors typically modify this process slightly to fit their needs.

In order to classify the diverse algorithms that can be found in the literature, a taxonomy broadly presented in a previous work (Marquez-Barja, Calafate, Cano, & Manzoni, 2010) is summarized next. The diagram given in Figure 5 illustrates it. As it is observed, the different phases appeal to several algorithms in order to process the information and finally make a multi-criteria decision:

- **Parameter selection algorithms:** This type of algorithms takes advantage of the context information, generating knowledge to make an accurate decision. Any

Figure 5. Handover algorithms taxonomy

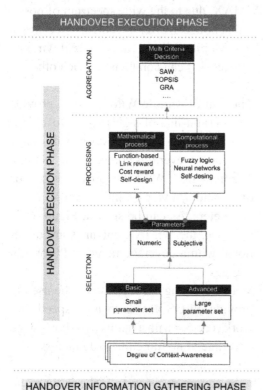

change in the mobile and network context triggers events and processes. Depending on the amount of parameters selected for processing, these algorithms can be considered as: *basic* or *advanced*.

- **Parameter processing algorithms:** The parameter processing algorithms are in charge of the processing of the chosen parameters and of the provision of the input information to the parameter aggregation algorithms. Different works in the literature use diverse functions to process the information depending on their nature. Therefore, the functions used can vary from pure mathematical to computational algorithms. Most mathematical algorithms are self-designed algorithms. Some authors propose their own self-design decision algorithms in order to satisfy their specific needs, based on the information available in their systems. Computational algorithms use Fuzzy Logic and Neural Networks techniques to interpret imprecise information, although authors usually apply their own self-designed algorithms to perform the interpretation task.

- **Parameter aggregation algorithms:** Since the decision process takes into account diverse metrics and parameters to evaluate the best candidate networks, there is a need for algorithms that are able to jointly handle multiple parameters and metrics. Consequently, Multi-Criteria Decision Making (MCDM) algorithms are adopted to fulfill this requirement by aggregating all these processed parameters. There are several approaches in the literature that follows these algorithms, such as *Analysis Hierarchy Process (AHP), Simple Additive Weighting (SAW)* or *Grey Relational Analysis (GRA)*, among others.

In the context of vehicular networks, information about location and mobility patterns are of utmost importance due to the high speeds involved. Thus, any handover decision scheme proposed should account for this information. The most appropriate VHDA scheme for vehicular networks must include advanced context information and, particularly, location-aware information. It is important to consider location and also location predictions in order to choose the best network candidate in the area. Nevertheless, context information adds valuable information to the VHDA. To combine the different sources of information, a fast multi-criteria decision making (MCDM) algorithm is recommended, being in charge of weighting the set of parameters and providing a fast decision on how to perform the handover at the best time and place. Nevertheless, a self-designed algorithm, defined according to the special characteristics of vehicular networks, can also be used to make decisions.

Finally, the handover execution phase performs the handover itself; besides performing the handover, the phase should also guarantee a smooth session transition process. In order to perform the handover, different handover strategies cooperate with control signaling, and the IP management protocols.

Concerning vehicular networks, the performance of each phase must focus on the distinctive characteristics and features of such types of networks. The information gathering phase must consider the dynamism of the available information at the devices and the network. Making decisions based on highly dynamic information with a given degree of the device's mobility requires a quick and reliable decision algorithm. Finally, the execution of the handover must be carefully controlled to achieve accuracy by considering the geographical location, the selected network and the precise time.

TESTBED

The challenge we face is creating a vehicular network testbed based initially on Mobile WiMAX, and WiFi in a near future, in order to establish an Internet access service using security mechanisms, extensible authentication and the dynamic establishment of security associations, thanks to IPsec, EAP and IKEv2, respectively. Mobility support is also added, thanks to the NEMO protocol (NEMO, 2010).

Deploying Wireless Infrastructure

Vehicular networks have special mobility needs that change depending on the speed of vehicles and the surrounding environment. There are several communication technologies that can be used in vehicular networks, as a previous work shows (Khaled, Tsukada, Santa, Choia, & Ernst, 2009), but this work focuses on WiFi and, above all, WiMAX, due to the wide spectrum of possibilities that both can offer in vehicular scenarios. WiFi and Mobile WiMAX are different wireless technologies that can complement each other:

- The aim of Mobile WiMAX is to provide NLOS (non-line-of-sight) access to a high-speed network service with a wide-range coverage (several kilometers in radius). Theoretically, WiMAX provides speeds of around 70 Mbps within a range of 15 kilometers. As can be seen in Figure 6, in our case, the WiMAX antennas are directional with a coverage range of 90 or 120 degrees.
- WiFi technology is supposed to be used to provide NLOS access to high speed network services with a radius of a short-range coverage of no more than 100 meters.

The important decision to make is where to use WiFi and where to use WiMAX, taking into account the mentioned mobility requirements.

The first step considered in the testbed was the deployment of the Mobile WiMAX in a real environment (Espinardo Campus, Murcia, SPAIN) and to analyze the coverage to ensure connectivity at least along the ring road surrounding the campus. In a first step, we decided to place the WiMAX antennas at key outdoor points in order to cover the whole ring surrounding the campus. See these locations on Figure 6. Next, a pre-deployed WiFi infrastructure was reused, which was mainly located inside the buildings. WiFi coverage complements the WiMAX coverage, which usually does not reach indoor locations. This WiFi deployment is currently operating as part of the Internet service offered to students in all the university, although handover tests between WiMAX and WiFi have not been carried out yet.

Our WiMAX infrastructure consists of five operational Alvarion Breeze Access VL base stations and several terminals that are mounted in vehicles. Although the working frequency of 4.9 GHz is supposed to be NLOS (it would not be necessary to have a direct vision between the client and the base station), there are obstacles that cannot be avoided, such as buildings or mountains. In order to ensure coverage of the entire campus ring, some coverage tests had to be performed using one of the clients. All WiMAX devices can be managed through their IP addresses, in order to operate them remotely via Telnet (Telecommunication Network) or SNMP (Simple Network Management Protocol). Using these protocols, a signal strength level indicator can be accessed. Therefore, we have created an automated system for taking signal strength level and geographical positions at the same time, and register these data with timestamps, in order to generate coverage maps. This requires a GPS device and a laptop with a WiMAX network interface that allow us to determine the signal strength (in decibels) and which base station is currently connected to. A reasonable set up for our scenario is to take a sample every 20 meters. The speed limit on the ring road is 30 Km/h, so the sample period is at least of 2.4 seconds.

Figure 6. WiMAX antenna locations

The collection of coverage samples should be performed for each installed antenna, disabling the rest for a while. In this way, a coverage map is obtained for each antenna individually, and all of them will let us check if there is enough coverage on the whole circuit, the size of overlapping zones, and make decisions of the orientation and position of the antennas. An example of these maps is shown in Figure 7. To study all possible handover scenarios, it is desirable for research purposes to have both big enough overlapping zones, to study pre-authentication scenarios, and no overlapping zones between antennas, in order to check the operation of the system when a connectivity gap occurs.

Providing Security

There are several alternatives to secure communications and establish access control to services. Due to the different technologies that are present in this heterogeneous wireless infrastructure, there could be different security mechanisms, one for each technology. In order to group security tasks in a uniform way, we have held them at the net-

work layer, through the use of IPsec, IKEv2 and its EAP transport support.

For this reason, a new security element must be added to the scenario, an enforcement point, which assures the presence of security mechanisms and prevents undesired accesses to the network. This element is called "Security Gateway" (SG). This SG will always be one of the end points of the IPsec tunnels, so it is necessary to install OpenIKEv2 on each SG. Every SG will have two interfaces, one connected to the Internet access network and the other one connected to an isolated network, where only the WiMAX base stations are present with unroutable IP addresses. On this isolated network we have configured another network with routable and accessible IP addresses, but only assigned to the end points of the IPsec tunnels, which protect traffic to or from the authenticated and allowed terminals. The routable IP addresses are automatically assigned by the IKEv2 protocol.

The schema of Figure 8 shows the setup, which works with both IPv4 and IPv6 protocols with an almost equivalent implementation, but only the IPv6 case is going to be analyzed in this chapter. In this way, all entities connected to the same network have auto-generated link-local addresses

Figure 7. Coverage map example

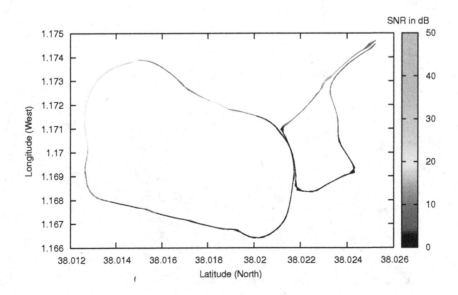

Figure 8. Security schema

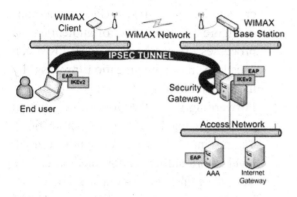

in order to provide direct connectivity between them. The Router Advertisement mechanism lets us know if a new Security Gateway is present.

Once a SG is detected, its link-local address is received; the mobile node can start an IKEv2 negotiation to create an IPsec tunnel between them by using their link-local addresses. In this negotiation, SG assigns a new IP address to the terminal. All the traffic that has this IP address as a source or destination will be secured and transported by IPsec between MN and SG. In addition, during this negotiation, an EAP-based authentication process is performed. As a reference implementation, the EAP-TLS (Transport Layer Security) authentication method has been chosen. For authentication purposes, another entity called "AAA" is needed. This is a Radius (Nelson & Dekok, 2007) server implemented by Free Radius (FreeRadius, 2010).

Providing Mobility

Imagine a vehicle in movement, connected to a network service provider. The vehicle has been assigned an IP address in order to use network services, like accessing the Internet. During the journey, the car needs to change its point of attachment (POA) due to coverage range limitations. When the change is performed, the infrastructure assigns a different IP address, resulting in con-

nectivity loss in a determined period of time. The applications would interrupt their open sessions and they would be forced to create new sessions from scratch using the new assigned IP address. As can be noted, handovers are not transparent to application layer in this case.

To solve this problem, an implementation of the NEMO protocol from UMIP is used (NEMO, 2010). Its duty is to create a scenario in which, at the application level, the customer always perceives the same IP address, while at the network level the IP address can change, according to the addressing scheme on the visited domain. In MIPv6 terminology, the IP address used by applications is the Home Address (HoA), which pertains to the home network where the user is registered, while the one that can be changed and is assigned by visited networks is the Care of Address (CoA). This mobility protocol needs the presence of an extra entity at the home network called Home Agent (HA), as you can see in Figure 9, which forwards all packets sent to the home address (HoA) in a communication with a Correspondent Node (CN). When NEMO is used, a complete mobile network changes its point of attachment, but only its mobile router (MR) is aware of this. In this way, the MR provides the mobility support,

Figure 9. Mobility schema

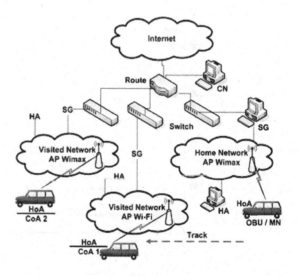

by maintaining the tunnel with the HA, and mobile network nodes (MNN) do not perceive network changes and, thus, do not require any change in the IP communication stack.

Although the combination of IKEv2 and NEMO covers security and mobility needs, they are not able to assure a seamless handover by themselves, due to the time needed to negotiate the new attachment point, authentication parameters and security associations. The authentication process takes a great part of this time, and this is the reason why further research is necessary to minimize this handover time. Two possible solutions include:

- Reducing the time spent by the authentication methods. Some authentication methods are being designed to reduce this authentication time as much as possible. This is the case of Fast EAP Re-authentication Method (EAP-FRM) (Marín, Pereñiguez, Bernal, & Skarmeta, 2009). This method

has been compared with EAP-TLS (slower) and pre-shared key (faster) methods in Figure 10, along a set of authentication processes. As can be seen, EAP-FRM can speed-up the authentication process by more than 300 ms.

- Forwarding the authentication negotiation before the handover (pre-authentication). Taking into account the signal strength level, a pre-authentication method can be started against the new access point using the current access point. It should be launched when the signal strength level reaches a certain threshold, before the complete signal losses.

Integration Issues between Security and Mobility Services

IKEv2 is unable to detect Router Advertisements (RA) on its own, so the NEMO and IKEv2 services

Figure 10. Comparison between authentication methods

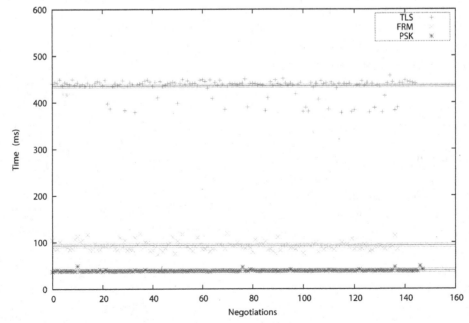

have to collaborate, because the IPsec tunnel has to be created before the mobility mechanism reacts to this RA. NEMO, which is always listening for RAs, has to notify IKEv2 to raise the IPsec tunnel. Then, IKEv2 also has to notify NEMO that the IPsec tunnel has been raised successfully or not. At this point, if IPsec tunnel has been raised, NEMO can continue with the BU/BA exchange in order to inform HA that the MN has changed its IP (CoA). In this way, all the traffic between MN an SG is protected.

With this bootstrapping process, we have established a transparent access control mechanism for the mobility service, which is not aware that the traffic is being protected by an IPsec tunnel through the SG. It can be said, in this case, that the mobility tunnel is inside the security tunnel, as can be seen in Figure 11. Therefore, it is important to note here the difference between this mechanism and the mechanism already available to protect NEMO mobility traffic using IPsec and IKEv2.

NEMO can also establish a tunnel between MR and HA using the Home Address. As a result, the tunnel never changes, despite the fact that the CoA changes. However, there is no way to provide access control by the visited network administrator since, in this case, only the MR and its HA are

involved. It can be said that the security tunnel is inside the mobility tunnel, as shown in Figure 11.

The handover procedure is initially triggered when the MR detects that a different router is available by means of Router Advertisements. In this case, the MR establishes a new complete IKEv2 negotiation against the new SG, establishing a new tunnel and getting a new IP address (CoA).

MOBILE ROUTER

The on-board unit (OBU), and concretely the equipment that implements the on-board mobile router, is a device installed in the vehicle intended to delegate the task of choosing the best access point and the best technology at every moment. Drivers cannot perform this task because they are driving and mobile network nodes inside the vehicles must be hidden from network changes. The MR hardware provides connectivity with different communication technologies and, by means of an additional mobility middleware; it can support vertical handovers (VHO) between them. It is important to remark that the MR is part of a more complex infrastructure that lets the handover process be performed automatically,

Figure 11. Sequence diagram of a handover procedure

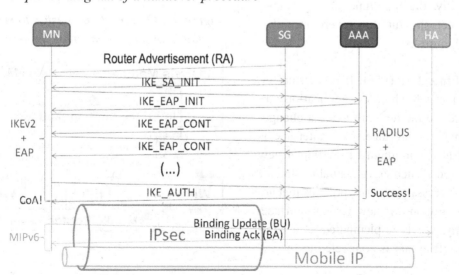

Figure 12. Two types of nesting tunnels to combine mobility and security

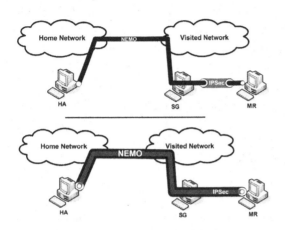

as was explained in the 802.21 overview at the beginning of the chapter.

In the frame of the testbed developed, all mobile router functionalities regarding mobility and security have been installed on a Mini ATX PC, provided with a VIA processor, 1 GB of RAM and a Linux Ubuntu distribution with kernel 2.6.32. A PCMCIA WiFi 802.11g interface has been added to enable the mobile router to connect with the WiFi infrastructure, and a Breeze Access VL client transceiver directly connected by an Ethernet interface provides connectivity to the deployed WiMAX infrastructure.

Conceptually, the MR functionality implemented has been structured in several modules, as shown in Figure 13:

- **Virtual interface (vIF):** It is a virtual interface through which the applications are connected to the network using a changeable physical interface. This interface is created at the moment of starting a new connection. When it is available, IKEv2 sets the necessary security policies that are applied only on this new virtual interface. Currently, vIF is implemented as a common interface that is connected to the ex-

ternal WiMAX device, which is managed through Telnet commands.

- **Statistics module (IM):** Its main task is to gather information from available network interfaces. Among the information gathered, the most important parameters are access points, signal strength and security protocols. This information is processed in order to make decisions based on pre-established rules, according to 802.21 mechanisms offered by the infrastructure. At the current stage, IM is implemented as a shell-script that gathers information from WiFi and WiMAX access points (signal strength, security mechanisms and communication standard used).

- **Rules Module (RM):** It contains rules that will be taken into account when the OBU selects a new network attachment point. Currently, these rules (later explained) are coded in the Analysis Module.

- **Analysis Module (AM):** Uses the information gathered by IM and the rules included in the RM, in order to make the final decision about what interface and network to choose. At this point, the system uses the information provided by the 802.21 MIIS in order to have an overview of the infra-

Figure 13. On-board unit design to support vehicular continuous communications

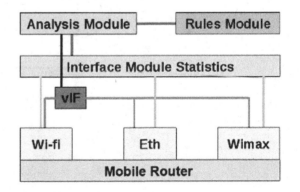

structure and make better decisions about when a handoff should be performed. AM has been implemented as a second shell-script that uses the data provided by IM about communication interfaces.

As can be noted, IM implements the functionality denoted as "Handover Information Gathering Phase" in Figure 4; while AM, together with RM, implements the "Handover Decision Phase", and trigger the "Handover Execution Phase", finally carried out by vIF. Among the rules considered in RM, which can modify the behavior of the handover process, the following have been initially considered:

- Right to access the service provider according to MR credentials.
- Technology that implements the interface used, to give priority to interfaces with higher data rates and low cost.
- Strength and signal quality, since it is desirable to choose a network that remains accessible for a long time.
- Maintenance of the same domain/technology. If a new candidate network belongs to the same domain than the current one, or the communication technology does not change in the new network, it might be preferable to choose this candidate network, instead of performing a vertical handoff to another.

All these rules can be adapted with the desired parameters to accommodate MR needs.

In this scenario, the mobile router is considered a module of the on-board equipment that, transparently to the user, performs handoffs between different networks to provide continuous IP connectivity (in the scenario considered IPv6), according to the available infrastructure and the preferences considered in the decision algorithm. One of the features that MR must meet is the ability to anticipate future changes in the network to

reduce the time in which communications can be interrupted (pre-authentication stage). Moreover, mobility can also be supported by the infrastructure through the information supplied by the MIIS service, since it can have a better knowledge of the network state, enabling certain management actions, such as load balancing.

FUTURE RESEARCH DIRECTIONS

Although handover techniques have been significantly improved in the past few years, there are still issues requiring further improvements such as QoS or quality of experience (QoE). Concerning QoS, handover techniques must consider multiple elements in order to choose the best candidate network that provides the QoS required by the different applications (Alcaraz, Vales, & Garcia, 2009) and supports a fast handoff (Jang, Jee, Jan, & Cha, 2008). Nevertheless, by offering not only QoS but also QoE, user satisfaction can be improved taking into account user preferences during the decision making process.

The heterogeneous infrastructure deployment presented in this work is certainly a necessary first step to open up further research possibilities, acting as a big testbed to check both emerging WiMAX technology itself and the protocols performance in situations where mobility and security are crucial factors. This is the case of the authentication methods, which can be analyzed in vehicular deployments in terms of performance, and can be adapted to the special mobility conditions of vehicular networks. We will continue analyzing and comparing authentication methods and enabling the pre-authentication mechanism in order to minimize the time spent on handovers.

Moreover, the information about the environment is critical to know when and where to handover. For example, the pre-authentication mechanism has to know what will be the next PoA in order to forward the authentication negotiation. This information is gathered from different sources like network interfaces and external entities in the frame of 802.21.

Another point of improvement focuses on considering not only infrastructure-based connectivity, but also vehicular ad-hoc networks (VANETs). If MR could choose between an infrastructure network and a VANET connected to Internet through a proper gateway, the flexibility of the system would be greatly improved, since deployment costs on infrastructure access points could be saved and vehicles could avoid the use of cellular networks. Moreover, by using VANETs, services with strident latency needs could be implemented, by means of route optimization techniques that avoid traversing the Internet (Lee, Chen, & Ernst, 2011). Finally, if the security mechanisms presented in this chapter are to be maintained when a VANET is used to reach the Internet, an IP support would be necessary over the ad-hoc protocol, since the proposal presented here focuses these tasks in the network layer. A work in this line can be seen in (Tsukada, et al., 2010).

CONCLUSION

WiFi and WiMAX technologies are perfect to cover indoor and outdoor areas respectively, so they are complementary solutions that can work together to provide a good experience while using provided services in vehicular scenarios. Both technologies have been combined in the proposal presented in this chapter in order to research handovers in heterogeneous scenarios, and to study the behavior of the various protocols involved in the platform in vehicular networks, where security and mobility are both key aspects. However, as we have stated in this chapter, the handover architecture proposed is ready to include other communication technologies that extend the current testbed. Protocols like IPsec, IKEv2, EAP and NEMO have been chosen to cover these requisites in a real scenario deployed at the University of Murcia. In addition, the use of EAP provides an

extensible authentication method which reduces the overall handover time.

Readers should also notice that this proposal is in line with current standardization works regarding communication architectures on vehicular cooperative systems (Kosch, et al., 2009), such as the ISO CALM (Communications Access for Land Mobiles) or the ETSI European ITS Communication Architecture. The work presented in this chapter supports several communication technologies to provide continuous connectivity in vehicles and covers an essential part of the CALM and ETSI standards. In fact, NEMO is currently being considered in these standards to provide IPv6 mobility, and some of the proposals given in this chapter regarding security, such as applying IPsec, IKE and authentication, have started to be discussed as possible extensions for the security and management modules of the current CALM/ETSI communication architecture for cooperative systems.

In order to provide mobility and security at the same time, some incompatibility issues have to be managed. Nesting tunnels is not as common as we imagine. For this reason, current open source solutions do not implement this feature properly. Therefore, a solution which combines mobility and security under nesting tunnels is provided in the chapter.

One of the most important phases of the handover process is the network selection phase. In vehicular environments, information about location and mobility patterns are of utmost importance due to the speed vehicles move. Thus, any handover decision scheme proposed should account for this information. Moreover, a decision scheme within vehicular environments must include advanced context information, particularly location-aware information.

Finally, collecting information from the surrounding environment is essential to predict when and where handovers are to be performed. On board communication equipment and the 802.21 standard can help us better manage this knowledge, always with the goal of providing vehicles with the best wireless connection available, and without the need to distract the user.

REFERENCES

Aboba, B., Blunk, L., Vollbrecht, J., Carlson, J., & Levkowetz, H. (2004). *Extensible authentication protocol (EAP)*. IETF RFC 3748. Retrieved September 10, 2010, from http://tools.ietf.org/html/rfc3748.

Alcaraz, J., Vales, J., & Garcia, J. (2009). Control-based scheduling with QoS support for vehicle to infrastructure communications. *IEEE Wireless Communications*, *16*(6), 32–39. doi:10.1109/MWC.2009.5361176

Blum, J., & Eskandarian, A. (2004). The threat of intelligent collisions. *IT Professional*, *6*(1), 24–29. doi:10.1109/MITP.2004.1265539

Chen, Y., Hsia, J., & Liao, Y. (2009). Advanced seamless vertical handoff architecture for WiMAX and WiFi heterogeneous networks with QoS guarantees. *Computer Communications*, *32*(2), 281–293. doi:10.1016/j.comcom.2008.10.014

Devarapalli, V., Wakikawa, R., Petrescu, A., & Thubert, P. (2005). *Network mobility (NEMO) basic support protocol*. IETF RFC 3963. Retrieved April 25, 2010 from http://www.ietf.org/rfc/rfc3963.txt.

Fang-Yie Leu, F., Huang, Y., & Chiu, C. (2010). *Improving security levels of IEEE802.16e authentication by involving Diffie-Hellman PKDS*. International Conference on Complex, Intelligent and Software Intensive Systems (CISIS).

FreeRadius. (2010). *The FreeRADIUS Project* (Version 2.1.10) [Computer software]. Retrieved from http://freeradius.org/.

3GPP-SAE. (2011). *Third Generation Partnership Project - System architecture evolution*.

Habib, M., & Ahmad, M. (2010). *A review of some security aspects of WiMAX and converged network*. Second International Conference on Communication Software and Networks.

Hubaux, J., Capkun, S., & Luo, J. (2004). The security and privacy of smart vehicles. *IEEE Security and Privacy*, *2*(3), 49–55. doi:10.1109/MSP.2004.26

IEEE 1609.2. (2006). *Standard for wireless access in vehicular environments - Security services for applications and management messages*. Version 2: Under Development.

IEEE P802.11u. (2010). *Interworking with external networks Task Group U*.

IEEE P802.16g. (2010). *Management plane procedures and services (MobileMan) Task Group*.

Jang, H., Jee, J., Jan, H., & Cha, J. (2008). *Mobile IPv6 fast handovers over IEEE 802.16e networks*. Retrieved on April 26, 2011, from http://tools.ietf.org/tools/rfcmarkup/rfcmarkup.cgi/draft-ietf-mipshop-fh80216e.

Johnson, D., Perkins, C., & Arkko, J. (2004). *Mobility support in IPv6*. IETF RFC 3775. Retrieved April 25, 2010, from http://www.ietf.org/rfc/rfc3775.txt.

Kaufman, C. (2006). *Internet key exchange (IKEv2) protocol*. IETF RFC 4306. Retrieved September 10, 2010, from http://tools.ietf.org/html/rfc2401.

Kent, S., & Atkinson, R. (1998). *Security architecture for the Internet protocol*. IETF RFC 2401. Retrieved September 5, 2010, from http://tools.ietf.org/html/rfc2401.

Khaled, Y., Tsukada, M., Santa, J., Choia, J., & Ernst, T. (2009). A usage oriented analysis of vehicular networks: From technologies to applications. *The Journal of Communication*, *4*(5), 357–368. doi:10.4304/jcm.4.5.357-368

Kosch, T., Kulp, I., Bechler, M., Strassberger, M., Weyl, B., & Lasowski, R. (2009). Communication architecture for cooperative systems in Europe. *IEEE Wireless Communication Magazine, 47*(5), 116–125. doi:10.1109/MCOM.2009.4939287

Lee, J. H., Chen, J., & Ernst, T. (2011). (in press). Securing mobile network prefix provisioning for NEMO based vehicular networks. *Mathematical and Computer Modelling.* doi:doi:10.1016/j.mcm.2011.02.023

Lee, S., Sriram, K., Kim, K., Kim, Y., & Golmie, N. (2009). Vertical handoff decision algorithms for providing optimized performance in heterogeneous wireless networks. *IEEE Transactions on Vehicular Technology, 58*(2), 865–881. doi:10.1109/TVT.2008.925301

Marín, R., Pereñiquez, F., Bernal, F., & Skarmeta, A. (2009). *Architecture for fast EAP re-authentication based on a new EAP method (EAP-FRM) working on standalone mode.* IETF draft. Retrieved September 07, 2010, from http://tools.ietf.org/html/draft-marin-eap-frm-fastreauth-00.

Marquez-Barja, J., Calafate, C. T., Cano, J. C., & Manzoni, P. (2010). An overview of vertical handover techniques: Algorithms, protocols and tools. *Computer Communications, 34*(8), 985–997. doi:10.1016/j.comcom.2010.11.010

Matthias, G. (2005). *VaneSe - An approach to VANET security.* In V2VCOM, 2005, San Diego, California, USA.

MIPSHOP. (2009). *IETF mobility for IP: Performance, signaling and handoff optimization.*

Nelson, D., & DeKok, A. (2007). *Common remote authentication dial in user service (RADIUS).* IETF RFC 5080. Retrieved from http://tools.ietf.org/html/rfc5080.

NEMO. (2010). *NEMO implementation.* Retrieved from http://www.umip.org/.

Olario, S., & Weigle, M. (2009). *Vehicular networks from theory to practice.* Chapman & Hall.

Parno, B., & Perrig, A. (2005). Challenges in securing vehicular networks. *Proceedings of the Fourth Workshop on Hot Topics in Networks (HotNets-IV).*

Pérez, A., Fernández, P. J., Marín, R., Martínez, G., Gómez-Skarmeta, A. F., & Taniuchi, K. (2008). OpenIKEv2: Design and implementation of an IKEv2 solution. *IEICE Transactions, 91-D*(5), 1319–1329. doi:doi:10.1093/ietisy/e91-d.5.1319

Raya, M., & Hubaux, J. P. (2005). The security of vehicular ad hoc networks. *Proceedings of the 3rd ACM Workshop on Security of Ad Hoc and Sensor Networks.* doi:10.1145/1102219.1102223

Raya, M., Papadimitratos, P., & Hubaux, J. (2006). Securing vehicular communications. *IEEE Wireless Communications Magazine, 13*(5), 8–15. doi:10.1109/WC-M.2006.250352

Samara, G., Al-Salihy, W., & Sures, R. (2010). *Security analysis of vehicular ad hoc networks (VANET).* 2010 Second International Conference on Network Applications Protocols and Services.

IEEE Std. 802.11g. (2003). *IEEE 802.11g-2003 IEEE standard for Information technology - Telecommunications and information exchange between systems - Local and metropolitan area networks - Specific requirements - Part 11: Wireless LAN medium access control (MAC) and physical layer (PHY) specifications - Amendment 4: Further higher-speed physical layer extension in the 2.4 GHz band.*

IEEE Std. 802.16. (2004). *IEEE standard for local and metropolitan area networks, Part 16: Air interface for fixed broadband wireless access systems.*

IEEE Std. 802.16e. (2005). *IEEE standard for local and metropolitan area networks part 16: Air interface for fixed and mobile broadband wireless access systems amendment for physical and medium access control layers for combined fixed and mobile operation in licensed bands.*

IEEE Std. 802.21. (2008). *IEEE standard for local and metropolitan area networks - Part 21: Media independent handover services.*

Sun, H., Lin, Y., Chen, S., & Shen, Y. (2007). *Secure and fast handover scheme based on pre-authentication method for 802.16/WiMAX infrastructure networks.* IEEE Region 10 Conference.

Tsukada, M., Ben-Jemaa, I., Menouar, H., Zhang, W., Goleva, M., & Ernst, T. (2010). *Experimental evaluation for IPv6 over VANET geographic routing.* 6th International Wireless Communications and Mobile Computing Conference.

UMTS. (2006). *3G/UMTS Evolution: Towards a new generation of broadband mobile services.* White paper, UMTS Forum.

Yi, L., & Miao, K. (2010). *WiMAX-WiFi unified network architecture, security, and mobility.* 12th IEEE International Conference on Communication Technology.

Zhou, P., Qin, Y., Xu, C., Guan, J., & Zhang, H. (2010). *Security investigation and enhancement of IKEV2 protocol.* 3rd IEEE International Conference on Broadband Network and Multimedia Technology (IC-BNMT).

KEY TERMS AND DEFINITIONS

Communication Tunnel: This is a common term used in computer communications, which stands for the process of encapsulating data packets transmitted using a protocol, inside packets of another protocol, with the aim of hiding communication end points of a change in the communication route or secure a segment of the network transparently, for instance.

Handoff: Also known as handover, it is the process of changing the network association of a terminal when changes its point of attachment to a different communication technology, a different network domain, or both.

IKEv2 (Internet Key Exchange): It is a protocol that provides a secure key exchange framework to establish a security association by means of IPsec.

IPsec (Internet Protocol security): It is a set of protocols that provide IP of authentication and confidentiality capabilities to secure data connections.

NEMO (Network Mobility): This is a protocol defined at IEFT that enables routers to act on behalf of a network to change its point of attachment to the Internet, hiding mobility to connected devices.

Terminal Mobility: Above all in wireless communications, devices connected with a network needs more and more an infrastructure support and a suitable communication stack which enable them to change between different networks without making the user aware of that.

WiMAX (Worldwide Interoperability for Microwave Access): This is a wireless communication technology that uses the IEEE 802.16 set of protocols to provide connectivity to terminals in the order of tens of Mbps within coverage areas in the order of tens of kilometres.

Chapter 15
Unpredicted Trajectories of an Automated Guided Vehicle with Chaos

Magda Judith Morales Tavera
Universidade Federal do Rio de Janeiro, Brazil

Omar Lengerke
Universidad Autónoma de Bucaramanga, Colombia

Max Suell Dutra
Universidade Federal do Rio de Janeiro, Brazil

ABSTRACT

Intelligent Transportation Systems (ITS) are the future of transportation. As a result of emerging standards, vehicles will soon be able to talk to one another as well as their environment. A number of applications will be made available for vehicular networks that improve the overall safety of the transportation infrastructure. This chapter develops a method to impart chaotic motions to an Automated Guided Vehicle (AGV). The chaotic AGV implies a mobile robot with a controller that ensures chaotic motions. This kind of motion is characterized by the topological transitivity and the sensitive dependence on initial conditions. Due the topological transitivity, the mobile robot is guaranteed to scan the whole connected workspace. For scanning motion, the chaotic robot neither requires a map of the workspace nor plans global motions. It only requires the measurement of the workspace boundary when it comes close to it.

INTRODUCTION

Today, robotics have become a key technology in many current industrial environments and are used in companies that require high degrees of automation. Robotics is an area that studies the link between perceptions and actions, and the robot is a device that performs tasks or activities similar to humans that are influenced by new customer requirements regarding the specific characteristics of products and services (quality, quantity and time). Important advancements have been made in the area of manipulators which are used in flexible manufacturing systems (FMS).

DOI: 10.4018/978-1-4666-0209-0.ch015

Their use has grown significantly because they are highly efficient in performing repetitive tasks (assembling, welding, and painting, among others). Their greatest disadvantage is displacement; they cannot physically move from one point to another within their environments because they possess limited movements to be performed in restricted spaces, which is quite different than what is expected from mobile robots. The nature of mobile robots permits them to move around a factory while avoiding obstacles, which makes them more flexible and increasingly demanded by industry.

Mobile robots are used in different environments (water, air, industrial, among others) and have been the object of development in the fields of mechanics, mechatronics, sensing, communications, navigation and movement optimization. The scope of mobile robots is not restricted to industry. It is significantly greater, reaching the areas of underwater exploration, oceanographic and planetary exploration, as well as military applications and logistics (distribution and warehousing). Currently, industrial projects conducted using mobile robotics have application mainly in manufacturing (cells and factories, flexible manufacturing systems), in the distribution chain logistics, storage and services. There are two fundamental types of systems in these fields of application: AS/RS (Automated Storage/Retrieval System) (Lowe, 2002) and AGVs (Automated Guided Vehicles) (Lengerke, et al., 2008). In recent years, there has been interest in developing technologies applied in AGVs, including the automation of tasks related to transportation, loading and unloading of materials or simple inspection tasks, which implies monitoring and controlling vehicle movements from a starting point to an endpoint, thus offering significant risk reduction, offset times and energy consumption. AGV systems are considered as one of the most appropriate methods to support the handling of materials in automated production environments. In general, AGV systems consists of a set of vehicles without drivers who operate cooperatively, carrying goods and materials between different workstations and storage locations, thus facilitating production. These vehicles usually follow a predetermined physical or virtual path that is incorporated in the layout of the manufacturing site and coordinated by a system of control which is based on centralized or distributed computers.

The movement of vehicles is based on the study of the various navigational techniques that use different types of sensors (infrared, ultrasonic, vision, optical, magnetic, etc.) or paths guided by wires as part of the equipment of the mobile robot.

Some of the advantages of this type of system are: increased flexibility of the forwarding of vehicles in the layout, improved use of space and security, as well as reduced operation costs (Reveliotis, 2000). The use of these vehicles has grown enormously since their introduction in 1973 in the Volvo vehicle production plant in Kalmar. The number of application areas and variation in types has increased significantly as warehouses and factories have increasing numbers of intersections and factory layouts, in general, become more complex with greater internal and external transport of material and handling of parts and products between workstations. Currently there are several applications used for repetitive tasks, such as transport manufacturing operations that work with average production volumes, including flexible manufacturing systems, storage and service industries. Also, these systems are used for various tasks such as mail sorting, luggage transport at airports, container cargo transport and tracking (Steenken et al., 2005), security, and even in hospitals (Ceric, 1990, Krishnamurthy & Evans, 1992).

Science has advanced a long way in making humans increasingly understand nature, enabling them to predict phenomena that occur in the near future, or reconstruct the past with the present information. However, the use of knowledge and of natural laws to forecast new phenomena and also to retrieve past events is not an easy one. What is the sense of humankind spoiling the environment in such a way that Mother Nature reactions are becoming so overwhelming?

It seems to us that the behavior of natural systems can be explained through chaos theory. Thus, the prediction of future events is possible; however, this forecast cannot be to infinity, but can only be extrapolated for a not too distant future, hence the term "deterministic chaos." Events that occurred in the past are certainly better determined when one has more data in the present (Baptista, 1996). Chaotic behavior is sensitive to initial conditions, which implies that the evolution of the system can be changed by small disturbances. Furthermore, the structure of a chaotic response is very rich, being associated with infinities unstable periodic orbits. These properties mean that chaotic behavior is very flexibility, making it of potential use in systems that need quickly react to certain disturbances. This is characteristic of natural systems where chaos, along with various regulatory mechanisms, provides unusual flexibility (Savi, 2006).

This chapter proposes implementing the chaotic nature of an Automated Guided Vehicles (AGV) for to inspect environments with non-defined trajectories, supported by sensor systems and intelligent vision. Chaos features a richer behavior and mysterious of nonlinear dynamical systems, characterized by the topology and transitive dependence on initial conditions. The chaotic behavior of the proposed AGV is achieved by incorporating the kinematic equations of robots, Arnold's equation, that is known as an equation that characterizes chaotic behavior.

AGV NAVIGATION CHAOTIC WITH OBSTACLES

Chaos theory is one of the richest and most mysterious behaviors of nonlinear dynamic systems. Much research has been conducted to establish the mathematical theory behind chaos; for example, chaos control and chaotic neural networks (Freeman, 1994) in search of simple rules.

This chapter presents a study for trajectories for AGVs based on dynamic characteristics of chaotic systems for their implementation on FMS (Martins-Filho & Macau, 2004, Jansri, et al., 2004). This is achieved by designing a motion controller with chaotic characteristics. A transitivity topology (property of chaotic movements) ensures full connection with the workspace (Nakamura & Sekiguchi, 2001). This method of construction of trajectories is slated to land exploration missions, with the specific purpose of observation or patrol, where a quick scan of the robot's workspace is needed. As a result, the trajectories of mobile robots seem highly opportunistic and unpredictable to external observers and characteristics of trajectories guarantee a quick exploration of spaces.

Mobile robotics, after decades of continuous development, continues to be a subject of intense research because of its increasing application in different areas and its technological and economic impact. Interesting applications can be seen in the execution of floor cleaning, industrial transport, and mining, scanning areas to find different types of materials and so on. This research discusses how mobile robots are used to transport materials in an area. For the mathematical modeling, let us assume a mobile robot like the one shown in Figure 1. Let linear velocity of the robot

Figure 1. Mobile robot

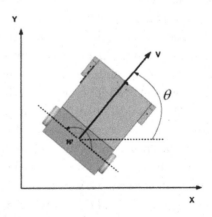

$v\left[\frac{m}{s}\right]$ and angular velocity $w\left[\frac{rad}{s}\right]$ are inputs of the system.

The state equation of the mobile robot is:

$$\begin{pmatrix} \dot{x} \\ \dot{y} \\ \dot{\theta} \end{pmatrix} = \begin{pmatrix} \cos\theta & 0 \\ \sin\theta & 0 \\ 0 & 1 \end{pmatrix} \begin{pmatrix} v \\ w \end{pmatrix} \qquad (1)$$

Where $\left(x[m], y[m]\right)$ is the position of the robot and $\theta[rad]$ is the angle of the robot. In order to make the robot move in a chaotic fashion, one system that can be used is the Arnold equation:

$$\begin{pmatrix} \dot{x}_1 \\ \dot{x}_2 \\ \dot{x}_3 \end{pmatrix} = \begin{pmatrix} A\sin x_3 + C\cos x_2 \\ B\sin x_1 + A\cos x_3 \\ C\sin x_2 + B\cos x_1 \end{pmatrix} \qquad (2)$$

The Arnold equation describes a steady solution to the three-dimensional Euler equation which expresses the behaviors of noncompressive perfect fluids in a 3-D torus space. It is known that the Arnold equation shows periodic motion when one of the constants, for example C, is 0 and shows chaotic motion when C is large.

These states evolve in a 5-D space, which includes 3-D subspaces of the Arnold flow. The states evolution in the 2-D complementary space is highly coupled with that in the 3-D subspace as seen in (3).

Figure 2. Poincaré section of Arnold flow

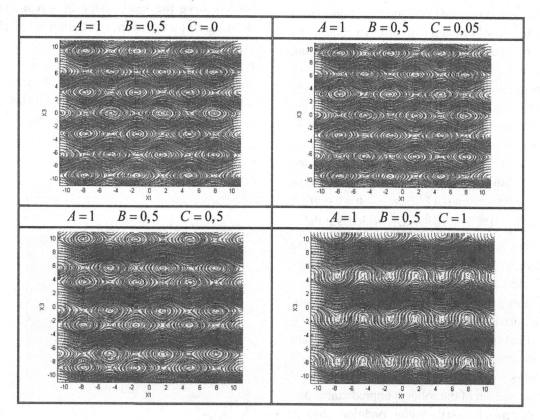

Figure 3. Trajectory of the mobile robot

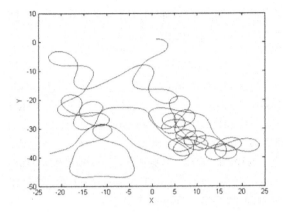

$$\begin{pmatrix} \dot{x}_1 \\ \dot{x}_2 \\ \dot{x}_3 \\ \dot{x} \\ \dot{y} \end{pmatrix} = \begin{pmatrix} A\sin x_3 + C\cos x_2 \\ B\sin x_1 + A\cos x_3 \\ C\sin x_2 + B\cos x_1 \\ v\cos x_3 \\ v\sin x_3 \end{pmatrix} \qquad (3)$$

The inputs applied to the robot are continuous since the Arnold equation describes a continuous system. We could have used the Rossler equation, the Lorenz equation, or even others well known continuous chaotic systems of lesser dimensions, but choosing Arnold's equation has the following advantages: (i) Arnold's equation and the mobile robot equation structures are similar, (ii) It is easy to deal with it because the state variables are limited within a 3-D torus space, (iii) The range of the input w becomes $-\left(|B|+|C|\right) \leq w \leq \left(|B|+|C|\right)$ which is suitable for robot input, and; (iv) The maximum of the state variables are determined by the parameters A, B and C.

Figure 3 shows an example of motions of a mobile robot with the proposed controller, obtained by numerical simulation. The initial conditions were chosen from a region where the Poincare section produces a closed path trajectory. It is observed that the motion of the robot is unpredictable and heavily dependent on the initial conditions chosen.

Figure 4. Mobile robot trajectories with boundaries

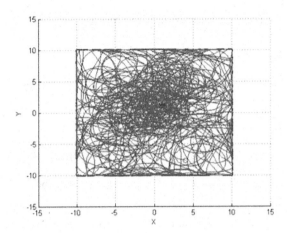

Automated Guided Vehicles moves in spaces with borders (or boundaries), such as walls or obstacles. To help overcoming this problem, an imaginary space is considered. This imaginary space is obtained by connecting two spaces whose borders have the same shape in a real space. Blowing air on the surface and allowing an elastic deformation allows the robot to move smoothly between the two sides of the border. The AGV moves on a imaginary surface (workspace) described by the mathematical model, while in the

Figure 5. Mobile robot trajectories with boundaries

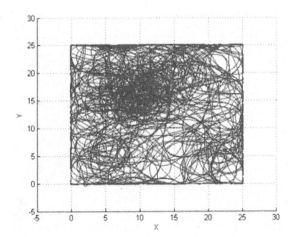

Figure 6. Mobile robot trajectories with boundaries and one obstacle

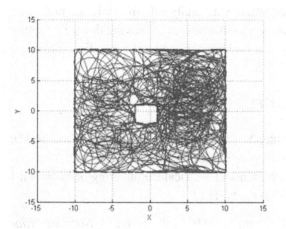

Figure 7. Mobile robot trajectory with boundaries and one obstacle

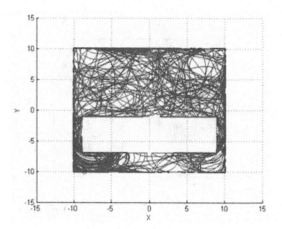

real space the robot movement is like it would be perceived from the top view of the imaginary space.

However, for observation, it is necessary to apply the transformation of coordinates of the left system to the right system. That is the reason it is called mirror mapping. In real space, the mobile robot moves and is reflected by the border. To avoid a barrier mirror mapping is considered (Bae, 2004) when robots approach walls or obstacles. Whenever the robot nears a barrier, the new position of the robot is calculated using the equations.

$$A = \begin{bmatrix} Cos\theta & Sin\theta \\ Sin\theta & -Cos\theta \end{bmatrix} \qquad (4)$$

$$A = \frac{1}{1+m} \begin{bmatrix} 1-m^2 & 2m \\ 2m & -1+m^2 \end{bmatrix} \qquad (5)$$

When the slope is infinitive, it is necessary to use Equation (4) and when the slope is not infinitive, it is possible to use Equation (5). The procedure employed is based on the principle of mirror mapping, with the variant that the robot's position will be directly recalculated. The coordinates x and y are necessary in order to allow

avoidance of obstacles or crossing the boundaries of the workspace. Examples of trajectories using mirror mapping are shown in Figures 4 and 5, with the coordinates initially set to the boundaries of the workspace for different value ranges. The processing time is 4.4903 seconds for Figure 4 and 4.8490 seconds for Figure 5.

To continue our analysis, we applied an obstacle with the same parameters shown in Figure 5. This generated Figure 6, but with a processing time of 3.4524 seconds, less than that obtained in

Figure 8. Mobile robot trajectory with boundaries and two obstacles

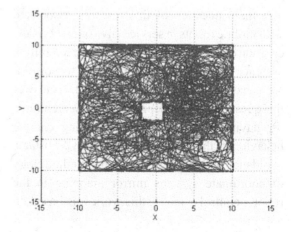

Figure 9. Mobile robot trajectory with boundaries and two obstacles

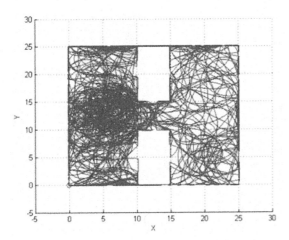

the simulation without an obstacle with the same parameters.

With a larger obstacle near the boundary, the robot maps the space as shown in Figure 7. With 8000 seconds in the simulation time the processing time is 5.0652 seconds.

Increasing the number of obstacles (Figure 8) and with a simulation time of 6000 seconds, the processing time increases significantly to 150.9973 seconds.

With different boundaries, Figure 9 is generated with a processing time of 165.0989 seconds.

CONCLUSION

The main question of this research associated with mobile robots in service environments is the creation of autonomous detection and recognition systems to improve navigation and to perform tasks that are more robust and efficient. To answer this question, this work proposes a new technique for navigation systems, incorporating chaotic behavior in the navigation to improve obstacle avoidance and also employing the methodology of coordinate systems mirror mapping in the robot´s control. Finally, this work was based on

the chaotic dynamics of the Arnold equation to integrate mobile robot and the behavior of the equation was analyzed. In addition, presented the controller design so that the dynamic mobile robot is characterized by the equation studied.

REFERENCES

Bae, Y. (2004). *Obstacle avoidance method in the chaotic robot*. Division Electronic Communication an Electrical Engineering of Yosu Nat'l University. IEEE.

Baptista, M. (1996). *Perturbando Sistemas Não-Lineares, Uma Abordagem ao Controle de Caos*. D.Sc. Brasil: Universidade de São Paulo.

Ceric, V. (1990). Simulation study of an automated guided-vehicle system in a Yugoslav hospital. *The Journal of the Operational Research Society*, *41*(4), 299–310.

Freeman, W. J. (1994). Neural networks and chaos. *Journal of Theoretical Biology*, *171*, 13–18. doi:10.1006/jtbi.1994.1207

Jansri, A., Klomkarn, K., & Sooraksa, P. (2004). On comparison of attractors for chaotic mobile robots. *The 30th Annual Conference of the IEEE Industrial Electronics Society Electronics Society*, (vol. 3, pp. 2536-2541).

Krishnamurthy, B., & Evans, J. (1992). Help-Mate: A robotic courier for hospital use. *IEEE International Conference on Systems, Man and Cybernetics*, (vol. 2, pp. 1630 – 1634).

Lengerke, O., Archila, J. F., & Dutra, M. S. (2008). Diseño Mecatrónico de un Robot Tipo AGV - Automated Guided Vehicle. *UIS Ingenierías - Facultad de Ingenierías Fisicomecánicas*, *7*(1), 63–74.

Lowe, D. (2002). *Dictionary of transport and logistics - Terms, abbreviations and acronyms. The Institute of Logistics and Transport*. Great Britain: Biddles Ltd, Guildford and King's Lynn.

Martins-Filho, L. S., & Macau, E. E. N. (2007). Patrol mobile robots and chaotic trajectories. *Mathematical Problems in Engineering*, Article ID 61543, v. 2007, 13 pages. Hindawi Publishing Corporation.

Nakamura, Y., & Sekiguchi, A. (2001). The chaotic mobile robot. *IEEE Transactions on Robotics and Automation, 17*(6), 898–904. doi:10.1109/70.976022

Reveliotis, S. A. (2000). Conflict resolution in AGV systems. *IIE Transactions, 32*(7), 647–659. doi:10.1080/07408170008967423

Savi, M. (2006). *Dinâmica Não-Linear e Caos*. Rio de Janeiro, e-papers.

Steenken, D. VOß, S., & Stahlbock, R. (2005). Container terminal operation and operations research – A Classification and literature review. In H. Günther, & K. H. Kim (Eds.), *Container terminals and automated transport systems - Logistics control issues and quantitative decision support*, (pp. 3 – 49). Berlin, Germany: Springer.

Compilation of References

3GPP-SAE. (2011). *Third Generation Partnership Project - System architecture evolution.*

80216-2004I.S. (2004). *IEEE standard for Local and metropolitan area networks-Part 16: Air interface for fixed broadband wireless access systems.* Retrieved from http://www.ncbi.nlm.nih.gov/pubmed/20715964

80216e. (2005). *I.S. Part 16: Air interface for fixed and mobile broadband wireless access systems.*

80216j. (2009). *I.S. IEEE standard for local and metropolitan area networks--Part 16: Air interface for broadband wireless access systems--Amendment 1: Multihop relay specification.*

Abhayawardhana, V. S., Wassell, I. J., Crosby, D., Sellars, M. P., & Brown, M. G. (2005). *Comparison of empirical propagation path loss models for fixed wireless access systems.* Paper presented at the Vehicular Technology Conference, 2005. VTC 2005-Spring. 2005 IEEE 61st.

Aboba, B., Blunk, L., Vollbrecht, J., Carlson, J., & Levkowetz, H. (2004). *Extensible authentication protocol (EAP).* IETF RFC 3748. Retrieved September 10, 2010, from http://tools.ietf.org/html/rfc3748

Acosta-Marum, G., & Ingram, M. (2007). Six time- and frequency-selective empirical channel models for vehicular wireless LANs. *IEEE Vehicular Technology Magazine, 2*(4), 4–11. doi:10.1109/MVT.2008.917435

Aggelou, G. (2005). *Mobile ad hoc networks: From wireless LANS to 4G networks.* New York, NY: McGraw-Hill.

Ahmed, A., Krishnamachari, B., & Psounis, K. (2008). IEEE 802.11p performance evaluation and protocol enhancement. *2008 IEEE International Conference on Vehicular Electronics and Safety*, (pp. 317-322).

Akki, A. (1994). Statistical properties of mobile-to-mobile land communication channels. *IEEE Transactions on Vehicular Technology, 43*(4), 826–831. doi:10.1109/25.330143

Akki, A., & Haber, F. (1986). A statistical model of mobile-to-mobile land communication channel. *IEEE Transactions on Vehicular Technology, 35*(1), 2–7. doi:10.1109/T-VT.1986.24062

Alam, N., Balaei, A. T., & Dempster, A. G. (2009). *Range and range-rate measurements using DSRC: Facts and challenges.* Paper presented at the IGNSS Symposium 2009, Surfers Paradise, Australia.

Alam, N., Balaei, A. T., & Dempster, A. G. (2010a). *Proceedings of the 72nd IEEE Vehicular Technology Conference Fall VTC 2010-Fall* (pp. 1-5). Ottawa. doi:10.1109/VETECF.2010.5594457

Alam, N., Balaei, A. T., & Dempster, A. G. (2010b). *Positioning enhancement with double differencing and DSRC.* Paper presented at the ION GNSS 2010, Portland, USA.

Alamouti, S. M. (1999). A simple transmit diversity technique for wireless communications. *IEEE Journal on Selected Areas in Communications, 16*(8), 1451–1458. doi:10.1109/49.730453

Alasmary, W., & Ashtiani, F. (2008). A modified 802.11-based MAC scheme to assure fair access for vehicle-to-roadside communications. *Computer Communications, 31*(12), 2898–2906. doi:10.1016/j.comcom.2008.01.030

Alasmary, W., & Zhuang, W. (2010). Mobility impact in IEEE 802.11p infrastructureless vehicular networks. *Ad Hoc Networks, 57*(1), 56–63. doi:doi:10.1016/j.adhoc.2010.06.006

Alcaraz, J., Vales, J., & Garcia, J. (2009). Control-based scheduling with QoS support for vehicle to infrastructure communications. *IEEE Wireless Communications, 16*(6), 32–39. doi:10.1109/MWC.2009.5361176

Al-Qutayri, M., & Yuen, C. (2010). Security and privacy of intelligent VANETs. In Ali, A.-D. (Ed.), *Computational intelligence and modern heuristics*. InTech.

Alsindi, N. A., Alavi, B., & Pahlavan, K. (2009). Measurement and modeling of ultrawideband TOA-based ranging in indoor multipath environments. *IEEE Transactions on Vehicular Technology, 58*(3), 1046–1058. doi:10.1109/TVT.2008.926071

Amadeo, M., Campolo, C., & Molinaro, A. (2010). Enhancing IEEE 802.11p/WAVE to provide infotainment applications in VANETs. *Ad Hoc Networks, Special Issue on Recent Advances in Analysis and Deployment of IEEE 802.11e and IEEE 802.11p Protocol Families*. Advance online publication. doi:10.1016/j.adhoc.2010.09.013

Amar, A., & Weiss, A. J. (2008). Localization of narrowband radio emitters based on doppler frequency shifts. *IEEE Transactions on Signal Processing, 56*(11), 5500–5508. doi:10.1109/TSP.2008.929655

America, I. T. (2009). *Intelligent Transportation Society of America*. Retrieved from http://www.itsa.org/

American Society for Testing and Materials. (2008). *ASTM E2213: Standard specification for telecommunications and information exchange between roadside and vehicle systems—5 GHz band dedicated short range communications (DSRC)-Medium access control (MAC) and physical layer (PHY) specifications*. Retrieved 22 September, 2008, from http://www.astm.org

Amin, R., & Wang, K. C. (2007). An integrated routing and scheduling approach for persistent vehicle communication in mobile wimax mesh networks. *Military Communications Conference*, (pp. 1-7).

Amin, R., Wang, K. C., & Ramanathan, P. (2008). An interference and QOS aware distributed scheduling approach for hybrid IEEE 802.16E mesh networks. *MILCOM 2008 IEEE Military Communications Conference*, (pp. 1-7).

Amundson, I., Koutsoukos, X., & Sallai, J. (2008). Mobile sensor localization and navigation using RF doppler shifts. In *Proceedings of the First ACM International Workshop on Mobile Entity Localization and Tracking in GPS-less Environments* (pp. 97-102). San Francisco, CA. doi:10.1145/1410012.1410034

Anderson, H. R. (2003). *Fixed broadband wireless system design*. West Sussex, England: Wiley. doi:10.1002/0470861290

Andrews, J., Ghosh, A., & Muhamed, R. (2007). *Fundamentals of WiMAX: Understanding broadband wireless networking*. Upper Saddle River, NJ: Prentice-Hall.

Aquino, R., Apolinar, V., Luis, A., & Crespo, A. J. (2009). Simulación de algoritmos para regular el flujo vehicular y la comunicación entre vehículos móviles autónomos utilizando redes Ad Hoc. *Revista Iberoamericana de Automatica e Informatica Industrial, 6*, 75–83.

Aquino, R., Potes, A., & Villaseñor, L. A. (2008). *Un nuevo algoritmo de enrutamiento para redes ad hoc vehiculares (A novel routing algorithm for vehicular ad hoc networks)* (pp. 120–131). Revista Facultad de Ingenieria Universidad de Antioquia.

Aquino, R., Rangel-Licea, V., & Edwards, A. (2008). Inter-vehicular communications using wireless ad hoc networks. *Ingeniería. Investigación y Tecnología, 9*, 319–328.

Aquino, S. R., & Edwards, B. A. (2006). A reactive location routing algorithm with cluster-based flooding for inter-vehicle communication. *Computación y Sistemas, 9*, 297–313.

Armstrong, L. (n.d.). *Dedicated short range communications (DSRC)*. Retrieved from http://www.leearmstrong.com/DSRC/DSRCHomeset.htm

Arthur, D. (2007). *HSPA and mobile WiMAX for mobile broadband wireless access- An independent report prepared for the GSM Association*.

Asenjo, A., & Gonzalez, E. (2006). Voz y datos digitales en el bus. Transportes Metropolitanos de Barcelona. *Comunicaciones World, 211*, 58.

Atkin, G. E., & Corrales, H. P. (1989). An efficient modulation/coding scheme for MFSK systems on bandwidth constrained channels. *IEEE Journal on Selected Areas in Communications, 7*(9), 1396–1401. doi:10.1109/49.44578

Ayyappan, K., & Dananjayan, P. (2008). Propagation model for highway communication system. *Ubiquitous Computing and Communication Journal, 3*(4), 6.

Bae, Y. (2004). *Obstacle avoidance method in the chaotic robot.* Division Electronic Communication an Electrical Engineering of Yosu Nat'l University. IEEE.

Bahillo, A., Prieto, J., Mazuelas, S., Lorenzo, R. M., Blas, J., & Fern, Ã. ¡ndez, P. (2009). IEEE 802.11 distance estimation based on RTS/CTS two-frame exchange mechanism. In *Proceedings of 69th IEEE Vehicular Technology Conference VTC-Spring09* (pp. 1-5). Barcelona. doi:10.1109/VETECS.2009.5073583

Bai, F., & Krishnamachari, B. (2009). Spatio-temporal variations of vehicle traffic in VANETs: Facts and implications. In *Proceedings of 6th ACM International Workshop on VehiculAr InterNETworking* (pp. 43-52). Bejing China.

Bai, F., & Krishnan, H. (2006). Reliability analysis of DSRC wireless communication for vehicle safety applications. *IEEE Intelligent Transportation Systems Conference 2006* (pp. 355-362). Toronto. doi: 10.1109/ITSC.2006.1706767

Bai, F., & Krishnamachari, B. (2010). Exploiting the wisdom of the crowd: Localized, distributed information-centric VANETS. *IEEE Communications Magazine, 48*(5), 138–146. doi:10.1109/MCOM.2010.5458375

Baker, D., Ephremides, A., & Flynn, J. (1984). The design and simulation of a mobile radio network with distribute control. *IEEE Journal on Selected Areas in Communications, 2*, 226–237. doi:10.1109/JSAC.1984.1146043

Baldessari, R., Festag, A.. & Lenardi, M. (2007). *C2C-C consortium requirements for NEMO route optimization.* IETF Draft draft-baldessari-c2ccc-nemo-req-01.

Baptista, M. (1996). *Perturbando Sistemas Não-Lineares, Uma Abordagem ao Controle de Caos. D.Sc.* Brasil: Universidade de São Paulo.

Barclay, L. (2003). *Propagation of radio waves.* London, UK: The Institution of Electrical Engineers.

Baron, M. (2006). *Probability and statistics for computer scientists.* Boca Raton, FL: Chapman & Hall/CRC.

Basagni, S. (1999). Distributed clustering for ad hoc networks. In *Proceedings of 4th International symposium on Parallel Architectures, Algorithms and Networks* (pp. 310-315)

Basu, K. N., & Little, T. (2001). A mobility based metric for clustering in mobile ad hoc networks. In *Proceedings of Conference on Distributed Computing Systems* (p. 413).

Belanovic, P., Valerio, D., Paier, A., Zemen, T., Ricciato, F., & Mecklenbrauker, C. (2010). On wireless links for vehicle-to-infrastructure communications. *IEEE Transactions on Vehicular Technology, 59*(1), 269–282. doi:10.1109/TVT.2009.2029119

Bellman, R. (1958). On a routing problem. *Quarterly of Applied Mathematics, 16*, 87–90.

Bello, P. (1963). Characterization of random time-variant linear channels. *IEEE Transactions on Communications, 11*(12), 360–393. doi:10.1109/TCOM.1963.1088793

Benslimane, A. (2005). Localization in vehicular ad-hoc networks. In *Proceedings of Systems Communications Conference,* Montreal, Canada. doi: 10.1109/ICW.2005.54

Berbineau, M., et al. (2006). *High data rate transmission for high speed trains. Dream or reality? Technical state of the art and user requirements.* Train-IPSAT Project - WP1 PREDIT 3 - CALFRANCE (Synthèse INRETS N° 51).

Bernstein, D., & Kornhauser, A. (1996). *An introduction to map matching for personal navigation assistants.* Newark, NJ: TIDE Center.

Bertolazzi, E., Biral, F., Da Lio, M., Saroldi, A., & Tango, F. (2010). Supporting drivers in keeping safe speed and safe distance: The SASPENCE Subproject Within the European Framework Programme 6 Integrating Project PReVENT. *IEEE Transactions on Intelligent Transportation Systems, 11*(3), 525–538. doi:10.1109/TITS.2009.2035925

Bétaille, D., & Bonnifait, P. (2000). *Road maintenance vehicles Location using DGPS, map-matching and dead-reckoning: Experimental results of a smoothed EKF.* Paper presented at the IAIN World Congress in Association with the U.S. ION 56th Annual Meeting, San Diego.

Bettstetter, C., Hartenstein, H., & Pérez-Costa, X. (2002). Stochastic properties of the random waypoint mobility model: Epoch time, direction distribution, and cell change rate. *Proceedings of the 5th International Workshop on Modeling Analysis and Simulation of Wireless and Mobile Systems*, (pp. 7-14).

Bilstrup, K., Uhlemann, E., Strom, E. G., & Bilstrup, U. (2008). Evaluation of the IEEE 802.11p MAC method for vehicle-to-vehicle communication. *2008 IEEE 68th Vehicular Technology Conference*, (pp. 1-5).

Bilstrup, K., Uhlemann, E., Ström, E. G., & Bilstrup, U. (2009). On the ability of the 802.11p MAC method and STDMA to support real-time vehicle-to-vehicle communication. *EURASIP Journal on Wireless Communications and Networking, 2009*. doi:10.1155/2009/902414

Biswas, S., Tatchikou, R., & Dion, F. (2006). Vehicle-to-vehicle wireless communication protocols for enhancing highway traffic safety. *IEEE Communications Magazine, 44*(1), 74–82. doi:10.1109/MCOM.2006.1580935

Blake-Wilson, S., & Brown, D. (2002). *RFC 3278*. Retrieved from http://www.ietf.org/rfc/rfc3278.txt

Blum, J., & Eskandarian, A. (2004). The threat of intelligent collisions. *IT Professional, 6*(1), 24–29. doi:10.1109/MITP.2004.1265539

Bohm, A., & Jonsson, M. (2009). Position-based data traffic prioritization in safety-critical, real-time vehicle-to-infrastructure communication. *IEEE Vehi-Mobi Workshop in IEEE International Conference on Communications (ICC)* (pp. 1-6). Dresden, Germany.

Bonnifait, P., Bouron, P., Crubille, P., & Meizel, D. (2001). Data fusion of four ABS sensors and GPS for an enhanced localization of car-like vehicles. In *Proceedings of IEEE International Conference on the Robotics and Automation* (pp. 1597-1602). Seoul. *Korea & World Affairs*. doi:doi:10.1109/ROBOT.2001.932839

Borgmann, M., & Bölcsei, H. (2005). Noncoherent space-frequency coded MIMO-OFDM. *IEEE Journal on Selected Areas in Communications, 23*(9), 1799–1810. doi:10.1109/JSAC.2005.853800

Borgonovo, F., Capone, A., Cesana, M., & Fratta, L. (2002). RR-ALOHA: A reliable R-ALOHA broadcast channel for ad-hoc inter-vehicle communication networks. In the *Proceedings of Med-Hoc-Net*.

Borsetti, D., & Fiore, M. (2009). *Cooperative support for localized services in VANETs*. International Symposium on Modeling Analysis and Simulation of Wireless and Mobile Systems. Tenerife, Spain: ACM.

Boukerche, A., Oliveira, H. A. B. F., Nakamura, E. F., & Loureiro, A. A. F. (2008). Vehicular ad hoc networks: A new challenge for localization-based systems. *Computer Communications, 31*(12), 2838–2849. doi:10.1016/j.comcom.2007.12.004

Briesemeister, L., Schäfers, L., & Hommel, G. (2000). Disseminating messages among highly mobile hosts based on inter-vehicle communication. *IEEE Intelligent Vehicle Symposium,* (pp. 522-527).

Brown, A. C., Cullen, E. J., Wu, J., Brackstone, M., Gunton, D. J., & McDonald, M. (2000). Vehicle to vehicle communication outage and its impact on convoy driving. *Proceedings of the IEEE Intelligent Vehicles Symposium 2000*, (pp. 528-533).

C2C-CC. (n.d.). Retrieved from http://www.car-to-car.org

C2R Consortium official website. (2011). *The COM2REACT project*. Retrieved April 15, 2011, from http://www.com2react-project.org/.

Calcev, G., Chizhik, D., Goransson, B., Howard, S., Huang, H., & Kogiantis, A. (2007). A wideband spatial channel model for system-wide simulations. *IEEE Transactions on Vehicular Technology, 56*(2), 389–403. doi:10.1109/TVT.2007.891463

CAMP Vehicle Safety Communications Consortium. (2005). DOT HS 809 859 [online] *Vehicle Safety Communications project task 3 final report: Identify intelligent vehicle safety applications enabled by DSRC*. Washington, DC: U.S. Department of Transportation. Retrieved from http://www.nhtsa.gov/DOT/NHTSA/NRD/Multimedia/PDFs/Crash%20Avoidance/2005/CAMP3scr.pdf

Camp, T., Boleng, J., & Wilcox, L. (2002). Location information services in mobile ad hoc networks. *International Communication Conference* (ICC), (pp. 1-7).

Canada, I. (2009). *Intelligent Transportation Systems Society of Canada*. Retrieved from http://www.itscanada.ca

Car2car Communication Consortium. (2010). Retrieved from http://www.car-to-car.org/

Casola, V., & Mazzoca, N. (2007). Static evaluation of certificate policies for GRID PKIs interoperability. *International Conference on Availability, Reliability and Security* (pp. 391-399). IEEE Computer Society.

Casola, V., Luna, J., Mazzeo, A., Medina, M., Rak, M., & Serna, J. (2010). An interoperability system for authentication and authorisation in VANETs. [IJAACS]. *International Journal of Autonomous and Adaptive Communications Systems*, *3*(2), 115–135. doi:10.1504/IJAACS.2010.031087

Casola, V., Luna, J., Oscar, M., Mazzocca, N., Medina, M., & Rak, M. (2007). Lecture Notes in Computer Science: *Vol. 4459. Interoperable grid PKIs among untrusted domains: architectural proposal*. New York, NY: Springer Verlag.

Casola, V., & Mazzeo, A. (2007). A security metric for Public Key Infrastructures. *Journal of Computer Security*, *15*(2).

Ceric, V. (1990). Simulation study of an automated guided-vehicle system in a Yugoslav hospital. *The Journal of the Operational Research Society*, *41*(4), 299–310.

Chan, Y. T., & Towers, J. J. (1992). Passive localization from Doppler-shifted frequency measurements. *IEEE Transactions on Signal Processing*, *40*(10), 2594–2598. doi:10.1109/78.157301

Chatterjee, M., Das, S. K., & Turgut, D. (2002). WCA: A weighted clustering algorithm for mobile ad hoc networks. *Journal of Clustering Computing*, *5*, 193–204. doi:10.1023/A:1013941929408

Chen, H., Martins, M. H. T., Huang, P., So, H. C., & Sezaki, K. (2008). Cooperative node localization for mobile sensor networks. In *Proceedings of The 5th International Conference on Embedded and Ubiquitous Computing EUC08* (pp. 302-308). Shanghai. doi: 10.1109/EUC.2008.166

Cheng, Y.-H., Lu, Y.-H., & Liu, C.-L. (2006). Adaptive channel equalizer for wireless access in vehicular environments. *International Conference on ITS Telecommunications*, (pp. 1102-1105). Chengdu.

Cheng, L., Henty, B., Stancil, D., Bai, F., & Mudalige, P. (2007). Mobile vehicle-to-vehicle narrow-band channel measurement and characterization of the 5.9 GHz dedicated short range communication (DSRC) frequency band. *IEEE Journal on Selected Areas in Communications*, *25*(8), 1501–1516. doi:10.1109/JSAC.2007.071002

Cheng, X., Wang, C., Laurenson, D., Salous, S., & Vasilakos, A. (2009). An adaptive geometry-based stochastic model for non-isotropic MIMO mobile-to-mobile channels. *IEEE Transactions on Wireless Communications*, *8*(9), 4824–4835. doi:10.1109/TWC.2009.081560

Chen, Y., Hsia, J., & Liao, Y. (2009). Advanced seamless vertical handoff architecture for WiMAX and WiFi heterogeneous networks with QoS guarantees. *Computer Communications*, *32*(2), 281–293. doi:10.1016/j.comcom.2008.10.014

Chiang, C., Wu, H., Liu, W., & Gerla, M. (1997). Routing in clustered multihop, mobile wireless networks with fading channel. *The IEEE Singapore International Conference on Networks*, (pp. 197-211).

Chiavaccini, E., & Vitetta, G. M. (2004). Maximum-likelihood frequency recovery for OFDM signals transmitted over multipath fading channels. *IEEE Transactions on Communications*, *52*(2), 244–251. doi:10.1109/TCOMM.2003.822706

Chiu, K. L., Hwang, R. H., & Chen, Y. S. (2009). A cross layer fast handover scheme in VANET. *IEEE International Conference on Communications* (pp. 1-5).

Choi, N., Choi, S., Seok, Y., Kwon, T., & Choi, Y. (2007). A solicitation-based IEEE 802.11p MAC protocol for roadside to vehicular networks. *IEEE Mobile Networking for Vehicular Environments*, (pp. 91-96). Anchorage, AK.

Chou, C., Li, C., Chien, W., & Lan, K. (2009). *A feasibility study on vehicle-to-infrastructure communication: WiFi vs. WiMAX*. Tenth International Conference on Mobile Data Management: Systems, Services and Middleware. Washington, DC: IEEE Computer Society. doi: 10.1109/MDM.2009.127

Ciurana, M., Barcelo-Arroyo, F., & Cugno, S. (2009). A robust to multi-path ranging technique over IEEE 802.11 networks. *Wireless Networks*, *16*(4), 1–11. doi:doi:10.1007/s11276-009-0180-3

Ciurana, M., Lopez, D., & Barcelo-Arroyo, F. (2009). Lecture Notes in Computer Science: *Vol. 5561. SofTOA: Software ranging for toa-based positioning of WLAN terminals* (pp. 207–221). Tokyo.

Clausen, T., Baccelli, E., & Wakikawa, R. (2010). *IPv6 operation for WAVE – Wireless access in vehicular environments*. (Tech. Rep. N°7383).

Clausen, T., & Jacquet, P. (2003). *RFC3626: Optimized link state routing protocol (OLSR)*. RFC Editor United States.

Cohen, L. (1995). *Time-frequency analysis*. Upper Saddle River, NJ: Prentice-Hall.

COMeSafety Project. (n.d.). Retrieved from http://www.comesafety.org/

Committee, I. T. S. (2007). *IEEE Std 1609.3 - IEEE Trial-Use Standard for Wireless Access in Vehicular Environments*. IEEE Vehicular Technology Society.

Communication for eSafety. (2010). Retrieved from http://www.comesafety.org

COOPERS Project. (n.d.). Retrieved from http://www.coopers-ip.eu

Correia, L. (Ed.). (2001). *Wireless flexible personalised communications. COST 259 Final Report*. Chichester, UK: Wiley.

COST. 231. (2007). *Final report*. Retrieved 19 April, 2007, from http://www.lx.it.pt/cost231/final_report.htm

Cox, T., & Cox, M. (1994). *Multidimensional scaling*. Chapman & Hall.

Cozzetti, H. A., & Scopigno, R. (2009). *RR-Aloha+: A slotted and distributed MAC protocol for vehicular communications*. In First IEEE Vehicular Networking Conference (VNC 2009).

Cozzetti, H. A., Scopigno, R., Casone, L., & Barba, G. (2009). *Comparative analysis of IEEE 802.11p and MS-Aloha in VANETs scenarios*. In the Second IEEE International Workshop on Vehicular Networking (VON 2009).

Cui, T., & Tellambura, C. (2007). Joint frequency offset and channel estimation for OFDM systems using pilot symbols and virtual carriers. *IEEE Transactions on Wireless Communications*, 6(4), 1193–1202. doi:10.1109/TWC.2007.348312

CVIS Project. (n.d.). Retrieved from http://www.cvis-project.org

Czarnecki, S. V., Johnson, J. A., Gray, C. M., Ver-Wys, G., & Gerst, C. (1999). *International Patent No. 5982164*, USA.

Daeinabi, A., Pour Rahbar, A. G., & Khademzadeh, A. (2010). VWCA: An efficient clustering algorithm in vehicular ad-hoc networks. *Journal of Network and Computer Applications*, 34, 207–222. doi:10.1016/j.jnca.2010.07.016

Danchik, R. J. (1998). An overview of transit development. [Applied Physics Laboratory]. *Johns Hopkins APL Technical Digest*, 19(1), 18–26.

Dang, Q., & Santesson, S. (2009). *From Internet X.509 public key infrastructure: Additional algorithms and identifiers for DSA and ECDSA*. Retrieved from http://tools.ietf.org/html/draft-ietf-pkix-sha2-dsa-ecdsa-06

Dao, T. S., Leung, K. Y. K., Clark, C. M., & Huissoon, J. P. (2007). Markov-based lane positioning using intervehicle communication. *IEEE Transactions on Intelligent Transportation Systems*, 8(4), 641–650. doi:10.1109/TITS.2007.908574

Dar, K., Bakhouya, M., Gaber, J., & Wack, M. (2010). Wireless communication technologies for ITS applications. *IEEE Communications Magazine*, 48(5), 156–162. doi:10.1109/MCOM.2010.5458377

Das, B., Sivakumar, R., & Bharghavan, V. (1997). Routing in ad hoc networks using a spine. *Proceedings in International Conference in Computer and Communication Networks*, (pp. 34-39).

de Fuentes, J. M., & Gonzalez-Tablas, A. I. (2010). Overview of security issues in vehicular ad-hoc networks. In Cruz-Cunha, M. M. (Ed.), *Handbook of research on mobility and computing*. Hershey, PA: IGI Global. doi:10.4018/978-1-60960-042-6.ch056

Deleuze, A. L., Martret, C. L., Ciblat, P., & Serpedin, E. (2004). Cramer-Rao bound for channel parameters in ultra-wide band based system. In *Proceedings of IEEE 5th Workshop on Signal Processing Advances in Wireless Communications* (pp. 140–144). Lisbon, Portugal. doi:10.1109/SPAWC.2004.1439220

Dellaert, F., Fox, D., Burgard, W., & Thrun, S. (1999). Monte Carlo localization for mobile robots. In *Proceedings of IEEE International Conference Robotics and Automation* (pp. 1322-1328). Detroit, Michigan. doi:10.1109/ROBOT.1999.772544

Delot, T., Cenerario, N., & Ilarri, S. (2010). Vehicular event sharing with a mobile peer-to-peer architecture. *Elsevier Transportation Research Part C: Emerging Technologies, 18,* 584–598. doi:10.1016/j.trc.2009.12.003

Devarapalli, V., Wakikawa, R., Petrescu, A., & Thubert, P. (2005). *Network mobility (NEMO) basic support protocol.* IETF RFC 3963. Retrieved April 25, 2010 from http://www.ietf.org/rfc/rfc3963.txt

Diggelen, F. V. (2009). *A-GPS: Assisted GPS, GNSS, and SBAS.* Boston, MA: Artech House.

Dijkstra, E. (1959). A note on two problems in connexion with graphs. *Numerischemathematik,* 269-271.

Ding, Y., & Xiao, L. (2010). SADV: Static-node-assisted adaptive data dissemination in vehicular networks. *IEEE Transactions on Vehicular Technology, 59,* 2445–2455. doi:10.1109/TVT.2010.2045234

Doetzer, F. (2005). *Privacy issues in vehicular ad hoc networks. Privacy Enhacing Technologies* (pp. 197–209). Lecture Notes in Computer Science Springer.

Doherty, L., Pister, K. S. J., & Ghaoui, L. E. (2001). Convex position estimation in wireless sensor networks. In *Proceedings of Twentieth Annual Joint Conference of the IEEE Computer and Communications Societies* (pp. 1655-1663). INFOCOM2001. doi:10.1109/IN-FCOM.2001.916662

Doshi, A., Shinko Yuanhsien, C., & Trivedi, M. M. (2009). A novel active heads-up display for driver assistance. *IEEE Transactions on Systems, Man, and Cybernetics. Part B, Cybernetics, 39*(1), 85–93. doi:10.1109/TSMCB.2008.923527

Edbauer, F. (1989). Performance of interleaved trellis-coded differential 8-PSK modulation over fading channels. *IEEE Journal on Selected Areas in Communications, 7*(9), 1340–1346. doi:10.1109/49.44579

EEA. (2006). *Technical report 9: Urban sprawl in Europe - The ignored challenge.* Copenhagen, Denmark: European Environmental Agency.

Efatmaneshnik, M., Balaei, A. T., Alam, N., & Dempster, A. (2009). A modified multidimensional scaling with embedded particle filter algorithm for cooperative positioning of vehicular networks. In *Proceedings of IEEE International Conference on Vehicular Electronics and Safety* (pp. 7-12). India. doi: 10.1109/ICVES.2009.5400202

Efatmaneshnik, M., Kealy, A., Lim, S., & Dempster, A. G. (2010). *Analysis of information fusion for low cost, precise and reliable vehicular cooperative positioning with DSRC.* Paper presented at the DSRC Workshop on the side of ICST QShine 2010, Houston, Texas.

EJBCA OCSP. (2011). Retrieved from http://www.prime-key.se/Products/EJBCA+PKI/EJBCA+OCSP/

El Najjar, M. E., & Bonnifait, P. (2005). A road-matching method for precise vehicle localization using belief theory and Kalman filtering. *Autonomous Robots, 19*(2), 173–191. doi:10.1007/s10514-005-0609-1

Er, I., & Seah, W. (2004). Mobility-based d-hop clustering algorithm for mobile ad hoc networks. In *Proceedings of IEEE Wireless Communications and Networking Conference* (pp. 2359-2364)

ERTICO ITS EUROPE. (2010). *ITS Europe project activities.* Retrieved June 15, 2010, from http://www.ertico.com/activities/.

ERTICO-a. (1998). *Intelligent city transport: A guidebook to intelligent transport systems.* Brussels, Belgium: ITS City Pioneers Consortium.

EstiNet website. (2011). *Estinet network simulator and emulator.* Retrieved February 14, 2011, from http://www.estinet.com/products.php

ETSI EN 302 665. (2010). *Intelligent transport systems (ITS): Communications architecture.*

ETSI ES 202 663 V1.1.0, (2010). *Intelligent transport systems (ITS)*. European Profile Standard for the Physical and Medium Access Control Layer of Intelligent Transport Systems Operating in the 5 GHz Frequency Band.

European Telecommunications Standards Institute (ETSI). (1997). *Universal mobile telecommunications system (UMTS): Selection procedures for the choice of radio transmission technologies of the UMTS.* (ETSI document UMTS 30.03, ver. 3.1.0, TR 101 112, v3.1.0, Section B.1.4.2).

European Transport Safety Council. (2008). *Road safety as a right and responsibility for all*. Brussels, Belgium: European Transport Safety Council (ETSC).

Falsi, C., Dardari, D., Mucchi, L., & Win, M. Z. (2006). Time of arrival estimation for UWB localizers in realistic environments. *EURASIP Journal on Applied Signal Processing, 2006*. doi:10.1155/ASP/2006/32082

Fan, P., Sistla, P., & Nelson, P. (2008). Theoretical analysis of directional stability-based clustering algorithm for VANET. In *Proceedings of ACM VANET* (pp. 80- 81).

Fang-Yie Leu, F., Huang, Y., & Chiu, C. (2010). *Improving security levels of IEEE802.16e authentication by involving Diffie-Hellman PKDS*. International Conference on Complex, Intelligent and Software Intensive Systems (CISIS).

Fan, P., Haran, J., Dillenburg, J., & Nelson, P. (2005). Cluster based framework in vehicular ad- hoc networks. *Lecture Notes in Computer Science, 3738*, 32–42. doi:10.1007/11561354_5

Farrell, J. A. (1998). *The global positioning system & inertial navigation*. New York, NY: McGraw-Hill.

Fazel, K., & Kaiser, S. (2003). *Multi-carrier and spread spectrum systems*. Chichester, UK: Wiley. doi:10.1002/0470871385

Fei, R., Yang, K., Ou, S., Zhong, S., & Gao, L. (2009). *International Conference on Scalable Computing and Communications; Eighth International Conference on Embedded Computing2009*, (pp. 200-205).

Festag, A., Noecker, G., Strassberger, M., Lubke, A., Bochow, B., & Torrent-Moreno, M. … Kunisch, J. (2008). NoW - Network on Wheels: Project objectives, technology and achievements. *Proceedings of 5rd International Workshop on Intelligent Transportation* (pp. 211 – 216). Hamburg, Germany.

Festag, A., Zhang, W., Le, L., & Baldessari, R. (2009). Geocast in vehicular networks. In Moustafa, H., & Zhang, Y. (Eds.), *Vehicular networks techniques, standards, and applications* (pp. 378–404). CRC Press.

Fischer, L., & Aijaz, A. (2006). *Secure revocable anonymous authenticated*. Workshop on Embedded Security in Cars.

Floyd, S., & Jacobson, V. (1994). The synchronization of periodic routing messages. *IEEE/ACM Transactions on Networking, 2*(2), 122–136. doi:10.1109/90.298431

Fonseca, E., & Festag, A. (2007). *Support of anonymity in VANETs - Putting pseudonymity into practice* (pp. 3400–3405). Hong Kong: WCNC.

FRAME Project. (n.d.). Retrieved from http://frame-online.net/

Franklin, D. B. (2003). Identity based encryption from the Weil pairing. *SIAM Journal on Computing, 32*(3), 586–615. doi:10.1137/S0097539701398521

Freeman, W. J. (1994). Neural networks and chaos. *Journal of Theoretical Biology, 171*, 13–18. doi:10.1006/jtbi.1994.1207

FreeRadius. (2010). *The FreeRADIUS Project* (Version 2.1.10) [Computer software]. Retrieved from http://freeradius.org/

Gallagher, B., Akatsuka, H., & Suzuki, H. (2006). Wireless communications for vehicle safety: Radio link performance & wireless connectivity methods. *IEEE Vehicular Technology Magazine, 1*(4), 4–24. doi:10.1109/MVT.2006.343641

Ganeriwal, S., Kumar, R., & Srivastava, M. B. (2003). Timing-sync protocol for sensor networks. In the *Proceedings of the 1st ACM International Conference on Embedded Networked Sensor Systems*, (pp. 138–149).

Garg, V. K. (2007). *Wireless communications and networking.* Amsterdam, The Netherlands: Elsevier Morgan Kaufmann.

GeoNet Project. (n.d.). Retrieved from http://www.geonet-project.eu/

Gerlach, M., Festag, A., Leinmüller, T., Goldacker, G., & Harsch, C. (2007). Security architecture for vehicular communication. In *Proceedings of the 5th International Workshop on Intelligent Transportation (WIT).*

Gerlach, M. (2006). *Assesing and improving privacy in VANETs.* Berlin: ESCAR.

Gesbert, D., Bolcskei, H., Gore, D., & Paulraj, A. (2002). Outdoor MIMO wireless channels: Models and performance prediction. *IEEE Transactions on Communications, 50*(12), 1926–1934. doi:10.1109/TCOMM.2002.806555

Ge, Y., Wen, S., Ang, Y. H., & Liang, Y. C. (2010). Optimal relay selection in IEEE 802.16j multihop relay vehicular networks. *IEEE Transactions on Vehicular Technology,* 2198–2206. doi:10.1109/TVT.2010.2044822

Ghareeb, I. (2005). Noncoherent MT-MFSK signals with diversity reception in arbitrary correlated and unbalanced Nakagami-*m* fading channels. *IEEE Journal on Selected Areas in Communications, 23*(9), 1839–1850. doi:10.1109/JSAC.2005.853877

Giordano, S., Stojmenovic, I., & Blazevic, L. (2003). Position based routing algorithms for ad hoc networks: A taxonomy. *Ad Hoc Wireless Networking Conference,* (pp. 103-136).

Godha, S., & Cannon, M. E. (2007). GPS/MEMS INS integrated system for navigation in urban areas. *GPS Solutions, 11*(3), 193–203. doi:10.1007/s10291-006-0050-8

Grace, D., & Mohorcic, M. (2010). *Broadband communications via high-altitude platforms.* John Wiley & Sons, 2010

Green, D. B., & Obaidat, A. S. (2002). *An accurate line of sight propagation performance model for ad hoc 802.11 wireless LAN (WLAN) devices.* Paper presented at the IEEE International Conference on Communications, New York.

Greenfeld, J. S. (2002). *Matching GPS observations to locations on a digital map.* Newark, NJ: Department of Civil and Environmental Engineering, New Jersey Institute of Technology.

Gunther, A., & Hoene, C. (2005). Measuring round trip times to determine the distance between WLAN nodes. In *Proceedings of NETWORKING 2005, Lecture Notes in Computer Science vol. 3462/2005,* (pp. 303-319). Waterloo, Canada. doi:10.1007/11422778_62

Guo, J., & Balon, N. (2006). *Vehicular ad hoc networks and dedicated short-range communication.* Universty of Michigan - Dearborn School Projects.

Guo, J., & Baugh, J. (2007). *A group signature based secure and privacy-preserving vehicular communication framework. Mobile Networking for Vehicular Environments* (pp. 103–108). MOVE.

Haas, J. J., & Hu, Y.-C. (2009). Design an analysis of a lightweight certificate revocation mechanism for VANET. *Proceedings of the 6th International Conference on VANETs.* Beijing, China: ACM.

Habib, M., & Ahmad, M. (2010). *A review of some security aspects of WiMAX and converged network.* Second International Conference on Communication Software and Networks.

Hara, Y., & Taira, A. (2005). System configuration for multiband MC-CDM systems. *Proceedings Fall Vehicular Tech. Conf.,* Dallas, TX.

Hata, M. (1980). Empirical formula for propagation loss in land mobile radio services. *IEEE Transactions on Vehicular Technology, VT-29*(3), 317–325. doi:10.1109/T-VT.1980.23859

Hide, C., Moore, T., & Smith, M. (2003). Adaptive Kalman filtering for low-cost INS/GPS. *Journal of Navigation, 56*(1), 143–152. doi:10.1017/S0373463302002151

Hochwald, B. M., & Marzetta, T. L. (2000a). Unitary space-time modulation for multiple antenna communications in Rayleigh flat fading. *IEEE Transactions on Information Theory, 46*(2), 543–564. doi:10.1109/18.825818

Hochwald, B. M., & Sweldens, W. (2000b). Differential unitary space-time modulation. *IEEE Transactions on Communications, 48*(12), 2041–2052. doi:10.1109/26.891215

Hofmann-Wellenhof, B., Lichtenegger, H., & Collins, J. (2001). *Global positioning system theory and practice* (5th ed.). New York, NY: Springer Wien. doi:10.1007/978-3-7091-6199-9

Hossain, E., Chow, G., Leung, V., McLeod, B., Misic, J., Wong, V., & Yang, O. (2010). Vehicular telematics over heterogeneous wireless networks: A survey. *Computer Communications*, *33*(7), 775–793. doi:10.1016/j.comcom.2009.12.010

Housley, R., Polk, W., Ford, W., & Solo, D. (2002). *RFC3280: Internet X. 509 public key infrastructure certificate and certificate revocation list (CRL) profile.* Retrieved from http://tools.ietf.org/html/rfc3280

Hou, T., & Tsai, T. (2001). An access-based clustering protocol for multihop wireless ad hoc networks. *IEEE Journal on Selected Areas in Communications*, *19*, 1201–1210. doi:10.1109/49.932689

Huang, C. J., Chen, Y. J., & Chen, I. (2009). An intelligent infotainment dissemination scheme for heterogeneous vehicular networks. *Expert Systems with Applications*, *36*, 12472–12479. doi:10.1016/j.eswa.2009.04.035

Huang, C. M. (Ed.). (2010). *Telematics communication technologies and vehicular networks: Wireless architectures and applications.* Hershey, PA: IGI Global.

Huang, C.-J., Chuang, Y.-T., Chen, Y.-J., Yang, D.-X., & Chen, I.-F. (n.d.). QoS-aware roadside base station assisted routing in vehicular networks. *The Engineering Applications of Artificial Intelligence*, *22*(8), 1292-1301. New York, NY. *ACM*. doi:doi:10.1016/j.engappai.2009.04.003

Hubaux, J., Capkun, S., & Luo, J. (2004). The security and privacy of smart vehicles. *IEEE Security and Privacy*, *2*(3), 49–55. doi:10.1109/MSP.2004.26

Hughes, B. L. (2000). Differential space-time modulation. *IEEE Transactions on Information Theory*, *46*(7), 2567–2578. doi:10.1109/18.887864

Hui Liu, H. L. (2010). *Efficient and secure authentication protocol for VANET.* International Conference on Computational Intelligence and Security.

IEEE 1609.0/D0.7. (2009). *Draft standard for wireless access in vehicular environments (WAVE) - architecture.*

IEEE 1609.2. (2006). *Standard for wireless access in vehicular environments - Security services for applications and management messages.* Version 2: Under Development.

IEEE 802.11 Working Group. (2007). *IEEE Std. 802.11-2007: Wireless LAN medium access control (MAC) and physical layer (PHY) specifications.*

IEEE 802.11p Working Group. (2010). *IEEE standard 802.11p: Wireless LAN medium access control (MAC) and physical layer (PHY) specifications: Amendment 6- Wireless access in vehicular environments.*

IEEE P1609.1 SWG. (2009). *IEEE P1609.1/D0.6, IEEE 1609.1: Trial-use standard for wireless access in vehicular environments (WAVE) – Resource manager.*

IEEE P1609.2 SWG. (2009). *IEEE P1609.2/D0.7, IEEE 1609.2: Trial-use standard for wireless access in vehicular environments (WAVE) – Security services for applications and management messages.*

IEEE P1609.3 SWG. (2010). *1609.3-2010: IEEE standard for wireless access in vehicular environments (WAVE) – Networking services.*

IEEE P1609.4 SWG. (2010). *1609.4-2010: IEEE standard for wireless access in vehicular environments (WAVE) – Multi-channel operation.*

IEEE P1609.4/D9. (2010). IEEE draft standard for wireless access in vehicular environments (WAVE) - Multi-channel operation.

IEEE P802.11u. (2010). *Interworking with external networks Task Group U.*

IEEE P802.16g. (2010). *Management plane procedures and services (MobileMan) Task Group.*

IEEE Std. 802.11g. (2003). *IEEE 802.11g-2003 IEEE standard for Information technology - Telecommunications and information exchange between systems - Local and metropolitan area networks - Specific requirements - Part 11: Wireless LAN medium access control (MAC) and physical layer (PHY) specifications - Amendment 4: Further higher-speed physical layer extension in the 2.4 GHz band.*

IEEE Std. 802.16. (2004). *IEEE standard for local and metropolitan area networks, Part 16: Air interface for fixed broadband wireless access systems.*

IEEE Std. 802.16e. (2005). *IEEE standard for local and metropolitan area networks part 16: Air interface for fixed and mobile broadband wireless access systems amendment for physical and medium access control layers for combined fixed and mobile operation in licensed bands.*

IEEE Std. 802.1D, (2004). Media access control (MAC) bridges.

IEEE Std. 802.21. (2008). *IEEE standard for local and metropolitan area networks - Part 21: Media independent handover services.*

IEEE. (2010). *1609.2: Trial use standard for wireless access in vehicular environments (WAVE) - Security services for applications and management messages.* Retrieved from vii.path.berkeley.edu/1609_wave/

IEEE. (2010). *1609: WAVE standards.* Retrieved from vii.path.berkeley.edu/1609_wave/

IEEE-SA Standards Board. (2009). *IEEE standard for local and metropolitan area networks part 16: Air interface for broadband wireless access systems. IEEE Computer Society and the IEEE Microwave Theory and Techniques Society.* New York, NY: IEEE.

Institute of Electrical and Electronics Engineers. (2001). *Channel models for fixed wireless applications.* (IEEE Broadband Wireless Access Working Group document IEEE 802.163c-01/29). Retrieved 11 September, 2009, from http://wirelessman.org/tg3/contrib/802163c-01_29r4.pdf

Institute of Electrical and Electronics Engineers. (2005a). *Channel models for IEEE 802.20 MBWA system simulations.* (IEEE document 802.20-03/48). Retrieved 28 March, 2005, from http://grouper.ieee.org/groups/802//20/Contribs/C802.20-03-48.pdf

Institute of Electrical and Electronics Engineers. (2005b). *IEEE 802.20 channel models (V1.0), IEEE 802.20 PD-08.* Retrieved 28 March, 2005, from http://grouper.ieee.org/groups/802//20/P_Docs/IEEE_802.20-PD-08.doc

Institute of Electrical and Electronics Engineers. (2007). *Channel models for fixed wireless applications.* (IEEE document 802.16.3c-01/29r4).

Institute of Electrical and Electronics Engineers. (2008). *IEEE wireless access in vehicular environments website.* Retrieved 23 September, 2008, from http://grouper.ieee.org/groups/802/11/Reports/tgp_update.htm

Institute of Electrical and Electronics Engineers. (2010). *IEEE wireless local area networks working group website.* Retrieved 20 October, 2010, from http://ieee802.org/11/

INTEGRAIL Project. (2008). Retrieved from http://www.integrail.info

International Telecommunications Union (ITU). (1999). *Document ITU-R P.1407-1: Multipath propagation and parameterization of its characteristics.*

ISO-21217-CALM-Architecture. (2010). *Intelligent transport systems - Communications access for land mobiles (CALM) - Architecture.*

iTETRIS Project. (n.d.). Retrieved from www.ict-itetris.eu

Itoua, S. M. (2008). *Effect of propagation models on ad hoc networks routing protocols.* Paper presented at the 2008 Second International Conference on Sensor Technologies and Applications.

ITU-R Report M.2072. (2006). *World mobile telecommunication market forecast.* Question ITU-R 229/8.

ITU-T Rec Y.154. (2008). *Network performance objectives for IP-based services amendment 3: Revised appendix VIII – Effects of IP network performance on digital television transmission QoS.*

ITU-T Rec. G.114. (2003). *One way transmission time.* ITU-T Recommendation G.114. 2003.

Jacquet, P., Laouiti, A., Minet, P., & Viennot, L. (2002). *Performance of multipoint relaying in ad hoc mobile routing protocols. Networking 2002* (pp. 1–12). Italy: Pise.

Jain, S., Fall, K., & Patra, R. (2004). Routing in a delay tolerant network. *ACM SIGCOMM Computer Communication Review, 34*(4), 145. doi:10.1145/1030194.1015484

Jakes, W. (1993). *Microwave mobile communication.* New York, NY: IEEE Press.

Jang, H., Jee, J., Jan, H., & Cha, J. (2008). *Mobile IPv6 fast handovers over IEEE 802.16e networks.* Retrieved on April 26, 2011, from http://tools.ietf.org/tools/rfcmarkup/rfcmarkup.cgi/draft-ietf-mipshop-fh80216e

Jang, H.-C., & Feng, W.-C. (2010). Network status detection-based dynamic adaptation of contention window in IEEE 802.11p. *IEEE Vehicular Technology Conference (VTC Spring)* (pp. 1-5). Taipei.

Jansri, A., Klomkarn, K., & Sooraksa, P. (2004). On comparison of attractors for chaotic mobile robots. *The 30th Annual Conference of the IEEE Industrial Electronics Society Electronics Society*, (vol. 3, pp. 2536-2541).

Japan, I. (2009). *ITS Japan*. Retrieved from http://www.its-jp.org/english/

Jerbi, M., Senouci, S., Rasheed, T., & Doudane, Y. (2007). An infrastructure- free traffic information system for vehicular networks. In *Proceedings of 66th IEEE Vehicular Technology Conference* (pp. 2086-2090).

Jiang, D., & Delgrossi, L. (2008). IEEE 802.11p: Towards an international standard for wireless access in vehicular environments. *IEEE International Symposium on Wireless Vehicular Communications (WiVec)*, Calgary, CA.

Jiang, D., Taliwal, V., Meier, A., Holfelder, W., & Herrtwich, R. (2006). Design of 5.9 GHz DSRC-based vehicular safety communication. *IEEE Communications Magazine, 44*(10), 36–43.

Jo, K. H., & Lee, J. (2007). Multi-robot cooperative localization with optimally fused information of odometer and GPS. In *Proceedings of International Conference on Control, Automation and Systems ICCAS 2007* (pp. 601-605). Seoul. doi:10.1109/ICCAS.2007.4407094

Jo, K., Lee, J., & Kim, J. (2007). Cooperative multi-robot localization using differential position data. In *Proceedings of IEEE/ASME International Conference on Advanced Intelligent Mechatronics* (pp. 1-6). Zurich. doi:10.1109/AIM.2007.4412548

Johnson, D., Maltz, D., & Hu, Y. (2004). *The dynamic source routing protocol for mobile ad hoc networks* (DSR). IETF Internet Draft (Work in Progress). Retrieved from http://www.ietf.org/internet-drafts/draft-ietf-manet-dsr-10.txt

Johnson, D., Perkins, C., & Arkko, J. (2004). *Mobility support in IPv6*. IETF RFC 3775. Retrieved April 25, 2010, from http://www.ietf.org/rfc/rfc3775.txt

Judge, P. (2005). *100 mph WiMAX hits the rails to Brighton*. Retrieved from Techworld.com

Kaplan, E. D., & Hegarty, C. J. (2006). *Understanding GPS principles and applications* (2nd ed.). Norwood, MA: Artech House Inc.

Karam, N., Chausse, F., Aufrere, R., & Chapuis, R. (2006a). Cooperative multi-vehicle localization. In *Proceedings of IEEE Intelligent Vehicles Symposium* (pp. 564-570). Tokyo. doi:10.1109/IVS.2006.1689688

Karam, N., Chausse, F., Aufrere, R., & Chapuis, R. (2006b). Localization of a group of communicating vehicles by state exchange. In *Proceedings of IEEE/RSJ International Conference on Intelligent Robots and Systems* (pp. 519–524). Beijing. doi:10.1109/IROS.2006.282028

Karedal, J., Tufvesson, F., Czink, N., Paier, A., Dumard, C., & Zemen, F. (2009). A geometry-based stochastic MIMO model for vehicle-to-vehicle communications. *IEEE Transactions on Wireless Communications, 8*(7), 3646–3657. doi:10.1109/TWC.2009.080753

Kargl, F., Papadimitratos, P., Buttyan, L., Muter, M., Schoch, E., & Wiedersheim, B. (2008). Secure vehicular communication systems: Implementation, performance, and research challenges. *IEEE Communications Magazine, 46*(11), 110–118. doi:10.1109/MCOM.2008.4689253

Käsemann, M., Hartenstein, H., Füßler, H., & Mauve, M. (2002). Analysis of a location service for position-based routing in mobile ad hoc networks. *Proceedings of the 1st German Workshop on Mobile Ad Hoc Networks*, (pp. 1-13).

Kaufman, C. (2006). *Internet key exchange (IKEv2) protocol*. IETF RFC 4306. Retrieved September 10, 2010, from http://tools.ietf.org/html/rfc2401

Kaul, S., Ramachandran, K., Shankar, P., Oh, S., Gruteser, M., Seskar, I., & Nadeem, T. (2007). *Effect of antenna placement and diversity on vehicular network communications*. IEEE Conference on Sensor, Mesh, & Ad Hoc Networks, San Diego, CA.

Kaygisiz, B. H., Erkmen, I., & Erkmen, A. M. (2004). GPS/INS enhancement for land navigation using neural network. *Journal of Navigation, 57*(2), 297–310. doi:10.1017/S037346330400267X

Kealy, A., Scott-Young, A., & Collier, P. (2004). *Improving land vehicle safety using augmented reality technologies*. Paper presented at the 4th International Symposium on Mobile Mapping Technology, Kunming, China.

Kent, S., & Atkinson, R. (1998). *Security architecture for the Internet protocol*. IETF RFC 2401. Retrieved September 5, 2010, from http://tools.ietf.org/html/rfc2401

Khaled, Y., Tsukada, M., Santa, J., Choia, J., & Ernst, T. (2009). A usage oriented analysis of vehicular networks: From technologies to applications. *The Journal of Communication, 4*(5), 357–368. doi:doi:10.4304/jcm.4.5.357-368

Khil, M., Bür, K., Tufvesson, F., & Aparicio, J. (2010). Simulation modeling and analysis of a realistic radio channel model for V2V communications. *IEEE ASNC 2010*, (pp. 981-988). Retrieved January 12, 2011, from http://ieeexplore.ieee.org/

Konrad, A., Zhao, B., Joseph, A., & Ludwig, R. (2003). A Markov-based model algorithm for wireless networks. *Wireless Networks, 9*, 189–199. doi:10.1023/A:1022869025953

Konstantinou, K., Kang, S., & Tzaras, C. (2008). A measurement-based model for mobile-to-mobile UMTS links. *Proceedings IEEE Spring Vehicular Technology Conference*, Singapore.

Kosch, T., Kulp, I., Bechler, M., Strassberger, M., Weyl, B., & Lasowski, R. (2009). Communication architecture for cooperative systems in Europe. *IEEE Wireless Communication Magazine, 47*(5), 116–125. doi:10.1109/MCOM.2009.4939287

Krajzewicz, D. (2008). *SUMO: From simulation of urban mobility*. Retrieved from http://sourceforge.net/apps/mediawiki/sumo/index.php?title=Main_Page

Krapichler, C. (2007). LTE, HSPA and mobile WiMAX: A comparison of technical performance. *Hot Topics Forum: LTE vs WiMAX and Next Generation Internet, 2007 Institution of Engineering and Technology*, (pp. 1-31).

Krishnamurthy, B., & Evans, J. (1992). HelpMate: A robotic courier for hospital use. *IEEE International Conference on Systems, Man and Cybernetics*, (vol. 2, pp. 1630 – 1634).

Krishna, P., Vaidya, N., Chatterjee, M., & Pradhan, D. (1997). A cluster-based approach for routing in dynamic networks. *ACM SIGCOMM. Computer Communication Review, 27*(2), 49–65. doi:10.1145/263876.263885

Kuklinski, S., & Wolny, G. (2009). Density based clustering algorithm for VANETs. In *International Journal of Internet Protocol Technology, 4*, 149–157. doi:10.1504/IJIPT.2009.028654

Kunisch, J., & Pamp, J. (2008). Wideband car-to-car radio channel measurements and model at 5.9 GHz. *Proceedings of the IEEE Fall Vehicular Technology Conference*, Calgary, Canada.

Kuran, M. S. (2007). A survey on emerging broadband wireless access technologies. *Computer Networks, 51*(11), 3013–3046. doi:10.1016/j.comnet.2006.12.009

Kuun, E., & Richard, W. (2004). Open standards for CCTC and CCTV radio-based communication. *Alcatel Telecommunications Review*, 243-252.

Landman, J., & Kritzinger, P. (2005). Delay analysis of downlink IP traffic on UMTS mobile networks. *Journal Performance Evaluation, 62*(1), 68–82. doi:10.1016/j.peva.2005.07.007

Lardennois, R. (2005). *Wireless communication for signalling in mass transit*.

LaSorte, N., Barnes, W. J., Zigreng, B., & Refai, H. (2009). *Performance evaluation of a deployed WiMAX system operating in the 4.9GHz public safety band*. Paper presented at the 6th IEEE Conference on Consumer Communications and Networking Conference.

Lebrun, J., Chuah, C., Ghosal, D., & Zhang, M. (2005). Knowledge- based opportunistic forwarding in vehicular wireless ad hoc networks. In *Proceedings of 61st IEEE Vehicular Technology Conference-Spring*, Vol. 4 (pp. 2289-2293).

Lee, B. G., & Choi, S. (2008). *Broadband wireless access and local networks: Mobile WiMax and WiFi*. Boston, MA: Artech House.

Lee, J. H., Chen, J., & Ernst, T. (2011). (in press). Securing mobile network prefix provisioning for NEMO based vehicular networks. *Mathematical and Computer Modelling*. doi:doi:10.1016/j.mcm.2011.02.023

Lee, S., Sriram, K., Kim, K., Kim, Y., & Golmie, N. (2009). Vertical handoff decision algorithms for providing optimized performance in heterogeneous wireless networks. *IEEE Transactions on Vehicular Technology, 58*(2), 865–881. doi:10.1109/TVT.2008.925301

Leinmuller, T., Schoch, E., & Maihofer, C. (2007). Security requirements and solution concepts in vehicular ad-hoc networks. *Forth Annual Conference on Wireless on Demand Network Systems and Services*, (pp. 84-91). Obergurgl. doi: 10.1109/WONS.2007.340489

Leng, S., Fu, H., Wang, Q., & Zhang Y. (2009). Medium access control in vehicular ad hoc network. *Wireless Communications and Mobile Computing.* Advance online publication. doi:10.1002/wcm.869

Lengerke, O., Archila, J. F., & Dutra, M. S. (2008). Diseño Mecatrónico de un Robot Tipo AGV -Automated Guided Vehicle. *UIS Ingenierías - Facultad de Ingenierías Fisicomecánicas, 7*(1), 63–74.

Lenoble, M., Ito, K., Tadokoro, Y., Takanashi, M., & Sanda, K. (2009). Header reduction to increase the throughput in decentralized TDMA-based vehicular networks. *IEEE Vehicular Networking Conference (VNC)*, (pp. 1-4), Tokyo, Japan.

Leontiadis, I., & Mascolo, C. (2007a). GeOpps: Geographical opportunistic routing for vehicular networks. In *Proceedings of IEEE International Symposium on World of Wireless, Mobile and Multimedia Networks* (pp. 1-6). Finland.

Leontiadis, I., & Mascolo, C. (2007b). Opportunistic spatio-temporal dissemination system for vehicular networks. In *Proceedings of 1st International MobiSys Workshop on Mobile Opportunistic Networking* (pp. 39-46). San Juan, Puerto Rico

Li, F., & Wang, Y. (2007, June). Routing in vehicular ad hoc networks: A survey. *IEEE Vehicular Technology Magazine, 2*(2), 12–22. doi:10.1109/MVT.2007.912927

Lin, C., Yuanqian, L., Siyuan, X., & Jianping, P. (2010). Scalable modulation for scalable wireless videocast. In *Proceedings of 29th IEEE International Conference on Computer Communications* (pp. 1-5). San Diego USA

Lin, X., Sun, X., Ho, P., & Xuemin, S. (2007). GSIS: A secure and privacy-preserving protocol for vehicular communications. *IEEE Transactions on Vehicular Technology, 56*(6), 3442–3456. doi:10.1109/TVT.2007.906878

Little, T., & Agarwal, A. (2005). An information propagation scheme for VANETS. In *Proceedings of 8th International Conference on Intelligent Transportation System* (pp. 155-160).

Liu, X., Fang, Z., & Shi, L. (2007). Securing vehicular ad hoc networks. *2nd International Conference on Pervasive Computing and Applications*, (pp. 424-429).

Liu, K., Guo, J., Lu, N., & Liu, F. (2009). *RAMC: A RSU-assisted multi-channel coordination MAC protocol for VANET* (pp. 1–6). Honolulu, HI: IEEE GLOBECOM Workshops.

Li, X. (2006). RSS-based location estimation with unknown pathloss model. *IEEE Transactions on Wireless Communications, 5*(12), 3626–3633. doi:10.1109/TWC.2006.256985

Li, Y., & Stuber, G. (2006). *Orthogonal frequency division multiplexing for wireless communications.* New York, NY: Springer. doi:10.1007/0-387-30235-2

Lomax, T., & Schrank, D. (2005). *Urban mobility study.* Texas: Texas Transportation Institute. Retrieved from http://mobility.tamu.edu/ums/report/

Lowe, D. (2002). *Dictionary of transport and logistics - Terms, abbreviations and acronyms. The Institute of Logistics and Transport.* Great Britain: Biddles Ltd, Guildford and King's Lynn.

Luo, C., Médard, M., & Zheng, L. (2005). On approaching wideband capacity using multitone FSK. *IEEE Journal on Selected Areas in Communications, 23*(9), 1830–1838. doi:10.1109/JSAC.2005.853803

Lv, T., Li, H., & Chen, J. (2005). Joint estimation of symbol timing and carrier frequency offset of OFDM signals over fast time-varying multipath channels. *IEEE Transactions on Signal Processing, 53*(12), 4526–4535. doi:10.1109/TSP.2005.859233

Maihofer, C. (2004). A survey of geocast routing protocols. *IEEE Communications Surveys and Tutorials, 6*(2), 32–42. doi:10.1109/COMST.2004.5342238

Makido, S., Suzuki, N., Harada, T., & Muramatsu, J. (2007). Decentralized TDMA protocol for real-time vehcile-to-vehicle communications. *IPSJ Journal, 48*(7), 2257–2266.

Mak, T. K., Laberteaux, K. P., Sengupta, R., & Ergen, M. (2009). Multichannel medium access control for dedicated short-range communications. *IEEE Transactions on Vehicular Technology, 58*(1), 349–366. doi:10.1109/TVT.2008.921625

Malaney, R. A. (2007). Nuisance parameters and location accuracy in log-normal fading models. *IEEE Transactions on Wireless Communications, 6*(3), 937–947. doi:10.1109/TWC.2007.05247

Mao, G., Anderson, B. D. O., & Fidan, B. (2007). Path loss exponent estimation for wireless sensor network localization. *Computer Networks, 51*(10), 2467–2483. doi:10.1016/j.comnet.2006.11.007

Marín, R., Pereñiquez, F., Bernal, F., & Skarmeta, A. (2009). *Architecture for fast EAP re-authentication based on a new EAP method (EAP-FRM) working on standalone mode.* IETF draft. Retrieved September 07, 2010, from http://tools.ietf.org/html/draft-marin-eap-frm-fastreauth-00

Marquez-Barja, J., Calafate, C. T., Cano, J. C., & Manzoni, P. (2010). An overview of vertical handover techniques: Algorithms, protocols and tools. *Computer Communications, 34*(8), 985–997. doi:10.1016/j.comcom.2010.11.010

Martínez-Silva, G., & Rodriguez-Henriquez, F. (2007). On the generation of X.509v3 certificates with biometric information. In H. R. Selim Aissi (Ed.), *International Conference on Security & Management* (pp. 52-57). Las Vegas, NV: CSREA Press.

Martins-Filho, L. S., & Macau, E. E. N. (2007). Patrol mobile robots and chaotic trajectories. *Mathematical Problems in Engineering*, Article ID 61543, v. 2007, 13 pages. Hindawi Publishing Corporation.

Maslekar, N., Boussedjra, M., Houda, L., & Mouzna, J. (2011). C-DRIVE: Clustering based on direction in vehicular environment. In *Proceedings of 4th IFIP New Technologies, Mobility and Security,* Paris.

Mathworks, I. (2008). *MATLAB help (Version 2008b).* Mathworks, Inc.

Matolak, D. (2006). *Wireless channel characterization in the 5 GHz microwave landing system extension band for airport surface areas.* Final Project Report for NASA ACAST Project, Grant Number NNC04GB45G, May 2006.

Matolak, D. (2010). *Wireless channel modeling: Fundamentals, quantification, and high-fidelity models for future communication systems.* University of Malaga Spring/Summer session School of Telecommunications short course, Malaga Spain, 14 & 23 June 2010.

Matolak, D. (2008). Channel modeling for vehicle-to-vehicle communications. *IEEE Communications Magazine, 46*(5), 76–83. doi:10.1109/MCOM.2008.4511653

Matolak, D., Sen, I., & Xiong, W. (2008). On the generation of multivariate Weibull random variates. *IET Communications Journal, 2*(4), 523–527. doi:10.1049/iet-com:20070133

Matolak, D., Sen, I., Xiong, W., & Apaza, R. (2007). Channel measurement/modeling for airport surface communications: Mobile and fixed platform results. *IEEE Aerospace & Electronics Magazine, 22*(10), 25–30. doi:10.1109/MAES.2007.4376108

Matolak, D., Wu, W., & Sen, I. (2010). 5 GHz band vehicle-to-vehicle channels: Models for multiple values of channel bandwidth. *IEEE Transactions on Vehicular Technology, 59*(5), 2620–2625. doi:10.1109/TVT.2010.2043455

Matthias, G. (2005). *VaneSe - An approach to VANET security.* In V2VCOM, 2005, San Diego, California, USA.

Matz, G. (2005). On non-WSSUS wireless fading channels. *IEEE Transactions on Wireless Communications, 4*(5), 2465–2478. doi:10.1109/TWC.2005.853905

Maurer, J., Fugen, T., Schafer, T., & Wiesbeck, W. (2004). A new inter-vehicle communications (IVC) channel model. *Proceedings of the IEEE Vehicular Technology Conference,* (pp. 9-13).

Maurer, J., Schäfer, M., & Wiesbeck, W. (2001). A realistic description of the environment for inter-vehicle wave propagation modeling. *IEEE Vehicular Technology Conference,* (vol. 3, pp. 1437-1441). Retrieved November 8, 2010, from http://ieeexplore.ieee.org/

Maurer, J., Schafer, T., & Wiesbeck, W. (2005). Physical layer simulations of IEEE 802.11a for vehicle-vehicle communications. *Proceedings of the IEEE Vehicular Technology Conference,* Dallas, TX.

Maurer, J., Sörgel, W., & Wiesbeck, W. (2005). Ray-tracing for vehicle to vehicle communications. *Proceedings of the International Union of Radio Science.* Retrieved November 24, 2010, from http://www.ursi.org/Proceedings/ProcGA05

Mauve, M. (2010). Information dissemination in VANETs. In Hartenstein, H., & Laberteaux, K. (Eds.), *VANET vehicular applications and inter-networking technologies* (pp. 49–80). Wiley&Sons Ltd.

Ma, X., Chen, X., & Refai, H. (2009). *Performance and reliability of DSRC vehicular safety communication: A formal analysis.* EURASIP Journal on Wireless Communications and Networking - Special Issue on Wireless Access in Vehicular Environments.

Mazuelas, S., Lago, F. A., Gonzalez, D., Bahillo, A., Blas, J., & Fernandez, P. (2008). Dynamic estimation of optimum path loss model in a RSS positioning system. In *Proceedings of IEEE/ION Position, Location and Navigation Symposium 2008* (pp. 679-684). Monterey, CA. doi:10.1109/PLANS.2008.4569988

McCrady, D. D., Doyle, L., Forstrom, H., Dempsey, T., & Martorana, M. (2000). Mobile ranging using low-accuracy clocks. *IEEE Transactions on Microwave Theory and Techniques, 48*(6), 951–957. doi:10.1109/22.846721

Medbo, J., Hallenberg, H., & Berg, J. (1999). Propagation characteristics at 5 GHz in typical radio-LAN scenarios. *Proceedings of IEEE Vehicular Technology Conference,* (vol. 1, pp. 185-189).

Melamed, R., Keidar, I., & Barel, Y. (n.d.). Octopus: A fault-tolerant and efficient ad-hoc routing protocol. *24th IEEE Symposium on Reliable Distributed Systems (SRDS'05),* (pp. 39-49).

Menouar, H., Filali, F., & Lenardi, M. (2006). A survey and qualitative analysis of MAC protocols for vehicular ad hoc networks. *IEEE Wireless Communications, 13*(5), 30–35. doi:10.1109/WC-M.2006.250355

Mina, T., & Faramarz, H. (2011). Disseminating a large amount of data to vehicular network in an urban area. *International Journal of Vehicular Technology,* ▪▪▪, 2010.

MIPSHOP. (2009). *IETF mobility for IP: Performance, signaling and handoff optimization.*

Mitelman, B., & Zaslavsky, A. (1999). Link state routing protocol with cluster based flooding for mobile ad-hoc computer networks. *Proceedings of the Workshop on Computer Science and Information Technologies CSIT '99,* (pp. 28-35).

Molisch, A. (Ed.). (2001). *Wideband wireless digital communications.* Upper Saddle River, NJ: Prentice Hall.

Molisch, A., Tufvesson, F., Karedal, J., & Mecklenbrauker, C. (2009). A survey on vehicle-to-vehicle propagation channels. *IEEE Wireless Communication Magazine, 16*(6), 12–22. doi:10.1109/MWC.2009.5361174

Montgomery, D. C., & Runger, G. C. (2003). *Applied statistics and probability for engineers* (3rd ed.). New York, NY: Wiley.

Morgan, Y. L. (2010). Notes on DSRC & WAVE standards suite: Its architecture, design, and characteristics. *IEEE Communications Survey & Tutorials, 12*(4), 1–15. doi:doi:10.1109/SURV.2010.033010.00024

Mousavi, S. M., Rabiee, H. R., Moshref, M., & Dabirmoghaddam, A. (2007). *MobiSim: A framework for simulation of mobility models in mobile ad-hoc networks.* The 3rd IEEE International Conference on Wireless and Mobile Computing, Networking and Communications.

MOWGLY Project. (2006). *Mobile wideband global link system.* Retrieved from http://www.mowgly.org

Msadda, I., Cataldi, P., & Filali, F. (2010). A comparative study between 802.11p and mobile WiMAX-based V2I communication networks. *2010 Fourth International Conference on Next Generation Mobile Applications, Services and Technologies* (pp. 186-191). Washington, DC: IEEE Computer Society. doi:10.1109/NGMAST.2010.45

Mui, L., Mohtashemi, M., & Halberstadt, A. (2002). A computational model of trust and reputation. In the *Proceedings of the 35th Hawaii International Conference on System Science* (HICSS).

Myers, M. (1999). *X.509 Internet public key infrastructure online certificate status protocol - OCSP.* Retrieved from http://www.ietf.org/rfc/rfc2560.txt

Nadeem, T., Shankar, P., & Iftode, L. (2006). A comparative study of data dissemination models for VANETs. In *Proceedings of 3rd Annual Conference on Mobile and Ubiquitous Systems: Networking & Services* (pp. 1-10). San Jose.

Nakagami, M. (1960). The m-distribution: A general formula of intensity of rapid fading. In *The Statistical Methods in Radio Wave Propagation: Proceedings of the Symposium at the University of California.* Permagon Press.

Nakamura, Y., & Sekiguchi, A. (2001). The chaotic mobile robot. *IEEE Transactions on Robotics and Automation, 17*(6), 898–904. doi:10.1109/70.976022

Narten, T., Nordmark, E., Simpson, W.. & Soliman, H. (2007). *Neighbor discovery for IP version 6* (IPv6). IETF RFC 4861.

Nekovee, M. (2009). Epidemic algorithms for reliable and efficient information dissemination in vehicular. *IET Journal Intelligent Transport Systems, 2*(3), 104–110. doi:10.1049/iet-its:20070061

Nelson, D., & DeKok, A. (2007). *Common remote authentication dial in user service (RADIUS).* IETF RFC 5080. Retrieved from http://tools.ietf.org/html/rfc5080

NEMO. (2010). *NEMO implementation.* Retrieved from http://www.umip.org/

Ni, Q. (2005). Performance analysis and enhancements for IEEE 802.11 wireless networks. *IEEE Network, 4*(19), 21–27. doi:doi:10.1109/MNET.2005.1470679

NS2. (2010). *The network simulator - NS2.* Retrieved from http://www.isi.edu/nsnam/ns/

NS-3 Project. (2011). *The NS-3 network simulator.* Retrieved April 10, 2011, from http://www.nsnam.org/.

Nundloll, V., Blair, G., & Grace, P. (2009, December). A component-based approach for (re)-configurable routing in VANETs. *Proceedings of the 8th International Workshop on Adaptive and Reflective Middleware.* Illinous: USA. doi: 10.1145/1658185.1658187

Ogunnaike, B. A. (2010). *Random phenomena: Fundamentals of probability and statistics for engineers.* Boca Raton, FL: CRC Press.

Olario, S., & Weigle, M. (2009). *Vehicular networks from theory to practice.* Chapman & Hall.

Omnet Community. (2011). *Omnet++ event simulation environment.* Retrieved April 5, 2011, from http://www.omnetpp.org.

OpenSSL. (2010). *The OpenSSL project.* From www.openssl.org/

Pack, S., Rutagemwa, H., Shen, X., Mark, J., & Park, K. (2007). Efficient data access algorithms for ITS-bsed networks with multihop wireless link. *IEEE International Conference on Communications* (pp. 4785 - 4790). Glasgow, UK: IEEE. doi: 10.1109/ICC.2007.790

Pahlavan, K., & Krishnamurthy, P. (2009). *Networking fundamentals: Wide, local, and personal area communications.* Chichester, UK: Wiley.

Paier, A., Karedal, J., Czink, N., Dumard, C., Zemen, T., & Tufvesson, F. (2009). Characterization of vehicle-to-vehicle radio channels from measurements at 5.2 GHz. *Wireless Personal Communications, 50,* 19–32. doi:10.1007/s11277-008-9546-6

Papadimitratos, P., Buttyan, L., Hubaux, J., Kargl, F., Kung, A., & Raya, M. (2007). Architecture for secure and private vehicular communications. *The 7th International Conference on ITS,* (pp. 1-6).

Papadimitratos, P., Buttyan, L., Holczer, T., Schoch, E., Freudiger, J., & Raya, M. (2008). Secure vehicular communication systems: Design and architecture. *IEEE Communications Magazine, 46*(11), 100–109. doi:10.1109/MCOM.2008.4689252

Papadimitratos, P., La Fortelle, A., Evenssen, K., Brignolo, R., & Cosenza, S. (2009). Vehicular communication systems: Enabling technologies, applications and future outlook on intelligent transportation. *IEEE Communications Magazine, 47*(11), 84–95. doi:10.1109/MCOM.2009.5307471

Papapanagiotou, K., Marias, G., & Panagiotis, G. (2008). A certificate validation protocol for VANETs. *IEEE Globecom Workshop,* (pp. 1 - 9).

Papazian, P. (2005). Basic transmission loss and delay spread measurements for frequencies between 430 and 5750 MHz. *IEEE Transactions on Antennas and Propagation, 53*(2), 694–701. doi:10.1109/TAP.2004.841391

Papoulis, A., & Pillai, U. (2001). *Probability, random variables, and stochastic processes* (4th ed.). New York, NY: McGraw-Hill.

Parker, R., & Valaee, S. (2006). Vehicle localization in vehicular networks. In *Proceedings of IEEE Vehicular Technology Conference* (pp. 679), Montreal, QC. doi:10.1109/VTCF.2006.557

Parker, R., & Valaee, S. (2007a). Vehicular node localization using received-signal-strength indicator. *IEEE Transactions on Vehicular Technology, 56*(6-I), 3371–3380. doi:10.1109/TVT.2007.907687

Park, Y., & Sur, C. (2010). An efficient anonymous authentication protocol. *Journal of Information Science and Engineering, 800*(3), 785–800.

Parno, B., & Perrig, A. (2005). Challenges in securing vehicular networks. *Proceedings of the Fourth Workshop on Hot Topics in Networks (HotNets-IV).*

Parsons, J. D. (2000). *The mobile radio propagation channel* (2nd ed.). New York, NY: John Wiley & Sons. doi:10.1002/0470841524

Patwari, N., Ash, J. N., & Kyperountas, S. III, A. O. H., Moses, R. L., & Correal, N. S. (2005). Locating the nodes, cooperative localization in wireless sensor networks. *IEEE Signal Processing Magazine, 22*(4), 54–69. doi:10.1109/MSP.2005.1458287

Patwari, N., Hero, A. O., Perkins, M., Correal, N. S., & O'Dea, R. J. (2003). Relative location estimation in wireless sensor networks. *IEEE Transactions on Signal Processing, 51*(8), 2137–2148. doi:10.1109/TSP.2003.814469

Patzold, M., Hogstad, B., & Youssef, N. (2008). Modeling, analysis, and simulation of MIMO mobile-to-mobile fading channels. *IEEE Transactions on Wireless Communications, 7*(2), 510–520. doi:10.1109/TWC.2008.05913

Pérez, A., Fernández, P. J., Marín, R., Martínez, G., Gómez-Skarmeta, A. F., & Taniuchi, K. (2008). OpenIKEv2: Design and implementation of an IKEv2 solution. *IEICE Transactions, 91-D*(5), 1319–1329. doi:doi:10.1093/ietisy/e91-d.5.1319

Perkins, C., Belding-Royer, E., & Das, S. (2003). *RFC3561: Ad hoc on-demand distance vector (AODV) routing.* Retrieved from http://portal.acm.org/citation.cfm?id=RFC3561

Peters, S. W., & Heath, R. W. (2009). The future of WiMAX: Multihop relaying with IEEE 802.16j. *IEEE Communications Magazine, 47*(1), 104–111. doi:10.1109/MCOM.2009.4752686

Petit, J. (2009). Analysis of ECDSA authentication processing in VANETs. *The 3rd International Conference on New Technologies, Mobility and Security (NTMS)*, (pp. 1-5).

Pilosu, L., Cozzetti, H. A., & Scopigno, R. (2010). *Layered and service-dependent security in CSMA/CA and slotted VANETs.* In 7th International ICTS Conference on Heterogeneous Networking for Quality, Reliability, Security and Robustness (QShine 2010).

Pinart, C., Lequerica, I., Barona, I., Sanz, P., García, D., & Sánchez-Aparisi, D. (2008). DRIVE: A reconfigurable testbed for advanced vehicular services and communications. *Proceedings of the 4th International Conference on Testbeds and Research Infrastructures for Development of Networks and Communities.* Brussels, Belgium: ICST.

Plossl, K., Nowey, T., & Mletzko, C. (2006). Towards a security architecture for vehicular ad hoc networks. *Proceedings of The First International Conference on Availability, Reliability and Security*, (p. 8).

Popescu-Zeletin, R., Radusch, I., & Rigani, M. (2010). *Vehicular-2-X communication: State-of-the-art and research in mobile vehicular ad hoc networks.* New York, NY: Springer.

Pre-Drive C2X Project. (n.d.). Retrieved from http://www.pre-drive-c2x.eu

Prieto Tejedor, J., Bahillo Martinez, A., Mazuelas Franco, S., Lorenzo Toledo, R. M., Fernandez Reguero, P., & Abril, E. J. (2009). Characterization and mitigation of range estimation errors for an RTT-based IEEE 802.11 indoor location system. *Progress in Electromagnetics Research B, 15*, 217–244. doi:10.2528/PIERB09050502

Proakis, J. (2010). *Digital communications* (4th ed.). Boston, MA: McGraw-Hill.

Pursley, M. (2002). *Random processes in linear systems.* Upper Saddle River, NJ: Prentice-Hall.

Qian, Y., & Moayeri, N. (2008). Design of secure and application-oriented VANETs. *Vehicular Technology Conference* (2794-2799). Singapore: IEEE. doi: 10.1109/VETECS.2008.610

Qiu, R. (2002). A study of the ultra-wideband wireless propagation channel and optimum UWB receiver design. *IEEE Journal on Selected Areas in Communications, 20*(9), 1628–1637. doi:10.1109/JSAC.2002.805249

Rai, V., Bai, F., Kenney, J., & Laberteaux, K. (2007). *IEEE 802.11 11-07-2133-00-000p: Cross-channel interference test results: A report from VSC-A project.*

Rajamani, R., & Shladover, S. (2001). An experimental comparative study of autonomous and co-operative vehicle-follower control systems. *Transportation Research Part C, Emerging Technologies, 9*(1), 15–31. doi:10.1016/S0968-090X(00)00021-8

Rappaport, T. (2002). *Wireless communications: Principles and practice* (2nd ed.). Upper Saddle River, NJ: Prentice-Hall.

Raya, M., & Hubaux, J. P. (2005). The security of vehicular ad hoc networks. *Proceedings of the 3rd ACM Workshop on Security of Ad Hoc and Sensor Networks.* doi:10.1145/1102219.1102223

Raya, M., & Hubaux, J.-P. (2007). Securing vehicular ad hoc networks. *Journal of Compputer Security, Special Issue on Security of Ad Hoc and Sensor Networks,* 39-68.

Reichardt, L., Fugen, T., & Zwick, T. (2010). Influence of antennas placement on car to car communications channel. *Proceedings of European Conference on Antennas & Propagation 2010*, Berlin, Germany.

Renaudin, O., Kolmonen, V., Vainikainen, P., & Oestges, C. (2011). Wideband measurement-based modeling of inter-vehicle channels in the 5 GHz band. *Proceedings of European Conference on Antennas & Propagation 2011*, Rome, Italy.

Renaudin, O., Kolmonen, V., Vainikainen, P., & Oestges, C. (2010). Non-stationary narrowband MIMO inter-vehicle channel characterization in the 5 GHz band. *IEEE Transactions on Vehicular Technology, 59*(4), 2007–2015. doi:10.1109/TVT.2010.2040851

Research and Innovative Technology Administration. (2008). *Transportation vision for 2030.* U.S. Department of Transportation. Retrieved from http://www.rita.dot.gov/publications/transportation_vision_2030/

Reveliotis, S. A. (2000). Conflict resolution in AGV systems. *IIE Transactions, 32*(7), 647–659. doi:10.1080/07408170008967423

RFC. 3820 - Internet X.509 Public Key Infrastructure (PKI). (2004). *RFC:3820 - Internet X.509 public key infrastructure (PKI) proxy certificate profile.* Retrieved from http://www.ietf.org/rfc/rfc3820.txt

Ritesh Kumar, K., Angolkar, P., Das, D., & Ramalingam, R. (2008). *SWiFT: A novel architecture for seamless wireless internet for fast trains.* Vehicular Technology Conference, 2008.VTC-2008 Singapore IEEE 67th. 10.1109/VETECS.2008.322

Ros, F. J., Ruiz, P. M., & Stojmenovic, I. (2010). Acknowledgment-based broadcast protocol for reliable and efficient data dissemination in vehicular ad-hoc networks. *IEEE Transactions on Mobile Computing, 11*(1).

Ross, S. M. (2004). *Introduction to probability and statistics for engineers and scientists* (3rd ed.). Amsterdam, The Netherlands: Elsevier Academic Press.

RSA Cryptography Standard. (2002). Retrieved from www.rsa.com

Ruesche, S. F., Steuer, J., & Jobmann, K. (2008). The European switch: A Packet-switched approach to a train control system. *IEEE Vehicular Technology Magazine, 3*(3), 37-46. ISSN: 1556-6072

SAFESPOT Integrated Project. (2010). Retrieved from http://www.safespot-eu.org/

Safety, C. F. (2009). *Make roads safe, a decade of action for road safety.* Commission for Global Road Safety. Retrieved from http://www.makeroadssafe.org/publications/Pages/homepage.aspx

Saha, A., Park, G. L., Ahn, K. J., Kim, C., Lee, B., & Rhee, Y. J. (2009). Data distribution of road-side information station in vehicular ad hoc networks (VANETs). *Proceedings of the International Conference on Computational Science and its Applications,* (pp. 503-512).

Sai, S., Niwa, E., Mase, K., Nishibori, M., Inoue, J., & Obuchi, M. (2009). Field evaluation of UHF radio propagation for an ITS safety system in an urban environment. *IEEE Communications Magazine*, *47*(11), 120–127. doi:10.1109/MCOM.2009.5307475

Sakagami, S., Aoyama, S., Kuboi, K., Shirota, S., & Akeyama, A. (1992). Vehicle position estimates by multibeam antennas in multipathenvironments. *IEEE Transactions on Vehicular Technology*, *41*(1), 63–68. doi:10.1109/25.120146

Salhi, I., Cherif, M., & Senouci, S. (2007). Data collection in vehicular networks. In *Proceedings of ASN Symposium.*

Samara, G., Al-Salihy, W., & Sures, R. (2010). *Security analysis of vehicular ad hoc networks* (VANET). 2010 Second International Conference on Network Applications Protocols and Services.

Sampigethaya, K., & Huang, L. (2005). CARAVAN: Providing location privacy for VANET. *Proceedings of ESCAR.*

Santesson, S., & Hallam-Baker, P. (2010). *OCSP algorithm agility.* Retrieved from http://tools.ietf.org/html/draft-ietf-pkix-ocspagility-09#page-4

Sardari, M., Hendessi, F., & Fekri, F. (2009). DMRC: Dissemination of multimedia in vehicular networks using rateless codes. In *Proceedings of the IEEE International Conference on Computer Communications (INFOCOM '09)*, (pp. 1–6).

Sarkar, T. (2003). *Smart antennas*. New York, NY: IEEE Press. doi:10.1002/0471722839

Saunders, S. R., & Aragón-Zavala, A. (2007). *Antennas and propagation for wireless communication systems* (2nd ed.). Chichester, UK: J. Wiley & Sons.

Savi, M. (2006). *Dinâmica Não-Linear e Caos*. Rio de Janeiro, e-papers.

Schafhuber, D., & Matz, G. (2005). MMSE and adaptive prediction of time-varying channels for OFDM systems. *IEEE Transactions on Wireless Communications*, *4*(2), 593–602. doi:10.1109/TWC.2004.843055

Schenato, L., & Gamba, G. (2007). A distributed consensus protocol for clock synchronization in wireless sensor network. In the *Proceedings of the 46th IEEE Conference on Decision and Control*, (pp. 2289–2294).

Schmidl, T. M., & Cox, D. C. (1997). Robust frequency and timing synchronization for OFDM. *IEEE Transactions on Communications*, *45*(12), 1613–1621. doi:10.1109/26.650240

Scopigno, R., & Cozzetti, H. A. (2009). *GNSS synchronization in VANETs*. In the Third IEEE International Conference on New Technologies, Mobility and Security (NTMS 2009).

Scopigno, R., & Cozzetti, H. A. (2009). Mobile slotted Aloha for VANETs. *IEEE Vehicular Technology Conference (VTC Fall)*, (pp. 1-5). Anchorage, AK.

Scopigno, R., & Cozzetti, H. A. (2010). *Evaluation of time-space efficiency in CSMA/CA and slotted VANETs*. In IEEE 71th Vehicular Technology Conference (VTC Fall 2010).

Scopigno, R., & Cozzetti, H. A. (2010). *Signal shadowing in simulation of urban vehicular communications*. In the 6th International Conference on Wireless and Mobile Communications (ICWMC 2010).

Seeber, G. (2003). *Satellite geodesy: Foundations, methods, and applications*. Berlin, Germany: Walter de Gruyter GmbH & Co.

Sen, I., Matolak, D., & Xiong, W. (2006). Wireless channels that exhibit "worse than Rayleigh" fading: Analytical and measurement results. *Proceedings of MILCOM 2006*, Washington, DC.

Sen, I., & Matolak, D. (2008). Vehicle-vehicle channel models for the 5 GHz band. *IEEE Transactions on Intelligent Transportation Systems*, *9*(2), 235–245. doi:10.1109/TITS.2008.922881

Sesia, S., Toufik, I., & Baker, M. (Eds.). (2009). *LTE: The UMTS long term evolution: From theory to practice*. West Sussex, UK: John Wiley & Sons. doi:10.1002/9780470742891

SEVECOM Project. (n.d.). Retrieved from http://www.sevecom.org

Seybold, J. S. (2005). *Introduction to RF propagation*. Hoboken, NJ: Wiley. doi:10.1002/0471743690

Shakkottai, S., Rappaport, T. S., & Karlsson, P. C. (2003). Cross-layer design for wireless networks. *IEEE Communications Magazine, 41*(10). doi:10.1109/MCOM.2003.1235598

Shibata, N., Terauchi, T., Kitani, T., Yasumoto, K., Ito, M., & Higashino, T. (2006). A method for sharing traffic information using inter-vehicle communication. In *Proceedings of 3rd Annual Conference on Mobile and Ubiquitous Systems: Networking & Services* (pp. 1-7). San Jose.

Shirahama, J., & Ohtsuki, T. (2008). RSS-based localization in environments with different path loss exponent for each link. In *Proceedings of IEEE Vehicular Technology Conference* (pp. 1509 - 1513). Singapore. doi:10.1109/VETECS.2008.353

Shladover, S. E., & Tan, S. K. (2006). Analysis of vehicle positioning accuracy requirements for communication-based cooperative collision warning. *Journal of Intelligent Transportation Systems: Technology, Planning, and Operations, 10*(3), 131–140. doi:10.1080/15472450600793610

Sichitiu, L. M., & Kihl, M. (2008). Inter-vehicle communication systems: A survey. *IEEE Communications Surveys, 10*(2), 88–105. doi:10.1109/COMST.2008.4564481

Sieskul, B. T., & Kaiser, T. (2005). Cramer-Rao bound for TOA estimations in UWB positioning systems. In *Proceedings of IEEE International Conference on Ultra-Wideband*, Zurich, Switzerland. doi:10.1109/ICU.2005.1570022

Sivakumar, R., Das, B., & Bharghavan, V. (1998). Spine routing in ad hoc networks. *ACM/Baltzer Cluster. The Computer Journal, 1*, 237–248.

Skordylis, A., & Trogoni, N. (n.d.). Delay-bounded routing in vehicular ad-hoc networks. *9th ACM International Symposium on Mobile Ad Hoc Networking and Computing* (pp. 341-350). New York, NY: ACM. doi:10.1145/1374618.1374664

Smith, J. O., & Abel, J. S. (1987). Closed -form least-squares source location estimation from range-difference measurements. *IEEE Transactions on Acoustics, Speech, and Signal Processing, ASSP-35*(12), 1661–1669. doi:10.1109/TASSP.1987.1165089

Sormani, D., & Turconi, G. (2006). Towards lightweight information dissemination in inter-vehicular networks. In *Proceedings of 3rd International Workshop on Vehicular Ad Hoc Networks* (pp. 20-29). Los Angeles.

Souza, E., Nikolaidis, I., & Gburzynski, P. (2010). A new aggregate local mobility (ALM) clustering algorithm for VANETs. In *Proceedings of IEEE International Conference on Communication* (pp 1-5). South Africa.

Spiegel, M. R., Hernández Heredero, R., & Abellanas, L. (1998). *Estadística* (2nd ed.). Madrid, Spain: McGraw-Hill.

Srivastava, V., & Motani, M. (2005). Cross-layer design: A survey and the road ahead. *Communications Magazine, IEEE, 43*, 112–119. doi:10.1109/MCOM.2005.1561928

Stampoulis, A., & Chai, Z. (2007). *A survey of security in vehicular networks*. Retrieved from http://zoo.cs.yale.edu/~ams257/projects/wireless-survey.pdf

Standard, I. E. E. E. 802.11p. (2010). *Wireless LAN medium access control (MAC) and physical layer (PHY) specifications: Amendment 6- Wireless access in vehicular environments*.

Steenken, D. VOß, S., & Stahlbock, R. (2005). Container terminal operation and operations research – A Classification and literature review. In H. Günther, & K. H. Kim (Eds.), *Container terminals and automated transport systems - Logistics control issues and quantitative decision support*, (pp. 3 – 49). Berlin, Germany: Springer.

Stein, S. (1987). Fading channel issues in system engineering. *IEEE Journal on Selected Areas in Communications, 5*(2), 68–89. doi:10.1109/JSAC.1987.1146536

Stephen, J. E. (2000). *Development of a GNSS-based multi-sensor vehicle navigation system*. University of Calgary.

Sterian, C. E. D., Ma, Y., Pätzold, M., Bănică, I., & He, H. (2011). New super-orthogonal space-time trellis codes using differential M-PSK for noncoherent mobile communication systems with two transmit antennas. *Annales des Télécommunications, 66*(3/4), 257–273. doi:10.1007/s12243-010-0191-1

Stibor, L., Zang, Y., & Reumerman, H. J. (2007). Evaluation of communication distance of broadcast messages in a vehicular ad-hoc network using IEEE 802.11p. *IEEE Wireless Communications and Networking Conference*, (pp. 254-257).

Strassberger, M., Schroth, C., & Lasowski, R. (2009). Data dissemination in vehicular networks. In Moustafa, H., & Zhang, Y. (Eds.), *Vehicular networks techniques, standards, and applications* (pp. 181–220). CRC Press.

Stuber, G. L. (2001). *Principles of mobile communication* (2nd ed.). Boston, MA: Kluwer Academic Publishers.

SUMO. (n.d.). *SUMO vehicles movement simulator.* Retrieved from http://sumo.sourceforge.net

Sun, H., Lin, Y., Chen, S., & Shen, Y. (2007). *Secure and fast handover scheme based on pre- authentication method for 802.16/WiMAX infrastructure networks.* IEEE Region 10 Conference.

Tadokoro, Y., Ito, K., Imai, J., Suzuki, N., & Itoh, N. (2008). *Advance transmission cycle control scheme for autonomous decentralized TDMA protocol in safe driving support system.* In the Intelligent Vehicles Symposium.

Talha, B., & Patzold, M. (2009). Statistical modeling and analysis of mobile-to-mobile fading channels in cooperative networks under line-of-sight conditions. *Wireless Personal Communications, 50*, 1–17.

Tank, T., & Linnartz, J.-P. (1997). Vehicle-to-vehicle communications for AVCS platooning. *IEEE Transactions on Vehicular Technology, 46*(2), 528–536. doi:10.1109/25.580791

Tao, J., Wu, J., & Xiao, C. (2009). Estimation of channel transfer function and carrier frequency offset for OFDM systems with phase noise. *IEEE Transactions on Vehicular Technology, 58*(8), 4380–4387. doi:10.1109/TVT.2009.2020066

Tarokh, V., & Jafarkhani, H. (2000). A differential detection scheme for transmit diversity. *IEEE Journal on Selected Areas in Communications, 18*(7), 1169–1174. doi:10.1109/49.857917

Tay, J. H., Chandrasekhar, V. R., & Seah, W. K. (2006). Selective iterative multilateration for hop count-based localization in wireless sensor networks. *In Proceedings of 7th International Conference on Mobile Data Management* (pp. 152 - 152). doi:10.1109/MDM.2006.139

Taylor, G., Blewitt, G., Steup, D., Corbett, S., & Car, A. (2001). Road reduction filtering for GPS-GIS navigation. *Transactions in GIS, 5*(3), 193–207. doi:10.1111/1467-9671.00077

Trees, H. L. V. (2003). *Detection, estimation, and modulation theory.* New York, NY: Wiley-IEEE.

Tse, D., & Viswanath, P. (2005). *Fundamentals of wireless communication.* Cambridge, UK: Cambridge University Press.

Tsukada, M., Ben-Jemaa, I., Menouar, H., Zhang, W., Goleva, M., & Ernst, T. (2010). *Experimental evaluation for IPv6 over VANET geographic routing.* 6th International Wireless Communications and Mobile Computing Conference.

Tureli, U., Liu, H., & Zoltowski, M. D. (2000). OFDM blind carrier offset estimation: ESPRIT. *IEEE Transactions on Communications, 48*(9), 1459–1461. doi:10.1109/26.870011

U.S Department of Transportation. (2006). *Vehicle safety communications project. Final Report.* National Highway Traffic Safety Administration, U.S Department of Transportation.

UMTS. (2006). *3G/UMTS Evolution: Towards a new generation of broadband mobile services.* White paper, UMTS Forum.

UNFPA. (2007). *Technical report: State of world population 2007: Unleashing the potential of urban growth.* New York, NY: United Nations Population Fundation. Retrieved from http://www.unfpa.org/swp/2007/english/introduction.html

Union Internationale des Chemins de Fer (UIC). (2006). *UIC Project EIRENE: Functional requirements specification.* Reference PSA167D005 v.7.0. UIC. EIRENE User Group. 2006.

Union Internationale des Chemins de Fer (UIC). (2006A). *UIC Project EIRENE: System requirements specification.* Reference: PSA167D006 Version:15.0. UIC. EIRENE Project Team. 2006.

Union Internationale des Chemins de Fer (UIC). (2007). *ERTMS/GSM-R quality of service specification reference O-2475 3.0.* UIC, QoS Working Group. UIC ERTMS/GSM-R Operators Group. 2007.

US Department of Transportation. (2010). *Intelligent transportation systems.* Retrieved 16 November, 2010, from http://www.its.dot.gov/index.htm

Uzcategui, R., & Acosta-Marum, G. (2009). WAVE: A tutorial. *IEEE Communications Magazine, 47*(5), 126–133. doi:10.1109/MCOM.2009.4939288

Varaiya, P. (1993). Smart cars on smart roads: Problems of control. *IEEE Transactions on Automatic Control, 38*(2), 195–207. doi:10.1109/9.250509

Vasilakos, A. (2011). *Delay tolerant networks: Protocols and applications (Wireless Networks and Mobile Communications).* CRC Press.

Vatalaro, F., & Forcella, A. (1997). Doppler spectrum in mobile-to-mobile communications in the presence of three-dimensional multipath scattering. *IEEE Transactions on Vehicular Technology, 46*(1), 213–219. doi:10.1109/25.554754

Venkatraman, S., Caffery, J. Jr, & You, H. R. (2004). A novel ToA location algorithm using LoS range estimation for NLoS environments. *IEEE Transactions on Vehicular Technology, 53*(5), 1515–1524. doi:10.1109/TVT.2004.832384

Vieira, P. (2009). *MRS logística switches to CBTC.* Railway Gazette, Marzo.

Vilalta, R., Apte, C., Hellerstein, J., Ma, S., & Weiss, S. (2002). Predictive algorithms in the management of computer systems. *IBM Systems Journal, 41*(3). doi:10.1147/sj.413.0461

Wada, T., Maeda, M., Okada, M., Tsukamoto, K., & Komaki, S. (1998). Theoretical analysis of propagation characteristics in millimeter-wave intervehicle communication system. *IEICE Transactions in Communication, 83*(11), 1116–1125.

Wang, S. Y., Chou, C. L., Liu, K. C., Ho, T. W., Hung, W. J., & Huang, C. F. … Lin, C. C. (2009). Improving the channel utilization of IEEE 802.11p/1609 networks. *IEEE Wireless Communications and Networking Conference (WCNC),* (pp. 1-6), Budapest.

Wang, Y. X., & Bao, F. S. (2007). An entropy-based weighted clustering algorithm and its optimization for ad hoc networks. In *Proceedings of IEEE 3rd International Conference on Wireless and Mobility, Networksing and Communications,* (p. 56). New York, USA.

Wang, Y., Ahmed, A., Krishnamachari, B., & Psounis, K. (2008). IEEE 802.11p performance evaluation and protocol enhancement. *IEEE International Conference on Vehicular Electronics and Safety (ICVES),* (pp. 317-322). Columbus, OH.

Wang, Y., Wu, T. Y., Lee, W., & Ke, C. (2010) A novel geographic routing strategy over VANET. In *Proceedings of AINA Workshops,* (pp. 873-879).

Wang, Z., Liu, L., Zhou, M., & Ansari, N. (2008). A position based clustering technique for ad hoc intervehicle communication. *IEEE Transactions on Systems, Man and Cybernetics- Applications and Reviews, 38,* 201-208

Wang, J. H., & Gao, Y. (2004). GPS-based land vehicle navigation system assisted by a low-cost gyro-free INS using neural network. *Journal of Navigation, 57*(3), 417–428. doi:10.1017/S037346330400284X

Wang, S., Chou, C., & Lin, C. (2010). *The GUI user manual for the NCTUns 6.0 network simulator and emulator. Network and System Laboratory, Department of Computer Science.* Taiwan: National Chiao Tung University.

Wang, X., Wang, Z., & O'Dea, B. (2003). A TOA-based location algorithm reducing the errors due to non-line-of-sight (NLOS) propagation. *IEEE Transactions on Vehicular Technology, 52*(1), 112–116. doi:10.1109/TVT.2002.807158

Watfa, M. (Ed.). (2010). *Advances in vehicular ad-hoc networks: Developments and challenges.* Hershey, PA: IGI Global. doi:10.4018/978-1-61520-913-2

Webb, W. (1999). *The complete wireless communications professional: A guide for engineers and managers.* Boston, MA: Artech House.

Website, R. I. T. A. (2010). *Department of Transportation research programs*. Retrieved October 13, 2010 from http://www.rita.dot.gov/rdt/dot_research_programs.html.

Wei, C., Zhiyi, H., & Tianren, Y. (2008). A street reference model of MIMO vehicle-to-vehicle fading channel. *IEEE Conference on Industrial Electronics and Application,* (pp. 275-278). Retrieved January 7, 2011, from http://ieeexplore.ieee.org/

Weiss, A. J. (2003). On the accuracy of a cellular location system based on RSS measurements. *IEEE Transactions on Vehicular Technology, 52*(6), 1508–1518. doi:10.1109/TVT.2003.819613

WiMAX Forum Report. (2008). *Deployment of mobile WiMAX networks by operators with existing 2G & 3G networks.*

Wischhof, L., Ebner, A., & Rohling, H. (2005). Information dissemination in self- organizing intervehicle networks. *IEEE Transactions on Intelligent Transportation Systems, 6*, 90–101. doi:10.1109/TITS.2004.842407

Wisitpongphan, N., Tonguz, O. K., Parikh, J. S., Mudalige, P., Bai, F., & Sadekar, V. (2007). Broadcast storm mitigation techniques in vehicular ad hoc networks. *IEEE Wireless Communications, 14*(6), 84–94. doi:10.1109/MWC.2007.4407231

Wolny, G. (2008). Modified DMAC clustering algorithm for VANETs. In *Proceedings of 3rd IEEE International Conference on Systems and Networks Communication* (pp. 268- 273).

Wymeersch, H., Lien, J., & Win, M. Z. (2009). Cooperative localization in wireless networks. *Proceedings of the IEEE, 97*(2), 427–450. doi:10.1109/JPROC.2008.2008853

Xiaoping Xue, J. D. (2011). LPA: A new location-based privacy-preserving authentication protocol in VANET. *Security and Communication Networks,* online version before print.

Xu, B., Ouksel, A., & Wolfson, O. (2004). Opportunistic resource exchange in intervehicle ad-hoc networks. In *Proceedings of IEEE International Conference of Mobile Data Management* (pp. 4-12)

Xu, A. Y. Z., Au, E. K. S., Wong, A. K. S., & Wang, Q. (2009). A novel threshold-based coherent TOA estimation for IR-UWB systems. *IEEE Transactions on Vehicular Technology, 58*(8), 4675–4681. doi:10.1109/TVT.2009.2020990

Xu, B., Shen, L., & Yan, F. (2009). Vehicular node positioning based on Doppler-shifted frequency measurement on highway. *Journal of Electronics, 26*(2), 265–269. doi:doi:10.1007/s11767-008-0110-z

Yang, X. Liu, J., Zhao, F., & Vaidya, N. (2004). A vehicle-to-vehicle communication protocol for cooperative collision warning. *The First Annual International Conference on Mobile and Ubiquitous Systems: Networking and Services,* (pp. 114-123).

Yang, K., Ou, S., Chen, H., & He, J. (2007). A multihop peer-communication protocol with fairness garantee for IEEE 802.16-based vehicular networks. *IEEE Transactions on Vehicular Technology, 56*(6), 3358–3370. doi:10.1109/TVT.2007.906875

Yi, L., & Miao, K. (2010). *WiMAX-WiFi unified network architecture, security, and mobility.* 12th IEEE International Conference on Communication Technology.

Yin, J., ElBatt, T., Yeung, G., Ryu, B., Habermas, S., Krishnan, H., & Talty, T. (2004). Performance evaluation of safety applications over DSRC vehicular ad hoc networks. *Proceedings of the first ACM Workshop on Vehicular Ad Hoc Networks,* (pp. 1-9).

Yu, Q., & Heijenk, G. (2008). Abiding geocast for warning message dissemination in vehicular ad hoc networks. In *Proceedings of IEEE Vehicular Networks and Applications Workshop (Vehi-Mobi)* (pp. 400-404). Beijing.

Zajic, A., & Stuber, G. (2008). Three-dimensional modeling, simulation, and capacity analysis of space-time correlated mobile-to-mobile channels. *IEEE Transactions on Vehicular Technology, 57*(4), 2042–2054. doi:10.1109/TVT.2007.912150

Zajic, A., Stuber, G., & Pratt, T. (2009). Wideband MIMO mobile-to-mobile channels: Geometry-based statistical modeling with experimental verification. *IEEE Transactions on Vehicular Technology, 58*(2), 517–534. doi:10.1109/TVT.2008.928001

Zang, Y., Stibor, L., Walke, B., Reumerman, H.-J., & Barroso, A. (2007). Towards broadband vehicular ad-hoc networks: The vehicular mesh network (VMESH) MAC protocol. *IEEE Wireless Communications and Networking Conference (WCNC)*, (pp. 417-422). Kowloon.

Zang, Y., Stibor, L., Orfanos, G., Guo, S., & Reumerman, H.-J. (2005). *An error model for inter-vehicle communications in highway scenarios at 5.9 GHz*. Montreal: ACM PE-WASUN.

Zeadally, S., Ray, H., Yuh-Shyan, C., Angela, I., & Aamir, H. (2010, December 9). *Vehicular ad hoc networks (VANETS): Status, results, and challenges*. Telecommunication Systems. Springer Science+Business Media. doi: 10.1007/s11235-010-9400-5

Zensus, J. A., Diamond, P. J., & Napier, P. J. (1995). *Very long baseline interferometry and the VLBA*. Orem, UT: Astronomical Society of the Pacific.

Zhang, J., & Matolak, D. (2008). FG-*MC-CDMA system performance in multi-band channels*. IEEE Communication Networks & Services Research Conference, Halifax, Nova Scotia, CA.

Zhang, W., Gui, L., Ma, W., Liu, B., & Xiong, J. (2008). The television broadcasting network of Chinese High Speed Railway. *IEEE International Symposium on Broadband Multimedia Systems and Broadcasting*, (pp. 1-4).

Zhang, X., & Su, H. (2006). Cluster-based multichannel communications protocols in vehicle ad hoc networks. *IEEE Wireless Communications*, *13*(5), 44–51. doi:10.1109/WC-M.2006.250357

Zhang, Y. (2009). *WiMAX network planning and optimization*. Boca Raton: CRC Press.

Zhang, Y., & Chen, H.-H. (2008). *Mobile WiMAX: Toward broadband wireless metropolitan area networks*. New York, NY: Auerbach Publications.

Zhao, J., & Cao, G. (2006). VADD: Vehicle-assisted data delivery in vehicular ad hoc networks. *Proceedings IEEE INFOCOM 2006. 25TH IEEE International Conference on Computer Communications*, (pp. 1-12).

Zheng, Y. R. (2006). A non-isotropic model for mobile to mobile fading channel simulations. *Proceedings of MILCOM '06*, Washington, DC.

Zhou, P., Qin, Y., Xu, C., Guan, J., & Zhang, H. (2010). *Security investigation and enhancement of IKEV2 protocol*. 3rd IEEE International Conference on Broadband Network and Multimedia Technology (IC-BNMT).

Zhuang, Y., Pan, J., Luo, Y., & Cai, L. (2011). Time and location-critical emergency message dissemination for vehicular ad-hoc networks. *IEEE Journal on Selected Areas in Communications*, *29*, 187–196. doi:10.1109/JSAC.2011.110118

Zhu, J., & Roy, S. (2003). MAC for dedicated short range communications in intelligent transport system. *IEEE Communications Magazine*, *43*(12), 60–67.

Zhu, Y., & Jafarkhani, H. (2006). Differential super-orthogonal space-time trellis codes. *IEEE Transactions on Wireless Communications*, *5*(12), 3634–3643. doi:10.1109/TWC.2006.256986

About the Contributors

Raúl Aquino Santos graduated from the University of Colima with a BE in Electrical Engineering, and received his MS degree in Telecommunications from the Centre for Scientific Research and Higher Education in Ensenada, Mexico in 1990. He holds a PhD from the Department of Electrical and Electronic Engineering of the University of Sheffield, England. Since 2005, he has been with the College of Telematics at the University of Colima where he is currently a Research-Professor in telecommunications networks. His current research interests include wireless and sensor networks.

Victor Rangel received the B.Eng (Hons) degree in Computer Engineering in the Engineering Faculty from the National Autonomous University of Mexico (UNAM) in 1996, the M.Sc in Telematics at from the University of Sheffield, U.K. in 1998, and the Ph.D. in Performance Analysis and Traffic Scheduling in Cable Networks in 2002, from the University of Sheffield. Since 2002, he has been with the School of Engineering, UNAM, where he is currently a Research-Professor in telecommunications networks. His research focuses on fixed, mesh and mobile broadband wireless access networks, QoS over IP, traffic shaping, and scheduling.

Arthur Edwards received his Master's degree in Education from the University of Houston in 1985. He has been a Researcher-Professor at the University of Colima since 1985, where he has served in various capacities. He has been with the School of Telematics since 1998. His primary areas of research are Computer Assisted Language Learning (CALL), distance learning, collaborative learning, multimodal leaning, and mobile learning. The primary focus of his research is presently in the area of mobile collaborative learning.

* * *

Marina Aguado holds a PhD in Telecommunications Engineering, Bilbao's Escuela Técnica Superior de Ingeniería (ETSI), University of the Basque Country (UPV/EHU). She has eight years of experience in the transportation industry, having held the positions of R&D Manager, Consultant, Project Manager, and Network Support Analyst. Furthermore, she has two years of experience in the automotive and quality sectors (Ford Motor Company, Dagenham - UK and Inasmet, San Sebastián – Spain). At present, she is a Senior Lecturer at ETSI (UPV/EHU) and is a member of the I^{2}T (Engineering and Research on Telematics) research group at the same university. Her current research interests include broadband wireless communication technologies, handover, and mobility management in the transportation scenario.

Nima Alam is pursuing his PhD in the field of "Vehicular Positioning Enhancement with DSRC" at the University of New South Wales, Sydney, Australia, commencing Feb. 2009. He achieved a Bachelor's degree in Telecommunication Systems from Sharif University of Technology, Tehran, Iran, in 1998. He obtained his Master's degree in Control Systems in 2000 from the same university. He has been involved in a variety of projects in the automotive industry including industrial robotics, moving robots, factory automation, machine vision, GPS navigation, and fleet management between 2000 and 2008. He is a certified project manager (PMP) by Project Management Institute, USA. He has managed more than 30 industrial and R&D projects before starting his PhD.

Asghar Tabatabaei Balaei completed the PhD (2008) in Global Navigation Satellite Interference at the University of New South Wales (UNSW), Sydney, Australia where he has also worked as a post-doctoral research fellow in the School of Surveying and Spatial Information Systems. His research is in the area of interference effects on the satellite navigation systems and also cooperative positioning systems in wireless networks. He is currently an Associate Lecturer in the Electrical Engineering and Telecommunication department of UNSW.

Marion Berbineau was born in Toulouse, France, on September 18, 1962. She received her degree in Electronics, Automatic and Metrology Engineering from Polytech'Lille (France) and her PhD in Electronics from the University of Lille 1989. She joined IFSTTAR (ex INRETS) as a full-time researcher in telecommunications in 1989. She is currently Research Director and Director of the LEOST laboratory. Dr. Berbineau's field of expertise include EM propagation, channel characterization and modeling for transport and complexes environments, particularly in tunnels, signal processing for wireless communication systems in multipath environment, and MIMO systems and wireless systems for ITS and for railway applications in the context of ERTMS (European Rail Traffic Management System). She is involved in several national and European projects. She has also authored and co-authored several publications and has registered patents. Dr. Berbineau is an IEEE member, affiliated to the VTS society.

Mounir Boussedjra has a Ph.D. in Computer Science from the University of Technology of Belfort-Montbéliard, France. The main goal of his Ph.D. work was to estimate the performance of intermodal transportation networks to provide real-time information about different modes of transportation. To reach this goal, he has studied the applications of multi objective and metaheuristic approaches. Currently, he is a researcher at IRSEEM and member of Intelligent Transportation System team. He works in collaboration with other researchers on the communication inter-vehicle team. At moment, Dr. Boussedjra works on addressing the issues in inter-vehicle communication to develop ITS safety and non-safety applications.

Claudia Campolo received a M.S degree in Telecommunications Engineering in October 2007 and a Ph.D. degree from the University Mediterranea of Reggio Calabria, Italy, in February 2011. She was a visiting PhD student at the Department of Electronics Engineering of Politecnico di Torino (May 2008-October 2008). She has been recipient of the Best Paper Award in Nets4Cars 2009. She serves as a technical reviewer of several international journals. She serves as Tutorial co-chair in ITST (International Conference on Intelligent Transport Systems Telecommunications) 2011 and as TPC member in several international workshops and conferences. Her major research interests are in the field of ad hoc and vehicular networking, and cooperation in heterogeneous wireless networks.

Hector Agustin Cozzetti was born in Buenos Aires (Argentina) on March 5, 1983. He received his Master's Degree in Telecommunications Engineering at Politecnico di Torino in April 2008 with a thesis on the "Application of SRTP to video streaming." He has worked in ISMB (Istituto Superiore Mario Boella) as a researcher since May 2008. His scientific interests include Vehicular Ad-hoc NETworks (VANETs), protocols and network simulations, Quality of Service, and content protection. He is an active member of the Car-to-Car Communication Consortium. He is author of papers on WiFi and mobile ad-hoc networks at IEEE international conferences and of two patent pending techniques for VANETs (on synchronous MAC and geo-routing protocol).

José Ramón Rodríguez Cruz received his Ph.D. in Electrical Engineering from CINVESTAV-IPN Zacatenco in August, 2000. Thereafter, he joined the Center for Electronics and Telecommunications at Instituto Tecnológico y de Estudios Superiores de Monterrey (ITESM), Campus Monterrey, Mexico. He was a member of SNI for 8 years. He participated in several government projects involving security and RF systems implementation. His line of research is joint source and channel coding and RF propagation channel modeling, among others.

Pedro Damián-Reyes is a Professor of Computer Science at the College of Telematics in University of Colima; he leads the Multimedia Laboratory. His research interests include ubiquitous computing, context-aware computing, and software development. He holds a BSc from the Instituto Tecnológico de Colima and MSc from the University of Colima and Phd from Student at the Centro de Investigación Científica y de Educación Superior de Ensenada (CICESE) in Baja California, México.

Andrew G. Dempster is Director of the Australian Centre for Space Engineering Research (ACSER), UNSW. He is also Director of Research in the School of Surveying and Spatial Information Systems and Director of Postgraduate Research in the Faculty of Engineering. He has a BE and MEngSc from UNSW and a PhD from University of Cambridge in Efficient Circuits for Signal Processing Arithmetic. He was System Engineer and Project Manager for the first GPS receiver developed in Australia in the late 80s and has been involved in satellite navigation ever since. His current research interests are in satellite navigation receiver design and signal processing, areas where he has six patents, and new location technologies. He is leading the development of space engineering research at ACSER.

Max Suell Dutra, Dr-Ing. in Robotics, obtained in 1995 (UNI-DUISBURG, Germany), M.Sc. in Mechanical Engineering in Robotics, obtained in 1990 (COPPE/UFRJ), is a Mechanical Engineer, graduated in 1987 (UFF, Brazil). He is Professor of COPPE/UFRJ, heading a research group in Automation and Robotics and Chief of the Robotics Laboratory (http://www.labrob.coppe.ufrj.br). More than 60 of his works have been published in national and international books, congresses, and journals in the last 3 years.

Mahmoud Efatmaneshnik is a research fellow at the School of Surveying and Spatial Information Systems, UNSW. He has a BE (1999) in Aerospace Engineering from the Tehran Polytechnic University and a ME (2005) in Manufacturing Management and Industrial Engineering from UNSW. He holds a PhD in the Mechanical School of UNSW on Complex Systems Engineering.

Pedro J. Fernández received an MSc in Computer Science Engineering in 2005 and an MSc on Advanced Information and Telematics Technologies in 2008, both from University of Murcia. Currently, he is a PhD student in the Information and Communications Engineering Department, at the University of Murcia. His research focuses on secure protocols like IKEv2 and IPsec, vehicular networks, and mobility and security in wireless communications.

Carlos Flores-Cortés holds a position as a full-time Lecturer at the University of Colima. His research interests include service discovery middleware, pervasive computing, ad hoc networking, and mobile data applications. He received his PhD in Computing from Lancaster University in UK.

Sergio Hernández Gaona graduated from the University of Guerrero, Mexico with a BScEd in Mathematics, received his MS degree in Computer Science from the University of Colima, Mexico in 2011. Since 1993, he has been with the CBTA 180 High School in Mexico, where he is currently a Professor in Computer Networks and TI. His current research interests include wireless networks.

Antonio F. Gómez-Skarmeta received his MSc degree in Computer Science from the University of Granada, Spain, and both the B.S. (Hons.) and the PhD degrees in Computer Science from University of Murcia, Spain. He is a Professor in the Department of Information and Communications Engineering at University of Murcia. Research interests include mobile communications, network security, and artificial intelligence.

Antonio Guerrero-Ibáñez is a Professor of Telecommunications and Networks at the College of Telematics in University of Colima, Colima, Mexico; he leads the research group *computer networks* at College of Telematics. His research interests include the areas of intelligent transportation systems for vehicular traffic control, wireless sensor networks, and heterogeneous wireless networks, with particular emphasis on the services and network management based on quality of service. He holds a BSc in Computer Systems Engineering (1996) and MSc in Telematics area (1999) from University of Colima, Colima, Mexico, and PhD in Telematics Engineering (2008) from Technical University of Catalonia (UPC), Barcelona, Spain.

Eduardo Jacob works as an Assistant Professor in the Department of Electronics and Telecommunications at the Faculty of Engineering of Bilbao in the University of the Basque Country (Spain), where he teaches Mobile Services and Networks and courses on Advanced Networks and Security in Wireless Networks. As director of his research group, he has directed several publicly funded R&D projects in the areas of security and distributed systems, and has participated in several European projects. His current interests include wireless communications for ITS applications and AAA in Neutral Access (or network access service provider independent) Networks with proposals that extend RFC2903 to these domains and authentication and authorization for privacy enhancing applications of IPv6-based low capacity sensors. He is currently a member of the advisory committee and he is an advisory member of the Information Systems of the University of the Basque Country Council of the Basque Agency for Data Protection.

Allison Kealy is a Senior Lecturer in The Department of Infrastructure Engineering at The University of Melbourne, Australia. She holds an undergraduate degree in Land Surveying from The University of the West Indies, Trinidad, and a PhD in GPS and Geodesy from the University of Newcastle upon Tyne, UK. Allison's research interests include sensor fusion, Kalman filtering, high precision satellite positioning, GNSS quality control, wireless sensor networks, and location based services. Allison is currently the co-chair of FIG Working Group entitled Ubiquitous Positioning.

Houda Labiod is an Associate Professor at Department INFRES (Computer Science and Network department) at Telecom ParisTech (previously named ENST) in Paris (France) since 2001. In 2005, she obtained her HDR (Habilitation à diriger les recherches). Prior to this, she held a research position at Eurecom Institute, Sophia-antipolis, France. She obtained her Ph.D. from the University of Versailles Saint-Quentin-en- Yvelines (France) in 1998. Her current research interests include mobile ad hoc networks, wireless LAN networks, sensor networks, wireless mesh networks, NEMO networks, Vehicular communications, QoS service provisioning, performance evaluation, modeling and security of large-scale distributed systems, cross layer design in wireless networks, and link adaptation mechanisms. Dr. Labiod has published four books and many research papers in these areas. She is a Founder of NTMS Conference on New Technologies, Mobility and Security (NTMS2007) and SecITS international workshop on Security in Intelligent Transportations Systems (SecITS'2011). She served as an Associate Editor and is on the editorial board for several journals.

Omar Lengerke earned his Ph.D in Mechanical Engineering in Robotics, obtained in 2010 (COPPE/UFRJ, Brazil), and an M. Sc. in Control and Automation of Manufacture Systems, obtained in 2002 (ITESM-CEM, Mexico). He is Computational Systems Engineer, graduated in 1999 (UNAB, Colombia). More than 30 of his works have been published in national and international congresses and journals in the last 5 years.

Nitin Maslekar is currently a PhD candidate at IRSEEM-Esigelec, and his degree is affiliated to University of Rouen, France. He received his B.E degree from University of Pune, India in Computer Engineering in 2005. He received his M.Tech degree from Manipal University, India in 2008 in Network Engineering. His research interests include wireless ad hoc networks, vehicular networking, and applications for intelligent transportation systems.

Pietro Manzoni received his MSc degree in Computer Science from the Universitá degli Studi, Milan, Italy, in 1989, and a PhD degree in Computer Science from the Polytechnic University of Milan, Italy, in 1995. He is a full Professor of Computer Science at Polytechnic University of Valencia. His research activity is related to wireless networks and protocol design, modelling, and implementation.

Joseph Mouzna graduate from St. Petersburg Polytechnic (Russia) in 1983 and received his Ph. D. degree in Physics from Univeriste Blaise Pascal France in 1987, where he began his career as Associate Professor in Applied Mathematics. Since 1992, he has worked on network and protocol design. His current research deals with Intelligent Transportation Systems, specifically Vehicle-to-vehicle and vehicle-to-infrastructure communications for safety and non-safety applications for traffic management. His research interests include metaheuristics, VANETs, and mobility, with application to Ad-Hoc and sensor networks. Since 2003, he is the head of Intelligent Transportation Systems division at IRSEEM-Esigelec. He has published several papers in international reviews and conferences, and has supervised several Ph. D. theses.

Cristian Nieto received an MSc in Web Engineering in 2007 from University Carlos III of Madrid and an MSc in Advanced Information and Telematics Technologies in 2008 from the University of Murcia, Spain. Currently, he is doing his PhD research in the Information and Communications Engineering Department at the University of Murcia. His research interests include context-aware handover and seamless mobility.

Jesús Luna received his Bachelor's degree in Telecommunications Engineering from the "Instituto Politécnico Nacional" (IPN, Mexico 1995), a Master's degree in Computer Science from the "Tecnológico de Monterrey" (ITESM CEM, Mexico 2002), and a PhD in Computer Architecture from the "Universidad Politécnica de Cataluña" (UPC, Spain 2008). He was a postdoctoral researcher with the CoreGRID Network of Excellence (Greece/Cyprus, 2008-2009) and has more than 15 years of experience in the field of computer security, working with public and private companies and universities in Mexico and southern Europe including "Banco de México," "Universidad Tecnológica de México," "SeMarket," and "Barcelona Digital CT." Since 2009, he is an active member of the "Cloud Security Alliance" (CSA), and in 2010, co-founded its Spanish Chapter (CSA-ES). Currently he works as a postdoc researcher with the DEEDS group at the "Technische Universität Darmstadt," and his topics of interest include security metrics, Cloud and Grid security, botnets mitigation, VANETs and WSN security+privacy, and PKI-related security.

David W. Matolak received the B.S. degree from Penn. State in 1983, the M.S. degree from Univ. of Massachusetts in 1987, and the Ph.D. degree from the Univ. of Virginia in 1995, all in Electrical Engineering. He has more than 20 years of experience in communication system research, development, design, and deployment, with private companies, government institutions, and academia, including AT&T Bell Labs, L3 Communication Systems, The MITRE Corp., and Lockheed Martin. He has dozens of publications, several patents, and expertise in spread spectrum, networking, wireless channel characterization, and their applications in both civil and military communication systems, including terrestrial, aeronautical, and satellite. He joined Ohio University School of EECS in 1999. His research interests are radio channel modeling and communication techniques for non-stationary fading channels, multicarrier transmission, and mobile ad hoc networks. Prof. Matolak is a member of Eta Kappa Nu, Sigma Xi, and a senior member of IEEE.

Johann Márquez-Barja received his Systems Engineering degree at Bolivia's Royal and Pontiff Saint Francisco Xavier of Chuquisaca Major University in 2002. He received his MSc in Science and Telematics from Echeverría Polytechnic University, Cuba, in 2004. He is currently a PhD candidate of the Department of Computer Engineering at the Polytechnic University of Valencia, Spain. His work focuses on vehicular networks and vertical handover communications.

Manel Medina is a Full Professor at the Technical University of Catalonia (UPC), since 1992. He was a Chief Innovation Officer of SeMarket, and Security Projects Officer of Barcelona Digital Technological Center. He was the Head of the Spanish Computer Emergency Response Team esCert-UPC and of the Internet Applications research center (UPC). He was the Head of cANet, research center of Internet Applications of the UPC and a full Member of ESRIF (European Security Research and Innovative Forum) (since 2006) to advise European Commission about security research topics in the R&D funding programs.

Antonella Molinaro received a Laurea degree in Computer Engineering in 1991 from the University of Calabria, a Master's degree in Information Technology in 1992 from CEFRIEL/Politecnico di Milano, and a Ph.D. degree in 1996. She has been an Assistant Professor of Telecommunications at the University of Messina and the University of Calabria. She is currently Associate Professor at the University Mediterranea of Reggio Calabria. She has been involved in organizing workshops and special sessions in international conferences and she has served as a guest editor for special issues of valuable international journals. She has published more than 150 publications in international conferences, journals, and book chapters, and she has received two Best-paper awards. Her current research interests are in the field of multi-hop wireless communications, vehicular ad hoc networks, and future Internet architectures.

Roberto Morales is a PhD candidate at the Technical University of Catalonia. Morales obtained a Bachelor's Degree in Computer Systems Engineering from the Technical Institute of Tuxtla Gutierrez (Chiapas, Mexico), in 1996. He achieved a Master of Sciences degree in Computer Science in the field of Distributed and Parallel Computing from the Computing Research Center (IPN, Mexico) in 2001. Currently he is working as a security researcher at esCert-UPC in the Network Security Group (NSG). His research interests are mobile computing, communication protocols, mobile application development, and tools for Internet services, and security and identity management for mobile environments.

Gabriel Alejandro Galaviz Mosqueda graduated from the University of Colima with a BE in Electrical Engineering, and received his MS degree in Computation from University of Colima. Since 2008, he has been as PhD student in Telecommunications at the Centre for Scientific Research and Higher Education in Ensenada. His current research interest includes vehicular ad-hoc networks and WiMAX.

Sergio David Villarreal Reyes received his M.S. in Information Technologies from the Instituto Tecnológico y de Estudios Superiores de Monterrey, México, in 2007. Since 2011, he has worked as research assistant on his Doctoral thesis at the Center for Electronics y Telecommunications, also at the Instituto Tecnológico y de Estudios Superiores de Monterrey, México. His current research interest is focused on Intelligent Transportation Systems and vehicle-to-vehicle communication networks.

David Muñoz Rodríguez received a B.S. in 1972, an M.S. in 1976, and a Ph.D. in 1979 in Electrical Engineering from the Universidad de Guadalajara, México, Cinvestav, México, and the University of Essex, Colchester, England, respectively. He is a Senior Member of the IEEE and was formerly Chairman of the Communication Department and Electrical Engineering Department at Cinvestav, IPN. In 1992, he joined the Instituto Tecnológico y de Estudios Superiores de Monterrey (ITESM), Campus Monterrey, México, where he became the Director of Center for Electronics y Telecommunications. His research interests include wireless systems and performance analysis.

José Santa received an MSc in Computer Science Engineering and an MSc in Advanced Information and Telematics Technologies in 2004 and 2008, respectively, and his PhD in Computer Science in 2009, all of them from University of Murcia, Spain. Currently, he is an Adjunct Professor in the Department of Information and Communication Engineering at University of Murcia. His research interests include context awareness, intelligent transportation systems, and indoor automation.

Jetzabel M. Serna-Olvera obtained her Bachelor's Degree in Computer Systems Engineering from the Technical Institute of Tijuana (Tijuana, Mexico), in 2001. She achieved a Master of Sciences degree in Computer Science and Communications Engineering from the Gerhard Mercator University (Duisburg, Germany), in 2006. She is currently pursuing her PhD at the Technical University of Catalonia in the Computer Architecture Department (Barcelona, Spain), and working as a security researcher at esCert-UPC in the Network Security Group (NSG). Her topics of interest are security, trust, and privacy in mobile environments.

Riccardo Scopigno (M.Sc. 1995 Summa cum Laude, Ph.D. 2005) has matured a 15-year working experience in the TLC field, obtaining, in the meantime, his Ph.D. His skills cover telecommunication architectures, from theory to practice, as matured from his variegate working experience. He was a hardware designer for TLC systems in Italtel-Siemens (1997-1999); in Marconi (2000-2003), he achieved a good expertise in IP network design (as certified network engineer). He is currently active in advanced research on wireless networks– he is Director of MultiLayer Wireless Dept. of ISMB. He is ISMB's representative in ETSI ITS (the working group on intelligent transportation systems) and within ERTICO and Car-to-Car Communication Consortium. He is author of papers on WiFi and vehicular communications at IEEE conferences, acting also as TPC and author of 3 patent pending techniques for VANETs (on synchronous MAC, georouting MapCast, and CSMA/CA QoS).

Corneliu Eugen D. Sterian (IEEE M'96-SM'98) was born in Bucharest, Romania, on April 30, 1947. He received the Dipl.-Ing. and Dr.-Ing. degrees in Electronics and Telecommunications Engineering from the University Politehnica of Bucharest. He is currently Associate Professor with the University Politehnica of Bucharest where he is teaching Information and Coding Theory, Communication Systems, and related matters. During the second half of the year 2000, he was the Telecommunications Engineer of UNMIK, Pristina, Kosovo. From the middle of 1997 to the end of 1998, he was Director General in the Ministry of Communications of his country. After the Ministry was replaced by the National Agency for Communications and Information Technology, he served as Head of Department and then Director. From 1992 to 1997, he was with ROMTELECOM, then the national telecommunications operator of Romania. From 1974 to 1992, he was with I.P.A. Research Institute, where he was promoted in 1991 to the highest degree of Principal Scientist. His research interests include information theory and more particularly channel coding.

Magda Judith Morales Tavera obtained her PhD in Mechanical Engineering in Robotics in 2010 (COPPE/UFRJ, Brazil), M.Sc. in Mechanical Engineering, in 2008 (COPPE/UFRJ, Brazil), and Mechatronics Engineer graduated in 2005 (UNAB, Colombia). She has more than 10 works published in national and international congresses and journals in the last 5 years.

Index